MOON

OAXACA

JUSTIN HENDERSON

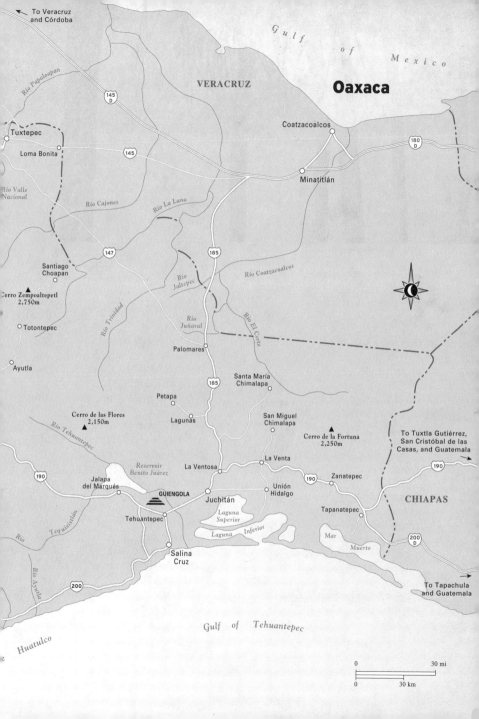

To Veracruz
and Córdoba

Gulf   *of*   *Mexico*

VERACRUZ

Oaxaca

Río Papaloapan

145
D

Coatzacoalcos

Tuxtepec

180
D

Loma Bonita

145

Minatitlán

Río Valle
Nacional

Río Cajones

Río La Lana

185

Río Coatzacoalcos

147

Santiago
Choapan

Río Jaltepec

Cerro Zempoaltepetl
2,750m

Río Trinidad

Río Juñaral

Río El Corte

Totontepec

Palomares

Santa María
Chimalapa

Ayutla

185

Petapa

San Miguel
Chimalapa

Cerro de las Flores
2,150m

Lagunas

Cerro de la Fortuna
2,250m

To Tuxtla Gutiérrez,
San Cristóbal de las
Casas, and Guatemala

Río Tehuantepec

La Ventosa

La Venta

190

Reservoir
Benito Juárez

190

Zanatepec

190

Jalapa
del Márqués

GUIENGOLA

Juchitán

Unión
Hidalgo

CHIAPAS

Tehuantepec

Laguna
Superior

Tapanatepec

Río Tequisistlán

200
D

Río
Ayuela

Salina
Cruz

Laguna   Inferior

Mar   Muerto

200

To Tapachula
and Guatemala

Gulf   of   Tehuantepec

Huatulco

0   30 mi

0   30 km

Contents

DISCOVER
Oaxaca

The state of Oaxaca offers the best of Mexico, both old and new. It has a vibrant, urban city, abundant indigenous arts and handicrafts, renowned native cuisine, fascinating history, natural wonders, and a rich cultural heritage, including 16 separate living languages.

Though honored by its designation as a World Heritage site by UNESCO, Oaxaca City is as much about the present as the past. By day, people linger at plaza-front sidewalk cafés. By night, the same central plaza comes alive with entertainment, from folkloric dance to orchestral music to a shifting cast of street performers. And in the blocks around the plaza, especially to the north, a new generation of Oaxacan chefs, hoteliers, designers, artists, and makers of *mezcal*, now offer travelers new ways to enjoy the city's pleasures.

Cultural wealth abounds outside the city. The surrounding Valley of Oaxaca is ringed by the ruins of ancient civilizations, including Mitla, celebrated for the unique Greca stone fretwork decorating its walls. The vibrant market of Zaachila coexists with the mysterious ruins of its pre-conquest old town. And on a western hill overlooking all, regal Monte Albán, Mesoamerica's first metropolis, still reigns from its mountaintop throne.

Clockwise from top left: cactus outside a Oaxacan cathedral; mineral waterfall at Hierve El Agua; a giant doll mask for a Guelaguetza dancer; an antique map of Oaxaca; embroidered blouses for sale; colorful church in Tamazulapan.

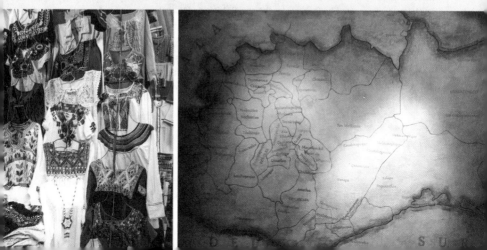

These ancient ghosts exist side by side with vibrant native markets offering everything from colorful carpets and pottery to embroidered dresses and *alebrijes,* Oaxaca's celebrated wooden animals. The less-traveled Mixteca region offers its share of magnificent Dominican churches, remote ancient kingdoms, and natural wonders, such as emerald waterfalls, limestone caves, and crystal springs. And southeast on the Isthmus, where the continent shrinks to a narrow land bridge, you can join the celebration at near-continuous festivals.

More contemporary recreational pleasures such as fishing, diving, stand-up paddleboarding, or simply lounging can be found on the golden strands of Pacific coastal resorts like Puerto Ángel, the Bahías de Huatulco, and Puerto Escondido. At Puerto Escondido, surfers challenge one of the world's fiercest breaks. Along the coast around Huatulco and Salina Cruz, a dozen mostly deserted surfing breaks provide every kind of wave imaginable.

Wherever you wander in this rich land, you'll find excitement, friendly people, relatively low prices, and a host of traditional Mexican delights.

Clockwise from top left: northern Oaxaca; handmade baskets for sale; a sunny day in Santa Cruz de Huatulco; dancers in action during the Guelaguetza.

Planning Your Trip

Where to Go

Oaxaca City
At the crossroads of the mountain-rimmed Valley of Oaxaca, the **capital city** offers virtually everything within its strollable downtown. Start from its charming central plaza to explore **baroque churches,** eclectic **handicrafts markets,** distinguished **galleries and museums,** a new wave of contemporary art galleries and shops, and inviting restaurants serving both **authentic Oaxacan** and **international cuisine.**

The Valley of Oaxaca
The banquet of old-Mexico experiences continues in the valley outside the city. Visit **native markets** with colorful arts and crafts at villages such as **Teotitlán del Valle** and **Tlacolula** on the east

side; **San Bartolo Coyotepec** on the south side; and **Zaachila, Arrazola,** and **Atzompa** in the southwest. Or seek out lost cultures at **Mitla** and **Monte Albán.** Don't miss the strangely compelling landscapes of **Hierve el Agua.**

Pacific Resorts and Southern Sierra
This long, lazy land of eternal summer is embellished by its resort trio: **Puerto Ángel** and **Huatulco,** on the east side, and **Puerto Escondido** on the west. Enjoy **beachcombing, sportfishing, swimming, snorkeling, surfing, kiteboarding, stand-up paddleboarding,** and **scuba diving.** On the Puerto Ángel-Huatulco side, add plenty of

sidewalk cafés around the *zócalo,* Oaxaca City

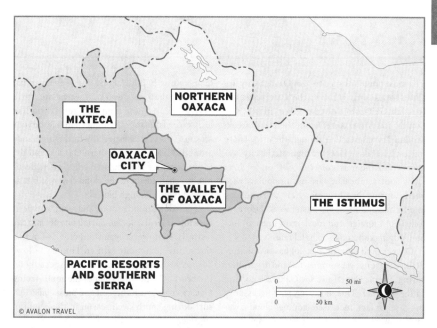

© AVALON TRAVEL

golf and **tennis, river rafting,** and **jungle coffee farms.** On the Puerto Escondido side, add abundant **wildlife-viewing** at **Laguna Manialtepec** and **Parque Nacional Lagunas de Chacahua.**

The Mixteca

This homeland of the **Mixtecs,** Oaxaca's "People of the Clouds," is a virtually **untouristed domain,** ripe for adventuring. Visit a monumental 16th-century Dominican ex-convent at **Yanhuitlán,** and the elegant open chapel at **Teposcolula.** Farther south, the cool, pine-tufted plateau of the High Mixteca offers groves of ancient *sabino* trees, plunging waterfalls, and **Tlaxiaco,** the "Paris of Oaxaca" with its splendid **Saturday market.** Even more is tucked in the Mixteca's hidden corners, especially the idyllic **Valley of Apoala.**

Northern Oaxaca

An exploration of northern Oaxaca begins in the villages of the **Sierra Juárez,** scarcely an hour

north from Oaxaca City. Farther north, past the towns of **Tuxtepec** and **Ixcatlán,** the highway climbs past the gigantic whale-back massif of the **Cerro Rabón,** the holy mountain of the Mazatec people, to the summit, at **Huautla de Jiménez,** their spiritual home. Stroll the native markets and shop for prized *huipiles* (traditional embroidered dresses). Or continue another half an hour to enjoy the **twin waterfalls of Las Regaderas,** or explore the **limestone cave** near **Eloxochitlán.**

The Isthmus

Nothing embodies the independent Isthmus spirit more than its **near-continuous menu of fiestas,** especially in **Tehuántepec** and **Juchitán,** where *istmeño* hearts beat fastest. Women dress in their spectacular floral *huipiles* and sway to the lovely, lilting melody of "La Sandunga," the song of the Isthmus. For surfers, kiteboarders, and other lovers of the wind and waves, the coast west of Salina Cruz offers a dozen world-class surf spots.

When to Go

The most popular times to visit Oaxaca City are **Christmas-New Year's,** the **Guelaguetza** (gay-lah-GET-zah) **dance festival** in July, and **Día de los Muertos** (Day of the Dead) week, around November 1. Although the crowds are biggest and hotel prices are highest, the city is at its merriest and most colorful.

By contrast, beaches are most popular twice yearly: during the Christmas-New Year's holiday and **Semana Santa,** pre-Easter week. Droves of folks, both foreign and local, crowd restaurants and lodgings and push up hotel rates.

Oaxaca (and most of Mexico) has two sharply defined seasons: wet summer-fall and dry winter-spring. People sometimes say Oaxaca is too hot in the summer. This, however, isn't necessarily the case. In fact, increased summer cloud cover and showers can actually create average daily temperatures in July, August, and September that are cooler than clear and very warm late April, May, and early June temperatures. If you like lush, green landscapes, summer-fall may be your season. This is true especially in the highlands around Oaxaca City, northern Oaxaca, and the Mixteca, where multicolored wildflowers decorate the roadsides and the clouds seem to billow into a 1,000-mile-high blue sky.

If you don't mind crowds and want to experience lots of local color, go during one of Oaxaca's festivals. If, however, you shun crowds but like the sunny, temperate winter, January, a low-occupancy season, is a good bet, especially on the beach. On the other hand, the south-facing Oaxaca coast gets its biggest and most consistent surf during south swell season in the height of summer.

sand painting on the Day of the Dead

Día de los Muertos

Instead of mourning the dead, Mexicans celebrate the deceased with a holiday, Día de los Muertos (Day of the Dead), which is, in all of Mexico and especially in Oaxaca, cause for a fiesta that goes on for a week. There is no better place to spend this magical week than Oaxaca. Here, the amazingly intricate altars created to welcome the dead, many constructed in "competitions" between schools and social organizations, can be found all over town. Additionally, the creation of sand tapestries, or tapetes de arena, has morphed from a Oaxacan mortuary custom into yet another expression of love and respect for the dead on the Day of the Dead. The most beautiful and elaborate works of art can be found in and outside of the Palacio de Gobierno. Other places to see the finest of these sand tapestries, and altars as well, include Escuela de Bellas Artes (across from La Soledad Church), at the Centro Cultural de Santo Domingo, and along the Alcalá pedestrian promenade.

Catrina Calavera, queen of the Day of the Dead

You can spend your entire week admiring altars and tapestries, and enjoying the party in Oaxaca City. Or you can head out into the valleys and hills, and celebrate the Day of the Dead, All Souls' Day, and All Saints' Days in a dozen different towns and villages. Every single one will have its own way of honoring their dead. People gather in their hometowns and villages to reunite with their loved ones. Around noon, on November 1, they arrive at the cemeteries and begin sweeping up the gravesites, polishing the tombstones, scattering flower petals, and lighting candles to mark the path. By early evening, all is ready. The graves are festooned with fruit, flowers, and glowing candles, and decorated with toys and candy for the *angelitos* (deceased little ones), and dishes loaded with the favorite foods and drinks of the deceased adults. Most importantly, everyone arrives; people drink, eat, and tell favorite family stories. As the evening wears on, people get sleepy and curl up beneath blankets and spend the night in a happy vigil to welcome their departed loved ones back into the family fold once again.

If you plan on coming to Oaxaca for El Día de Los Muertos, book early and be prepared to pay a premium for your hotel room. This is one of the biggest weeks of the year for visitors in Oaxaca.

October, November, and the first half of December are also good times to go (except possibly for the crowded, expensive high-holiday Día de los Muertos week). Hotel prices are cheapest, the landscape is lush and green, beaches are beautifully uncrowded, and it's cooler and not as rainy as July, August, and September.

Before You Go

Passports, Tourist Cards, and Visas

Your passport (or birth or naturalization certificate) is your positive proof of national identity. Mexican authorities won't let U.S. and Canadian citizens, including children, enter Mexico without one, and U.S. Immigration rules require that **all U.S. citizens must have a valid passport in order to re-enter the United States.**

For U.S. and Canadian citizens, entry by air into Mexico for a few weeks could hardly be easier. Desk clerks check your passport, airplane attendants hand out **tourist cards** *(tarjetas turísticas),* and officers make them official by stamping them at the immigration gate. Business travel permits for 30 days or fewer are handled by the same simple procedures.

Immunizations and Precautions

A good physician can recommend the proper preventatives for your Oaxaca trip. If you are going to stay pretty much in town, your doctor will probably suggest little more than updating your basic typhoid, diphtheria-tetanus, hepatitis, and polio shots.

For remote tropical areas (below 1,200 meters/4,000 ft.), doctors often recommend a gamma-globulin shot against **hepatitis A** and a schedule of chloroquine pills against **malaria.** Use other measures to discourage mosquitoes and other tropical pests. Common precautions include mosquito netting and rubbing on plenty of pure **DEET** (N,N dimethyl-meta-toluamide)

"jungle juice," mixed in equal parts with rubbing alcohol (70 percent isopropyl). Less toxic alternatives are out there, but they simply do not work as well as your basic poison, DEET. With dengue fever now well-established if not an epidemic along stretches of Mexico's tropical coast, mosquito deterrence can be critical.

Transportation

The majority of visitors reach Oaxaca **by air,** and a large fraction of those through **Mexico City.** There, travelers transfer to flights bound for either **Oaxaca City, Puerto Escondido,** or **Huatulco.**

But **bus travel** rules in Mexico. Hundreds of sleek luxury- and first-class bus lines roar out daily from the border, headed south. The route to Oaxaca along the Pacific shore, although the longest, requiring one or two transfers and at least three full 24-hour days, is the most scenic. Within Oaxaca, a host of lines connect virtually every town and most villages. Three distinct levels of service—luxury or super-first class, first class, and second class—are generally available.

If you're adventurous, but still want to have all the comforts of home, you may enjoy driving your **car or RV** to Oaxaca. On the other hand, the cost, risk, wear on both you and your vehicle, and the congestion hassles in towns may change your mind. Oaxaca car rentals are not cheap. With a 15 percent or more "value added" tax tacked on and **mandatory Mexican car insurance,** they run more than in the United States.

The Best of Oaxaca

This itinerary focuses on Oaxaca's most compelling and attractive places, beginning with the crown jewel, Oaxaca City, one of the most beautiful and charming cities in Mexico. First-time visitors will want to spend at least 2-4 days in Oaxaca City before heading out into the Valley of Oaxaca. The valley, with its fascinating archaeological sites and myriad colorful market towns, is well worth another 3-4 days of exploring. Finally, travel by car or plane to Huatulco or Puerto Escondido on Oaxaca's long, sun-drenched coast, and enjoy a few days chasing waves, paddleboarding through the bays, or chilling by the pool at a high-end resort. When you've had enough of the beach, there are bird-filled lagoons to explore, coffee plantations and mountain waterfalls to enjoy, and rivers to run. This semi-epic 15-day journey does not cover all of Oaxaca's regions—you'll have the Mixteca and northern Oaxaca to look forward to on another trip. But, it will immerse you in the best Oaxaca has to offer for the two-week traveler.

Oaxaca City

DAY 1

Once you're settled into your hotel, head out to the *zócalo* (central plaza). This is the heart of Oaxaca, and the best possible place to begin your peregrinations through the city. Visit the imposing **Catedral de Oaxaca,** and have a look at the mysterious Santa Cruz de Huatulco. Afterwards, spend some time roaming the lively plaza.

For lunch, try the east side of the *zócalo*, which features a row of sidewalk cafés, the best among them being **Terranova.** Afterwards, pay a visit to the **Museo de los Pintores Oaxaqueños.**

For dinner, taste some classic Oaxacan food at **Casa de la Abuela,** on the northwest corner of the *zócalo*. After dinner you'll find a lively late night mix of locals and tourists up the pedestrian promenade, Macedonio Alcalá, at **La Cantinita.**

DAY 2

Start your day with breakfast at **Primavera** on the plaza. Then wander over and plunge into

Catedral de Oaxaca anchors the *zócalo* in Oaxaca City.

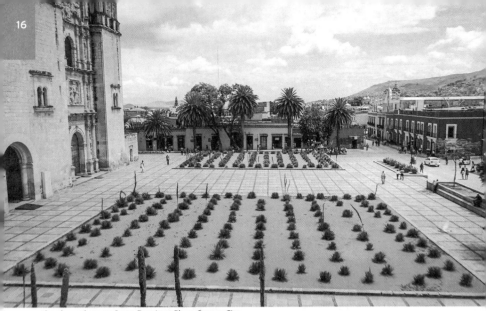

the elegantly spare Santo Domingo Plaza, Oaxaca City

Mercado Juárez for an hour or more of intense, colorful shopping and people-watching. You might even stick around for lunch, as there are dozens of small food stalls in the market. Don't miss the adjacent **Templo y Ex-Convento San Juan de Dios,** dating from 1703. From here, head to **Mercado de Artesanías,** where you can immerse yourself in arts and crafts and wonderful handmade clothes.

After the market, stroll back a few blocks to the magnificent **Basilica de Nuestra Señora de la Soledad,** the church of the patron saint of Oaxaca. Admire the church inside and out, and have a look at the church museum across the street. If you still have an hour before your next round of eating and drinking, check out the contemporary photography at the nearby **Centro de Fotografía Manuel Alvarez Bravo.**

For dinner, try Oaxacan food re-imagined in the hands of one of the city's great new chefs. **Zandunga** offers contemporary food inspired by the traditions of the Isthmus. Alternately, **Zicanda,** does something similar with traditional Oaxacan fare. They are both exquisitely designed dining spaces and usually full of lively crowds of Oaxacans and tourists.

After dinner, slip into the tiny, magical confines of **Mezcaleria Los Amantes,** where you can sample locally-distilled, artisanal *mezcal.* For more nightlife, head down the Alcalá to **Bar la Pasion,** the rocking late-night club.

DAY 3

Have your morning coffee on or near the plaza at the **Italian Coffee Company, Oaxacan Coffee Company,** or **Café Brújula.** Then head up the **Alcalá,** and take some time to explore some of the many art galleries, clothing stores, jewelry and craft stores, and other retail outlets that line the Alcalá and its side streets. Take an hour, at least, to explore the **Museo de Arte Contemporaneo on the way up the Alcalá.**

Take lunch at **Hostería Alcalá** or dive into the mole experience at **Los Pacos.** After lunch, stop in at the **botanical gardens** behind the **Museo de las Culturas de Oaxaca.** Head into the Museo itself, and spend a couple of hours here and at the adjacent **Iglesia y Ex-Convento de**

Santo Domingo, getting acquainted with the history and culture of this most magical region of Mexico. If you have time afterwards, the **Instituto de Artes Gráficos de Oaxaca,** across the street, is a fine showcase for more contemporary work. Next door, try a refreshing tequila and mango sorbet or some other wild concoction at the **Ice Cream Museum (Museo de las Nieves),** a unique ice cream shop right next door.

Drop into **Café Central** for a *mezcal* sampling before dinner. You can then meander back up García Vigil or Alcalá for an amazing dinner at **Pitiona** or **Los Danzantes.** For some live music after dinner, head to **El Barracuda** for rock, or the stylish **El Piano y El Sofa** for jazz and blues.

DAY 4

On your last full day in Oaxaca City, explore some slightly less busy yet entirely compelling neighborhoods, museums, and attractions. This day calls for a lot of walking, but still, it's a small city and these distances are manageable.

Start with breakfast at the tradition-steeped **Restaurant Tayu.** From Tayu, walk to the

Museo Arte Prehispánico de Rufino Tamayo. The fabled Mexican artist possessed one of the great private collections of pre-Colombiana, and it is all here.

If you're feeling particularly energetic, make your way up the **Escalera del Fortín** to the Guelaguetza auditorium; it's a fascinating piece of architecture and a great viewpoint over the city. Head back down the stairs and walk to **Mercado Sánchez Pasqua.** Enjoy a low budget lunch in the form of tamales or *memelas* from any of the market's many food stalls.

Walk a few blocks to the charming **Los Arquitos** neighborhood. Then enjoy the stroll back down hill to the *zócalo*. Spend an hour at the **Palacio de Gobierno.** Take a snack break at **Del Jardín** or anywhere on the plaza before heading east, to view the **Teatro Alcalá** and visit the **MARO** store and the **Ex-Convento de Santa Catalina.** *Mezcal*-tasting time or coffee-sipping recovery time can be spent at **La Condesa Coffee Bar.**

Finally, get thee to the **Hotel Monte Albán** or the **Camino Real** for dinner and a Guelaguetza folkloric dance performance.

a panoramic view of Monte Albán and Oaxaca Valley

the weekly *tianguis* (market) in Zaachila

a roadside waterfall on the road to Puerto Escondido

The Valley of Oaxaca

All of the places mentioned in these 4-5 days of valley tripping can be visited easily in 2-3 days with organized tour groups, who travel the countryside in vans and have the art of getting several great destinations done in a day without rushing anybody. Autonomy has its advantages, but so does getting chauffeured around.

DAY 5

Drive, bus, or take a group tour leaving early from the city heading to **Zaachila**'s large and bustling Thursday market. The archaeological site across the plaza from the market is well worth visiting as well. For lunch, try one of the great pork dishes at the market or try **Restaurant la Capilla.**

Afterwards, return on the road that takes you through **Culiapan de Guerrero** to visit the church, and the alebrijes craft town of **Arrazola.**

You'll be back in time for dinner at **La Flor de Oaxaca,** a tradition-steeped restaurant on Oaxaca City's south side with plenty of rich moles on the menu. Night owls can then head up to **La Tentacion** for late-night salsa or DJ dance music.

DAY 6

If it's a Friday, it is market day in **Ocotlán,** so you'll want to drive or take a tour down route 175 to Ocotlán. Afterwards, take short side trips to **Santo Tomás Jalieza** for embroidery and **San Martín Tilcajete** for *alebrijes*. On the way back to the city, **San Bartolo Coyotepec** beckons with its market full of locally-made and strikingly-beautiful black pottery.

In the evening, go relatively low budget with some fine seafood at **Restaurant La Red.** Afterwards, if you still have the mojo, head up to **Tlaxaparta,** a hookah bar by day and a very lively dance club after midnight.

DAY 7

From the city, take a tour or drive to **Monte Albán,** Oaxaca's most important and impressive archaeological site. The site and on-site museum are well worth a half day of your time, so bring a lunch or plan on dining at the café.

In the afternoon, head to **Santa María Atzompa** to peruse their green-glazed pottery and other ceramics for sale. After all that hard work viewing the ruins, another fine meal is in

Mezcal and Mole

Aside from arts and crafts, *mezcal* and mole are what visitors want to take home from Oaxaca. So, where do you get the best?

MOLE

First, immerse yourself in mole while in Oaxaca. Your first stop should be **Restaurant los Pacos,** a restaurant in Oaxaca City that serves a sampler of six of the seven types of Oaxacan mole. For those who think "chocolate" when they hear the word mole, know that only three of the seven Oaxacan moles use chocolate in the mix. For take-home moles, there's a great selection at the **Mayordomo chocolate stores** (at Aldama 209, 20 de Noviembre 219, and Alcalá 302). Or head into the **Mercado Juárez** to puesto **Tonita** (no. 80) for a great selection of mole pastes. Just add water or stock for a perfect, made-at-home mole sauce. The following are the names of Oaxaca's seven moles (the first three use chocolate, the rest do not): *negro, rojo, coloradito, amarillo, verde, chichilo,* and *manchamantel.*

MEZCAL

Mezcal is a growth "industry" right now in Oaxaca—witness the countless acres of agave you see growing practically everywhere outside the city limits, and the countless brands of *mezcal* on display in stores all over town. Trying to figure out which *mezcal* you like, or might want to take home, can be daunting. A few facts might help: most *mezcal* is made from Espadin, a specific type of agave (although other agaves get in the mix, which never happens with tequila), and like tequila it is served *blanco* (white or young), *reposado* (rested), or *añejo* (aged). But you can get *mezcals* made from other types of agaves, even wild ones. It is usually drunk straight up with a slice of orange and *sal gusano* (salt with chile and ground-up worms—trust me, it's very tasty!) on

Oaxacans drink *mezcal* with *sal gusano* and orange slices.

the side, but many bartenders are beginning to mix it up. Just go to any bar in Oaxaca and try a few rounds. Most have plenty of brands on the shelf.

Some favorite *mezcal* stops in Oaxaca City include **Mezcaleria Los Amantes** and **La Biznaga,** or park yourself at the late-night hot spot **Café Central** if Los Amantes is too small and sedate for your taste. But, there are dozens and dozens of *mezcals* available in every bar in Oaxaca City, and at countless stores and distilleries in small towns and in the countryside. As for which are the best there are many opinions. There are plenty of great *mezcals* to sample, the best invariably being small batch, artisanal brands, such as **Mezcal Unión, Yuu Baal** (made from wild agave), **Los Siete Misterios,** or **Pierde Almas.**

Avoid the major labels. Mass production and *mezcal* don't mix. Your best bet is not so much to shop around as to sip around. Sample your way to the ones you like, find out where to get them, and pick up a few bottles. Every sip you take back home will deliver Oaxaca back into your heart.

the offing at **Restaurant La Toscana** or **Casa Oaxaca.** There are several late night bars and clubs within strolling distance of Casa Oaxaca. Follow the sound of music.

DAYS 8-9

Head east on an overnight journey. En route, stop to admire the enormous tree at **Santa María del Tule,** with its pretty adjacent church and topiary-festooned plaza. Continue east; archaeology buffs will want to make time for a stop at **Dainzu** or **Lambityeco,** or head to **Tlacolula,** where the Sunday market will be in full swing and the *mezcal* will be flowing.

At this point, there are three or four more places you'll want to visit; you can try to cram them all in, or you can take it easy, and meander up to **Hierve El Agua,** and after touring the site, spend the night at the ecotourism *cabañas* on site. The next day, visit **Mitla,** an impressive archaeological site, which is a must on all itineraries. Here you can spend at least an hour or

three before stopping at **Restaurant La Choza** for a buffet lunch.

In the afternoon, visit the rug-weaving towns of **Teotitlán del Valle** and **Santa Ana del Valle,** where you can see carpets being made using age-old methods and organic dyes. You can also buy them from the people that make them. There are good community museums in both towns. At the end of the day, head back to Oaxaca City for one last night, with a quiet dinner at **Café La Olla.**

The Isthmus and the Pacific Coast

After all this cultural immersion and shopping, it's time to hit the beach. Highway 190 will take you from Oaxaca City to Tehuántepec in roughly 5-6 hours. Or you can take a half-hour flight to Huatulco or Puerto Escondido.

DAY 10: TEHUÁNTEPEC

Even if you've been driving for six hours, take a

Mitla, Valley of Oaxaca

little time to visit the **Tehuántepec Market,** ruled by women, most of them dressed in elegant and colorful traditional garb. You can't miss the enormous *La Tejuana* sculpture as you come into town; after dark, go back for another look, the lighting is striking. Take a stroll around town, dine at **Restaurant Scaru,** and spend the night at **Hotel Guiexhoba.**

DAYS 11-13: SALINA CRUZ TO HUATULCO TO PUERTO ÁNGEL
Surfers will want to find their surf camp in **Salina Cruz,** dial into the waves, and stay a few days riding local waves before heading up to **Barra de la Cruz** and **Huatulco.**

Non-surfers will want to check out Huatulco; if you're into luxe, find a beachfront hotel at **Bahía Tangolunda** and chill. If you want to leave the high end for a slightly more rustic experience, continue up to **Puerto Ángel** and find the low-budget beach hotel of your dreams.

Visit the **Centro Mexicano de la Tortuga** at **Playa Mazunte,** the protected lagoon with crocodiles at **Playa La Ventanilla,** or head up into the hills to visit the magic mushroom town of **San José del Pacífico.**

DAYS 14-15: PUERTO ESCONDIDO
Eventually everybody ends up in **Puerto Escondido,** where surfers take on the monster waves, and everybody else watches the drama. But there are great beginner and intermediate waves in the area at **La Punta** and **Carrizalillo,** excellent **bird-watching lagoons** at **Chacahua** and **Manialtepec, coffee farms** and **ecological adventures** to pursue, and, even **rivers** to run in season.

After all this excitement, fly back to Oaxaca City, or if you are in a car, take one of the two mountain roads that connect Puerto Escondido (Route 131) and Puerto Ángel (Route 175) with Oaxaca City. Either way, you'll climb way high into the Sierra and witness some stunning scenery en route back to Oaxaca City.

Ecotourism Lodges

Cabañas ecoturísticas offer a unique opportunity for visitors weary of the tourist rush who desire more contact with local people and Oaxaca's unique mountain cultures. Many of the participating communities produce fine handicrafts and enjoy scenic, wildlife-rich locations. For modest fees, these local communities furnish guides who lead visitors along scenic trails, past springs, caves, meadows, and mountain vistas, identifying useful plants and animals along the way. Some communities rent mountain bikes and offer instruction in rappelling and rock climbing and other outdoor diversions.

Given the city and valley's wealth of cultural attractions, and that endless sunshine coast, it can be easy to overlook the natural beauty of Oaxaca's mountainous regions. Those who take the time to explore the more rugged side of Oaxaca will be amazed and impressed at the state's seemingly endless expanses of mountainous forests and jungles. Relatively few people take to the hills in Oaxaca; in many regions, you can hike or bike all day and not see a soul other than those you're traveling with. What adds to the appeal is the diversity of options, ranging from relatively easy roadside *cabañas* to lodges deep in the hills, reachable only by long days' hikes or mountain bike rides. You can get a taste of these deep and endless mountains just by taking a drive from Oaxaca City a couple of hours in almost any direction.

The **Oaxaca Federal-State Department of Tourism (SEDETUR)** first built tourist cabin complexes on the east side of the Valley of Oaxaca during the 1990s. Although five of the original nine are not being used, several more *cabañas ecoturísticas* have been built, mostly in Northern Oaxaca and the Mixteca, raising the total to about 14 operating complexes. About two dozen Oaxaca communities now invite visitors to stay in their community tourist lodging.

The *cabañas* are government constructed but locally managed, modern but usually rustic. Each bungalow typically sleeps four, with private hot-water shower-baths and toilet, and perhaps a kitchenette. The following are the locales for the best *cabañas ecoturísticas* and their highlights.

The Valley of Oaxaca

Santa Ana del Valle: Master weavers' shops, museum, lake, scenic views, hikes.

San Sebastián de las Grutas: Limestone caves, hikes, riverside picnicking, groves of grand old *sabino* trees.

Hierve El Agua: Hikes, scenic vistas, mineral springs, frozen stone cascades.

The Mixteca

Apoala: Idyllic village, wild canyon, cave, cascade, springs, camping.

Yosocuta: Reservoir, boating, fishing, RV and tent camping.

San Martín Huamelulpan: Ruined city, museum, hikes to other archaeological sites.

San Miguel Tequixtepec: Museum, hike to hieroglyphic rock paintings, palm weaving, restored 17th-century church.

Northern Oaxaca

Ixtlán de Juárez: Cloud forest, wildlife-viewing, Benito Juárez's birthplace and museum, limestone cave.

Santa Catarina Ixtepeji: Hiking trails, campground, colonial-era church.

Benito Juárez: Cool pine-scented air, camping, panoramic views.

Cuajimoloyas: Mountain-top village, hiking, rock climbing.

Llano Grande: Woodland hikes, wildflowers.

Valle Nacional, Balnearios Monte Flor: Forest picnicking, kayaking, swimming in natural spring.

Reservations

Two agencies handle reservations for most of the *cabañas*. The **Oaxaca state ecotourism** (703 Av. Juárez, tel./fax 951/516-0123, www.aoaxaca. com) reserves Santa Ana del Valle, Hierve El

Oaxacan weaver

Tianguis: Native Markets

Most important Oaxaca towns have a public outdoor market every day, but a *tianguis* (tee-AHN-gees) only once a week. The word *tianguis* is an ancient native expression, synonymous with "awning," the colorful tarpaulins that shade the mini-mountains of fruits, vegetables, crafts, and merchandise. Native people flock to *tianguis* everywhere in Oaxaca to buy and sell.

Although trade appears to be the prime mover, people really come to *tianguis* for human contact, not only in the buying and selling itself, but for gossip, entertainment, flirtation—all of the other diversions that make life worth living.

OAXACA CITY

- Abastos: Saturday
- Juárez: every day

THE VALLEY OF OAXACA

- Tlacolula: Sunday
- Etla: Wednesday
- Ejutla: Thursday
- Zaachila: Thursday
- Ocotlán: Friday

PACIFIC RESORTS AND SOUTHERN SIERRA

- Juquila: Friday, Saturday, and Sunday
- Pinotepa Nacional: Monday
- Pochutla: Monday
- Jamiltepec: Thursday

THE MIXTECA

- Nochixtlán: Sunday
- Yosundua: Sunday
- Putla: Sunday
- Huajuapan: Wednesday, Saturday
- Tamazulapan: Wednesday
- Chalcatongo: Thursday

- Juxtlahuaca: Thursday, biggest on Friday
- Tonalá: Friday
- Tlaxiaco: Saturday

NORTHERN OAXACA

- Cuicatlán: Saturday and Sunday
- Huautla: Sunday
- Ixtlán de Juárez: Sunday
- Tuxtepec: Sunday
- Valle Nacional: Sunday
- Teotitlán del Camino: Wednesday and Sunday
- Jalapa de Díaz: Thursday and Sunday

THE ISTHMUS

- Juchitán: every day
- Salina Cruz: every day
- Tehuántepec: Wednesday and Sunday

Agua, Ixtlán de Juárez, Santa Catarina Ixtepeji, Apoala, and Yosundua. They also publish an informative *Guía Ecoturística* (Ecotourism Guidebook), written in Spanish.

The other reservations agency, **Expediciones Sierra Norte** (M. Bravo 210, tel./fax 951/514-8271, www.sierranorte.org.mx), handles *cabaña* reservations for the several communities collectively organized as the **Pueblos Mancomunados:** Benito Juárez, Cuajimoloyas, and Llano Grande, and three neighboring communities, Santa Catarina Lachatao, La Guacamaya, and San Miguel Amatlan.

You can also make the reservations yourself, by phone (in Spanish), or email. Even without a prior reservation, you can nearly always rent a *cabaña* if you arrive by 5pm or 6pm (especially on non-holiday weekdays).

Outdoor Adventures

Oaxaca abounds with outdoor adventures, from the extreme challenge of wave-riding at Puerto Escondido to the relaxing activity of lounging by a natural spring swimming pool at El Zuzul in northern Oaxaca. Those in search of outdoor action will find hiking, climbing, kayaking, rafting, fishing, caving, bird-watching, surfing, and much more all over the state of Oaxaca. Get out and go for it.

Hiking, Biking, and Horseback Riding

In Oaxaca City, walk uphill to the top of breezy **Cerro del Fortín,** or, at **Hierve El Agua** in the Valley of Oaxaca (best by tour), follow the *sendero peatonal* (footpath) that circuits the entire fascinating site. From outposts and guest ranches like **Rancho Pitaya** in Tlacolula Valley, take an overnight horseback ride into the Sierra Madre— or a leisurely half-day ride around in the valley. Make arrangements at their office in Oaxaca City.

waterfalls at Las Regaderas, near Huautla

There are dozens of great surf spots along Oaxaca's coast. The Oaxacan town that has long been synonymous with surfing is **Puerto Escondido** because of its great surfing spot Playa Zicatela. In summer, which is low season for tourism in most of Oaxaca, the south-facing beaches of Oaxaca's coast are swamped with swells. Getting good waves in Oaxaca in the summertime is close to a sure thing.

From the east to the far western border, here are a few (by no means all) of the best Oaxacan surfing options:

- **Chacahua:** By the jetty on the beach near the national park of Laguna Chacahua, this great right point break has long been ridden by locals and a few lucky vagabond surfers (page 177).

The Oaxacan Coast has some of the best surfing spots in Mexico.

- **Carrizalillo:** On the west side of Puerto Escondido, this gorgeous little bay has an excellent beginner's wave on its east side, and a more challenging wave on its west side. This right side break is a locals' wave, so don't ride it if there are more than a few people in the water (page 158).

- **Playa Zicatela:** Puerto Escondido is home to one of the most challenging waves in the surfing world, comparable in energy and danger to the Pipeline on Oahu's north shore. At the east end of Zicatela, three miles down the beach, find **La Punta,** a lefthander off a rocky point that can get big but is usually smaller and far less intimidating than the main break of Zicatela (page 157).

- **Playa Zipolite:** By Puerto Ángel, this lovely stretch of sand serves up a macking beach break that can be deceptively powerful. Beginners beware. Don't take a lesson or paddle out unless you know what you're doing or the waves are small. Watch out for riptides (page 113).

- **La Joya:** On Barra de la Cruz's beach, 15 minutes east of Huatulco, a rocky headland forms a point break, but the bottom is sand, and on a good day this is one of the longest, fastest tubes in the Americas, if not the world (page 137).

- **Between Barra de la Cruz and Salina Cruz:** There are at least half-a-dozen excellent surf spots here—some beach breaks, some point breaks. To access these breaks, such as **Punta Chivo** and **Punta Conejo,** you'll likely require local knowledge, four-wheel-drive vehicles, and/or the services of a surf camp/surf safari guide. There are several of these guides and camps in and around Salina Cruz, and at least one—Café Surf—in Huatulco (page 259).

In Huatulco, follow the forest paths to **Bahía El Organo** and **Bahía Cacaluta,** hike or ride horseback along the **Río Copalita,** or hike to the coffee farm downhill from **Pluma Hidalgo.**

The Mixteca abounds with unforgettable walks. For example, in **Apoala,** follow the spectacular trail into the gorge of **Las Dos Peñas Colosales** to the hidden valley of the **La Peña Donde Murió El Aguila con Dos Cabezas.**

Oaxaca's northern mountains offer plenty of hiking and mountain biking, beginning not far from Oaxaca City, around the pine-scented **Benito Juárez, Cuajimoloyas,** and **Ixtlán de Juárez** villages. There are adventure companies offering multi-day camping, hiking, and mountain biking holidays that start near Oaxaca City and end all the way on the other side of the mountains, at Puerto Escondido. There are half-day rides, four-day rides, and plenty in-between for the serious biker or the occasional rider.

River Rafting and Kayaking

When the water conditions are right (usually in the fall), outfitters take parties for rafting on the **Río Copalita** near Huatulco. A number of other coastal rivers, notably (moving from east to west) the **Ríos Zimatán, Colotepec, Verde,** and **Arena,** appear negotiable during the fall and early winter seasons for skilled rafters and kayakers with their own equipment.

Fishing

Fish thrive all along Pacific Oaxaca. From the beach or shoreline rocks, pluck them out of the surf with a net or rod and tackle at Huatulco's **Bahía Chahue,** at the **Bahía Puerto Ángel,** and at **Bahía Carrizalillo** near Puerto Escondido. For deep-sea fishing, either launch your own boat or rent a launch in Huatulco, Puerto Ángel, or Puerto Escondido. You can also rent a fully equipped fishing boat at either Huatulco or Puerto Escondido.

If you prefer to go after freshwater fish, such as *mojarra* (bass) or tilapia, launch at either **Yosocuta Reservoir** in the Mixteca or **Temascal** reservoir in northern Oaxaca.

a hiker at Hierve El Aqua, Valley of Oaxaca

Playa Zicatela, Puerto Escondido

Caverns, Waterfalls, and Natural Springs

In the Valley of Oaxaca, start your exploring at the limestone cavern complex near **San Sebastián de las Grutas** down Highway 131, south of Zimatlán.

Around the Mixteca, visit **Apoala** to explore the limestone cavern, natural spring, and waterfall.

In northern Oaxaca and on the Isthmus, most spectacular are the crystalline springs **Monte Flor** and **El Zuzul** and the limestone cavern **Nindo-Da-Gé**, near Huautla de Jiménez.

Kayaking

At Huatulco, for easy bay boating or kayaking, start out from the sheltered **Bahía Chahue marina** with your own boat or by kayak from **Playa Entrega** in the Bahía Santa Cruz or the beach at **Bahía El Maguey.** More challenging kayaking opportunities abound in the less-sheltered Huatulco bays of **El Organo, Cacaluta,** and **San Agustín.** Near Puerto Escondido, easy boating or kayaking is possible from the landings at **Las Hamacas, La Alejandria,** or **Isla El Gallo** in Laguna Manialtepec.

Surfing and Stand-Up Paddleboarding

Puerto Escondido has been a destination for world-class surfers for a couple of decades now. They are drawn to the powerful, even dangerous beach break barrels that have made this surf spot famous. However, in more recent years a dozen other breaks, none quite so heavy as Puerto but several featuring world-class waves, have been "discovered" in Oaxaca. Surf camps and safaris are now on offer, primarily from the Salina Cruz area, to several of these high-quality, as-yet-uncrowded surfing breaks. Among the top choices are **Chacahua, Punta Conejo,** and **Barra de la Cruz.** There are also beginner-friendly waves, and surf instructors, at **Carrizalillo** in Puerto Escondido. In **Santa Cruz de Huatulco,** paddleboards and paddling instructors are available for tours and lessons.

Best Beaches

Playa Bachoco, Puerto Escondido

BEST OVERALL

- Playa San Agustinillo (Puerto Ángel, page 114)
- Playa Entrega (Bahías de Huatulco, page 135)
- Playa Manzanillo (Puerto Escondido, page 158)

BEST SURF-FISHING

- Bahía Chahue (Bahías de Huatulco, page 133)
- Playa Bachoco (Puerto Escondido, page 158)

BEST SNORKELING

- Playa Estacahuite (Puerto Ángel, page 113)
- Playa Manzanillo (Puerto Escondido, page 158)

BEST SURFING

- Playa Zipolite (Puerto Ángel, page 113)
- Playa Zicatela (Puerto Escondido, page 157)
- Punta Conejo (Salina Cruz, page 260)
- Barra de la Cruz (Bahías de Huatulco, page 137)

BEST SUNSETS

- Playa Zipolite (Puerto Ángel, page 113)
- Playa La Ventanilla (Puerto Ángel and vicinity, page 117)

- Bahía Tangolunda (Bahías de Huatulco, page 133)
- Playa Zicatela (Puerto Escondido, page 157)

BEST FOR KIDS

- Playa Panteón (Puerto Ángel, page 113)
- Bahía El Maguey (Bahías de Huatulco, page 137)
- Playa Principal (Puerto Escondido, page 157)

BEST FOR CAMPING

- Playa Zipolite (Puerto Ángel, page 113)
- El Playon at Bahía San Agustín (Bahías de Huatulco, page 138)

MOST PRISTINE

- Playa La Ventanilla (Puerto Ángel, page 117)
- Bahía Chachacual (Bahías de Huatulco, page 138)
- Bahía Carrizalillo (Puerto Escondido, page 158)

MOST INTIMATE

- Bahía El Organo (Bahías de Huatulco, page 136)
- Bahía Carrizalillo (Puerto Escondido, page 158)

MOST SPECTACULAR

- Bahía Cacaluta (Bahías de Huatulco, page 138)

Oaxaca City

Look for ★ to find recommended sights, activities, dining, and lodging.

Highlights

© AVALON TRAVEL

★ **Basilica de Nuestra Señora de la Soledad:** Five pounds of gold and 600 diamonds crown Oaxaca's adored patron, and a fascinating adjacent museum preserves her beloved legacy (page 38).

★ **Andador Macedonio Alcalá:** In the blocks surrounding the junction of the pedestrian promenade and Centro Cultural, dozens of great new bars, restaurants, galleries, and all manner of unique retail stores have opened, turning this area into the city's most vibrant neighborhood for visitors (page 38).

★ **Ex-Convento de Santa Catalina:** Wander the tranquil inner courtyards of this richly restored ex-convent, now a distinguished hotel (page 40).

★ **Centro Cultural de Santo Domingo:** Explore the celebrated duo: the art-swathed Iglesia y Ex-Convento de Santo Domingo and the adjacent Museo de las Culturas de Oaxaca, with its golden treasure of Monte Albán's Tomb 7 (page 40).

★ **Los Arquitos:** The original 18th-century aqueduct still stands in Oaxaca City's uptown northwest corner, in a quaint string of arches. The surrounding neighborhood is ripe for strolling winding village lanes and lingering at a sprinkling of shops, small cafés, and an all-natural Saturday food market (page 42).

★ **MARO:** Do a major part of your Oaxaca handicrafts shopping at this store, run by a remarkable group of native Oaxacan women artisans (page 50).

★ **Mercado Juárez:** A regiment of stalls offers the best traditional Oaxaca merchandise, from *huipiles* to mountain-gathered remedies and spit-roasted chickens (page 35).

★ **Catedral de Oaxaca:** The restored facade and the inner chapel, which enshrines one of the four replicas of the Holy Cross of Huatulco, highlight a visit to this plaza-front gem (page 37).

The city of Oaxaca (wah-HAH-kah; pop. 400,000, elev. 1,778 meters/5,110 feet) is both the governmental capital of Mexico's fifth-largest state by area (about tenth largest by population) and the de facto capital of Mexico's southern indigenous heartland. And Oaxaca is southern indeed. It lies farther south than all of Mexico's state capitals save one, Tuxtla Gutiérrez, the capital of Chiapas. Oaxaca nestles in a temperate highland valley, blessed with a year-round balmy, spring-like climate, prized by both residents and visitors.

Every year, starting in mid-July, Oaxaca City becomes the focus of the extraordinary diversity of its entire state. In the celebrated Guelaguetza (gay-lah-GAY-tzah; The Giving) festival, indigenous Oaxaca people, speaking 16 unique languages and representing hundreds of Oaxaca's ethnic groups, converge in the city for a grand two-week party of food, dancing, music, and general merrymaking.

The Guelaguetza, like virtually all of Oaxaca's civic revelries, starts at the *zócalo* (central plaza), ringed by relaxing sidewalk cafés and bordered by the porticoed Palacio de Gobierno on its south side and the distinguished baroque bulk of the Catedral de Oaxaca on its north side.

With some exceptions, this north side of Oaxaca City is more welcoming and exciting to tourists and locals alike, with most of the better new restaurants, stores, and bars located "uptown," along the pedestrian walkway known as the Andador Macedonio Alcalá (hereafter referred to as the Alcalá) and other streets such as Allende, García Vigil, and Bravo. There is plenty to do farther south, for that is where the city's great traditional markets can be found, but uptown is where most of the younger Oaxacans like to spend their time.

From the *zócalo,* the city's street grid spreads south past the town's vibrant pair of central markets, the Mercado Juárez and the Mercado San Juan de Dios, and north, uphill, along the Alcalá. The walkway connects the *zócalo* with Oaxaca's uptown monuments, most notably Oaxaca's jewel, the Centro

---

Previous: facade of Catedral de Oaxaca; Santo Domingo cathedral and plaza. **Above:** Museo de las Culturas de Oaxaca.

Oaxaca City

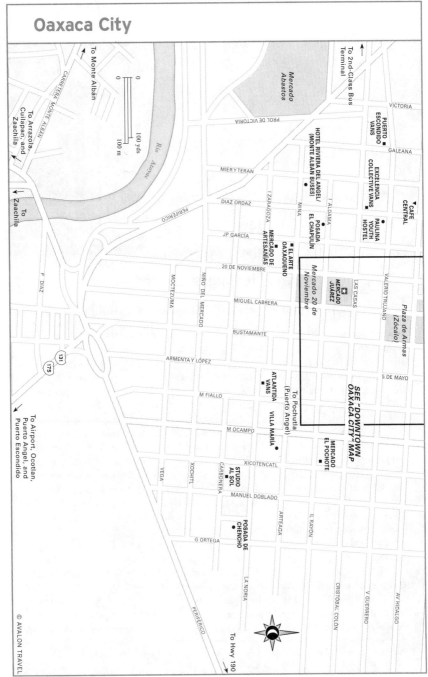

© AVALON TRAVEL

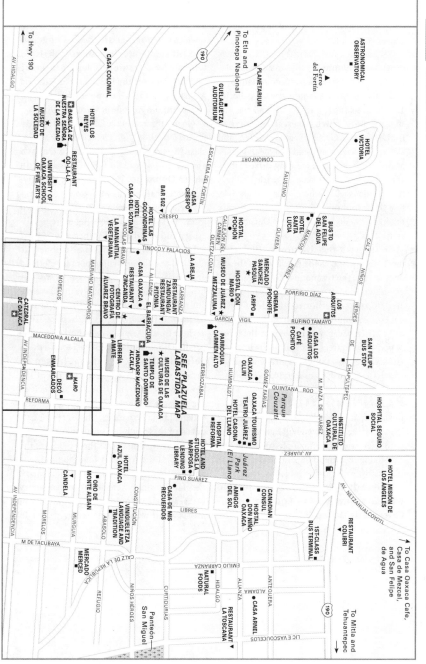

SEE "PLAZUELA LABASTIDA" MAP

Cultural de Santo Domingo, made up of the Iglesia y Ex-Convento de Santo Domingo and the adjacent magnificent Museo de las Culturas de Oaxaca.

Where Andador Macedonio Alcalá meets the Centro Cultural, a lively street life has developed, with dozens of bars and restaurants, and a number of contemporary art galleries and stores selling fine crafts from all over the state, beautiful jewelry, *mezcal* from myriad individual distilleries, organic coffee, and clothes, especially high-end designer fashions. Many of the designers creating these clothes synthesize colorful Oaxacan fabric and textile traditions with contemporary urban style. For those looking for a hip and lively mix of old and new Oaxaca—call it Oaxacan fusion—this is ground zero.

To the west, the city streets climb even more steeply, and as the Guelaguetza throng does in July, the westbound streets reach the grand outdoor dance stage and amphitheater atop Oaxaca's storied hillside of Cerro del Fortín. This hill, originally known as the hill of Huaxyacac, was named for the forest of pod-bearing trees that still covers its slope. Huaxyacac was the city's original name, which the Spanish transliterated as Oaxaca.

PLANNING YOUR TIME

In about four fairly relaxed days, you can take in most of the downtown highlights. Start out with a leisurely day of people-watching and café-lounging around the old *zócalo*. Explore the nearby Palacio de Gobierno, the colorful Mercado Juárez, the baroque Templo y Ex-Convento de San Agustín, and the Catedral de Oaxaca.

Spend your second day in the multitude of shops along the Andador Macedonio Alcalá, at the Museo de Arte Contemporaneo, and in the Ex-Convento de Santa Catalina, now restored as the Hotel Camino Real. Be sure to enjoy lunch on the relaxing patios of the Danzantes or Hostería Alcalá restaurants. Or try one of the great new restaurants on Allende or García Vigil.

On day three, visit the Centro Cultural de Santo Domingo, which includes the world-class Museo de las Culturas de Oaxaca and the lovely Iglesia y Ex-Convento de Santo Domingo. Have a look at the adjacent botanical gardens while you're upstairs.

Spend your fourth day following your own interests, such as investigating more handicrafts and retail stores, especially MARO (Mujeres Artesanías de las Regiones de Oaxaca) and the new contemporary clothing and textile stores along Cinco de Mayo; visiting small museums, notably, the Casa de Juárez and the Museo Arte Prehispánico de Rufino Tamayo; or taking in sights, such as the intimate Arquitos neighborhood or the gemlike Basilica de Nuestra Señora de la Soledad and adjacent museum, Museo de la Soledad. Alternately, visit some of the newer contemporary art galleries, such as the Galería 910 Arte Contemporaneo and Galería Linda Fernandez. There are at least a dozen of these galleries open now, and most of them are within two or three blocks of the junction of the Andador Macedonio Alcalá and the Centro Cultural. For the most part, they are showing art created by contemporary Oaxacan artists, and there are a number of artists whose work is worth seeing.

Sights

ORIENTATION

The streets of Oaxaca still run along the same simple north-south grid the city founders laid out in 1529. If you stand at the center of the old zócalo and look out toward the *catedral* across Avenida Hidalgo, you will be looking north. Diagonally left, to the northwest, you'll see the smaller plaza, **Alameda de León,** and directly beyond that, in the distance, the historic hill of Huaxyacac, now called **Cerro del Fortín.** Along the base of Cerro del Fortín, the Pan American Highway (National Highway 190) runs generally east-west through the northern suburbs.

Turn around—we're still standing in the zócalo—and you'll see the porticoed facade of the former **Palacio de Gobierno,** now a museum. This main entry side of the palacio has been occupied by radical unionists for years—their banners and billboards have taken on a wearily permanent look—but everybody has learned to live with them. If you find a clear vantage point, you'll see the hill of **Monte Albán** looming above the southwest horizon.

The venerable restored downtown buildings and streets, some converted to traffic-free promenades, make a delightful strolling ground for discovering traditional Mexico at its best. The shady old *zócalo,* officially called Jardín Juárez, basks at the heart of it all, a perfect place for taking a seat at one of many sidewalk cafés and watching the world glide by. Its portals, clockwise from the west side, are named Flores, Clavería, Juárez, and Mercaderes.

It is useful to know that almost all of the streets running east-west, and most of the north-south ones as well, change their names as they cross major arteries. For example, Calle Constitución in the northwest quadrant of downtown turns into Calle Allende as it crosses the Alcalá. And north-south Porfirio Díaz becomes 20 de Noviembre as it crosses Avenida Morelos. These name changes, which are not consistent in terms of where they happen, can take some getting used to.

AROUND THE ZOCALO
Palacio de Gobierno

Give the guards a cheery *"buenos días"* or *"buenas tardes"* at the temporary entrance (the long-term occupation of the front entrance by radicals is ongoing) near southwest zócalo corner, on Flores Magón, of the former statehouse-now-museum **Palacio de Gobierno** (south side of the zócalo, 951/501-1662, 10am-7pm Mon.-Sat., 10am-5pm Sun., $2), and step inside. City fathers first built a city hall on the same site in 1576. Repeated earthquakes led to reconstructions, until 1948, when the present building, a modernized and strengthened version of the previous 1884 structure, was finished.

Inside, you'll find a beautifully renovated museum, highlighted by dramatic historic murals by Arturo Bustos in the stairwell area, and an excellent 2nd-floor science and natural history sub-museum. In the center of the Bustos mural is Oaxaca's favorite son and Mexico's revered *presidente,* Benito Juárez, and his wife, Margarita Maza.

★ Mercado Juárez

The traditional **Juárez market** (most shops open by 8am and close by 6pm daily) occupies the one-block square that begins just one block south and one block west of the zócalo. Dozens of stalls offer traditional Oaxaca merchandise—such as dresses, *huipiles,* woven blankets, serapes, and herbs.

While at the market, be sure to step to the southwest corner of 20 de Noviembre and Rayón for a history lesson in art inside the **Templo y Ex-Convento de San Juan de Dios,** which stands on the site of Oaxaca's oldest church. The present structure, completed in 1703, replaced the former earthquake-damaged 1535 town cathedral, which

Downtown Oaxaca City

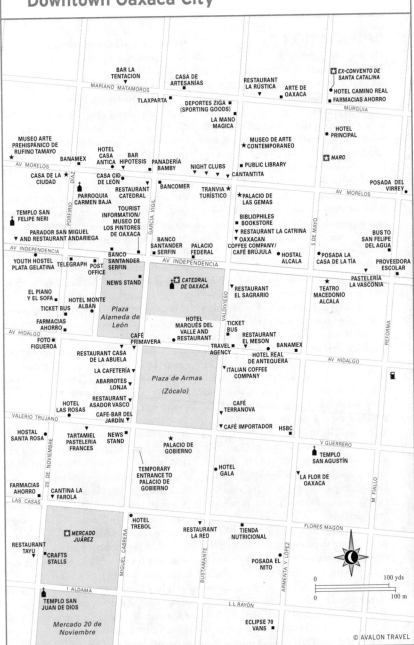

BAR LA TENTACION
MARIANO MATAMOROS
CASA DE ARTESANÍAS
RESTAURANT LA RÚSTICA
ARTE DE OAXACA
EX-CONVENTO DE SANTA CATALINA
HOTEL CAMINO REAL
FARMACIAS AHORRO
MURGUIA

TLAXPARTA
DEPORTES ZIGA (SPORTING GOODS)
LA MANO MAGICA

HOTEL PRINCIPAL

MUSEO ARTE PREHISPÁNICO DE RUFINO TAMAYO
BANAMEX
HOTEL CASA ANTICA
BAR HIPOTESIS
PANADERÍA BAMBY
NIGHT CLUBS
MUSEO DE ARTE CONTEMPORANEO
PUBLIC LIBRARY
MARO

AV MORELOS
CANTANTITA

CASA DE LA CIUDAD
CASA CID DE LEÓN
RESTAURANT CATEDRAL
BANCOMER
TRANVIA TURÍSTICO
PALACIO DE LAS GEMAS
POSADA DEL VIRREY

PARROQUIA CARMEN BAJA
AV MORELOS

PORFIRIO DÍAZ

TEMPLO SAN FELIPE NERI
TOURIST INFORMATION/ MUSEO DE LOS PINTORES DE OAXACA
BIBLIOPHILES BOOKSTORE
RESTAURANT LA CATRINA
BUS TO SAN FELIPE DEL AGUA

PARADOR SAN MIGUEL AND RESTAURANT ANDARIEGA
BANCO SANTANDER SERFIN
PALACIO FEDERAL
OAXACAN COFFEE COMPANY/ CAFÉ BRÚJULA
HOSTAL ALCALÁ
POSADA LA CASA DE LA TÍA
PROVEEDORA ESCOLAR

AV INDEPENDENCIA
BANCO SANTANDER SERFIN
AV INDEPENDENCIA

GARCIA VIGIL

5 DE MAYO

YOUTH HOSTEL PLATA GELATINA
TELEGRAPH
POST OFFICE
NEWS STAND
PASTELERÍA LA VASCONIA

CATEDRAL DE OAXACA
RESTAURANT EL SAGRARIO
TEATRO MACEDONIO ALCALA

EL PIANO Y EL SOFA
HOTEL MONTE ALBÁN
Plaza Alameda de León
VALDIVIESO

TICKET BUS
FARMACIAS AHORRO
CAFÉ PRIMAVERA
HOTEL MARQUÉS DEL VALLE AND RESTAURANT
TICKET BUS
RESTAURANT EL MESON
BANAMEX

AV HIDALGO
AV HIDALGO

FOTO FIGUEROA
RESTAURANT CASA DE LA ABUELA
TRAVEL AGENCY
HOTEL REAL DE ANTEQUERA
ITALIAN COFFEE COMPANY

REFORMA

LA CAFETERÍA
ABARROTES LONJA
Plaza de Armas (Zócalo)

HOTEL LAS ROSAS
RESTAURANT ASADOR VASCO
CAFÉ TERRANOVA

VALERIO TRUJANO
CAFE-BAR DEL JARDÍN
CAFÉ IMPORTADOR
HSBC

HOSTAL SANTA ROSA
TARTAMIEL PASTELERIA FRANCES
NEWS STAND
PALACIO DE GOBIERNO
V GUERRERO
TEMPLO SAN AGUSTÍN

20 DE NOVIEMBRE

FARMACIAS AHORRO
CANTINA LA FAROLA
TEMPORARY ENTRANCE TO PALACIO DE GOBIERNO
HOTEL GALA
LA FLOR DE OAXACA

LAS CASAS

M FIALLO

HOTEL TREBOL
RESTAURANT LA RED
TIENDA NUTRICIONAL
FLORES MAGON

MERCADO JUÁREZ

MIGUEL CABRERA

RESTAURANT TAYU
CRAFTS STALLS
POSADA EL NITO

BUSTAMANTE

ARMENTA Y LÓPEZ

0   100 yds
0   100 m

I ALDAMA
TEMPLO SAN JUAN DE DIOS

Mercado 20 de Noviembre
ECLIPSE 70 VANS
L L RAYÓN

© AVALON TRAVEL

itself replaced the original 1521 adobe structure. Large, luminous paintings lining the nave walls depict landmarks in Oaxaca's religious history.

Templo y Ex-Convento de San Agustín

Off-*zócalo* side streets are studded with Oaxaca's old church gems. One of the most precious and most accessible is the San Agustín church and ex-convent (on Calle Guerrero), one block due east from the Palacio de Gobierno. One of the few Oaxacan works of the Augustinian order, the original adobe church on this site was finished in 1596, but it was seriously damaged by subsequent earthquakes. The present church, finished in 1722, replaced the original.

★ Catedral de Oaxaca

Return to the *zócalo*'s north side for a look at the present cathedral. It replaced the 1550 original, demolished by an earthquake in 1696. Finished in 1733, the present cathedral is distinguished by its Greek-marble main altar, where a polished Italian bronze Virgin of the Ascension is being drawn upward to the cloud-tipped heavenly domain of the Holy Spirit (the dove) and God (the sunburst).

Of considerable historical interest is the Santa Cruz de Huatulco (Holy Cross of Huatulco), enshrined in a chapel at the middle, south (right) side of the nave. The cross, about two feet high, in the glass case atop the chapel altar, is one of four made in 1612 by Oaxaca bishop Juan Cervantes from the original mysterious cross worshipped by the natives on the southern Oaxaca coast long before the conquest. An explanation, in Spanish, gives three versions of the story of the cross, which, as the natives reported to the conqueror Pedro Alvarado in 1522, was erected long before by a strange, white-robed holy man who soon departed and never returned. Bishop Cervantes sent the three other copies of the cross, respectively, to authorities at Santa María Huatulco municipality, Mexico City, and Rome.

NORTHWEST OF THE *ZÓCALO*

Templo de San Felipe Neri

Just two blocks west of Catedral de Oaxaca rises the distinguished facade of the Templo de San Felipe Neri (on Independencia, corner of Tinoco and Palacios, open for worship 8am-11pm daily). The building is immediately notable, for it faces south, unlike the great

herbal remedies for sale, Mercado Juárez

majority of Oaxaca's churches, which follow tradition and face west.

Its builders finished the structure, once a convent of the order of San Felipe Neri, and dedicated it to the Virgin of Patrocinio in 1773. The subsequent 1795 earthquake caused extensive damage, which was not completely repaired until the 20th century. Unfortunately, more earthquakes, in 1928 and 1931, inflicted additional destruction. The present restoration was completed in 1985.

Museo Arte Prehispánico de Rufino Tamayo

Just one block farther north, **Museo Arte Prehispánico de Rufino Tamayo** (503 Morelos, tel. 951/516-4750, 10am-2pm and 4pm-7pm Mon. and Wed.-Sat., 10am-3pm Sun., $3) exhibits the brilliant pre-Columbian artifact collection of celebrated artist Rufino Tamayo (1899-1991). Displays include hosts of animal motifs—Colima dogs, parrots, ducks, snakes—whimsically crafted into polychrome vases, bowls, and urns.

★ Basilica de Nuestra Señora de la Soledad

Continue three blocks west, past the University of Oaxaca School of Fine Arts and the airy Plaza of Dances, to the baroque **Basilica de Nuestra Señora de la Soledad** (Calle Morelos, at the Plaza de las Danzas, tel. 951/516-5076, 9am-2pm and 4pm-6pm daily, free admission). Inside, the Virgen de la Soledad (Virgin of Solitude), the patron of Oaxaca, stands atop the altar with her five-pound solid golden crown, encrusted with 600 diamonds.

Step into the **Museo de la Soledad** (Calle Morelos, at the Plaza de las Danzas, tel. 951/516-5076, 9am-2pm and 4pm-6pm daily, free admission) at the downhill side of the church, on the rear end. A multitude of objects of adornment, including shells, paintings, and jewelry, crowd cabinets, shelves, and aisles of musty rooms.

the Basilica de Nuestra Señora de la Soledad

★ ANDADOR MACEDONIO ALCALÁ

The **Andador Macedonio Alcalá** pedestrian mall, named after the composer of the Oaxacan hymn "Dios Nunca Muere" ("God Never Dies"), leads north from the *zócalo*. Paved with Oaxaca green stone in 1985 and freed of auto traffic one block north of the *zócalo*, the mall connects the *zócalo* with a number of not-to-be-missed Oaxaca sights.

The neighborhood around Andador Macedonio Alcalá is now home to a colorful assortment of crafts and clothing stores, bars, restaurants, and art galleries. You'll find a lineup of galleries on Calle Gurrión, by the Santa Domingo plaza, and around the corner on Cinco de Mayo. These galleries feature the work of contemporary Oaxacan artists, and much of it is world-class. However, exploring the retail clothing stores on Cinco de Mayo and the Andador itself can be even more intriguing. It is here that Oaxacan designers are reinventing the Oaxacan traditions—textiles

© AVALON TRAVEL

and styles of clothing—for contemporary women and men. There are also half a dozen great restaurants nearby, where a new wave of chefs is doing the same for food what the designers are doing for threads. There are also bars for every kind of drinker, from late-night rock and roll dives to tiny little rooms devoted to a particular, and particularly refined and flavorful, brand of *mezcal*.

Teatro Alcalá

Christened by a 1909 opening performance of *Aida*, the **Teatro Alcalá** (900 Independencia, tel. 951/516-8312 or 951/516-8344, 9am-5pm Mon.-Fri., admission free, except during events) houses a treasury of Romantic-era art. Above the foyer, a sumptuous marble staircase rises to a bas-relief medallion allegorizing the triumph of art. Inside, soaring above the

orchestra, a heavenly choir of muses, representing the arts, decorates the ceiling.

To get to the theater from the back of the Catedral de Oaxaca head right one block along Independencia to the corner of Independencia and Cinco de Mayo.

Museo de Arte Contemporaneo de Oaxaca

Continuing north along Andador Macedonio Alcalá past the bookstore (which sells some English-language history, art, and travel books), you soon reach the **Museo de Arte Contemporaneo de Oaxaca** (Macedonio Alcalá 202, tel. 951/514-1055, www.museomaco.com, 10am-6pm daily, free admission). Exhibitions feature works of local and nationally known modern artists.

For a change of pace, enjoy an airy

45-minute ride around town on the motorized trolley **Tranvia Turístico** (corner of Macedonio Alcalá and Morelos, $3 pp), which takes off hourly, half a block downhill from the Museo de Arte Contemporaneo.

★ Ex-Convento de Santa Catalina

Continue uphill and, at Murguia, detour right again, to the **Ex-Convento de Santa Catalina** (Cinco de Mayo 600, tel. 951/516-0611, public tours 5pm Tues.-Fri., free), the second-oldest women's convent in New Spain, founded in 1576. Although the quarters of the first novitiates were spare, the convent grew into a sprawling chapel and cloister complex decorated by fountains and flower-strewn gardens. Juárez's reforms drove the sisters out in 1862; the building has since served as city hall, school, and movie theater. Now it stands beautifully restored as the Hotel Camino Real. Note the native-motif original murals that the renovation revealed on interior walls.

★ Centro Cultural de Santo Domingo

Return to the Andador Macedonio Alcalá and continue another block uphill to Oaxaca's pride, the **Centro Cultural de Santo Domingo** (corner of Macedonio Alcalá and I. Allende, tel. 951/516-2991 or 951/516-3721, free admission), which contains two main parts, side by side: the Museo de las Culturas de Oaxaca and the Iglesia y Ex-Convento de Santo Domingo, both behind the broad Plaza Santo Domingo maguey garden and pedestrian square.

Inside, the **Iglesia y Ex-Convento de Santo Domingo** (7am-1pm and 5pm-8pm daily) glows with a wealth of art. Above the antechamber spreads the entire genealogical tree of Santo Domingo de Guzmán, starting with Mother Mary and weaving through a score of noblemen and women to the saint himself over the front door. Continuing inside, the soaring, Sistine Chapel-like nave glitters with saints, cherubs, and Bible-story paintings.

Next door, the **Museo de las Culturas de Oaxaca** (10am-6:15pm Tues.-Sun., admission $4, audio tour $5) occupies the completely restored convent section of the Santo Domingo church. Exhibitions begin on the bottom floor in rooms adjacent to the massive convent cloister, restored in 1998 to all of its original austere beauty. A downstairs highlight is the long-neglected but now safely preserved **Biblioteca de Francisco Burgoa,**

The Catedral de Oaxaca looms over the city's central plaza.

which you can walk right through and examine some of the more important works on display. The earliest work in the collection of 23,000 titles is a 1484 commentary on the works of Aristotle by Juan Versor.

A Museo sign points you upstairs via a glittering, restored, towering, domed chamber, adorned overhead with the Dominican founding fathers, presided over by Santo Domingo de Guzmán himself.

The museum also includes a jardín etno-botánico (ethno-botanical garden; enter at northwest corner of Reforma and Constitución, tel./fax 951/516-5325 or 951/516-7915; tours in Spanish 5pm Fri. and Sat., $5 pp; tours in English 11am Sat., $10 pp) in its big backyard. The staff conducts tours regularly and there is an announced schedule, but the schedule seems to change often. Inquire (check for the tour schedule on the door) at the ethno-botanical library at the garden entrance, two blocks behind the Santo Domingo churchfront. Visitors are not allowed to explore the gardens on their own; you have to take the tour. Or, easier, observe the garden from above, from the adjacent cultural center. There are fine views, and unless you're a botanist or determined to bond with the garden, you'll probably get enough of a look.

Small Museums

Back outside, step across the Alcalá, a few doors uphill, into the rust-colored old building now restored as the museum of the Instituto de Artes Gráficos de Oaxaca (Macedonio Alcalá 507, tel. 951/516-6980, 10am-8pm daily, free admission). Inside, displays exhibit mostly contemporary etchings, wood-block prints, and paintings by artists of both national and international renown.

Head west one block (along the Plazuela del Carmen, off the Macedonio Alcalá across from the museum) to the Casa de Juárez museum (609 García Vigil, tel. 951/516-1860, 10am-7pm Tues.-Sun., $3). The modest but beautifully restored house was the home of Juárez's benefactor, priest, and bookbinder: Father Antonio Salanueva.

Later, if you have time, return to the Santo Domingo church plaza and continue east past the church along Constitución to the Museo Filatelia de Oaxaca (Reforma 504, just uphill from the corner of Constitución, tel. 951/514-2366 or 951/514-8028, www.mufi.org.mx, 10am-8pm Tues.-Sun., $2). This elegant, little, modern museum displays the noted collection of José Cosino y Cosio—a library of international postal paraphernalia—and other postal-themed artworks. It's a surprisingly engaging institution.

the library of Franicisco Burgoa in the Museo de las Culturas de Oaxaca

Return a block and a half down Reforma and turn right at Abasolo, which, past Macedonio Alcalá, becomes M. Bravo. Continue a block to the **Centro de Fotografía Manuel Alvarez Bravo** (M. Bravo 116, corner of García Vigil, tel. 951/516-9800, 9am-8pm Wed.-Mon., free admission). Galleries display the work of both locally prominent and internationally acclaimed photographers, while instructors in classrooms conduct photography classes for children, adult beginners, and professionals.

Back downhill, at the north edge of the *zócalo* stands a regally restored colonial-era house, formerly the Oaxaca state tourism headquarters, now home to the **Museo de los Pintores Oaxaqueños** (Museum of Oaxacan Painters; corner of Independencia and García Vigil, tel. 951/516-5645, 10am-6pm Tues.-Sun., $2, free Sun.). It houses an eclectic, revolving collection of modern art on two floors around a central patio. Presently, the state *Turismo* agency maintains a tourist information desk to the left as you enter the museum.

★ LOS ARQUITOS

Long ago, Oaxaca's city founders provided for a permanent local water supply. They tapped the bountiful natural springs flowing from the mountains rising directly north of the city, topped by the towering Cerro San Felipe (elev. 3,100 meters/10,200 feet). The aqueduct they built gave rise to the name San Felipe del Agua, the foothill village where the aqueduct begins. Although now replaced by underground steel pipes, the original 18th-century aqueduct still stands, paralleling the downhill road from San Felipe and ending in a quaint string of arches, called **Los Arquitos,** in the city neighborhood several blocks northwest of Iglesia y Ex-Convento de Santo Domingo.

Walking Tour

The following is a one- or two-hour stroll through the relatively close-in Los Arquitos neighborhood.

Starting from the Santo Domingo churchfront, at the corner of Macedonio Alcalá and Allende, walk north, uphill along Macedonio Alcalá three blocks to Humboldt. Turn left and continue two blocks to busy Porfirio Díaz, where, across the street rises a towering fig tree that marks the **Mercado Sánchez Pasqua.** Continue past the tree to the entrance of the market. Inside, you'll first find dry goods, clothes,

Los Arquitos

and handicrafts shops, and then a mix of colorful fruit and vegetable stalls. Soon you'll arrive at the *fondas* (food stalls), for which Mercado Sánchez Pasqua is famous. Here you can enjoy a homestyle breakfast or a special lunch treat.

Retrace your steps back outside, across Porfirio Díaz, to Humboldt one block and turn left at García Vigil. Continue north to the corner of Calle Xolotl (show-LOH-tuhl), where García Vigil changes to Calle Rufino Tamayo. Pass (on the left, above the street), the art-film **Cinema El Pochote** (García Vigil 817, tel. 951/514-1194, films at 6pm and 8pm Tues.-Sat.).

Continue uphill along Tamayo, paralleling the arches for three blocks, until you reach busy east-west thoroughfare Calzada Niños Héroes. Don't miss the little shrine built beneath one arch, at Tamayo 802, and also the tiny café, El Pavito (The Little Peacock), beneath another. Be sure to explore some of the side lanes, such as the one opposite Tamayo 818 that heads beneath an arch and opens into a tiny plaza presided over by Archangel Gabriel.

Entertainment and Events

AROUND THE *ZÓCALO*

The Oaxaca *zócalo*, years ago relieved of traffic, is ideal ground for spontaneous or unexpected diversions, such as the young American modern dance troupe and their Oaxacan students who put on a sterling performance in the middle of the zócalo in a rainstorm in June 2014. Such events transpire all the time, I'm told. Regular concerts serenade from the *zócalo* band kiosk beginning around 6pm virtually every evening: the Oaxaca state band, Tuesday and Thursday; Marimba band, Wednesday (at 6:30pm); and the Oaxaca orchestra, Sunday. Furthermore, the Oaxaca state band also plays Wednesdays and Saturdays, at noon. (Schedules may change; verify with Oaxaca state tourism, 703 Av. Juárez, tel. 951/516-0123.)

FESTIVALS

There seems to be a festival somewhere in the Valley of Oaxaca every week of the year. Oaxaca's wide ethnic diversity explains much of the celebrating. Each of the groups celebrates its own traditions. Sixteen languages, in dozens of dialects, are spoken within the state. Authorities recognize around 500 distinct regional costumes.

The Guelaguetza

All of this ethnic ferment focuses in the city during the July **Lunes del Cerro** (Mondays on the Hill) festival, so named because it kicks off on the first Monday following July 16—the **Día de la Virgen de Carmen** (Virgin of Carmen day)—and continues for two weeks, when Oaxaca City is awash with both travelers, and native Oaxacans in costume from all seven traditional regions of the state.

This gathering was known in pre-Hispanic times as the **Guelaguetza** (gay-lah-GAY-tzah, or "offering"), a time of feasting, when tribes reunited for rituals and dancing in honor of Centeotl, the god of corn. The ceremonies, which climaxed with the sacrifice of a virgin who had been fed hallucinogenic mushrooms, were changed to tamer, mixed Christian-native rites by the Catholic Church. Lilies replaced marigolds—the flower of death—and saints sat in for the indigenous gods.

During recent times, the Guelaguetza festival has grown to include a grand crafts exposition at the *zócalo* and an agricultural fair. Festivities climax on each of the two Mondays at the Guelaguetza dance amphitheater on the Cerro del Fortín hill northwest of the city. Thousands of spectators thrill to the whirling, stomping, and swaying performances of dozens of brightly costumed troupes, which wow the crowd by throwing offerings of fruit, candy, and handicrafts from the stage.

If you're coming, bring sunglasses and a hat for shade, and make hotel reservations several months ahead of time. Hotels customarily offer packages that include tickets (about $40) for each Guelaguetza performance. Alternatively, local Ticketmaster outlets usually sell tickets, adding a fee of about $15. For more information, contact the **Oaxaca state tourist information office** (703 Av. Juárez, tel. 951/516-0123, www.aoaxaca.com, 8am-8pm daily) on the west side of El Llano park.

Note: If the first Monday after July 16 happens to fall on July 18, the anniversary of Benito Juárez's death, the first Lunes del Cerro shifts to the succeeding Monday, July 25.

On the Sunday before the first Lunes del Cerro, Oaxacans celebrate their history and culture at the Plaza de Danzas, adjacent to the Iglesia de la Virgen de la Soledad. Events include a big sound, light, and dance show and depictions in tableaux of the four periods of Oaxaca history.

If you miss the Lunes del Cerro festival, some towns and villages stage smaller Guelaguetza celebrations year-round. A number of hotels do as well, most frequently the

Hotel Monte Albán (Alameda de León 1, tel. 951/516-2777, usually 8:30pm daily, $7), adjacent to the *zócalo;* or most elaborately, the hotel **Camino Real** (Cinco de Mayo 300, tel. 951/516-0611, www.caminoreal.com/Oaxaca, 7pm Fri., $28 show with buffet, not including drinks). Also, **Restaurant Casa de Cantera** (on northside Calle Dr. Federico Armengal, at the top of Av. Porfirio Díaz, tel. 951/514-7585 or 951/514-9522, www.casadecantera.com, 9pm several nights a week, $15 pp, including a snack) has staged a popular Guelaguetza show for years.

Day of the Dead

Instead of mourning the dead, Mexicans celebrate the deceased with a holiday, **El Día de los Muertos** (The Day of the Dead), which is, in all of Mexico and especially in Oaxaca, cause for a fiesta that goes on for a week and culminates with the three days that comprise El Día de los Muertos. Some say that this holiday, which takes place from October 31 to November 2, should be called Día con los Muertos, for it is not so much that the dead are honored but rather that they come to visit.

The roots of this festival go back some 3,000 years, to an ancient Aztec festival dedicated to Mictecacihuatl, the guardian-goddess

Steps lead down from the Guelaguetza dance amphitheater into the city.

of the dead, celebrated by pre-Hispanic Mexicans during the month of August (later moved to its current dates by the Catholics, to coincide with their own holy days of All Saints Day and All Souls Day). With its relatively intact pre-Hispanic cultures, Oaxaca celebrates this mixed indigenous and Christian holiday with more fervor, solemnity, and gaiety than any other part of Mexico.

In Oaxaca City the festivities begin a week prior to November 1, when every market spills over with all the decorations, foods, and materials required for the arrival of the dead. Flowers are gathered, especially marigolds *(cempasuchil),* and then, on October 31 and the following two days, altars are constructed in homes and plazas and countless locations. These often-elaborate altars are loaded up with aromatic foods favored by the dead: Oaxacan mole, corn jelly *(nicuatole),* pumpkin with black sugar, stone ground chocolate, and the sweet bread of the dead *(pan de muerto).* Fruits are also heaped on the altars. Candles are placed and lit, and marigolds are added as the final decorative touch, all over the altars and, also, often leading up to it, for their sweet aroma is said to help the dead find their way. Of course many altars contain photographs and memorabilia of the dead family members who will come to visit. A final touch is a glass or gourd of fresh water, for the dead will be thirsty after their long journey back.

Día de los Muertos amounts to a joyous reunion of all family members—both living and dead. Death is part of the inevitable flow of life, and in Mexico, on this special day, the truth of this is acknowledged and lived.

Guadalupe, Soledad, and Navidad

The month of December in Oaxaca nearly amounts to a nonstop fiesta that kicks off with celebrations leading up to Mexico's patron day, **Virgen de la Guadalupe** (Dec. 12), after which Oaxacans continue feting their own patron, the **Virgen de la Soledad** (Dec. 16-18). Festivities, which center around the Virgin's basilica (on Independencia, six

blocks west of the *zócalo),* include fireworks, dancing, food, and street processions of the faithful, bearing the Virgin's gold-crowned image decked out in her fine silks and satins.

Soon comes the **Fiesta de los Rábanos** (Festival of the Radishes; Dec. 23), when celebrants fill the Oaxaca *zócalo,* admiring amazing displays of plants, flowers, and whimsical figures crafted of giant radishes. Ceremonies and prizes honor the most innovative designs. Food stalls nearby serve traditional delicacies, including *buñuelos* (honey-soaked fried tortillas), plates of which are traditionally thrown into the air before the evening is over.

Oaxacans culminate their pre-Christmas week on **Nochebuena** (Christmas Eve) with candlelit processions from their parishes, accompanied by music, fireworks, and floats. They converge on the *zócalo* in time for a midnight cathedral mass.

Other Festivals

Besides the usual national holidays, a number of other locally important fiestas liven up the Oaxaca calendar. The first day of spring, March 21, kicks off the **Juegos Florales** (Flower Games). Festivities go on for 10 days, including the crowning of a festival queen at the Teatro Alcalá, poetry contests, and performances by renowned artists and the National Symphony.

On the second Monday in October, residents of Santa María del Tule venerate their ancient tree in the **Lunes del Tule** festival. Locals in costume celebrate with rites, folk dances, and feats of horsemanship beneath the boughs of their beloved great cypress.

ARTS EVENTS

Many Oaxaca institutions, such as the **Museo de Arte Contemporaneo de Oaxaca** (Macedonio Alcalá 202, tel. 951/514-1055, www.museomaco.com), the **Teatro Alcalá** (900 Independencia, tel. 951/516-8312 or 951/516-8344), the **Instituto de Artes Gráficos de Oaxaca** (across Macedonio Alcalá, tel. 951/516-6980), and the art-film **Cinema El Pochote** (García Vigil 817, tel.

Catrina, Queen of the Day of the Dead

Catrina Calavera, stylish queen of the Day of the Dead

While Día de los Muertos has its roots in Aztec rituals several thousand years old, and other elements draw on Catholic holidays and ceremonies imported by the Spanish, some of the imagery and activity associated with this most beloved of Mexican holidays is of a newer vintage.

Take Catrina, for example. All those skeletal women with fancy hats and dresses you'll see, either live, in paper mache, or perhaps in a candy version around November 1, are all versions of Catrina, whose origins lie not in pre-Hispanic Mexico but in the 19th century. A famous Mexican illustrator named José Guadalupe Posada created a print of a figure he called La Calavera Catrina (The Elegant Skull). Meant as a parody of an upper-class Mexican woman (striving to be as white-skinned as possible), the figure of Catrina, with her gown and usually impossibly fancy hat, soon took on a life of her own.

Today, the well-costumed female with a skeleton face and a fancy hat has become a ubiquitous presence on Dia de los Muertos. Girls who want to dress up on this holiday often turn themselves into Catrina, with faces painted to look like skulls, big hats, and elaborate gowns. You'll find Catrina comes in all shapes and sizes all over Oaxaca and indeed all over Mexico on November 1.

951/514-1194, films at 6pm and 8pm Tues.-Sat.), sponsor first-rate cultural events, as do the owners of Oaxaca's premier bohemian hipster bar, **Café Central** (Hidalgo 302, tel. 951/514-2042, colectivocentral.com, 9pm-2am Wed.-Sat.), who offer free movies of an independent persuasion on Wednesday evenings.

Local sources of events information include resident Diane Barclay's top-notch website (www.oaxacacalendar.com), the weekly Spanish *El Grito,* events newsletter of the **Oaxaca State Secretary of Culture** (www.cultura.oaxaca.gob.mx), and **Oaxaca state tourist information office** (703 Av. Juárez, west side of El Llano park, www.aoaxaca.com).

NIGHTLIFE

When lacking an official fiesta, you can create your own at a number of nightspots around town.

Some sidewalk cafés around the *zócalo* regularly have live music. Just follow the sound to either café **Terranova** (tel. 951/516-4747) or **El Importador** (southeast *zócalo* corner, tel. 951/514-3200) next door, or the marimba band in front of the café **Del Jardín** (southwest corner, tel. 951/516-2092).

Founded in 1916, **Bar La Farola** (20 de Noviembre 314, corner of Las Casas, tel. 951/516-5352, 11am-2am daily), a block west and a block south of the *zócalo*, claims to be Oaxaca's longest-running cantina. The Farola's dignified old-style-pub ambience attracts a middle-to-upper-class local clientele, some young, some old, who come to relax over food, drinks, and the rhythms of a live Latin-jazz-salsa trio.

One of the most intense in-town nightspots is **Candela** (Murguia 413, corner of Pino Suárez, tel. 951/514-2010, from about 10pm Thurs.-Sat.), which jumps with hot salsa and African-Latin rhythms. Arrive at 10pm for dance lessons; call to confirm.

Very popular among twentysomethings is **Bar La Pasion** (tucked beyond the rear of Restaurant Mayordomo, Macedonio Alcalá 302, tel. 951/514-4363 or 951/516-6113, noon-3am daily), with giant flat-screen TVs, studio lighting, and loud, live music.

La Condesa Coffee Bar (Cinco de Mayo 413, on the corner of Adolfo Gurrion, tel. 951/514-1806) is a high-ceilinged, multi-room hangout—coffee bar by day, drinking bar by night—for Oaxacan and visiting hipsters of all ages. The style is ultra-cool, the music is loud, and the lighting is intense, but if this is your kind of thing this is one good place to do it. Hours are flexible, credit cards are accepted, and there are plenty of excellent *mezcals* on the menu.

El Barracuda (García Vigil 416, no phone listed, late hours) is a hard core rock n' roll bar that opens late and stays open later.

For a taste of a great, single distillery *mezcal*—in several different styles—don't miss a stop at **Mezcaleria Los Amantes** (Allende 107, 4pm-10pm daily, tel. 951/501-0687, losamantes.com), one of Oaxaca City's most interesting little "bars." More like a mini-museum, Los Amantes is the work of mezcalero Horacio Arenas. He's the guy who comes in almost every night and plays acoustic guitar and sings beautiful Mexican songs. You can do a sampling of *blanco, reposado,* and *añejo* for about $8. The tiny room is a work of art, as are the mezcals Arenas cooks up at his distillery. This place is one of a kind! (If you happen to be in New York City, drop by the Casa Mezcal at 86 Orchard Street and get a little taste of Los Amantes without going south of the border.)

Café Central (Hidalgo 302, tel. 951/516-8505, 9pm-2am Wed.-Sat.) is the art-bar project of Oaxacan artist Guillermo Olguín, who shows independent films for free on Wednesdays, offers live music on Thursdays and Fridays ($3), and turns the whole place into a rocking, free-entry dance club on Saturdays.

For a more subdued atmosphere, try the luxury hotels, which host live dance music in their lobby bars, especially on weekends and holidays. Call to confirm programs at **Camino Real** (Cinco de Mayo 300, tel. 951/516-0611, www.caminoreal.com/Oaxaca) and **Hotel Victoria** (Km 545, Blvd. Adolfo Ruiz Cortínez 1306, Carretera Panamericana, tel. 951/515-2633, www.hotelvictoriaoax.com.mx).

Tlaxaparta (Matamoros 206, tel. 951/514-4305) serves as hookah club by day (with a good low priced set lunch) and kicks into gear as a dance club around midnight. It's a lively scene for all ages, visitors and locals alike.

La Cantinita (Macedonio Alcalá 303, tel. 951/516-8961) draws plenty of tourists and a smattering of locals due to its prime location on the Alcalá. The joint is liveliest on weekends, with live music many nights, otherwise a DJ keeps the beat. Throw in free *botanas* (snacks) and bottle service (buy a whole bottle instead of a series of cocktails), and you've got yourself a party.

At **La Divina** (Adolfo Gurion 104, tel. 951/582-0508) local and visiting bands churn out heavy metal and other forms of hard, live rock and roll, drawing young visitors and locals into the club's surrealist interior until the wee hours.

La Tentacion (Matamoros 101, tel. 951/514-9521, $1-3 cover) offers another late night scene: after 10pm the salsa band kicks in and the crowd cuts loose. When the band is not on, the DJ is, mixing Mexican and international pop. People wait in line to get in here.

La Casa de Mezcal (Flores Magón 209, tel. 951/156 4285) has been open since 1935, earning it accolades as one of Oaxaca City's original taverns. Mezcal-lovers take note: this bar specializes in mezcal made from a wild agave called Tobala, which grows only at high altitudes in the shade of oak trees.

If you are looking for gay Oaxacan nightlife, Bar 502 (Porfirio Díaz 502, no phone) is open weekend nights, and draws a mixed gender clientele who arrive late and dance until dawn.

El Piano y El Sofa (20 de Noviembre #103A, tel. 951/191-3060) is a bar and dance club that offers live jazz and blues rather than rock. The style is vintage chic, but the mood is utterly contemporary.

For great international food with an Italian slant, and live music in one package, try El Sol y La Luna (Reforma 502, tel. 951/514-8069), where jazz, salsa, merengue, and all manner of Latin music is played live several nights a week. Call to see who's on the bill.

Sports and Recreation

MOUNTAIN BIKING

For adventurous types, a fantastic way to explore the mountains of Oaxaca is with the guides from Bicicletas Pedro Martinez Tours (Aldama 418, tel. 951/514-5935, bicicletgaspedromartinez.com), a mountain biking company with offices located on the southwest side of town a few blocks from the Mercado Juárez. Martinez is a former Mexican Olympic team cyclist so he knows his stuff. Private and group biking and hiking tours can range from half-day trips to multi-day tours encompassing trails all over the state with serious trans-Sierra climbs involved. Food, water, guides, support vehicles (which will haul people up the hard hills if need be), and well-maintained bikes are included. Contact the office or tour the website for details on the company's many interesting and unusual trips.

The shortest trips are half-day or full-day rides in the Valle de Tlacolula or up into Llano Grande or around Monte Albán, or up into the Hierve de Agua region: the full-day trips cost about $100 per person for two people or $90 per person for four including bikes, guide, lunch, water, and transportation to starting points and back to Oaxaca City. For ultra-adventurous souls, the company offers a four-day tour that starts in Oaxaca and ends

in Puerto Escondido, with a mix of camping and hotels along the way through the mountains. Bikes, gloves, guides, meals, and transportation back to Oaxaca provided for prices ranging from $400 to $500 per person, depending on the size of the group and the state of the peso. You will see parts of Oaxaca that no tourists ever see, except those on bikes.

HORSEBACK RIDING

There are a number of guest ranchos just outside Oaxaca City that offer horseback riding adventures in the countryside around Oaxaca Valley. One that comes highly recommended is Rancho Pitaya in the Tlacolula Valley. Their short version is a half-day trip, for about $70, that includes round-trip transport from their office in Oaxaca City (Murguia 403, tel. 951/199-7026 in Oaxaca, tel. 310/929-7099 from the U.S.) and a two-hour ride with an English-speaking guide. Longer versions include full-day and multi-day rides with overnight stays at the rancho or at cabins up in the mountains, at costs up to $525 per person. Everything is discounted for larger parties. This is another off-the-road option for experiencing Oaxaca's ruggedly gorgeous backcountry while avoiding the hordes of high-season tourists.

SWIMMING, TENNIS, AND GOLF

Swimmers can do their laps and laze the afternoon away by the big pool (unheated but usually swimmable) at in-town **Hotel Rivera del Ángel** (Mina 518, tel. 951/516-6666, $10 adults, $5 kids ages 5 and under).

For both tennis (about seven courts) and a nine-hole golf course, go to the relaxed country club-style **Club Brenamiel** (intersection of Hwy. 190 and Calle San Jacinto, tel. 951/512-6822, clubbrenamiel@hotmail.com), about three miles north of the town center, on the left just past the Hotel Villas del Sol. Alternatively, on the other side of town, try the well-equipped (half a dozen tennis courts, two pools, gymnasium) YMCA-like **Deportivo Oaxaca** (Km 6.5, Carretera a El Tule, tel. 951/517-5271, 951/517-5974, or 951/517-7312), off Highway 190 on the way to El Tule, about four miles east of town. *Note:* Although both Club Brenamiel and Deportivo Oaxaca are membership organizations, they do accept day guests for a fee.

You can also take a swim at **Balneario Vista Hermosa** (Hidalgo 18 San Agustín Etla, tel. 951/521-2049), or play a round of golf at **Club de Golf Vista Hermosa** (Carretera a San Agustín Etla, tel. 951/547-1177), in the nearby town of San Agustín Etla, about half an hour north of the city.

For both swimming and tennis, you can also stay at either the **Hotel Victoria** (Km 545, Blvd. Adolfo Ruiz Cortínez 1306, Carretera Panamericana, tel. 951/515-2633, www.hotelvictoriaoax.com.mx) or the **Hotel Misión de los Angeles** (Porfirio Díaz 102, tel. 951/502-0100, www.misiondelosangeles.com).

WALKING

For an invigorating in-town walk, climb the **Cerro del Fortín.** Your reward will be a panoramic city, valley, and mountain view. The key to getting there through the maze of city streets is to head to the **Escalera del Fortín** (staircase), which will lead you conveniently to the instep of the hill. For example, from the northeast *zócalo* corner, walk north along the Macedonio Alcalá mall. After five blocks, in front of the Iglesia de Santo Domingo, turn left onto Allende, continue four blocks to Crespo, and turn right. After three blocks, you'll see the staircase on the left. Continue uphill, past the sprawling Guelaguetza open-air auditorium, to the road (Av. Nicolas Copernicus) heading north to the **Planetario Nundehui** (tel. 951/514-5379, 8am-3pm and 7pm-9pm daily Nov.-May, $1.50 adults, $1 kids, check the events schedule), where you can enjoy the panoramic city and valley view. (Besides daytime movies and star shows, the planetarium is customarily open for evening telescopic viewings of the moon, planets, and stars.) Past the planetarium, you can keep walking along the hilltop for at least another mile. Wear a hat and bring water. The round-trip from the *zócalo* is a minimum of two miles; the hilltop rises only a few hundred feet. Allow at least a couple of hours.

Shopping

The city of Oaxaca is renowned as a handicraft shopper's paradise. Prices are moderate, quality is high, and sources—in both large traditional markets and many dozens of private stores and galleries—are manifold. In the city, however, vendors do not ordinarily make the merchandise they sell. They buy wholesale from family shops in town, the surrounding valley, and remote localities all over the state of Oaxaca and Mexico in general. If your time is severely limited, it's best to buy from the good in-town sources, many of which are recommended here.

TRADITIONAL MARKETS

The original town market, **Mercado Juárez,** covers the entire square block just one block south and one block west of the *zócalo.* Many dozens of stalls offer everything; cotton and wool items—such as dresses, *huipiles,* woven blankets, and serapes—are among the best buys. Despite the overwhelming festoons of merchandise, bargains are there for those willing to search them out.

Before diving into Juárez market's cavernous interior, first orient yourself by looking over the lineup of stalls on the market's west side, along the block of 20 de Noviembre, between Las Casas and Trujano. Here, you'll be able to select from a reasonably priced representative assortment—*alebrijes* (fanciful wooden animals), black and green pottery, cutlery, filigree jewelry, *huipiles,* leather goods, pewter, tinware—of much that Oaxaca offers.

If organic food and produce suits your style, visit the modest **Pochote Market** (411 Rayon, corner of Xicotencatl, most shops 9am-4pm daily), four blocks east and two blocks south of the *zócalo*'s southeast corner. A sprinkling of vendors from all over the Valley of Oaxaca offer fruit, vegetables, homemade mezcal, honey, delicious hot tecate (tay-KAH-tay) chocolate-flavored drink, and lots of fresh food cooked on the spot.

After your Juárez market tour, walk along Aldama, a block west, to J. P. Garcia, then left, one and a half blocks south, to between Mina and Zaragoza, for a look inside the **Mercado de Artesanías** (handicrafts market). Here, you'll find a ton of textiles—fetching *huipiles* and *camisas* (shirts), flowery *blusas* (blouses), fine wool *tapetes* (carpets), colorful *alfarería* (pottery), whimsical *alebrijes,* festive handmade masks, and much more.

PRIVATE HANDICRAFTS SHOPS

Although pricier, the private shops generally offer the choicest merchandise. Here you can select from the very best: *huipiles* from San Pedro de Amusgos and Yalalag; richly embroidered "wedding" dresses from San Antonino Castillo Velasco; rugs and hangings from Teotitlán del Valle and Santa Ana del Valle; pottery (black from San Bartolo Coyotepec and green from Atzompa); carved *alebrijes* from Arrazola; whimsical figurines by the Aguilar sisters of Ocotlán; mezcal from Tlacolula; and masks from Huazolotitlán.

Most of the best individual shops lie scattered along three streets—Cinco de Mayo, Macedonio Alcalá, and García Vigil, which run uphill, north of the *zócalo.*

★ MARO

Somewhere along your handicrafts route, you must take a serious look around **MARO, Mujeres Artesanías de las Regiones de Oaxaca** (Craftswomen of the Regions of Oaxaca; 204 Cinco de Mayo, tel./fax 951/516-0670, 9am-7:30pm daily). From behind Oaxaca Cathedral, walk uphill, along Macedonio Alcalá, first passing Independencia; one block farther, at Morelos, turn right, continue a block and turn left on Cinco de Mayo, and walk half a block uphill to MARO, on the right.

Here, a remarkable all-Oaxaca grassroots movement of women artisans sell their goods and demonstrate their manufacturing techniques. The artisans are native Mexicans from all parts of Oaxaca, and their offerings reflect their unique effort. The shelves of several rooms are filled with hosts of gorgeous handicrafts: wooden masks, toys, carvings; cotton *traje* (native clothing), such as *huipiles, pozahuancos,* and *quechquémitles;* wool serapes, rugs, and hangings; woven palm hats, mats, and baskets; fine steel knives, swords, and machetes; tinplate mirrors, candlesticks, and ornaments; and leather saddles, briefcases, wallets, and belts. Don't miss it. Better still, do a major part of your Oaxaca shopping at this store.

Other Private Shops

South of the *zócalo,* head up J. P. Garcia and visit the unique private store **El Arte Oaxaqueño** (Mina 317, corner of J. P. Garcia, tel. 951/516-1581, 10am-8pm Mon.-Sat., 10am-5pm Sun.). The diverse, carefully selected offerings run from lovely wool weavings and bright one-of-a-kind pottery to fetching wooden toys and precious metal Christmas ornaments. Each piece comes with a detailed explanation of its history and a description of the craftsperson that made it.

Continue north on Macedonio Alcalá for a block and step into **La Mano Mágico** (Macedonio Alcalá 203, on the west side, just below corner of Murguia, tel./fax 951/516-4275, 10:30am-3pm and 4pm-8pm Mon.-Sat.). The shop offers both a colorful exposition of crafts from all over Mexico and a patio workshop where artisans work, dyeing wool and weaving examples of the lovely, museum-quality rugs and serapes that adorn the walls.

Take a one-block detour west along Matamoros to **Casa de Artesaniás** (Matamoros 105, corner of García Vigil, tel. 951/516-5062, 9am-9pm Mon.-Sat., 10am-6pm Sun.). Here, a cooperative of about six dozen Oaxaca artisan families offers a wide handicrafts selection, including rainbows of fantastic *alebrijes,* from Tilcajete and Arrazola, a treasury of glistening black pottery from Coyotepec, and preciously embroidered dresses from San Antonio Castillo Velasco.

Return and continue uphill on Macedonio Alcalá, a block farther north, to the Plaza Alcalá complex (southwest corner of M. Bravo), which has both an outstanding courtyard restaurant, Hostería Alcalá, and some good shops. Best among them is an exceptional bookstore, **Librería Amate** (307 Macedonio Alcalá, tel. 951/516-6960 or 951/516-7181, amatebooks@prodigy.net.mx, 10:30am-7:30pm Mon.-Sat., 2pm-7pm Sun.). Personable owner Henry Wangeman stocks an expertly selected library of English-language books about Mexico, including archaeology, cookbooks, ethnography, guides, history, literature, maps, postcards, and much more.

If you're interested in fine weavings, step directly across Macedonio Alcalá at the corner of Gurrion to **Tapetes de Teotitlán**

(Macedonio Alcalá, tel. 951/516-1675, 11am-7:30pm Mon.-Sat., 1pm-7pm Sun.), the shop of the Martínez family from the famous Teotitlán del Valle weaving village. Here, you're looking at the real thing: fine, mostly traditional designs, made of all-natural dyes.

Half a block farther uphill, be sure to look inside jewelry store **Oro de Monte Albán** (Macedonio Alcalá 403, tel. 951/514-3813, 10am-8pm Mon.-Sat., noon-8pm Sun.), across from the Iglesia de Santo Domingo. This extraordinary family-run enterprise carries on Oaxaca's venerable goldsmithing tradition as the sole licensed manufacturer of replicas from the renowned treasure of Monte Albán Tomb 7. Besides the luscious, museum-quality reproductions, Oro de Monte Albán offers a fine assortment of in-house silver and gold earrings, charm bracelets, necklaces, brooches, and much more. There are now three of these **Oro de Monte Albán** shops within a block of each other along the Alcalá; one does jewelry only, the others offer jewelry plus a wide selection of T-shirts and sweatshirts with often dazzling Oaxacan-inspired imagery printed on them.

CLOTHING AND TEXTILES

While you're on Macedonio Alcalá, be sure to peruse the colorful outdoor displays of for-sale local paintings and native-style women's *blusas, enredos, vestidos* (blouses, skirts, dresses), and *huipiles* that decorate **Plaza Labastida,** just south, across Abasolo, from the Santo Domingo church.

And if you want to know what's up with contemporary Oaxacan textile and clothing design, there are at least half a dozen retail stores within a few blocks, most run by their owner/designers, offering collections of one-of-a-kind, tradition-grounded clothes and textiles. These stores are for the most part not inexpensive, but you might find something—one thing—that is just perfect, an inspired interpretation of vintage Oaxaca with style enough for New York or Paris. The following is a sample: there are many others in the neighborhood worth visiting.

Huizache (Murguia 101 at Alcalá, tel. 951/501-1282, 10am-8pm daily) is a large, lovely store offering work from a collective of about 100 Oaxacan artisans, clothing designers, and craftspeople from all over the country. It's well worth a visit to check out the beautiful clothes as well as the pottery. A loom and a spinning wheel on site allow shoppers an opportunity to see how the fabric is made.

Fabiola Calvo Arte Textil (Cinco de Mayo 101, Macedonio Alcalá 501, tel. 951/516-0445, 10am-6pm) does the new-old mix with panache. The designs are ultra-chic and sexy, but the patterns of the textiles are traditional.

At **Reallstmo** (Cinco de Mayo 315-A, Murguia 101-5, tel. 951/515-1174 or 951/205-4516) find beautifully-rendered modern clothing, shoes, handbags, and other accessories done in the bright, colorful fabrics of Tehuantepec (in the Isthmus, hence the name). High-topped lace-up tennies, done Tehuantepec style? Why not? They look great.

Designer Odilon Merino Morales of **Arte Amuzgo** (Cinco de Mayo 217-B, tel. 951/516-9104 or 951/210-4089) works with the traditional textiles of the Amuzco people, who occupy a small piece of territory on the Oaxaca-Guerrero border. The patterns are geometrically-inspired and quietly colorful; she has reinterpreted the traditional in a fresh, modern way.

FINE ART GALLERIES

The tourist boom has stimulated a Oaxaca fine-arts revival. Several downtown galleries bloom with the sculpture and paintings of masters, such as Rufino Tamayo, Rudolfo Morales, Francisco Toledo, and a host of up-and-coming local artists. Besides **La Mano Mágico** (Macedonio Alcalá 203, on the west side, just below corner of Murguia, tel./fax 951/516-4275, 10:30am-3pm and 4pm-8pm Mon.-Sat.), one of the private handicrafts shops, a number of galleries stand out. Foremost among them is **Arte de Oaxaca** (Murguia 105, between Macedonio Alcalá

and Cinco de Mayo, tel. 951/514-0910, www.artedeoaxaca.com, 11am-3pm and 5pm-8pm Mon.-Fri., 11am-6pm Sat.), the gallery of the Rudolfo Morales Foundation.

Also outstanding is **Galería Quetzalli** (Constitución 104, between Reforma and Cinco de Mayo, tel. 951/514-2606, fax 951/514-0735, www.galeriaquetzalli.com, 10am-2pm and 5pm-8pm Mon.-Sat.), local outlet for celebrated artist Francisco Toledo. It's located opposite the south flank of Iglesia de Santo Domingo.

There are several other galleries in the neighborhood of Quetzalli; they primarily exhibit contemporary art by Oaxacan painters, sculptors, and artists in other media. For the most part these galleries open at 10am and close at 8pm daily; some take a mid-day break. In our most recent visit we found interesting contemporary work at all of the following galleries: **Galería 910 Arte Contemporaneo** (Alcalá 305 interior 3 y 4—upstairs, tel. 951/516-9862); **Galería Linda Fernandez** (Gurríon 104-1, tel. 951/171-6205); **Didier Mayés** (Cinco de Mayo 409-B, tel. 951/501-2352, didiermayes.com). We found some great work in the gallery that is next door to and operated by the owners of the **Decó Enmarcados art supply store** (Reforma 407-A, tel. 951/205-0597) as well. If you are in the neighborhood, you'll find other galleries that might have something you can take home. Oaxaca is currently a hotbed of contemporary art. There is fine work in styles ranging from abstract to surreal to expressionist and everything in between, and, for the most part, the work is not at all overpriced.

CURIOSITY SHOPS

A few blocks away from the fine arts galleries is the longtime coin, antique bric-a-brac, and art store **Monedas y Antiguidades** (Coins and Antiques; Abasolo 107, between the upper end of Cinco de Mayo and Reforma, tel. 951/516-3935, 11am-3pm and 6pm-9pm Mon.-Sat.). Browsers enjoy a potpourri of art, from kitsch to fine, plus a for-sale museum of dusty curios, from old silver coins and pioneer clothes irons to revolutionary photos and Porfirian-era tubas.

CUTLERY AND METALWORK SHOPS

Oaxaca is well known for its fine metal crafts. A few families produce nearly everything. A couple of the families sell their wares from their own shops. While in Mercado Juárez, stop by stall number 5 to see the fine swords, knives, and scissors of **Miguel Martínez** and family (Mercado Juárez, tel. 951/514-4868, 9am-9pm Mon.-Sat., 9am-6pm Sun.). Walk a few blocks west and south to see an even wider selection, plus artisans at work, at **Guillermo Aragon**'s street-front shop (J. P. Garcia 503, tel. 951/516-2658, 10:30am-3pm and 4pm-8pm Mon.-Sat.).

SPORTING GOODS AND CLOTHES

A modest sporting goods and clothing selection (no tennis rackets at this writing, however) is available at **Deportes Ziga** (southwest corner of Macedonio Alcalá and Matamoros, next to La Mano Mágico handicrafts shop, tel. 951/514-1654, 9am-3pm and 4pm-9pm Mon.-Sat., 11am-2pm Sun.). There is at least one **Walmart** on Oaxaca's outskirts these days. You'll pass it coming into town from the airport. No doubt they stock plenty of underpriced sporting goods and clothes.

Accommodations

Oaxaca offers a wide range of good lodgings. Air-conditioning is not particularly necessary in temperate Oaxaca, although hot-water showers (furnished by all lodgings listed here, though the budget hotels and hostels often have warm rather than hot water, with sketchy water pressure) feel especially comfy during cool winter mornings and evenings. Many of the less expensive hotels, which generally do not accept credit cards, are within easy walking distance of the colorful, traffic-free *zócalo*. Every hotel we have listed offers free Wi-Fi: most often, you will get it, however slow, in your room, but in some cases you might have to go to a lobby area.

During holidays and festivals (pre-Easter week, July, August, late October-early November, December 15-January 6), most Oaxaca hotels and bed-and-breakfasts raise their prices 10-50 percent above the rates listed here. Several of the following lodgings and many more not listed here are advertised on **websites,** such as www. hotelesdeoaxaca.com for **hotels,** www. oaxacabedandbreakfast.org for **bed-and-breakfasts,** and www.vrbo.com (**Vacation Rentals by owner**) for long-term house and apartment rentals.

All accommodations listed in this section are positive recommendations, grouped by location in relation to the *zócalo,* and listed, within each location group, in ascending order of double-occupancy price. Almost all of the hotels listed have tour offices or people on staff who can help you plan tours to Oaxaca Valley destinations.

The number of Oaxaca bed-and-breakfast-style lodgings has increased in response to the influx of North American visitors. From only a scant few a generation ago, Oaxaca has blossomed with perhaps two dozen attractive bed-and-breakfasts located mostly on the north side, uphill from the town center. As a group, they are not particularly economical, since they are a North American transplant that appeals to foreign visitors who are accustomed to paying somewhat elevated prices. The recommendations that follow present a sampling of several of the most solid, long-standing Oaxaca bed-and-breakfasts. For even more choices, check out the good website, www. oaxacabedandbreakfast.org.

NEAR THE *ZÓCALO*
Under $50

For economy and value, consider **Hotel El Chapulin** (Aldama 317, tel. 951/516-1646, hotelchapulin@hotmail.com, $16 s, $20 d, $24 t), one of Oaxaca's fine budget lodgings. The welcoming owners carefully tend to the eight rooms, which are tucked away from street traffic noise. The result: a restful, clean, two-story retreat climaxed by an airy rooftop patio with a superb view of town, and the towering Monte Albán ridge above the southern horizon as the backdrop. All of this plus private shower-bath, Wi-Fi, and inviting lobby-sitting room is available for less than $25.

Head northeast a few blocks east of the *zócalo's* northeast corner to the busy, budget traveler-favorite, the 39-room **Posada del Virrey** (1001 Morelos, tel. 951/516-5555, fax 951/516-2193, $35 s or d in one bed, $45 d in two beds, $50 t). Only four blocks (five minutes) east of the *zócalo,* the authentically colonial Posada del Virrey offers two floors of rooms surrounding a spacious inner restaurant patio. The rooms are comfortably furnished, including one, two, or three double beds. Rooms come with cable TV, phone, fan, and parking (9pm-9am); MasterCards are accepted.

Even closer in, just half a block west of the *zócalo's* southwest corner, is the popular **Hotel Las Rosas** (Trujano 112, tel./fax 951/514-2217, $41 s, $47 d, $53 t). Climb a flight of stairs to the small lobby, relatively tranquil by virtue of its 2nd-floor location. Beyond that, a double tier of rooms surrounds a homey inner patio. Adjacent to the lobby is a cheery sitting room with a tropical aquarium and a TV, usually kept at subdued volume. In the rear, guests enjoy an airy terrace for reading and relaxing. The rooms themselves, although plainly furnished, are clean and tiled. Prices are very reasonable for such a well-located hotel. Discounts are negotiable for a one-week stay. No credit cards, parking, or wheelchair access, however.

A block west of the *zócalo's* southwest corner, find the **Hotel Santa Rosa** (Trujano 201, tel. 951/514-6714 or 951/514-6715, fax 951/514-6715, hostalsantarosa@hotmail.com, $40 s, $48 d). The streetside lobby leads past an airy restaurant to the rooms, recessed along a meandering inner passageway and courtyard. Inside, the rooms are comfortably furnished and decorated in pastels. Rates continue to be reasonable except during festivals and holidays, when they might rise as much as 40 percent. Hotel Santa Rosa offers TV, phones, parking, limited wheelchair access, and an in-house travel-tour agency, but credit cards are not accepted.

$50-100

Just a block south of the *zócalo's* southwest corner, the ★ **Hotel Trebol** (Flores Magón 201, tel./fax 951/516-1256, www.oaxaca-mio. com/trebol.htm, $50 s or d in one bed, $70 d in two beds, $80 t) remains an enduring, brightly-painted jewel among Oaxaca's moderately priced hotels. Guests can choose from about 40 rooms, artfully sprinkled in three stories around an airy, plant-decorated inner patio. The rooms are comfortably furnished with rustic tile, hand-hewn wooden furniture, table lamps, color-coordinated bedspreads, and shower-baths. Rooms include fans, telephone, cable TV, and Wi-Fi; there's also a travel agent and a good restaurant in the hotel.

Ideally situated just east of the *zócalo's* northeast corner, the best-buy colonial-era **Hotel Real de Antequera** (Hidalgo 807, tel. 951/516-4635, fax 951/516-7511, www.oaxaca-mio.com/real.htm, $45 s, $55 d, $65 t) offers plenty for reasonable rates. The 29 comfortable rooms, in two stories around an inviting old world-style restaurant-patio, include breakfast, bath, fans, cable TV, Internet in most rooms, phones, and parking (8:30pm-8:30am), and credit cards are accepted.

Just a few doors south of the *zócalo's* southeast corner, consider the popular 1980s-mod **Hotel Gala** (Bustamante 103, tel. 951/514-2251 or 951/514-1305, fax 951/516-3660, Mex. toll-free 800/712-7316, www.gala.com.mx, $60 s, $68 d, $76 t, $86 junior suite). Guests enjoy comfortable, modern, deluxe accommodations at relatively moderate prices right in the middle of the *zócalo* action. The 36 rooms, although tastefully decorated and carpeted, are smallish. Get one of the quieter ones away from the street. Rooms include private shower-baths, phones, TVs, and fans; conveniently, the downstairs has a restaurant, and there is parking (10pm-8am); credit cards are accepted.

Return just two blocks west of the *zócalo's* northwest corner to the class-act ★ **Parador San Miguel** (Independencia 503, tel./fax 951/514-9331, www.paradorsanmigueloaxaca. com, $100 s or d, $110 t). Here, little seems to have been spared in transforming a colonial-era mansion into a lovely hotel. Inside, a plethora of old-world details—leafy, tranquil inner patio; sunny upstairs corridors; brilliant stained glass-decorated staircase; scrolled wrought-iron railings; handsome, hand-carved wooden doors—are bound to please lovers of traditional refinement. A correspondingly elegant restaurant, the Andariega, completes the picture. The 19 rooms and four suites are no less than you'd expect, attractively furnished with custom-woven bedspreads and curtains, handcrafted bamboo and leather furniture, elegantly tiled shower-baths, and a choice of king, single, or double beds. Add about 50 percent to price during festivals and holidays. All rooms come with air-conditioning, cable TV, phones, and wireless Internet. Credit cards are accepted.

NORTH AND EAST OF THE *ZÓCALO*
Under $50

With its rustic, stone-floored lobby and bustling atmosphere, the **Hotel Posada La Casa De La Tia** (Cinco de Mayo 108, tel. 951/514-1963, posadalacasadelatia.com, $30 s, $35 d, $40 t) is a welcoming low-budget option two blocks northeast of the *zócalo*. The clean, well-lit, and comfortable rooms are finished with traditional textile bedspreads, and come relatively cheap considering the fine location. Amenities include Wi-Fi, security lockers, a computer for guest use, cable TV, tour desk,

auto rental service, and a restaurant/bar on the premises.

Nearby stands another well-located, moderately-priced choice, the **Hotel Villa de León** (Reforma 405, tel. 951/516-1958 or 951/516-1977, www.hotelesdeoaxaca.com/ hotelvilladeleon.html, $30 s, $40 d, $50 t), adjoining the back side of the Iglesia de Santa Domingo grounds. Past the reception and inner-courtyard restaurant, about half of the 20 rooms encircle an upstairs balcony; the remainder are tucked in the rear, fortunately removed from street and restaurant noise. All rooms have tile floors, handmade wooden furniture, and private shower-baths. Credit cards are accepted. Reserve a room away from the heavily trafficked street.

One of the most popular modestly-priced options, ★ **Casa Arnel** (Aldama 404, Colonia Jalatlaco, tel./fax 951/515-2856, www. casaarnel.com.mx, $45 s, $50 d, $55 t) is also farthest north from the *zócalo*. Casa Arnel stands at the edge of downtown, so removed from the urban bustle that it feels as if it's embedded in another era. In front of Casa Arnel, the streets are cobbled with stone, and across from it stands the ancient church, San Matias Jalatlaco, beside its shady neighborhood plaza. The neighborhood is perking up, with a couple of other new hotels and restaurants, and is also home to Toscana, one of Oaxaca's Italian dining gems. Casa Arnel is a family home that grew into a hotel, with about 20 attractively-furnished rooms with baths, around a jungly garden blooming with birdcalls and flowers. Additional amenities include a broad roof deck with umbrellas, tables, and chairs for sunning and relaxing, a couple of big tables on the patio for communal breakfasting, and on-site tour planning.

$50-100

Behind (east of) the Iglesia de Santo Domingo block, find **La Casa de Rosita** (Reforma 410, tel. 951/516-1982 or 951/514-9815, www.lac-asa-de-rosita.com, $60/night, $400/week), formerly La Casa de los Abuelos (House of the Grandparents). This charmingly quirky colonial-era complex is the life project of personable owner-builder Luis Arroyo Nuñez, who inherited it from his *abuelos* (grandparents). This former priests' residence for Iglesia de Santo Domingo was confiscated by the government after the *cristero* revolt of the late 1920s. Luis's six completely renovated apartments, built around two quiet inner patios, are replete with unique details, such as exposed original brick walls, old family photos, bric-a-brac, and sturdy wooden staircases leading up to bedroom lofts. Rentals include invitingly furnished living-dining rooms, kitchenettes, queen-size beds, and shower-baths. Asking rates are negotiable by the month; apartments come with fans, TV, purified bottled water, and Wi-Fi.

In the Santo Domingo neighborhood, discerning travelers should consider the low-key but inviting **Hotel Maela** (Constitución 206, tel./fax 951/516-6022, www.hotelesdeoaxaca.com/maela.htm, $41 s, $51 d, $61 t, suites for four $70), one block east of the Iglesia de Santo Domingo compound. Inside, just past reception, the ceilings are gracefully high, and the 23 rooms and three suites, in two stories, are spacious, with private shower-baths and attractive handmade wood dressers, beds, and end tables. Rooms

come with fans or air-conditioning, TV, Wi-Fi, and parking.

On the northwest side, about three blocks west of the Iglesia de Santo Domingo, is the very inviting ★ **Hotel Las Golondrinas** (Tinoco y Palacios 411, tel. 951/514-3298, hotellasgolondrinas.com.mx, $50 s, $55 d, $60 t). Rooms surround an intimate garden, lovingly decorated with festoons of hothouse verdure. Leafy bananas, bright bougainvillea, and platoons of potted plants line pathways that meander past a fountain patio in one corner and lead to an upstairs panoramic vista sundeck in the other. The care also shows in the rooms, which, although smallish, are immaculate and adorned with pastel earthtoned curtains and bedspreads, and natural wood furniture. Guests additionally enjoy use of laundry facilities, a TV room, Wi-Fi, a shelf of paperback books, and a breakfast café (8am-10am) in the garden. In addition to the 27 regular rooms, two honeymoon suites rent for about $60 each.

Right across the street from Las Golondrinas you'll find ★ **Hotel Casa del Sotano** (Tinoco y Palacios 414, tel. 951/516-2494, hoteldelsotano.com, $57-77 s, $69-88 d, $77-97 t), another beautifully put-together small hotel in our medium price range. All 21

a garden patio at Hotel Las Golondrinas

rooms and two suites are finished and furnished in the rich mix of traditional and contemporary style that defines Oaxaca today. The higher rates are for the upper-floor rooms, which have better views of the city. Down below, however, the rooms encircle a lovely patio with plantings and an elegant and soothing water feature. An on-premises café serves breakfast and lunch, remaining open into the afternoon and evening, seasonally. The café specializes in chocolate and mezcal, two Oaxacan favorites. The rooftop deck puts the city on display. Rooms have phones, fans, cable TV, safes, and hair dryers; the hotel will organize tours. Wi-Fi is available in the lobby only.

Several blocks north of Iglesia de Santo Domingo stands the **Hotel Casona de Llano** (Av. Juárez 701, tel. 951/514-7719 or 951/514-7703, fax 951/516-2219, www.hotelcasonadellano.com, $60 s, $70 d, $80 t). This hotel is a favorite of visitors who enjoy the shady, untouristed ambience of Oaxaca's big Sunday park, officially called Parque Paseo Juárez, but popularly referred to as El Llano (YAH-noh, Plain or Flat Place). The 28 rooms include fans, TV, and phones. Parking is available and credit cards are accepted.

On the other side and a block south of El Llano, step into ★ **Hotel Casa Vertíz** (Reforma 404, tel. 951/516-2525, www.hotelvertiz.com.mx, $100 s, $110 d, $140 t), one of the most inviting small hotels in Oaxaca. Here you find a masterfully rebuilt former colonial house with air, light, and space that encourages lingering. Inside the entrance, guests enjoy a refined, airy patio restaurant and a tropical rear garden. All 14 rooms are tucked away from the busy street. Upstairs, rooms open onto a terrace. Accommodations are luxuriously appointed with designer-rustic tile floors, earth-toned bedspreads and curtains, deluxe tiled baths (four rooms have tubs), and queen-size beds. Rentals include cable TV, phone, Wi-Fi, air-conditioning, and parking; credit cards are accepted.

Just south of El Llano park, ★ **Hotel and Studios Las Mariposas** (Pino Suárez 517, tel. 951/515-5854, from U.S./Can. direct tel. 619/793-5121, www.lasmariposas.com.mx, $45 s, $50 d, rate includes breakfast) is strongly recommended as either a bed-and-breakfast, hotel, or apartment rental. Welcoming and knowledgeable owner Teresa Dávila offers 13 rooms (with baths, but no kitchenettes) in her restored 19th-century family house. She also rents five comfortable studio kitchenette suites with private baths

the lively exterior of the Hotel Casa del Sotano

($45 s, $50 d without breakfast). Besides the happy customers, pluses include Wi-Fi, coffee, TV, and use of credit cards (Visa only) for stays of a week or more; kids under 12 are not welcome.

For another worthy, moderately-priced option, check out the **Casa los Arquitos** (Rufino Tamayo 816, tel. 951/132-7951, www.casalosarquitos.com, $65-130), where a welcoming Mexican couple have converted their modest home into an inviting small bed-and-breakfast tucked into the heart of the charming north-end Los Arquitos neighborhood. Their five immaculate rooms with bath, simply but attractively decorated, offer a choice of either one single bed, two single beds, or one king-size bed with full kitchenette, including refrigerator, stove, microwave oven, dishes, and utensils, and a private patio to boot. Amenities include Wi-Fi and a generous continental breakfast with choice of savory organic coffee, hot chocolate, or tea, and breads, yogurt, granola, and fresh seasonal fruit.

Much closer in, just two blocks behind Iglesia de Santo Domingo, you'll find **Casa de las Bugambilias** (Reforma 402, tel./fax 951/516-1165, U.S./Can. toll-free 866/829-6778, www.lasbugambilias.com, $65-95 s, $75-105 d), with seven rooms and one suite, artfully tucked behind its good street-front restaurant. Several rooms open onto a lovely rear garden. Rules include a minimum three-night stay, $50 cancellation fee, children over 12 only, no pets, and no smoking. Amenities include private bath, breakfast, Wi-Fi, a *temazcal* hot room (at extra cost); credit cards are accepted, but parking is not included. The 21 members of the Cabrera-Arroyo family operate this and two other B&Bs nearby; you'll find all three—the others are El Secreto and Casa de los Milagros—elegant and inviting.

Another promising bed-and-breakfast in the same north-side neighborhood (but a few blocks west of El Llano park) is ★ **Bed-and-Breakfast Oaxaca Ollin** (oh-YEEN; Quintana Roo 213, tel. 951/514-9126, U.S./Can. tel. 619/787-5141, www.oaxacaollin.com, $85-135), the project of guide Judith Reyes López and her husband Jon McKinley. Judith and Jon offer 11 comfortable double rooms in their large house, located on a quiet side street a block north and a block east of the Centro Cultural de Santo Domingo. Rooms are comfortably appointed with natural wood furniture, reading lamps, and lovely Talavera-tile bathrooms. Extras abound, such as a swimming pool (not heated, however) and patio, living room, library, reading room, Wi-Fi and local phone calls, and much more. Prices include a hearty Oaxaqueño breakfast.

Back on the northeast side, from Casa de las Bugambilias, go east two blocks and turn north a block to the bed-and-breakfast gem **Casa de Mis Recuerdos** (House of My Memories, Pino Suárez 508, tel. 951/515-8483 or 951/515-5645, www.misrecuerdos.net, U.S. toll-free 877/234-4706, $60-80 s, $95-105 d). Enter the front gate and continue through a bougainvillea-festooned garden to the home of the Valenciana family, which has been accommodating students and foreign visitors for a generation. The rented rooms occupy rear and front sections. The four front rooms, immaculate, spacious, and lovingly decorated with folk art and furnished with handmade wooden furniture, have two bathrooms between them. They are closer to the busy streetfront than the five similarly furnished rear rooms, which, although they have private baths, are smaller.

Over $100

For genuine urbane class, try Oaxaca's most distinguished downtown hotel, the ★ **Camino Real** (Cinco de Mayo 300, tel. 951/516-0611, toll-free U.S./Can. tel. 800/722-6466, fax 951/516-0732, www.caminoreal.com/Oaxaca, $300 d), which occupies the lovingly restored former convent of Santa Catalina, four blocks north and one block east of the *zócalo*. Flowery, secluded courtyards, massive arched portals, soaring beamed ceilings, a big blue pool, and impeccable bar and restaurant service combine to create a refined but relaxed old-world atmosphere. Rooms are large, luxurious, and invitingly decorated with antiques and folk crafts and furnished with a plethora of modern conveniences. The hotel entertains guests and the paying public (about $35 pp) with a weekly class-act, in-house buffet and folkloric dance performance. Rooms have phones and cable TV, but parking is not included; credit cards are accepted.

A more modern take on Oaxacan tradition can be found at the ★ **Hotel Azul** (Abasolo 313, tel. 951/501-0016, hotelazuloaxaca.com, $178-540), where 21 colorful and inviting contemporary rooms and suites surround a stone and cactus patio with a fountain designed by Oaxacan artist Francisco Toledo. Standard rooms with king or two twin beds come with air-conditioning, Wi-Fi, LCD TV, minibar, hair dryer, designer bath products, and telephone. The five suites are designed by different Oaxacan artists; each is unique and wonderful. The in-house restaurant features cuisine from Oaxaca's eight regions, with an emphasis on seafood; the rooftop bar offers inspired views of the heart of the city.

Hotel Misión de Los Angeles (Porfirio Díaz 102, tel. 951/502-0100, fax 951/502-0111, www.oaxaca-mio.com/misiondelosangeles. htm, $140 d, junior suites $155) rambles like a hacienda through a spreading oak- and acacia-decorated garden-park two blocks uphill from Calzada Niños Héroes (Hwy. 190), about a mile uphill, north, of the city center. After a rough few days on the sightseeing circuit, this is an ideal place to kick back beside the big pool or enjoy a set or two of tennis. The 162 rooms and suites are spacious and comfortable, decorated in earth tones and pastels. Many but not all have big garden-view windows or balconies. Additional amenities include phones, air-conditioning, parking, and a restaurant; credit cards are accepted.

The **Hotel Victoria** (Km 545, Blvd. Adolfo Ruiz Cortínez 1306, Carretera Panamericana, tel. 951/5020850, www.hotelvictoriaoax.com. mx, rooms $125, villas $150, junior suites $240) spreads over a lush hillside garden of panoramic vistas and luxurious resort ambience. The 1960s-modern lobby extends from an upstairs bar, downhill past a terrace restaurant, to a flame tree and jacaranda-decorated pool patio. Rooms come in three grades, all comfortably deluxe, that vary by size and location. The smallest are the rooms in the original hotel building; somewhat larger are the villas downstairs around the pool; and most spacious are the junior suites, in the newer wing detached from the lobby building. The 150 rooms come with cable TV, phones, air-conditioning, Wi-Fi, tennis courts, live music seasonally, handicrafts shop, parking, and wheelchair access; credit cards are accepted.

Cooler, breezier San Felipe village, in the foothills north of Oaxaca town, is home to a number of restful luxury lodgings. Choicest among them, ★ **Hacienda Los Laureles** (Hidalgo 21, San Felipe del Agua, tel. 951/501-5300, www.hotelhaciendaloslaureles.com, or agent Mexico Boutique Hotels toll-free U.S./ Can. tel. 800/728-9098, www.mexicoboutiquehotels.com, deluxe rooms $300 s or d, superior deluxe $330 s or d) is the labor of love of personable German expatriate owner-managers Ligia and Peter Kaiser. During the late 1990s they rebuilt a venerable hacienda, tenaciously preserving its rustic old-world essence while installing the best of the new. Now, Hacienda Los Laureles's centerpiece is its lush interior garden of grand tropical trees and climbing vines that, at night, is transformed by shadowed lighting and the serenades of crickets and tree frogs into an enchanted forest. The Hacienda's 25 rooms are decorated in elegant simplicity, with high ceilings, handsome tile floors, and hand-hewn mahogany furniture. Bathrooms are likewise luxurious and comfortable. Suites for 3-6 or more people are also available. All come with air-conditioning, cable TV, pool with whirlpool tub, and breakfast at their excellent terrace restaurant. A *temazcal* ceremonial hot room and a menu of spa services are also available at an extra cost.

Elegant **Hotel Casa Oaxaca** (García Vigil 407, tel. 951/514-4173, www.casa-oaxaca.com, $180 s or $242-263 d for the four smallest, yet spacious units, $330 s or d for a larger suite,

$260-407 for a two-story apartment above the rear courtyard) is straight uphill four blocks and a world apart from the *zócalo*. Its sky-blue colonial facade reveals nothing of its singularly unique interior. The lobby, which appears more like an art museum foyer than a lodging entrance, provides the first clue. Past that, you enter a spacious, plant-decorated courtyard, with the wall plaster artfully removed here and there to reveal the brick underlay. Continue to a rear courtyard, which centers on a blue designer pool and a *temazcal*. All six rooms, which border the courtyards, are luxuriously austere and uniquely appointed with antiques, crafts, and contemporary wall art. Rates include gourmet continental breakfast, Wi-Fi, and parking; credit cards are accepted. *Temazcal* treatments, complete with native healer, run about $50 per person.

Apartments

About five blocks north of the *zócalo*, right in front of Iglesia de Santo Domingo, is **Departmentos del Fraile** (Macedonio Alcalá 501, tel./fax 951/516-4310, humberto-benitezc@yahoo.com, $550/month). Family owner-managers offer four compact, modern, and historic (former Santo Domingo priests') apartments, hidden behind a street-front wall and tucked within a quiet, leafy inner courtyard. The renovated units have one bedroom, a bathroom, and a kitchenette. Rentals are monthly only.

SOUTH AND WEST OF THE *ZÓCALO*
$50-100

Only a few bed-and-breakfast lodgings dot the south and west sides of town. Here are two gems.

Start several blocks southeast of the *zócalo* with **Posada de Chencho** (4ta Privada de la Noria 115, tel./fax 951/514-0043, www.mex-online.com/chencho.htm, $37 s, $49 d, 54 t, without breakfast, add about $6 with breakfast). Chencho is in his 90s and retired now, but his son Antonio carries on the welcoming tradition. Twenty-two immaculate rooms

in two stories surround an inviting garden patio. The rooms themselves are comfortably and thoughtfully decorated, with Western-standard baths. Downstairs, guests enjoy a dining room and a big sitting room/library, as well as patio nooks for reading and relaxing.

On the west edge of downtown, about 10 blocks due west of the *zócalo*, stands **Casa Colonial** (Calle Miguel Negrete 105, tel./fax 951/516-5280, toll-free U.S./Can. tel. 800/758-1697, www.casa-colonial.com, $45-110). Personable owner Jane Robison, who seems to know everyone in town, calls her 13-room domain the "posada with no sign," because she doesn't advertise and only accepts guests with reservations. Upon arrival, you immediately see why Casa Colonial is such a favorite among savvy visitors. Low-rise rooms and apartments envelop a spacious, gracefully lovely inner garden. Guests enjoy the use of a living room with a fine library and Wi-Fi. Room prices vary according to size and elegance; there's a 10 percent discount if you pay in cash. For information on Casa Colonial Tours, visit the website.

APARTMENTS

Many Oaxacans offer apartment or house rentals and lodging in their homes. If you're interested, be sure to see the classified sections of the English-language newspaper *Oaxaca Times,* either online (www.oaxacatimes.com) or at their editorial office (Macedonio Alcalá 307, tel. 516-3443), or check out the excellent website www.vrbo.com (Vacation Rentals by Owner). If you'd like to experience a homestay with a Mexican family, ask for information at one of the several Oaxaca language schools that arrange homestays.

Just three blocks from the *zócalo*, find the secluded and attractive, **Casa Luz María** (1002 Morelos, tel. 951/514-6280 or 951/516-2378, luzmago30@hotmail.com, $450/month for two). The sprightly, grandmotherly owner, who retired from running her lodging as a bed-and-breakfast, now offers four smallish furnished apartments around a pair of flowery interior patios. The apartments include a kitchenette, a double bed, a shower-bath (either private or shared), and in-house Internet. The owner prefers monthly rentals.

HOSTELS

Oaxaca's best hostel might be the beautifully restored ★ **Paulina Youth Hostel** (V. Trujano 321, tel. 951/516-2005, www.paulinahostel.com, dorms $14 pp, rooms $27 s, $29 d, $44 t, $58 q), just three blocks west of the *zócalo*. The owners created the best of all possible hostelling worlds, with a good cafeteria and inviting, spacious common areas. With 100 beds in six private rooms and 10 dorms, the comfortable, squeaky-clean rooming options include separate male and female dorms and private rooms with shower-baths, all with comfortable orthopedic mattresses, roof terrace, hot water, and hearty breakfast thrown in for free. Get your reservations in early.

Also worthy are two hostels in the picturesque Los Arquitos neighborhood on the far northwest side of downtown. First, consider **Hostal Pochón** (Callejon del Carmen 102, tel. 951/516-1322, www.hostalpochon.com, dorms $12 pp, rooms $14-20 d, includes breakfast), two blocks west and nine blocks north (15 min.) from the *zócalo*'s northwest corner. The owners offer lodging for about 30 guests in three separate dorms, three rooms with shared bath, and one suite with private bath. Amenities include Wi-Fi, library, use of phone, cable TV, free popcorn, and more.

In the same northwest neighborhood is the very worthy **Posada Don Mario** (Cosijopi 219, tel./fax 951/514-2012, www.posadadonmario.com, rooms with shared bath $31 s, $41 d, $60 t, rooms with private bath $41 s, $54 d) on a quiet side street. Hardworking owner Norma Moran offers 10 rooms and a dormitory, tucked around an intimate downstairs patio and an airy upstairs porch, furnished with comfy chairs and couches for reading and relaxing. Continental breakfast and in-house Internet are included.

A number of hostels have opened on the north side in recent years, catering to the new generation of low-budget travelers who have discovered Oaxaca City's allure. Among the best, combining low prices, modern and comfortable facilities, and good location are the following pair: **Hostel Alcalá** (Valdivieso 120—this is the one block between the zócalo and Macedonio Alcalá not closed to traffic—tel. 951/501-0289, hostelalcala.hostel.com, dorms $8-11, private rooms $27 d, $35 t) offers dorm-style sleeping arrangements and a couple of private rooms for 2-3 people. Enter by climbing the spiral stairs at the back of Cafecito (same address). Secure lockers, Wi-Fi, table games, flat screen cable TV, and free coffee and continental breakfast come with the very low price of a bed.

Farther north and east find **Hostel Don Nino Oaxaca** (Pino Suarez 804, tel. 951/502-5336, hosteldonnino.com, dorms $12, private rooms and suites $38-50 s, $46-50 d, $60 t, all include breakfast) overlooking tranquil El Llano park. A modern hostel tucked into a vintage Oaxaca building, Don Nino's offers men's, women's, and mixed dorms and private rooms along with an on-site restaurant and bar, tour packages, a shared kitchen, table games, computers, Wi-Fi, and a terrace.

TRAILER PARKS AND CAMPING

The **Oaxaca Trailer Park** (900 Av. Violetas, tel. 951/515-0376, hookups $15, tents $10) lies at the far northeast side of town. Once a very popular facility, the Oaxaca Trailer Park has been partly converted to offices and apartments during the past few years. Nevertheless, it lives on, still with dozens of all-hookup spaces and tent spaces remaining. Amenities include big shade trees, diagonal parking spaces for the largest rigs, clean hot-water showers and toilets, a manager-watchperson, and the original sturdy security fence. Get there by turning left at Violetas, marked by the big green Colonia Reforma sign over the highway, a block or two past the baseball stadium, several blocks east of the first-class bus terminal on Highway 190. Continue uphill six long blocks to the trailer park entrance on the left.

Food

AROUND THE ZÓCALO

Cafés

Recent years have seen an explosion of coffee houses, shops, and bars all over Oaxaca City, along with cafés specializing in chocolate drinks and chocolate snacks of all kinds. The Oaxacan version of Starbucks is the **Italian Coffee Company** with several locations around town. The one with the best location is on the northeast corner of the *zócalo,* at Valdivieso and Hidalgo.

Snacks and Food Stalls

The cost of meals at many of Oaxaca's popular restaurants has risen during the past few years. Nevertheless, plenty of tasty, reasonably priced food is out there for the discerning diner to enjoy. Read on for a plethora of possibilities.

During fiestas, snack stalls along Hidalgo, at the cathedral-front Alameda de León square, abound with local delicacies. Choices include *tlayudas,* giant pizza-like crisp tortillas loaded with avocado, tomato, onions, and cheese; and *empanadas de amarillo,* huge tacos stuffed with cheese and red salsa. For dessert, have a *buñuelo,* a crunchy, honey-soaked wheat tortilla.

At non-fiesta times, you can still fill up on the sizzling fare of tacos, *tortas,* hamburgers, and hot dogs (eat 'em only when they are served hot) at stands that set up in the same vicinity, especially in the late afternoon and evenings.

Restaurants

Oaxaca visitors enjoy a number of reasonably priced eateries right on or near the *zócalo.* In fact, you could spend your entire time enjoying the fare of the several *zócalo*-front sidewalk cafés, but then, if you did, you'd miss out on the real story of Oaxacan cuisine, which is taking place a few blocks uptown.

But first, the *zócalo.* Of the eight cafés at street level, several offer recommendable food and service. Possibly the best of the lot is **Terranova** (tel. 951/516-4747) on the east side, for professionally prepared and served lunch and dinner entrées. For good, reasonably priced breakfasts, try **Primavera**, at the northwest (Hidalgo) corner. The adjacent west-side **La Cafetería** and **Del Jardín** (tel. 951/516-2092) rate OK for food, but their service can be spotty. **El Importador** (tel. 951/514-3200) is trying harder with entertaining, not-too-loud live music, and passably good food, at lower prices than neighboring Terranova. They all are open long hours, about 8am-midnight daily, and have typical menus: morning breakfasts ($2-5); soups and salads ($3-6); pasta, meat, poultry, and fish ($5-12).

As for *zócalo* restaurants with a view from upstairs, serious-eating longtimers return to **El Asador Vasco** (Portal Flores 10A on the 2nd Fl. balcony above Del Jardín, tel. 951/514-4755, 1pm-midnight daily, $25-35). The menu specializes in hearty Basque-style country cooking: salty, spicy, and served in the decor of a medieval Iberian manor house. Favorites include fondues (bean, sausage, and mushroom), garlic soup, salads, veal tongue, oysters in hot sauce, and the carnes asadas (roast meats) house specialties.

Longtimers also swear by the Oaxacan specialties at **Casa de la Abuela** (Grandmother's House; above the Primavera café, tel. 951/516-3544, 10am-11pm daily, $7-20) at the *zócalo's* northwest corner. Here you can enjoy tasty, professionally prepared regional dishes and airy *zócalo* vistas from the balcony. Call for reservations and a table with a view.

For fine Oaxacan specialties in a graceful, old-world setting, try **Andariega Restaurant** (Independencia 503, tel./fax 951/514-9331, 7:30am-9pm daily, $8-14) in the Parador San Miguel, two blocks west of Catedral de Oaxaca. Here's one of your best chances to try some of Oaxaca's moles, such as *almendrado* (almond), *verde* (greena), *amarillo* (yellow), or *negro* (black), over chicken, beef, or pork. Other favorites are *chiles rellenos,* stuffed with cheese and *picadillo* (spiced meat), and red snapper in orange sauce. An excellent daily four-course *comida* (set lunch) runs about $8.

Moving uphill, the **Restaurant Catedral** (García Vigil 105, tel. 951/516-3285, 9am-midnight Mon.-Fri., 8am-2am Sat.-Sun., $8-16), two blocks north of the zócalo, at the corner of Morelos, serves as a tranquil daytime business and middle-to-upper-class refuge from the street hubbub. The refined ambience—music playing softly in the background, tables set around an airy, intimate fountain patio crowned by the blue Oaxaca sky above—is half the show. The finale is the attentive service and quality food for breakfast, lunch, or supper. The Aguilar family owners are especially proud of their moles that flavor their house specialties. These include fillets, both meat and fish, and regional dishes, such as banana leaf-wrapped tamales Oaxaqueños.

More good, eating, in a genteel, relaxed atmosphere, awaits you at the very popular **Restaurant El Sagrario** (120 Valdivieso, tel. 951/514-0303 or 951/514-3319, 8am-midnight daily, $7-14), behind Oaxaca Cathedral. Mostly local, youngish, upper-class customers enjoy a club/bar atmosphere (lower level), pizza parlor booths (middle level), or restaurant tables (upper level). At the restaurant level, during the evening, you can best take in the whole scene around you—chattering, upbeat crowd; live guitar, flute, jazz, or salsa melodies; and elegantly restored colonial details. Then, finally, comes the food, beginning, perhaps, with an appetizer, continuing with a soup or salad, then an international or regional specialty, which you top off with a light dessert and a savory espresso. Music volume goes up later in the evening.

Groceries and Wine

For simple, straightforward grocery shopping, plus a small selection of good wines, go to handily located **Abarrotes Lonja** (8am-9:30pm daily), on the zócalo's west side, next to La Cafetería café.

NORTH OF THE *ZÓCALO*
Cafés and Desserts

For coffee and dessert, you have a number of additional downtown choices, notably **Coffee Beans** (Cinco de Mayo 400, no phone, 8am-11pm daily), five blocks north of the zócalo, or nearby **Restaurant La Antigua** (a block east at Reforma 401, tel. 951/516-5761, noon-11pm daily, $3-8), just uphill from Abasolo.

A few blocks up Macedonio Alcalá find the tiny **Oaxacan Coffee Company** (100 Alcalá, no phone, 8am-9pm daily), serving organic brew and morning croissants. They also sell beans by the bag, and chocolate flavored with berries and spices. The service is take-out only. They also have main store and roasting facility (Constitución 108, tel. 951/218-1939). And for those who might be staying up in Xochimilco on the north side of Highway 190, the **A.M. Siempre Café** (Jose Lopez Alavez 1355, Xochimilco, tel. 951/515-6160, 8am-9pm daily) offers great coffee and pastries in the morning and sandwiches and lunch all day long. Try the chocolate cake—it's great!

An admirable coffee "chain" is ★ **Café Brújula** (various locations including García Vigil 409, 8am-10pm Mon.-Sat.; Macedonio Alcalá 104, no phone, 8am-10pm Mon.-Sat., 9am-10pm Sun.), roasting and serving coffee in Oaxaca since 2006. They work with the 21st of September Coop, which produces shade-grown organic coffee, and they roast their beans northern Italian style, good and dark. The shops are entertainingly decorated with visual puns, and the coffee is great.

Continue clockwise, north of the zócalo a block, to **Panadería Bamby** (northwest corner of García Vigil and Morelos, 6am-9pm Mon.-Sat.). A block east of the zócalo, stop by ★ **Pastelería and Café La Vasconia** (Independencia 907, between Cinco de Mayo and Reforma, tel. 951/516-2677, 8am-9pm daily, $2-6), with an inviting arched interior patio and a luscious selection of pastries, cakes, salads, and sandwiches. Another new addition to the many outstanding bakeries around the plaza is **Boulenc** (Porfirio Díaz 222-A, tel. 951/514-0582, 8:30am-8:30pm Mon.-Fri., 8:30am-5pm Sat., $1-7). The three young guys that run this place make great croissants in the morning, with or without chocolate, and pizzas, breads, chocolate chip cookes, and all kinds of great baked stuff all day long. For another kind of sweet treat, try ★ **Museo de las Nieves** (Alcalá 709-A at Humboldt, tel. 951/143-9253, museodelas-nieves.com, $2 and up), where you can indulge in organic sorbet, ice cream, or gelato in all sorts of interesting flavors, not only the usual fruits and spices, but, say, cheese with basil and *mezcal* ice cream, or atun (cactus fruit) sorbet.

Snacks and Food Stalls

On the northwest side of downtown, take a look around the **Mercado Sánchez Pasqua** (8am-2pm Mon.-Sat.) for some pleasant surprises. (To get there, from the *zócalo* cathedral, walk uphill along García Vigil seven blocks to Humboldt and turn left a block to Porfirio Díaz. It's the market across the street, past the gigantic wild fig tree.) Here, you can enjoy the town's tastiest *comal* (charcoal-fired griddle) cooking. Enjoy a hearty, homestyle breakfast (perhaps *huevos a la mexicana* with hot tortillas, or hotcakes with honey and bacon).

For a special lunchtime treat, ask for ★ **Carmen Hernández Ramírez** and order her *memelas* (big, thick, open-face tortillas smothered in beans, $1.50) or the luscious, plump tamales ($1.50) of **Señora Catalina Minerva Paz.**

Much farther up the economic scale, sample the delicious offerings of ★ **Hostería Alcalá** (Macedonio Alcalá 307, 8:30am-11pm daily, $5-15), four blocks north of the *zócalo.* The airy, tranquil patio ambience is ideal for a relaxing refreshment or lunch break from sightseeing along the Macedonio Alcalá pedestrian mall.

Restaurants

Devotees of light, vegetarian-style (and economically priced) cuisine get what they're hungering for at ★ **La Manantial Vegetariana** (corner of west-side Calle Tinoco y Palacios 303, tel. 951/514-5602, 9am-9pm Mon.-Sat., lunch $6, dinner $8), located just north (uphill) of Matamoros, two blocks west and three blocks north of the *zócalo.* A tranquil patio ambience sets the tone for the house specialty, a set lunch *comida.* Typically they might offer soup (onion or cream of zucchini), salad (mixed greens or tomato cucumber), stew (mushroom or soya steak), bread, fruit drink, dessert, and coffee or tea.

Another northside budget vegetarian restaurant, **Calabacitas Tiernas** (Alcalá 802, tel. 951/201-2582, 1pm-5pm Mon.-Fri., 2pm-5pm Sat., $7), offers great, healthy lunch fare in the form of a five-course, fixed-price menu with fresh ingredients. This is a vegetarian and vegan oasis with a hip, young professional clientele.

Step into the unpretentiously elegant, vine-hung atrium-courtyard of the ★ **Hostería Alcalá** (307 Macedonio Alcalá, tel. 951/516-2093 or 951/514-0820, 8am-11pm Mon.-Sat., 7am-10pm Sun., $12-14), and choose from a long menu of professionally prepared and presented salads, soups, pasta, meats, and fish. The Hostería provides an invitingly cool and soothing refuge on a warm afternoon. Find it one block downhill from the Santo Domingo church-front.

Right across from the Santo Domingo church, enjoy some relief from high restaurant prices at **Nostrana** (Macedonio Alcalá 501A, tel. 951/514-0778, 1pm-11pm daily, $7-12). In the cozy, five-table, old-country Italian dining room, relax and choose from a long menu of genuine Napolitano (the owners are Italian immigrants) country cooking. Choices include prosciutto, salads, plenty of pizza, and superb pasta, all washed down by good red wine.

A few doors west of Nostrana you'll find ★ **Pitiona** (Allende 108, tel.951/514-0690, pitiona.com, $7-40), one of Oaxaca's most talked about new restaurants (a write-up in the *New York Times* didn't hurt). Yes, this stylish place could hold its own in New York, both visually and gastronomically. Nor is it low budget. But Oaxacan-born chef Jose Manuel Baños Rodriguez, from Pinotepa, is busy reinventing traditional Oaxacan cuisine in a lively new fashion. Venison with yellow mole, goat hip stew, river mussel tamales, and mango tacos with pear mousse are but a few of the unusual gems on this menu.

Around the corner from Pitiona on García Vigil—uptown Oaxaca's new "restaurant row"—find three more restaurants offering variations on this same theme of reinvented tradition. Call it Oaxacan fusion. First, Zandunga (García Vigil 512-E, tel. 951/516-2265, $3-$15), named for the beloved theme song from Oaxaca's isthmus, features contemporary versions of that regional cuisine. The pulled pork with potato puree is pure dining pleasure.

Second, don't miss La Biznaga (García Vigil 512, tel. 951/516-1800, labiznaga.com.mx, $6-12), home of very slow food, as the website proclaims. That's all right, it's a lively room, with plenty of mezcal options to sample while you wait for the slow food, which includes such delights as fried squash blossoms

in poblano chile sauce, shrimp with garlic, chile, and tamarind mole, and an array of unique and original soups.

Last but not least, down the block find Zicanda (García Vigil 409-A, tel. 951/501-0715, $8-26), where cocinero (chef) Yiannis Roja Pozos works his magic in a visually stunning dining room with a glowing bar at the back featuring, of course, several dozen flavors and brands of mezcal. Try the grilled octopus, spicy watermelon salad, or plantain dumplings with mole negro.

If you're unfamiliar with (or unconvinced about) Oaxaca's mole sauces, erase your doubt by walking two blocks east of the front of Iglesia de Santo Domingo to Restaurant los Pacos (Abasolo 121, tel. 951/516-1704, 10am-10pm daily, $12-14). Your meal automatically comes with a mole appetizer sampler, which treats you to six—*coloradito, verde, negro, estofado, Amarillo,* and *chichilo*—of Oaxaca's moles right off the bat. It only gets better after that, especially if you continue with one of the good salads, from Caesar to tomato, then follow up with a traditional Oaxaca specialty, such as *enchiladas coloradito con picadillo, espinazo de puerco con mole verde,* or *entomatadas,* either *solas* (alone) or with beef.

Also behind Santo Domingo, half a block

art and design on display in lobby of the restaurant Zandunga

north of Abasolo, **Café La Olla** (Reforma 402, in front of Casa de las Bugambilias bed-and-breakfast, tel. 951/516-6668, 8am-10pm daily, $6-15) enjoys a loyal following of longtime North American residents and visitors. Here, the dark-beamed ceiling, subdued spotlighting of the art-decorated walls, quiet music, and candlelight set a refined, romantic tone. Select from a long but light menu of skillfully prepared and presented soups (Aztec soup is nearly a meal in itself), salads, Oaxacan specialties, and meats. (Café La Olla's main drawback is street noise, which you can minimize by taking an upstairs table.)

Right across the street is **Café La Antigua** (Reforma 401, tel. 951/516-5761, 9am-11pm Mon.-Sat., $3-10), enjoyed by a long list of loyal patrons for entirely different reasons. Here, the main course is conversation and fine on-site roasted Oaxaca "Pluma" coffee (from the farms around Pluma Hidalgo village, in the sierra above Huatulco). Along with their savory lattes, cold cappuccinos, and mocha frappés, patrons can enjoy fresh baked goods, crepes, sandwiches, eggs, and juices. The prime mover behind all this is friendly coffee grower and owner Diego Woolrich Ramírez.

A few blocks north and west of the *zócalo*, discriminating diners will seek out **Luvina Cocina de Taller** (Mártires de Tacubaya 517, tel. 951/132-5912, luvinaoaxaca.wix.com/luvina#!bar/c16fk, 1pm-11pm Tues.-Sat., 1pm-8pm Sun., $5-15), the dining "workshop" inspired by the writer Juan Rulfo. The space is light and wonderful, and the Oaxacan fusion menu offers yet another new expression of the meaning of Oaxacan cuisine. The location is in an alleyway off the small street called Cosijoeza, north of the street called La Constitición, and a little hard to find, but if you take the time you won't regret it.

Finally, if you're hankering for good seafood, take a table in the relaxing garden of northeast-side **Mariscos Jorge** (on Pino Suárez, across from El Llano park, tel. 951/513-4308, 8am-6:30pm daily, $8-16), the standout standby of local middle- and upper-class patrons. Choose from a long menu: 14

cocktail selections including shrimp, squid, and clams; salads and soups; and entrées, including fish fillets, from breaded and baked to *a la diabla*, octopus, and much more. It's also a good place to go for breakfast.

Due east of the south side of the *zócalo*, **Café Bistrot Epicuro** (Vicente Guerrero 318, tel. 951/514-9750, 1pm-11pm Wed.-Mon., $9-19) provides an Italian break from Oaxacan cuisine. Many claim Bistrot has the best pizza in Oaxaca, for what it's worth (and it's worth something, as there are quite a few pizza places here). They also serve pastas, Italian specialties (the owners are from Genoa), and some Mexican dishes as well. The room is so pretty and pleasant that the rooftop deck with its retractable roof goes unused at times.

Groceries, Wine, and Natural Food

Local devotees go to **Xiguela** café and natural food store (Hidalgo 104C, corner of Cinco de Mayo, in the northeast-side Jalatlaco district, no phone, 9am-6pm Mon.-Fri., 9am-3pm Sat.). There they stock up with healthy goodies, teas (arnica, anise, manzanilla), organic grains, granola, yogurt, honey, jams, and a ton more.

SOUTH OF THE *ZÓCALO*
Bakeries

For baked goods, try the sweet offerings of **Tartamiel Pastelería Frances** (on Trujano, half a block west from the southwest corner of the *zócalo*, tel. 951/516-7330, 7am-8pm Mon.-Sat., 8:30am-7pm Sun.).

Snacks and Food Stalls

For economical sit-down meals, visit the acre of food stalls inside the **Mercado 20 de Noviembre**, two blocks south and one block west of the *zócalo*'s southwest corner. Adventurous eaters will be in heaven among a wealth of succulent *chiles rellenos;* piquant moles; fat, banana leaf-wrapped *tamales Oaxaqueños;* and savory *sopas* (soups) and *guisados* (stews). Insist, however, that your selection be served hot.

Restaurants

Only a few good sit-down restaurants sprinkle the neighborhoods south of the zócalo. A trio of them, two well known for Oaxacan cuisine, and one for seafood, stand out.

Local folks strongly recommend the no-nonsense, country-style (but refined) La Flor de Oaxaca (Armenta y López 311, tel. 951/516-5522, 7:30am-10pm Mon.-Sat., 9am-3pm Sun., $8-10), a block east and half a block south from the zócalo's southeast corner. The mole-smothered regional specialties come mostly in four styles: con tasajo (thin broiled steak), con pollo (chicken), con cecina (roast pork), or sola (without meat). Besides those, you can choose from an extensive menu of equally flavorful items, such as tamales Oaxaqueños (wrapped in banana leaves), pork chops, several soups, spaghetti, and much more. Credit cards are accepted.

A block west and two blocks south of the zócalo's southwest corner, ★ Restaurant Tayu (20 de Noviembre 416, tel. 951/516-5363, 8am-6pm Mon.-Sat., $3-7) allows you to step in to Oaxaca "as it used to be." Take a table and relax in the refined, old-world, TV-free ambience. In the mornings, select from a host of tasty breakfasts; in the afternoons, choose one of their four-course $6 comidas that include a choice between several hearty entrées, such as short ribs, chicken, chiles rellenos, with soup, rice, and dessert included. Arrive in the afternoon, 2:30pm-4:30pm, and enjoy their live instrumental music.

Lovers of fresh seafood can join the loyal brigade of local folks who frequent the airy and unpretentious Restaurant La Red (The Net; corner of Bustamante and Colón, tel. 951/514-8840, noon-9pm daily, $10-16), one of five Oaxaca branches, located one block south of the zócalo's southeast corner. Customers get their heart's delight of generous seafood cocktails, heaping bowls of shrimp, fish fillets, octopus, and much more.

Fine Dining

The Oaxaca visitor influx during the 1990s nurtured a crop of fine restaurants. If at all possible, visit the elegant ★ Los Danzantes (Macedonio Alcalá 402, tel. 951/501-1184 or 951/501-1187, 1:30pm-11:30pm daily, $20 lunch, $35 dinner), where everything seems designed for perfection. We were lucky to enjoy a surprisingly economical ($10 until 6pm) set lunch, which, when offered, changes daily. In the airy dining atrium, beneath blue sky and sunlight filtering through curtains artfully draped overhead, waiters scurried, starting us off with chilled artichoke soup, and continuing with savory spinach lasagna with Oaxaca requesón cheese, accompanied by delicious pressed guava-apple juice. They topped it all off with delectable dark-Oaxaca chocolate mousse and espresso coffee. Bravo! After such an introduction, you'll be tempted to return on another day. Reservations are strongly recommended.

Hotel manager and chef Alejandro Ruiz of Casa Oaxaca (García Vigil 407, tel. 951/516-8889, $25-35) now has new venues to work his culinary wonders. While the Casa Oaxaca remains at its original address, the restaurant and its new sister café have moved to a couple of different locations. The vine-draped and breezily casual Casa Oaxaca Café (Jasmines 518, corner of. Sabinas, tel. 951/502-6017, casa-oaxacacafe.com, $10-25) offers much of the same great cuisine as the restaurant, but opens for all three meals and charges slightly lower prices. Ruiz puts his all into blending the best of old and new cuisine at the elegant new location of the Casa Oaxaca Restaurant (Constitución 104-A, tel. 951/516-8531, casa-oaxacaelrestaurante.com, 1pm-11pm Mon.-Sat., 1pm-9pm Sun., $23-30), with its rooftop bar. For example, start off with duck pâté and continue with flor de calabaza, stuffed with cheese and accompanied by tostaditas (toasted corn) and guacamole. Follow through with broiled shrimp in their juice with lentils, or baked robalo (snook) with lemon, all accompanied with a bottle of white wine from their extensive list. Finish off with baby coconut custard, mango pie, or guanabana mousse, or a sampling of all three. Reservations are mandatory.

In the far northeast corner of downtown, showplace **Restaurant La Toscana** (corner of Cinco de Mayo and Alianza, tel. 951/513-8742, 2pm-10pm daily, $10-20), in the old northeast-side Jalatlaco neighborhood, offers a long, elegant Mediterranean menu, spiced with a dash of traditional Oaxaca. Although it would be hard to go wrong with most anything here, I enjoyed the lettuce and tomato salad with goat cheese, shrimp fettuccine, leg of *jabalí* (wild pig), and, for dessert, croquettes of coconut and banana. Reservations are recommended. Note that this is a different Cinco de Mayo from the one near Santo Domingo—note as well that this restaurant is located in a beautifully fading old building with no signage.

Groceries, Wine, and Natural Food

For fruits and vegetables, the cheapest and freshest are in Mercado Juárez, which takes up the square block immediately southwest of the *zócalo.*

Information and Services

TOURIST INFORMATION

The state tourism secretariat maintains an **information office** (703 Av. Juárez, tel./fax 951/516-0123, www.aoaxaca.com, 8am-8pm daily) on the west side of El Llano park. They also staff a town center **information desk** (on Independencia, corner of García Vigil, tel. 951/516-5645, 10am-6pm Tues.-Sun.) at their former headquarters (now the Museum of Oaxacan Painters), at the north edge of the *zócalo,* half a block north of the cathedral-front.

Furthermore, the city (Coordinaciñn de Turismo Municipal) also maintains a town-center **tourist information office** (102 Matamoros, tel. 951/516-9901 or 951/516-8365, 9am-6pm Mon.-Sat.). Follow García Vigil two blocks north of the *zócalo,* turn left (west), and continue half a block.

Travel and Tour Agencies and Guides

Lohbi Tours and Travel (corner of Valdivieso and Independencia, tel. 951/514-3165, lohbitour@yahoo.com.mx, 9am-2pm Mon.-Sat.), one block northeast of the *zócalo,* behind the cathedral, is a good source for most travel services, especially air tickets.

Other agencies are likewise experienced, especially with tours. Among them is **Viajes Xochitlán** (García Vigil 617, tel. 951/514-3271, www.xochitlan-tours.com.mx, 9am-2pm and 4pm-7pm Mon.-Sat.). Travel in comfort to Oaxaca City and Valley sites and villages, such as Monte Albán, Mitla, Teotitlán del Valle, Tlacolula, and much more. They specialize in individuals and groups, tourist and business services, and travel agent services, such as air and bus tickets and hotel bookings.

Another reliable, long-time travel and tour agent is **Viajes Turísticos Mitla** (Mina 501, tel. 951/516-6175 or 951/501-0220). The office is three blocks west and three blocks south of the *zócalo*'s southwest corner, near the departure points for several tour bus companies. They also provide very economical bus-only tourist transportation to a plethora of Valley of Oaxaca sites, with multiple daily departures to Monte Albán.

There are literally dozens of these tour agencies around downtown Oaxaca, all offering tours for small to medium-sized groups, usually on a given schedule that covers 3-6 Oaxaca Valley destinations in a half- or full-day of touring with a bilingual guide. Given Oaxaca's not-so-great traffic management and the cost of a rental car, this is probably the best and most economical way to see the sights in the Valley of Oaxaca. The prices are generally in the $12-15 price range for a four- to six-hour tour, but this does not include entry fees at the destinations, or the price of lunch at a restaurant of the driver's choosing.

A Oaxaca regiment of private individual guides also offers tours. Among the most highly recommended is the fluent-in-English Juan Montes Lara (Prol. de Eucaliptos 303, Colonia Reforma, tel./fax 951/513-0126, jmonteslara@yahoo.com, $25/hour), backed up by his wife Karin Schutte. Besides cultural sensitivity and extensive local knowledge, Juan and Karin also provide comfortable transportation in a big Chrysler van.

Moreover, satisfied customers rave about guide Sebastian Chino Peña (home tel. 951/562-1761, cell tel. 044-951/508-1220 in Oaxaca City, sebastian_oaxaca@hotmail.com, $20/hour). He offers tours by car of anywhere you would like to go in the city or valley of Oaxaca.

More athletic travelers might enjoy the services of Zona Bici (García Vigil 409, tel. 951/516-0953, www.bikeoaxaca.com), five blocks due north of the *zócalo,* which rents bikes and also conducts bike tours into the countryside.

For even more extensive backcountry adventure bicycling, hiking, and camping in the mountains just north of the Valley of Oaxaca, contact Expediciones Sierra Norte (M. Bravo 210, tel./fax 951/514-8271, www.sierranorte.org.mx).

You might inquire for a guide recommendation at the state tourist information office (703 Av. Juárez, tel./fax 951/516-0123, www.aoaxaca.com, 8am-8pm daily). They maintain a list of officially-sanctioned and certified guides.

HEALTH AND EMERGENCIES

If you get sick, ask your hotel desk to recommend a doctor. Otherwise, go to the 24-hour Clinica Hospital Carmen (Abasolo 215, tel./fax 951/516-0027), staffed by English-speaking IAMAT Doctors Horacio Tenorio S. and Germán Tenorio V. Alternatively, go to the highly-recommended northside Hospital Reforma (Reforma 613, tel. 951/516-6100), a block west of El Llano park.

For routine medicines and drugs, go to one of many pharmacies, such as the Farmacia Ahorros (on Cinco de Mayo, near the northeast corner of Murguia, 7am-11pm daily), one block east and two blocks north of the cathedral. After hours, call Farmacia Ahorros's free 24-hour delivery service (tel. 951/515-5000). Most pharmacies in Oaxaca, indeed in all of Mexico, have on staff at least one pharmacist who is well-versed in medicine, and can help you figure out what ails you and what you need to cure it.

For fire or police emergencies, call the emergency number 066, or take a taxi to the municipal police station (*policia municipal;* Morelos 108, tel. 951/516-0455), or call the firefighters (*bomberos;* tel. 951/506-0248).

BOOKSTORES AND PUBLICATIONS

The best source for English-language books about Mexico is the Librería Amate (Alcalá 307, ground floor of Plaza Alcalá, tel. 951/516-6960, fax 951/516-7181, www.amatebooks.com, 10am-8:30pm Mon.-Sat., 2pm-7pm Sun.), four blocks north of the *zócalo.*

The interesting Librería de Bibliofiles de Oaxaca (Bibliophiles' Bookstore of Oaxaca; Macedonio Alcalá 104, tel. 951/516-9901, 10am-9pm daily), downhill from Iglesia de Santo Domingo, offers a big collection of new, mostly Spanish books, with a good number of art, crafts, archaeology, and cultural books in English.

Pick up a copy of the good daily English-language *News,* from Mexico City, available late mornings, except Sunday, at the newsstand near the *zócalo*'s southwest corner, a few steps south on Cabrera.

Also, you can print out copies of the useful tourist newspapers, *Oaxaca Times* (www.oaxacatimes.com) and *Go-Oaxaca* (www.go-oaxaca.com) on the Internet. Pick up the *Oaxaca Times* paper edition at hotels, shops, travel agents, the local tourist information offices, or at the publisher (Macedonio Alcalá 307, upstairs, tel./fax 951/516-3443).

MONEY EXCHANGE

Several banks, all with ATMs, sprinkle the downtown area. (*Note:* Remove your ATM card promptly; some local machines are known to "eat" them if left in for more than about 15 seconds after the transaction is finished.) One of the most convenient is the Banamex ATM (on Valdivieso, directly behind Oaxaca Cathedral, 9am-4pm Mon.-Fri.). As of this writing, many ATMs in Mexico are frequently the targets of fraud, as in guys who'll set up the machine to steal your PIN and then drain your account. We recommend using ATMs located inside or adjacent to banks, where access is controlled.

The best-bet, full-service bank with long hours is HSBC (one block north, one block east of the *zócalo* corner of Guerrero and Armenta y López, tel. 951/514-7040 or 951/516-9754, 8am-6pm Mon.-Fri., 9am-6pm Sat.).

A full-service Banamex branch (Hidalgo at Cinco de Mayo, tel. 951/516-5900, 9am-4pm Mon.-Sat.) nearby receives customers just one block due east of the *zócalo.* If Banamex is too crowded, go to HSBC or Banco Santander (on the Independencia corner, north of the Oaxaca Cathedral, tel. 951/516-1100, 9am-4pm Mon.-Sat.); they change U.S. and Euro currencies and travelers checks.

If banks are closed, try moneychanger Ce Cambio (on Valdivieso, corner of Independencia, tel. 951/516-3399, 9am-6pm Mon.-Fri., 9am-5pm Sat.), just north of the *zócalo,* behind the Oaxaca Cathedral. Although it may pay about a percent less than the banks, it changes many major currencies. There are numerous other money changers on most of the streets around the *zócalo,* all offering pretty much the same services at the same rates. If you have the option, you'll do better withdrawing cash from an American account from a safely located ATM, since you'll get the

bank rate rather than the money changer rate. And within reason, take as much money out as you need, since you'll pay the same fee for a 1,000-peso withdrawal as you will for a 5,000-peso withdrawal.

COMMUNICATIONS

The Oaxaca post office (*correo;* corner of Alameda de León plaza and Independencia, tel. 951/516-1291, 8am-7pm Mon.-Fri., 10am-5pm Sat.) is across from the cathedral-front. Mail service in and from Mexico ranges from abominable to painfully slow. Don't rely on it for anything important. A block west of the post office, the telecomunicaciones (corner of Independencia and 20 de Noviembre, tel. 951/516-4902, 8am-7:30pm Mon.-Fri., 9am-4pm Sat., 9am-noon Sun.) offers money orders, telephones, and public fax machines.

For long-distance and local telephone service, buy a Ladatel phone card (widely available in stores; look for the yellow Ladatel sign) and use it in public street telephones.

Answer your email and access the Internet at any one of a number of spots around the *zócalo.* For example, try the small shop behind the cathedral (Valdevieso 120, tel. 951/514-9227, 9am-11pm daily). Most Oaxaca hotels have free Wi-Fi, though it may be a little slow and you might have to sit near the reception desk.

LIBRARIES

Visitors starving for a good read in English will find satisfaction at the Oaxaca Lending Library (Pino Suárez 519, tel. 951/518-7077, www.oaxlibrary.org, 10am-2pm and 4pm-7pm Mon.-Fri., 10am-1pm Sat.), about five blocks north of the *zócalo* on the west side of Pino Suárez, a block north of Constitución.

The city biblioteca (public library; corner of Morelos and Macedonio Alcalá, tel. 951/516-1853, 9am-8:30pm Mon.-Fri., 10am-2pm Sat.), two blocks north of the *zócalo* in a lovingly restored former convent, is worth a visit, if only for its graceful, cloistered Renaissance interiors and patios. The library holdings are nearly all in Spanish.

CONSULATES AND IMMIGRATION

The **U.S. Consulate** (Macedonio Alcalá 407, tel. 951/514-3054 or 951/518-2853, fax 951/516-2701, 11am-4pm Mon.-Thurs.) is upstairs at Plaza Santo Domingo, across from the Santo Domingo church. In an emergency, call the **U.S. Embassy** (tel. 01-55/5080-2000). The **Canadian Consulate** (700 Pino Suárez, local 11B, tel. 951/513-3777, fax 951/515-2147, 11am-2pm Mon.-Fri.) services Canadian citizens. In an emergency, call the **Canadian Embassy in Mexico City** (toll-free Mex. tel. 800/706-2900).

Other consulates that may be available in Oaxaca are the **Italian Consulate** (Macedonio Alcalá 400, tel. 951/516-5058) and the **Spanish Consulate** (Porfirio Díaz 340, Colonia Reforma, tel. 951/515-3525 or 951/518-0031). For more information, look for consulate contact numbers in the *Oaxaca Times* or the telephone directory Yellow Pages, under *Embajadas, Legaciones, y Consulados*, or call the U.S. or Canadian consulates for information.

If you lose your tourist permit, make arrangements with **Migración** (at the airport, tel. 951/511-5733, 7am-9pm daily) at least several hours before your scheduled departure from Mexico. Bring with you proof of your arrival date in Mexico—stamped passport, airline ticket, or copy of the lost permit.

LAUNDRY

Get your laundry done at conveniently located **Super Lavandería** (corner of Hidalgo and J. P. Garcia, tel. 951/514-1181, 8am-8pm Mon.-Sat.), two blocks west of the *zócalo*'s northwest corner.

PHOTOGRAPHY

Good photo stores in downtown Oaxaca include **Foto Figueroa** (Hidalgo 516, corner 20 de Noviembre, tel. 951/516-3766, 9am-8pm Mon.-Sat.). With plenty of Kodak digital accessories, it offers quick digital and develop-and-print services. Another store with the same range of services and accessories is **Central Fotografía** (Rayón 117, tel. 951/514-4479, 951/516-9517, 9am-6pm Mon.-Sat., closed Sun.).

VOLUNTEER WORK AND DONATIONS

Local residents and visitors have banded together to provide help for Oaxaca's street children and poor single-parent families. A formerly grassroots organization, **Centro de Esperanza Infantil** (Crespo 308, tel. 951/501-1069, www.oaxacastreetchildren-grassroots.org, 9am-4pm Mon.-Fri., 9am-2pm Sat.) operates cooperatively out of its center, about four blocks north and three blocks west of the *zócalo*. The all-volunteer organization raises money for food, schoolbooks and uniforms, housing, foster care, and much more for homeless children and destitute single mothers and their children. They welcome donations and volunteers, and visitors are always welcome. Check the website for an address for sending donations within the United States or Canada.

LANGUAGE INSTRUCTION AND COURSES

A long list of satisfied clients attest to the competence of the language instruction of the **Instituto Cultural de Oaxaca** (northside corner of Calz. Niños Héroes/Hwy. 190 and Av. Juárez, tel. 951/515-3404, fax 951/515-3728, www.icomexico.com), in a lovely garden campus.

Also very highly recommended is the **Becari Language School** (M. Bravo 210, tel./fax 951/514-6076, www.becari.com.mx). Offerings include small-group Spanish instruction, as well as cooking and dancing classes. If you desire, the school can arrange homestays with local families.

Similarly experienced is the **Vinigulaza Language and Tradition School** (Vinigulaza Idioma y Tradición; Abasolo 503, corner of Los Libres, about six blocks east, four blocks north of the plaza, tel. 951/513-2763, www.vinigulaza.com), associated with the local English-language Cambridge Academy. Offerings include informative (and even fun), small-group Spanish instruction. Schedules are flexible, and prices are reasonable.

Alternatively, for more lightweight instruction, try **Español Interactivo** (Interactive Spanish; Armenta y López 311B, tel./fax 951/514-6062, www.studyspanishinoaxaca.com), one block east and half a block south of the *zócalo*, by Iglesia de San Agustín. The school offers several levels that provide 15-40 instructional hours per week. Classes have a maximum of five students.

All the language schools also arrange **homestays** with Oaxaca families and often offer classes in folkloric and salsa dancing, weaving, and painting on clay and wood.

Inexpensive Spanish instruction is customarily available from volunteers at the **Oaxaca Lending Library** (Pino Suárez 519, tel. 951/518-7077, www.oaxlibrary.org), about

five blocks north of the *zócalo* and a block north (uphill) from Constitución.

OAXACAN COOKING AND CULTURE

Susana Trilling, Oaxaca resident and author of *My Search for the Seventh Mole* (as in MOH-lay), offers an unusual mix of Oaxacan culture, cooking, and eating, with a lodging option, at her **Seasons of My Heart cooking school** (Rancho Aurora; in Oaxaca, local cell tel. 044-951/508-0469; in Mexico, long-distance 045-951/508-0469; from Canada or U.S. 011-52-1-951/508-0469; www.seasonsofmyheart.com) in the Etla Valley, north of the city. Susana's simplest offering is a half-day cooking lesson ($50). She also offers a one-day group cooking adventure ($75), which includes a morning trip to a local native market to buy food, then preparing and eating at Susana's ranch. Farther-ranging cooking courses (six days, $1,500) regularly include trips to outlying parts of Oaxaca, such as the Isthmus of Tehuántepec or northern Oaxaca, around Tuxtepec.

Transportation

AIR

The Oaxaca airport (code-designated OAX) has several daily flights that connect with Mexico City and other Mexican and international destinations. Many of the Mexico City flights allow same-day connections between Oaxaca and many U.S. gateways.

Continental Airlines, (toll-free in Mex. tel. 800/900-5000) fortunately, has eliminated the stop in Mexico City en route to Oaxaca and now flies nonstop to and from Houston (flight time only 2.5 hours).

Aeroméxico (reservations toll-free in Mex. tel. 800/021-4000, tel. 951/516-1066, 951/516-7101, or 951/516-3765; flight information tel. 951/511-5055 or 951/511-5044) has flights that connect daily with Mexico City.

Budget carrier **Volaris Airlines** (toll-free in Mex. tel. 800/122-8000 and 800/865-2747) currently offers a direct Tijuana-Oaxaca connection, which is especially handy for southern California travelers.

Alternatively, light charter airlines (in the general aviation terminal, the building to the right as you face the main terminal) connect Oaxaca City with various points within Oaxaca. **Aerotucan** (tel. 951/502-0840, toll-free in Mex., outside Oaxaca tel. 800/640-4148, www.aerotucan.com.mx) regularly connects Oaxaca City with Puerto Escondido, Huatulco, and sometimes with Tuxtla Gutiérrez and Puebla.

The Oaxaca airport provides a modicum of services, such as a few shops for last-minute purchases; an international newsstand (seasonally only) with magazines and paperback novels; car rentals; a cafeteria in the waiting/boarding area, a mailbox (*buzón;* downstairs by the staircase to the restaurant); public Ladatel card-operated telephones; and an ATM downstairs.

Travel to and from the Airport

Arrival transportation for the 10-kilometer (six mi) trip into town is easy, aside from traffic jams. Buy tickets at the booth at the far right end of the terminal as you exit. Fixed-fare *colectivo* (shared taxi) tickets run about $5 per person for downtown ($7 to northside Hotels Misión de los Angeles, Fortín Plaza, and Victoria). For the same trip, a *taxi especial* (private taxi) ticket runs about $15 for four people; larger Nissan Vans cost $17 and $28 (depending on destination) for up to eight passengers. No public buses run between the airport and town.

Car rental agents stationed regularly at the Oaxaca airport are: **Alamo** (tel. 951/511-8534, toll-free in Mex. tel. 800/002-5266, tel./fax 951/514-8534, oaxalamo@hotmail.com); **Europcar** (tel. 951/516-8258, 951/516-9305 or 951/143-8340, toll-free in Mex. tel. 800/201-1111 or 800/201-2089, Oaxaca office Matamoros tel. 951/516-9305, www.europcar.com.mx), and **Economy Rent a Car** (Oaxaca office Cinco de Mayo 203, tel. 951/514-8534, economyrentacar.com). Economy offered the best prices on our last go-round and their employee pointed out to us that if you rent in town instead of at the airport, you pay 10 percent less. This is worth knowing if you are renting for more than a few days.

For **departure,** save taxi money by getting your *colectivo* airport transportation ticket ahead of time, at **Transportacion Terrestres** (on the west side of Plaza Alameda de León, across from the cathedral, tel. 951/514-4350, 9am-2pm and 5pm-8pm Mon.-Sat.).

If you lose your tourist permit, take proof of your arrival date in Mexico, such as a stamped passport, airline ticket, or copy of lost permit, to airport **Migración** (tel. 951/511-5733, 8am-9pm daily) a minimum of several hours prior to departure from Mexico.

CAR OR RV

Paved (but long, winding, and sometimes potholed) roads connect Oaxaca City with all regions of Oaxaca and neighboring states.

Four routes connect Oaxaca City south to the Pacific coast; two of them, via Highways 175 and 131, connect directly south over the super-scenic but rugged Sierra Madre del Sur. Especially during the June-October rainy season, travelers are subject to landslides and bridge washout delays. The longer but less rugged (and most dependable in bad weather) route connects Oaxaca via Highway 190 southeast to Tehuántepec, and from there to the Pacific coast Highway 200 west. The fourth route, also less direct, but still rugged and winding, travels west from Oaxaca, via Highway 190, and then south to the Pacific coast, via Highway 125.

The most direct route, narrow national **Highway 175,** runs along 238—winding, sometimes potholed—kilometers (148 mi), with its junction with coast Highway 200 at Pochutla (from there, it's 10 km/6 mi to Puerto Ángel). The road climbs to more than 2,700 meters (9,000 ft.) through winter-chilly pine forests and indigenous Chatino and Zapotec villages. Under dry, daylight conditions, count on about seven hours at the wheel if heading south from Oaxaca to Puerto Ángel, or about eight hours in the opposite direction. This is not a white-knuckle drive—not quite.

About the same is true for the paved **National Highway 131** route south from Oaxaca, which splits off of Highway 175 three kilometers (two mi) south of San Bartolo Coyotepec. On your way out of town, fill up with gasoline at the Oaxaca airport Pemex. Continue, via Zimatlán and Sola de Vega (fill up with gas again), over the pine-clad Pacific crest, a total of 254 kilometers (158 mi) to Puerto Escondido. Under dry, daylight conditions, allow about seven hours southbound, or about eight hours in the opposite direction. Gasoline is available mid-route at the Sola de Vega Pemex.

Highway 190 connects Oaxaca City southeast with Tehuántepec, along 250 kilometers (155 mi) of well-maintained but winding highway. Allow about 4.5 hours to Tehuántepec (downhill), or 5 hours in the opposite direction.

At Tehuántepec, connect west with Highway 200, via Salina Cruz, to the Oaxaca Pacific coast, and Bahías de Huatulco (161 km/100 mi, three hours), Pochutla-Puerto Ángel (200 km/124 mi, four hours), and Puerto Escondido (274 km/170 mi, five hours) via paved, lightly-traveled but secure Highway 200. All of the roads in coastal Oaxaca are undergoing great improvements as the tourism industry seeks to bring more people in, and these are, for the most part, easy drives.

The very long but super-scenic 368-kilometer (229 mi) Highway 190-Highway 125 route connects Oaxaca southwest with coastal Pinotepa Nacional, via the Mixtec country destinations of Yanhuitlán, Teposcolula, and Tlaxiaco. Although winding most of the way, the generally uncongested road is safely drivable (subject to some potholes, however) from Oaxaca in about 10 driving hours if you use the *cuota autopista* northwest of Oaxaca City (exit to old Highway 190 at Nochixtlán). Add an hour for the 2,100-meter (7,000 ft.) climb in the opposite direction.

The 564-kilometer (350 mi) winding Highway 190-Highway 160 from Oaxaca to Cuernavaca, Morelos, and Mexico City via Huajuapan de León requires a very long day, or better two days for safety. Under the best of conditions, the Mexico City-Oaxaca driving time runs 11 hours either way. Take it easy and stop overnight en route. (Make sure you arrive in Mexico City on a day when your car is permitted to enter. There are restrictions in place to reduce smog and traffic congestion in the city.)

Alternatively, you can cut your Mexico City-Oaxaca driving time significantly via the Mexico City-Puebla-Oaxaca *autopista,* combined 150D-131D, which, southbound, takes off from the southeast end of Mexico City's Calzada General Ignacio Zaragoza. Northbound, follow the signs on Highway 190 a few miles north of Oaxaca. Allow about six hours driving time at a steady 100 kph (60 mph). Tolls, which are worth it for the increased speed and safety, run about $30 for a car, much more for a big RV.

Car Rentals

Car rentals offer a convenient means of exploring Oaxaca City and environs. Although town and valley roads present no unusual hazards, drive defensively, anticipate danger, and keep a light foot on the accelerator. Also be aware that road hazards—animals, people, potholes, barricades, rocks—are much more dangerous at night. Traffic in Oaxaca City is like traffic in every city these days: slow-moving. Renting a car is not recommended if your itinerary is limited to Oaxaca City and the Valley of Oaxaca. Let tour company drivers do the work.

To rent a car, all you need is a current driver's license and a credit card. However, car rentals, which by law must include adequate Mexican liability insurance—that extra $12 a day you have pay, no matter what credit card you have—are expensive, running upwards of $40 per day in high season. Save *mucho dinero* by splitting the tariff with others. Rent in town instead of the airport and save 10 percent.

Get your rental through either a travel agent or, before departure, through U.S. and Canadian toll-free car rental numbers, or in Oaxaca locally: Alamo (tel. 951/511-6220, tel./fax 951/514-8534, fax 951/514-8686, Alamo.com); Europcar (at airport, or at Matamoros 101, tel./fax 951/143-8340, toll-free tel. in Mexico 800/201-1111 or 800/201-2084, europcar.com); Economy Rent a Car (at airport and at Cinco de Mayo 203, tel. 951/514-8534, toll-free 01-800/002-5266, economyrentacar.com).

VAN

Eight-to-sixteen-passenger vans, although less comfortable than first-class buses, provide faster service (at a much cheaper price). They are becoming increasingly popular for medium-distance connections, especially for the Pacific coast destinations of Pochutla-Puerto Ángel and Huatulco, northwest destinations in the Mixteca, and Northern Oaxaca destinations in the Sierra Norte, the Cañada, and around Tuxtepec.

At least two operators provide Oaxaca-Pochutla connections, from stations about one block east, three blocks south of the *zócalo*'s southeast corner. The first option is **Eclipse 70** (tel. 951/516-1068, Pochutla $12), which departs about every half hour during the day from Armenta y López 540. Alternatively, around the second left downhill corner, you can ride **Atlantida** (Noria 101, tel. 951/514-7077, $12) every two hours for the same price.

For a direct Huatulco connection, try competent carrier **Van 2000** (Hidalgo 208, westside, near Soledad Church, tel. 951/516-3154), which offers about eight daily departures, connecting with Crucecita on the Huatulco coast.

The northwest (Nochixtlan, Teposcolula, Tlaxiaco, Putla) van connection is **Excelencia** (Díaz Ordaz 305, tel. 951/516-3578), three blocks west, one block south, from the *zócalo*'s southwest corner.

For northern Cañada (Cuicatlan and Teotitlan del Camino) and Sierra Mazateca (Huautla de Jiménez) destinations, go by **Transportes Turistico Oaxaca-Cañada** vans (600 Trujano, five blocks west of the *zócalo*, tel. 951/378-1080).

BUS
Luxury and First Class

In contrast to vans, buses are much more comfortable and remain a popular option, especially for longer trips. Oaxaca's major luxury- and first-class carriers, Autobuses

del Oriente and Omnibus Cristóbal Colón and their associated minor carriers, operate out of their **terminal** (toll-free in Mex. tel. 800/702-8000, Calz. Héroes de Chapultepec 1036, at Carranza, on the north side of town) on Highway 190. Bus lines accept credit cards for luxury- and first-class bookings. Passengers enjoy some amenities, such as Ladatel-card public telephones (on the terminal south end), snack stands, luggage lockers, air-conditioned first- and luxury-class waiting rooms, and cool, refined Restaurant Colibri across the street.

Moreover, all of the carriers that use the Héroes de Chapultepec terminal cooperate through the joint agency **Boletotal** (formerly Ticket Bus, toll-free in Mex. tel. 800/702-8000 or 800/009-9090, www.boletotal.com.mx, 8am-10pm Mon.-Sat. and 8am-9pm Sun.), which sells tickets at three town-center offices: on the *zócalo*'s south side, by the **Internet store** (tel. 951/513-3773); a block west of the *zócalo* (20 de Noviembre 103D, tel. 951/514-6655); and behind the Oaxaca Cathedral (corner of Independencia, tel. 951/502-0560).

Omnibuses Cristóbal Colón (OCC) offers first- and luxury-class connections with many Oaxaca and national destinations. Buses connect northwest with the Mixteca destinations of Nochixtlán, Tamazulapan, and Huajuapan de León, then continuing on to Puebla and Mexico City. Westerly, they connect with the Mixteca Alta, via Teposcolula, Tlaxiaco, Juxtlahuaca, Putla de Guerrero, and Pinotepa Nacional. Southerly, they connect (via the surer, but 11-hour long, Isthmus route) via Salina Cruz, with Huatulco, Pochutla-Puerto Ángel, and Puerto Escondido; and southeasterly, with Tehuántepec, Juchitán, Tapachula, Tuxtla Guitiérrez, and San Cristóbal de las Casas.

Autobuses del Oriente (ADO) also offers both first- and luxury-class Oaxaca connections, mostly along the Highway 190 corridor. First-class buses connect northwest with Mexico City (Tapo Tasqueña and Norte stations), via Nochixtlán and Huajuapan de León, and southeast with Tehuántepec and Salina Cruz. Other departures connect northeast with Coatzacoalcos, Villahermosa, Palenque, and Mérida; others connect north, with Tuxtepec, Veracruz, and Tampico.

ADO luxury-class buses mostly connect with Mexico City: ADO Platino (Platinum-class) connects, nonstop northwest, with Mexico City's Tapo and Norte stations, and southeast, with Tuxtla Gutiérrez in Chiapas. Furthermore, ADO GL luxury-class buses connect northwest, with Mexico City's Tapo and Tasqueño stations; southeast, with Tuxtla Gutiérrez and San Cristóbal de las Casas; and north, with Veracruz.

Also, first-class **Estrella de Oro** departures connect with Acapulco, via Huajuapan de León in the Mixteca, and Chilapa and Chipancingo in Guerrero.

Regional first-class **Cuenca** buses connect with northern Oaxaca points along Highway 175, including Ixtlán de Juárez, Valle Nacional, Tuxtepec, and Tierra Blanca, continuing all the way to Veracruz.

Note: Although first-class **Sur** and **Autobuses Unidos** (AU) tickets for reserved seats are sold at the Héroes de Chapultepec first-class station, they nevertheless depart from the Oaxaca Second-Class terminal. (Be sure to double-check your departure station when you buy Sur or AU tickets.)

Sur departures connect with Mexico City's Tapo station, along old Highways 190 and 160, via Huajuapan de León, Izucar de Matamoros, Puebla, and Cuatla, Morelos.

Autobuses Unidos departures connect with either Mexico City along the fast *autopista* expressway via Nochixtlán, Coixtlahuaca, and Puebla; or along the old Highway 131 via Cuicatlán, Teotitlán del Camino, Tehuacán, and Puebla.

Second Class

A swarm of long-distance second-class buses runs from the *camionera central segunda clase* (second-class bus terminal), south-west of downtown, just north of the Abastos

market. Get there by taxi or by walking due west about eight blocks from the *zócalo* to the west end of Calle Las Casas. Take care crossing the busy *periférico* straight across the railroad tracks. Keep walking the same direction, along the four-lane street for two more blocks, to the terminal gate on the right. Inside, you'll find an orderly array of snack stalls, a cafeteria, luggage lockers, a long-distance telephone and fax, and a lineup of *taquillas* (ticket booths).

With one exception all ticket booths line up along the terminal to your left as you enter. **Fletes y Pasajes** (tel. 951/516-2270) dominates the terminal, with three separate ticket booths. All three Fletes y Pasajes booths sell tickets to most of their destinations. They offer very broad second-class service, connecting with nearly everywhere in Oaxaca except north: westerly, with Mixteca destinations of Nochixtlán, Tamazulapan, Huajuapan, and Tlaxiaco, connecting all the way via Highway 125 to Pinotepa Nacional on the coast; easterly, with Mitla and Mixe destinations of Ayutla, Zacatepec, and Juquila Mixes; and southeasterly, with Isthmus destinations of Tehuántepec, Juchitán, and Salina Cruz. Besides all of the above, Fletes y Pasajes offers luxury-class "super" expressway connections with Mexico City.

In approximate consecutive order, moving left from the entrance, first find **Transportes Oaxaca Istmo** (tel. 951/516-3664). Departures connect with dozens of destinations east and south. These include the east Valley of Oaxaca destinations of Tlacolula and Mitla, continuing to the Isthmus destinations of Tehuántepec, Juchitán, and Salina Cruz. From Tehuántepec and Salina Cruz, they connect west, with the Pacific coast destinations of Huatulco, Pochutla-Puerto Ángel, and Puerto Escondido.

Cooperating **Auto Transportes Oaxaca-Pacífico** (tel. 951/516-2908) and **Autobuses Estrella del Valle** travel the Highway 175 north-south route between Oaxaca and

Pochutla-Puerto Ángel. Both lines continue, connecting along east-west coastal Highway 200 with Bahías de Huatulco, Puerto Escondido, and Pinotepa Nacional.

Estrella Roja del Sureste and **Trans Sol** (tel. 951/516-0694), with some first-class buses, connect directly with Puerto Escondido along Highway 131 north-south via Sola de Vega (with a side-trip to Juquila pilgrimage shrine). From Puerto Escondido, you can make coastal connections with Pochutla-Puerto Ángel, Bahías de Huatulco, Jamiltepec, and Pinotepa Nacional.

Several other semi-local lines connect mostly with Valley of Oaxaca points: **Choferes del Sur,** with the northwest Valley of Oaxaca, ranging from San Felipe del Agua north of the city to Etla northwest; **Autobuses de Oaxaca** connects south with Cuilapan and Zaachila; and **Sociedad Cooperativa Valle del Norte** connects west with Teotitlán del Valle and Tlacolula. Lastly, if you hanker for a long, sometimes rough but scenic back-roads adventure, ride **Flecha de Zempoaltépetl** northeast to the remote Zapotec mountain native market towns of Villa Alta and Yalalag, via Tlacolula and Cuajimoloyas.

Finally, to the right of the entrance as you enter, **Pasajeros Benito Juárez** buses climb the mountains edging the Valley of Oaxaca's north side to the cool, pine-shadowed mountain-top communities of Benito Juárez and Cuajimoloyas (koo-ah-hee-moh-LO-yahs).

The Valley of Oaxaca

The cultural and economic riches of the city of Oaxaca flow largely from its surrounding hinterland, the Valley of Oaxaca, a mountain-rimmed patchwork expanse of fertile summer-green (and winter-dry) fields, pastures, and reed-lined rivers and streams. The Valley of Oaxaca consists of three subvalleys—the Valley of Tlacolula, the Valley of Ocotlán, and the Valley of Etla—that each extend about 30 miles east, south, and northeast of Oaxaca City. It is unique in a number of ways. Most important, the inhabitants are nearly all indigenous Zapotec-speaking people.

The Valley of Oaxaca's vibrant and prosperous native presence flows from a fortunate turn of history. During the mid-1800s, Mexico's Laws of the Reform forced the sale of nearly all church lands throughout the country. In most parts of Mexico, rich Mexicans and foreigners bought up much of these holdings, but in Oaxaca, isolated in Mexico's far southern region, there were few rich buyers, so the land was bought at very low prices by the local people, most of them indigenous farmers. Moreover, after the Revolution of 1910-1917, progressive federal-government land-reform policies awarded many millions of acres of land to campesino communities, notably to Oaxaca Valley towns Teotitlán del Valle and Santa Ana del Valle, whose residents now conserve many thousand acres of rich valley fields and foothill forests.

Although the grand monuments, fascinating museums, good restaurants, and inviting handicrafts shops of Oaxaca City alone would be sufficient, a visit to Oaxaca is doubly rich because of the manifold wonders of the surrounding Valley of Oaxaca. The must-see highlights of the valley are the timeless Mitla and Monte Albán archaeological sites, the unique crafts—wool weavings, pearly black pottery, floral-embroidered blouses and dresses, and *alebrijes* (wood-carved animals)—and last but not least, the natural wonders at El Tule, Hierve El Agua, and San Sebastián de las Grutas.

You might even let the valley's *tianguis* (literally, "shade awnings" and synonymous with "native markets") guide you along your

Previous: Monte Albán; rugs for sale at the Zaachila *tianguis*. **Above:** a weaver at work in Teotitlán del Valle.

Look for ★ to find recommended
sights, activities, dining, and lodging.

Highlights

© AVALON TRAVEL

prized product of dozens of local family workshops and stores in this valley town (page 85).

★ **Mitla:** Explore the monumental plazas and columned buildings, handsomely adorned by a treasury of painstakingly placed Greca stone fretwork (page 89).

★ **Hierve El Agua:** The beautiful and the bizarre commingle here, where mineral water has pushed up from underground for centuries, creating an otherworldly landscape—with views to die for and an inviting mineral water pool to play in (page 92).

★ **San Bartolo Coyotepec:** Don't miss this small city where roadside workshops and a must-see museum display the pearly black pottery pioneered by celebrated potter Doña Rosa a generation ago (page 94).

★ **San Sebastián de las Grutas:** The idyllic setting is enough to please anyone. The presence of eerie caves only adds to the allure of this pristine hideaway in the foothills south of Oaxaca City (page 97).

★ **Zaachila:** Its monumental archaeological zone and riotously colorful *tianguis* (native market) make Zaachila a Thursday destination of choice in Oaxaca (page 99).

★ **Monte Albán:** Any day is a good day to visit Mesoamerica's earliest true metropolis, which to some still rules from its majestic mountain-top throne (page 101).

★ **Santa María del Tule:** Townsfolk have literally built the town around their gigantic beloved El Tule tree, a cousin of the giant redwood trees of California (page 83).

★ **Teotitlán del Valle:** Fine wool carpets and hangings, known locally as *tapetes*, are the

The Valley of Oaxaca

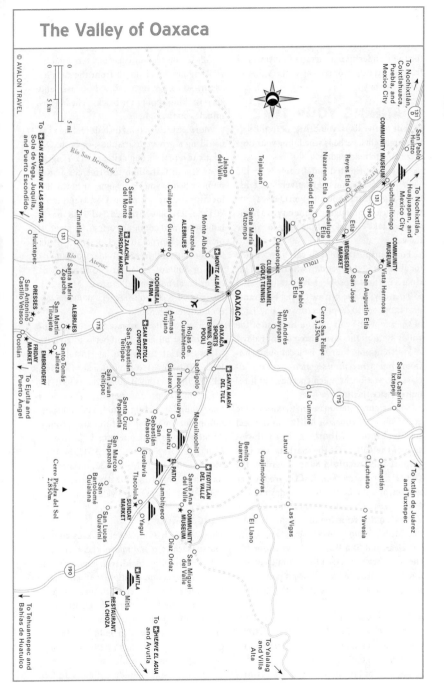

© AVALON TRAVEL

0   5 mi
0   5 km

excursion path. Beneath the shadowed market canopies and the shops of Oaxaca's welcoming local people, you can look, select, and bargain for the wonderful handicrafts that travelers from all over the world come to the Valley of Oaxaca to buy.

PLANNING YOUR TIME

In four or five days, you can soak in the valley's highlights, perhaps scheduling your time according to market days.

Given the limited hotel choices in the Valley of Oaxaca and the relatively short distances (16-48 km/10-30 mi) from Oaxaca City, you can use your lodging in the city as a home base and take excursions from there to explore the valley.

For transportation, you can hire a guide for about $150-200 per day, which should include a car for 4-5 people; rent a car for around $50 per day; or use private tourist bus transportation for $10-20 per person per day. Each of these options can get you to most of the valley's highlights over three or four days. A fourth option, touring by local public bus from *camionera central segunda clase* (second-class bus station) is much cheaper, but it requires twice the time.

Some sights you won't want to miss are the archaeological zones of **Mitla,** on the east side, and **Monte Albán,** on the southwest side of the valley. Of the markets, the biggest are the **Tlacolula** Sunday market, the **Ocotlán** Friday market, the **Etla** Wednesday market, and the **Zaachila** Thursday market. Fascinating crafts villages along the way are **Teotitlán del Valle** (on the way to Tlacolula and Mitla); Santo Tomás Jalieza, San Martín Tilcajete, and **San Bartolo Coyotepec** (on the way back to Oaxaca City from Ocotlán); and the **Santa María Atzompa** pottery village (on the way to or from Monte Albán).

GETTING AROUND
Taxis, Buses, and Rental Cars
For Oaxaca Valley touring, the cheapest (but not quickest) option is to ride a bus from the west-side Abastos market *camionera central*

segunda clase (second-class bus terminal). The buses run everywhere in the Valley of Oaxaca and beyond.

Get to the second-class bus terminal by walking one block south from the *zócalo's* southwest corner, turn right at Las Casas, and keep walking about nine blocks. The big terminal is on the right.

More leisurely options include renting a car or riding a private tourist bus, or both. Get your car rental through either a travel agent or U.S. and Canadian toll-free car rental number before you leave home, or in Oaxaca locally: **Alamo** (at airport or Matamoros 203, tel. 951/503-3618, 951/501-2188, oaxalamo@hotmail.com); **Europcar** (at airport, or at Matamoros 101, tel. 951/143-8340, 951/5169305, toll-free tel. in Mexico 800/201-1111 or 800/201-2084); or **Economy Rent a Car** (at airport and at Cinco de Mayo 203, tel. 951/514-8534, toll-free tel. 800/002-5266, economyrentacar.com).

For economical private transportation-only tourist buses, a good bet is to go with **Viajes Turísticos Mitla** (at Hóstal Santa Rosa, Trujano 201, main office at Mina 501, tel. 951/516-6175 or 951/501-0220, fax 951/514-3152, vmitla@prodigy.net.mx). They offer many tours, including a guide and transportation, for small- or medium-size groups. Another good tour operator is **Santours** (Porfirio Díaz 102-C, tel. 951/514-1617, Morelos 802, tel. 951/514-0732, turismosantours.com), offering half-day, full-day, and private tours to all Oaxaca Valley destinations.

Guided Tours
Websites such as discover-Oaxaca.com or toursoaxaca.com and many others will provide a certified guide/driver, a comfortable van to ride in, and multiple tours to choose from. Shop the Internet, or, if you are already in Oaxaca, find the tour offices dotting the streets around the *zócalo* and in many hotel lobbies. There are also many individual guides; often your hotel or B&B can connect you with a bilingual guide.

One great guide guide option is **Judith**

Reyes López (Bed-and-Breakfast Oaxaca Ollin, Quintana Roo 213, tel./fax 951/514-9126, www.oaxacaollin.com), who operates through her Art and Tradition tours. Judith offers tours ranging from half-day city tours and whole-day Valley of Oaxaca archaeological and crafts-village outings to farther-reaching explorations of the art and architecture of venerable Dominican churches in the Mixteca. Contact her at her bed-and-breakfast, Oaxaca Ollin, a block north and a block east of the Centro Cultural de Santo Domingo.

On the other hand, travelers interested in the diverse natural world of Oaxaca might go with biologist Fredy Carrizal Rosales, owner-operator of **Tourism Service in Ecosystems** (tel. 951/515-3305, in-town cell tel. 044-951/164-1897, ecologiaoaxaca@yahoo.com.mx).

Customized explorations of Oaxaca's indigenous communities, traditions, and natural treasures are the specialty of native Zapotec guide Florencio Moreno, who operates **Academic Tours in Oaxaca** (Nieve 208A, Colonia Reforma, home tel. 951/518-4728, in-town cell tel. 044-951/510-2244, www.academictoursoaxaca.com). Florencio's tours reflect his broad qualifications: fluency in native dialects, historical knowledge, cultural sensitivity, personal connections with indigenous crafts communities, and expertise in wildlife-watching and identification. His excursions can be designed to last a day or a week and include any region of Oaxaca.

Commercial guided tours also provide a hassle-free means of exploring the Valley of Oaxaca. Travel agencies, such as **Viajes Turisticos Mitla** (at Hóstal Santa Rosa, Trujano 201, tel./fax 951/514-7800 or 951/514-7806, fax 951/514-3152), **Viajes Xochitlán** (M. Bravo 210A, tel. 951/514-3271 or 951/514-3628, www.xochitlan-tours.com.mx, 9am-2pm and 4pm-7pm Mon.-Sat.), and others, offer such tours for about $12-15 for a half day and $18-20 for a full day, meals and entry fees not included.

For an extensive list of guide recommendations, check at the **Oaxaca state tourist information office** (703 Av. Juárez, west side of El Llano park, tel. 951/516-0123, www.aoxaca.com, 8am-8pm daily).

The Textile Route

The host of colorful enticements along this path could tempt you into many days of exploring. For example, on Saturday you could head out, visiting the great El Tule tree and the weavers' shops in Teotitlán del Valle and continuing east for an overnight at Mitla. Next morning, explore the Mitla ruins, then return, stopping at the hilltop Yagul archaeological site and the Sunday market at Tlacolula.

One more day would allow time to venture past Mitla to the remarkable mountainside springs and limestone mineral deposits at Hierve El Agua. Stay longer and have it all: a two- or three-day stay in a colorful market town, such as Tlacolula, with a side trip to visit the textile market and community museum at Santa Ana del Valle.

Alternately, you could sign up for a tour that takes in El Tule, Teotitlán del Valle, Mitla, a *mezcal* distillery, and Hierve El Agua in a single long day with a stop for lunch. These six- to eight-hour tours run less than $20 per person (entry fees at sites and meals not included) and the driver-guides are usually fairly knowledgeable, cheerful, and bilingual.

EL TULE AND TLACOCHAHUAYA
★ Santa María del Tule

El Tule is a gargantuan Mexican *ahuehuete* (cypress) tree, possibly the most massive in Latin America, with a gnarled, house-sized trunk supporting a forest of limbs rising up

15 stories overhead. Down at ground level, the small town of Santa María del Tule has a crafts market, church, and topiary-bedecked plaza encircling this magnificent tree. Every year on October 7 the town celebrates El Tule's 2,000 plus years of existence by throwing a grand fiesta. This is an awe-inspiring tree, well worth the 14-kilometer (nine mi) trip east from Oaxaca City on Highway 190.

Tlacochahuaya

At San Jerónimo Tlacochahuaya, seven kilometers (four mi) east of El Tule, stands the 16th-century Templo y Ex-Convento de San Jerónimo, built by Dominican friars and their indigenous acolytes over a few decades beginning in 1586. If you love old churches, by all means drop in for an hour and have a look around. This recently-restored church houses several exquisite paintings, especially the group depicting the legend of the Virgin of Guadalupe. You'll find the town most interesting in the last week of September, when the annual fiesta takes places, climaxing on September 30, the feast day of San Jerónimo.

DAINZU AND LAMBITYECO ARCHAEOLOGICAL SITES

Among the several Valley of Oaxaca buried cities, Dainzu and Lambityeco, both beside Highway 190, are the most accessible. Dainzu comes first, on the right, about nine kilometers (six mi) east of El Tule. Though there is not that much to actually see, and nothing dramatic at all, these two sites are relatively easy to get to. The amateur or professional archaeologist will assuredly find them interesting, the rest of us less so. They're worth a stop if you are in a rental car or on a private tour. They are not on most of the tour itineraries.

Dainzu

Dainzu ("Hill of the Organ Cactus" in Zapotec; Hwy. 190, no phone, 10am-5pm daily, $3) spreads over an approximate half-mile square, consisting of a partly restored ceremonial center surrounded by clusters of unexcavated mounds. Beyond that, on the west side, a stream runs through fields, which at Dainzu's apex (around AD 300) supported a town of about 1,000 inhabitants.

cypress tree El Tule

Town Names

Town names in Oaxaca (and in Mexico) generally come in two pieces: an original native name accompanied by the name of the town's patron saint. Very typical is the case of San Jerónimo Tlacochahuaya, a sleepy but famous little place. Combining both the saint's name (here, San Jerónimo) and the native name (here, Tlacochahuaya) often makes for very unwieldy handles; so, many towns are known only by one name, usually the native name. Thus, in the west side of the Valley of Oaxaca, San Jerónimo Tlacochahuaya, Santa María del Tule, Tlacolula de Matamoros, and San Pablo Villa de Mitla, for example, are commonly called Tlacochahuaya, El Tule, Tlacolula, and Mitla, respectively.

Nevertheless, sometimes a town's full name is customarily used. This is especially true when a single name—such as Etla, northwest of Oaxaca City—identifies an entire district, and thus many towns, such as San Agustín Etla, San Sebastián Etla, and San José Etla, must necessarily be identified with their full names. In this book, although we may mention the formal name once on a map or in the text, we generally conform to local, customary usage for town names.

Lambityeco

Ten kilometers (six mi) farther, **Lambityeco** (Hwy. 190, no phone, 10am-5pm daily) is on the right, a few miles past the Teotitlán del Valle side road. The excavated portion, only about 100 square yards, is a small but significant part of Yegui ("Small Hill" in Zapotec), a large buried town dotted with hundreds of unexcavated mounds covering about half a square mile. The name "Lambityeco" may derive from the Arabic-Spanish *alambique,* the equivalent of the English "alembic," or distillation or evaporation apparatus. This would explain the intriguing presence of more than 200 local mounds. It's tempting to speculate that they are the remains of *cujetes,* raised leaching beds still used in Mexico for concentrating brine, which workers subsequently evaporate into salt.

★ TEOTITLÁN DEL VALLE

Teotitlán del Valle (pop. 5,000), 14 kilometers (nine mi) east of El Tule, at the foot of the northern Sierra, means "Place of the Gods" in Nahuatl; before that, it was known, appropriately, as Xa Quire (shah KEE-ray), or "Foot of the Mountain," by the Zapotecs who settled it at least 2,000 years ago (by archaeologists' estimate).

Present-day Teotitlán people are relatively well off, not only from sales of their renowned *tapetes* (wool rugs), but from their rich communal landholdings. Besides a sizable swath of valley-bottom farmland and pasture, which every Teotitlán family is entitled to use, the community owns a dam and reservoir and a small kingdom of approximately 100,000 acres of sylvan mountain forest and meadow, spreading for about 32 kilometers (20 mi) along the Valley of Oaxaca's lush northeastern foothills.

Textile Shops

Nearly every Teotitlán house is a mini-factory where people card, spin, and color wool, often using hand-gathered natural dyes. The weaving, on traditional handlooms, is the final, satisfying part of the process. The best weaving is generally the densest, typically packing in about 18 strands per centimeter (45 strands per inch); ordinary weaving incorporates about half that.

Visiting at least one workshop-store should be on your itinerary, and will be if you sign up for a tour. The artisans are well-versed at demonstrating their techniques for dye-making, spinning, and weaving, and the sales pitch that follows is generally low-key. These home workshops, once confined to the town center, now sprinkle nearly the entire mile-long entrance road.

Community Museum

Allow enough time to visit the community museum **Balaa Xtee Guech Gulal** (Hidalgo, tel. 951/524-4463, 10am-6pm Tues.-Sun., $3), whose name translates from the local Zapotec as "Shadow of the Old Town." It's on the north side of Hidalgo, about a block east of Juárez. Step inside and enjoy the excellent exhibits that illustrate local history, industry, and customs. One display shows the wool-weaving tradition (introduced by the Dominican padres), which replaced the indigenous cotton-weaving craft. Sources of some natural dyes—*cochinilla* (red cochineal), *musgo* (yellow moss and lichens), *anil* (dark blue indigo), and *quizache* bean (black)—are part of the exhibit.

Teotitlán Church

Built over an earlier Zapotec temple, the **Teotitlán church,** known as the Templo de la Precioso Sangre de Cristo (Church of the Precious Blood of Christ), contains many interesting pre-Columbian stones, which the Dominican friars allowed to be incorporated into its walls. Outside, behind the church, lies the reconstructed foundation corner, on the street, downhill, of the original **Zapotec temple.** Note the Zapotec stone fretwork,

similar to the famous *Greca* (Grecian-like) remains at Mitla, 32 kilometers (20 mi) farther east.

Accommodations and Food

Sample Teotitlán's best at the traditional **Tlamanalli** restaurant (on Juárez, about a block south of Hidalgo, no phone, 1pm-4pm daily, possibly longer hours on Mon. and Thurs. when more people stop by, $5-10). Their menu of made-to-order Zapotec specialties, such as *sopa de calabaza* (squash soup) and *guisado de pollo* (chicken stew) is limited but highly recommended by Oaxaca City chefs.

Alternatively, for a lunch or early dinner treat, stop at **Restaurant El Patio** (Hwy. 190, 1.2 km/0.8 mi east of the Teotitlán entrance road, tel. 951/514-4889, 10am-6pm Tues.-Sun.). The restaurant centers around an airy patio, decorated by antique country furniture and a fetching gallery of scenes from the 1940s-era films of the Mexican Golden Age of cinema. The ambience is wonderful; the food, which can be inconsistent, consists of tasty traditional Oaxacan dishes, such as *ensalada Oaxaqueña* and Zapotec soup.

Getting There

You can go to Teotitlán del Valle by car, tour,

woven rugs on display in a shop in Teotitlán del Valle

taxi, or bus. Drivers: Simply turn left from Highway 190 at the signed Teotitlán del Valle side road, 14 kilometers (nine mi) east of El Tule. By bus: Ride a Fletes y Pasajes Tlacolula- or Mitla-bound bus from the *camionera central segunda clase* (in Oaxaca City by the Abastos market at the end of Las Casas, past the *periférico* west of downtown).

TLACOLULA

The Zapotec people who founded Tlacolula (pop. 15,000, 38 km/24 mi east from Oaxaca City) around AD 1250 called it Guichiibaa ("Place Between Heaven and Earth"). Besides its beloved church and chapel and famous Sunday market, Tlacolula is also renowned for *mezcal*, a Tequila-like alcoholic beverage distilled from the fermented hearts of maguey, also known as agave. *Mezcal* is Oaxaca's obsession, pride, and joy, and getting out to see where it is made is now a big part of the Oaxaca experience—and well worth it, since you not only get to witness the process, you can try a few samples of the smoky brew. Get a good free sample at the friendly Pensamiento shop (Juárez 9, tel. 951/562-0017, 9am-7pm daily), about four blocks from the highway gasoline station (along Juárez) toward the market.

Just before the market, take a look inside the main town church, the 1531 Parroquia de la Virgen de la Asunción. Although its interior is distinguished enough, the real gem is its attached chapel, Capilla del Señor de Tlacolula, which you enter from the nave of the church. Every inch of the chapel's interior gleams with sculptures of angels and saints, paintings, and gold scrollwork.

The big gate bordering the church grounds leads you to the Tlacolula market. One of Oaxaca's biggest and oldest, the Tlacolula market draws tens of thousands from all over the Valley of Oaxaca every Sunday. Wander around and soak it all in—the diverse crowd of buyers and sellers, and the equally manifold galaxy of merchandise.

For food and accommodations, try the basic but clean downtown Tlacolula lodging, the Hotel and Restaurant Calenda (Juárez 40, tel. 951/562-0660, entrées $3-8, lodging $20 s or d, $30 t). They offer about 30 rooms with fans and hot-water shower-baths in three floors around an interior restaurant courtyard. Their restaurant serves a wholesome country menu that, although specializing in *barbacoa pollo, chivo,* or *borrego* (barbecue chicken, goat, or lamb), offers many more hearty choices, such as

A shop owner explains the creation of natural dyes for rugs in Teotitlán del Valle.

Mezcal Magic

Hundreds of small distilleries produce and market mezcal in Oaxaca.

"Para todo mal, mezcal, y para todo bien también" ("for everything bad, *mezcal;* for everything good, the same"). This saying reflects the integral role *mezcal* plays in Oaxacan culture. With agave growing in hundreds of small-scale family plots, *mezcal* is a modern-day cultural phenomenon in Oaxaca—one with deep historical roots. Some argue (especially after eating the worm found at the bottom of many bottles of *mezcal*) that this liquor has psychedelic properties. It does not, and bears no chemical or psychic relationship to mescaline, which comes from a mushroom, or peyote, which comes from a different sort of cactus. *Mezcal* is merely a flavorful and potent form of alcohol.

Mezcal has been the "national" drink of the state of Oaxaca for centuries. Like its more famous cousin, tequila (tequila is a *mezcal, mezcal* is not a tequila), *mezcal* is made from the maguey, a.k.a. agave, cactus, but there is a huge difference: tequila is always made from a single distinct species of agave, while *mezcal* can be made from any of the 30 or so types of agave (most commonly it is made from the one called Espadin). Although it can be drunk new, rested, or aged, just like tequila, the flavor is smokier and more complex. It is not recommended for mixed drinks, although various iterations of *mezcal* martinis are popping up on restaurant menus in Mexico and the United States. The Oaxacans generally savor it straight up, drinking slowly, biting into a slice of fresh orange coated with a combination of *sal gusano* (salt, chile, and freshly ground worms) after each sip.

Mezcal-making follows a series of steps that have been the same for centuries. Though perhaps more mechanized than in the past, it is mostly the same hands-on, handmade operation: using machetes, *mezcaleros* cut the plants, weighing up to 90 pounds, by hand. They hack the leaves off, leaving the heart, or piña, which does resemble an oversized pineapple. The piñas are cooked for three days, in a pit oven over piles of hot rocks. Hence the smoky flavor. The piñas are then crushed and mashed, and their juices are left to ferment in vats or barrels of water. In time, it is bottled, and you have *mezcal: blanco, reposado,* or *añejo* (white/young, rested, or aged, respectively).

For a serious trip into the world of Oaxacan *mezcal*, take a *mezcal* tour with Alvin Starkman, author of a book on the subject. You can reach him to set up a tour or explore the world of *mezcal* online through http://www.oaxaca-mezcal.com.

pork chops, spaghetti, eggs, fish, and chiles rellenos.

The Sunday market is usually "bundled" with a tour that might include, say, El Tule and Mitla, in a half day, or some other combination, with a well-spent hour or so dedicated to exploring the market. Ask around at any of the many tour offices in Oaxaca City to find a tour that best suits your interests, be they markets, churches, or archaeology; most of the organized tours out of Oaxaca City offer a sampling of all three.

YAGUL ARCHAEOLOGICAL ZONE

The remains of Yagul (Zapotec for "Old Tree"; 45 km/28 mi east of Oaxaca City, just north of Hwy. 190, no phone, 10am-5pm daily, $3) preside atop their volcanic hilltop. Although only 12 kilometers (7.5 mi) from Mitla and sharing architectural details, such as Mitla's famous *Greca* (Grecian-like) fretwork, the size and complexity of Yagul's buildings suggest that Yagul was an independent city-state in its own right. Locals call the present ruin the Pueblo Viejo (Old Town) and remember it as the forerunner of the present town of Tlacolula. Archaeological evidence, which indicates that Yagul was occupied for

about a thousand years, at least until around AD 1100 or 1200, bears them out.

One of Yagul's major claims to fame is its Palace of Six Patios, actually three nearly identical but separate complexes of two patios each. In each patio, rooms surround a central courtyard.

South of the palace sprawls Yagul's huge ball court, the second largest in Mesoamerica, shaped in the characteristic Oaxaca I configuration. Southeast of the ball court is Patio 4, consisting of four mounds surrounding a courtyard. A boulder sculpted in the form of a frog lies at the base of the east mound.

★ MITLA

The ruins at Mitla (Hwy. 176, about 57 km/35 mi east of Oaxaca City, no phone, 8am-5pm daily, $5) are a "must" for Valley of Oaxaca sightseers. Mitla (Liobaa in Zapotec, the "Place of the Dead") flowered late, reaching a population of perhaps 10,000 during its apex around AD 1350. It remained occupied and in use for generations after the conquest.

Exploring the Site

In a real sense, Mitla lives on. The ruins coincide with the present town of San Pablo

Mitla's striking architectural style is both Zapotec and Mixtec.

Mitla

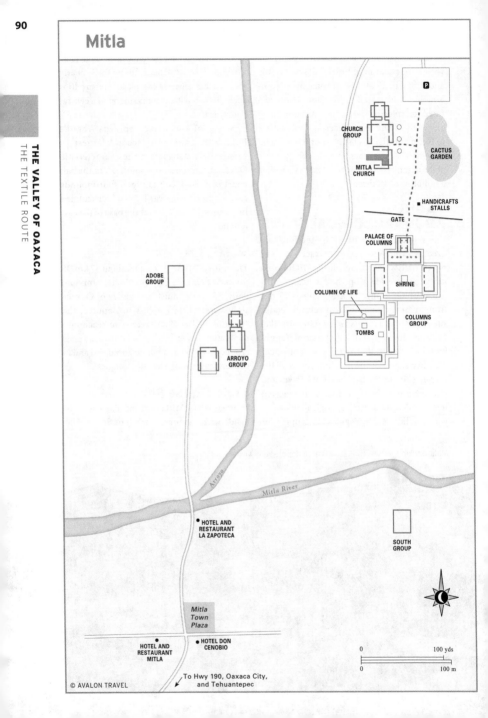

P

CHURCH GROUP

MITLA CHURCH

CACTUS GARDEN

HANDICRAFTS STALLS

GATE

PALACE OF COLUMNS

SHRINE

ADOBE GROUP

COLUMN OF LIFE

COLUMNS GROUP

TOMBS

ARROYO GROUP

Arroyo

Mitla River

HOTEL AND RESTAURANT LA ZAPOTECA

SOUTH GROUP

Mitla Town Plaza

HOTEL AND RESTAURANT MITLA

HOTEL DON CENOBIO

To Hwy 190, Oaxaca City, and Tehuantepec

0   100 yds
0   100 m

© AVALON TRAVEL

Villa de Mitla, whose main church occupies the northernmost of five main groups of monumental ruins. Virtually anywhere archaeologists dig within the town they hit remains of the myriad ancient dwellings, plazas, and tombs that connected the still-visible landmarks.

On the main entrance path, continue past the tourist market and through the gate to the **Columns Group.** Of the five ruins clusters, the best preserved is the fenced-in Columns Group. Its exploration requires about an hour. Inside, two large patios, joined at one corner, are each surrounded on three sides by elaborate apartments. A shrine occupies the center of the first patio. Just north of this stands the **Palace of Columns,** the most important of Mitla's buildings. It sits atop a staircase, inaccurately reconstructed in 1901.

The interesting **Church Group** (marked by the monumental columns that you pass first on your right after the parking lot) is on the far north side of the Palace of Columns. Builders used the original temple stones to erect the church here.

Shopping

Instead of making handicrafts, Mitla residents concentrate on selling them, mostly at the big handicrafts market adjacent to the archaeological zone parking lot. Here, you can sample from a concentrated all-Oaxaca assortment, especially textiles: cotton *huipiles,* wool hangings and rugs, onyx animals and chess sets, fanciful *alebrijes* (wooden animals), and leather huaraches, purses, belts, and wallets.

Accommodations and Food

Restaurant La Choza (Carretera Oxaca-Mitla km 3.5, tel. 225-7878, $10 lunch buffet, credit cards accepted), on the right side of the road going in to Mitla, is where many tour bus operators bring their troops of passengers for lunch between destinations. The dining room is large, airy, and busy, and the food is done buffet style, with myriad options available in big pots and trays along the side and back walls. While some of the cooked items are overcooked for obvious reasons, there are plenty of fresh fruits and vegetables available, and enough good main courses—just about anything and everything that says Oaxacan or Mexican cuisine is here in some form or other—to make the price seem reasonable since you will likely be tanking up for a long day, between visiting Teotitlán and driving to Mitla and/or Hierve El Agua.

Alternatively, closer to the archaeological

The town's Catholic church was built atop a pyramid at Mitla.

zone, try the family-run ★ **Hotel and Restaurant La Zapoteca** (Cinco de Febrero 12, tel. 951/568-0026, ivettsita_revelde@hotmail.com, restaurant 8am-6pm daily; lodging $15 s, $20 d, $27 t), on the right just before the Río Mitla bridge. The spic-and-span restaurant, praised by locals for "the best mole negro and chiles rellenos in Oaxaca," is fine for meals, and the 20 clean, reasonably priced rooms, with hot water, in-house Internet, and parking, are good for an overnight.

Getting There

Bus travelers can get to Mitla from Oaxaca City by Fletes y Pasajes or Oaxaca-Istmo bus from the *camionera central segunda clase* (second-class bus station). Drivers get here by forking left from main Oaxaca Highway 190, at the big Mitla sign, onto Highway 176. Continue about 3.2 kilometers (two mi) to the Mitla town entrance, on the left. Turn left, and head straight past the town plaza. Continue across the bridge over the (usually dry) Río Mitla, and, after about 1.6 kilometers (one mi), arrive at the archaeological site.

This destination is included in countless half- and full-day tours out of Oaxaca City, and most of the drivers and/or guides are fairly well-versed in Mitla lore. Half-day tours generally run 10am-2pm, full days 10am-6pm, with meals and entry fees not included in the $12-15 half-day, $15-18 full-day tour fee. If you want to look at some options in advance of traveling, check the website gooaxaca.com, which offers all the basic tours out of Oaxaca City into the Valley. There's no need to reserve, however: there are plenty of tour packages available once you're on the ground in Oaxaca.

★ HIERVE EL AGUA

Although the name of this place translates as boiling water, the springs that seep from the side of a limestone mountain less than an hour's drive east of Mitla aren't hot. Instead, they are loaded with minerals. These minerals over time have built up into rock-hard deposits, forming great algae-painted slabs in level

the mineral waterfall at Hierve El Agua

spots and, on steep slopes, accumulating into what appear to be grand frozen waterfalls.

The Springs

At **Hierve El Agua** (no phone, 9am-6pm daily, $2) the first thing you'll see after passing the entrance gate is a lineup of snack and curio stalls at the cliff-side parking lot. A trail leads downhill to the main spring, which bubbles from the mountainside and trickles into a huge basin that the operators have dammed as a swimming pool. Bring your bathing suit: if the weather is good it's a wonderful place for a dip.

Part of Hierve El Agua's appeal is the panoramic view of mountain and valley. On a clear day, you can see the tremendous massif of Zempoatepetl (saym-poh-ah-TAY-pehtl), the grand holy mountain range of the Mixe people, rising above the eastern horizon.

From the ridge-top park, agile walkers can hike farther down the hill, following deposits curiously accumulated in the shape of miniature limestone dikes that trace the mineral water's downhill path. Soon you'll glimpse a towering limestone formation, like a giant petrified waterfall, appearing to ooze from the cliff downhill straight ahead, on the right.

Hikers can also enjoy following a *sendero peatonal* (footpath) that encircles the entire zone. Start your walk from the trailhead beyond the bungalows or at the other end, at the cliff edge between the parking lot and the entrance gate. Your reward will be an approximately one-hour, self-guided tour, looping downhill past the springs and the great frozen rock cascades and featuring grand vistas of the gorgeous mountain and canyon scenery along the way.

Accommodations and Food

The Hierve El Agua tourist ★ *cabañas ecoturísticas* ($10 pp, $40 up to six people in a bungalow) are fine for a restful one-night stay. There are several clean and well-maintained housekeeping bungalows, with shower-baths and hot water, as well as bungalows for up to groups of six, with refrigerator, stove, and utensils. For information about cabaña reservations, contact the **Oaxaca state tourist information office** (Av. Juárez 703, west side of El Llano park, tel. 951/516-0123, www.aoxaca.com, 8am-8pm daily).

For food, you can bring and cook your own in your bungalow or rely upon the strictly local-style beans, carne asada (roast meat), tacos, tamales, and tortillas offered by the parking-lot food stalls.

Getting There

Get there by riding an Ayutla-bound Fletes y Pasajes bus east out of either Oaxaca City (departing from *camionera central segunda clase*) or from Mitla on Highway 179 just east of town. Get off at the Hierve El Agua side road, about 18 kilometers (11 mi) past Mitla. Continue the additional eight kilometers (five mi) by taxi or the local bus marked San Lorenzo.

Many tour operators operating out of Oaxaca City, such as **Verde Antequara Travel** (Murguía 100, tel. 951/514-8624) and **Monte Albán Tours** (Macedonio Alcalá 206-F, tel. 951/514-1385, 951/514-1976), include about a one- or two-hour visit to Hierve El Agua in their full-day tour packages, which run about $15-18 per person, meals and entry fees not included. The longish drive precludes its inclusion in half-day tours, but the spectacular scenery and the unusual nature of the site make this destination well worth visiting either on a tour or in a rental car should you have one.

natural mineral swimming pool at Hierve El Agua

The Crafts Route

Travelers who venture into the Valley of Oaxaca's long, south-pointing fingers, the Valleys of Zimatlán and Ocotlán, can discover a wealth of crafts, history, and architectural and scenic wonders. These are all accessible as day trips from Oaxaca City by car or combinations of bus and taxi. Most reachable are the renowned crafts villages of San Bartolo Coyotepec, San Martín Tilcajete, Santo Tomás Jalieza, and others along Highway 175, between the city and the colorful market town of Ocotlán (best to plan a visit to all on Friday, Ocotlán's market day; start at Ocotlán early and work your way north back to Oaxaca City). Another day, you can either continue farther south, off the tourist track, to soak in the feast of sights at the big market in Ejutla, or fork southwest, via Highway 131 through Zimatlán, to the idyllic groves, crystal springs, and limestone caves hidden around San Sebastián de las Grutas. The most renowned of the crafts villages have been included in quite a few tour itineraries, so if you

dread driving, let someone else do it: shop around at any of the Oaxaca City-based tour companies previously listed, or ask at your hotel. You'll no doubt find one that includes at least a few of these destinations.

★ SAN BARTOLO COYOTEPEC

San Bartolo Coyotepec (Hill of the Coyote), on Highway 175, 23 kilometers (14 mi) south of Oaxaca City, is famous for its black pottery, the renowned *barro negro*. Sold all over Mexico, here it is available at the signed Mercado de los Artesanias market on the right and at a number of cottage factory shops (watch for signs) off the highway, scattered along the left (east side) of Calle Juárez, marked by a big Doña Rosa sign. Doña Rosa, who passed away in 1980, pioneered the technique of crafting lovely, big, round jars without a potter's wheel. With their local clay, Doña Rosa's descendants and neighbor families regularly turn out acres of glistening black

Mercado de los Artesanias, San Bartolo Coyotepec

Building Churches

Although European architects designed nearly all of Mexico's colonial-era churches, embellishing them with Old-World Gothic, Renaissance, baroque, and Moorish decorations, native artists blended their own geometric, floral, and animal motifs. The result was a hybrid that manifested in intriguing variations all over Mexico. This was especially true in Oaxaca, where faithful droves worship before gilded altars and flowery ceilings built and decorated by their long-gone ancestors. Local materials further distinguish Oaxacan churches from others in Mexico. The spectrum of soft pastels of local *cantera* volcanic stone, from yellow through gray, including green in Oaxaca City, marks Oaxacan walls and facades.

THE LAYOUT

Mexican church design followed the Egypto-Greco-Roman tradition of its European models. Basically, architects designed their churches beginning with the main space of the nave, in the shape of a box, lined with high lateral windows. Depending on their origin and function, the churches fit into three basic groups: the monk's *convento* (monastery or convent); the bishop's *catedral* (cathedral); and the priest's *templo* or *parroquia* (parish church).

In Oaxaca, faced with the constant threat of earthquakes, the Dominican padres built massively thick walls supported on the exterior with ponderous buttresses. Key elements were naves, with or without *cruceros* (transepts), cross spaces separating the nave from the altar, making the church layout resemble a Christian cross. They placed the *coro* (choir) above and just inside the entrance arch.

At the opposite, usually east (or sunrise) end of the church, builders sometimes extended the nave beyond the transept to include a *presbiterio* (presbytery), which was often lined with seats where church officials presided. The building ended past that at the *ábside* (apse), the space behind the altar, frequently in semi-circular or half-octagonal form. Within the apse rose the gilded *retablo* (retable or altarpiece), adorned with sacred images, attended by choirs of angels and cherubs.

THE FACADE

Outside, in front, rises the *fachada* (facade), sometimes in a uniform style, but just as often with a mixture of Renaissance, Gothic, and baroque, with some *mujedar* (Moorish) worked into the mix. A proliferation of columns nearly always decorates Oaxacan church facades, from the classic *Toscano, Dórico, Jónico,* and *Corintio* (Etruscan, Doric, Ionic, and Corinthian) pillars to spiraled *Salomónico* (Solomonic) barber's poles and bizarre *estipites.*

CONVENTS

The monastery- or convent-style churches included, in addition to all of the above, living and working quarters for the members of the order, typically built around a columned patio called the *claustro* (cloister). A corridor through an arched *portería* (porch) adjacent to the nave usually leads to the cloister, from which monks and nuns could quickly reach the dining hall, or *refectorio* (refectory), and their private rooms, or *celdas* (cells).

The Oaxacan missionary fathers always designed their churches with an eye to handling the masses of natives whom they hoped to convert. Padres included an *atrio* (atrium), a large exterior courtyard in front of the facade, for the potential large audience. For the partly initiated natives, they often built a *capilla abierta* (open chapel) on one side of the atrium. Conversions also occurred at smaller open chapels called *pozas,* built at the corners of the atrium.

plates, pots, bowls, trees of life, and fetching animals for very reasonable prices.

San Bartolo Museum

Across the highway from the town church, on the town plaza's southern flank, stands the large, new **Museo Estatal de Arte Popular** (Plaza Principal, tel. 951/551-0036, 10am-6pm Tues.-Sun., $4). Although the main event is a fine exposition of San Bartolo Coyotepec's famed black pottery, the museum also exhibits a surprisingly innovative range of some of the best crafts that the Valley of Oaxaca offers. Besides Doña Rosa's classic pearly-black examples, a host of other pieces—divine angels, scowling bandidos, fierce devils—reveal the remarkable talent of Doña Rosa's generation of students and followers.

SAN MARTÍN TILCAJETE AND SANTO TOMÁS JALIEZA

San Martín Tilcajete (teel-kah-HAY-tay; Hwy. 175, not far north of the Hwy. 131 fork), about 37 kilometers (21 mi) south of Oaxaca City, is a prime source of *alebrijes,* fanciful wooden creatures occupying the shelves of crafts stores the world over. Both it and **Santo Tomás Jalieza** (Hwy. 175, south of the Hwy. 131 fork), a mile or two farther south, can be visited as a pair on any day.

The label *alebrije,* a word of Arabic origin, implies something of indefinite form, and that certainly characterizes the fanciful animal figurines that a generation of Oaxaca woodcarvers has been crafting from soft copal wood. Dozens of factory-stores sprinkle San Martín Tilcajete.

Santo Tomás Jalieza, on the other hand, is known as the town of embroidered *cinturones* (belts). Women townsfolk, virtually all of whom practice the craft, concentrate all of their selling in a single, many-stalled **market** (Centro de Artesanias, Plaza Principal, no phone, 9am-5pm daily) in the middle of town.

A couple of local restaurants are recommended. Although it caters to the tourist crowd, the food is good and innovative at **Restaurant Azucena** (on the Tilcajete entrance road, tel. 951/524-9227). On the other hand, for truly rustic, ranch-style ambience, complete with old wagon wheels, wooden picnic-style tables, and plenty of savory barbeque, stop by **Restaurant Huamuches** (on the highway, by the Santo Tomás Jalieza entrance road, no phone).

OCOTLÁN

The main **Ocotlán** attraction is the huge **Friday market** (Centro district, between the central park and temple). Beneath a riot of colored awnings, hordes of merchandise—much modern stuff, but also plenty of old-fashioned goodies—load a host of tables and street-laid mats.

Since markets are best in the morning, you should make Ocotlán your first Friday stop. Drivers could get there by heading straight south out of the city, arriving in Ocotlán by mid-morning. Spend a few hours, then begin your return in the early afternoon, stopping at the sprinkling of crafts villages along the road back to Oaxaca. Bus travelers could hold to a similar schedule by riding an early Autobuses Estrella del Valle, Autotransportes Oaxaca-Pacífico, or Choferes del Sur from the *camionera central segunda clase* (second-class bus station), then returning, in steps, by bus, or more quickly by taxi, stopping at the crafts villages along the way.

Casa de Cultura Rudolfo Morales

During the 1980s and 1990s, Ocotlán came upon good times, largely due to the late Rudolfo Morales, the internationally-celebrated, locally-born artist who dedicated his fortune to improving his hometown. The Rudolfo Morales Foundation has been restoring churches and other public buildings, reforesting mountainsides, and funding self-help and educational projects all over Ocotlán and its surrounding district. The bright colors of the plaza-front *presidencia municipal* and the big church nearby

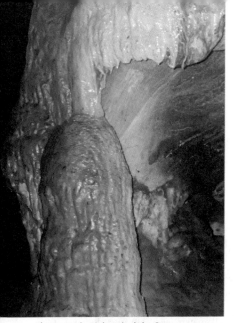

the cave at San Sebastián de las Grutas

result from the good works of Rudolfo Morales.

The Morales Foundation's local efforts radiate from the **Casa de Cultura Rudolfo Morales** (Morelos 108, tel. 951/571-0198, 9am-2pm and 5pm-8pm Mon.-Fri., 9am-3pm Sat.), in the yellow-painted mansion three doors north from the Ocotlán plaza's northwest corner. In the Casa de Cultura's graceful, patrician interior, the Morales family and staff manage the foundation's affairs, teach art and computer classes, and sponsor community events.

The foundation staff welcomes visitors. For advance information, contact the foundation's **headquarters in Oaxaca City** (Murguia 105, between Macedonio Alcalá and Cinco de Mayo, tel. 951/514-2324 or 951/514-0910, www.artedeoaxaca.com, 11am-3pm and 5pm-8pm Mon.-Sat.).

Templo de Santo Domingo

Local people celebrate Rudolfo Morales's brilliant restoration of their beloved 16th-century **Templo de Santo Domingo** (Juarez, next to the park). Gold and silver from the infamous Santa Catarina Minas (mines), in the mountains east of Ocotlán, financed the church's initial construction. When overwork and disease tragically decimated the local native population by around 1600, the mines were abandoned, and work on the church stopped. Although eventually completed over the succeeding three centuries, it had slipped into serious disrepair by the 1980s.

Fortunately, the Templo de Santo Domingo is now completely rebuilt, from its bright blue, yellow, and white facade to the baroque gold glitter of its nave ceiling.

Practicalities

Free yourself of the Friday downtown crowd at the rustic-chic restaurant **La Cabaña** (Hwy. 175, tel. 951/571-0201, 8am-7pm daily, $4-10), an open-air *palapa* by the *gasolinera* on the highway, at the north, Oaxaca, side of town.

If you decide to linger overnight in Ocotlán, the newish, clean, and modern **Hotel Rey David** (16 de Septiembre 248, tel. 951/571-1248, $13 s or d in one bed, $22 d or t in two beds) can accommodate you. The hotel offers about 20 comfortable, attractively decorated rooms. Find it on the south-side Highway 175 ingress-egress avenue, Avenida 16 de Septiembre, where it runs east-west, about three blocks east of the market and central plaza.

Do your money business at the Ocotlán **Banamex** (9am-4pm Mon.-Fri.), with ATM, on the north side of the town plaza.

★ SAN SEBASTIÁN DE LAS GRUTAS

It's hard not to fall in love with this idyllic hidden corner of the Valley of Oaxaca. The turnoff lies 73 kilometers (45 mi) south of Oaxaca City on Highway 131. After 0.4 kilometers (0.25 mi) toward the *grutas* (caves), the road becomes a gently winding, sylvan, creekside drive. The jade-green brook (muddy in the rainy season) gurgles downhill, pausing here and there in picture-perfect swimming holes.

Meanwhile, overhead, a regal host of towering, gnarled *sabinos* (bald cypress trees; *tules* or *ahuehuetes*) shades the creek, appearing every bit as ancient and grand as their northern cousins, the California redwoods. When you reach the edge of the village, you'll see farmers plowing their land with paired oxen, not tractors.

About 12 kilometers (seven mi) after the Highway 131 turnoff, and half a mile past San Sebastián de las Grutas village (pop. 900), you reach the cave area. The creek emerges clear and pristine, as if by magic, from beneath a big rock at the foot of a mountain.

Several hundred yards uphill—the climb is steep but paved and easy to manage—are the caves, which you can tour for a fee of about $2. A guide, armed with strong flashlights, will lead you on an easy, mostly level walk through the cave's several chambers, which vary from about 6 meters (20 ft.) to more than 60 meters (200 ft.) in height. The guide is used to receiving a tip of about $2 per person.

Practicalities

Spend the night in one of a dozen rustic wooden *cabañas ecoturísticas* (tel. 951/488-4640, $25 d, $30 t or q), with hot-water shower-bath, accommodating up to six people in an inviting, forest and meadow creekside setting at the foot of the trail leading to the cave.

The shady streamside park, furthermore, appears ripe for camping ($15), either in your tent or (self-contained) RV. For food and drinking water, bring your own or go to stores in the village. A small restaurant is included in the new buildings. It will open when and if there is enough business to sustain it.

Get there by bus via the Trans-Sol or Estrella Rojo del Sureste bus from the *camionera central segunda clase* (second-class bus station) next to the Abastos market on the southwest side of Oaxaca City. The Trans-Sol buses, some of which may (ask when you buy the ticket) go right to the caves, leave several times a day, beginning around 6am. The Estrella Rojo del Sureste may only drop you at the intersection, 13 kilometers (eight mi) from the caves. Take a taxi or *colectivo* van or truck from there. Drivers, follow Highway 131, a total of 76 kilometers (53 mi) south of Oaxaca City. Allow about two hours' driving time. In the reverse, north direction, the *grutas* (caves) are 190 kilometers (119 mi) north of Puerto Escondido.

tourist cabinas at Las Grutas, San Sebastián

SOUTHWEST SIDE
★ Zaachila

About 16 kilometers (10 mi) south of Oaxaca City, Zaachila (pop. 30,000), like Mitla, overlies the ruins of its ancient namesake city, which rose to prominence after the decline of Monte Albán. Although excavations have uncovered many Mixtec-style remains, historical records nevertheless list a number of Zapotec kings (including the greatest, Zaachila Yoo, for whom the town is named) who ruled Zaachila as a virtual Zapotec capital during the 14th and 15th centuries.

The big forested hill that rises north of the market plaza is topped by the Zaachila pyramid (no phone, 8am-5pm daily, $4). Several unexcavated mounds and courtyards dot the hill's north and south flanks.

In 1962, archaeologist Roberto Gallegos uncovered a pair of unopened tombs beneath the summit of the pyramid. They yielded a trove of polychrome pottery, gold jewelry (including a ring still on a left hand), and jade fan handles. Tomb 1 descends via a steep staircase to an entrance decorated with a pair of cat-motif heads. On the antechamber walls a few steps farther are depictions of owls and a pair of personages inscribed respectively with the name-dates 5-Flower and 9-Flower.

The Thursday *tianguis* (native market) is Zaachila's weekly main event. It spreads for blocks below the archaeological site and church. Thousands of Zapotec-speaking country people stream into town to buy, sell, gossip, flirt, and fill up with their favorite delicacies. If you're in the mood for food, wholesome country fare is available at the regiment of *fondas* in the roofed section of the market. Pork is a Zaachila ("Town of Pork") specialty, and any one of a small acre of pork stalls will be ready to barbeque a pork chop for you on the spot. Alternatively, enjoy lunch at the showplace ★ Restaurant La Capilla (tel. 951/528-6115, 7am-7pm daily, $5-10). Get there on foot or by asking your *moto-taxi* driver to let you off at La Capilla (kah-PEE-yah), on the main east-west Oaxaca ingress street, a few blocks west of the market.

By bus, get to Zaachila via Autobuses de Oaxaca, from the *camionera central segunda clase* (second-class bus station) in Oaxaca City, or by private tourist bus.

By car from Oaxaca City, head south from downtown to the *periférico*. Do not continue south via the airport Highway 131-175. Instead, from the *periférico* a block west of the airport-highway intersection (watch for the Monte Albán sign), follow the four-lane

Zaachila

boulevard that angles southwest, away from the *periférico,* across the Río Atoyac bridge. Just after crossing the bridge, do not continue straight ahead toward Monte Albán, but take the second left (south) onto the old (scenic route) Zaachila road, which also passes Cuilapan de Guerrero and Arrazola. These roads are in good condition and their signage is clear and easy to follow. You won't get lost out there.

Cuilapan de Guerrero and Arrazola

Southwest of Oaxaca City, on the old road between Zaachila and Arrazola, **Cuilapan de Guerrero** is famous for its elaborate but unfinished **Ex-Convento de Santiago** (Saint Jame, 9am-5pm daily). It's visible from the Oaxaca City-Zaachila Highway (via Xoxocotlan). This is where Vicente Guerrero, father of the Mexican republic, was infamously executed in 1831. Although construction began in 1535, the cost of the basilica and associated monastery began to balloon. In 1550, King Philip demanded humility and moderation of the builders, whose work was finally ended by a 1570 court ruling. The extravagances—the soaring, roofless basilica, magnificent baptismal font, splendid Gothic cloister, and elaborate frescoes—remain as national treasures. Extravagance has its value.

Arrazola, a few miles farther north, toward Oaxaca City, is one of the sources (along with San Martín Tilcajete) of the intricately painted *alebrijes* (ah-lay-BREE-hays)—fanciful

fruit and herbs for sale, Zaachila *tianguis*

wooden creatures that decorate the shelves of handicrafts shops all over Mexico and foreign countries. Bus travelers: Get here either by second-class bus or by tourist bus from Oaxaca City. Drivers: Turn west (left) onto signed Highway 145 a few miles north of Cuilapan de Guerrero or, traveling south, turn right 5.1 kilometers (3.2 mi) south of the Río Atoyac bridge in Oaxaca City. Pass through San Javier village and continue from the turnoff a total of five kilometers (three mi) to the Arrazola town plaza.

Monte Albán and the Archaeological Route

★ MONTE ALBÁN

Monte Albán ranks among Mesoamerica's most spectacular ruined cities. Known in ancient times by its Zapotec name, Danni Dipaa, the site's present "Monte Albán" label was probably coined by a local Spaniard because of its resemblance to a similarly named Italian hilltop town.

The great city atop the hill reigned for at least 1,200 years, between 500 BC and AD 750, as the capital of the Zapotecs and the dominant force between Teotihuacán in the Valley of Mexico and the Maya kingdoms of the southeast. Archaeologists have organized the Valley of Oaxaca's history from 500 BC to the conquest into five periods, known as Monte Albán I-V. Over those centuries, the hilltop city was repeatedly reconstructed with new

steps at Monte Albán

walls, plazas, and staircases, which, like layers of an onion, now overlie earlier construction.

Remains from Monte Albán Period I (500 BC-AD 1) reveal an already advanced culture, with gods, permanent temples, a priesthood, a written language, numerals, and a calendar. Sharply contrasting house styles indicate a differentiated, multilayered society. Monte Albán I ruins abound in graceful polychrome ceramics of uniquely Zapotec style.

Concurrent Olmec influences have also been found, notably in the buildings known as the Danzantes (Dancers), decorated with unique bas-reliefs similar to those unearthed along the Veracruz and Tabasco coasts.

The people who lived during Monte Albán Period II (AD 1-300), by contrast, came under heavy influence from Chiapas and Guatemala in the south. They built strange, ship-shaped buildings, such as Monte Albán's mysterious Building J, and left unique remains of their religion, such as the striking jade bat-god now on display in the Anthropology Museum in Mexico City.

Monte Albán reached its apex during the classical Period III (AD 300-800), attaining a population of perhaps 40,000 in an urban zone of about eight square kilometers (three sq mi), which spread along hilltops (including the El Gallo and Atzompa archaeological sites) west of the present city of Oaxaca.

Vigorous Period III leaders rebuilt the main hilltop complex as we see it today. Heavily influenced by the grand style of the Teotihuacán structures in the Valley of Mexico, the buildings were finished with handsome sloping staircases, corniced walls, monumental carvings, ball courts, and hieroglyph-inscribed stelae depicting gods, kings, and heroic scenes of battle.

In AD 800, Monte Albán, mysteriously cut off from the rest of Mesoamerica, was

Monte Albán

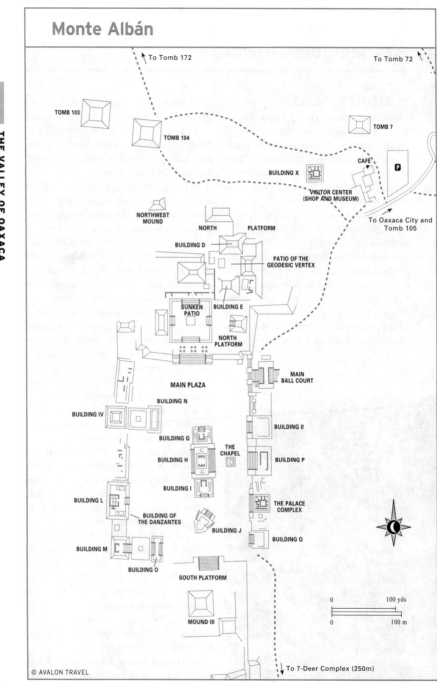

To Tomb 172

To Tomb 72

TOMB 103

TOMB 104

TOMB 7

BUILDING X

CAFÉ

P

VISITOR CENTER
(SHOP AND MUSEUM)

To Oaxaca City and
Tomb 105

NORTHWEST
MOUND

NORTH   PLATFORM

BUILDING D

PATIO OF THE
GEODESIC VERTEX

SUNKEN
PATIO

BUILDING E

NORTH
PLATFORM

MAIN
BALL COURT

MAIN PLAZA

BUILDING N

BUILDING IV

BUILDING II

BUILDING G

THE
CHAPEL

BUILDING H

BUILDING P

BUILDING I

BUILDING L

THE PALACE
COMPLEX

BUILDING OF
THE DANZANTES

BUILDING J

BUILDING Q

BUILDING M

BUILDING O

SOUTH PLATFORM

MOUND III

0   100 yds

0   100 m

© AVALON TRAVEL

To 7-Deer Complex (250m)

declining in population and power. By AD 1000, the city was virtually abandoned. The reasons—whether drought, disease, or revolt—and the consequent loss of the necessarily imported water, wood, salt, and food supplies remain an enigma.

During Periods IV and V, Mixtec peoples from the north invaded the Valley of Oaxaca. They warred with valley Zapotecs and, despite their relatively small numbers, became a ruling class in a number of valley city-states. The blend of Mixtec and Zapotec art and architecture sometimes led to new forms, especially visible at the west valley sites of Yagul and Mitla.

Exploring the Site

Visitors to **Monte Albán** (tel. 951/516-9770, 8am-5pm daily, entrance $5) enjoy a panoramic view of green mountains rising above the checkerboard of the Valley of Oaxaca. Allow at least two hours for your visit.

A good **guide** (about $10 pp for a two-hour tour) can certainly enhance your Monte Albán visit. Many are licensed by the authorities. You can often hire someone on the spot.

Past the visitor's center, as you enter the Main Plaza, north will be on your right, marked by the great **North Platform,** topped

by clusters of temples. The **Ball Court** will soon appear on your left. Twenty-foot-high walkways circumscribe the sunken I-shaped playing field. This, like all Oaxacan ball courts, had no stone ring (for supposed goals), but rather four mysterious niches at the court's I-end corners.

The **Main Plaza,** 1,000 feet long and exactly two-thirds that wide, is aligned along a precise north-south axis. Probably serving as a market and civic/ceremonial ground, the monumentally harmonious Main Plaza was the Zapotec "navel" of the world.

Monte Albán's oldest monumental construction, the **Danzantes** building (surmounted by newer Building L, on the west side of the plaza between Buildings M and IV), dates from Period I. Its walls are graced with a host of personages, known commonly as the *danzantes* (dancers) from their oft-contorted postures—probably chiefs vanquished by Monte Albán's armies. Their headdresses, earplugs, bracelets, and necklaces mark them among the nobility, while glyphs around their heads identify each individual.

Building J (circa AD 1), one of the most remarkable in Mesoamerica, stands nearby in mid-plaza at the foot of the South Platform. Speculation has raged since excavators

Monte Alban's Building J

The Tragic Story of Princess Donaji

The fabled marriage of King Cosijoeza (koh-see-hoh-AY-zah) of the Zapotecs to Coyollicatzin (koh-yoh-yee-KAH-tseen), daughter of Emperor Moctezuma II of the Aztecs, around 1490, was a happy one. It resulted in five children, the youngest of whom was a charming little girl.

The king asked his soothsayers what their divinations told of his little daughter's future. They replied that her life would be filled with tragic events and that she would finally sacrifice herself for her people. The king, saddened by the news but happy that she would turn out to be so selfless, named her Donaji (Great Soul).

Earlier, Cosijoeza, who ruled the Zapotec Isthmus domains from his capital at present-day Tehuántepec, had been an uneasy ally of his old enemy, King Dzahuindanda (zah-ween-DAHN-dah) of the Mixtecs. In 1520, with the Aztec threat diminished by the Spanish invasion, Cosijoeza recklessly attacked the fierce Mixtecs, losing the initial battle and then nearly his life as the Mixtecs pressed their advantage.

However, the Spanish, in the person of Hernán Cortés's lieutenant, Francisco Orozco, soon imposed a Mixtec-Zapotec treaty in which Dzahuindanda received Princess Donaji as a hostage to guarantee the peace.

Having Donaji as a prisoner at Monte Albán (known as Danni Dipaa in those days) was not exactly an advantage to Dzahuindanda, for he suspected that she was as much a spy as a hostage. His guess was right. Donaji gleaned intelligence vital to the Zapotec counterattack her father Cosijoeza was planning. At the moment Dzahuindanda's forces were most vulnerable, she sent her father a secret message to attack, which he did, with complete success, except for one thing.

With the treaty broken, the outraged Mixtecs decided to do away with Donaji. They decapitated her and buried her body before her father could rescue her. Later, some Zapotecs found Donaji's remains on the bank of the Atoyac river. They were surprised to see a lovely violet wild iris blossoming from her blood. Even more surprising, they found the flower's roots growing around her head, which was without any sign of decomposition.

Three hundred years later, the Oaxaca government decided to honor the heroine who sacrificed herself for her people by adding an image of Donaji's head to the Oaxacan coat of arms, where it remains to the present day.

---

unearthed its arrow-shaped base generations ago. It is not surprising that Alfonso Caso, Monte Albán's original principal excavator, theorized it was an astronomical observatory (it does point in the direction of the setting sun at its winter solstice).

Aficionados can't resist claiming that Building J represents some other-worldly influence. They assert that the figure, visibly inscribed on the building's upper northwest corner, is an extraterrestrial wearing a space helmet. Expert professionals refute this with a more earthly explanation, that the figure simply represents a ball player wearing the customary protective leather helmet.

The **South Platform** affords Monte Albán's best viewing point, especially during the late afternoon. Starting on the right-hand, Palace-complex side, **Building II** has a peculiar tunnel on its near side, perhaps covertly used by priests for privacy or some kind of magical effect.

The South Platform itself is only marginally explored. Looters have riddled the mounds on its top side. Its bottom four corners were embellished by fine bas-reliefs, two of which had their engravings intentionally buried from view. You can admire the fine sculpture and yet-undeciphered Zapotec hieroglyphs on one of them, along with others, at the South Platform's plaza-edge west side.

On Monte Albán's northern periphery stand a number of tombs that, when excavated, yielded a trove of artifacts, now mostly housed in museums. Walking west from the

Northern Platform's northeast base corner, you will pass Mound X on the right. A few hundred yards farther comes the Tomb 104 mound, presided over by an elaborate ceramic urn representing Cocijo, the Zapotec god of rain. Just north of this is Tomb 172, which has its skeletons and offerings left intact from when it was first opened.

Heading back along the northernmost of the two paths from Tomb 104, you will arrive at Tomb 7 a few hundred feet behind the visitors center. Here, around 1450, Mixtec nobles removed the original eighth-century contents and reused the tomb, burying a deceased dignitary and two servants for the netherworld. Along with the bodies, they left a fabulous treasure in gold, silver, jade, alabaster, and turquoise, now visible at the museum at the Centro Cultural de Santo Domingo in Oaxaca City.

A few hundred feet toward town on the opposite side of the road from the parking lot is a trail leading past a small ball court to the Cerro de Plumaje (Hill of Plumage), site of Tomb 105. A magnificent entrance door lintel, reminiscent of those at Mitla, welcomes you inside. Past the patio, descend to the mural-decorated tomb antechamber. Inside the cruciform tomb itself, four figures walk in pairs toward a great glyph, flanked by a god and goddess, identified by their name-dates.

Visitors Center

The Monte Albán Visitors Center (tel. 951/516-9770, 8am-5pm daily) has an excellent museum, good café with airy terrace, and information counter. Also, a well-stocked bookstore (tel. 951/516-9180) offers many books on Mesoamerica, including travel, histories, art, and folklore books. In the bookstore, you might purchase a copy of the very useful *Guide to Monte Albán*, by Monte Albán's director, Neli Robles. You could also pick up a copy of the very authoritative, in-depth *Oaxaca, the Archaeological Record*, by archaeologist Marcus Winter.

Getting There

Get to Monte Albán economically and very conveniently by one of the several tourist buses run by Hotel Rivera del Ángel (Mina 518, tel. 951/516-6666) and Viajes Turísticos Mitla (Mina 501, tel. 951/516-5327). Find them three blocks south and four blocks west of the *zócalo* in Oaxaca City. The aptly-named Monte Albán Tours (tel. 951/514-1976, montealbantours.com) is one of many Oaxaca-based tour companies that

THE VALLEY OF OAXACA
MONTE ALBÁN AND THE ARCHAEOLOGICAL ROUTE

Santa María Atzompa is renowned for green-glazed pottery.

send a bus to Monte Albán every day, for a four-hour visit ($12 pp).

By car, get to Monte Albán via the most scenic route. Start from Oaxaca City's south side, at the *periférico,* past the end of southbound Calle M. Cabrera. Cross the *periférico,* then bear right and immediately cross over the Río Atoyac bridge. Continue ahead, following other Monte Albán signs, about eight kilometers (five mi), uphill, to Monte Albán.

Alternatively, get to Monte Albán by following Highway 190 northwest from downtown Oaxaca City. After three kilometers (two mi) from the city center, curve left, around the big monument and traffic circle, reversing your direction, then immediately turn right (west) and continue across the Río Atoyac bridge. Follow the signs about 10 more kilometers (six mi) uphill to Monte Albán.

SANTA MARÍA ATZOMPA

The present-day town of Santa María Atzompa (pop. 5,000) spreads somewhat chaotically over the western end of the greater Monte Albán archaeological complex, overlying hundreds of acres of unexplored ancient remains. The majority of modern Atzompans, however, have little time for the past. They are busy producing Atzompan pottery, famous all over Mexico and the world.

Along with their distinctive pottery creations—attractive emerald green-glazed cooking pots, bowls, baking dishes, plates—the local potters have turned to creating multicolored vases, some with artfully cut holes for placing dried or fresh flowers, as well as lily-adorned crosses, vases, plates, and red pottery, inscribed with fetching floral motifs. There is some beautiful stuff here, but also a lot of modern-day, made-for-tourists kitsch.

The work can be seen and purchased at the **Mercado de Artesanías** (Handicrafts Market, tel. 951/558-9232, or local cell tel. 044-951 516-5062, 9am-7pm daily), on the entrance road (right side) after a long initial line of private stores. Each of the *mercado* displays contains the name and address of the artist, whom you can contact nearby in town.

For lunch at the handicrafts market, try the adjacent ★ **Restaurant Patio** (no phone, 11am-6pm daily, $4). They offer a menu of many Mexican specialties, including a number of moles (with chicken) and the reliable favorite, chiles rellenos.

Pacific Resorts and Southern Sierra

Look for ★ to find recommended
sights, activities, dining, and lodging.

Highlights

★ **Playa Estacahuite:** This intimate cove, sheltered by friendly offshore rocks, and teeming with colorful fish, ranks among Oaxaca's loveliest beaches (page 113).

★ **Playa Zipolite:** A little bit for everyone—surf, sun, and plenty of clean, golden sand—makes Zipolite a choice spot for a relaxing day, week, or even a season (page 113).

★ **Centro Mexicano de la Tortuga:** Far-seeing government action and community cooperation has converted a former turtle processing factory into a center for the recovery of Oaxaca's Pacific sea turtles (page 115).

★ **Barra de la Cruz and La Joya:** Barra de la Cruz is the town en route to the surf spot known as La Joya, one of the best right point breaks in Mexico (page 137).

★ **Cascadas Mágicas:** Enjoy a day of strolling, swimming, picnicking, and admiring bubbling blue waterfalls in the foothill forest not far from Huatulco (page 152).

★ **Playa Zicatela:** The two types of Zicatela waves—large and larger—make for lots of excitement, for both the intrepid surfers and the spectators on the beachfront. At the far east end, surfers have created a South Seas surf village (page 157).

★ **West-Side Beaches: Manzanillo, Carrizalillo, and Bachoco:** Rewarding snorkeling, golden sand, gentle waves, and *palapa* restaurants make these three playas the local favorites for Sunday family outings (page 158).

★ **Laguna Manialtepec:** Mirror-smooth water and dozens of bird species make this a prime adventure ground for kayakers, boaters, and campers (page 172).

★ **Santuario de Nuestra Señora de Juquila:** Images of the beloved patron are accessible to the hundreds of thousands of adoring pilgrims who arrive in Juquila yearly (page 175).

Historically, Oaxaca's southern coastal residents have both earned their livelihoods and sought their connections with the outside world by the Mar del Sur (the Southern Sea), the traditional Mexican name for the Pacific Ocean.

The southern coast was isolated by the towering, cloud-capped wall of the Sierra Madre del Sur (Mother Range of the South). Oaxaca's high southern Sierra, always remote and mysterious, was finally unveiled in its majesty only in the 1980s, when satellite photo measurements revealed that Cerro Quiexobra (kee-ay-SHOW-brah), at 3,750 meters (12,300 ft.), was by far Oaxaca's tallest mountain massif, a scarce 64 kilometers (40 mi) due north of the Bahías de Huatulco.

From such high, cool, pine-crested summits along its entire 320-kilometer (200 mi) rampart, the Sierra Madre del Sur plunges precipitously downward through lush, vine-hung canyon and foothill forest to the Pacific shore, an acacia-tufted expanse of endless summer.

There, as if forced southward by the weight of the high mountains, the coastline bulges to Oaxaca's most southerly point, near Puerto Ángel. From there, the Oaxaca coastline bends northerly—on its east side toward the Isthmus, and on its west side toward the Mixtec Coast, often called the Costa Chica (Little Coast) in southern Mexico.

During the 1970s and 1980s, paved highways and airlines ended the Oaxaca coast's isolation and brought Mexican and foreign visitors to the region. The government recognized the area's potential and began developing a new, ecologically correct vacationland at the Bahías de Huatulco. Meanwhile, visitors were discovering the South Seas village resorts of Puerto Ángel and Puerto Escondido, the latter offering expert surfers one of the most challenging waves in the world.

Now the steady stream of vacationers can choose from a growing menu of outdoor diversions, from strolling the sand and snorkeling in hidden coves to rescuing sea turtle eggs, splashing in upland waterfalls, and lodging comfortably overnight at rustic jungle coffee farms.

Previous: beach umbrellas, Puerto Escondido; beach at Puerto Ángel. **Above:** surfer in Puerto Escondido.

Pacific Resorts and Southern Sierra

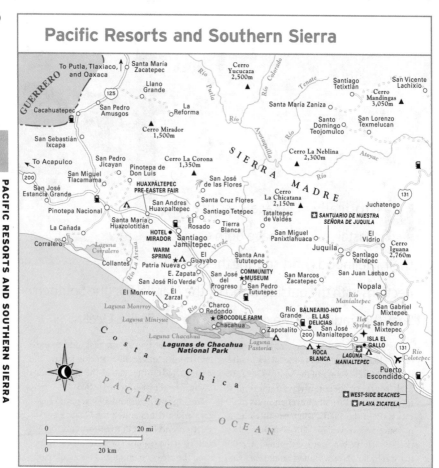

PLANNING YOUR TIME

Where you go and how much time you spend on Oaxaca's sun-drenched southern coast depends on what you prefer. The prime resorts of Puerto Ángel (and its neighboring villages Zipolite and Mazunte), the Bahías de Huatulco, and Puerto Escondido each have their distinct charms. Puerto Ángel is heaven for those who prefer sleepy Mexico beach-village ambience. Puerto Escondido has the awesome breakers of Playa Zicatela, the most famous (and most challenging) surfing beach in Mexico; plenty of handicrafts shopping; a pair of lovely hidden

coves, and a couple of other nearby surfing breaks. The up-to-date Bahías de Huatulco resort has the widest range of hotels, from modest to luxurious; several very good restaurants; and a small kingdom of sylvan forests that enfold its nine bays. Between Huatulco and the industrial port of Salina Cruz, and also in the Parque Nacional Lagunas de Chacahua National Park to the west, surfers have discovered half a dozen world-class breaks, and Oaxaca's reputation as a surfing destination now includes not only Puerto Escondido but points both east and west.

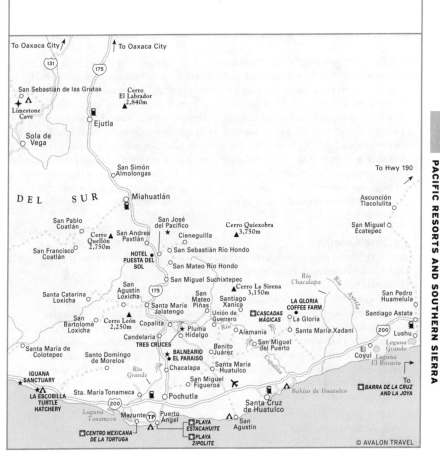

To Oaxaca City
To Oaxaca City
131
175
San Sebastián de las Grutas
Limestone Cave
Ejutla
Cerro El Labrador 2,840m
Sola de Vega
San Simón Almolongas
To Hwy 190
DEL SUR
Miahuatlán
Ascunción Tlacolulita
San Pablo Coatlán
San José del Pacífico
Cerro Quiexobra 3,750m
San Miguel Ecatepec
Cerro Quellón 2,750m
San Andres Paxtlán
Cieneguilla
San Francisco Coatlán
HOTEL PUESTA DEL SOL
San Sebastián Río Hondo
San Mateo Río Hondo
Río Chacalapa
Río Ayula
San Agustín Loxicha
175
San Mateo Piñas
San Miguel Suchixtepec
Cerro La Sirena 3,150m
Santa Catarina Loxicha
Santa María Jalatengo
Santiago Xanica
LA GLORIA COFFEE FARM
San Pedro Huamelula
San Bartolomé Loxicha
Cerro León 2,250m
Copalita
Unión de Guerrero
CASCADAS MÁGICAS
La Gloria
Santiago Astata
Candelaria
Pluma Hidalgo
Río
Alemania
Santa María Xadani
200
Lushu
TRES CRUCES
Benito Juárez
San Miguel del Puerto
Copalita
Laguna Grande
Santa María de Colotepec
Santo Domingo de Morelos
BALNEARIO EL PARAISO
Chacalapa
Santa María Huatulco
El Coyul
Laguna El Rosario
IGUANA SANCTUARY
Río Grande
San Miguel Figueroa
Bahías de Huatulco
BARRA DE LA CRUZ AND LA JOYA
LA ESCOBILLA TURTLE HATCHERY
Sta. María Tonameca
Pochutla
Santa Cruz de Huatulco
Laguna Tonameca
Mazunte
Puerto Ángel
San Agustín
CENTRO MEXICANA DE LA TORTUGA
PLAYA ESTACAHUITE
PLAYA ZIPOLITE

© AVALON TRAVEL

If you have a week, you could spend it all at one place, spending half of your time on the beach, in the water, and by the pool. With the rest of your week, in Puerto Ángel, spend two or three days on excursions, to **Playa Estacahuite,** the **Centro Mexicano de la Tortuga** in Mazunte, and **Playa La Ventanilla** for bird- and crocodile-watching. Maybe continue for a day upcountry at the the pine-scented sierra summit at **San José del Pacífico.** In Huatulco, you can easily spend a day on a catamaran or stand-up paddleboard tour exploring the bays, another day rafting or kayaking the Río Copalita, and a third day visiting **La Gloria coffee farm** and the **Cascadas Mágicas** in the tropical foothill forest. In Puerto Escondido be sure to spend a day wildlife-viewing at **Laguna Manialtepec.** Continue farther afield to explore **Parque Nacional Lagunas de Chacahua.** Finally, if you have the time and desire, heading a few hours uphill into the Chatino indigenous heartland to visit the **Santuario de Nuestra Señora de Juquila** pilgrimage shrine.

Puerto Ángel and Vicinity

In the 1960s, Puerto Ángel was still a sleepy little spot connected by a single frail land link—a tortuous cross-Sierra dirt road—to the rest of the country. Adventure travelers saw it at the far south of the map and dreamed of a South Seas paradise. They came and were not disappointed. Although that first tourist trickle has grown steadily, it's still only enough to support the sprinkling of modest lodgings and restaurants that now dot the beaches and hillsides around Puerto Ángel's tranquil little blue bay.

Getting Oriented

Puerto Ángel is at the southern terminus of Highway 175 from Oaxaca City, about nine kilometers (six mi) downhill from its intersection with Highway 200. It's a small place, where nearly everything is within walking distance along the beach, which a rocky bayfront hill divides into two parts: Playa Principal, the main town beach; and sheltered west-side Playa Panteón, the tourist favorite. A scenic boulder-decorated shoreline *andador* (walkway) connects the two beaches.

A paved road winds west from Puerto Ángel along the coastline a couple of miles to Playa Zipolite, lined by a colony of beachfront *cabañas,* popular with an international cadre of budget-minded seekers of heaven on earth. Continuing west, the road passes the former turtle-processing village beaches of Playa San Agustinillo and Playa Mazunte. From there it goes on another 6.4 kilometers (four mi), past the joining with Highway 200 (and thence Puerto Escondido) at San Antonio village at Kilometer 198.

The major local service and transportation center is **Pochutla** (pop. 35,000), a mile north along Highway 175 from its Highway 200 junction.

Getting Around

Local *colectivo* taxis ferry passengers frequently between Pochutla and Puerto Ángel (fare around $1) from about 7am until 8pm, stopping at the Highway 200 intersection. Some taxis continue to Zipolite after stopping on Bulevar Virgilio Uribe, Puerto Ángel's main bayfront street. To continue to Playa San

the bay and pier in Puerto Ángel

Agustinillo and Playa Mazunte, you must transfer to another *colectivo* (arriving from the opposite direction) in Zipolite. Private taxis also routinely make runs between Puerto Ángel and either Zipolite or Pochutla for about $7.

You can also get around (much more expensively) by boat. Captains routinely take parties of up to eight for sightseeing, snorkeling, and picnicking to a number of nearby beaches. Bargain at Playa Panteón: The rate should run about $30/hour for a whole boat rented privately for 6-8 people or about $15 per person per day for a shared boat.

Tours and rental cars are other options for getting around.

SIGHTS AND BEACHES
Playas Principal and Panteón
Playa Principal's 400 yards of wide golden sand decorate most of Puerto Ángel's bayfront. Waves can be strong near the pier, where they often surge vigorously onto the beach and recede with a sometimes-strong undertow. Swimming is always more tranquil at the sheltered west end toward Playa Panteón. The clear waters are good for casual snorkeling around the rocks on both sides of the bay.

Sheltered Playa Panteón (Cemetery Beach) is Puerto Ángel's sunning beach, lined with squadrons of beach chairs and umbrellas in front of beachside restaurants. Playa Oso (Bear Beach) is a little dab of sand beside a rugged seastack of rock beyond Playa Panteón.

★ Playa Estacahuite
Decorating the rocky shoreline, about half a mile outside the opposite (east) side of Puerto Ángel bay, Playa Estacahuite (ay-stah-kah-WEE-tay) is actually two beaches in one: a pair of luscious coral-sand nooks teeming with fish grazing the living reef just offshore. Several *palapa* restaurants perched picturesquely above the beaches provide food and drinks. Get there in less than a mile by taxi ($3) or on foot via the dirt road (watch for sign) that forks right off the highway, about 400 yards uphill from beachfront Bulevar Uribe.

★ Playa Zipolite
Playa Zipolite (see-poh-LEE-tay), a wide, mile-long strand of brilliant golden sand enfolded by headlands and backed by palm groves, is simply stunning. It stretches from the intimate little cove and beach of Playa

Playa Zipolite

Puerto Ángel and Vicinity

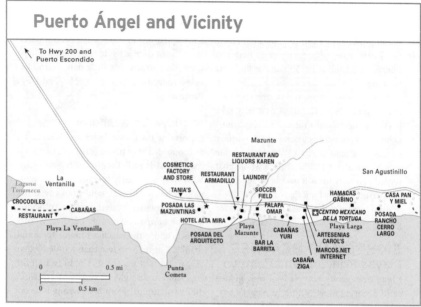

del Amor, tucked on its east side, to towering cactus-festooned sea cliffs rising behind the new-age Shambala retreat on the west end.

Although often good for wading and for casual swimming (with care), Playa Zipolite's surf, usually tranquil in the mornings (but always with significant undertow), can turn thunderous by the afternoon, especially when offshore storms magnify both the swells and the undertow. Experienced surfers love these times, when everyone but experts should stay out.

Playa Zipolite has evolved from a lineup of stick and thatch beachfront *cabañas* to mostly concrete hotels, most with oceanfront *palapa* restaurants. Many of these hotels share a new, paved, two-block streetfront known locally as the **adoquín** (ah-doh-KEEN), along with a procession of homegrown restaurants and small businesses, from grocery and pharmacy to surf shop, laundry, and Internet stores. All of this, in a neighborhood known as **Colonia Roca Blanca,** is now Playa Zipolite's town center. Get there, heading west from Puerto Ángel, by turning left, past Piñ Palmera, the children's school.

Good surfing notwithstanding, Playa Zipolite's renown stems from its status as one of the very few nude beaches in Mexico. Bathing *au naturel*, practiced nearly entirely by visitors and a few local young men, is tolerated only grudgingly by local people, many of whose livelihoods depend on the nudists. If you're discreet and take off your clothes at the more isolated west end (behind the big rock), no one will appear to mind (and women will largely avoid voyeuristic attention from Mexican boys and men).

Playas San Agustinillo and Mazunte

About a mile west of Playa Zipolite, a wide, mile-long, yellow-sand beach curves past the village of **San Agustinillo.** On the open ocean, but partly sheltered by offshore rocks at the west, its surf is much like that of Playa Zipolite, varying from gentle in the morning to rough in the afternoon, depending mostly upon wind and offshore swells. Small village groceries and beachside *palapa* restaurants supply food and drinks to the occasional Playa Zipolite overflow as well as to local families

© AVALON TRAVEL

on weekends and holidays. Fishing is excellent either in the surf from nearby rocks, by rented *panga*, or from your own boat launched from the beach. Beach camping is customary, especially in front of beachfront restaurants.

The half-mile-long, yellow-sand **Mazunte Beach,** like San Agustinillo, is semi-sheltered and varies from tranquil to rough. Fishing is likewise good, beach camping is customary, and local stores and seafood *palapa* restaurants sell basic supplies and food.

San Agustinillo and Mazunte people, including a group of European (many Italian) resident-entrepreneurs, have been renovating their houses and building hotels and *cabañas* to accommodate an increasing number of visitors. Signs along the road and at the beach advertise their lodgings and restaurants.

★ Centro Mexicano de la Tortuga

The former turtle-processing plant at Mazunte lives on as the **Mazunte Turtle Museum** (on the main road, east end of the village, tel./fax 958/584-3376, www.centro-mexicanodelatortuga.org, www.tomzap.com/

turtle.html, 10am-4:30pm Wed.-Sat., 10am-2:30pm Sun., $4). At the museum, which includes an aquarium, study center, and turtle hatchery, you can peruse displays illustrating the ongoing turtle research and conservation program and see members of most of Mexico's turtle species paddling in tanks overlooking the beach where their ancestors once swarmed. Guided tours are offered in a number of foreign languages, including English, German, and Italian.

Fábrica Ecología de Cosméticos Naturales de Mazunte

About half a mile farther west along the main road through Mazunte village is a **cosmetics factory and store** (tel. 958/587-4860, www.cosmeticosmazunte.com, 9am-5pm daily). Initially funded partly by the Body Shop Foundation and spearheaded by the local community, the project has grown into an important local industry, with dozens of workers and a sizable shop filled with thousands of bottles of locally produced all-natural shampoo, skin cream, hair conditioner, and much

Puerto Ángel

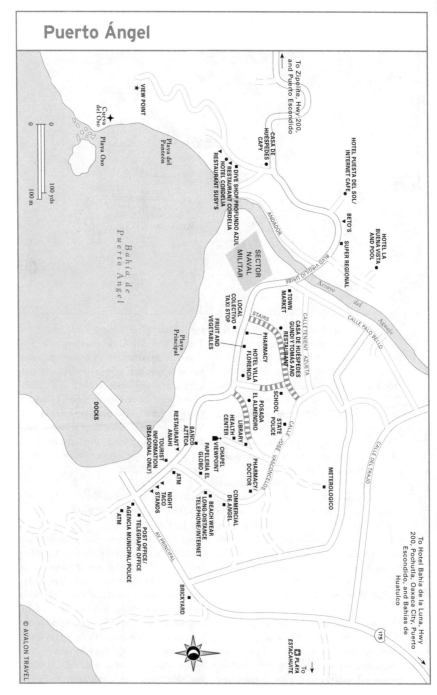

To Zipolite, Hwy. 200, and Puerto Escondido

VIEW POINT

Cueva del Oso

Playa Oso

Playa del Panteón

Bahia de Puerto Ángel

0   100 yds
0   100 m

DIVE SHOP PROFUNDO AZUL
RESTAURANT CORDELIA
HOTEL CORDELIA
RESTAURANT SUSY'S

CASA DE HUÉSPEDES CAPY

HOTEL PUESTA DEL SOL/ INTERNET CAFÉ

BETO'S

SUPER REGIONAL

HOTEL LA BUENA VISTA AND POOL

ANDADOR

BLVD VIRGILIO URIBE

Arroyo del Aguaje

SECTOR NAVAL MILITAR

TOWN MARKET

LOCAL COLLECTIVO TAXI STOP

FRUIT AND VEGETABLES

STAIRS

CALLE TENIENT AZUETA

CASA DE HUÉSPEDES GUNDI Y TOMAS AND RESTAURANT

PHARMACY

HOTEL VILLA FLORENCIA

POSADA EL ALMENDRO

SCHOOL

STATE POLICE

CALLE PALO BELLO

CALLE JOSÉ VASCONCELOS

CALLE DEL TRAJO

Playa Principal

DOCKS

RESTAURANT ANAHI

TOURIST INFORMATION (SEASONAL ONLY)

BANCO AZTECA

HEALTH CENTER

LIBRARY

CHAPEL VIEWPOINT

PAPELERIA EL GLOBO

PHARMACY/ DOCTOR

METEROLOGICO

ATM

NIGHT TACO STANDS

COMMERCIAL DE ANGEL

BEACH WEAR
LONG-DISTANCE TELEPHONE/INTERNET

POST OFFICE/ TELEGRAPH OFFICE

AGENCIA MUNICIPAL/POLICE

ATM

AV. PRINCIPAL

BRICKYARD

To Hotel Bahía de la Luna, Hwy. 200, Pochutla, Oaxaca City, Puerto Escondido, and Bahías de Huatulco

175

To PLAYA ESTACAHUITE

more. The staff is working hard to assure that the effort continues to grow, so that locally grown products such as coconut, corn, and avocado oils and natural aromatics will form the basis for a thriving cottage cosmetics industry.

Playa La Ventanilla

Continue about 2.4 kilometers (1.5 mi) west along the main road over the low hill west of Mazunte and turn left at the signed dirt road to pristine wildlife haven **Playa and Laguna La Ventanilla** (cocodrilianos@hotmail.com, 8am-6pm daily). Now protected by local residents, swarms of birds, including pelicans, cormorants, and herons, and a population of wild *cocodrilos* and *lagartos* is making a comeback in a bushy mangrove wetland.

Boat workers headquartered at the sturdy **visitors center** *palapa,* past the beach village road's end parking lot, guide visitors on a two-hour **ecotour** (adults $4, kids $2), which includes a stop for refreshment at a little mid-lagoon island. The boat workers are known for their wildlife sensitivity and allow no motor vehicles within 100 yards of their communally owned lagoon-sanctuary.

The Playa La Ventanilla community has taken responsibility for protecting the turtles that arrive on their beach against poachers. During both February and June-October, hundreds of sea turtles come ashore to lay eggs. If necessary, community volunteers help the exhausted turtles up the steep beach, where they lay their eggs. Volunteers then gather the eggs and rebury them in a secure spot. After the hatchlings emerge about a month and a half later, volunteers nurture them for about three months and release them safely back into the ocean. For more information and photos, visit www.tomzap.com/ventanil.html.

Besides lagoon tours and saving turtles, La Ventanilla cooperative maintains the excellent beach-view **Restaurant Maiz Azul** (8am-7pm daily, $2-6), run by half a dozen dedicated women. They specialize in local recipes, such as savory banana-leafed-wrapped tamales, baked turkey smothered in mole sauce, and chiles rellenos. They also sell their own home-ground fresh peanut butter.

Furthermore, the Ventanilla community invites visitors to stay in their very rustic **accommodations** (tel. 958/108-7288, cocodrilianos@hotmail.com, *cabañas* $35 s or d, dorms $15 pp). They offer two options: either four clean *cabañas* (on the left as you enter), with choice of one king-size bed, two double beds, or one double bed, all with mosquito nets and private hot-water shower-bath; or, a four-room dormitory-style *cabaña,* each room with two bunk beds for a total of four people per room, with shared toilets and showers.

ENTERTAINMENT AND EVENTS

Nightlife

Puerto Ángel's entertainments are mostly spontaneous. If anything exciting is going to happen, it will most likely be on the beachfront Bulevar Uribe, where people often congregate during the late afternoon and evenings. A small crowd may accumulate by the food stalls and the pier for tacos, talk, and beer.

For livelier nightlife, in Zipolite, follow the youthful folks who (especially on Saturdays) crowd into **Disco La Puesta** (on the Zipolite *adoquín*, 9pm-late Tues.-Sat. high season, Fri.-Sat. only in low season).

Similar diversions go on at salsa-rock disco **La Barracuda** (near the west end of the Zipolite *adoquín,* no phone, most nights of the week in season, until midnight).

Festivals

Puerto Ángel's major scheduled event is the big **Fiesta de San Miguel Arcangel** (Oct. 1 and 2). Then the *mascaritas* (masked children) dancers romp, carnival games and rides light up the streetfront, and a regatta of fishing boats parades around the bay.

Mazunte folks enjoy more than their share of fiestas. The year kicks off with the exciting **Fiesta Popular** (around Jan. 15), an old-fashioned carnival, complete with ferris wheel, loop-the-loop, a platoon of coin-tossing, bottle-knocking, balloon-popping games, and loads of popcorn, tacos, and hot dogs, all topped off by a colorful riot of fizzing, whirling, and booming fireworks.

Día de la Marina (June 1) honors the Mexican navy with bigwigs on a bandstand, flowers in the bay, basketball and volleyball tourneys, and a traditional dance.

Día del Pescador (Aug. 5) offers a full day's celebration beginning with a 25k foot race followed by competitive sports, boat races, diving, and swimming. The evening includes a community dinner followed by dancing, singing, and even poetry reading.

Curanderos (traditional healers) converge from all over to celebrate the beginning of spring with a feast of **traditional healing arts** (Mar. 21). They offer treatments, from temazcal hot room, native herb potions and poultices, to massage and spine straightening by the *curanderos de huesos* bone healers.

Finally, Mazunte celebrates the fall with an all-Oaxaca **Jazz Festival** around the end of November.

RECREATION
Swimming and Surfing
Swimming provides cooler exercise opportunities, especially in the sheltered waters off of **Playa Panteón.** Off of **Playa Zipolite,** bodysurfing, boogie boarding, and surfing can be rewarding, depending on wind and swells. The waves in this part of Mexico tend to be bigger, scarier, and more dangerous in summer, when the swells come from the south. For those who don't know the ocean well, be wary out here. There are riptides and very forceful waves. This is also an unofficial (meaning officially illegal but unenforced) nude beach and there are plenty of European tourists who take advantage of this. For **surfing lessons** contact expert and friendly surfers **Bastián and Fabián López at Casa de Huéspedes Gundi y Tomás** (tel. 958/584-3068, localsur_13@hotmail.com or gundtoma@hotmail.com, $20 for two hours). They will be able to judge the safety of the water and whether or not lessons should be offered.

Snorkeling and Scuba Diving
Rocky shoals at the edges of Puerto Ángel Bay, especially just off **Playa Panteón,** are fine for casual snorkeling. **Playa Estacahuite,** on the open ocean just beyond the bay's east headland, is even better. Snorkel rentals are available on the beach, at both Playa Estacahuite and Playa Panteón.

Puerto Ángel divers enjoy a well-equipped,

A rock-lined path links Puerto Ángel's two main beaches.

professional scuba diving shop, **Profundo Azul** (Deep Blue; at Playa Panteón, tel. 958/584-3109, tel. 958/584-3015 at Zipolite, www.tomzap.com/azulprofundo.html), run by very experienced Juan José de Nova Reyes, known locally as Chepe. He offers snorkel trips ($15 pp), scuba dives (two tanks, for certified scuba divers, $100), and scuba instruction, from the basics (beginners, $70) all the way up to a complete open-water advanced certification course (3-5 days, $350).

Fishing

Puerto Ángel's Playa Principal, Playa Panteón, and Playa Zipolite are the best places to bargain for a boat and captain to take you and your friends out on a fishing excursion. Prices depend on season, but you can figure on paying around $60 for a half-day excursion for three or four people with bait and two or three good rods and reels.

During a three-hour outing a few miles offshore, a competently captained boat will typically bring in three or four big, good-eating *dorado* (mahi-mahi), *huachinango* (snapper), *atún* (tuna), or *pez de gallo* (roosterfish). If you're uncertain about what's biting, go down to the Playa Principal in Puerto Ángel around 2pm or 3pm and see what the boats are bringing in.

Experienced scuba instructor Chepe at **Profundo Azul** (Deep Blue; at Playa Panteón, tel. 958/584-3109, tel. 958/584-3015 at Zipolite, www.tomzap.com/azulprofundo.html) also offers fishing trips (three hours in motor *lancha* for $100, including tackle and bait, for up to four people). Experienced swimmer and surfer Bastián López at **Casa de Huéspedes Gundi y Tomas** (tel. 958/584-3062, gundtoma@hotmail.com) offers about the same.

SHOPPING
Market

The biggest local market is the Monday *tianguis,* which spreads along the Pochutla main street, Highway 175, about seven miles from Puerto Ángel, one mile inland from the Highway 200 junction. It's mostly a place for looking rather than buying, as throngs of vendors from the hills line the sidewalks, even crowding into the streets, to sell their piles of onions, mangoes, forest herbs, carrots, cilantro, and jícama.

In Puerto Ángel, the freshest fruit and vegetables are available at the tiny **fruit and vegetable store** (on the main beachfront street, west end, 8am-9pm daily) by the pharmacy. Alternately, go to the smallish **Puerto Ángel market** (near the corner of main beachfront street Bulevar Uribe and the westside bridge).

Handicrafts

For fine custom-made **hammocks,** visit local craftsman Gabino Silva at his country shop, off a jungly stretch of the road between Zipolite and San Agustinillo. Watch for his sign labeled Hamacas and Cabaña on the beach side of the road, 6.7 kilometers (4.2 mi) from the Puerto Ángel village center.

A handful of handicrafts have arrived in Puerto Ángel at **La Carey beachware** (on Vasconcelos, directly uphill from the pier, tel. 958/584-3251, 9am-10pm daily).

In Mazunte, stop by **Artesanias Carol's** (across from the turtle museum, no phone, 9am-6pm daily) for a carefully selected assortment of mostly women's wear, including *huipiles*, resort wear, straw hats, shells, bathing suits, black Oaxaca pottery, interesting bamboo drinking cups, and *palos de lluvia* ("rain sticks") to restore your jangled nerves.

ACCOMMODATIONS

The Puerto Ángel area offers a good selection of modest, homegrown, guesthouse-style lodgings. The successful ones have given their legion of savvy repeat customers what they want: clean, basic, tepid-water accommodations in tranquil, television-free settings where Puerto Ángel's natural isolation and tropical charm set the tone for long, restful holidays.

Visitors have their choice of several neighborhoods. In Puerto Ángel itself, hotels and guesthouses dot the hillside above the main town beach, the pier, and the single main business street. The Playa Panteón lodgings, by contrast, are on the sleepier west side of the bay, above the lineup of rustic *palapa* restaurants along petite Playa Panteón.

Outside of Puerto Ángel visitors also have many choices, mostly right on the beach, but some atop breezy hillsides, above the beachfront hamlets of Zipolite, San Agustinillo, and Mazunte.

Unless otherwise specified, prices listed here are year-round rates, excepting Christmas-New Year's and Easter holiday seasons, when rates customarily rise 25-50 percent, depending on demand.

Puerto Ángel: Main Town
$25-50

Puerto Ángel's most welcoming lodging is the exceptional ★ Casa de Huéspedes Gundi y Tomás (tel. 958/584-3068, www.puertoangel-hotel.com, $25-40 for 2, depending on room), the life project of personable German-born Gundi Ley and her sons, Bastián and Fabián López. Their homey, rustic-aesthetic complex rambles up a leafy hillside to a breezy bay-view *palapa,* where patrons relax, socialize, and enjoy food and drink from the kitchen. Below and above that, guests enjoy two rows of several clean, colorfully furnished rooms, shaded by two hammock-strewn view porches. Bastián and Fabián, both accomplished surfers, offer surfing lessons in English, German, or Spanish, and take parties out for beach tours in their sturdy boat.

Their accommodations, which also include the Almendro tropical-garden *posada* (lodging) near the beach downhill, consist of 14 rooms—some shared shower and toilets, some private—and one bungalow (50 percent discount for a one-week rental), all with fans and a good restaurant. Get there via the lane (see the sign, uphill side) that stair-steps uphill near the west end of Puerto Ángel's main beachfront street.

Travelers who enjoy being right in the middle of the Puerto Ángel beachfront street scene choose the Hotel Villa Florencia (Blv. Virgilio Uribe, tel./fax 958/584-3044, villaserenaoax@hotmail.com, $23 s, $30 d, $35 t, add $3 for a/c). Here, in the shady interior lobby-patio, past the porch-front café, is tranquility. Upstairs, the approximately 15 rooms with bath are decorated with local art and handicrafts.

Enjoy the variety and luxury of west-side (two blocks past the bridge), hilltop castle-in-the-palms at solid long-time Hotel Puesta del Sol (Barrio del Sol, tel. 958/584-3096, 958/584-3315, www.puertoangel.net/puesta_del_sol.html, $25-50 d). Luxuriant tropical verdure festoons a sunny inner patio, leading up to the main building, with 14 immaculate, semi-deluxe rooms, appointed with ruffled bedspreads and curtains (with private baths, two with hot water). A dining room serves breakfast. The owners also offer three apartments near the Puerto Ángel lighthouse, five minutes by car from the beach for those seeking longer-term rentals. Each comes with a double and single bed, kitchenette, and Wi-Fi.

Another worthy west-side Puerto Ángel accommodation is Hotel La Buena Vista (Calle Palo Bello, tel./fax 958/584-3104, www.labuenavista.com, $50-70), tucked on the hillside that rises just west of the mid-town Arroyo de Aguaje bridge. The hotel's five accommodations levels stair-step artfully up the forested slope. The 1st- and 2nd-level rooms look out onto verdure-framed garden forest views. On the 3rd level are more rooms and a luxuriously airy restaurant *palapa* that opens to a bay vista. The hotel climaxes with several, large, onyx-tile-floored 4th- and 5th-floor rooms that share an entire private view patio with hammocks. There, the owners have provided a luxurious view pool-patio for their guests ($3 entrance for non-guests). All rooms are immaculate, light, and simply but tastefully furnished, with spotless bathrooms. Several of the 23 rooms have private, hammock-hung, view balconies, and some have kitchenettes; all rooms come with fans, mosquito curtains, and breakfast and supper at the restaurant (in season only, $4-14), but with room-temperature water only.

Playa Panteón
UNDER $25
Heading around the curve of the bay to the Playa Panteón neighborhood, you'll find one of Puerto Ángel's old standby budget lodgings, **Casa de Huéspedes Capi** (Playa Panteón, tel./fax 958/584-3002, $12 s, $18 d in one bed, $22 d, $25 t in two beds), perched on the bay-view hillside by the road fork to Playa Zipolite. Rooms are stacked in two stories, many of which enjoy views toward the beach. The rooms are basic but clean, with fans and cool-water private baths. The upper rooms open to an airy bay-view porch. The restaurant, with TV, is handy for breakfast.

$25-50
Downhill stands Puerto Ángel's only truly beachfront lodging, **Hotel Cordelia's** (right on Playa Panteón, tel. 958/584-3021, azul_profundomx@hotmail.com, $40 s or d, $60 d, $90 t, some credit cards accepted). The Cordelia's seven rooms, most with expansive bay views, are pleasingly decorated with rustic, whitewashed walls, attractive native floor tiles, natural wood furniture, and artful tile touches in the bathrooms. Amenities include Wi-Fi, fans, air-conditioning, hot water, and handy beachfront restaurant for breakfast downstairs.

Bahía de la Luna (Playa La Boquilla)
$50-200
Visitors who long for the delights of a hidden South Seas hideaway can have it at **Bahía de la Luna** (on the coast about two miles east of Puerto Ángel, tel. 958/589-5020, www.bahiadelaluna.com, $85 s, $90 d, $150 suite, $160-270 villa). New owners have revitalized this mini-paradise, set on a palm-shaded half-moon strand called Playa La Boquilla, lapped by gentle waves and enfolded by rocky headlands. They offer about a dozen comfortable rustic-chic thatched, adobe *cabañas*, some with panoramic views, on the forested hillside above the beach, and others, tucked in the leafy shade, right on the beach below. *Cabaña* rentals feature one room with a big bed, reading lamps, and private, tepid-water shower-bath. Two larger similarly comfortable units—a suite accommodating four, and a villa accommodating eight—are also available. All include a hearty breakfast in the beachfront restaurant. There, guests enjoy shady beach *palapas* with recliners, hammocks for snoozing, kayaks for exploring, and snorkeling equipment.

Get there via the signed side road, east off of Highway 175, about eight kilometers (five mi) downhill from the Highway 200 Pochutla junction, or three kilometers (two mi) uphill from Puerto Ángel. After about two miles from the turnoff, the road steepens. It's best to go by taxi unless you are a fearless driver.

Playa Estacahuite
OVER $200
Nestled on the west flank of Playa Estacahuite, **Casa Bichu** (Playa Estacahuite, tel. 958/584-3489, -90, -91, from Canada or U.S. toll-free direct 877/223-9590, www.casabichu.com, $350-500 d) is graced by an abundance of natural, hand-fashioned decor created by Mexican architect Monia Vizcarra. From inlaid mahogany floors and luxuriously thick thatched roofs, to polished liana vine handrails and stunning ocean views, nothing has been spared at Casa Bichu to create heaven on earth. All nine rooms and suites are large and superbly furnished with all possible amenities, including comfy king-size beds, soft couches, and garden and vine-framed ocean-view windows, all of which blend to create a feeling of luxurious seclusion.

Accommodations, all called "villas," come in three variations, Garden ($350), Deluxe ($460), and Resort ($500), depending upon size and location. All villas come with breakfast, exercise machines, sauna, Wi-Fi, and the opportunity to dine at the gourmet restaurant

($10-35). Spa services, such as massage and temazcal ceremonial hot room, are extra. Pets ($50 extra) and young adults 16 and over are welcomed.

Zipolite
UNDER $25

The *cabañas* of Lo Cósmico (Playa Zipolite, no phone, www.locosmico.com, $12-25 d) nestle on a cactus-decorated rocky knoll at Playa Zipolite's sheltered west end. White spheres perched on their thatched-roof peaks lend a mystical Hindu-Buddhist accent to the *cabañas'* already picturesque appearance. In the restaurant atop the knoll, you're likely to find Antonio Nadurille, Lo Cósmico's Mexican owner-manager. He watches after the *cabañas* and the restaurant, specializing in a dozen varieties of tasty crêpes. His hillside and beach-level *cabañas* are clean, candlelit, and equipped with hammocks and concrete floors, with shared bath and toilets. Recently, Antonio has built a number of sturdy, rock-walled, hurricane-proof designer rooms with baths and views on his hilltop. *Note:* All of Lo Cósmico's very clean shared toilet and shower facilities are separate from the accommodations and a short walk downhill.

$25-50

Shambhala (Playa Zipolite, tel. 958/584-3152, fax 958/584-3151, www.advantagemexico.com/shambhala, $25-50), which shares the same forested, west-side headland as Lo Cósmico, is—as it sounds—a tranquil, Buddhist-style retreat. Shambhala's driving force is the articulate owner-community leader Gloria Esperanza Johnson, who arrived in Zipolite by accident in 1970 and decided to stay, eventually adopting Mexican citizenship.

Gloria has built Shambhala from the ground up; she now offers five rustic *cabañas* on a no-reservation, first-come-first-served basis only. Choices include one large beachfront *cabaña* with kitchen, accommodating four with shared toilet and shower, and a second beachfront *cabaña* for two with shared toilet and shower. Also in the leafy (green in summer-early winter) uphill forest overlooking lovely Zipolite beach, are a pair of smaller *cabañas,* each with private toilet and shower-bath, and a larger-view *cabaña,* accommodating three, with shared toilet and shower. All *cabañas* come with fans and mosquito nets.

Get to both Shambhala and Lo Cósmico by turning toward the beach from the main Puerto Ángel-Zipolite road onto the signed dirt driveway at Zipolite's west end (where the

Relaxing at Shambhala can be a cosmic experience.

colectivos stop to transfer passengers). Bear right at the first fork, then left at the next for Lo Cósmico or right for Shambhala.

$50-100

Bungalows ★ **Las Casitas** (Playa Zipolite, tel. -958/100-9234, www.las-casitas.net, $50-100) are also on Zipolite's far west end near Shambhala. Las Casitas is the labor of love of friendly Italian builders-owners Daniela and Bruno Canibus, who have created their vision of paradise in Zipolite's summer-green tropical forest. They offer five rustic housekeeping bungalows, hand-built of all-natural materials, in a naturalistic garden of meandering stone pathways and sea views. A new version of the house restaurant, La Providencia, should be open next high season.

The five unique bungalows come with kitchenettes equipped with gas stove, utensils, and purified water. Two of the bungalows, El Organo and La Tortuga, are spacious studios, furnished with one double bed and private toilet and shower-bath. The other two bungalows, Los Platanos and La Ceiba, accommodate six and nine people, respectively, in three separate bedrooms with shared kitchen and bathroom facilities. The Los Platanos bungalow has rooms for one, two, and three people each. The rooms in the larger La Ceiba bungalow are for two, three, and four people each. A fifth large and luxurious bungalow, El Sueño, is the most expensive and comes with kitchen and private bath. Be sure to bring mosquito repellent.

Get to Las Casitas via the dirt road to Lo Cósmico and Shambhala, which you will pass along the way. Continue uphill about 200 yards more to the Las Casitas gate.

San Agustinillo
$25-50

A number of lodgings sprinkle the San Agustinillo beachfront and hillside above the road. Here, you can enjoy it all: charming Mexican beach village ambience; stores and small restaurants nearby; hammock-hung verandas with gorgeous views of the foaming San Agustinillo surf; and hundreds of yards of golden sand to wander upon.

One of the most popular options, where you can walk out your door right onto the sand, is **Mexico Lindo** (Playa San Agustinillo, no phone, faustojasso@gmail.com, $40 d), at the west end of the village. Italian-born owner-manager Fausto offers five spacious individually decorated *cabañas* in two stories, with soft beds and private shower-baths. Amenities include fans and Fausto's good restaurant next door.

$50-100

In the middle of San Agustinillo is **Casazul** (tel. 958/584-6489, casazulplus@hotmail.com, $35-85), uphill two long blocks, at the end of a driveway signed "Casa Azul." This hillside-perched, stucco-and-tile, art-decorated complex offers four lodgings, including a rustic whitewashed *cabaña* in-the-round, with queen-size bed, small refrigerator, and private bath, by the swimming pool. Two casitas each come with a double bed and kitchenette, sharing a panoramic ocean-view veranda. One two-bedroom kitchenette apartment has two double beds and one bath, and a patio with a view. Extras include breakfast service at additional cost, mosquito nets, and a lovely blue lap pool.

If you prefer the beach, consider **Posada La Termita** (Playa San Agustinillo, local cell tel. 044-958/589-3046, www.posadalatermita.com, $70-80), right on the dazzling San Agustinillo beachfront. Italian-born owner Isabel Bresci offers four comfortable upstairs rooms, with choice of one king-size bed, one queen-size bed, or two queen-size beds, with private hot-water shower-bath, fan, mosquito net, in-house Internet, and a downstairs ocean-view restaurant, with good cappuccino, breakfasts, and pizza.

OVER $100

★ **Casa Pan de Miel** (about 0.3 mile west of San Agustillo village, tel. 958/584-3509, www.casapandemiel.com, $100-225), the lifelong dream-come-true of French-born co-owner Anne Gillete, perches on its airy hilltop above the blue Pacific. Only superlatives can describe the architecturally designed amenities: spacious veranda breakfast restaurant; a blue designer pool; soft couches and chairs for sitting inside; lounge chairs and umbrellas by the pool; and panoramic ocean views east, toward San Agustinillo, south, out to sea, and west, toward Mazunte's gracefully curving strand. Guests enjoy eight spacious, comfortable, and artfully decorated deluxe rooms, with private view porches, hot-water bathrooms, fans, air-conditioning, and credit cards accepted, but no children under 12.

Mazunte

Mazunte offers a number of lodgings, from rough beachfront *cabañas* to semi-deluxe, architecturally-designed thatched *palapas*.

$25-50

Very popular among the Mazunte beachfront accommodations is ★ **Posada Ziga** (Mazunte, tel. 958/583-9295, www.posadaziga.com, $30-73), just west of the Mazunte Turtle Museum, with 15 rooms in three floors and a palm-shaded beach-view restaurant, just above the waves. The plainly decorated, spacious, and clean tile-floored rooms come with fans, Wi-Fi, a safe, and mosquito nets.

Also invitingly rustic (frequented mostly by youthful international travelers) on the palm-shadowed Mazunte beachfront is **Posada del Arquitecto** (Calle Rinconcito, Mazunte, no phone, www.posadadelarquitecto.com, $25-45 s or d, $6 pp dorm or camping). The owner offers about 10 *palapa*-sheltered *cabañas* atop a palm-shaded ocean-view knoll. All lodgings include mosquito nets, fans, and private, room-temperature shower-baths. Also available are dormitory bunks and a beach-level campground with *palapa* shelters and hammocks. Find it at the beach end of Calle Rinconcito, a block west of the bridge in Mazunte. Amenities include Wi-Fi, massage and yoga classes (fees apply), and on-site restaurant with an ocean-view terrace.

The fanciest accommodation in Mazunte, and sister to the Hotel La Buena Vista in Puerto Ángel, is the lovely hillside ★ **Alta Mira Bungalows** (make reservations via the Hotel La Buena Vista in Puerto Ángel, tel./fax 958/584-3104, www.labuenavista.com/alta_mira, $50-60 d). Guests enjoy a beautiful ocean-view hillside setting with restaurant, and a stepped path (5-10 minutes) down to glorious Mazunte beach. The approximately 10 separate *cabañas* have comfortable, rustic-chic decor, including handcrafted furniture, soft beds, and hurricane lamps. Rentals include private shower-baths and mosquito nets.

Get to Alta Mira Bungalows from the main through-town road. A block west of the bridge, turn toward the beach at the side road, Calle Rinconcito. Continue about a block, where you turn right at a signed uphill fork road. Continue 300 yards to Alta Mira's signed driveway on the left.

Trailer Parks and Camping

The **Trailer Park La Palmera Fernando's** (958/584-0646, trailerparkfernandos@hotmail.com, $5 pp tent, $12-20 RV) has about 20 parking (big rigs possible) and camping spaces beneath a shady, tufted grove by the road at the east end of Playa Zipolite. A spirit of camaraderie often blooms among the tents and assorted RVs of travelers from as far away as Miami, Medicine Hat, and Murmansk. RV rates get you a space for two people, including electricity, water, shared dump station, shower, and toilets.

Alternatively, park or camp at Zipolite's former hacienda and now shady paradise RV and camping park, ★ **Rancho Los Mangos** (tel. 958/109-1316, Mex. toll-free 800/546-4693, $20 RV, $50 hotel room, $150 bungalow). Soak in the lush, tropical, garden ambience; bask in the swimming pool and patio; and feast on all the mangos you can eat in season, April-June. The RV rate includes electricity, water, and drainage. Also available are two deluxe, two-bedroom bungalows, sleeping up to five, with living room, kitchen, and air-conditioning, and two comfortable hotel rooms with bath and air-conditioning. Find it on the Puerto Ángel-San Agustinillo main road, at a signed driveway about half a mile past the Zipolite-*Adoquín*-Roca Blanca intersection.

FOOD
Puerto Ángel

Cheap eats abound, especially in Puerto Ángel **food stalls** (around noon-midnight daily, $2-3), on the beachfront street by the pier. Although tacos are the favorite, fish, *carnitas* (roast pork), chicken, beef, *pozole* (savory pork and hominy soup), *guisados* (chicken, pork, or beef stew), and delicious Oaxaca-style tamales are also common.

Even though its list of sit-down restaurants has dwindled in recent years, Puerto Ángel still offers some good choices. Most welcoming of all Puerto Ángel places to eat is the relaxingly simple restaurant at ★ **Casa de Huéspedes Gundi y Tomás** (tel. 958/584-3068, 8am-9pm daily, $4-8). It's uphill on the west end of Puerto Ángel's beachfront street; see the streetside sign. Owner Gundi Ley and her family offer hearty breakfasts, light lunches, and a couple of tasty dinner entrées.

Of the *palapa* restaurants right on the beach, the best is **Anahi** (tel. 958/584-3142, 8am-9pm daily, breakfast $3, seafood $6). Here you'll find a cool, palm-shaded, beach-view spot for breakfast (fresh orange juice, fruit salad, ham and eggs) and super-fresh seafood (conch salad, dorado filet, grilled shrimp, seafood pasta Alfredo).

Most visible along the beachfront main street is the café at the **Hotel Villa Florencia** (Blv. Virgilio Uribe, tel./fax 958/584-3044, 8am-11pm daily, $5-12). Lulu, the wife of the late Italian-born owner-chef, carries on his tradition, specializing in antipasti, salads, and meat and seafood pastas.

Playa Estacahuite

Finally, you can top everything off by enjoying a splurge gourmet dinner at **Casa Bichu** (Playa Estacahuite, tel. 958/584-3489,-90,-91, reservations mandatory, about $40 pp including wine). Although the innovative menu often derives from Oaxaca-style cuisine, you can also anticipate seafood, such as super-fresh lobster, shrimp, or fish, or the tenderest filet mignon, or maybe the crispest possible Caesar salad.

Zipolite

Zipolite also has some good eating places. For tasty macrobiotic fare and a breezy beach view, go to the restaurant at **Shambhala** (on the Playa Zipolite west-end headland above the beach, 8am-8pm daily, $3-6). Personable owner Gloria Johnson runs a very tidy kitchen, which serves good breakfasts, soups, salads, and sandwiches. There is no alcohol at this restaurant.

A regiment of satisfied patrons of ★ **Restaurant El Alquimista** (on far west-side of Zipolite beachfront, tel. 958/587-8961, www.el-alquimista.com, 8pm-10pm daily, $6-12) choose from a seemingly mile-long menu of appetizers (hummus, guacamole), soups (onion, cream of carrot), salads (Greek, romaine), *tortas* (egg, ham, cheese), fish (10 styles of fillet), pastas (*al burro,* cream, Bolognese), hamburgers (fish, beef, chicken), and much, much more.

The restaurant of **Posada Mexico** (on the beach, a few steps from Zipolite's *adoquín* main-street, in Colonia Roca Blanca, tel./fax 958/584-3194, 8am-9pm daily, $6-9) is among the best. In a beachfront candlelit setting, the food seems especially good. Menu items include breakfast eggs and pancakes, salads (Mediterranean), seafood (shrimp brochette), pasta (fetuccini arabiata), and steak (T-bone). *Bravissimo!*

San Agustinillo and Mazunte

In San Agustinillo, try the shady beachfront *palapa* **Restaurant Mexico Lindo** (at the east, Mazunte end of the beach, no phone, 8am-10pm daily, closed Sept.-Oct., $5-10). Owner Fausto and his wife serve from a short but tasty menu of salads, sandwiches, tacos and tostadas, and seafood.

In Mazunte, tasty vegetarian-style goodies are the specialty at **Tania's** (on the west end, uphill from the cosmetics factory-store, tel. 958/101-8455, 9am-11pm daily, $5-12). Besides super-fresh seafood, Tania offers plenty of tasty juices, salads, and burgers, both meat and soy.

A fortunate addition to Mazunte's list of good restaurants is bakery and restaurant **Armadillo** (Calle Rinconcito, tel. 958/101-3834, armadillo.mazunte@yahoo.com.mx, 8am-11pm daily high season, 3pm-11pm daily low season, $9). Armadillo is the life project of a personable Mexican-French husband-wife team, Raoul and Beatrix, who, beneath their sculpture-decorated *palapa* (he's the sculptor), offer a delicious, eclectic menu (she's the chef), including breakfasts (omelets), lunch (tuna salad), and, for dinner, the Armadillo specialty, stuffed fish fillet. Find them a block and a half down Calle Rinconcito, the street that heads toward the beach, a block west of the Mazunte bridge.

INFORMATION AND SERVICES

Money Exchange, Banks, and Tourist Information

In Puerto Ángel, only a few shopkeepers change money. For example, manager Bastián López, at the **Casa de Huéspedes Gundi y Tomás** (uphill on the west end of Puerto Ángel's beachfront street, tel. 958/584-3068, www.puertoangel-hotel.com), changes U.S. dollars. You can also change U.S. dollars at the local **Banco Azteca** (which is not a real bank, only a high-fee credit and money-wiring agency), but their fee, around 10 percent, is excessive.

The best Puerto Ángel money source is the pair of 24-hour **ATMs,** a Bancomer machine (on Bulevar Uribe at the corner of Vasconcelos), by the taco stands, and HSBC (a block east, behind the agencia municipal).

For more complete banking services, go to the real banks in **Pochutla.** Your best bet is **HSBC** bank (on the Pochutla main street, Lázaro Cárdenas, tel. 958/584-0699, 8am-5pm Mon.-Fri.). Alternatively, go to **Bancomer**

(corner of Lázaro Cárdenas and Av. 3A Norte, tel. 958/584-0053, 8:30am-4pm Mon.-Fri.), or, a few doors south, **Scotiabank Inverlat** (Lázaro Cárdenas, tel. 958/584-0145, 9am-5pm Mon.-Fri.).

Pochutla tourism runs a seasonal **information office** (upstairs at the foot of the Puerto Ángel pier, 9am-2pm and 4pm-8pm daily in season).

Health and Emergency

Puerto Ángel's **doctor** is Dr. Constancio Aparicio Juárez, who is available at the **pharmacy** (Calle Vasconcelos, tel. 958/584-3058, 9am-2pm and 5pm-9pm Mon.-Sat., 9am-2pm Sun.) on the left side of Calle Vasconcelos, a block uphill from the pier. For serious illness requiring diagnostic specialists, Dr. Juárez recommends you go to the government **Hospital Regional in Pochutla** (tel. 958/584-0236) or the **Seguro Social in Crucecita** (Bahías de Huatulco, tel. 958/587-1182).

Another option is to go to Puerto Ángel's small government **Centro del Salud** health clinic, which concentrates on preventative rather than diagnostic medicine, on the hill behind the church. Go up Vasconcelos on a long curving block, go left at the first corner, and continue past the library to the health center (by the church).

For police emergencies, contact the **state police** (uphill on Vasconcelos, tel. 958/584-3207), or call or go to the **Agencia Municipal** (at the foot of Hwy. 175., tel. 958/584-3101) at the end of the beachfront main street, past the pier in Puerto Ángel.

Communications

The Puerto Ángel **correo** and **telecomunicaciones** stand side by side at the Agencia Municipal (at the foot of Hwy. 175., tel. 958/584-3101, 9am-3pm Mon.-Fri.).

The Puerto Ángel **larga distancia** telephone, fax office, and **Gela Net** Internet access is on Calle José Vasconcelos (on Vasconcelos, just uphill from the pier, tel. 958/584-3046 or 958/584-3054, fax

958/584-3210, shenalo@hotmail.com, 8am-10pm daily).

Internet access is also available in Puerto Ángel, at **Cyber Zone Café** (uphill, about a block west of the Blv. Uribe bridge, tel. 958/584-2034, 9am-10pm daily).

Internet access has also arrived in Zipolite, at **Danydoquin** (at the far end of the *adoquín*, tel. 958/584-3363, 9am-9pm daily), with fax, copies, and public telephone. In Mazunte, answer your email at **Marcos Internet** (10:30am-8pm daily) on the main road through town, about a block west of the turtle museum.

Most of the hotels in the area now have Wi-Fi in-house, either in the lobby and/or restaurant, or in guest rooms as well.

TRANSPORTATION

Air

Scheduled flights to Mexican and international destinations connect daily (in high season) with airports at **Huatulco,** 30 kilometers (19 mi) east, or **Puerto Escondido,** 71 kilometers (44 mi) west, by road from Puerto Ángel.

Car or RV

National highways connect Puerto Ángel to the west with Puerto Escondido and Acapulco, north with Oaxaca, and east with the Bahías de Huatulco and the Isthmus of Tehuántepec.

Highway 200 connects westward with Puerto Escondido in an easy 71 kilometers (44 mi), continuing to Pinotepa Nacional (217 km/135 mi, three hours) and Acapulco in a total of seven hours (469 km/291 mi) of driving. In the opposite direction, Bahías de Huatulco (actually Crucecita town), 45 kilometers (28 mi) away, is reachable in about 45 minutes. The continuation to Salina Cruz stretches another 148 kilometers (92 mi), or around 2.5 additional hours of driving time.

North to Oaxaca, paved but narrow and winding National Highway 175 connects 238 kilometers (148 mi) over the Sierra Madre del Sur from its junction with Highway 200 at Pochutla. The road climbs to around 9,000 feet through cool (chilly in winter) pine forests and hardscrabble Chatino and Zapotec native villages. Fill up with gas in Pochutla. Unleaded gasoline is available at the Pochutla Pemex stations, both on through-town Highway 175. Allow about eight hours behind the wheel from Puerto Ángel to Oaxaca, about seven in the opposite direction.

Bus and Van

All long-distance bus connections must be made in Pochutla. Operating out of separate stations, several long-distance bus lines and two van shuttle services connect with points west, east, and north. The stations cluster less than a mile north from the Highway 200 junction along Avenida Lázaro Cárdenas, the Highway 175 main street into Pochutla.

As you enter the Pochutla business district, first you'll come to combined first-class **Omnibus Cristóbal Colón** and second-class **Sur** station (Av. Lázaro Cárdenas 84, tel. 958/584-0274) on the left. From there, several departures per day connect east with Huatulco at Crucecita. Some continue east, connecting with Salina Cruz and Tehuántepec, continuing to Chiapas destinations of Tuxtla Gutiérrez San Cristóbal and Tapachula, at the Guatemala border. A few buses connect north with Oaxaca via the relatively level, long (10-hour) Isthmus route, via Salina Cruz and Tehuántepec. During the dry season, buses also connect with Oaxaca, via the shorter (eight-hour) trans-Sierra Highway 175. One bus continues to Puebla and Mexico City daily. A few buses also connect daily west with Puerto Escondido.

Next, **Estrella Blanca** (94 Lázaro Cárdenas, tel. 958/584-0380) and subsidiary-line buses (such as first-class Elite, luxury-class Turistar and Futura) connect west daily with Puerto Escondido, continuing to Acapulco, where connections are available for the entire Mexican Pacific coast, all the way to the U.S. border. They also connect east (many per day) with the Bahías de Huatulco destination of Crucecita, and Salina Cruz on the Isthmus. A few "plus" (pronounced "ploos") luxury-class buses connect daily, all the way to Mexico City, via Acapulco.

About a block farther, across Lázaro Cárdenas street, **Autobuses Estrella del Valle, Autobuses Oaxaca Pacífico,** and **Fletes y Pasajes** (tel. 958/584-0138) operate out of their joint central bus station *(central de autobus)*. Frequent second-class and some first-class service is offered, connecting west with Puerto Escondido and Pinotepa Nacional; north with Oaxaca, Puebla, and Mexico City; and east with Bahías de Huatulco.

Farther north, **Atlantida** shuttle vans (Av. Lázaro Cárdenas 62, tel. 958/584-0116) connect north, via Highway 175, about every two daylight hours, with Oaxaca. Next door, **Eclipse** vans (Av. Lázaro Cárdenas, tel. 958/584-0840) also offer frequent Oaxaca connections.

SAN JOSÉ DEL PACÍFICO

This is a little mountaintop town with a tremendous view, so high that the Pacific Ocean is clearly visible far below. The climate is brisk and dry, and pine-clad mountains rise all around, an ideal setting for a few days away from the tropics. What's just as good—the village has a pair of decent restaurants and an invitingly rustic hotel. This town is also a center for the seasonal use of hallucinogenic mushrooms like those celebrated by the late Maria Sabina and her followers at Huautla. They are technically illegal but during the season from July to October, you'll find them very available.

Little was spared to create the ★ **Hotel Puesta del Sol** (on Hwy. 175, from the U.S tel. 011-52-1-951/100-8678, in Mexico long distance tel. 045-951/100-8678, local tel. 044-951/100-8678, www.sanjosedelpacifico.com, www.tomzap.com/sjose.html, $26-55 s or d), about a quarter mile north of town. Gardens lead downhill, past the hotel restaurant, to clean and cozy knotty-pine rooms and *cabañas* with fireplaces, all with private hot-water shower-baths.

Food is available either at Hotel Puesta del Sol's **restaurant** (tel. 044-951/100-8678, 8am-8pm daily, $3-10), with its lovely view, or at the attractively rustic, inexpensive restaurant **Rayito del Sol (Little Sunbeam)** (in the village on the highway nearby, tel. 951/547-4225) with live karaoke nightly.

The main local diversions are natural, such as basking in the sun, hiking mountain trails to panoramic viewpoints, observing wildlife, watching spectacular sunsets, resting or reading by the fireplace, and/or eating those mushrooms. The Puesta del Sol management arranges guided local walks and tours.

Get to San José del Pacífico by bus or car via Highway 175, either 105 kilometers (65 mi) north of Pochutla or 130 kilometers (81 mi) south of Oaxaca City.

Bahías de Huatulco and Vicinity

The nine azure bays of Huatulco (ooah-TOOL-koh) decorate a couple dozen miles of acacia-plumed rocky coastline east of Puerto Ángel. Between the bays, the ocean joins in battle with jutting, rocky headlands, while in their inner reaches the ocean calms, caressing diminutive crescents of coral sand. Inland, a thick hardwood forest stretches in a continuous carpet to the Sierra.

Ecologists shuddered when they heard that these bays were going to be developed. Fonatur, the government tourism development agency, says it has a plan, however. Relatively few hotels will occupy the beaches; other development will be confined to a few inland centers. The remaining 70 percent of the land will be kept as pristine ecological zones and study areas.

Although this story sounds sadly familiar, Fonatur, which developed Ixtapa and Cancún,

Bahías de Huatulco and Vicinity

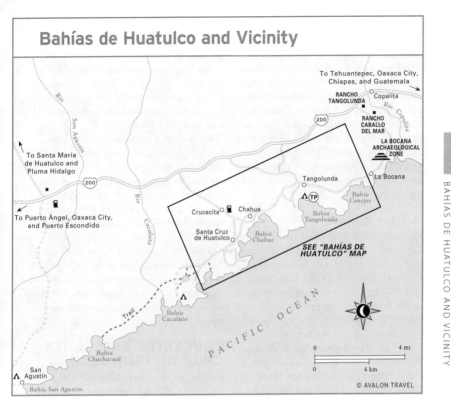

seems to have learned from its experience. Up-to-date sewage treatment was installed *ahead of time;* logging and homesteading were halted; and helicopters patrol the beaches, spotting turtle poachers. Development is expected to be completed in 2020. If all goes according to the plan, the nine Bahías de Huatulco and their 100,000-acre forest hinterland will be both a tourist and ecological paradise, in addition to employing thousands of local people. If this Huatulco dream ends as well as it has started, Mexico should take pride while the rest of the world should take heed.

Getting Oriented

With no road to the outside world, the Bahías de Huatulco remained virtually uninhabited and undeveloped until 1982, about the time that coastal Highway 200 was pushed through. A few years later, the Bahías de Huatulco's planned initial kernel of infrastructure was complete, centering on the brand-new residential service town, Crucecita (pop. 10,000), and nearby Santa Cruz de Huatulco boat harbor on Bahía Santa Cruz.

The bays of Huatulco decorate the coastline both east and west of Santa Cruz. To the east, a paved road links Bahías Chahue, Tangolunda, and Conejos. To the west lie Bahías El Organo, El Maguey, and Cacaluta. Of the latter three, only Bahía El Maguey is accessible by paved road. El Organo and Cacaluta are accessible only with the help of a guide; the former on foot or by horseback, the latter by truck or SUV. Isolated farther west are Bahías Chachacual and San Agustín, with no road from Santa Cruz (although a good dirt road runs to San Agustín from Highway 200 near the airport).

Besides Bahía Santa Cruz, the only other

bays that have been extensively developed are Chahue, a mile east, and Tangolunda, four miles east. Chahue now has a marina and a sprinkling of small-to-medium-size, medium-priced hotels. Tangolunda has a golf course, small restaurant/shopping complex, and seven major resort hotels (Las Brisas, Quinta Real, Crown Pacific, Barceló Huatulco, Club Gala Resort, Dreams Huatulco, and Camino Real Zaashila). A couple of smaller hotels have joined the Tangolunda fray in recent years, providing travelers with a few less overwhelming options.

Getting Around

Frequent public **collective taxis** connect Crucecita and Bahías Santa Cruz, Chahue, and Tangolunda. Find the terminal, on Guamuchil, two blocks east of the plaza, at curbside, in front of the Madero shopping center. Private *(especial)* taxis make the same trips for about $3 by day, $4 at night. No public transportation is available to the other bays. Taxi drivers are willing to drive you for a picnic to west-side Bahía El Maguey, or Playa Entrega (a popular beach on Bahía Santa Cruz), for about $5 one-way, from Crucecita or Tangolunda; it's about the same to Bahía Conejos.

For a half-day trip, taxis will take you to all road-accessible bays for about $15 per hour. On the other hand, you can rent your own car for about $50 per day. Call **Thrifty** (tel. 958/581-9000), **Hertz** (958/581-9092 or 958/581-0588), or **Europcar** (tel. 958/581-9094 or 958/581-0551).

Another option is to go by boat. The **local boat cooperative** (Sociedad Cooperativa Turístico Tangolunda; for reservations call the dock office: tel. 958/587-0081) runs a daily excursion on the 100-passeger catamaran **Fiesta** and, in season, the gigantic 300-passenger **Reventón** (around 10:30am, $20 pp, kids 4-9 half price) to all nine bays, including soft drinks, bilingual guide, and snacks; snorkeling is $5 extra. Alternatively, tour by the similarly big catamaran **Tequila** (from the same dock, tel. 958/587-2303),

or contact a travel agent such as **Paraíso Huatulco** (tel. 958/587-0190) or **Prometur** (tel. 958/587-0413).

The cooperative also rents entire boats for all-day tours for up to 10 people for about $100. Drop-off runs to the nearest beach are about $10 per boat round-trip; to the more remote beaches, around $20-30.

Local travel agents offer other tour options: several hours of sunning, swimming, picnicking, and snorkeling at a couple of Bahías de Huatulco beaches cost around $20 per person; tours to Puerto Ángel, Puerto Escondido, and wildlife-rich lagoons go for $30-50 per person. For reservations, call Paraíso Huatulco or Prometur.

Another option is to get your own guide. An economical option is to hire an English-speaking taxi driver to take you wherever you want to go for several hours, or up to a whole day, for about $15 per hour, depending on the season.

CRUCECITA AND SANTA CRUZ DE HUATULCO

Despite its newness, **Crucecita** (Little Cross, pop. 10,000) resembles a traditional Mexican town, with life revolving around a central plaza and adjacent market. Crucecita is where the people who work in the Bahías de Huatulco hotels, businesses, and government offices live. Although pleasant enough for a walk around the square and a meal in a restaurant, and perhaps an evening at a bar or disco, it's mostly a place whose modest hotels and restaurants accommodate business travelers and weekenders who can't afford the plush hotels near the beach. Ironically, Crucecita is the most "Mexican" of towns around Huatulco because there has been little to draw tourists there, until recently. However, with its shady, tidy central plaza ringed by good bars and gourmet restaurants, Crucecita is a quieter, less pricey place to stay, and a great place to get a fine meal, while visiting the Huatulco area. It's a squeaky clean Mexican town with a sweet central plaza and home to a bunch of really

Crucecita

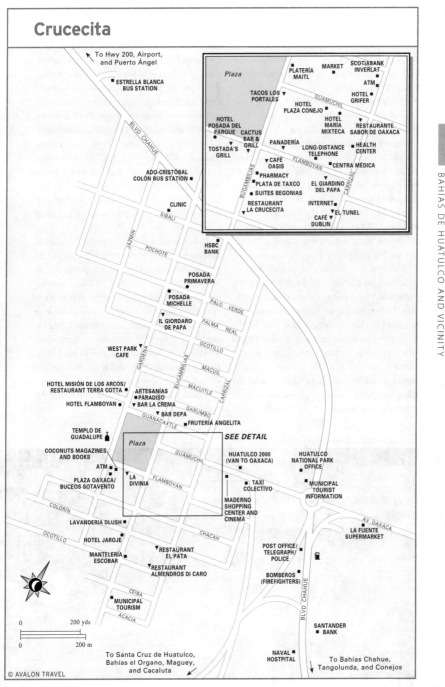

To Hwy 200, Airport, and Puerto Ángel

ESTRELLA BLANCA BUS STATION

BLVD CHAHUE

ADO-CRISTÓBAL COLÓN BUS STATION

CLINIC

SIBALI

JAZMIN

POCHOTE

HSBC BANK

POSADA PRIMAVERA

POSADA MICHELLE

PALO VERDE

IL GIORDARO DE PAPA

PALMA REAL

WEST PARK CAFE

GARDENIA

OCOTILLO

HOTEL MISIÓN DE LOS ARCOS/ RESTAURANT TERRA COTTA

ARTESANÍAS PARADISO

BUGAMBILIAS

MACUIL

MACUITLE

CARRIZAL

HOTEL FLAMBOYAN

BAR LA CREMA

BAR DEPA

GARUMBO

GUANACAXTLE

FRUTERÍA ANGELITA

TEMPLO DE GUADALUPE

SEE DETAIL

COCONUTS MAGAZINES AND BOOKS

Plaza

GUAMUCHIL

HUATULCO 2000 (VAN TO OAXACA)

HUATULCO NATIONAL PARK OFFICE

ATM

PLAZA OAXACA/ BUCEOS SOTAVENTO

LA DIVINIA

FLAMBOYAN

TAXI COLECTIVO

MUNICIPAL TOURIST INFORMATION

COLORÍN

MADERNO SHOPPING CENTER AND CINEMA

AV. OAXACA

LAVANDERIA DLUSH

CHACAH

LA FUENTE SUPERMARKET

OCOTILLO

HOTEL JAROJE

MANTELERÍA ESCOBAR

RESTAURANT EL PATA

POST OFFICE/ TELEGRAPH/ POLICE

RESTAURANT ALMENDROS DI CARO

BOMBEROS (FIREFIGHTERS)

CEIBA

MUNICIPAL TOURISM

BLVD CHAHUE

ACACIA

0   200 yds

0   200 m

SANTANDER BANK

To Santa Cruz de Huatulco, Bahías el Organo, Maguey, and Cacaluta

NAVAL HOSTPITAL

To Bahías Chahue, Tangolunda, and Conejos

© AVALON TRAVEL

Detail:

Plaza

PLATERÍA MAITL

MARKET

SCOTIABANK INVERLAT

ATM

TACOS LOS PORTALES

GUAMUCHIL

HOTEL GRIFER

HOTEL PLAZA CONEJO

HOTEL POSADA DEL PARQUE

CACTUS BAR & GRILL

HOTEL MARÍA MIXTECA

RESTAURANTE SABOR DE OAXACA

PANADERÍA

LONG-DISTANCE TELEPHONE

HEALTH CENTER

TOSTADA'S GRILL

CAFÉ OASIS

FLAMBOYAN

CENTRA MÉDICA

BUGAMBILIAS

PHARMACY

PLATA DE TAXCO

EL GIARDINO DEL PAPA

SUITES BEGONIAS

CARRIZAL

RESTAURANT LA CRUCECITA

INTERNET

EL TUNEL

CAFÉ DUBLIN

great Italian restaurants! Possibly inspired by a 1992 Italian movie called *Puerto Escondido,* Italians have been showing up on the Oaxaca coast ever since. They have colonized the hotel and restaurant scene in the area, and Crucecita especially.

While in Crucecita, before finding your perfect pasta or seafood risotto, be sure to step into the church on the plaza's west side to admire the heavenly **ceiling mural** of the Virgin of Guadalupe. The mural, the largest of Guadalupe in Mexico, is the work of local artists José Ángel del Signo and Marco Antonio Contreras, whose for-sale art is on display locally. Besides the heavenly Virgin overhead, the muralists decorated the space above the altar with the miraculous story of Don Diego and the Virgin of Guadalupe.

The few hotels and the mostly travel-oriented businesses of **Santa Cruz de Huatulco** (on Bahía Santa Cruz, south, about two miles from Crucecita) cluster near the boat harbor. Fishing boats, tour boats, and cruise ships come and go, vacationers sun themselves on the tranquil, yellow-sand Playa Santa Cruz, while T-shirt and fruit vendors and boat workers hang around the quay watching for prospective customers. After the sun goes down, not much usually

happens in Santa Cruz de Huatulco. Tourists quit the beach for their hotels and workers return to their homes in Crucecita, leaving the harbor and streets pretty quiet. However, there is a little new life here yet, during the day, especially with the stand-up paddleboard and surf shop right in town, the great coffee bar under the bandstand, and **Café Juanita** (tel. 958-105-1671). At the paddleboard shop, **Café Surf** (Calle Mitla 402 on the La Cruz plaza, tel. 958/585-0222, 958/105-1806 www.huatulcosurftrip.com), you can rent a board and the guides will take you down to the beach and out to sea to explore the bays, or off to another part of the coast, on a surfing expedition.

Before you leave Santa Cruz de Huatulco, however, be sure to visit the big **Chapel of the Santa Cruz of Huatulco,** on the shoreline side, past the boat harbor. The venerated object on the altar is one of the four smaller crosses, made from the historic original large shoreline cross that had been worshipped for centuries before the Spanish conquistadors arrived at the bays of Huatulco in the 1520s. Climb the altar steps and look through the viewing hole of the shoreline, where a replica (albeit smaller) of the original stands, facing the sea.

the boat harbor at Santa Cruz de Huatulco

Santa Cruz de Huatulco

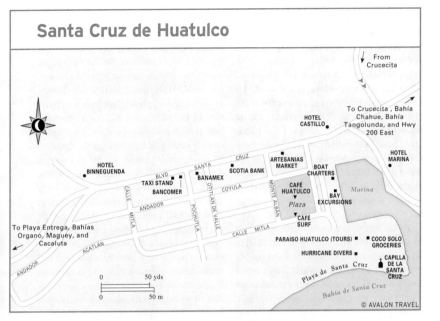

From Crucecita

To Crucecita, Bahía Chahue, Bahía Tangolunda, and Hwy 200 East

HOTEL CASTILLO

HOTEL MARINA

HOTEL BINNEGUENDA

BLVD SANTA CRUZ

TAXI STAND

BANCOMER

SCOTIA BANK

BANAMEX

COYULA

OTTLAN DE VALLE

ARTESANIAS MARKET

BOAT CHARTERS

CAFÉ HUATULCO

Plaza

BAY EXCURSIONS

Marina

MONTE ALBAN

CAFÉ SURF

CALLE MITLA

To Playa Entrega, Bahías Organo, Maguey, and Cacaluta

ACATLÁN

ANDADOR

CALLE MITLA

POCHUTLA

ANDADOR

PARAISO HUATULCO (TOURS)

HURRICANE DIVERS

COCO SOLO GROCERIES

CAPILLA DE LA SANTA CRUZ

Playa de Santa Cruz

Bahía de Santa Cruz

0   50 yds
0   50 m

© AVALON TRAVEL

EXPLORING THE BAHÍAS DE HUATULCO

Isolation has left the Huatulco waters blue and unpolluted, the beaches white and clean. Generally, the bays are all similar: tropical; deciduous (green in the rainy season, July-Jan.); forested, rocky headlands enclosing yellow-white coral sand crescents. The water is clear and good for snorkeling, scuba diving, sailing, kayaking, stand-up paddleboarding, and kiteboarding during the often-calm weather. Beaches, however, are typically steep, causing waves to break quickly near the sand, and generally unsuitable for bodysurfing, boogie boarding, or surfing.

Your preparations depend on which bays you plan to explore. For the five developed or partially developed bays—Santa Cruz, Chahue, Tangolunda, El Maguey, and San Agustín—you'll need nothing more than transportation, a hat, and sunscreen. Restaurants and stores can supply everything else.

By contrast, the four undeveloped Huatulco bays of El Organo, Cacaluta, Chachacual,

and Conejos have neither restaurants, stores, drinking water, nor lots of shade; they're so pristine even coconut palms haven't gotten around to sprouting on them. When exploring, bring food, drinks, hats, sunscreen, and mosquito repellent.

East Side

Bahía Chahue, about a mile from both Crucecita and Santa Cruz, is wide and blue, with a steep yellow dune above the beach, stretching to the marina jetty at the east end. With waves that break quickly near the shore, and recede with strong undertow, Playa Chahue is not good for swimming, boogie boarding, or surfing.

About four miles farther east is the breezy and broad **Bahía Tangolunda.** Although hotels front much of the beach, a signed Playa Pública public access road (the parking lot does double duty as a trailer park) borders the western edge of the golf course (turn right just past the creek bridge). Except for its east end, the Tangolunda beach is steep and the waves break quickly right at the sand.

Over the headland about two miles

farther east, **Punta Arena** (Sand Point), a forested thumb of land, juts into wide **Bahía Conejos.** Three separate, steep beaches spread along the inner shoreline. The main entrance road arrives at high-duned Playa Punta Arena. Playa Tejoncito (Little Coatamundi) is beyond the rocks far to the right; Playa Conejos (Rabbits) is to the left on the other side of Punta Arena. A few palm-frond branches for shade and a saltwater flush toilet lavatory occupy the Playa Punta Arena dune. Trees behind the dunes provide a few shady spots for RV or tent campers. Playa Conejos is now home to a single large resort hotel called Secrets.

At **La Bocana,** a signed driveway leads to a parking lot. Walk downhill past that, to a breezy beach and view of the Río Copalita emptying into the sea. Beyond that, a broad beach with oft-powerful surfing rollers (novices beware) stretches for at least a mile east. By the parking lot, restaurants serve drinks and very fresh seafood and a shop rents surfboards for about $14 per day. A spring-fed lagoon above the beach (bring your kayak) appears ripe for wildlife-viewing. A small housing development with some rentals available has taken hold on the west side of the river mouth, by the restaurants.

Archaeological Zone

Just past La Bocana, a signed driveway on the right leads to a parking lot and the **Bocana-Río Copalita Archaeological Zone** (no phone, 8am-4:30pm daily, $4), where INAH (National Institute of History and Archaeology) investigators have uncovered an early (circa 500 BC) town. The zone itself, which occupies about 80 acres, which stretch about half a mile along the Copalita riverbank, may have supported as many as 2,000 people. Scores of dwelling foundations, about 80 burial sites, and a number of large structures, including ceremonial plazas, at least one ball court, and an 18-meter-high (60 ft.) *templo mayor,* have been excavated. From their research so far, archaeologists reckon that the structures bear architectural resemblance to structures found in southern (Mixe Zoque and Mayan) zones. From radiocarbon dating, archaeologists believe that the site was occupied at least until AD 1000, and maybe even until the conquest, when it would have been part of the Aztec village of Copalitlán (Place of Copal). A museum, opened in October 2010, displays a general panorama of the site, and a number of the many intriguing artifacts, recovered during the excavations.

The Bahías de Huatulco offer many tranquil coves.

Much of the Huatulco coast remains wild and untouristed.

After La Bocana, the road bends inland, paralleling the **Río Copalita wildlife sanctuary,** perfect for adventurous exploring. Several operators guide visitors on river ecotours. A highly recommended guide for river tours is **Mario Cobos** (tel. 958/587-1833, mariocobos.com). Options include bird- and animal-watching walks along riverine forest trails, kayaking river rapids, rafting, and mud baths at a riverside ranch. Furthermore, **Rancho Caballo del Mar** (entrance on the road, before the Hwy. 200 intersection, tel. 958/584-6545, 958/587-0366, 958/107-8211) offers horseback rides along the river for around $25 per person.

West Side

Bahía Santa Cruz has a pair of inviting beaches: **Playa Entrega** and, the most visited, **Playa Santa Cruz,** beyond the shops and restaurants, to the right (facing the ocean) of the boat harbor. With the boat harbor infrastructure, this is far from a rustic beach. There is a cruise ship pier,

as well as parking areas, pedestrian malls, and other structures directly behind it. But Playa Santa Cruz remains a very pleasant stretch of sand. Especially during the high winter season and weekends, kids play and vacationers improve their tans at this beach, and two or three days a week cruise liners dock (and discharge hundreds of tourists ashore) at the adjacent, east side, maritime terminal dock. Pick up a paddleboard at **Café Surf** (Calle Mitla 402 on the La Cruz plaza, tel. 958/585-0222, 958/105-1806 www.huatulcosurftrip.com), the shop in town, and head out for an exploration. It's just about the best way to see any bay, when the wind isn't blowing.

Playa Entrega is a small, hidden stretch of sand slipped into the west side of Bahía Santa Cruz. It is the infamous spot where, on January 20, 1831, Vicente Guerrero, president and independence hero, was brought ashore in custody of arch-villain Francisco Picaluga and sent to be executed in Cuilapan, near Oaxaca City, a few months later.

Quarter-mile-long Playa Entrega is the ideal Sunday beach, with calm, clear water and clean yellow sand. Swimming, kayaking, and often snorkeling, sailing, and kiteboarding possibilities are excellent. A number of shoreline restaurants serve fresh seafood plates and drinks until around 8pm daily.

Hikers and drivers get there via the main east-west street, Boulevard Santa Cruz, which passes the inland edge of the Santa Cruz boat harbor. Continue west, bearing left, at the Y intersection at the renovated and reopened Hotel Binneguenda on the right. Mark your odometer. After 1.3 kilometers (0.8 mi) the road bends left and winds uphill, past panoramic viewpoints above Bahía Santa Cruz. Follow the signs and you'll soon be at Playa Entrega.

If, instead of curving left to Playa Entrega, you follow the highway that continues straight ahead at the same spot, you'll be headed for the Bahías El Maguey, El Organo, Cacaluta, and Chachacual (Chah-chah-KOOAHL). At this writing, the planned roads to the latter

Bahías de Huatulco

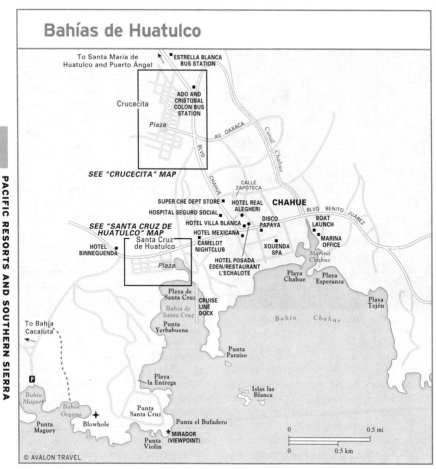

To Santa María de Huatulco and Puerto Ángel

ESTRELLA BLANCA BUS STATION

Crucecita

ADO AND CRISTOBAL COLON BUS STATION

Plaza

AV. OAXACA

Canal Chahue

BLVD

CHAHUE

SEE "CRUCECITA" MAP

CALLE ZAPOTECA

SUPER CHE DEPT STORE

HOSPITAL SEGURO SOCIAL

HOTEL REAL ALEGHERI

CHAHUE

BLVD BENITO JUAREZ

SEE "SANTA CRUZ DE HUATULCO" MAP

HOTEL VILLA BLANCA

DISCO PAPAYA

BOAT LAUNCH

Santa Cruz de Huatulco

HOTEL MEXICANA

HOTEL BINNEGUENDA

CAMELOT NIGHTCLUB

XQUENDA SPA

MARINA OFFICE

Marina Chahue

Plaza

HOTEL POSADA EDEN/RESTAURANT L'ECHALOTE

Playa Chahue

Playa Esperanza

Playa de Santa Cruz

CRUISE LINE DOCK

Bahía de Santa Cruz

Punta Yerbabuena

Bahía Chahue

Playa Tejón

To Bahía Cacaluta

Punta Paraíso

Playa la Entrega

Islas las Blanca

Bahía Maguey

Bahía Órgano

Punta Santa Cruz

Punta el Bufadero

Punta Maguey

Blowhole

MIRADOR (VIEWPOINT)

Punta Violin

0   0.5 mi
0   0.5 km

© AVALON TRAVEL

three of these four bays are still not completed. Until authorities get around to finishing them, land access to the bays of El Organo, Cacaluta, and remote Chachacual will be achievable only by hikers or experienced drivers in off-road vehicles who can navigate the several dirt tracks that wind through the tropical deciduous forest west of Santa Cruz. If in doubt, hire a jeep and a guide (or at least a taxi), or take a boat tour.

Bahía El Organo is closest. About 1.8 kilometers (1.1 mi) along the highway from the Hotel Binneguenda. Look for (or ask a taxi driver to show you) the easy, unofficial 0.8-kilometers (0.5 mi) foot trail to El Organo that

takes off downhill through the forest from the road.

The beach is isolated, intimate, and enfolded by rocky shoals on both sides, and sprinkled with driftwood and green verbena vines. Stroll the quarter-mile-long beach, enjoy the antics of the spouting blowhole on the left-side shoal, and, with caution, swim beyond the close-in surf. Surf fishing appears to be fine here. Some trees behind the dune provide shade. Bring food, water, and everything else, including insect repellent.

Back out on the road, continuing straight ahead, the paved highway forks again (about

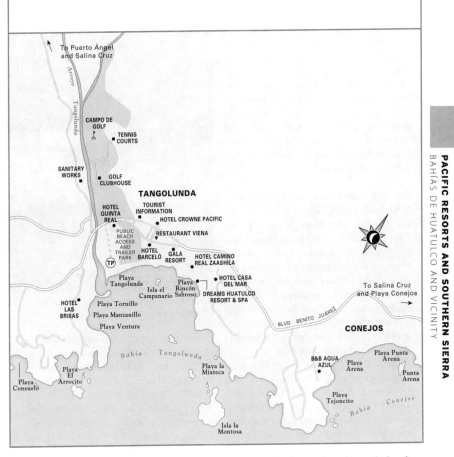

2.9 km/1.8 mi from the hotel). Either continue straight ahead downhill to El Maguey, or fork right to Cacaluta. The sandy crescent of **Bahía El Maguey** is bordered by tide pools tucked beneath forested headlands. Facing a protected fjord-like channel, the Maguey beach is usually calm, nearly waveless, and fine for swimming, snorkeling, diving, and sailing. It would be a snap to launch a kayak, a paddleboard, or a rubber boat here for fishing in the bay. Beach access is on foot only, via a downhill staircase. A procession of permanent seafood *palapas* line the beach. Most days, especially weekends and holidays, picnickers arrive and banana towboats and *aguamotos* (mini motor boats) buzz the beach and bay.

★ **Barra de la Cruz
and La Joya**

You'll see a **Barra de la Cruz** turnoff a few miles south of Huatulco. Surfers, by all means take it, and even non-surfing beach-lovers should have a look. Pass through town, pay a small fee, and head to the beach. A couple of *palapa* restaurants overlook a beach that stretches east for miles; and right in front of the *palapas* you'll find **La Joya,** which on a good day offers one of the fastest and most spectacular right-breaking barrels in Mexico.

When the wave "goes off," it offers one of the longest and most exciting tube rides in the world. Unusual rock formations on the headland form the point that shapes the waves. I wouldn't be giving up this location except that it is pretty well-known in the surfing community at this point. In any case, if you're wandering this stretch of Oaxaca with boards on the car, have a look. If you're in Huatulco, the guys at the **Café Surf** (Calle Mitla 402 on the La Cruz plaza, tel. 958/585-0222, 958/105-1806 www.huatulcosurftrip.com) will safari you down for a reasonable fee.

Bahías Cacaluta, Chachacual, and San Agustín

The paved road that forks right toward **Bahía Cacaluta** ends at a steel barrier, about 1.1 kilometers (0.7 mi) past the fork, at an unsigned sandy but firm track, negotiable by car, bicycle, or on foot. It continues past the barrier and winds and bumps ahead through the shady tropical forest, past two signed forks that, if you bear left all the way, will lead you to Playa Cacaluta after about 1.9 kilometers (1.2 mi) from the pavement's end.

There, the bay spreads along a mile-long, heart-shaped beach, beckoningly close to a cactus-studded offshore islet. Swimmers beware, for waves break powerfully, surging upward and receding with strong undertow. Many shells—limpets and purple- and brown-daubed clams—speckle the beach. Surf-fishing prospects, either from the beach itself or from rocks on either end, appear excellent.

Bahía Chachacual, past the Río Cacaluta, about four miles farther west from Bahía Cacaluta, is a sand-edged azure nook accessible only with a guide, via forest tracks.

Bahía San Agustín, by contrast, is popular and easily reachable by a Pochutla-bound bus, then by the good dirt road just across the highway (one-way taxi from the highway runs about $8, *colectivo* van $2) from the fork to Santa María Huatulco (at Km 236, a mile west of the airport). After about seven miles along a firm track, accessible by all but the bulkiest RVs, bear right to the road's end to

A rocky headland shapes a beautiful right point wave at La Joya.

a modest but very crowded village of *palapas* at the bay's sheltered west end. From there, the beach curves eastward along two miles of forest-backed dune.

Besides good swimming, sailing, and fishing prospects, Bahía San Agustín offers some self-contained RV or tent camping options. On your way in, follow the first of two left forks immediately before the road's end. After about a mile, you arrive at **El Playon** (Big Beach). Facilities, besides a long, lovely curving beach, include several beachfront *palapa* restaurants and several sandy lots, ripe for RV and tent camping.

Back on the entrance road, if you follow the second left fork, after a soccer field, you arrive at **El Sacrificio,** a sheltered, family-friendly beach, lapped by gentle waves, lined by *palapa* restaurants, and picturesquely decorated by big, friendly rocks.

Adventure Tours

Rancho Tangolunda (on the Bocana-Hwy. 200 road, tel. 958/587-2126, www.

The road to La Joya, the beautiful surfing beach at Barra de la Cruz.

(tel. 958/587-1833, www.mariocobos.com). Although Mario's first love is bird-watching, he also offers fishing excursions and back-country ecotours. His fee begins at $50 per day, for one or two people, with your wheels (with jeep rental, figure a minimum of about $50 extra).

Veteran guide **Alberto Chavez** (tel. 958/587-0671, spain1965@hotmail.com) is also highly recommended. He routinely guides small groups on wildlife-viewing excursions, especially in the lush Sierra foothills above the Bahías de Huatulco.

ENTERTAINMENT
Nightlife

Bahías de Huatulco entertainment centers on the Crucecita plaza. Although the hubbub cools down on weekdays and during the low season (and hot clubs seem to change as often as the Huatulco breeze), many spots heat up significantly during the winter high season.

A growing platoon of visitors and local expatriates gather for a little bit of Ireland in Huatulco at **Café Dublin** (Calle Carrizal, no phone, noon-after midnight daily low season, 6am-2am daily high season), a block east and half a block south of the Crucecita plaza's southeast corner. Good imported beer, Irish coffee, spaghetti and meatballs, hamburgers, satellite TV, and good fellowship keeps the customers happy. In a cozy upstairs room, patrons settle in for the evening, socializing, enjoying recorded music, and watching videos.

Next door to the Café Dublin is the very worthy low- to medium-volume jazz, Latin rock, and karaoke vocal nightspot **El Tunel** (Calle Carrizal 504, cell tel. 044-958/587-6986, 7pm-11pm Mon.-Sat.).

One of the longest lasting Crucecita nightclubs is the **La Crema Restaurant-Bar** (at the plaza's northwest corner, tel. 958/587-0702, 6pm-2am Tues.-Sun.). In high season, it's open nightly, with food and drink, videos, flashing lights, and high-volume salsa music for dancing.

A pair of promising nightspots draws crowds in Chahue. The original was the

ranchotangolunda.com) offers a number of options for the adventure-minded visitor. Although most of their clients are in their teens or twenties, there's no age limit. Actvities vary from a half-day to a full three days and nights, and from hiking, rapelling, zip-lining through the forest canopy, rafting (both beginning and advanced), and more. The **Xtreme Team** (Conjunto Marina #6, Benito Juárez corner Mitla, Huatulco, tel. 958/587-2878, 958/583-4105, ParaisoHuatulco.com) offers the following activities: flyboarding, Jet Skiing, sport fishing, private yacht charter, night snorkeling, and kayaking. Their other business, called **ParaisoHuatulco** (Conjunto Marina #6, corner of Benito Juárez and Mitla, Huatulco, tel. 958/587-2878, 958/583-4105, ParaisoHuatulco.com), books ATV jungle trips, river rafting, waterfall swimming, ecotours, and various boat and city trips.

Guides
Savvy local folks recommend the services of ecologically-sensitive guide **Mario Cobos**

fancifully decorated disco El Igloo (in the basement of the Hotel Real Aligheri, on Zapoteco, about a block north of main Av. Benito Juárez, tel. 958/589-4489), fixed up to resemble an ice-bound Eskimo house. Programs include mostly salsa, tango, and 1970s and 1980s rock. Hotter still is Disco Papaya (on main east-west Av. Benito Juárez, beach side, approximately two blocks east of the intersection to Crucecita, tel. 958/587-2589, 10pm-3am Thurs.-Sat.).

Sunset Cruise, Live Music, and Tourist Shows

Lovers of quieter diversions might enjoy going on a wine, snack, and soft-music sunset cruise on the sailboat Luna Azul (tel. 958/587-0509). For higher-volume entertainments with your sunset view, go by the catamaran Tequila (tel. 958/587-2303) from the Santa Cruz de Huatulco boat harbor.

The Dreams Huatulco Resort (Av. Benito Juárez 4, tel. 958/583-0400, www. dreamsresorts.com) in Tangolunda is one of the more reliable sources of hotel nightlife. Live music often plays before dinner (about 6pm-8pm) in the lobby bar, and "Dreams Night" tourist buffet and shows rev up at least weekly year-round. Contact a travel agent or call the hotel directly for details and reservations (about $55 pp for the "Dreams Night" buffet and show). Other hotels, such as the Hotel Crown Pacific (Av. Benito Juárez 8, tel. 958/581-0044, toll-free Mex. tel. 800/711-0044, fax 958/581-0221, reservaciones@crownpacifichuatulco.com) and Barceló Huatulco ("Caribe Tropical" and "Broadway" nights; Av. Benito Juárez, tel. 958/583-1440, www.barcelohuatulco.com), customarily offer similar buffet and show entertainments in season.

SPORTS AND RECREATION
Swimming, Snorkeling, and Scuba Diving

Swimming is ideal in the calm corners of the Bahías de Huatulco. Especially good swimming beaches are located at Playa Entrega in Bahía Santa Cruz and Bahía El Maguey.

Generally clear water makes for rewarding snorkeling off the rocky shoals of all of the bays of Huatulco. Local currents and conditions, however, can be hazardous. Novice snorkelers should go on trips accompanied by strong, experienced swimmers or professional guides. Although rentals are generally available, it's best to be prepared with your own equipment.

Huatulco scuba divers enjoy the services of the well-equipped and professional scuba shop Hurricane Divers (tel. 958/587-1107, fax 958/587-2576, www.hurricanedivers. com, 9am-6pm Mon.-Fri., 9am-4pm Sat.), in the small complex between the Santa Cruz main beach and boat harbor. They start novices out with a pool mini-course, followed by a three-hour ($95) resort dive in a nearby bay. Snorkelers go for about $40, with good equipment furnished. Hurricane Divers' (PADI) open-water certification course takes about four days and runs about $340. With your open-water certificate, you are qualified for the advanced (two-tank $120) dives. After that, you may be ready for more advanced trips, which might include local shipwrecks, night dives, and marine flora, fauna, and ecology tours.

Alternatively, try very experienced (since 1988 in Huatulco) Buceos Sotavento (at Plaza Oaxaca complex, upstairs, shop #18, on the Crucecita plaza, southwest corner of Flamboyan and Gardenia, tel./fax 958/587-2166, www.tomzap.com/sotavento.html, beginning lesson and dive $75, snorkeling $20, two-tank certified dive $75, three-day open water certification $250), which offers similar (PADI) services at very reasonable rates.

Surfing and Stand-Up Paddleboarding

Café Surf (Calle Mitla 402 on the La Cruz plaza, tel. 958/585-0222, 958/105-1806 www. huatulcosurftrip.com) is home base for Gil Cardenas' surf school and his stand-up paddleboard excursion and surf safari business. Gil takes paddlers of all persuasions from beginner to expert on tours of Huatulco bays, and takes people on surf trips designed for wave riders of all skill levels. Experienced surfers will want to head to Barra de la Cruz and La Joya with Gil: La Joya is an awesome wave with a beautiful beach to watch from, and a low-priced *palapa* restaurant to fuel up you surfers. Anybody from novice to expert can enjoy climbing on a paddleboard to explore the Huatulco bays. Programs include three-hour surf classes, two-hour paddleboarding lessons, three-hour paddle and snorkel tours, and three-hour boat trips with snorkeling and paddling.

Fishing and Boat Launching

For a fishing launch *(lancha)* with two or three lines and bait, figure on paying about $25 per hour, for a minimum five-hour excursion. For big-game fishing, best rent a big 30-40 foot boat, with lines and equipment for 4-6, for about $350 for a full day. More reasonable prices might be obtained by asking around among the individual fisherfolk at the Santa Cruz boat harbor or the village at San Agustín. For example, the local boat cooperative **Sociedad Servicios Turísticos**

Bahía Tangolunda (ticket office at the Santa Cruz harbor, tel. 958/587-2303 for catamaran *Tequila*) takes visitors out for fishing excursions from the Santa Cruz boat quay.

Some of the guides already recommended arrange custom fishing outings. Check with **Mario Cobos** (tel. 958/587-1833, www. mariocobos.com) and **Alberto Chavez** (tel. 958/587-0671, spain1965@hotmail. com). Likewise, both **Hurricane Divers** (tel. 958/587-1107, fax 958/587-2576, www.hurricanedivers.com) and **Buceos Sotavento** (at Plaza Oaxaca complex, upstairs, shop #18, on the Crucecita plaza, southwest corner of Flamboyan and Gardenia, tel./fax 958/587-2166, www.tomzap.com/sotavento.html) also arrange fishing trips.

A number of local boat captains are highly recommended for their experience and skill. For details, contact **Valentin Garcia** (local cell tel. 044-958/589-2015, www.tomzap.com/valentino.html, $60/hr for four), with a 20-foot outboard *lancha*, or Abun**dio Vasquez Lavarraga** and his partner **Efrain Cortez** (tel. 958/109-7170, efrain999@yahoo.com, about $350 for full day), with a 33-foot fishing yacht.

Huatulco's best **boat-launching site** is at easily-reachable Bahía Chahue marina, with

paddleboards and surfboards available for rent

about 40 slips and an excellent heavy-duty boat ramp. Go to the **marina office** (tel. 958/587-2652, 9am-3:30pm and 4pm-7pm Mon.-Fri.) for permission to launch ($15) and slip rental information. Slip rates run about $0.55 per foot per day (between 35 and 80 feet) at the dock. Electricity and water cost extra. Find the marina from the east-west Chahue beachfront boulevard; follow the sign for *remolques* (trailers) to the big parking lot and ramp.

Tennis, Golf, and Spa

If you're planning on playing lots of tennis, it's best to stay at one of the Tangolunda luxury resorts, such as the **Barceló Huatulco** (Av. Benito Juárez, tel. 958/583-1440, www.barcelohuatulco.com) or the **Hotel Las Brisas Huatulco** (Lote 1, tel./fax 958/583-0200, fax 958/583-0240, toll-free Mex. tel. 800/227-4727, toll-free U.S./Can. tel. 888/559-4329, www.brisas.com.mx). Otherwise, the **Tangolunda Golf Course** (tel. 958/581-0037, fax 958/581-0059, tennis courts $10/hour) rents tennis courts. The tennis courts are next to the clubhouse on the knoll at the east side of the golf course.

The breezy green Tangolunda Golf Course (greens fee: $100 for 18 holes, $80 for 9 holes, cart $35, club rental $17, caddy $25), designed by the late architect Mario Chegnan Danto, stretches for 6,851 yards down Tangolunda Valley to the bay. The course starts from a low building complex (watch for bridge entrance) off the Highway 200-Tangolunda highway across from the sanitary plant.

The luxury **Xquenda** (sh-QUEN-dah, "soul" in Zapotec; tel. 958/583-4448 or 958/583-4449, www.huatulcospa.com, 9am-7pm daily) spa and athletic club, in Chahue, west side, on the Santa Cruz-Tangolunda road, offers tennis, paddle tennis, and a lap swimming pool. Spa services include massage, facials, *temazcal* ceremonial hot room, and more.

Horseback Riding

Rancho Caballo del Mar (tel. 958/584-6545 or 958/587-4886, local cell tel. 044-958/107-8211) guides horseback trips along the ocean-view forest trail that stretches from its corral through the eco-preserve zone by the Río Copalita. The four-mile tour, which costs about $25 per person, begins at the ranch site (best go by car or taxi) on the road several miles east past Tangolunda, about a mile before (south of) Highway 200.

SHOPPING
Market and Handicrafts

Crucecita has a small traditional **market** (officially the Mercado 3 de Mayo) east of the plaza, between Guanacastle and Guamuchil. Although produce, meats, and clothing occupy most of the stalls, a few offer Oaxaca handicrafts. Items include black pottery, hand-crocheted Mixtec and Amusgo *huipiles,* wool weavings from Teotitlán del Valle, and whimsical duck-motif wooden bowls carved by an elderly but sharp-bargaining local gentleman.

One of the few local handicrafts workshops is the charmingly traditional **Mantelería Escobar** (Ocotillo 217, tel. 958/587-0532, 9am-8pm daily) at the corner of Bugambilias, three blocks south of the Crucecita plaza. This factory uses century-old looms to create lovely, all-cotton *manteles* (tablecloths). Besides their own work, they also sell plenty of blouses, skirts, *huipiles* (traditional dresses), and ceramics from all over Oaxaca.

Another worthwhile Crucecita handicrafts option is **Artesanías Paradiso** (on Gardenia, corner of Guarumbo, tel. 958/587-0268, 9am-10pm Mon.-Sat., 5pm-10pm Sun.), just past the plaza's northwest corner. Among the many carefully selected treasures, find masks from Huazaolotitlán, black pottery from San Bartolo Coyotepec, dolls from San Miguel de Allende, *alebrijes* (wood-carved animals) from San Martín Tilcajete, and a whole roomful of fetching one-of-a-kind dresses, blouses, and skirts ranging from traditional to chic.

ACCOMMODATIONS

In Huatulco as in other resorts, hotels on the beach are the priciest. Tangolunda's are most expensive, Santa Cruz and Chahue hotels fall in between, and Crucecita's hotels are the cheapest. Virtually all Huatulco lodgings are modern standard, with private baths with hot water. Many, but not all, have air-conditioning, a plus, especially in the warm spring. More information about most of the hotels listed here is available through the **Huatulco Hotel and Motel Association** (toll-free U.S. and Canada tel. 866/416-0555, local tel. 958/581-0486, fax 958/581-0487, www.hoteleshuatulco.com.mx).

Huatulco accommodation rates are highly seasonal. Hotels recommended here are arranged by the customary low-season rates, which rise anywhere between 20 and 100 percent, according to demand, during the high Christmas-New Year's and Easter seasons and some *puente* (bridge) 3-5-day holiday weekends.

Crucecita

Nearly all Crucecita lodgings are within a few blocks of the central plaza. They are generally clean, well-managed posada-style hotels.

$25-50

The economy **Posada Primavera** (Palo Verde 5, corner of Gardenia, tel./fax 958/587-1167, fax 958/587-1169, $30 s or d in one bed, $35 d or t in two beds), a few blocks north of the plaza, offers six simply furnished but clean, light, high-ceilinged upstairs rooms with baths. Windows look out onto the palmy, bougainvillea-adorned surrounding neighborhood. Rooms come with fans.

On Calle Guamuchil, just half a block east of the plaza, the ★ **Hotel Los Conejos** (Guamuchil 208, tel./fax 958/587-0054, www.hotelconejoplaza.com, $30 s, $40 d, $55 t or q) offers 10 rooms built around the upstairs balcony of a tranquil, intimate interior patio. The rooms are decorated with ceramic tile floors, white stucco walls, and color-coordinated curtains and bedspreads. Rooms come with choice of air-conditioning or fans; all have cable TV, private hot-water shower-baths, but no parking.

One of Crucecita's loveliest is ★ **Hotel María Mixteca** (Guamuchil 204, tel. 958/587-2336 or 958/587-2337, fax 958/587-2338, www.travelbymexico.com/oaxa/mariamixteca, $45 d), a block east of the plaza. The 14 rooms are situated around an inviting, tranquil inner patio. Reflecting the owner's love of the Mixteca region, all rooms are named individually, mostly for Mixteca towns, such as Juquila, Tlaxiaco, and Juxtlahuaca. Rooms are

Antique looms are still in use in Crucecita.

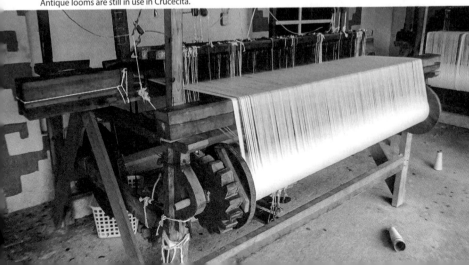

high-ceilinged and attractively decorated in pleasant pastels, tile, and native art. One room has a queen-size bed, the rest have two double beds, and many have private balconies. Rates include air-conditioning, cable TV, Wi-Fi, and parking; credit cards are accepted.

$50-100

The finest Crucecita hotel is the ★ **Hotel Misión de los Arcos** (Gardenia 902, tel. 958/587-0165, fax 958/587-1903, www.misiondelosarcos.com, $55-65 d), a block north of the plaza's northwest corner. The owners offer 14 spacious, rustic-chic rooms and suites. Guests in many rooms enjoy views of the leafy park next door. Some rooms have airy balconies and/or private patios, and all come with large luxurious baths, cable TV, and air-conditioning. Credit cards are accepted. The restaurant is highly recommended. Parking is only available on the street.

Santa Cruz de Huatulco

Although no Santa Cruz hotels are actually on the beach, they all have inviting pool patios on their own grounds and are within a five-minute walk of the lovely golden strand of Playa Santa Cruz.

$50-100

Consider the inviting 63-room **Hotel Marina** (Tehuántepec 112, tel. 958/587-0963, fax 958/587-0830, www.hotelmarinaresort.com, $80 d) that perches on the east side of the Santa Cruz harbor-marina. Rooms are comfortable and deluxe, and come with phones, air-conditioning, and cable TV. The hotel has a bar, restaurant, inviting pool patio, and parking; credit cards are accepted.

On the main Boulevard Santa Cruz, a block inland from the boat harbor, the popular long-time **Hotel Castillo Huatulco** (Blv. Santa Cruz 303, tel. 958/587-0135 or 958/587-0144, fax 958/587-0131, www.hotelcastillohuatulco.com, $90 d) offers a recommendable alternative. Its 106 white stucco and tile neo-colonial-motif rooms are deluxe and comfortable with high-ceilings. Amenities include, phone, cable

TV, air-conditioning, a palmy pool patio, restaurant, beach club, and parking; credit cards are accepted.

Chahue

The Bahía Chahue vicinity has, in recent years, acquired a number of new hotels that dot the mostly undeveloped land a few blocks from the beach. At present, however, underdevelopment and isolation make Chahue a less attractive beach neighborhood than either Santa Cruz de Huatulco or Tangolunda. Nevertheless, if you can get a low promotional rate, you might consider staying at one of the hotels recommended here.

$50-100

A block inland from the bayfront boulevard, about four blocks from the beach, find the semi-deluxe **Hotel Real Aligheri** (Calle Zapoteco, tel. 958/587-1242, toll-free Mex. tel. 800/737-0783, www.bushhuatulco.com, $55 d). It offers about 20 clean, comfortable rooms with pool, air-conditioning, cable TV, and beach club access.

Nearby, on the same quiet side street, find the small-scale ★ **Posada Eden Costa** (Calle Zapoteco, tel./fax 958/587-2480, www.edencosta.com, $80 d). Here, the husband-wife owners—he's French, she's Southeast Asian—set the international theme. The nine rooms and three kitchenette suites, all with a pair of double beds, are simply beautiful, with rustic-chic tile floors and gorgeous Talavera-accented bathrooms. Rooms come with cable TV, fans, attractive pool patio, and an outstanding on-site restaurant, L'Echalote.

Tangolunda

Several luxury resort hotels spread along the Tangolunda shoreline. The emphasis of all Tangolunda resorts is on facilities, such as multiple pools, bars, and restaurants, full wheelchair access, live music, discos, shows, and sports, including tennis, golf, sailing, kayaking, snorkeling, diving, and swimming. Other amenities may include shops, babysitting, children's clubs, and Spanish and arts and crafts instruction.

$100-200

Perched at the west end of Bahía Tangolunda, the **Hotel Las Brisas Huatulco** (Lote 1, tel./fax 958/583-0200, fax 958/583-0240, toll-free Mex. tel. 800/227-4727, toll-free U.S./Can. tel. 888/559-4329, www.brisas.com.mx, $200 s or d), formerly Club Med, is now owned and operated by the highly respected Mexican Las Brisas hotel chain. The place is huge, spreading from its grand open-air lobby, from which carts ferry guests to hundreds of spartan-deluxe view rooms, equipped with all modern amenities. Hotel facilities include many sports, three pools, a gym, secluded beaches and coves, kiddie activities, and much more. Two kids under age 12 stay for free with parents; breakfast is included.

OVER $200

The ★ **Dreams Huatulco Resort** (Av. Benito Juárez 4, tel. 958/583-0400, fax 958/581-0220, toll-free U.S. tel. 866/237-3267, fax 958/581-0220, www.dreamsresorts.com, $120 pp all inclusive), originally built and operated by the competent Mexican Club Maeva chain, ranks among Mexico's better all-inclusive resorts. The beach setting is gorgeous, and bright bedspreads, immaculate bathrooms, and private oceanview balconies grace the accommodations. Kids 7 years or under stay for free; ages 8-11 go for half-price.

At the ★ **Camino Real Zaashila Huatulco** (Av. Benito Juárez 5, tel. 958/583-0300, toll-free Mex. tel. 800/910-2300, toll-free U.S./Can. tel. 800/722-6466, fax 958/581-0468, www.caminoreal.com, $250-450 d) designers succeeded in creating a modern luxury hotel with an intimate feel. This begins at the reception *palapa,* where arriving guests sit in soft chairs while being attended to by personable clerks seated behind rustic designer desks. Outside, you walk to your room through manicured tropical gardens, replete with gurgling fountains, splashing brooks, and green lawn terraces. A few steps downhill,

past the big, meandering pool, comes the superb beachfront: acres of luscious, billow-washed yellow sand, intimately enclosed between wave-sculpted rocks on one side and a jungly headland on the other. Some units have their own pool; all have access to water sports, tennis, golf, and three restaurants.

Playa Conejo
$100-200

A personable North American couple, Richard and Brooke Gazer, have built ★ **Villa Agua Azul** (overlooking Playa Conejos, tel. 958/581-0265, www.huatulco.com.mx/aguaazul, $120-140 s or d year-round), with six elegant, lovely, and comfortable guest rooms, into their home. The luxuriously private accommodations stair-step down from the main house to an airy ocean-vista garden pool patio. Rates include a hearty breakfast. For the Christmas-New Year's holiday, add 25 percent. Rooms come with fans and air-conditioning; only nonsmoking adults 18 and over are welcome. It's a short downhill walk to a private beach.

Camping

Authorities permit tent camping and RV parking at some of the Bahías de Huatulco. Self-contained RV parking and tenting is allowed in the **Bahía Tangolunda** public beach access park for about $5 per person per day. Although the beach is beautiful and the partly palm-shaded lot is pleasant enough, facilities are limited to toilets and cold-water showers. Get there along the road that goes along the beach to Tangolunda. Turn right at the signed Playa Pública public access road bordering the western edge of the golf course. It's a two-minute hike through a mangrove swamp to the beach.

Other Huatulco beaches, such as Playa El Maguey, may be available for RV or tent camping. For more information, visit the **Huatulco National Park office** (three blocks east of the Crucecita central plaza, corner of Blv. Chahue, tel. 958/587-0849, 9am-2pm and 4pm-6pm Mon.-Fri.), which issues camping permits *(permisos)*.

FOOD

Aside from the Tangolunda hotels, most of the good Bahías de Huatulco eateries are either on or near the Crucecita plaza.

Crucecita

BREAKFAST, SNACKS, AND BAKERY

For inexpensive, homestyle cooking, try the *fondas* (food stalls) at the Crucecita *mercado* (market), between Guamuchil and Guanacastle, half a block off the plaza.

The market stalls are good for fresh fruit during daylight hours, as is the **Frutería Angelita** (just across Guanacastle, 7am-9pm daily).

Also nearby, the **Panadería San Alejandro** (at the southeast plaza corner of Flamboyan and Bugambilias, tel. 958/587-0317, 6am-10pm daily) offers mounds of scrumptious baked goodies.

Located on the main street leading into La Crucecita, ★ **West Park Café** (Gardenia 1302, tel. 958/587-2551, thewestparkcafe.blogspot.mx, 8:45am-4pm, $2-10) sounds American or Canadian but is run by an Italian named Max, who bakes the best croissants in Oaxaca if not all of Mexico, every day. And the best brioche, cinnamon rolls, and whole grain bread. Or so his satisfied customers proclaim. Max and his crew also offer a full breakfast menu, and lunch as well, all of it generously portioned and reasonably priced. Aside from the fabulous breakfast pastries, the menu mixes Asian, Spanish, and Italian influences. The coffees are stellar.

The crowd of satisfied customers will lead you to Crucecita's best-bet snack shop, ★ **Los Portales Taco and Grill** (corner of Guamuchil and Bugambilias, right on the plaza, tel. 958/587-0070, 8am-midnight daily, $2-6). Breakfasts, a dozen styles of tacos, Texas chili (or, as in Mexico, *frijoles charro*—cowboy beans), and barbecued ribs are the specialties. Beer is inexpensive, to boot.

MEXICAN AND INTERNATIONAL

The refined ambience of **Cafe Oasis** (at the southeast plaza corner of Flamboyan and Bugambilias, tel. 958/587-0045, 8am-midnight daily, $4-12) has made it Crucecita's plaza-front restaurant of choice. Beneath cooling ceiling fans, customers watch the passing scene while enjoying a full bar and a professionally prepared and served menu of breakfast, good espresso, fruit and salads, hamburgers, Mexican and international specialties, and much more.

Diagonally across the plaza, half a block north of the plaza's northwest corner, step into the cool, airy interior of ★ **Restaurant Terra Cotta** (at the Hotel Misión de los Arcos, Gardenia 902, tel. 958/587-0165, 8am-11pm daily, $7-12). Kick back and enjoy the bay-window plaza view while you choose from a list of tasty breakfasts (eggs any style, omelets, waffles), salads (Caesar), baguettes (barbequed pork loin), and Mexican specialties (*mole negro* on chicken, baby back ribs with luscious tamarind sauce).

Good, economically priced, local-style food in an open-air, TV-free setting is the specialty of refined but relaxing ★ **Restaurant La Crucecita** (501 Bugambilias, corner of Chacah, tel. 958/587-0906, 8am-11pm Thurs.-Tues., lunch $5), one block south of the plaza. A platoon of loyal local customers arrives daily to enjoy the afternoon five-course *comida corrida* (fixed-price menu). Pick an entrée (such as *guisado de res, costilla en mole verde,* or chiles rellenos) and you get bottomless fruit *agua* (choice of lemon, orange, jamaica, pineapple), soup, rice, cooked veggies or salad, and dessert. The *comida corrida* is served between noon and about 4:30pm.

ITALIAN

Lovers of fine Italian cuisine can't miss enjoying a meal at Crucecita's first, and still, some say, best Italian restaurant, ★ **El Giardino del Papa** (The Pope's Garden; Flamboyan 204, tel. 958/587-1763, 2pm-midnight daily, $17), brainchild of owner Rossana Pandolfini, of Amalfitano, Italy, and chef Mario Saggese of Salerno, who actually was once the pope's bodyguard. He immigrated to Mexico to follow his passion for cooking. Although Mario's suggestions include *calamari criollo, scampi al brandy,* and Caesar salad (highly recommended), most everything is tasty. Call for reservations, especially during the winter. Find the restaurant one block west of the plaza's southwest corner.

Santa Cruz de Huatulco
CAFÉ

For a relaxing drink or a sandwich in Santa Cruz de Huatulco, go to the **Cafe Huatulco** (at the bandstand in the shady Santa Cruz town plaza, a block west of the marina embarcadero, tel. 958/587-1228, cafehuatulco@hotmail.com, 8am-10pm daily). The mission of the friendly owner, Salvador López de Toledo, and his wife (who operates the kitchen) is to promote the already well-deserved popularity of Huatulco's mountain-grown coffee, which they grind fresh daily for their good cappuccinos and café lattes. Furthermore, Salvador is a good source of information on Huatulco coffee and the mountain *fincas cafeteleras* (coffee farms) where it's grown.

INTERNATIONAL

Fine dining in Huatulco has received a big boost at ★ **Restaurant L'Echalote** (on Calle Zapateco behind the big Hotel Villablanca in Chahue, tel. 958/587-2480, info@edencosta.com, 2pm-11pm Tues.-Sun., soups and salads $7-9, fondue for two $22). Although the cooking of owner-chefs Thierry Faivre and his Laotion wife, Tina, derives from an entire world of cuisine experience, their creations invariably come with a French touch. Ask Thierry to put on Edith Piaf and it will be better than Paris. Everything they serve is good, from the soup *(caldo camarón),* salad with goat cheese, and Thai fondue for two. *Vive la France!* Reservations are highly recommended.

★ **Restaurant Viena** (Tangolunda, across from the Barceló Huatulco hotel, cell tel. 044-958/106-0855, 5pm-11pm Mon.-Sat., $13-17) of chef Helmut Miklin embellishes the growing Huatulco fine-food tradition. His eclectic and variable menu often includes Grecian- or Tuscan-style salad, goulash, Viennese-style schnitzel with potatoes, pork cordon bleu, *filete de robalo* (snook), and apple strudel. Yum!

INFORMATION AND SERVICES
Tourist Information Offices

The Huatulco office of the **Oaxaca Secretary of Tourism** (tel./fax 958/581-0176, 8am-5pm Mon.-Fri. high season only) is in the Tangolunda hotel zone, inland side, west edge of the hotel-shopping complex.

For year-round information, go to **Huatulco Municipal Tourism** (corner of Guamuchil and Blv. Chahue, tel. 958/587-2880, tel./fax 958/587-2741, www.huatulco.gob.mx, 9am-5pm Mon.-Fri., 9am-2pm Sat.), three blocks east of the plaza.

Health and Emergency

Among the better of the Huatulco private clinics is **Clínica Médico** (403 Sibali, corner of Gardenia, about eight blocks north of the Crucecita plaza, tel. 958/587-0600 or 958/587-0687), with 24-hour emergency service.

For an English-speaking, U.S.-trained doctor, go to IAMAT (International Association for Medical Assistance to Tourists) member and general practitioner **Dr. Andrés González Ayvar** (Av. Benito Juárez, at the Barceló Huatulco hotel, tel. 958/581-0055 or cell tel. 044-958/587-6065, 11am-1pm and 8:30pm-11pm Mon.-Sat.).

Alternatively, go to the 24-hour government clinic, **Centro de Salud** (Calle Carrizal, tel. 958/587-1421), a block east of the Crucecita plaza, or the big modern-standard hospital, **Seguro Social** (tel. 958/587-1182 or 958/587-1183), in Crucecita, on the boulevard to Tangolunda, a quarter mile south of the Pemex gas station.

For routine medications, Crucecita has many pharmacies, such as **Farmacia del Centro** (plaza corner of Flamboyan and Bugambilias, tel. 958/587-0232, 8am-10pm Mon.-Sat., 9am-2pm and 5pm-10pm Sun.), at street level, below the Hotel Begonias.

For police and fire emergencies, call the Crucecita policía (tel. 958/587-0047) and the fire department (tel. 958/587-0847), both are at the Agencia Municipal behind the post office, across the boulevard from the Pemex gasolinera.

Newspapers, Books, and Magazines

The small newsstand (tel. 958/587-0279, 8am-10pm daily) at the southwest Crucecita plaza corner may seasonally stock some North American magazines and newspapers, such as Newsweek, People, USA Today, and the daily News from Mexico City.

Also, pick up a copy of Huatulco Magazine (office: Cerrada de Tlacolula no. 3, tel. 958/587-0342, www.huatulco.magazzine. net), the handy commercial tourist booklet, at your hotel, a store or travel agent, or at the magazine's office in Santa Cruz de Huatulco.

Money Exchange

For cash, you may either use the ATMs available at all of Huatulco's banks, or go inside. In Crucecita, try HSBC (corner of Bugambilias and Sibali, tel. 958/587-0324, 8am-5pm Mon.-Fri.), eight short blocks north of the plaza. Otherwise, go to Scotiabank Inverlat (corner of Guamuchil and Carrizal, tel. 958/587-0394, 9am-4pm Mon.-Fri.), with shorter hours, a block west of the plaza. After hours, use either the Banamex ATM (on Carrizal a block west of the plaza a few doors north of the Hotel Grifer) or the Bancomer ATM (on the Crucecita plaza's southwest corner by the newsstand).

You'll find other banks in Santa Cruz de Huatulco: Banamex (Av. Benito Juárez, corner of Pochutla, tel. 958/587-0071, 9am-4pm Mon.-Fri.) exchanges both U.S. and Canadian travelers checks; Bancomer (tel. 958/587-0305, 8:30am-4pm Mon.-Fri.), on the adjacent corner, across Pochutla, does about the same thing.

Post and Telecommunications

The Huatulco correo (post office; tel. 958/587-0551, 8am-4pm Mon.-Fri.), with its slower than snail mail service, and telecomunicaciones Telecom (tel. 958/587-0894, 8am-7pm Mon.-Fri., 9am-12:30pm Sat.) stand side by side, across east-side Blv. Chahue from the Pemex gas station three blocks from the plaza.

For telephone, buy a Ladatel telephone card and use it at public street telephones, or go to one of the larga distancias on Carrizal, such as Caseta Telefónica Gemenis (Carrizal, tel. 958/587-0735 or 958/587-0736, 9am-8pm daily) near the Hotel Grifer.

Immigration and Customs

Both Migración (tel. 958/581-9003 or 958/587-0760) and the Aduana (customs) are at the Huatulco airport. If you lose your tourist permit, try to avoid trouble or a fine at departure by presenting Migración with proof of your date of arrival—stamped passport, an airline ticket, or preferably a copy of your lost tourist permit—a day (or at least three hours) before your scheduled departure.

Supermarket and Photography

The supermarket La Fuente (on east-side Av. Oaxaca in Crucecita, tel. 958/587-0222, 8am-10pm daily), a block east of the Pemex station, offers a large stock of groceries, an ice machine, and a little bit of everything else.

For quick digital and film processing and printing, go to Foto Conejo (tel. 958/587-0054, 9am-8pm Mon.-Sat., 9am-5pm Sun.), just off the Crucecita plaza, across Guamuchil from the market. Besides a photo-portfolio of the Bahías de Huatulco, the friendly owner stocks point-and-shoot cameras and both film and digital supplies and accessories.

Ecology Association

Local ecologists and community leaders monitor Huatulco's development through their informal Green Globe association. They gather weekly at the resort, Camino Real Zaashila Huatulco, in Tangolunda. For more information, please contact one of the local Green

Globe activists, **Yvonne Kraak** (at the Camino Real Zaashila Huatulco, tel. 958/583-0300, Yvonne.kraak@caminoreal.com.mx).

TRANSPORTATION
Air

The **Huatulco airport** (officially the Aeropuerto Internacional Bahías de Huatulco, code-designated HUX) is just off Highway 200, 13 kilometers (8 mi) west of Crucecita and 31 kilometers (19 mi) east of Puerto Ángel. The terminal recently expanded, with ticketing and airline offices in a handsome new building under a large *palapa* roof. Amenities include snack bars, handicrafts shops, and a modest seasonal book and magazine store, with some English-language paperback novels.

A number of scheduled air carriers connect with Mexican and international destinations: The most direct U.S. flight is via **Continental Airlines** (toll-free Mexico tel. 800/900-5000, airport check-in desk tel. 958/581-9103), which connects daily non-stop with Houston.

In the meantime, a number of reliable carriers make Huatulco connections to and from North American gateways, via Mexico City. **Magnicharters** (tel. 958/587-1435 or 958/587-1436, www.magnicharters.com.mx) is the most frequent, connecting Huatulco with Mexico City daily.

Interjet (toll-free Mexico tel. 800/001-2345 or 800/911-4538, www.interjet.com.mx), the up-and-coming Mexican airline, also connects Huatulco with Mexico City daily.

Likewise, **Aeromar** (reserve online, www.aeromar.com.mx) connects Huatulco with Mexico City.

A number of winter-spring seasonal charter flights connect Huatulco with U.S. and Canadian destinations. At this writing, one of the most active is charter airline **Sunwing** (reserve online, www.sunwing.ca), which connects Huatulco directly with Toronto, returning via Puerto Vallarta.

Also, experienced local light charter airline **Aerotucan** (Mexico toll-free tel. 800/640-4148, Huatulco local tel. 958/587-2427, www.aerotucan.com.mx) regularly connects Huatulco with Oaxaca City.

Huatulco air arrival is simple and straightforward. After the typically quick immigrations and customs checks in the new terminal building, arrivees have a choice of efficient **ground transportation** to town. Agents sell tickets for collective vans (about $10 pp) to Crucecita, Santa Cruz de Huatulco, and Tangolunda. A private *taxi especial* outside the airport gate only, for three, possibly four passengers, runs about $15 to the same destinations. Prices to the Puerto Ángel vicinity run more than double these, and to Puerto Escondido even more.

Car or RV

Paved highways connect Huatulco east with the Isthmus of Tehuántepec, west with Puerto Ángel and Puerto Escondido, and north with Oaxaca.

A few **car rental** agents are usually on duty for flight arrivals: **Thrifty** (tel. 958/587-0010, or Mex. toll-free tel. 800/021-2277, www.thrifty.com); **Hertz** (at airport, tel. 958/581-9092, in Tangolunda tel. 958/581-0588, Mexico toll-free tel. 800/709-5000, www.hertz.com); **Europcar** (at airport tel. 958/581-9094, in Crucecita tel. 958/581-0551, www.europcar.com); or **Dollar** (tel. 958/581-0532, www.dollar.com).

Highway 200, the east-west route, runs an easy 161 kilometers (100 mi) to Tehuántepec, where it connects with Highway 190. From there, it continues northwest to Oaxaca or east to Chiapas and the Guatemala border. (A new $2 toll cutoff—fork left about five miles west of, before, Salina Cruz—cuts the time to Tehuántepec and, thence Oaxaca, by at least half an hour.)

In the opposite direction, the Highway 200 route is equally smooth, connecting Huatulco with Pochutla (Puerto Ángel), 40 kilometers (25 mi) west, and Puerto Escondido, 113 kilometers (70 mi), continuing to Acapulco in a long 519 kilometers (322 mi). Allow about 3 hours to Tehuántepec, 1.5 hours to Puerto

Escondido, and to Acapulco, a full 9 hours' driving time, in either direction.

Highway 175, the cross-Sierra connection north with the city of Oaxaca, although paved, is narrow, winding, and can be potholed, with few services in the 129-kilometer (80 mi) high Sierra stretch between its junction with Highway 200 at Pochutla (35.4 kilometers west of Crucecita) and Miahuatlán in the Valley of Oaxaca. The road climbs to 9,000 feet into pine-tufted, winter-chilly Chatino and Zapotec country. Allow eight hours northbound, seven hours southbound, for the entire 282-kilometer (175 mi) Huatulco-Oaxaca trip. You can save an hour by taking the new shortcut, from Highway 200, a couple of miles west of the Huatulco airport, via Santa Cruz de Huatulco and Pluma Hidalgo, to Highway 175 and thence to Oaxaca.

Bus

Several long-distance bus lines connect Huatulco with destinations east, west, and north. They depart from two separate new terminals in Crucecita.

From the **ADO Terminal** (Rescadillo 108, corner of Blv. Chahue), nine blocks north of the Crucecita plaza, across Bulevar Chahue, luxury-class **Autobuses del Oriente** (ADO GL), first-class **Omnibus Cristóbal Colón** (OCC), second-class **SUR,** and economy-class **Ecobus** connect with points east, west, and north. For all of these buses, tickets are purchased through the same venue (toll-free Mex. tel. 800/702-8000, www.ticketbus.com.mx).

ADO GL luxury-class buses connect east with Isthmus points of Salina Cruz and Tehuántepec, thence either northwest, with Oaxaca, Puebla, and Mexico City Tapo terminals, or east, with Tehuántepec and Juchitán, thence north with Veracruz.

OCC first-class buses connect west with Pochutla (Puerto Ángel) and Puerto Escondido. OCC buses also connect east with Salina Cruz and Tehuántepec on the Isthmus. From there they connect east, either with Tuxtla Gutierrez and San Cristóbal las Casas or Tapachula in Chiapas; or northwest with

Oaxaca City, Puebla, and Mexico City (North, Tapo, and Tasqueña) terminals.

SUR second-class buses connect both west with Pochutla and Puerto Escondido, and east, with Salina Cruz, Tehuántepec, and Juchitán.

Finally, economy-class Ecobus departures connect east with Salina Cruz, Tehuántepec, and Juchitán, thence north with Minatitlán, Coatzocoalcos, and Villahermosa.

About one kilometer (0.6 mi) north along Bulevar Chahue (turn off right, one block) at the Crucecita general **Camionera Central** (Central Bus Terminal), a number of lines also offer western, eastern, and northern connections.

Estrella Blanca affiliate, luxury-class **Turistar** (tel. 958/587-1560) connects west, with Pochutla, Puerto Escondido, Pinotepa Nacional, thence north, to Mexico City Sur and Norte terminals.

Also Estrella Blanca affiliate, first-class **Elite** (tel. 958/587-1560) connects both east with Salina Cruz, and west, with Pochutla, Puerto Escondido, Pinotepa Nacional, and Acapulco, where connections may be made via Puerto Vallarta and Mazatlán, all the way, to either Nogales or Tijuana, at the U.S. border.

First-class independent **Costeño** buses (tel. 958/587-0680) connect east with Salina Cruz, and west with Pochutla, Puerto Escondido, Pinotepa Nacional, and Acapulco (Ejido terminal), thence north, with Mexico City Tasqueña terminal.

Furthermore, a number of first- and second-class buses of the **Lanesco** cooperative line (combined Estrella del Valle and Autobuses Oaxaca Pacífico, tel. 958/587-2554 and 958/583-4499) connect daily with Oaxaca City by the winding trans-sierra Highway 175 via Pochutla. Under good conditions, the trip runs a minimum of eight hours.

Van

Although not as comfortable (they're bumpier and often crowded), travel by van is quicker, cheaper, and much more frequent than buses. Competent carrier **Van 2000** (on Guamuchil, two blocks east of the Crucecita plaza, tel. 958/587-2910) offers about eight departures, connecting with Oaxaca City (terminal at Hidalgo 208, tel. 951/516-3154). The trip, about seven hours, takes a shortcut through Pluma Hidalgo in the mountains above Huatulco.

COFFEE COUNTRY

A century before the Bahías de Huatulco development was even on the drawing board, the cooler, greener Huatulco uplands were home to a community of farmers and fruit and coffee ranchers. Bypassed by the new Highway 200 and the coastal resort development, the foothill region above the Bahías de Huatulco is a treasury of traditional Oaxaca life and natural diversions—wildlife to view, springs and waterfalls to splash in, and jungle coffee ranches to visit.

Ecotouring and Guides

Local tour operators and guides lead tours of archaeological zones, rapelling, fishing trips, river rafting, coffee farms, forest wildlife-viewing, springs, waterfalls, and much more. The following rank among the most experienced and long-lasting of Huatulco tour operators and guides. Although their websites display a number of standard tours, tell them what you want and they can also arrange something special for you.

- **Bahías Plus:** Carrizal 704, Crucecita, tel. 958/587-0216 or 958/587-0932, www.bahiasplus.com; snorkel, bay tour, crocodiles and turtles, Cascadas Mágicas, coffee farms.
- **Paraiso Huatulco:** Plaza Bonita, local 5, Santa Cruz de Huatulco, tel. 958/587-2878 or 958/583-4105, www.paraisohuatulco.com, office also at hotels Barceló Huatulco and Zaashila; horseback ride, sunset cruise, bay tour, rappel, mountain biking, sportfishing, rafting, Cascadas Mágicas, coffee farm.
- **Prometur:** Sabali 304, Crucecita, tel. 958/587-0413, 958/587-1435, www.todo-huatulco.com/prometur; bay tour, rafting,

rapelling, horseback, Cascadas Mágicas, coffee farm.

You might also hire one of these two excellent guides: **Mario Cobos** (tel. 958/587-1833, www.mariocobos.com) and **Alberto Chavez** (tel. 958/587-0671, spain1965@hotmail.com).

Pluma Hidalgo

This mini-metropolis of Oaxaca's southern Sierra owes its fame to the excellent coffee, produced by a competent cadre of local *fincas cafeteleras* (coffee farms) sprinkled in the cool, vine-hung mountain forests that surround the town. The original impulse for Oaxaca coffee growing dates back to President Benito Juárez's efforts to encourage upcountry coffee growing and shipping via the newly built port of Puerto Ángel around 1870. Although the shipping is now all done by highway, the deep, rich flavor of Pluma Hidalgo coffee is prized by brew fanciers all over Mexico and the world.

SIGHTS

The town of Pluma Hidalgo (pop. 3,000, elev. 1,470 meters/4,830 feet) nestles on a lush mountainside 26 kilometers (16 mi) by paved road uphill from Santa María de Huatulco. The name "Pluma" originates from the feather-like cloud (thus "plume") that often forms over the verdant ridge above the town.

The main town-center sights are the plaza, the colonial-era church, and the town market, which is best on Sunday. Just below the market on the north side is one of the most unusually picturesque basketball courts in Mexico. From anywhere on the court (which is fenced in by netting so the ball will not get lost over the adjacent cliff), expansive vistas spread, both up to the Sierra summit and down-valley to the Pacific shore.

The must-do Pluma Hidalgo activity is visiting a coffee farm. On the plaza, on the left as you face the church, is **Abarrotes Ulilsis** (Plaza Principal 2, tel. 958/525-8110, speak in Spanish, 9am-8pm daily), the store of coffee grower and dealer Filadelfo Ramirez Ordaz, who sells top-quality organically-grown

Pluma coffee for about $5 per half-kilo bag, as well as his locally made coffee liqueur.

An on-the-spot alternative would be to visit one of the coffee *fincas* (farms) immediately on foot. Beginning at the plaza, walk past the Posada Isabel hotel and continue downhill along the road to the *panteón* (cemetery). From the cemetery you can enjoy views in three directions across lush mountain-framed river valleys. Past the cemetery, the downhill road leads three kilometers (two mi) past coffee farms, marked by the shiny dark-green-leafed coffee bushes beneath the shady overhead forest canopy. At valley bottom, arrive at a river and a high, 60-meter (200 ft.) gushing cascade on your left.

After a cooling dip in the pond beneath the waterfall and perhaps a picnic lunch, visit the **Tres Cruces** coffee *finca* (no phone, 9am-noon Mon.-Fri., free admission), a fraction of a mile back uphill. There you can see where the coffee pickers bring the harvested beans and watch the beans get weighed and recorded in the logbook by the overseer, and then washed and set out to dry. Other *fincas* (farms) that you may visit in the area are La Providencia, San Francisco, and Margaritas. Be sure to wear long pants and carry insect repellent to deter mosquito and no-see-um attacks.

ACCOMMODATIONS AND FOOD

Overnighters can stay at the working coffee farm **El Refugio** (off the Santa María de Huatulco-Pluma Hidalgo road, at about mile 5 from Santa María watch for the sign, tel. 958/583-5021, local cell tel. 044-529/587-7181, www.ecoturismoenoaxaca.com/hotelrefugio.html, $23 s, $46 d). Ensconced in a luscious foothill tropical forest, the hotel offer 25 clean, comfortable rooms with private bath, home-cooking restaurant, a tour around the farm, a small spring-fed panoramic-view patio and swimming pool, an events salon, and a guide and airport pickup (at additional cost).

If instead you choose to stay in Pluma Hidalgo town, you have the option of the **Hotel Posada Isabel** (Calle Guerrero, tel. 958/525-8113, joesue24-7@yahoo.com, $20 s, $25 d). The Posada Isabel, located just southwest of the church, offers six clean rooms, some with view balconies, and all with two double beds, private hot-water bathrooms, TV, and parking.

For dining, friendly family-owned **Restaurant Luria** (Av. Hidalgo 16, tel. 958/525-8022, 6am-9pm daily, $4) offers hearty Mexican country specialties. Besides Mexican breakfasts, food offerings often include chicken smothered in *mole negro, mole coloradito* (spicy chile usually over pork or chicken), or *estofado* (meat and vegetable stew).

Alternatively, try plaza-front **Restaurant La Flor del Café** (Calle Guerrero 1, no phone, 6am-9pm daily, $3-6), which offers traditional Mexican plates, such as *guisado de res* (beef stew) and *chilaquiles* (spicy baked tortillas and cheese).

Get to Pluma Hidalgo from the coast via Santa María de Huatulco. Ride with Oaxaca City shuttle **Van 2000** (on Guamuchil, two blocks east of the Crucecita plaza, tel. 958/587-2910) or *colectivos* that leave frequently from the Santa María de Huatulco turnoff on Highway 200, west of the Huatulco airport entrance (in Santa María you may have to transfer to a Pluma Hidalgo-bound *colectivo*); taxis run uphill from there (about $15 for up to four people). **By car,** turn north off Highway 200 at the Santa María de Huatulco crossing, west of the airport. At the town center, turn left at the (Hwy. 178) Pluma Hidalgo-marked sign. Pass over a scenic, mountain-framed river gorge just outside of town. Continue half an hour (26 km/16 mi) uphill to the Pluma Hidalgo right-hand turnoff.

★ Cascadas Mágicas

The foothill destination of **Cascadas Mágicas** (or Cascadas Llano Grande for the village where they're located) makes a superb day trip by car or tour. By bus, you might need two days, including an overnight at the La Gloria coffee farm. Along the way, nature lovers will enjoy the leafy foothill country, laced with rivers and springs, gurgling through sylvan, vine-hung woodland, rich with birds, mammals, and butterflies.

Your first destination, which is a Huatulco must-do, should be the tropical foothill headwaters of the Río Copalita, where you first hike a forest trail and then climb, passing the gorgeous procession of bubbling aqua-blue Cascadas Mágicas waterfalls. You walk past a hanging rope swing, and finally dive in and paddle through the cool, crystal-clear current.

La Gloria Coffee Farm

About seven kilometers (three mi) back from the Cascadas, you'll pass **La Gloria** (Apdo. Postal 220, Bahías de Huatulco, Oaxaca 70989, tel. 958/587-0697, www.ecoturismoenoaxaca.com.fincalagloria.html, $20 pp for lunch and tour, $50 pp overnight and three meals), a little German farm in the jungle. The parents of La Gloria's owner-operator Gustav Sherenberg arrived from the wreckage of World War II, seeking a new life in Mexico. The dream that they carved out remains with Gustav (now Gustavo), who, with his son Max, continues to improve on it. (Lately, however, La Gloria has stopped producing coffee, hopefully they will resume when prices rise again.)

The centerpiece, a whitewashed farmhouse and its antique furnishings—polished oak wall telephone, heirloom Old-World sideboard, 1940s-vintage shortwave radio—endure for guests to admire and enjoy. The owners invite you to enjoy their farm with them, either for an afternoon, including lunch, or for an overnight, including comfortable and cozy jungle- *cabaña* lodging with lunch, dinner, and breakfast included.

The easiest way to enjoy the Cascadas Mágicas and La Gloria coffee farm is by guide or tour from Huatulco. If you're going independently, you should first head for Xadani, accessible via the signed side road on the north side of Highway 200, 11.4 kilometers (seven mi) west of the Río Copalita bridge and Copalita village (which has a store, *palapa* restaurants, a basic hotel, long-distance telephone; 66 km/41 mi east of Pochutla, 119 km/74 mi west of Salina Cruz).

If by car, set your odometer as you turn off the highway. Continue immediately through a Zimatán village along a good gravel road, paralleling the gorgeous vine-hung, butterfly-decorated Río Zimatán valley. Continue through Xadani to the church (20.4 km/12.7 mi). Proceed, bearing left around the right rear side of the church, then straight ahead another 8.7 kilometers (5.4 mi) to La Gloria coffee farm and about 4.8 kilometers (3 mi) more to the Cascadas Mágicas entrance gate ($5 per car) past El Llano village.

By bus, take a local or long-distance bus from Pochutla or Crucecita, which will take you at least to Copalita, or better, to the Xadani Highway 200 turnoff. From there, you can catch a taxi or a *colectivo* truck ride (offer to pay) to Xadani, thence to La Gloria and Cascadas Mágicas.

Puerto Escondido and Vicinity

Puerto Escondido (Hidden Port) got its name from the rocky Punta Escondida that shelters its intimate half-moon cove, which perhaps would have remained hidden if local farmers had not discovered that coffee thrives beneath the cool forest canopy of the lush seaward slopes of the Sierra Madre del Sur. They began bringing their precious beans for shipment when the port of Escondido was established in 1928.

When the coast highway was pushed through during the 1970s, Puerto Escondido's then-dwindling coffee trade was replaced by a growing trickle of vacationers, attracted by the splendid isolation, low prices, and high waves. With one of the most challenging

Puerto Escondido

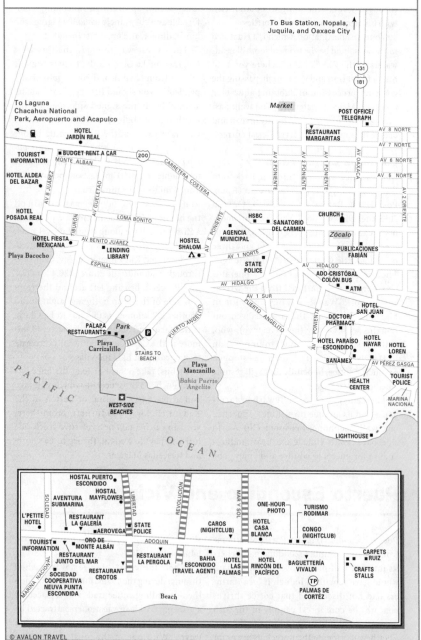

To Bus Station, Nopala,
Juquila, and Oaxaca City

131
181

Market

To Laguna
Chacahua National
Park, Aeropuerto and Acapulco

POST OFFICE/
TELEGRAPH

RESTAURANT
MARGARITAS

AV 8 NORTE
AV 7 NORTE
AV 6 NORTE
AV 5 NORTE

AV 3 PONIENTE
AV 2 PONIENTE
AV 1 PONIENTE
AV OAXACA
AV 2 ORIENTE

HOTEL
JARDÍN REAL

TOURIST
INFORMATION

BUDGET RENT A CAR

200

MONTE ALBAN

CARRETERA COSTERA

HOTEL ALDEA
DEL BAZAR

AV 8 JUÁREZ

AV GUELETAO

LOMA BONITO

HOTEL
POSADA REAL

HSBC

SANATORIO
DEL CARMEN

CHURCH

Zócalo

TIBURON

AV BENITO JUÁREZ

HOTEL FIESTA
MEXICANA

LENDING
LIBRARY

HOSTEL
SHALOM

AGENCIA
MUNICIPAL

PUBLICACIONES
FABIÁN

Playa Bacocho

ESPINAL

AV 5 PONIENTE

AV 1 NORTE

STATE
POLICE

AV HIDALGO

ADO-CRISTÓBAL
COLÓN BUS

ATM

AV HIDALGO

AV 1 SUR

HOTEL
SAN JUAN

PUERTO ANGELITO

DOCTOR/
PHARMACY

PALAPA
RESTAURANTS

Park

Playa
Carrizalillo

P

STAIRS TO
BEACH

PUERTO ANGELITO

Playa
Manzanillo

Bahía Puerto
Angelito

AV 1 PONIENTE

HOTEL PARAÍSO
ESCONDIDO

HOTEL
NAYAR

HOTEL
LOREN

BANAMEX

AV PÉREZ GASGA

TOURIST
POLICE

HEALTH
CENTER

MARINA
NACIONAL

P A C I F I C

WEST-SIDE
BEACHES

LIGHTHOUSE

O C E A N

HOSTAL PUERTO
ESCONDIDO

HOSTAL
MAYFLOWER

AVENTURA
SUBMARINA

L'PETITE
HOTEL

RESTAURANT
LA GALERÍA

AEROVEGA

SOLEDAD

OCÉANO

LIBERTAD

REVOLUCIÓN

STATE
POLICE

CAROS
(NIGHTCLUB)

MAR Y SOL

ONE-HOUR
PHOTO

HOTEL
CASA
BLANCA

TURISMO
RODIMAR

CONGO
(NIGHTCLUB)

CARPETS
RUIZ

TOURIST
INFORMATION

ORO DE
MONTE ALBÁN

RESTAURANT
JUNTO DEL MAR

ADOQUIN

RESTAURANT
LA PERGOLA

BAHÍA
ESCONDIDO
(TRAVEL AGENT)

HOTEL
LAS
PALMAS

HOTEL
RINCÓN DEL
PACÍFICO

BAGUETTERÍA
VIVALDI

CRAFTS
STALLS

MARINA NACIONAL

SOCIEDAD
COOPERATIVA
NEUVA PUNTA
ESCONDIDA

RESTAURANT
CROTOS

TP

PALMAS DE
CORTÉZ

Beach

© AVALON TRAVEL

STATE POLICE

HOTEL SANTA FE

TABACHIN APARTMENTS

HORSES FOR RENT

BUNGALOWS ACALI

CINE MAR

ABARROTES MERLIN

HOTEL ARCO IRIS

INFRAGANTE

TP

CAFÉ CASA BABYLON/ BOOK EXCHANGE

LAUNDRY LA PLAYA

RESTAURANT LOS MANGOS

BUNGALOWS AQUARIO/GYM

AV DEL MORRO

CENTRAL SURF

MONEY EXCHANGE

FARMACIA OLLIN

PLAYA ZICATELA

BEACH HOTEL INÉS

AGENCIA DE VIAJES DIMAR

MONEY EXCHANGE

CAFECITO

200

CASA OLGA

AV 4 ORIENTE

AV 3 ORIENTE

AV 4 NORTE

AV 3 NORTE

AV 2 NORTE

AV 1 NORTE

AV HIDALGO

AV BENITO JUÁREZ (AV 1 SUR)

CARRETERA COSTERA

LIBERTAD

SEE LEFT DETAIL

ADOQUIN

PEREZ GASGA

Laguna Agua Dulce

Playa Principal

Playa Marinero

Andador

SEE RIGHT DETAIL

INFRAGANTE

VILLA TEMAZCALLI

PLAYA ZICATELA

AV DEL MORRO

200

To La Punta, Puerto Ángel, Bahías de Huatulco, and Tehuantepec

0   100 yds
0   100 m

waves in North America pounding down daily on Playa Zicatela (especially in summertime), a permanent surfing colony soon was established. This led to more nonsurfing visitors, who, by the 1990s, were arriving in droves to enjoy the comfort and food of a string of small hotels and restaurants lining Puerto Escondido's still-beautiful but no longer hidden cove.

Getting Oriented

Puerto Escondido (pop. 45,000) seems like two towns separated by Highway 200, which runs along the bluff above the beach. The upper town is where most of the local folks live and go about their business. In the town below the highway, most of the restaurants, hotels, and shops spread along a single, touristy, beachfront street mall, **Avenida Pérez Gasga** (known locally as the *adoquín,* ahdoh-KEEN), where motor traffic is allowed only before noon during the high season. In the afternoon, chains go up, blocking cars at either end. Beyond the west-end chain, Avenida Pérez Gasga leaves the beach, winding uphill. Note that beachfront locations are described as being on the *adoquín,* while hillside locations are described as being on Avenida Pérez Gasga.

Avenida Pérez Gasga winds up to the highway, where it enters the upper town at the *crucero,* Puerto Escondido's main intersection. From there, Avenida Pérez Gasga continues into the upper town as Avenida Oaxaca, also known as National Highway 131.

Getting Around

In town, walk or take a taxi, which should run no more than $4 to anywhere in town. For longer excursions, such as to Lagunas Manialtepec and Río Grande (near National Park Lagunas de Chacahua, westbound), and as far as Pochutla (near Puerto Ángel, eastbound), ride one of the very frequent *urbano* buses that stop at the *crucero,* or rent a car from **Budget** (Av. Benito Juárez, at the corner of Monte Alban, tel./fax 954/582-0312 or 954/582-0315, budget33@hotmail.com) in the Bachoco suburb by the airport. Alternatively, try Gabriel at **Economica Rent-a-Car** (Las Brisas 7, tel. 954/582-2557) on the downhill street, from Highway 200, at the south end of the Playa Zicatela development. Gabriel also rents out motorbikes.

Safety Concerns

Occasional knifepoint robberies and muggings mar the once-peaceful Puerto Escondido

a pathway near the beaches of Puerto Escondido

nighttime beach scene. Walking alone can be unsafe, especially along Playa Bachoco and the unlit stretch of Playa Principal between the east end of Avenida Pérez Gasga and the Hotel Santa Fe. If you have dinner alone at the Hotel Santa Fe, avoid the beach by returning by taxi or walking along the highway to Avenida Pérez Gasga back to your hotel.

Fortunately, such problems seem to be confined to the beach. Visitors are quite safe on the Puerto Escondido streets, often more so than on their own city streets back home.

BEACHES AND ACTIVITIES

Puerto Escondido's bayfront begins at the sheltered rocky cove beneath the wave-washed lighthouse point, Punta Escondida. The shoreline continues easterly along Playa Principal, the main beach, curving southward at Playa Marineros, and finally straightening into long open-ocean Playa Zicatela. The sand and surf change drastically, from narrow sand and calm ripples at Playa Principal to a wide beach pounded by gigantic rollers at Zicatela.

Playa Principal

The best place to appreciate Puerto Escondido is not from the cluttered *adoquín,* but from one of the shady restaurants (such as Los Crotos or Junto del Mar) that front **Playa Principal.** It's here that Mexican families love to frolic on Sunday and holidays and sun-starved winter vacationers doze in their chairs and hammocks beneath the palms. The sheltered west side is very popular with local people who arrive in the afternoons with nets and haul in small troves of silvery fish. The water is great for wading and swimming, clear enough for casual snorkeling, but generally too calm for anything else in the cove. However, a few hundred yards east around the bay the waves are generally fine for bodysurfing and boogie boarding, with a minimum of undertow. Although it's not a particularly windy location, kiteboarders do occasionally bring their own equipment and practice here.

Fishing is fine off the rocks or by small boat, easily launched from the beach.

Playa Marinero

As the beach curves toward the south, it increasingly faces the open ocean. **Playa Marinero** begins about 100 yards from the "Marineros," the east-side rocky outcroppings in front of the landmark Hotel Santa Fe. The rocks' jutting forms are supposed to resemble visages of grizzled old sailors.

★ Playa Zicatela

Past the Marinero rocks you enter Mexico's hallowed ground of surfing, **Playa Zicatela.** The wide beach, of fine golden-white sand, stretches south for miles to a distant cliff and point. The powerful Pacific swells arrive unimpeded, crashing to the sand with awesome, thunderous power. Both surfers and nonsurfers congregate year-round, waiting for the renowned Puerto Escondido "pipeline," where grand waves curl into whirling liquid tunnels, which expert surfers blast through like trains in a subway. At such times, the spectators on the beach outnumber the surfers by as much as 10 or 20 to one. Don't try surfing or swimming at Zicatela unless you're an expert.

If you want to watch the surfers go at it, on the edge of wide Playa Zicatela and across the street as well, a number of restaurants and bars provide wave watchers with plenty of comfortable spots to enjoy food and drink while watching the surfers. It's a great show! And it's not to be missed if you visit Puerto Escondido.

Another surfing wave, called **La Punta,** breaks off the east end of Playa Zicatela. This wave, mostly a lefthander, is very mellow compared to Zicatela's thunderous main beach break. Plenty of surfers have discovered it and make the daily trek on foot or in a cab down to ride this more manageable wave. A small colony of restaurants, bars, cheap rooms, and mini-supers has grown up just off the beach in response to the growing popularity of this spot, so low-budget wave-chasers can set up shop here and live the vagabond life for weeks on end for very little money. It's a surfer's dream come true—good waves, warm water, and a cheap place to stay, and if that surfer gets in enough practice he or she can wander three miles up the beach and try to paddle out at Zicatela's notorious main break. The vibe at La Punta is like the main break at Zicatela was 20 years ago—low key, downscale, and uncrowded—only with an easier wave to ride.

★ West-Side Beaches: Manzanillo, Carrizalillo, and Bachoco

About a mile west of town, the picture-postcard little blue bays of Bahía Puerto Ángelito and Bahía Carrizalillo nestle beneath the seacliff. Their sheltered gold-and-coral sands are perfect for tranquil picnicking, sunbathing, and swimming. Here, snorkeling and scuba diving are tops, among shoals of bright fish grazing and darting among the nearby coral shelves and submerged rocky outcroppings. Get there by launch from Playa Principal or by taxi. On foot (take a sun hat and water), follow the street that heads west from Avenida Pérez Gasga, uphill across from the Hotel Nayar. Continue to the second street on the left, Avenida 1 Poniente, turn left and go a long block to Avenida 5 Sur. Turn right and

continue straight ahead for about a half mile to Bahía Puerto Angelito, which shelters **Playa Manzanillo** at its inner edge. Follow the steps down the cliff. Even more pristine **Playa Carrizalillo,** a petite strip of golden sand with a few *palapa* restaurants, is another mile farther west. Here, surfers of less advanced skill levels, and beginners as well, will find a mellow, easy-to-ride lefthander, and several locals offering surfing lessons and board rentals. There is also a righthander a hundred yards to the west of the left, on the other side of the bay, but this is pretty much a locals-only spot, and non-locals will not feel welcome. Surfers are territorial and this particular territory has been claimed, so you don't want to go after this wave if there are more than two or three people in the water.

Playa Bachoco, yet another mile farther west, down the bluff from the Hotel Posada Real, is a long, scenic strip of breeze-swept sand, with thunderous waves and correspondingly menacing undertow. Swimming is much safer in the inviting pool of the adjacent Hotel Posada Real beach club.

If you're strong, experienced, and can get past the breaking waves, snorkeling is good around the little surf-dashed rocky islet 100 yards offshore.

The sculpted hands honor those who've saved lives in the waters of Puerto Escondido.

The Perilous Barrels of Puerto Escondido

Playa Zicatela

Puerto Escondido's famously fast and heavy barrel-shaped waves break in shallow water over a hard sand bottom, and it is the speed and power of these waves that attract surfers. This wave has broken many a board and quite a few bodies as well. It is not for the surfer of even moderate skill, and definitely not for beginners.

The Puerto barrels were first seen by wandering California surfers in the 1950s, but the heavy longboards of that era were in no way equipped to handle such powerful waves. It wasn't until the shortboard revolution of the early 1970s that surfers actually began riding the so-called Mexican Pipeline. The timing was propitious, as at that time the quintessential surfing experience shifted from the mellow, point break mode developed at Malibu and Rincon in southern California, to the faster, more challenging tube-riding style originated by Gerry Lopez at the Banzai Pipeline in Hawaii. The barrels of Zicatela soon became a hard-core surfing mecca, and surfers began showing up, first in a trickle, and then, as access improved and word got out, in a bit of a flood.

Puerto's (in)famous barrels remain one of the supreme surfing challenges on our planet, and every year, hundreds of surfers come from all over to test themselves. The wave they encounter is a natural creation—the beach faces south so every south (summer) swell hits it dead on. Offshore, a canyon formed by the convergence of tectonic plates funnels the swells and magnifies them into the monster tubes that pound along Playa Zicatela.

A whole generation of local Mexican wave riders have grown up on these epic waves, and ride them fearlessly alongside the many surfing tourists who come during the summer season. It's a magnet for these testosterone-driven enthusiasts—and if you should find yourself in the neighborhood during a big south swell, don't miss a chance to watch great surfers challenged by some of the most dangerous and exciting waves in the world. Even if you haven't a clue about surfing, you'll know, just by watching, that this is the real deal: fearless surfers charging into scarily dangerous waves.

Although Playa Bachoco's rock-sheltered nooks appear inviting for beach camping, local people don't recommend it because of occasional *rateros* (thugs and drunks) who roam Puerto Escondido beaches at night.

Beach Walking

The *andador* (concrete walkway), which circles the lighthouse point, provides a pleasant, breezy afternoon (or sunset) diversion. From the west chain, follow the street, Marina

Nacional, that heads toward the beach. Immediately on your left, stairs head down onto the beach cove, where, on the rocks that shelter the cove, at the Capitania del Puerto building, the *andador* heads left along the rocks. It continues, above the spectacularly splashing surf, for about half a mile. Return by the same route, or loop back through side streets to Avenida Pérez Gasga.

For a longer walk, you can stroll as far out of town along Playa Zicatela as you want, in outings ranging from an hour to a whole day. Avoid the heat of midday, and bring along a sun hat, sunglasses, shirt, drinks, and snacks if you plan on walking more than a mile past the last restaurant down the beach. Your rewards will be the acrobatics of surfers challenging the waves, swarms of shorebirds, and occasional finds of driftwood and shells. After about three miles you will reach a point beneath a cliff and a sea arch where you can scamper through at low tide to the beach on the other side, **Playa Barra de Colotepec.**

Playa Barra de Colotepec's surf is as thunderous as Zicatela's and the beach even more pristine, being a nesting site for sea turtles. The beach continues for another mile to the jungle-fringed lagoon of the Río Colotepec, where, during the dry winter season, a host of birds and wildlife, both common and rare, paddle and preen in the clear, fresh water.

Boat Tours

Travel agencies; the local boat cooperative, **Sociedad Cooperativa Turística Nueva Punta Escondida;** and some individuals offer trips from the town beach. The minimum one-hour trip visits a number of sandy little coves west of town, including Carrizalillo (Little Reeds), Puerto Ángelito and its beach, Playa Manzanillo (Little Apple), Coral, and Puesta del Sol (Sunset). Take drinks, hats, sunscreen, and sunglasses, and don't go unless your boat has a sunroof. Trips can be extended (about $15 per additional hour) to your heart's content of whale-, dolphin-, and turtle-watching, beach picnicking, snoozing,

and snorkeling. For more details, visit www.tomzap.com/pe-coop.html.

Alternatively, very competent family-run **Omar's Sportfishing** (local cell tel. 044-954/559-4406, long distance tel. 045-954/559-4406, www.oaxaca-mio.com/omarsportfishing_eng.htm) offers excursions, including dolphin-, whale-, and turtle-watching. You can find Omar on the beach at Puerto Ángelito.

ENTERTAINMENT AND EVENTS
Nightlife

The amusements along the *adoquín* mall and Playa Zicatela are Puerto Escondido's prime after-dinner entertainment source. You'll find them by following your ears. Right in the middle of the *adoquín* is karaoke bar **Congo** (beach side, open nightly). Those who prefer to gyrate, go to open-air, high volume disco **Tarros** (across from the Hotel Las Palmas).

For quieter offerings, check out the guitarists who play evenings at the **Hotel Santa Fe restaurant-bar** (Av. del Morro, Zicatela side of the bay, tel. 954/582-0170, 7:30am-11pm daily), or go to **Casa Babylon** (Calle El Morro, no phone, 10:30am-2pm and 8pm-midnight daily), right in the middle of Playa Zicatela, for coffee, conversation, and table games.

For more entertainment suggestions, ask friendly and helpful **Gina Machorro** (on the *adoquín,* west end, beach side, tel. 954/582-0276 or 954/582-1186, ginainpuerto@yahoo.com, 9am-2pm and 4pm-6pm Mon.-Fri.), who staffs the Avenida Pérez Gasga information booth.

Sunsets and Happy Hours

Many bars have sunset happy hours, but not all of them have good sunset views. Since the Oaxaca coast faces south (and the sun sets in the west), bars and restaurants along west-facing Playa Zicatela, such as **Hotel Santa Fe** (Av. del Morro, tel. 954/582-0170), **Hotel Arco Iris** (Av. del Morro, Colonia Marinero, tel./fax 954/582-1494 or 954/582-0432), and

Restaurant Cafecito (south end, next to Bungalows Acuario, tel. 954/582-0516,), are the only ones that can offer unobstructed sunset horizons.

If, on the other hand, you prefer solitude, stroll the bayfront *andador* (walkway) that begins on the Playa Principal, west side, on the rocks on the outer western edge of the bay, past the Capitán del Puerto office. The path leads west, past a succession of breezy sunset viewpoints above the waves, about half a mile, to steps that continue uphill to city streets near the lighthouse.

Festivals

Puerto Escondido pumps up with a series of fiestas during the surfing season (also excellent for all around vacationing) with the **Fiestas de Noviembre** (usually Nov. 10-Dec. 10). The main events invariably include surfing and usually sportfishing, cooking, beauty contests, and notably, the dance festival, **Fiesta Costeño,** when a flock of troupes from Pochutla, Pinotepa Nacional, Jamiltepec, Tehuántepec, and more perform regional folk dances.

Visitors who hanker for the old-fashioned color of a traditional patronal fiesta should be sure to arrive in Puerto Escondido by December 8, when seemingly the whole town takes part in the fiesta of the **Virgen de la Soledad.** Besides being the patron saint of the state of Oaxaca, the Virgen de la Soledad is also protectress of fishermen. To honor her, around 3pm the whole town accompanies the Virgin by boat out to the bay's far reach, and then returns with her to the church plaza for dancing, fireworks, and bullfights.

If you can't be in Puerto Escondido in time to honor the Virgin in December, perhaps you may be able enjoy either Puerto Escondido's **Carnaval** or take a day trip a couple of hours west of Puerto Escondido. There, at **Pinotepa Nacional** (or one of the small towns nearby) you can enjoy the traditionally colorful native Carnaval fiestas with parades, fireworks, and masked traditional dances, on the weekend before Ash Wednesday, the beginning of Lent.

SPORTS AND RECREATION
Surfing, Snorkeling, and Scuba Diving

Although surfing is *de rigueur* for the skilled in Puerto Escondido, beginners usually learn by starting out with bodysurfing and boogie boarding. Boogie boards and surfboards are for sale and rent ($10/day) at a few shops along the *adoquín* and Zicatela beach. The most experienced shop is **Central Surf** (on Zicatela, by the Bungalows Acuario, tel. 954/582-2285, www.centralsurfshop.com, 9am-9pm daily). Beginners with boogie boards and body surfers should not, however, swim or paddle out in big waves at Zicatela. These waves are not for play unless you are a surfing master. Beginners and surfers of intermediate skill levels can go to Carrizalillo to practice or take lessons. Though not for beginners when there is a big swell, La Punta, at the calmer east end of Zicatela, is also an easier wave to manage for intermediate surfers, and beginners as well when the swell is small.

Beginners practice on the gentler billows of **Playa Principal** and adjacent **Playa Marinero,** while advanced surfers go for the powerful waves of **Playa Zicatela,** which regularly slam foolhardy inexperienced surfers onto the sand with backbreaking force.

Local aficionados organize spontaneous **surfing tournaments** during the summer-fall surfing season, when the surf happens to be up. For information, it's best to contact friendly **Gina Machorro** (on the *adoquín,* west end, beach side, tel. 954/582-0276 or 954/582-1186, ginainpuerto@yahoo.com), who staffs the Avenida Pérez Gasga information booth.

Clear blue-green waters, coral reefs, and swarms of multicolored fish make for good local snorkeling and diving, especially in little **Puerto Ángelito** and **Carrizalillo** bays just west of town. A number of *adoquín* stores sell serviceable resort-grade snorkeling equipment. Beginners can also learn to surf or boogie board in the gentle waves of Carrizalillo.

A professional dive shop, **Aventura**

Submarina (Av. Pérez Gasga 601 A, local cell tel. 954/582-2353, asubmarina@yahoo.com. mx, 9am-2pm daily), at the *adoquín* west end, has gained a foothold in Puerto Escondido. It's run by welcoming veteran PADI instructor Jorge Pérez Bravo. The introductory lesson, including two offshore dives, runs about $80, including equipment. For certified openwater divers (bring your certificate), a onetank night dive costs about $65; a one-tank day dive, about $60.

Alternately, check out equally professional **Puerto Dive Center** (a block farther east on Av. Pérez Gasga, across from the Libertad steps, tel. 954/582-3421, www.puertodivecenter.com). They offer a beginner's lesson and dive, $70; certificated one- and two-tank dives, $60 and $80 respectively; open water certification, $320; and snorkeling $25.

Sportfishing

Puerto Escondido's offshore waters abound with fish. Launches go out mornings from Playa Principal and routinely return with an assortment including big tuna, mackerel, snapper, sea bass, and snook. The sheltered west side of the beach is calm enough to easily launch a mobile boat with the help of usually-willing beach hands.

The local **Sociedad Cooperativa Turística Nueva Punta Escondida** (tel. 954/582-1678, www.puertoescondidoinfo. com/pefishing.html or www.tomzap.com/ pe-coop.html), which parks its boats right on Playa Principal, regularly takes fishing parties of three or four out for about $25 an hour, including bait and tackle. Check with boat workers right on the beach, or at their Restaurant Pescador, at the west end of the main town beach (where they will cook up a dinner of the fish you catch).

Individual captains also offer sportfishing excursions. Check out highly recommended **Capitán Carlos Guma** (tel. 954/582-1303, guerra445@hotmail.com, $25/hour with four-hour minimum). He has a 25-foot boat, fine for catching big, fine-eating *dorado* (mahi mahi), tuna, and *pez gallo* (roosterfish).

Alternatively **Omar's Sportfishing** (local cell tel. 044-954/559-4406, omarsportfishing-1@hotmail.com) offers fishing excursions, for about the same prices, with bait and tackle included. You can find Omar on the beach at Puerto Ángelito.

Additionally, travel agencies, such as the reliable **Viajes Dimar** (Av. Pérez Gasga 905, tel. 954/582-0734 or 954/582-1551, in Zicatela tel. 954/582-2305, viajesdimar@hotmail.com), arrange fishing trips and much more.

Eco-Projects

Locally-grown ecological efforts well worth visiting are the two reptile sanctuaries east of Puerto Escondido.

Another local eco-project is the famously successful **turtle sanctuary at Playa Escobillo** (Hwy. 200, Kilometer 181, cell tel. 044-958/587-9882 or 958/589-5908, santuarioescobillo@yahoo.com), about 32 kilometers (20 mi) east of Puerto Escondido. There, a cadre of SEMARNAT (Secretariat of Marine Natural Resources) professionals and volunteers are rescuing, hatching, and returning baby turtles to the ocean. Over the past 20 years, they have helped many hundreds of thousands of baby turtles. They welcome visitors with tours ($10 pp), a restaurant, campground (tent $10 for two), and rustic beachfront- *cabaña* lodging ($20-25 d).

Halfway back from Playa Escobillo to Puerto Escondido, a lovely **bird-watching estuary** lies at the mouth of the Río Colotepec. A small, locally-run restaurant, La Luna Azul, provides a great spot from which to watch some 37 species of local birds and a couple of dozen migratory species, including the fabulous, and famously pink, roseate spoonbill. Though the trail system was badly damaged by Hurricane Carlotta in 2012, hikes through the mangrove swamps are still possible. For access to the Colotepec estuary, take a *colectivo* from Highway 200 marked Barra de Navidad; if you're driving, follow the signs to Barra de Navidad. If you take the *colectivo*, you'll have a 30-40 minute walk from the bus stop.

A few miles east of the rivermouth, and best accessed by car, lies the **Laguna Palma Sola,** where visitors are invited to view some of the over 350 crocodiles (last count) living in the lagoon. View them from non-motorized watercraft with guides from a local cooperative of indigenous families. This co-op works with various national commissions to ensure the preservation of the ecosystem, and to create ecotourism as a viable economic basis for these local indigenous peoples. Look for the Embarcadero Palma Sola sign along the road. After the tour, a fresh fish lunch can be had at La Ballena, the co-op's beachfront restaurant. New cabins have recently been constructed; check for prices and availability on arrival.

Barra de Navidad is also home to an **Iguana Sanctuary** (left side of the road into La Barra, tel. 954/544-1551, donations requested, not required) operated by a gentleman named Don Galo and his family. He also has crocodiles, parrots, snakes, turtles, and other critters under his protection, all of which visitors are welcome to view.

Meditation and Massage

Healing is the mission of partners Patricia Heuze and Alejandro Villanuevo, who operate **Villa Temazcalli** (Av. Infragante, tel. 954/582-1023, www.temazcalli.com) meditation and massage center, on the southeast end of town, past the army barracks, two blocks uphill from the highway. Facilities include rustic hot baths, an indigenous-style *temazcal,* and massage room in an invitingly tranquil tropical garden setting. Prices run about $55 each for massage and the hot tub, and about $25 for one, $50 for two, and $60 for three, for the *temazcal.*

SHOPPING
Market and Handicrafts

As in most Mexican towns, the place to begin your Puerto Escondido shopping is the local *mercado* (Av. 10 Norte), one long block west of the big electric transformer station on upper Avenida Oaxaca. Although produce occupies most of the space, a number of stalls at the south end offer authentic handicrafts. These might include Guerrero painted pottery animals; San Bartolo Coyotepec black pottery; masks from Guerrero and Oaxaca with jaguar, devil, and scary human-animal motifs; the endearing multicolored pottery animals from Iguala and Zitlala in Guerrero; and beautiful crocheted *huipiles* from San Pedro Amusgos.

Back downhill on the *adoquín,* the prices

fruit stall in Puerto Escondido

increase along with the selection. Perhaps the most fruitful time and place for handicraft shopping is during the cooler evenings, within the illuminated cluster of crafts stalls just beyond the *adoquín* east-end. Among the finest bargains that, with effort, you will find are the gorgeous handwoven rugs and serapes from Teotitlán del Valle and Santa Ana del Valle near Oaxaca City. The highest-quality examples are the most tightly woven—typically about 20 strands per centimeter (50 per inch).

Oaxaca's venerable gold jewelry tradition is well represented at the very professional **Oro de Monte Albán** (*adoquín* west end, by Restaurant Junto del Mar, tel. 954/582-0530, 10am-2pm and 6:30pm-10:30pm Mon.-Sat.). They have authentic museum-grade replicas of the celebrated Mixtec trove discovered in Monte Albán's Tomb 7.

Next door, the Uribe silversmithing family well represents Taxco tradition at its **Plateria Ixtlán** (*adoquín* west end, tel. 954/582-1672, 10am-10pm Mon.-Sat.). Choose from a host of fetching floral, animal, and abstract designs, in silver and turquoise, garnet, jade, and other semiprecious stones.

ACCOMMODATIONS

With a few exceptions, the successful hotels in Puerto Escondido are appropriate to the town itself: small, moderately priced, and near the water. They dot the beachfront from Playa Zicatela around the bay and continue up Avenida Pérez Gasga to the highway. Most are either on the beach or within a stone's throw of it, which makes sense, because it seems a shame to come all the way to Puerto Escondido and not stay where you can soak up all the scenery.

Rates for the hotels are listed in ascending order of customary low season room rates. These prices, unless noted, are in effect most of the year, except for **high season** (Christmas-New Year's, Easter, some long weekend holidays, and sometimes July and August), when they may rise 10-30 percent, depending upon availability.

Avenida Pérez Gasga-*Adoquín*
UNDER $50

Moving downhill, from the highway, first find the immaculate, best-buy ★ **Hotel San Juan** (Felipe Merklin 503, tel. 954/582-0518, tel./fax 954/582-0612, www.sanjuanhotel.com.mx, $32 per room). For those who like saving money and don't mind (or would enjoy) a 10-minute downhill walk to the beach, this is the place. Rooms, in four levels, enclose an intimate inner pool patio. They are invitingly furnished with wall paintings, reading lamps, and color-coordinated drapes and bedspreads. Amenities include private hot-water shower-baths, fans, Wi-Fi, morning coffee, a restaurant, and parking. For a splurge, add $13 for air-conditioning with a luxuriously private ocean-view balcony.

The popular **Hotel Loren** (Av. Pérez Gasga 507, tel. 954/582-0057, $38 s or d, $41 t or q), just two blocks uphill from the beach, offers approximately 30 rooms spread through two three-story buildings. Guests in the front-building rooms enjoy private ocean-view balconies. (However, all rooms, especially the bathrooms, could use a good scrubbing.) The good news is the hotel's inviting blue pool patio and the short five-minute walk to the beach. Reserve a *cuarto con vista* ("a room with a view") in the front building. Reservations are often necessary, especially in the winter. The rooms are basic but comfortable. Add $10 for air-conditioning; parking is available and credit cards are accepted.

$50-100

Tucked in its own corner, away from the tourist mall bustle, the compact ★ **Le P'tit Hotel** (at the west-end intersection of Soledad and the *adoquín*, tel. 954/582-3178, www.oaxaca-mio.com/leptit.htm, $50 s or d a/c, $10 per extra person) offers an attractive lodging option. Personable, French-born owner-builder Michel Kobryn offers 18 rooms and thatched South Seas-style bungalows, all lovingly adorned with colorful tile, original wall art, decorator reading lamps, and sparkling bathrooms. Amenities include cable TV, restaurant, wireless Internet, and an inviting small pool patio; credit cards are accepted.

Back uphill, two blocks below the highway on a short side street off Avenida Pérez Gasga, is the **Hotel Paraíso Escondido** (Calle Union 1, tel. 954/582-0444, fax 954/582-2767, www.hotelpe.com, $57 s or d, suite $65). A tranquil colonial-chic refuge, the hotel abounds in traditional artistic touches—Mixtec stone glyphs, tiny corner chapels, stained glass, and Old-World antiques—blended into the lobby, corridors, and patios. The two levels of rooms nestle around a spacious pool and restaurant patio. The rooms themselves are large, with view balconies, designer tile bathrooms, wrought-iron fixtures, and handcrafted wooden furniture. The 24 rooms include air-conditioning, pool, kiddie pool, and parking, but credit cards are not accepted.

Playa Zicatela

Beach lovers and surfing enthusiasts enjoy staying on Playa Zicatela, the creamy strand that stretches east and south of the busy *adoquín.* Here, folks relax in street-side cafés and restaurants and stroll and sun on the beach as they watch the surfers conquer (or try to conquer) Zicatela's awesome waves.

UNDER $50

Back at the beginning of Playa Zicatela's north-end, find ★ **Bungalows Acali** (Av. del Morro, tel. 954/582-0754, casadanycarmen@escondido.com.mx, $32 s, $35 d, $40 t, $55 with a/c). Here, a small colony of rustic *cabañas* clusters around a blue pool in a banana, palm, and mango mini-jungle. The *cabañas* themselves, like a vision out of a South Seas tale, are built with walls made of sticks and sturdy plank floors, raised above ground level. Rentals are clean, fan-equipped, with mosquito nets and good bathrooms. Rooms have a fan or air-conditioning, a hot-water shower, and a small refrigerator; parking is available and credit cards are accepted.

Additionally, Bungalows Acali offers three rustic hammock-hung, sunset-view

kitchenette bungalows ($45 for 1-4 guests, fan only; $70 with a/c) perched on its leafy bamboo- and mango-decorated hillside.

About two long blocks south down the beach, **Beach Hotel Inés** (Av. del Morro, tel. 954/582-0416 or 954/582-0792, info@hotelines.com, $25-120 d) is the life project of German expatriate Peter Voss and his daughter, Inés. Their 45 units occupy the palmy periphery of a lush, pool-café-garden layout, which climaxes with an attractive, stuccoed, two-story complex of rooms at the backside. Most of the rentals are hotel-style rooms, in deluxe and super-deluxe grades, with clean, light interiors, comfortable furnishings, and well-maintained bathrooms. They rent four levels of accommodation, from smallish, but comfortable, hotel-style rooms, to larger *cabañas,* deluxe apartments, and large super-deluxe suites.

It's easy to miss the ★ **Hotel Flor de María** (at Primera Entrada Playa Marinero, Colonia Marinero, tel. 954/582-0536, fax 954/582-2617, www.mexonline.com/flordemaria.htm, $45 d), tucked on a quiet side street above east-side Playa Marinero. Rooms rise in two stories around a tranquil, leafy interior patio. At rooftop, a breezy sundeck-bar, with a small but inviting pool and a hammock-hung *palapa,* overlooks a beach-and-bay vista. The approximately dozen immaculate deluxe rooms each have two double beds, hot-water shower-baths, and Wi-Fi. Additionally, the hotel offers a pair of spacious 2nd-floor ocean-view suites and a very good restaurant.

$50-100

Head about three blocks south along Avenida del Morro, which runs along Playa Zicatela, to the three-story **Hotel Arco Iris** (Av. del Morro, Colonia Marinero, tel./fax 954/582-1494 or 954/582-0432, www.hotel-arcoiris.com.mx, $70 s or d). A shady green garden surrounds the hotel, leading to a gorgeous rear pool and patio. The Arco Iris's proximity to the famous Puerto Escondido "pipeline" draws both surfers and surf-watchers to the

3rd-floor restaurant La Galera, which seems equally ideal for wave-watching at breakfast and sky-watching at sunset.

OVER $100

Puerto Escondido's class-act hostelry is the ★ **Hotel Santa Fe** (Av. del Morro, Playa Marinero, tel. 954/582-0170 or 954/582-0266, fax 954/582-0265, from U.S. toll-free tel. 888/649-6407, Mex. toll-free tel. 800/712-7057, www.hotelsantafe.com.mx, $113-260 d). Built in pleasing neocolonial style, with gracefully curving staircases, palm-shaded pool patios, and flower-decorated walkways, the Santa Fe achieves an ambience both intimate and luxuriously private. Its refined but relaxed restaurant, wonderful for morning ocean-view breakfasts, serves a delicious menu, featuring a number of traditional Oaxacan specialties.

The accommodations—spacious, high-ceilinged, and comfortable—are appointed with hand-painted tile, rustic wood furniture, and regional handicrafts. Moreover, the newest room wing has enhanced the hotel's ambience, with an airy and tranquil elevated-view pool-patio that connects gracefully with the original hotel section. The approximately 50 accommodations come in standard, junior, and master-suite grades; there are also 10 kitchenette bungalows that sleep four (kids under 12 are free). All accommodations come with air-conditioning, phones, parking, and credit cards accepted, but no TV.

Apartments and Long-Term Rentals

If you're planning on a stay of two weeks or more, you may be able to save money and yet have all the comforts of home in an apartment rental. Look over the classifieds in the English-Spanish newspaper *El Sol de la Costa* (tel./fax 954/582-2230, www.elsoldelacosta.com), edited by Warren Sharpe.

Alternatively, for rentals, you might also contact Nolan Van Way, of **PEP Realty** (tel. 954/582-0085, www.pep-realty.com). Try AirBnB and/or VRBO.com as well; both of these websites have dozens of Puerto Escondido rentals available.

Trailer Parks, Camping, and Hostels

Occasional muggings and robberies on the beach have eliminated virtually all camping on Puerto Escondido beaches (with the possible exception of Easter week, when such large crowds flock into town that they spill onto the beaches).

Nevertheless, beachfront camping space is available in the small, palm-shaded trailer park, once closed but now re-opened, **Palmas de Cortés** (east side of Puerto Escondido's Playa Principal, tel. 954/582-3234, cortes@ptoescondido.com.mx, $15-25 for RVs, $5 pp for tents), by the crafts stalls, half a block downhill by the beach. Facilities include security fence, a guard at night, brand-new showers and toilets, hook-ups, and room for about a dozen RVs and maybe some tents.

A good alternative for tenters and hostelers is **Shalom Hostel** (on the east end of Av. Benito Juárez, tel. 954/582-3234, www.hostalshalom.com, $7 pp tents, $17 pp *cabañas*, $6 pp dorms), in the Rinconada subdivision, west side of town. Besides tenting in their shady, green, back garden, with heavenly pool-patio, they offer rustic *cabañas* with shared baths and dorm beds. There's a snack restaurant and parking out front. Proximity to Playa Crazalillo is an added amenity.

For a central location, the best hostel-type choice seems to be **Hotel and Youth Hostel Mayflower** (Andador Libertad, tel. 954/582-0367, fax 954/582-0422, www.tomzap.com/mayflower.html, rooms $35 d, $9 pp dorms). Find it half a block uphill on Andador Libertad, the stair-stepped walkway a block east of the *adoquín*'s west end. Here you can choose from 14 plain but clean hotel rooms with bath, or hostel dorm beds. Extras include communal kitchen, in-house Internet, and lots of local information.

Alternatively, nearby, you might consider the smaller, bare-bones but clean **Hostal Puerto Escondido** (Andador Libertad, tel.

954/582-3455, www.mexonline.com/pehostal. htm, $5 pp), also on Andador Libertad, within a block of the *adoquín*. Facilities (communal kitchen and Internet access) are spare, but the price is right.

FOOD
Breakfast and Snacks

In the mornings, you can enjoy breakfast with the baked offerings from the **patisserie** (Playa Zicatela, south end, next to Bungalows Acuario, no phone, 7am-9pm daily), where you can savor a cappuccino as you watch the surfers conquering the waves.

Baguettería Vivaldi (middle of beachfront Av. Pérez Gasga, across the street from the Hotel Casa Blanca, tel. 954/582-0800, 7:30am-11pm daily) is the labor of love of friendly Jenny Sinnhuber, who, besides lots of homemade bread, serves a wide selection of delicious breakfasts, and sandwiches for lunch.

You can also get your day started right with breakfast, while watching the beachfront scene, at either airy patio **Restaurant Danny's** (at Hotel Rincón del Pacífico, Av. Pérez Gasga 900, tel. 954/582-0056 or 954/582-0193, www.rincondelpacifico. mx, $4-15), or **Restaurant Los Crotos** (on the *adoquín*, west end, tel. 954/582-0025, 8am-11pm daily, $4-20), a block from the end of the beach.

Upper Town and *Adoquín*

Many of Puerto Escondido's good restaurants line the *adoquín*. One major exception is immaculate, strictly home-cooking-style ★ **Margaritas** (Ave. 8 Norte, few doors east of Calle 2 Poniente, tel. 954/582-0212, 8am-6pm daily, $6-12, set lunch $3.50), where all you need is to love good Mexican food. Find it in the upper town, near the market. Although the long country menu, including eggs in several styles, tacos, tamales, quesadillas, fish and shrimp any style, and broiled steaks reveals nothing unusual, everything arrives to your table delicious. The day's main event is the *comida corrida* (set lunch). The set lunch includes an entrée (for example, savory beef or pork *guisado* stew, or mole chicken, or chiles rellenos); dessert; and drink, chosen from a half dozen delicious fruit *aguas* (strawberry, lemonade, melon, orange, and more).

Among three longstanding restaurants on the *adoquín*, west end block, where the main beach begins, is **Restaurant La Galería** (on the inland side, tel. 954/582-2039, 8am-11pm daily, $5-14), which usually has customers even when most other eateries are empty. The reason is the excellent Italian fare—crusty, hot pizzas, rich pastas and lasagna, bountiful salads, and satisfying soups—which the European-expatriate owner puts out for her batallion of loyal customers.

For a refined beachfront option, try the excellent, **Restaurant Junto del Mar** (Beside the Sea; *adoquín*, west end, tel./fax 954/582-1803, 7:30am-11pm daily, $12-15). The menu offers good breakfasts plus many delectable lunch and dinner options. Breakfasts include rich bottomless coffee, fresh fruit, omelets, and French toast. Lunch and dinner specialties include shrimp-stuffed fillets, lobster and shrimp brochettes, and whole garlic-stuffed fish. Mornings are brightened by the always-changing beach scene; in the evenings, the setting turns romantic, with soft candlelight and strumming guitars. Credit cards are accepted.

Start the day off right: Go for breakfast at beachfront **Restaurant Los Crotos** (*adoquín*, a block from the end of the beach, tel. 954/582-0025, 8am-11pm daily, $4-20) and sit at shaded tables, enjoying the fascinating morning scene. (The restaurant is named for its lovely garden of reddish Crotos plants, famously known in Hawaii as *ti*.) Later, at lunch and dinner, the attractively-presented and delicious house specialties of jumbo shrimp, broiled lobster, and super-fresh *huachinango* (snapper) and *robalo* seem like an added bonus.

At the *adoquín* east end, some local Italian resident entrepreneurs have founded a modest spaghetti and pizza gourmet ghetto. In some cases, the results are excellent. For example, be sure to try the tasty creations of owner-chef Bendito, at his completely unpretentious

★ **Restaurant Bendito** (*adoquín* east end, no phone, 8am-midnight daily, $7-14). Bring a group of people and enjoy sampling his delicious Napoli-style specialties, such as spaghetti puttanesca, spinach raviolis, mushroom fettuccine, and pizza *zavarieta*.

A few doors farther east, restaurant **András** (*adoquín* east end, tel. 954/582-1534, 4:30pm-11pm daily, $8) is another good Italian option. In a romantic atmosphere of soothing Italian melodies and gently whirring ceiling fans, the owner-chef offers a long and varied menu, featuring plenty of good pizza, but also salads (such as, *mixta* with ham), pasta (such as spinach-stuffed raviolis or fettucini de András), and desserts (like the lemon pie).

Playa Zicatela

If you have dinner at the restaurant of the ★ **Hotel Santa Fe** (Av. del Morro, Zicatela side of the bay, tel. 954/582-0170, 7:30am-11pm daily, $9-11), you may never go anywhere else. Savory food, impeccably served beneath a luxurious ocean-view *palapa*, with evenings accompanied by softly strumming guitars, brings travelers from all over the world. Although everything on the menu is delicious, the restaurant is proudest of its Mexican favorites, such as rich tortilla soup, bountiful plates of chiles rellenos, and succulent snapper, Veracruz style.

Restaurant Mangos (farther south on Playa Zicatela, next to Hotel Acuario, tel. 954/582-3805, 8am-midnight daily, $7) packs in a steady stream of youthful customers, with a long menu of innovative breakfasts (crepes, three-egg omelets), salads (plenty of alfalfa sprouts), sandwiches (*cuerno*, large horn croissant), and Mexican specialties (fish-stuffed chiles rellenos).

Farther south, **Restaurant El Cafecito** (a few blocks down the Zicatela beachfront on Av. Del Morro, tel. 954/582-0516, 6:30am-10pm daily, $5-10) is headquarters for a loyal platoon of local surfers and Canadian and American residents who crowd in for bountiful breakfasts, hamburgers, and fresh seafood plates. (Unfortunately, Cafecito's popularity is both a boon and a burden; the customer crowd is sometimes simply too large and noisy for both comfort and good service.)

INFORMATION AND SERVICES

Tourist Information Offices

Most months of the year, Gina Machorro staffs an **information booth** (on the *adoquín*, west end, beach side, tel. 954/582-1186 or 954/582-0276, ginainpuerto@yahoo.com, 9am-2pm and 4pm-6pm Mon.-Fri.). Gina also gives a **walking tour** of Puerto Escondido, including the Puerto Escondido archaeological zone.

Otherwise, you can consult the well-informed staff at the *oficina de turismo* (tel./fax 954/582-0175, 8am-3pm Mon.-Fri.), who distribute a map of Oaxaca. They are located just off Highway 200, in the little office on the beach side of the highway, a couple of blocks east of the airport Pemex gas station.

Travel Agent

One of the most respected travel agents in town is **Viajes Dimar** (Av. Pérez Gasga 905, tel. 954/582-0734 or 954/582-1551, in Zicatela tel. 954/582-2305, viajesdimar@hotmail.com). They offer a wide range of travel services, especially ecotours, air and bus tickets, fishing excursions, and more.

Health and Emergencies

If you need a doctor, go to the private hospital, **Sanatorio del Carmen** (Calle 3 Poniente, between Calles 2 and 3 Norte, tel. 954/582-1876 or 954/582-0174), three blocks west of the *crucero*, uphill from the highway. There are a number of doctors on call, including general practitioners and specialists, such as a pediatrician, family medicine doctor, an opthamologist, and an internist, plus a pathology laboratory.

Another medical option is the 24-hour government *centro de salud* (Av. Pérez Gasga, tel. 954/582-2360), below the Hotel Nayar, by Banamex.

Get over-the-counter remedies and

prescriptions at one of the good tourist-zone pharmacies, such as the 24-hour **Farmacia La Moderna** (Av. Pérez Gasga, tel. 954/582-0698, 24 hours daily) of Dr. José Luis Esparzar, a block below the *crucero.*

For police emergencies, call the **municipal police** (Hwy. 200, tel. 954/582-0498); ride a taxi to the headquarters in the Agencia Municipal on Highway 200, about four blocks west of the Avenida Pérez Gasga *crucero.* Alternatively, contact the **state tourist police** (*adoquín,* west side, tel. 954/582-0721) at the Libertad steps. For fire emergencies, call the *bomberos* (cell tel. 044-954/104-2494) or the police.

Publications, Library, and Movies

One of the few local outlets of English-language newspapers or magazines in Puerto Escondido is **Publicaciones Fabian** (corner of main-street Av. Oaxaca and Calle 1 Norte, tel. 954/582-1334, 8am-9pm Mon.-Sat.) in the uphill town. Usually available are the daily Mexico City *News* and magazines such as *Time, Newsweek,* and *Scientific American,* and maybe some new paperback novels.

The local English-Spanish newspaper, *El Sol de la Costa,* provides a load of useful information, including community events listings, informative cultural features, emergency numbers, apartment rental listings, and many service advertisements. Pick up a free copy in one of its many advertiser-businesses along the *adoquín.* If you can't find a copy, contact editor Warren Sharpe (tel. 954/582-2230, elsol@escondido.com.mx, 9:30am-4pm Mon.-Fri., 9:30am-2pm Sat.).

English-language books are available at many hotels, plus at least three spots in Puerto Escondido. On Playa Zicatela, browse the used-paperback **Book Exchange** (at Casa Babylon, next to the Bungalows Acuario) as well as the collection at **Cine Mar** (also on Playa Zicatela, no phone, 10am-11pm Thurs.-Tues.).

Cine Mar's friendly proprietor, Dove Sussman, lives out his bliss by also renting,

selling, and screening videos. Three screenings, of hits such as *Inception, True Grit,* and *Social Network,* begin at 7pm daily.

Furthermore, a **lending library** (in the west-side Rinconada district, on east-west Av. Benito Juárez, contact Sheila Clarke tel. 954/582-0276; 10am-2pm Mon., Wed., and Sat., high season; 10am-noon Wed. and Sat, low season) is maintained by the International Friends of Puerto Escondido (IFOPE).

Money Exchange

Banamex (Av. Pérez Gasga 314, tel. 954/582-0626, 9am-4pm Mon.-Fri., 10am-2pm Sat.), with ATM, uphill from the Hotel Nayar, changes U.S. and Canadian cash and travelers checks. Moreover, **HSBC** (Av. 1 Norte in the upper town, tel. 954/542-1825, 8am-5pm Mon.-Sat.) also changes money.

After bank hours, a small *casa de cambio* (no phone, 8am-8pm Mon.-Sat.), on Playa Zicatela, next to Viajes Dimar, changes U.S., Canadian, and Euro currency and travelers checks.

Communications

The *correo* (Av. 7 Norte, tel. 954/582-0959, 8am-3pm Mon.-Fri., 9am-1pm Sat.) and *telégrafo* (Av. 7 Norte, tel./fax 954/582-0232, 8am-7:30pm Mon.-Sat., 9am-noon Sun.) stand side by side on Avenida 7 Norte, at the corner of Avenida Oaxaca, seven blocks into upper town from the *crucero.*

For local and long-distance telephone, buy a Ladatel public telephone card at one of several *adoquín* stores and use it in street telephones. First dial 001 for calls to the United States and Canada, and 01 for long-distance calls within Mexico.

On Playa Zicatela, use either the public street phones, or the public long-distance telephone at the desk of the Bungalows Acuario.

Beware of certain prominently situated "Call Home Collect" or "Call Home with Your Credit Card" telephones. Tariffs on these phones can run $10 or more per minute, with a three-minute minimum, costing $30 whether you talk three minutes or not.

Ask the operator for the rate; if it's too high, take your business elsewhere.

Internet connection, fax, and long-distance telephone are available at **Coffee Net** (*adoquín*, tel. 954/582-0797, 11am-10:30pm daily), in the middle of the *adoquín*. Also, on Playa Zicatela, Internet access is available at the store next to the Bungalows Acuario (tel. 954/582-0788, 9am-11pm daily). Most hotels these days offer in-house Wi-Fi, although you might have to hang around the lobby to get a signal.

Laundry

Get your laundry done at either **Lavandería Pérez Gasga** (Av. Pérez Gasga, no phone, 8am-8pm Mon.-Sat., 8am-5pm Sun.) by Banamex, about two blocks uphill from the west-end chain; or **Lavandería Playa** (on Playa Zicatela, next to Casa Babylon, tel. 954/582-1542, 9am-10pm Mon.-Sat.).

Groceries

At the east end of the *adoquin,* on the inland side, **Abarrotes Lupita** (10am-11pm daily), a fairly well-stocked small grocery, sells meat, milk, ice, and vegetables. Out on Playa Zicatela, a few stores, such as **Abarrotes Merlin** (tel. 954/582-1130, 8am-11:30pm daily), offer a modest grocery and wine selection.

Photography

On Playa Zicatela, **Centro Photografico** (tel. 954/582-3307, 9am-9pm Mon.-Sat., 10am-7pm Sun.) offers a modest selection of film, cameras, accessories, and color and black-and-white developing and printing services.

Spanish Instruction

The very experienced **Puerto Escondido Language Institute** (tel. 954/582-2055, www.puertoschool.com) offers private or group lessons, homestays, tours, rock climbing, and more, across the highway from Cruz Azul cement store, above Playa Zicatela.

Newcomer **Centro de Idiomas Agua Marí** (Agua Zarca 210, tel. 954/582-0321, www.callilanguageschool.com) offers a very professional and flexible menu of both individual and group Spanish instruction. Find it in the upper town, two blocks west of the market.

TRANSPORTATION
Air

The small jetport, officially the **Aeropuerto Puerto Escondido** (code-designated PXM), is just off the highway a mile west of town. The terminal, consisting of a plain waiting room with check-in desks, has no services save a small bar and snack counter. Out in front, *colectivos* ($3 pp) shuttle people to hotels in town. Arrivees with a minimum of luggage, however, can walk a block to the highway and flag down one of the many eastbound local *colectivos,* which all stop at the main town highway crossing. Arrive with a hotel in mind (better yet a hotel reservation in hand), unless you prefer letting your taxi driver choose one, where he will probably collect a commission for depositing you there.

Although car rental agents do not ordinarily meet flights, they will meet you if you have a reservation. Contact **Budget** (tel. 954/582-0312 or 954/582-0315, budget33@hotmail.com).

If you lose your tourist card, avoid trouble or a fine by taking your passport and some proof of your arrival date (such as a stamped passport, a copy of your lost tourist card, or an air ticket) to **Migración** (at the airport, tel. 954/582-3369), for help *before* your day of departure.

A few regularly scheduled flights connect Puerto Escondido with other Mexican destinations.

Up-and-coming **Aeromar** airlines (tel. 954/582-0977, in Mexico toll-free tel. 800/237-6627, www.aeromar.com.mx) connects daily with Mexico City.

Alternatively, you can try experienced, local, air-taxi service **Aerovega** (tel./fax 954/582-0151; in Oaxaca City tel. 951/515-4982, www.oaxaca-mio.com/aerovega.htm), which connects with Oaxaca City.

You can also fly with reliable charter airline **Aerotucan** (tel./fax 954/582-3461; in Oaxaca City tel. 951/502-0532 or 951/502-0840, tel. 951/501-0530 or 951/502-0532, or toll-free Mex. tel. 800/640-4148, www.aerotucan.com.mx), which routinely runs Oaxaca-Puerto Escondido flights, depending upon passenger demand.

Puerto Escondido is also accessible via the Huatulco airport, one hour east by road.

Bus

Several long-distance bus lines serve Puerto Escondido from two separate bus stations: the mostly first-class **Autobuses del Oriente** (ADO) terminal on Highway 200, and the (first- and second-class) Puerto Escondido **Camionera Central** (central bus station) on Highway 131, uphill, a mile beyond the north edge of town.

At the latter, **Estrella Blanca** (tel. 951/582-0086) and subsidiary lines (luxury and first-class Futura and Elite and others) travel the Highway 200 Acapulco-Isthmus route. More than two dozen daily *salidas de paso* (buses that travel long distances with many stops along the way) come through en route both ways between Ixtapa-Zihuatanejo, Acapulco and Pochutla, Huatulco (Crucecita), and Salina Cruz. Additionally, a few departures also connect north to Mexico City, via Acapulco.

Cooperating lines **Autobúses Estrella del Valle** and **Autotransportes Oaxaca Pacífico** (tel. 954/582-0050) provide both first- and second-class connections east to Pochutla, thence north, connecting to Oaxaca City and Mexico City, via Highway 175.

Both **Autobúses Estrella Roja del Sureste** (tel. 954/582-0875) and **Linea Dorada,** formerly La Solteca, second-class bus lines connect north with Oaxaca City (with some departures via pilgrimage town Juquila) along Highway 131 direct from Puerto Escondido.

An additional pair of second-class bus lines, **Transportes Oaxaca-Istmo** and **Fletes y Pasajes,** connect east, via Highway 200, with Pochutla, Huatulco (Crucecita), Salina Cruz, Tehuántepec, and Juchitán.

Operating from the bright, new, steel-and-glass **ADO bus terminal** (tel. 954/582-1073, on Hwy. 200, half a block west of the *crucero* signal), **Autobuses del Oriente** (ADO) and cooperating bus lines **Cristóbal Colón** (OCC), intermediate-class **Sur,** and second-class **Ecobus** provide broad service east, northeast, north, and northwest.

Luxury-class ADO GL express buses connect east with Salina Cruz, thence north via Acayucan on the Gulf Coast, all the way to Veracruz.

First-class OCC buses connect with the Isthmus, via Highway 200 with the Oaxaca east coast and Isthmus, connecting all the way east with Tuxtla Gutiérrez and San Cristóbal las Casas in Chiapas and Tapachula, at the Guatemala border, and with the Gulf of Mexico destinations of Coatzacoalcos and Veracruz, northwest, and Villahermosa, northwest. Intermediate OCC destinations include Pochutla, Huatulco (Crucecita), and Salina Cruz. At Huatulco and Salina Cruz, passengers can transfer to Cristobal Colón Oaxaca City-bound buses. At Oaxaca City, at least one of these continues, northwest, via Puebla, to Mexico City (both Tapo and Norte terminals).

Intermediate-class SUR connects east with Pochutla, and Huatulco, thence Isthmus destinations of Salina Cruz, Tehuántepec, and Juchitán.

Second-class Ecobus connects east, via Pochutla and Huatulco, with Tehuántepec and Juchitán, thence north with Minatitlan and Villahermosa on the Gulf of Mexico.

Car or RV

National Highway 200, although sometimes winding, is generally smooth and uncongested between Puerto Escondido and Pinotepa Nacional (143 km/89 mi, 2.5 hours) to the west. From there, continue another 258 kilometers (160 mi, 4.5 hours) to Acapulco.

Traffic sails between Puerto Escondido and Puerto Ángel, 71 kilometers (44 mi) apart, in an easy hour. (Actually, Pochutla is immediately on Highway 200; Puerto Ángel is an additional six miles to the right, downhill from the Pochutla junction.) Puerto Ángel is alternatively accessible via the very scenic paved shortcut, via Mazunte and Zipolite, from Highway 200, at San Antonio village, Kilometer 198. Huatulco (Crucecita) is an easy 45 kilometers (27 mi) farther east from the Pochutla junction.

To or from Oaxaca City, all paved (but sometimes potholed during the summer rainy season) National Highway 131 connects directly north, along main street Avenida Oaxaca, via its winding but spectacular 254-kilometer (158 mi) route over the pine-clad Sierra Madre del Sur. The route, which rises 7,000 feet through Chatino foothill and mountain country, can be chilly in the winter and has few services along the lonely 161-kilometer (100 mi) middle stretch between San Gabriel Mixtepec and Sola de Vega. Allow about seven hours at the wheel from Puerto Escondido, six hours the other way, from Oaxaca City. Fill up with gasoline at either end before heading out. Unleaded gasoline is consistently available only at the Sola de Vega Pemex *gasolinera* en route. (On the other hand, you could make this drive more leisurely with an overnight at the fascinating pilgrimage town of Juquila en route.)

EXCURSIONS FROM PUERTO ESCONDIDO

Whether you go independently or by escorted tour, outings away from the Puerto Escondido resort can reveal rewarding glimpses of flora and fauna, local cultures, and idyllic beaches seemingly half a world removed from the *adoquín* tourist hubbub.

Farthest afield, to the west of Puerto Escondido, are the colorful festivals, markets, and handicrafts of the indigenous Mixtec towns of **Jamiltepec** and **Pinotepa Nacional** and the crystalline beaches and wildlife-rich mangroves of the **Parque Nacional Lagunas de Chacahua.** To the

east lie the hidden beaches of **Mazunte, Zipolite,** and the picture-book **Bahía de Puerto Ángel,** with its turtle museum, au naturel sunbathing on Playa Zipolite, and very accessible off-beach snorkeling at Puerto Ángel. A bit farther beckon the nine breezy Bahías de Huatulco, ripe for swimming, scuba diving, wildlife-viewing, biking, and river rafting.

Closer at hand, especially for wildlife lovers and beachgoers, are the jungly lagoons and pristine strands of the west-side **Laguna Manialtepec,** the nearby hot spring and Chatino sacred site of **Atotonilco,** and a duo of homegrown **reptile conservation sanctuaries.**

★ Laguna Manialtepec

Sylvan, mangrove-fringed **Laguna Manialtepec,** about 10 miles west of Puerto Escondido, is a repository for Pacific Mexico wildlife. Unlike Lagunas de Chacahua, Laguna Manialtepec is relatively deep and fresh most of the year, except occasionally during the rainy season when its main source, the Río Manialtepec, breaks through its sandbar and the lagoon becomes a tidal estuary. Consequently lacking a continuous supply of ocean fry for sustained fishing, Laguna Manialtepec has been left to local people, a few Sunday visitors, and its wildlife.

Laguna Manialtepec abounds with birds. Of the hundreds of species frequenting the lagoon, 40 or 50 are often spotted in a morning outing. Among the more common are the olivaceous cormorant and its relative, the anhinga; and herons, including the tricolored, green-backed, little blue, and the black-crowned night heron. Other common species include ibis, parrots, egrets, and ducks, such as the Muscovy and the black-bellied whistling duck. Among the most spectacular are the huge great blue herons, while the most entertaining are the northern *jacanas,* or lily walkers, who scoot across lily pads as if they were the kitchen floor.

Manialtepec tours are conveniently

Laguna Manialtepec

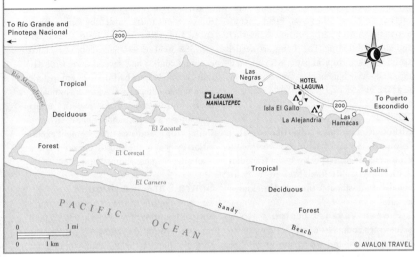

To Río Grande and
Pinotepa Nacional

© AVALON TRAVEL

arranged through travel agencies in Puerto Escondido. If, however, you prefer to organize your own Manialtepec excursion by bus or car, you might find yourself tempted to linger. Manialtepec is ripe for kayaking, boating, and RV and tent camping along its mangrove- and palm-decorated shoreline. A handful of shaded restaurant and lodging compounds along the shore offer the essentials for a week of Sundays in paradise.

ACCOMMODATIONS

About half a mile past the dormant mini-resort of Las Hamacas at the near (east) end of Laguna Manialtepec is the sleepy little family-run pocket Eden of **La Alejandria** (local cell tel. 044-954/108-3290, tents $10, RVs $15, *cabañas* $25), which nestles along its 100 yards of lakefront, shaded by palms and great spreading trees. It's so idyllic that the *Tarzan* TV series picked La Alejandria for its setting, adding a rustic lake treehouse (now destroyed by hurricanes) to the already gorgeous scene. Embellishing all this is a homey restaurant/ bar (with a long Mexican-style menu, with familiar breakfasts and lots of seafood, $3-10),

screened-in from bugs, decorated with animal trophies, and reminiscent of an old-time East African safari lodge.

La Alejandria rents about six palm-shaded RV spaces with electricity and water (be prepared with your own long extension and hose). Camping spaces are also available. In addition, they rent some rough but serviceable South Seas *cabañas* with private toilet and tepid water; check for mildew and see if everything is working before moving in, however.

Another kilometer west of La Alejandria, find lakefront restaurant and dock ★ **Isla El Gallo** (local cell tel. 044-954/107-5718), perfect for a day or a week of exploring the lagoon. Consider swimming, kayaking, bird-watching along the mangrove-decorated shoreline, launching your own canoe or boat, or hiring one of El Gallo's boat workers to take you on a lagoon excursion from the dock ($9/hr).

If you decide to linger, next door is resort-style **La Laguna** hotel (tel. 954/582-1997, fax 954/582-0335, U.S. toll-free tel. 800/528-1234, Mex. toll-free tel. 800/713-0204, www.best-western.com, $60 d), which offers 15 modern, invitingly furnished lakefront hotel rooms.

The lower rooms' windows, unfortunately, don't open for fresh air. Ask for one of the upper-floor rooms, with doors opening to private balconies and lake views. Tariffs include hot-water shower-baths, in-house Internet, and air-conditioning. The rooms are nestled around a green tropical patio, with a restaurant and lovely blue pool. A short path leads to a lake-view dock.

TOURS

Although most tours advertise so-called "ecotours," a pair of genuinely worthwhile ecotours are led, respectively, by Canadian ornithologist Michael Malone and his equally professional former student, known as Lalo.

Hidden Voyages Ecotours (www. peleewings.com, $40-65 pp per day) of the Canadian husband-wife team of Michael Malone and Joan Walker (he's an ornithologist; she's an artist-ecologist) lead unusually informative tours seasonally, December-March. Besides their excellent bird-watching and animal-viewing boat tour at Laguna Manialtepec, they also offer a Lagunas de Chacahua wildlife tour and a sunset tour. Contact them in Puerto Escondido, December 1-April 1, through the competent **Viajes Dimar travel agency** (Av. Pérez Gasga 906, tel. 954/582-0734 or 954/582-1551 or 954/582-2305, viajesdimar@hotmail.com or michael@peleewings.ca). In the off-season, contact them in Canada (tel. 519/326-5193).

Other Viajes Dimar travel agency tours include a full-day jaunt east to the turtle museum at Playa Mazunte, continuing to Playa Zipolite, where you can stop for lunch and an afternoon of snorkeling around Puerto Ángel. In the evenings, during the dark of the moon, trips can include night snorkeling ($50 pp) when algae coat everything underwater with an eerie bioluminescent glow. Additionally, they offer an all-day hiking, picnic, and swimming excursion ($50 pp; or $95 for two days, one night, minimum four persons) at a luxuriously cool mountain river and cascade in the sylvan Sierra Madre foothill jungle above Pochutla.

Alternatively, you could also try one of the excellent tours guided by very experienced and well-equipped **Lalo Tours** (tel. 954/582-3050 or 954/582-3060, www.laloecotours.com). Their several tours (full-day tours about $45 pp, half-day $25 pp) include Laguna Manialtepec bird-watching by boat or kayak; bird-watching by footpath in Laguna Manialtepec's barrier sandbar forest; an ocean sunset cruise; and a fascinating night exploration by boat of the ghostly glow of Laguna Manialtepec's phosphorescent waters.

Santa Catarina Juquila

Much of the life in the Chatino mountain town of Juquila (hoo-KEE-lah, pop. 25,000) revolves around its renowned patron, the Virgin of Juquila, the object of adoration for multitudes who begin converging on the town around the first of December.

The reason for all the hubbub is a small, frail figurine scarcely more than a foot tall, which was donated to Juquila by a priest, Father Jordán de Santa Catalina, of the neighboring town of Amialtepec, in 1713. Father Jordán feared that the image, which was already locally adored, deserved a more secure home than his rude *jacal* (thatched country house).

The love the faithful show for the Virgin of Juquila has grown over the centuries. Somehow, she strikes chords of sympathy in the hearts of Mexicans, perhaps partly because of her frailty and also because she's a simple figurine of a native woman, not unlike a pre-conquest goddess idol.

She was first revered by the Chatino people of Amialtepec during the 16th century when she resided in the town church. But in 1633, the entire town of Amialtepec burned down, and one of the sole remembrances left intact was the Virgin, who from that point forward became a symbol of hope for Chatino people.

A word of caution: if you don't mind doing

battle with crowds of Mexicans intent on adoring the Virgin of Juquila, by all means go during a festival. You should also note that this is an arduous 3.5-hour drive from Pochutla, which puts you in the car for 7 long hours if you choose to do it on a day trip. A more practical approach is to stop in for an hour (doable during non-festival times) en route from the coast to Oaxaca City, or vice versa, and have a look around.

★ SANTUARIO DE NUESTRA SEÑORA DE JUQUILA

The Juquila town plaza is *the* place to appreciate Juquila and the town's beloved patron. Getting there requires some doing, however, especially during festivals. If you're driving, park your car in the lot of the Hotel del Carmen (on the right-hand side of Av. Antonio Valdez, half a block before the plaza) and check in at the desk or order breakfast or lunch, if the restaurant is open. If busing, walk or ride a taxi from the Juquila station about 1.6 kilometers (one mi) ahead along Avenida Antonio Valdez to the plaza.

Step inside the church, where the tiny Virgin presides above the main altar, surrounded by flowers and encircled by a halo of blue fluorescent light. The diminutive figure is decorated with a pearl-garnished silk cape. Her face is of brown complexion, and upon her head rests a regal, native-style crown. In front of the altar stand boxes for donations and personal letters to the Virgin.

LA CAPILLA DEL PEDIMENTO

Despite the supernumerary virgins in the downtown plaza church itself, another nearby hilltop shrine, locally known as La Capilla del Pedimento, also draws multitudes of pilgrims. It is a necessary second devotional stop for Juquila pilgrims, who adorn the life-size replica image of the Virgin of Juquila with dozens of *milagros* (metal wish tokens). You'll find it at a signed left turn into a parking lot, about five kilometers (three mi) back, east along the highway out of town.

FESTIVALS

The big Friday, Saturday, and Sunday *tianguis* (native town market), spreading from the northeast corner of the plaza, is Juquila's main regular event. It swells to a 15-day marathon blowout during the December **Fiesta de la Virgen de Juquila.** The celebration begins quietly in late November with early-morning masses and religious processions; builds with a street carnival, floats, and fireworks; and climaxes around December 8 with traditional and modern dances, tapering off after the December 12 Virgin of Guadalupe festival.

SHOPPING

Stalls on Avenida Revolución past the plaza's northeast corner offer a variety of local handicrafts and food delicacies. Handicrafts include embroidered *huipiles, cinturones* (belts), *manteles* (tablecloths), and embroidered *servilletas* (napkins). Food includes coffee, coconut candy, and *panela* (brown sugar).

ACCOMMODATIONS

Juquila's probable best-bet hotel is the **Hotel del Carmen** (Av. Antonio Valdez, tel./fax 954/524-0004, $30 s or d, one bed, $40 d or t two beds), at the town center. With an entrance driveway leading steeply downhill to a rear parking lot, this is an especially convenient option for drivers in congested Juquila. The approximately 40 rooms are clean enough for an overnight, with hot-water shower-baths, cable TV, an acceptable restaurant, and parking.

Other options, some cheaper, are available around the plaza, half a block uphill. The best of these is the homey, family-run **Posada los Ángeles** (Av. Benito Juárez 2, Barrio Grande, tel. 954/524-0073, $23 s or d with one or two beds, $30 t), at the plaza's southeast corner. The approximately 20 rooms are clean, simply furnished, and well-maintained, with shaded (as opposed to bare-bulb) lamps. Rooms vary; if possible, get one with a balcony for a plaza-front view.

FOOD

Several sources around the plaza offer food. For fruits and vegetables, go to the market on the plaza's north side. A convenient grocery source is **Abarrotes El Centro** (tel. 954/524-0060, 8am-10pm daily), on the plaza's northeast corner across Avenida Revolución from the market. Hearty country-style food, always wholesome if hot, is available at *fondas* (food stalls) in the market.

A sprinkling of restaurants serves Juquila visitors. Very convenient is the restaurant in the **Hotel del Carmen** (Av. Antonio Valdez, tel. 954/524-0004, about 7:30am-10pm daily seasonally, $3-7), half a block north of the church, with a good standard menu of soups, sandwiches, meats, poultry, and Mexican specialties.

Highly recommended, especially for breakfast, is the eco-conscious **Restaurant Sierra** (no phone, 8am-1pm daily, $3-5), a block west of the plaza's northeast corner or half a block west of the Hotel del Carmen. Here, for breakfast, you can feast on ham and eggs, toast, coffee, orange juice, and pancakes with maple syrup (*miel maple*); or, if you prefer Mexican style, chilaquiles, enchiladas, or quesadillas. The portions are huge, enough for two.

SERVICES

Juquila, the capital of the big southern Sierra Juquila governmental district, offers some basic services (but unfortunately no bank as of this writing). The *correo* and the *telecomunicaciones* (tel. 954/524-0023, both 9am-3pm Mon.-Fri.) are in the rebuilt *palacio municipal*, on the south side of the plaza. A public telephone office, **Caseta Mimitel** (tel. 954/524-0277, 7am-9pm daily), inside at the rear of the market, offers long-distance and public fax service.

For routine medicines and drugs, try the plaza-front **Farmacia Dolores** (opposite the church). If you get sick, follow the recommendation of your hotel desk or hire a taxi to take you to the local **Hospital Civil** (Carretera Rio Grande, Km 1.5, tel. 954/524-0228, 954/524-0225, 954/524-0221, or 954/524-0223). Alternatively, near the plaza, consult with general practitioner Dr. José Luis Zavaleta, on Avenida Revolución, uphill side, at two locations: either at his **Clinica San Juanito** (104 Chapultepec, tel. 954/512-2875) or his **doctor's office** (on the 2nd Fl. above Abarrotes Zavaleta, tel. 954/524-0237), directly across the plaza from the church.

TRANSPORTATION

A pair of long-distance second-class bus lines serve Juquila from both Oaxaca City and Puerto Escondido. From the Oaxaca City *camionera central segunda clase* near the westside Abastos market, ride either **Dorado** or **Estrella Roja del Sureste** to Juquila. The same lines connect with Juquila from the **Puerto Escondido central bus station** (tel. 954/582-0875). *Note:* Not all buses make the 30-kilometer (19 mi) detour to Juquila from the El Vidrio crossing. In such a case, get off the bus at El Vidrio and catch a local *colectivo* taxi for the remaining 30 kilometers.

Juquila is accessible from Puerto Escondido, north via paved but sometimes potholed Highway 131, which starts off as the main north-south street through Puerto Escondido. Fill up with gasoline, then follow the winding 88-kilometer (55 mi) route, climbing past the cool, 2,100-meter (7,000 ft.) summit to the El Vidrio crossing (where there is a gas station and rough truck-stop *comedores*). There, drivers fork left and continue another 30 kilometers (19 mi) west to Juquila. For safety, allow about 3.5 hours for the entire curvy uphill trip.

The same is approximately true heading south from Oaxaca City. Fill up with gasoline at the airport Pemex station south of town and continue to about three kilometers (two mi) south of Coyotepec, where you fork right on to Highway 131. Continue, winding uphill and down, past Sola de Vega (roadside hotel, restaurant, and unleaded gasoline) to the El Vidrio summit crossing (166 km/103 mi). Turn right at the fork and continue the remaining mostly paved but sometimes bumpy 30 kilometers (19 mi) west to Juquila.

Parque Nacional Lagunas de Chacahua

The Parque Nacional Lagunas de Chacahua spreads for about 20 miles of open-ocean beach shoreline and islet-studded jungly lagoons midway between Pinotepa Nacional and Puerto Escondido. Tens of thousands of birds typical of a host of Mexican species fish the waters and nest in the mangroves of the two main lagoons, Laguna Pastoría on the east side and Laguna Chacahua on the west.

The fish and wildlife of the lagoons, over-fished and overhunted by local people during the 1970s and 1980s, have largely recovered. Commercial fishing is now strictly licensed. Crocodiles were hunted out during the 1970s, but the government is restoring them with a hatchery on Laguna Chacahua.

For most visitors, mainly Mexican families on Sunday outings, access is by boat, except for one unpaved road (passable in the dry season; marginally so in the wet). The boats go from east-side Zapotalito village, where the local fishing cooperative offers full- and half-day excursions to the beaches: Playa Hermosa on the east side and Playa Chacahua on the west.

EXPLORING LAGUNAS DE CHACAHUA

Zapotalito, on the eastern shore of Laguna Pastoría, is the busiest quick access point to the Lagunas de Chacahua. Get there from the Zapotalito turnoff at Kilometer 82, 82 kilometers (51 mi) from Pinotepa and 65 kilometers (41 mi) from Puerto Escondido. (Taxis and

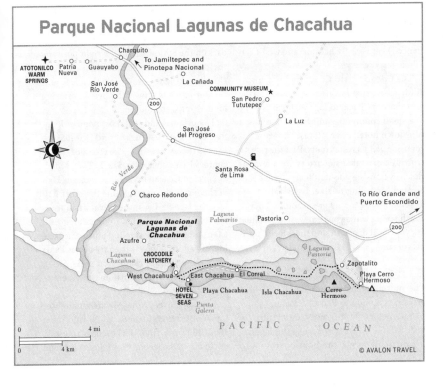

Parque Nacional Lagunas de Chacahua

Charquito

ATOTONILCO WARM SPRINGS

Patria Nueva

Guauyabo

To Jamiltepec and Pinotepa Nacional

San José Río Verde

La Cañada

COMMUNITY MUSEUM

San Pedro Tututepec

La Luz

San José del Progreso

Santa Rosa de Lima

Charco Redondo

To Río Grande and Puerto Escondido

Laguna Palmarito

Pastoria

Parque Nacional Lagunas de Chacahua

Azufre

Laguna Chacahua

CROCODILE HATCHERY

Laguna Pastoría

Zapotalito

West Chacahua

East Chacahua

El Corral

HOTEL SEVEN SEAS

Playa Chacahua

Isla Chacahua

Cerro Hermoso

Playa Cerro Hermoso

Punta Galera

Río Verde

PACIFIC OCEAN

0   4 mi

0   4 km

© AVALON TRAVEL

local buses run from Río Grande all the way to Zapotalito on the lagoon, while second-class buses from Puerto Escondido and Pinotepa Nacional will drop you on the highway.)

From the Zapotalito landing, the fishing cooperative, Sociedad Cooperativa Turística Escondida, enjoys a near-monopoly for transporting visitors on the lagoons. The boat workers used to make their living by fishing; now they mostly ferry tourists. Having specialized in hauling in fish, most are neither wildlife sensitive nor wildlife knowledgeable. Canopied powerboats, seating about 10, make long, full-day round-trips across the lagoon to lovely Playa Chacahua and village ($110/boat for 10 people, $70/boat for 5). It's best to arrive before 11am. Cheaper half-day excursions (about $30) take visitors to nearby **Playa Cerro Hermosa** at the mouth of Laguna Pastoría for a couple of hours' beach play and snorkeling (bring your own snorkeling gear).

(*Note:* There are two Chacahua villages, on opposite—east and west—sides of Laguna Chacahua. To distinguish them, they are referenced here as east-Chacahua and west-Chacahua, respectively.)

The **Cocodrilario Chacahua** is a crocodile hatchery at west-Chacahua village, on the west shore of Chacahua lagoon. It's also home to a small community of *costeño* families, a run-down hotel, a few stores, and some lagoonside *palapa* restaurants. Past the rickety crocodile caretaker's quarters are a few enclosures housing about 100 crocodiles segregated according to size, from hatchlings to six-foot-long toothy green adults. They're worth seeing while you're at west-Chacahua; ask your boat driver to stop there for 10 minutes or so.

Boat Excursion to Chacahua

The more expensive, but quick, full-day private excursion to Playa Chacahua, about 23 kilometers (14 mi) away, unfortunately necessitates a fast trip across the lagoon. It's difficult to get the boat operators to slow down. They roar across broad Laguna Pastoría, scattering flocks of birds ahead of them. They wind among the islands, with names such as Escorpión (Scorpion), Venados (Deer), and Pinuelas (Little Pines), sometimes slowing to view multitudes of nesting pelicans, herons, and cormorants. They pick up speed again in the narrow jungle channel between the lagoons, roaring past idyllic, somnolent El Corral village, and break into open water again on Laguna Chacahua.

East-Chacahua Village and Playa Chacahua

The excursion climaxes at the east-lagoon half of Chacahua village across Laguna Chacahua. The main attraction here is **Playa Chacahua,** lovely *because* of its isolation. The unlittered golden-white sand, washed by gently rolling waves, seems perfect for a host of beach diversions. You can snorkel off the rocks nearby, fish in the breakers, and surf the intermediate breaks that angle in on the west side. During big swells, when the sand bars on the bottom are in the right position, the surf here can be spectacular, with long right-breaking waves. Once only a few, now several *palapas* crowd the beach, offering food, drinks, and lodging.

The original and still most popular lodging here is the **Restaurant and Hotel Siete Mares** (Seven Seas, tel. 954/114-0062, www.lagunasdechacahua.com, $25 d). The 13 *cabañas* occupy Chacahua's choicest location. Half of them face the beach, while the other half face the lagoon. For more privacy and tranquility, choose the latter. Rooms come with a fan and private shower and toilet. The Siete Mares's added bonus is friendly owner Doña Meche's restaurant (8am-9pm daily, $3-8), which keeps satisfied customers returning year after year.

Furthermore, Doña Meche's daughter Juana also rents *cabañas*. You'll find them about 100 yards from the beach, as you walk north along the lagoon-front. Juana is proud of her 17 semi-deluxe **Cabañas Delfines** (tel. 954/132-8054, $23 d with fan, shower-bath, and toilet, $35 d with a/c added, camping $5 pp per night). She also welcomes tenters to her campground, including hammock-hung *palapa* shelters and showers.

If these accommodations are full, you can also take a look at **El Piojo** *cabañas* (on the beach, tel. 954/559-5073) and those of **Isabel Ortíz** (on the beach, tel. 954/588-6656).

Also, some groceries and fruits and vegetable are available at **Abarrotes Nayeli** (8am-9pm daily), on the lagoonfront, between Juana's and Reynaldo's *cabañas*.

The Mixteca

The homeland of the Mixtecs, Oaxaca's "People of the Clouds," spreads over an immense domain stretching northward from the tropical Pacific coast over the high, cool, pine-tufted Sierra to the warm, dry "Land of the Sun" along Oaxaca's northern border. The Mixteca's vastness and diversity have led Oaxacans to visualize it as three distinct sub-regions: Mixteca Alta, Mixteca Baja, and Mixteca de la Costa. These labels reflect the geographical realities of the Mixteca's *alta* (high) and *baja* (low) mountains and the tropical Pacific *costa* (coastal plain and foothills).

The Mixteca Alta comprises the Mixteca's highest, coolest country: all or part of the governmental districts of Nochixtlán, Coixtlahuaca, Teposcolula, and Tlaxiaco. The Mixteca Baja includes, on the other hand, the warm, dry districts of Huajuapan, Silacayoapan, and parts of Juxtlahuaca along Oaxaca's northern frontier. The Mixteca de la Costa lies south of all this, encompassing the tropical coastal districts of Putla and Jamiltepec on Oaxaca's southwest border.

PLANNING YOUR TIME

The Mixteca is a large and fascinating region, rich in history and natural wonders, quickly accessible by tour, bus, or car from Oaxaca City. You can get a quick glimpse of the Mixteca on a day trip, visiting the grand restored 16th-century Dominican churches at Yanhuitlán and Teposcolula and returning to Oaxaca City in the afternoon. If you add a day for a Friday overnight in Tlaxiaco, you could soak in the sights and sounds of the big, colorful **Tlaxiaco Saturday** *tianguis* (native town market) before returning back to Oaxaca City.

Add two days to the above and you'll have time en route to Yanhuitlán for a rewarding two-day side-trip from Nochixtlán for a hotel or camping overnight in the lovely, rustic **Valley of Apoala.** Soak in Apoala's tranquil, bucolic ambience while exploring the limestone Cave of Serpent, the towering canyon of the Two Colossal Rocks, and the Serpent's Tail waterfall.

Previous: Cerro de las Minas Archaeological Zone; Templo y Ex-Convento de Santo Domingo de Guzmán in Yanhuitlán. **Above:** main altar, Templo y Ex-Convento de Santo Domingo de Guzmán in Yanhuitlán.

The Mixteca

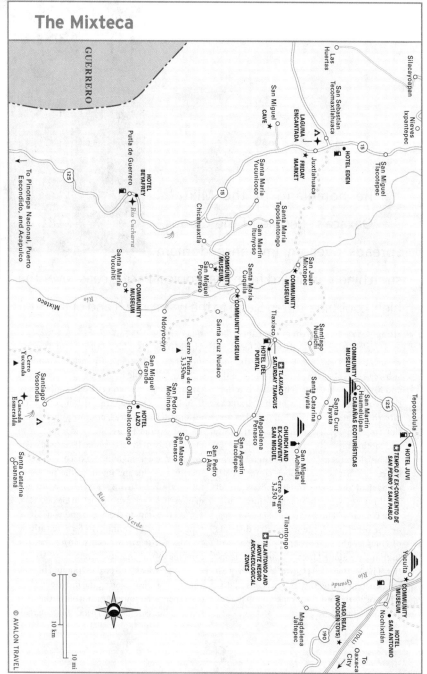

GUERRERO

Silacayoapan

Las Huertas

Nieves Ixpantepec

San Sebastian Tecomaxtlahuaca

San Miguel Tlacotepec

San Miguel CAVE

LAGUNA ENCANTADA

Juxtlahuaca

HOTEL EDEN

FRIDAY MARKET

Santa Maria Yucunicoco

Santa Maria Teposlantongo

Putla de Guerrero

HOTEL BEVAFREY

Río Cachurra

Chicahuaxtla

Santa Maria Itunyoso

San Juan Mixtepec

COMMUNITY MUSEUM

To Pinotepa Nacional, Puerto Escondido, and Acapulco

Santa Maria Cuquila

COMMUNITY MUSEUM

COMMUNITY MUSEUM

Santiago Nuidichi

COMMUNITY MUSEUM

Huamelulpan

CABAÑAS ECOTURISTICAS

San Martin Tayata

Teposcolula

Santa Maria Yucuhiti

San Miguel Progreso

Río Mixteco

Ndoyocoyo

Santa Cruz Nudaco

Tlaxiaco

HOTEL DEL PORTAL

TLAXIACO SATURDAY TIANGUIS

Santa Cruz Tayata

San Martin Tayata

HOTEL JUVI

TEMPLO Y EX-CONVENTO DE SAN PEDRO Y SAN PABLO

Cerro Yucunda

Santiago Yosondua

Cascada Esmeralda

Cerro Piedra de Olla 3,350m

San Miguel Grande

San Pedro Molinos

HOTEL LAZO

Chalcatongo

San Mateo Peñasco

Magdalena Peñasco

Santa Catarina Tayata

San Miguel Achiutla

CHURCH AND EX-CONVENT SAN MIGUEL

Santa Catarina Cuananá

San Pedro El Alto

San Agustin Tlacotepec

Cerro Negro 3,250 m

Tilantongo

TILANTONGO AND MONTE NEGRO ARCHAEOLOGICAL ZONES

Río Verde

Río Grande (Grande)

Magdalena Jaltepec

PASO REAL (WOODEN TOYS)

COMMUNITY MUSEUM

HOTEL SAN ANTONIO

Nochixtlan

To Oaxaca City

Yucuita

0   10 km

0   10 mi

© AVALON TRAVEL

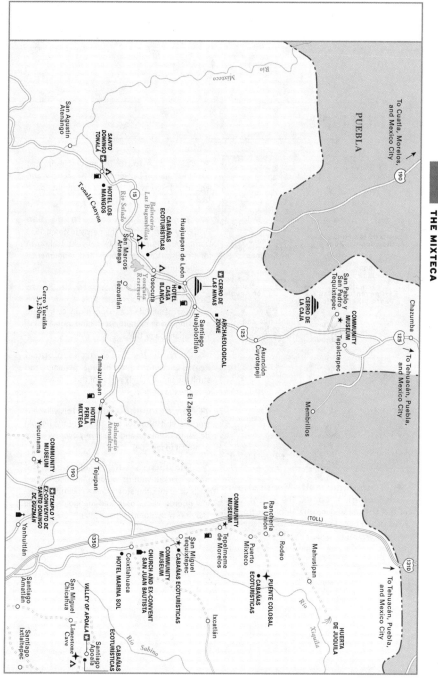

Look for ★ to find recommended
sights, activities, dining, and lodging.

Highlights

★ **Valley of Apoala:** This mountain-rimmed Oaxacan Shangri-La, replete with scenery and legends, deserves at least an overnight (page 189).

★ **Templo y Ex-Convento de San Pedro y San Pablo:** The newly restored 1538 Dominican church and ex-convent is known for its historical significance and monumental architecture (page 194).

★ **Templo y Ex-Convento de Santo Domingo de Guzmán:** This is one of the grandest of all Oaxaca's Dominican cathedrals, a striking stone monument shining atop a hill in Yanhuitlán (page 196).

★ **Cerro de las Minas Archaeological Zone:** Climb to the top of regal pyramids and stroll the broad stately plazas of this archaeological zone (page 197).

★ **Santo Domingo Tonalá:** This village is worth a visit both for the 16th-century Templo de Santo Domingo and the lovely cypress grove behind it (page 204).

★ **Tlaxiaco Saturday *Tianguis*:** This native market, with its winding, awning-draped stalls of scarlet tomatoes, green cucumbers, yellow gourds, lilies, roses, and marigolds, may be Oaxaca's most colorful (page 207).

★ **Tilantongo and Monte Negro Archaeological Zones:** The ancient capital of the Mixteca and nearby Monte Negro, with ruins dating back to 500 BC, make a memorable one-day excursion (page 189).

NOCHIXTLÁN

Nochixtlán (noh-chees-TLAN, pop. 11,000), busy capital of the governmental district of Nochixtlán, is interesting for its colorful market and festivals and especially as a jumping-off point for exploring the wonders of the idyllic mountain valley of Apoala and the remains of the ancient Mixtec kingdoms of Tilantongo and Yucuita.

Sights

Nochixtlán town itself spreads out from its plaza, which is directly accessible from Highway 190, from the Oaxaca side by north-south street Calle Progreso and, from the adjacent, Tamazulapan side, by east-west Calle Porfirio Díaz. The streets intersect at the northwest corner of the central plaza. From there, you can admire the distinguished 19th-century twin-towered **Templo**

Nochixtlán's charming central gazebo

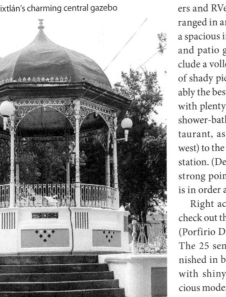

de La Asunción rising on the plaza's opposite side. Adjacent, to the right of the church, the *presidencia municipal* spreads for a block along Calle Hidalgo. At the plaza's northeast side is the big market, which expands into a much larger *tianguis* (native town market) on Sunday, when campesinos from all over northwest Oaxaca crowd in to peruse, haggle, and choose from a small mountain of merchandise.

Accommodations

The town's three recommendable hotels are all on Highway 190, which curves past the edge of town.

For room for parking and a green inner patio, check out the family-friendly **Hotel Santillan** (Porfirio Díaz 88, tel./fax 951/522-0351, norbertpcl@hotmail.com, $20 s or d, $27 d in two beds, $29 t), on the highway's west (Tamazulapan) side, convenient for drivers and RVers. The motel-style rooms are arranged in an L-shaped, two-story tier around a spacious inner parking lot, with kiddie pool and patio garden. Additional amenities include a volleyball/basketball court and a pair of shady picnic *palapas*. Upper rooms, probably the best choice, are plainly furnished, but with plenty of light. All come with hot-water shower-baths, parking, and a family-run restaurant, as well as proximity (half a block west) to the Omnibus Cristóbal Colón-Sur bus station. (Details, however, are not the family's strong point. Inspect your room to see if all is in order and functional before moving in.)

Right across from the main bus station, check out the brand-new **Hotel San Antonio** (Porfirio Díaz 112, no phone, $20-40 s or d). The 25 semi-deluxe rooms, invitingly furnished in beige-tone bedspreads and drapes, with shiny hot-water bathrooms and spacious modern-standard wash basins and commodes, are stacked in three stories above the bottom-floor parking garage. More expensive

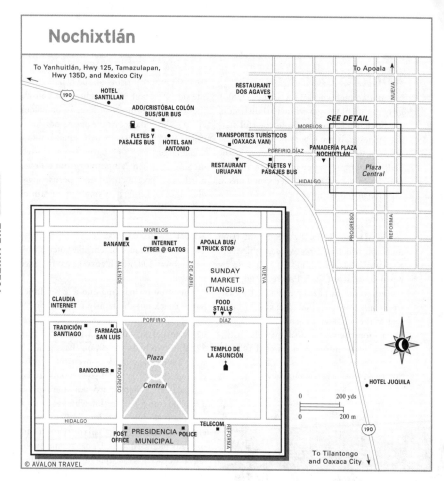

Nochixtlán

To Yanhuitlán, Hwy 125, Tamazulapan, Hwy 135D, and Mexico City

To Apoala

HOTEL SANTILLAN

ADO/CRISTÓBAL COLÓN BUS/SUR BUS

FLETES Y PASAJES BUS

HOTEL SAN ANTONIO

RESTAURANT DOS AGAVES

TRANSPORTES TURÍSTICOS (OAXACA VAN)

MORELOS

PORFIRIO DÍAZ

SEE DETAIL

PANADERÍA PLAZA NOCHIXTLÁN

RESTAURANT URUAPAN

FLETES Y PASAJES BUS

HIDALGO

Plaza Central

NUEVA

PROGRESO

REFORMA

MORELOS

BANAMEX

INTERNET CYBER @ GATOS

APOALA BUS/ TRUCK STOP

ALLENDE

2 DE ABRIL

SUNDAY MARKET (TIANGUIS)

NUEVA

CLAUDIA INTERNET

FOOD STALLS

TRADICIÓN SANTIAGO

FARMACIA SAN LUIS

PORFIRIO

DÍAZ

TEMPLO DE LA ASUNCIÓN

BANCOMER

PROGRESO

Plaza

Central

HOTEL JUQUILA

0   200 yds

0   200 m

HIDALGO

POST OFFICE

PRESIDENCIA MUNICIPAL

TELECOM

POLICE

REFORMA

To Tilantongo and Oaxaca City

190

© AVALON TRAVEL

THE MIXTECA
NORTHWEST FROM OAXACA CITY

rooms come with king-size beds and whirlpool tubs.

On the diagonally opposite, Oaxaca, side of town, find the newish **Hotel Juquila** (Hwy. 190, Km 1, tel. 951/522-0581, $26 s or d in one bed, $32 d or t in two beds) on the highway, about 0.8 kilometers (0.5 mi) from the center of town, a few doors from the ADO bus stop. The hotel's name comes from the owner's devotion to the Virgin of Juquila, for whom he keeps a candle burning in front of a picture of the Virgin on the hotel front desk. Upstairs, the rooms are sparcely decorated but very clean. Many are dark, however. Ask for one with *mas luz* (more light).

Rooms all come with TV, hot-water showers, and a restaurant downstairs. If you're sensitive to noise, come prepared with ear plugs; the passing trucks and buses may be a problem here.

Food

Nochixtlán offers a sprinkling of budget meal and bakery options. For wholesome country-style meals, go to the *fondas* (food stalls) in the market, on the north side of the plaza.

In the evenings the action spreads to the market streetfront, across from the church, where a line of stalls does big business serving a small mountain of tacos, *tortas*

Templo de La Asunción

190, tel. 951/522-0495, 8am-9:30pm daily, $3-5). Offerings include especially good Mexican-style breakfasts with fruit; a hearty afternoon four-course *comida corrida* with tasty entrées, such as *guisado de res* (savory beef stew), and soup, rice, and dessert; and à la carte omelets, tacos, quesadillas, tamales, and much more for supper.

Information and Services

Find the *correo* (tel. 951/522-0309, 8am-4:30pm Mon.-Fri., 8am-noon Sat.) at the plaza's southwest corner, west end of the *presidencia municipal.* Skip uphill east, half a block past the *presidencia municipal,* to *telecomunicaciones* (corner of Hidalgo and Reforma, tel. 951/522-0053, 9am-3pm Mon.-Fri.).

For economical local or long-distance telephone access, buy a widely available Ladatel telephone card and use it in one of the several downtown street telephones. Otherwise, use the long-distance public phone and also connect to the **Internet**, at **Claudia's restaurant** (Porfirio Díaz, tel. 951/522-0190, 9am-11pm daily). Find it on the north side of Porfirio Díaz, a block west of the plaza.

Stock up with pesos at **Bancomer** (tel. 951/522-0154, 8:30am-4pm Mon.-Fri.), in the middle of the plaza's west side, with a 24-hour ATM.

A number of attractive all-Oaxaca handicrafts are for sale at the small **Tradición Santiago** (Porfirio Díaz 49, tel. 951/522-0294, 9am-9pm daily). Offerings include fetching embroidered *huipiles* from remote source villages (such as Yalalag and Tehuacán), genuine homegrown Oaxaca *mezcal,* and the famous green pottery from Atzompa.

Furthermore, beside the toll expressway between Nochixtlán at Km 209, about 16 kilometers (10 mi) past the Huitzo toll gate, watch for the bright toys beside the road. A close look reveals a charming treasury of handmade wooden toys, from windmills and angels to trucks and tractors. They're made by the local members of **Paso Real Toy cooperative** (8am-8pm daily, toys $2-10).

(sandwiches), quesadillas, and especially the Oaxaca specialty, *tlayudas* ($3-6): giant pizza-sized crisp tortillas loaded with everything from beans and cheese to spicy chorizo sausage, cabbage, boiled eggs, and more.

Freshly baked offerings are plentiful at **Panadería Plaza** (Porfirio Díaz, no phone, 7am-9:30pm daily), a block and a half west of the plaza.

Nochixtlán's restaurant of choice is **Dos Agaves** (local cell tel. 044-951/160-4399, 8am-8pm daily, set lunch $2.50). Although breakfast is fine here, they specialize in hearty four-course *comidas corrida* (set lunch; for example, fresh strawberry punch, rice, cream of carrot soup, and scrumptious meat balls in sauce). Find them on the west side of downtown. From the highway, walk east along Porfirio Díaz a block, turn left and go one block to Morelos and continue a fraction to Dos Agaves (which looks like a rustic cowboy bunkhouse) on the left.

Alternatively, try **Restaurant Uruapan** (southwest corner of Porfirio Díaz and Hwy.

Simple, over-the-counter remedies and prescriptions are available at the big well-stocked drug store, **Farmacia San Luis** (tel. 951/522-0484, 7am-11:30pm daily), at the plaza's northwest corner.

As for doctors, you can visit the **Centro de Especialidades** (Melchor Ocampo 10, tel. 951/522-0594, 9am-7pm Mon.-Sat.) of Dr. José Manuel Sosa Bolanos.

For **police** and **fire** emergencies, dial tel. 951/522-0430, or go to the *policía municipal,* at their plaza-front station, at the east end (across from the church) of the *presidencia municipal.*

Getting There and Away

Several long-distance bus lines serve Nochixtlán. Luxury and first-class **Autobuses del Oriente** (ADO), first-class **Omnibus Cristóbal Colón** (OCC), and second-class **Sur** (operating jointly out of their west-side station on Porfirio Díaz, Hwy. 190, tel. 951/522-0387) provide broad service southeast with Oaxaca City; northwest both along Highway 190, with the Mixteca Baja (Tamazulapan, Coixtlahuaca, Huajuapan), and along the autopista 135D,

continuing to Puebla, Veracruz, and Mexico City Tapo and Tasqueña terminals; and west with Teposcolula, Tlaxiaco, Juxtlahuaca, Putla, and intermediate points in the Mixteca Alta.

Additionally, second-class **Fletes y Pasajes** (Porfirio Díaz, corner of Hwy. 190, tel. 951/522-0585) offers connections northwest with Mexico City via Tehuacán and Puebla and southeast, with Oaxaca.

Enterprising **Transportes Turísticos de Nochixtlán** (Porfirio Díaz 72, tel. 951/522-0503, 6am-9pm daily, $15), on the west-side highway, offers fast and frequent Suburban van rides to and from Oaxaca City. In Oaxaca City, contact them downtown (Galeana 222, tel. 951/514-0525). They also rent Suburban station wagons for $15 per hour; negotiate for a cheaper daily rate. This would be especially handy for a family or group visit to Apoala.

Drivers can cover the 80 kilometers (50 mi) from Oaxaca City in an easy hour via the *cuota autopista.* If you want to save the approximately $6 car toll (more for big RVs and trailers), figure about two hours via the winding old Highway 190 *libre* (free) route.

Nochixtlán's municipal market

★ TILANTONGO AND MONTE NEGRO ARCHAEOLOGICAL ZONES

The **Tilantongo archaeological zone** is the town itself (pop. 4,000), which sits smack on top of storied ancient Tilantongo. In the old days, around AD 1050, Tilantongo was the virtual capital of the Mixteca, ruled by the ruthless but renowned Mixtec king 8-Deer of the Tiger Claws. Carved stones built into the Tilantongo town church wall attest to Tilantongo's former glory.

The town government commissioned a mural, now on the outside wall of the *presidencia municipal,* which dramatically portrays the legendary Mixtec Flechador del Sol (Bowman of the Sun) and copies of pages from the Codex Nuttall, a pre-conquest document in blazing color that records glorious events in Mixtec pre-conquest history.

At least as important and more rewarding to explore is the much older **Monte Negro archaeological zone** atop the towering, oak-studded **Monte Negro** (Black Mountain), visible high above Tilantongo. A graveled road, passable by ordinary cars, easier for high-clearance trucks or jeep-like vehicles, allows access to the top in about an hour. You must obtain permission from authorities at the *presidencia municipal* (tel. 951/510-4970), who require that a local guide accompany you; they will furnish the guide (fee about $10, plus lunch).

Getting There

Bus passengers can go by the Tilantongo-Nochixtlán bus, which makes the trip about three times a day from Calle Porfirio Díaz, in front of the Nochixtlán market. Drivers: Follow Highway 190 (old *libre* route) to the Jaltepec paved turnoff about 13 kilometers (eight mi) southeast (Oaxaca City direction) from Nochixtlán. Mark your odometer at the turnoff. The road is paved to the Jaltepec plaza (8.2 km/5.1 mi), where you turn right. The road is dirt and gravel, often rough, after that. Follow the Tilantongo (or Teozocoalco)

signs. Turn left at a church (17.7 km/10.8 mi) at Morelos villages, and right after a river bridge (23.8 km/14.8 mi). You'll pull up to the Tilantongo plaza after 29 kilometers (18 mi) and about an hour of steady, bumpy driving.

★ VALLEY OF APOALA

The **Valley of Apoala,** tucked in the mountains north of Nochixtlán, nestles beneath towering cliffs far from the noise, smoke, and clutter of city life. Apoala is no less than a Oaxacan Shangri-La: a farming community replete with log-cabin houses, men plowing the field with oxen, women sitting and chatting as they weave palm-leaf sombreros, dogs barking, and burros braying faintly in the warm dusk. The spring-fed river assures good crops; people, consequently, are relatively well off and content to remain on the land.

Exploring Apoala

A tour of Apoala begins at the **Cave of Serpent,** translated from the local Mixtec dialect. Just before the cave, you pass a crystalline spring welling up from the base of a towering cliff.

Entering the cave, you see why your guide is so important: The guide carries a large battery and light to illuminate the way. In the first of the cave's two galleries, bats flutter overhead as your guide reveals various stalactites and then flashes the light on the subterranean river gurgling from an underground dark lagoon, unknown in extent. What *is* known, however, is that the water from the lagoon arrives at the springs at Tamazulapan, more than 50 kilometers (30 mi) away. Someone long ago dropped some oranges into the cave lagoon in Apoala, and they bobbed to the surface later in Tamazulapan.

After the cave, you'll head up-valley between a pair of cliffs that tower vertically at least 150 meters (500 ft.). Soon, above and to your left, you'll see the towering 600-meter (2,000 ft.) burnt-yellow rampart, **La Peña Donde Murió El Aguila con Dos Cabezas** (The Rock Where the Eagle with Two Heads Died). No kidding. It seems that, once upon a time, a huge eagle that actually had two heads lived in one of the many caves in the rock face. The problem was, it was killing too many lambs, so one day one of the villagers shot it. The Eagle with Two Heads, however, lives on in the community memory of Apoalans.

Finally, after about 20 minutes of walking, the climax arrives: a narrow, river-cut breach in the canyon, like some antediluvian giant had cut a thin slice through a mountain of butter. The slice remains, between a pair of vertical rock walls called **Las Dos Peñas Colosales** (The Two Colossal Rocks).

The grand finale, down-valley about 1.6 kilometers (one mi), is the waterfall **Cola del Serpiente** (The Serpent's Tail). You walk down a steep, forested trail that looks out on a gorgeous mountain and valley panorama. At the bottom, the Río Apoala, having already tumbled hundreds of feet, pauses for spells in several pools, and finally plummets nearly 90 meters (300 ft.) in a graceful arc to an emerald green pool surrounded by a misty, natural stone amphitheater.

Accommodations and Food

Camping ($15 per day per group, pay at the *cabaña ecoturística*), by self-contained RV or tent, is superb here. The community has set aside a choice grassy riverside spot, across the river from the cave at the upper end of town; it's heavenly for a few days of camping. Clear, pristine spring water wells up at the foot of the cliff at the road's end nearby.

Non-campers shouldn't miss staying in Apoala's fine *cabaña ecoturística* ($15 pp), where you probably first met your guide. This is a model of Oaxaca's improved, second-generation, government-built, locally-managed tourist accommodation. Besides three very clean and comfortable rooms with either one or two double beds, it features a light, spacious solarium-sitting room and snack café, serving water, beer, and sodas, as well as breakfast, lunch, and early supper.

Overnight reservations are recommended. Reserve directly with Apoala through their satellite phone connection (in Mexico long-distance tel. 01-55/5151-9154; in Mexico City, simply dial as a local call, tel. 5151-9154; from the U.S. tel. 011-52-55/5151-9154). Alternatively, you can get information and lodging reservations in Oaxaca City at the government **tourism office** (703 Av. Juárez, tel. 951/516-0123, www.aoaxaca.com).

Getting There and Away

Like Shangri-La, Apoala isn't easy to get to. *Colectivo* passengers have it easiest. The Apoala community provides an Apoala-marked *colectivo* ($5), which leaves from Calle 2 de Abril near the corner of Morelos, Nochixtlán (a block north of the plaza's northeast corner). It departs daily, arriving in Apoala around 3pm. It departs Apoala for Nochixtlán on the same days at around 6:30am. Check locally for the Apoala *colectivo* schedule with stores or bus or truck drivers parked along Calle 2 de Abril, as it varies from low to high season. To check in advance, call the Apoala satellite phone number: Dial long distance tel 01-55/5151-9154. Otherwise, taxis ($18) and passenger trucks ($4-6) make the same trip hourly until about 5pm from the same spot.

For **drivers,** the 42-kilometer (26 mi) rough dirt and gravel road is a challenge, especially in an ordinary passenger car. The route heads north from downtown Nochixtlán; turn left from Calle Porfirio Díaz (the street that borders the plaza's north side) at the street just past (east) the market. Follow the road signs all the way.

Dominican Route South

Of the four missionary orders—Franciscans, Jesuits, Augustinians, and Dominicans—who established an important presence in New Spain, the Dominicans were dominant in Oaxaca. Their legacy remains vibrant to this day. More than 90 percent of Oaxacans consider themselves Catholics, and lovely old Dominican ex-convent/churches decorate the Oaxacan countryside. Some of these outstanding venerable monuments, notably at **Yanhuitlán, Teposcolula, Tlaxiaco,** and **Coixtlahuaca,** grace the Mixteca Alta, not far from the modern town of Tamazulapan, making it a natural base for exploration of what has become known as Oaxaca's Dominican route.

TAMAZULAPAN AND VICINITY

Tamazulapan (tah-mah-soo-LAH-pahn, pop. 5,000), partly by virtue of its crossroads

Templo de la Natividad

position on the National Highway 190, has eclipsed its more venerable, but isolated, neighbor towns and become the major service and business center for the Teposcolula district. You know you're in Tamazulapan immediately as you pass its town plaza, which proudly displays a semicircular columned monument right by the highway in honor of Benito Juárez, "Benemérito de las Américas."

Sights

The portaled *presidencia municipal* stands across the **Plaza Constitución.** Beyond the storefronts along plaza-front Calle Independencia rise the cupolas of the 18th-century Dominican **Templo de la Natividad.** Bordering the plaza on the other side are the stores and services along Calle Constitución. Don't miss the amusing topiary animals in the churchyard.

Tamazulapan townsfolk love their resort, **Balneario Atonaltzin** (tel. 951/502-1200, 9am-6pm daily, adults $3, kids $2). Natural sulfur water springs are channeled into a huge swimming pool. It's a family-friendly spot and usually crowded with locals on hot days. Drive, take a taxi, or walk the 2.5 kilometers (1.5 mi) north along the road to Tepelmeme (east plaza-front Calle Independencia) to get there. Soon after a bridge, you'll see the *balneario* (resort) on the right.

Accommodations

Of Tamazulapan's acceptable hotels, most prominent is the four-story **Hotel Dom Pedro** (Cristóbal Colón 24, tel./fax 953/533-0736, $14 s or d in one bed, $16 d in two beds, $18 t), a few doors north of the plaza. The 25 plain but clean upstairs rooms (no elevator) come with toilets and hot-water showers, TV, and parking, but no phone except the long-distance phone at the hotel desk. Credit cards are not accepted.

The star of Tamazulapan hotels is the

Tamazulapan

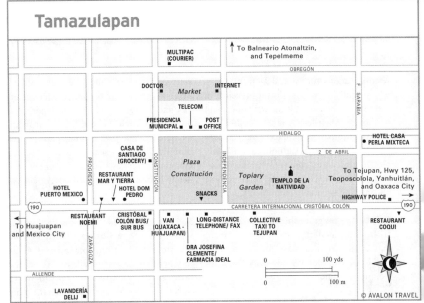

deluxe, newish ★ **Hotel Casa Perla Mixteca** (Calle 2 de Abril 3, tel./fax 953/533-0280, toll-free Mex. tel. 800/717-3956, $25 s, $28 d, and $33 t). A major plus here is the hotel's quiet location, removed from the noisy highway truck traffic. Take your pick of 10 designer-decorated rooms, with rustically lovely tile floors, handwoven bedspreads, reading lamps, and bathrooms with hot-water showers.

Food

For inexpensive prepared food, try the *fondas* (food stalls) inside the market and the nighttime taco stands or one of the several sit-down snack bars along the highway by the plaza.

As for restaurants, **Hotel Puerto Mexico** (Carr. Cristóbal Colon 12, tel. 953/533-0044 or 953/533-0778) offers basic meals for breakfast, lunch, and dinner. However, ★ **Restaurant Noemi** (Cristóbal Colón 16, tel. 953/533-0595, 8am-11pm daily, $2-7), a few steps west, between Hotel Puerto Mexico and Hotel Dom Pedro is a much

better option. The owner puts out Mexican home-style breakfasts, lunches, and suppers, including savory *café de la olla* (pot-brewed coffee, with cinnamon).

Information and Services

For telephone service, go to the *larga distancia* across the highway from the plaza, or one of the three or four Ladatel card-operated public phones sprinkled along the highway and near the plaza.

At least two **doctors** near the plaza offer consultations and medicines. Choose either **Dra. Josefina Clemente** at her **Farmacia Ideal** (on the highway directly opposite the plaza, tel. 953/533-0224; pharmacy: 8am-9pm Mon.-Sat.; consultations: 4pm-8pm Mon.-Fri.); or **Dr. Fidel A. Cruz Ramírez** (a block and a half north from the highway, on the west Constitución side of the market, no phone; consultations: 9am-3pm and 5pm-9pm Mon.-Fri.).

For a police emergency, contact either the **Delegación de Transito highway police** (half a block east of the plaza, on the same side as the highway, tel. 953/533-0472, on duty 24 hours) or the **municipal police** (at the *presidencia municipal,* tel. 953/533-0017).

Get your laundry done at handy **Lavandería Delij** (on Zaragoza, 9am-8pm Mon.-Sat.), a block and a half south (uphill) from the Hotel Puerto Mexico on the highway.

Getting There and Away

Bus lines **Omnibus Cristóbal Colón** and **Sur** (both across from the plaza, tel. 953/533-0699) operate jointly out of their highway-front station. Their buses connect southeast with Oaxaca City via Nochixtlán; northwest via Huajuapan and Cuautla (Morelos), with Mexico City (Tapo); and south with Teposcolula, Tlaxiaco, and Juxtlahuaca.

Good paved roads connect Tamazulapan with all the important Mixteca and Oaxaca destinations: southeast, via Highway 190, 133 kilometers (84 mi), two hours, with Oaxaca City; northwest, 41 kilometers (25 mi), 45 minutes, with Huajuapan; north, by paved (but potholed) secondary road via Tejupan, 35 kilometers (22 mi), 45 minutes, with Coixtlahuaca; and south via Highway 190-Highway 125, 35 kilometers (22 mi), 45 minutes, with Teposcolula.

Frequent (10 per day) **Transportes**

Atolzín vans (cell tel. 044/117-8800) connect southeast with Oaxaca City, and northwest with Huajuapan. Check for departures at their small office across the highway from the plaza's southwest corner.

Servicios Turísticos Teposcolula vans connect south with Mixteca destinations of Teposcolula and Tlaxiaco, and west with Huajuapan. They stop for passengers on the highway, by the plaza.

TEPOSCOLULA

Although smaller in population than Tamazulapan, **Teposcolula** (pop. 2,000) continues to outrank it as district capital, a distinction it gained way back in 1740. Its history, however, reaches back much further. When the Spanish arrived in the 1520s, they found well-established Mixtec towns on the hillsides above a beautiful lake-filled valley. They drained the lake for farmland and moved the population down to Teposcolula's present location. Abiding by common practice, the Spanish kept the Mixtec name, Teposcolula (Place Surrounded by Springs), tacking on the Catholic patronal title San Pedro y San Pablo. This produced a name so long that practically no one refers to the official San Pedro y San Pablo Teposcolula.

A statue of Benito Juarez presides over Plaza Constitución in Tamazulapan.

★ Templo y Ex-Convento de San Pedro y San Pablo

Most visitors head right over to the venerable 1538 Dominican church and ex-convent, one of Oaxaca's most important, not only for its historical significance, but also for its monumental architecture. Here rises the famous, recently-restored **Capilla Abierta** (Open Chapel), with massive, soaring arches and gigantic buttresses. Visitors often wonder why such a huge outdoor chapel was needed right next to an equally massive indoor church. The adjacent grassy expanse provides the reason. It's the **atrium,** the extension of the outdoor chapel, the largest in Mexico, where the Dominican builders imagined 10,000 native faithful gathering for mass.

Before you leave town, be sure to visit the **carcel** (jail) at the *presidencia municipal* on the plaza. There, the prisoners make and sell handicrafts, such as leather belts, leather-covered *mezcal* flasks, and miniature-shoe key rings.

Accommodations and Food

Teposcolula's **Hotel Juvi** (Hwy. 125, tel. 953/518-2064, $13 s, $15 d in one bed, $16 d in two beds, $18 t, $20 q) now makes an overnight stay possible here. The hotel's layout remains unique: 12 rooms around a parking courtyard containing the last remnant, a grain storage crib, of the ancient family homestead.

You can buy basic food supplies at a plaza-front *abarrotes* (grocery); a *panadería* (bakery; on Iturbide, tel. 953/537-8683, 8am-8pm daily), a block behind the *presidencia municipal*; or treat yourself to a hearty afternoon *comida* (set lunch) at the town's good (but pricey) **Restaurant Eunice** (tel. 953/518-2017, 8am-8pm Sun.-Fri., $4-12), a block behind the east side of the *presidencia municipal*.

Information and Services

If you're sick, consult Dr. Brigido Vidal in his **Farmacia Nelly** (on the plaza-front east side, a few doors from the highway, tel. 953/518-2072; consultations: 3pm-10pm Mon.-Sat.); pharmacy: 9am-2pm and 5pm-9pm Mon.-Sat.). Alternatively, go to the **Centro de Salud** (doctor available 8am-2pm and 4pm-6pm daily, 24 hours in emergency). Get there via Calle Madero, uphill, passing the *presidencia municipal*'s west side. After two blocks, turn left, and continue three long blocks to the *centro de salud*, on the right.

For **police** or **fire** emergencies, contact the police at the *presidencia municipal,* north side of the plaza.

topiary creatures at play in a Tamazulapan churchyard

To mail a letter or make a phone call, go either to the *telcomunicaciones* (on Madero, upstairs, half a block north of the plaza's northwest corner, tel. 953/518-2070, 9am-3pm Mon.-Fri.) or the *correo* (on Madero, downstairs, 11am-4pm Thurs. only). Or go to the "Mr. Marbo" office (across the highway from the plaza, tel. 953/518-2103, 7am-10:30pm daily).

Getting There and Away

Bus transportation to and from Teposcolula is easy and frequent. Bus passengers arrive at and depart from the bus station (Autobuses Sur, Omnibus Cristóbal Colón, and Fletes y Pasajes; on Hwy. 125, tel. 953/518-2000), half a block east from the plaza. Buses connect southeast with Oaxaca City; north with Tamazulapan, Huajuapan, and Mexico City; and south with Tlaxiaco, Juxtlahuaca, and Putla (where connections are available with Pinotepa Nacional on the Pacific coast).

Long-distance vans Servicios Turísticos Teposcolula (local cell tel. 044-953/110-9288) connect frequently with Oaxaca and Tlaxiaco, from the small station directly across the highway from the town plaza.

For drivers, Highway 125 runs right past Teposcolula's town plaza, about 13 kilometers (eight mi) southwest of its junction with the Oaxaca City-Mexico City Highway 190. To or from Oaxaca City, using the *cuota autopista* (toll expressway), drivers should allow around two hours to safely cover the approximately 125-kilometer (78 mi) Oaxaca City-Teposcolula distance; add at least another hour if going by the old Highway 190 *libre* (free) route via Yanhuitlán. To or from Tamazulapan in the north, allow about 45 minutes for the 35 kilometers (22 mi) via Highway 190-Highway 125 and about an hour for the 47 kilometers (29 mi) along Highway 125 to or from Tlaxiaco in the south.

YUCUNAMA

Yucunama (pop. 600) is attractive partly *because* of its small size. From the diminutive plaza, cobbled streets pass rustic stone houses and continue downhill to verdant fields, which, in the distance, give way to lush oak and pine-tufted woodlands.

Yucunama's beauty is probably one reason that Mixtec people have been living there for at least 4,000 years. Its name, which means Hill of Soap, perhaps reflects the town's spic-and-span plaza, clean-swept streets, and newly painted public buildings. It's a pure Mixtec town, for although Yucunama is part of the Teposcolula district, Spanish settlers never lived here.

The remarkable must-see Bee Nu'u (House of the People) community museum should be your first stop. The museum now only opens by appointment. Try talking to someone at the dignified, porticoed *presidencia municipal,* across the plaza from the museum.

Exhibits include the original of the Lienzo Yucunama, an *amate* (wild fig bark paper) document from the 1300s that details the 35 tribute payments of a Yucunama Mixtec noblewoman with the name-date 5-Eagle, and her first and second husbands, 12-Flower and 10-Eagle, to her father, who lived in a nearby town. In the cabinet below the *lienzo* stands a copy of the famous Codex Nuttall (folded like an accordion), which details, in full color, the exploits of the renowned Mixtec lord 8-Deer.

After the museum, stroll down Calle Independencia (from the museum, follow the left side of the plaza, past the *presidencia municipal*) about three long blocks east to the picture-perfect town fountain, fed by the old town aqueduct. A block south and a couple more blocks downhill east, at the end of Calle Libertad, marvel at Yucunama's oldest resident, the gigantic 1,000-year-old Tule, or *ahuehuete* tree (Mexican bald cypress, *Taxodium mucronatum*).

Getting There and Away

Yucunama is about nine kilometers (six mi) northwest of the Highway 125-Highway 190 intersection. Drivers: Follow the signed, graded gravel road that takes off from the north corner of the intersection. By bus: Ride an **Omnibus Cristóbal Colón, Sur,** or **Fletes y Pasajes** bus to the Highway 125-Highway 190 intersection, then hike the nine kilometers (six mi) or ride a *colectivo* van or truck from there.

YANHUITLÁN

It sometimes seems a miracle that the Dominican padres, against heavy odds and isolated as they were in the far province of Oaxaca, were able to build such masterpieces as their convent and church in Yanhuitlán. When Father Domingo de la Cruz began the present church, in 1541, Yanhuitlán retained the prosperity and the large skilled population that it had when it was a reigning Mixtec kingdom prior to the arrival of the Spanish. For a workforce, de la Cruz used the labor of thousands of Mixtec workers and artisans, who deserve much of the credit for the masterfully refined monuments that they erected.

An ancient arch frames a view of the Templo y Ex-Convento de Santo Domingo de Guzmán.

And monuments, indeed, they still are. Approaching Yanhuitlán from the northwest, the road reaches a hilltop point where the entire Yanhuitlán Valley spreads far below. In the bright afternoon sun, the white-shining, massively buttressed Yanhuitlán church and adjacent atrium (now soccer field), big enough for 15,000 indigenous faithful, dwarfs everything else in sight.

★ Templo y Ex-Convento de Santo Domingo de Guzmán

The Templo y Ex-Convento de Santo Domingo de Guzmán is as much a museum of national treasures as it is a place of worship. In fact, it is divided so: The ex-convent, which you enter on the right, has been converted to a **museum** (no phone, 9am-4pm daily, $4). Inside, you begin to appreciate the gigantic proportions of the place as you circle the cloister, passing beneath ponderous but delicately designed arches that appear to sprout and spread from stone cloister columns like branches from giant trees.

The nave glows with golden decorations. Overhead, stone rib arches support the ceiling completely, without the need of columns, creating a single soaring heavenly space. Up front, above the altar, Santo Domingo de Guzmán presides, gazing piously toward heaven, his forehead decorated by a medallion that appears remarkably like a Hindu *tilak.*

Getting There and Away

Get to Yanhuitlán, on Highway 190, by car, van, or Sur, Fletes y Pasajes, or Omnibus Cristóbal Colón bus. By car, from Nochixtlán, head 19 kilometers (12 mi) north along Highway 190 (100km/62 mi from Oaxaca via the toll expressway, allow 1.5 hours), or about 37 kilometers (23 mi) south from Tamazulapan (or about the same from Teposcolula via Hwys. 125 and 190).

The Mixteca Baja: Land of the Sun

Although its name implies a lowland, the Mixteca Baja is high, seasonally dry, sunny country. It comprises the 900-1,600-meter (3,000-5,000 ft.) mountain valley and plateau land of northwest Oaxaca. Before the conquest, this land was richer and much more densely populated than today. Irrigated, stone-terraced fields graced the hillsides, and busy market towns supported large populations of Mixtec-speaking people in the fertile valleys. However, after the conquest, the Spanish soldiers and settlers forcibly congregated the indigenous people into more controllable villages and introduced sheep and goats, which quickly ate up much of the natural grassland. Their way of life changed forever; the people abandoned most of their irrigated fields, and their terraces fell into ruin.

HUAJUAPAN DE LEÓN AND VICINITY

Huajuapan de León (pop. 50,000), with good hotels, restaurants, and many services, makes a comfortable base for enjoying the Mixteca Baja.

The town itself has much to offer. For first-time arrivals, untouristed Huajuapan de León is a pleasant surprise. The town center, including plaza, church, and *presidencia municipal,* is removed a few blocks south of the Highway 190 clutter and bustle. Although the present town dates only from colonial times, the surrounding region, which city hall boosters call Tierra del Sol (Land of the Sun), has been inhabited for many millennia. The extensive Cerro de las Minas (Hill of the Mines) archaeological zone, just 1.6 kilometers (one mi) north of the present town, was a ceremonial, market, and governmental center for thousands of inhabitants during its apex, around AD 500.

The Plaza

The town's choice people-watching spot is the tranquil, old-fashioned town plaza, **Plaza Central Antonio de León,** bordered by the *presidencia municipal* on its west side. On the plaza's north side stands a distinguished bronze statue of General Antonio de León (1794-1847). Also on the north side, across the street from the plaza, rise the twin spires of the late-19th-century **Catedral de la Virgen de Guadalupe.**

Inside, a brilliantly illuminated Virgin of Guadalupe occupies the main front altar, while in the right-side chapel, the **Capilla del Sagrario del Señor de los Corazones,** a painted celebration of baroque glitter climaxes in the beloved, dark-complexioned Señor hanging limply above the altar.

★ Cerro de las Minas Archaeological Zone

Be sure to investigate the remains of **Cerro de las Minas,** a major urban-stage (AD 300-800) Mixtec town. Artifacts uncovered on this hill just north of town during the 1980s demonstrate characteristics of so-called Ñuiñe glyphs, which archaeologists recognize as one of the five unique writing systems of ancient Mesoamerica.

Similar finds unearthed at contemporaneous Mixteca Baja ruined cities, such as Tequixtepec, Chazumba, Miltepec, Suchitepec, Lunatitlán, and Mixtlahuaca, led archaeologists to name the style by the Mixtec label, Ñuiñe (nyoo-EE-nyay), for the "Hot Country," the Mixteca Baja, where they were discovered.

EXPLORING THE SITE

Get to the ruins by driving, hiking, or hailing a taxi. From the town center, follow Nuyoo north across the highway and three blocks past the uphill church. Continue straight ahead, up a steep track and turn right to the parking lot, marked by a Zona Arqueología sign. From there, on foot, scramble uphill

Huajuapan de León

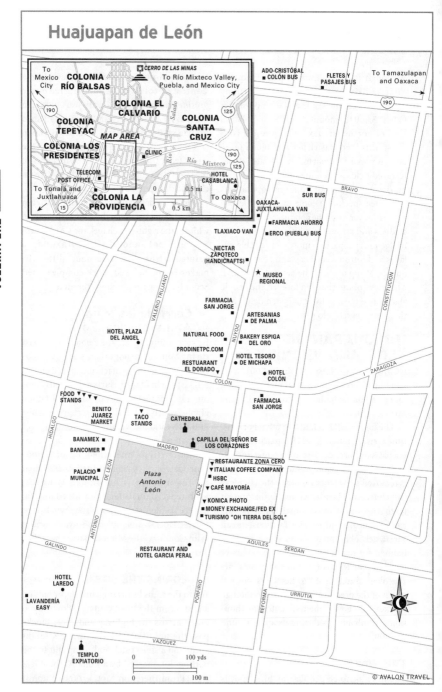

past the retaining wall to the highest point, **Mound 1,** on the east side.

From the top, the entire Huajuapan Valley spreads in all directions. On the south side, in the distance, rise the downtown cathedral's ruddy twin towers. Far behind them stand the cloud-draped heights of the Mixteca Alta. On the opposite, north side, flat-topped Cerro Yucunitza, the site of another hilltop ruined city, towers over the valley. Below Yucunitza's right shoulder, the Río Mixteco meanders below the high brushy hills of the Mixteca Baja.

Unrestored Mound 1, most certainly a former pyramid, slopes downhill past some reconstructed walls and stairs to a wide ceremonial courtyard. On its north side are the previously excavated Tombs 4 and 5. On the south side, a staircase descends to a smaller courtyard complex of what appear to be residential walls and patios. To the west is **Mound 2,** a partly reconstructed ceremonial pyramid. A partially excavated **ball court** lies about a hundred yards down the slope.

Shopping

If it's Wednesday or Saturday, the days of Huajuapan's huge *tianguis* (native town market), which is so big that the local government had to move it to the western outskirts of town, it's best to get there by taxi ($3). Stroll beneath the acres of shady *tianguis* (literally, awnings) for your pick of the best, from mounds of luscious bananas, tomatoes, cucumbers, and squashes. During the summer and fall, you'll also see plenty of pears, peaches, guavas, and grapes. Also admire the piles of deep-red chilies and bright-yellow *flor de calabaza* (squash flower) used for flavoring soups and stews. Here and there, you'll glimpse piles of old-fashioned items, such as corn husks (for wrapping tamales), *cal* (lime or quicklime) for soaking corn, red *jamaica* (hah-MAHEE-kah) petals for delicious drinks, nopal (cactus leaves), *tamarindo* and *guaje* pods, yellow *manzanilla* (chamomile) flowers, and hunks of *panela* (brown sugar). Throughout your walk, take note that the women vendors are definitely in charge, although few wear *traje* (traditional indigenous dress).

You'll also find some **handicrafts.** Locally made items include red- and black-streaked pottery, in practical shapes such as *ollas* (pots), bowls, and *comales* (griddles); and stone, carved into *manos* (rollers), *metates* (basins), and *molcajetes* (mortar and pestle) for grinding corn and chilies. Local folks also

Cerro de las Minas was a thriving Mixtec town from 300-800 AD.

sell plenty of items woven from palm. These include sombreros, *bolsas* (purses), *petates* (mats), and *cestas* (baskets).

Accommodations
UNDER $25
The budget hotels (none of which accept credit cards) dot the downtown, along Nuyoo and Colón, near the second-class bus stations. **Hotel Colón** (Colón 10, tel./fax 953/532-0817 or 953/532-1860, $15 s, $22 d one bed, $28 d two beds, $31 t), on the north side of the church, is probably the best super-budget choice. It offers about 20 clean but smallish dark rooms, with cable TV, hot-water shower-baths, and a restaurant on site.

$25-50
High marks go to suburban resort-style ★ **Hotel Casa Blanca** (Amatista 1, Colonia Sta. Teresa, tel. 953/532-0779 or 953/532-9364, fax 953/532-0979, $26 s or d in one bed, $50 d in two beds, $60 t), on Highway 190, Oaxaca City side, about 1.6 kilometers (one mi) east of downtown. This is a comfortable option for drivers anxious to avoid downtown traffic and save money. The Casa Blanca's 70 semi-deluxe rooms, in a pair of two-story wings in a spacious garden complex, are carpeted and comfy. Amenities include hot-water shower-baths, cable TV, fans and air-conditioning, relaxing pool-patio, good, airy restaurant, parking, and phones; credit cards are accepted.

OVER $50
Visitors who enjoy soaking up Mexico in comfort should choose the immaculate, class-act ★ **Hotel Garcia Peral** (Porfirio Díaz 1, tel. 953/532-0777 or 953/532-0742, fax 953/532-2000, www.garciaperalhotelrestaurant.com, $41 s, $53 d, $70 t), by the southeast corner of the central plaza. The 37 rooms in three floors surround an inviting pool patio blooming with tropical plants and birdsong. Rooms are comfortably furnished, with beige bed covers, reading lamps, attractively rustic tile floors, and modern-standard bathrooms. Amenities include fans, a good restaurant-bar, pool and sauna, and parking; credit cards are accepted.

Food
Huajuapan's best grocery, vegetable, fruit, and economy meals source is the downtown **Mercado Benito Juárez** (west, on Trujano), two blocks north from the plaza's northwest corner. For wholesome cooked specialties,

government building in Huajuapan de León

visit the airy **andador de fondas** walkway on the Benito Juárez market's north side.

On the other hand, health food fanciers can get plenty of honey, grains, juices, soya, vitamins, supplements, granola, and yogurt at **Natura** (Nuyoo 18, tel. 953/532-2538, 9am-9pm Mon.-Sat.), a block uphill from the cathedral. Satisfy your hankering for cake, pie, and cookies at the bakery, **Espiga de Oro** (Nuyoo 9, tel. 953/532-3432, 7am-10pm daily), half a block uphill from the cathedral.

Relaxing courtyard ambience, quiet music, and genteel conversation draw a steady stream of middle- and upper-class patrons to ★ **Cafetería Pasticel** (two doors south of Zona Zero, next to HSBC, tel. 953/532-2161, 8am-10pm daily, $3-7). Here, diners start off the day with strong Oaxaca espresso coffee and hearty breakfasts (hotcakes, eggs), and enjoy lunches and suppers of American-style sandwiches (hamburgers, hot dogs, and club) and hearty Oaxacan-style specialties (chicken enchiladas, chilaquiles, tacos).

Information and Services

A number of banks around the plaza, all with ATMs, change money. Best for its long hours is **HSBC** (on Porfirio Díaz, tel. 953/532-0169, 9am-6pm Mon.-Fri., 9am-3pm Sat.), across from the plaza's northeast corner, south of the church.

Banamex (tel. 953/532-1282, 9am-4pm Mon.-Fri.) can be found at the plaza's northwest corner.

Get to the *correo* (5 de Febrero 16, on the south side, tel. 953/532-0692, 8am-4pm Mon.-Fri., 9am-noon Sat.) from the plaza's southwest corner, by walking south on de León three blocks to 5 de Febrero; turn right and continue another two blocks to the post office on the left side of the street. The *telecomunicaciones* (on Galindo, between Hidalgo and Matamoros, tel. 953/532-0584 or 953/532-3577, 8am-7:30pm Mon.-Fri.), with money orders, telephone, and fax, is southwest of the plaza. From the plaza's southwest corner, walk a block south, turn right at Hidalgo, and walk a block and a half.

Long-distance telephone and fax are readily available at the **money exchange** (on the plaza, west side, tel. 953/532-2908, 9am-4pm Mon.-Fri., 9:30am-2:30pm Sat.-Sun.); it's also a Federal Express and copy shop.

If you get sick, one of the best places to go for a doctor is the **Centro de Especialidades de la Mixteca** (Zaragoza 24, tel. 953/532-1355, consultations: 9am-8pm Mon.-Sat.), three blocks west of the plaza. It has about 15 specialists on call, from gynecologist and pediatrician to internists and a cardiologist.

For routine remedies and prescriptions, go to one of the several pharmacies near the plaza, such as **Farmacia San Jorge** (on Colón, behind the church, tel. 953/532-1399, 8am-11pm daily), or its second branch (Nuyoo 20, half a block north from the church, tel. 953/532-1123 or 953/532-1584, 8am-11:30pm daily).

Although Huajuapan has a city *turismo office* on the upper floor of the *presidencia municipal* on the west side of the plaza, you might get more good information by consulting friendly José Flores Cubas, owner of the **Turismo "Oh Tierra del Sol"** (at the plaza's southeast corner, tel./fax 953/532-4555, ohtierradelsol@hotmail.com, 8:30am-7pm Mon.-Sat.).

Get your wash done at **Lavandería Easy** (on Hidalgo, 8am-8pm Mon.-Sat., 9am-8:30pm Sun.), one block west, one block south from the plaza's southwest corner.

Getting There and Away

Several first- and second-class bus lines operate out of various terminals, providing direct connections with many Oaxacan and national destinations. The busy, nearly all-first-class **bus terminal** (Hwy. 190 intersection with Nuyoo, tel. 953/532-9309), six blocks north of the plaza, is the hub for **Omnibus Cristóbal Colón, Autobuses del Oriente (ADO), Sur,** and **Autobuses Unidos (AU)** ticket sales, arrivals, and departures. Principal connections, including many intermediate destinations, are southeast with Nochixtlán and Oaxaca City; south via Highway 182 and Tonalá with

Juxtlahuaca, where you can transfer on to Tlaxiaco, Putla, and Pinotepa Nacional; and northwest with Puebla and Mexico City.

Second-class **Fletes y Pasajes** (on the highway, across the street, west from the ADO station) offers a broad range of connections in Oaxaca, approximately the same as Sur. **Autobuses Erco** (Linea Oro, Nuyoo 19, tel. 953/532-1513) offers first-class express connections with northern destinations of Izucar de Matamoros, Puebla, and Mexico City.

A pair of long-distance van services also provide oft-frequent fast connections. **Servicios Turísticos Huajuapan** (Nuyoo, tel. 953/554-0813) provides broad connections, southeast, with Highway 190, to the destinations of Tamazulapan, Nochixtlán, and Oaxaca; and south, along Highway 182, with Tonalá and Juxtlahuaca.

Furthermore, **Servicios Turísticos Teposcolula** (Nuyoo, local cell tel. 044-953/110-4025) provides connections southeast with Tamazulapan, thence south along Highway 125, with Teposcolula and Tlaxiaco. Find them both on Nuyoo, about three blocks north of the church, across from the big Farmacia Ahorros.

Drivers have their pick of four major paved highways radiating from Huajuapan. Northwest, Highway 190 connects with Mexico City: 316 kilometers (196 mi) via Cuautla, Morelos. Two winding lanes and numerous big trucks along the way usually slow traffic on the route. Figure about seven hours under good conditions, in either direction. A quicker alternative is to first head northeast via Highway 125, 118 kilometers (74 mi), two hours, to Tehuacán, Puebla. There, connect with the *cuota autopista,* which will whisk you in another three hours, via Puebla, to Mexico City.

For Oaxaca City, follow Highway 190 for 113 kilometers (70 mi), two hours, southeast to Nochixtlán. Continue via the *cuota autopista* to Oaxaca City, another 80 kilometers (50 mi), about one additional hour.

SOUTH OF HUAJUAPAN: ALONG THE HIGH ROAD TO THE MIXTECA ALTA

This lightly traveled, all-paved route, National Highway 182, branches south from Huajuapan, opening a scenic back door to Oaxaca's cool, green, and culturally rich Mixteca Alta. Along the way, you'll cross rushing mountain rivers, wind through fertile farm valleys, and climb to high ridges where you can gaze back down upon it all.

Pleasant surprises along the way include boating, fishing, camping, and lakeside bungalows at Yosocuta Reservoir, and riverside hiking and wilderness camping in spectacular Tonalá Canyon. A few miles farther, at colonial-era Tonalá town, you can enjoy a cool, shady walk, and a picnic in the town's grand old *sabino* (bald cypress tree) grove.

Yosocuta Reservoir

This big artificial lake, 13 kilometers (eight mi) south of Huajuapan, confined by the government-built Yosocuta dam on the Río Salado, rises and falls with the seasons. From February through June, the reservoir drains, nourishing irrigated crops downstream. Its level consequently falls, leaving an ugly bathtub-like lakeshore ring. However, by October, the lake usually refills to its brim, gently lapping the shoreline at **Parador Yosocuta,** the major lakeside access point.

If it's off-season and half full or Lake Yosocuta doesn't suit you, stop instead at the **Balneario las Bugambilias** (no phone, 10am-6pm daily, $6 adults, $3 under 12), a family paradise of pools, water slides, a merry-go-round, restaurant, and campground. The *balneario* (resort) is located on the highway, past the town of San Marcos, about eight kilometers (five mi) west of the reservoir.

Also along the road, at San Marcos village, you must stop for a treat at ★ **Panadería San Marcos** (no phone, 7am-8pm daily), on the highway at the south edge of San Marcos village, a few kilometers past (west of) Yosocuta (but before the *balneario*). Here,

Cohetes: Bangs, Flashes, and Hisses in the Night

a flaming *cohete*

Like everyone, Mexicans love celebrations, and every one of them, humble or grand, must be accompanied by *cohetes*. Although *cohetes* literally means "rockets," folks always associate them with the myriad other booming, flaring, whooshing, banging, and whirling incendiary devices that traditionally go along with *cohetes*. And while in most of the United States, bland "Safe and Sane" fireworks are all that ordinary folks set off on the Fourth of July and maybe New Year's, the sky seems to be the only limit during the seemingly innumerable fiestas that Mexicans celebrate everywhere.

Celebrating peaks during the several weeks before Easter Sunday, when folks start out with a rip-roaring Carnaval (Mardi Gras) and then parade the six succeeding Friday afternoons to the cannonades of *cohetes de trueno* (thunder rockets) overhead, ending with a grand explosive bash on Easter Sunday.

Whatever the occasion, the *coheteros* (rocketeers) have plenty of tricks up their sleeves, from the familiar, colorfully brilliant *cohetes de luces* (rockets of lights) to a dozen other strictly Mexican varieties. These include *toritos*, a bull-shaped frame, decorated with papier mâché and loaded with flares and firecrackers, that some daredevil wheels or carries on his back through the crowds of merrymakers.

Sometime after that, someone usually scatters some *buscapies* (heel-chasers) that go whizzing, whirling, and shrieking under the feet of the crowd.

Finally, the *cohetero* lights up the *castillo*, a grand framework laced with pinwheels, flares, and smoke bombs, from which a spinning *corona* finally swishes skyward, scattering a trail of stars in the inky firmament overhead.

you can savor what has to be the Mixteca's, if not all of Oaxaca's, best pastries.

Tonalá Canyon

Past a high, pine-studded ridge and pass, Highway 182 winds down to the fertile, green Tonalá valley. There, 43 kilometers (27 mi) south of Huajuapan, beneath the foot of **Puente Morelos,** a steel-arch highway bridge, the Río Salado issues through the deep defile of **Cañon de Tonalá** (known locally as El Boquerón, "Big Mouth").

A trail (and aqueduct) cut into the canyon wall leads to a diversion dam about

1.6 kilometers (one mi) upstream. The trail begins at some stairs not far from the bridge's north footing. It continues spectacularly, above the river along the diversion canal, winding beneath towering 300-meter (1,000 ft.) moss-mottled cliffs, green-tufted like a classical Chinese painting.

★ Santo Domingo Tonalá

The sleepy farm community of **Santo Domingo Tonalá** (pop. 3,000) owns a pair of gems: its 16th-century Dominican-founded church and ex-convent, the **Templo de Santo Domingo,** and the shady, sylvan *sabinera* (cypress grove) behind the church, home to an intriguing portrait of Angel Gabriel holding the scales of justice, deciding which of a cluster of beseeching souls will be admitted to Paradise. Farther on stands an image of the beloved African Dominican padre San Martín de Porres.

You'll find the *sabinera* two blocks behind the church. Stroll around and soak in the cathedral-like loveliness beneath the ancient trees. At the grove's far west end (left as you enter), find the rugged old grandparent of them all, 4.5 meters (15 ft.) in diameter and 15 meters (50 ft.) around.

ECOTOURISM

Santo Domingo Tonalá has been increasingly welcoming to visitors. Besides camping, hiking, and wildlife-viewing opportunities in Tonalá Canyon, you can enjoy guided tours of local archaeological sites. These include a cave with *pinturas rupestres* (prehistoric hieroglyphic rock paintings), and walls of ancient crumbling temples (from a time long ago, when the local population is said to have migrated from present Chiapas state).

For information on all this, drop by the local **ecotourism office** (in the Tonalá *presidencia municipal,* tel. 953/531-0023, in Spanish), where Artemio Cruz is in charge. They now have hiking trails for guided tours, navigable either on foot or by mountain bike; and in Tonalá Canyon, there's a riverside campground and *cabañas* for overnight accommodations.

ACCOMMODATIONS AND FOOD

Consider Tonalá's one hotel, the homey **Los Mangos** (Lázaro Cárdenas 27, tel. 953/531-0023, $15 s, $18 d in one bed, $22 d or t in two beds), marked by a tall mango tree, on the entrance road from the highway. The owners offer 10 rooms beside a flowery garden and the loveliest of crimson-blossomed *tabachínes* (flame trees). Check the rooms before moving in; mildew can be a problem here, especially during the rainy summer. Ask for fresh linens if necessary. All rooms have baths, with 24-hour hot water, and all the mangos you can eat, in season.

INFORMATION AND SERVICES

Most of Tonalá's essential services are on Lázaro Cárdenas, near the town plaza. For example, if you're sick, go to the *centro de salud* (8am-2pm and 4pm-6pm Mon.-Sat.), downhill a block past the church. Alternatively, consult with Doctora Aracel Orate at her **Farmacia Diana** (across from the *centro de salud,* 8am-9pm Mon.-Sat., 8am-3pm Sun.).

Find both the *correo* (9am-2pm Mon.-Fri., 9am-1pm Sat.) and the *telecom* (8am-3pm Mon.-Fri.) on the plaza, by the *presidencia municipal.* For long-distance telephone and fax go to the *larga distancia* (Lázaro Cárdenas, 9am-9pm daily), a block downhill from the church, on the right.

For lots of digital photo services, go to **Foto Studio Tonalá** (local cell tel. 044-953/531-0307, 10am-4pm and 5pm-9pm Mon.-Sat.), a block south of the plaza.

Getting There and Away

Bus passengers can reach Yosocuta, Tonalá Canyon, and Tonalá town by second-class **Sur** (choose Sur) or **Boquerón** buses, either northbound for Huajuapan or southbound for Juxtlahuaca. By van, **Servicios Turísticos Huajuapan** picks up southbound

Easter Calendar

Although Christian religious denominations' Easter calendars vary, virtually all Western Christian churches follow the same calendar as the Roman Catholic version, universally used in Mexico. This calendar originated with the Council of Nicaea, which, in AD 325, set Easter as the first Sunday after the first full moon of spring (or, more precisely, the first full moon after the vernal equinox, which the church authorities fixed as March 21).

The Easter season customarily kicks off with **Carnaval,** a rip-roaring party that runs the few days preceding **Miercoles de Ceniza** (Ash Wednesday), when all merriment ceases. Ash Wednesday, in turn fixed as the 46th day before Easter Sunday, occurs most often in February, and marks the beginning of **Lent,** a period of penitence and fasting. The gravity of Lent is literally rubbed in via ashes that the faithful get smeared onto their foreheads during solemn Ash Wednesday Christian church ceremonies worldwide.

In Mexico, religious processions and sober observances continue on each of the subsequent six Fridays. **Domingo de Ramos** (Palm Sunday) immediately follows the fifth Friday, and finally, after the sixth, or **Viernes Santa** (Good Friday), **Domingo Gloria** (Easter Sunday) breaks the fast of Lent as folks celebrate the risen Christ with joy and feasting.

(Juxtlahuaca) or northbound (Huajuapan) passengers.

From Huajuapan, drivers should first take the Mexico City direction along Highway 190 to a signed Highway 182 Juxtlahuaca (or Tonalá) left turn, about 1.6 kilometers (one mi) west of the city center. After another 1.6 kilometers (one mi) turn right at the main street, Avenida Mina, and head out another 13 kilometers (eight mi) to Yosocuta. After a total of 43 kilometers (27 mi), arrive at Tonalá Canyon; continue another 5 kilometers (3 mi) to Tonalá town, continuing to Juxtlahuaca, a total of 100 kilometers (62 mi) to Juxtlahuaca. Heading in the reverse direction, north from Juxtlahuaca, the distances total approximately 51 kilometers (32 mi) to Tonalá, 56 kilometers (35 mi) to Tonalá Canyon, and 87 kilometers (54 mi) to Yosocuta. Figure about two hours at the wheel, either direction.

The Mixteca Alta

The Mixteca Alta, Oaxaca's temperate Mixtec highland, is a land poor in gold but rich in scenic and cultural assets: Airy mountain vistas, colorful village markets, pine-scented breezes, beloved old churches, tumbling waterfalls, ancient ruins, and crystalline springs await the traveler who ventures into the Mixteca Alta.

Moreover, travel within the Mixteca Alta is not difficult. Tlaxiaco, with its hotels, restaurants, bus connections, and services, is a good base for exploring the Mixteca Alta. From Tlaxiaco, roads lead out east past cool green mountain vistas to the enigmatic ruins at Huamelulpan and Achiutla, south over the airy Chalcatongo plateau to the Cascada Esmeralda at Yosundua, and west to the friendly little Mixtec-speaking museum towns of Cuquila and San Miguel Progreso.

ASUNCIÓN TLAXIACO

Tlaxiaco (Place of the Ball Game) is the economic capital of the entire Mixteca Alta, a magnet for many hundreds of vendors from all over central and southern Mexico and thousands more native folks who swarm into town for the **Saturday** *tianguis* (native town market), second only to the big Saturday market in Oaxaca City.

The Dominican missionary padres understood Tlaxiaco's importance as early as

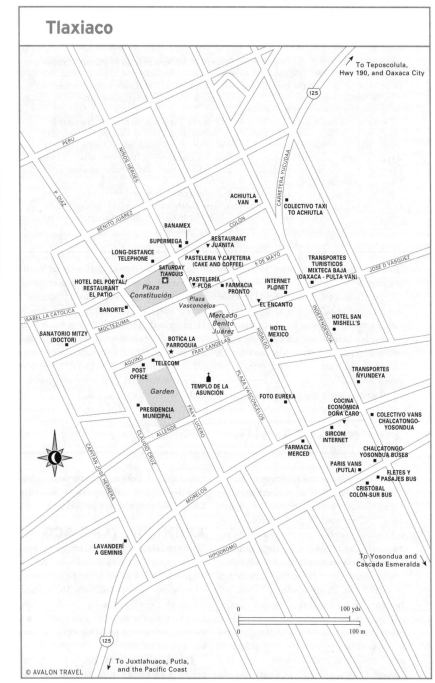

Tlaxiaco

To Teposcolula,
Hwy 190, and Oaxaca City

125

PERU

NIÑOS HEROES

P. DIAZ

CARRETERA YUCUDAA

ACHIUTLA
VAN

COLECTIVO TAXI
TO ACHIUTLA

BENITO JUAREZ

COLON

BANAMEX

SUPERMEGA

RESTAURANT
JUANITA

LONG-DISTANCE
TELEPHONE

PASTELERIA Y CAFETERIA
(CAKE AND COFFEE)

5 DE MAYO

TRANSPORTES
TURISTICOS
MIXTECA BAJA
(OAXACA - PULTA VAN)

JOSE D VASQUEZ

SATURDAY
TIANGUIS

PASTELERÍA
FLOR

FARMACIA
PRONTO

INTERNET
PL@NET

HOTEL DEL PORTAL/
RESTAURANT
EL PATIO

Plaza
Constitución

Plaza
Vasconcelos

EL ENCANTO

ISABEL LA CATOLICA

BANORTE

MOCTEZUMA

Mercado
Benito
Juárez

HOTEL
MEXICO

HIDALGO

INDEPENDENCIA

HOTEL SAN
MISHELL'S

SANATORIO MITZY
(DOCTOR)

BOTICA LA
PARROQUIA

FRAY CANDELAS

AQUINO

TELECOM

POST
OFFICE

TEMPLO DE LA
ASUNCIÓN

PLAZA VASCONCELOS

TRANSPORTES
ÑYUNDEYA

Garden

FOTO EUREKA

COCINA
ECONÓMICA
DOÑA CARO

PRESIDENCIA
MUNICIPAL

CLAUDIO CRUZ

FRAY LUCERO

ALLENDE

SIRCOM
INTERNET

COLECTIVO VANS
CHALCATONGO-
YOSONDUA

CAPITAN JOSE HERRERA

FARMACIA
MERCED

PARIS VANS
(PUTLA)

CHALCATONGO-
YOSONDUA BUSES

FLETES Y
PASAJES BUS

MORELOS

CRISTÓBAL
COLÓN-SUR BUS

LAVANDERÍ
A GEMINIS

HIPODROMO

To Yosondua and
Cascada Esmeralda

0   100 yds

0   100 m

125

To Juxtlahuaca, Putla,
and the Pacific Coast

© AVALON TRAVEL

1550, when Friar Francisco Marín began building the monumental town church, the Templo de la Asunción. Scholars have identified details in the church's decorations that resemble those of the main church in the city of Caceres, Spain. This link has added a piece to one of the puzzles of Oaxaca's great Dominican churches: Where did the Dominican clerics, presumably isolated in the Oaxaca hinterlands, acquire the skill to create the masterpiece churches of Yanhuitlán, Teposcolula, Coixtlahuaca, and Tlaxiaco? The answer may lie in a previously unknown connection between the Dominican friars and the noted Rodrigo Gil de Montañon, master of Spanish Gothic-Plateresque architecture and builder of the Caceres church.

★ Tlaxiaco Saturday *Tianguis*

Make sure to arrive in Tlaxiaco by noon on Saturday, in time to soak in its spreading, colorful, **Saturday *tianguis***. Especially interesting are the time-tested handmade goods: *calabazas* (gourds) cut and carved into bowls, utensils, and musical instruments; extensive assortments of forest-gathered roots, seeds, bark, dried flowers, and nuts, ready to brew into teas to relieve dozens of illnesses; traditional clothes—hand-embroidered *huipiles* and *blusas* from all over Oaxaca; *canastas* (reed baskets), *tenates* (sturdy woven palm-leaf baskets), *petates* (mats); soft sombreros, not unlike famed "panama hats" also from palm; and leather *cinturones* (belts), *bolsas* (bags), purses, and *billeteras* (billfolds).

While you're people-watching in front of the church, the **Templo de la Asunción,** take a break and step into its cool, calm interior. Although begun in 1550, the church, once a Dominican convent, has been continually modified and strengthened since that time. Towering overhead, a network of unreinforced (no steel: all stone and mortar) Gothic arches have, amazingly, supported the entire ceiling for more than 400 years.

Botica la Parroquia

Just across the street, north, from the church-front, the **Botica la Parroquia** (Porfirio Díaz, at the corner of Fray Candelas, tel. 953/552-0008, 8am-9pm daily) is as much a museum as a pharmacy. Its 150 years of continuous operation, begun by the present owner's great-grandfather and handed down through the family, has resulted in a vast and venerable collection of antique bottles, flasks, urns, mortars and pestles, and a regiment of drawers stuffed with locally gathered barks, leaves, mosses, grasses, flowers, mushrooms, seeds, minerals, and animal parts for compounding into remedies to relieve a host of ailments. For example, you can get *siete aguas* (seven waters) for relief of *mal aire* (bad air), a folk name for a common ailment with symptoms of weakness and fever; often, but not always, modern doctors diagnose *mal aire* as malaria. You can also get *catalan* and arnica for aches and pains; and, for whatever else ails you, homemade herbal brandy is dispensed in two-peso portions from a gallon jug on the front counter.

The present owner explains his pharmacy's history and mission: "Grandad was the town doctor. Everyone came to him when they were sick. He hand-prepared all of his prescriptions. My mom still does it."

Accommodations

UNDER $25

A block and a half west of Plaza Constitución stands the downscale old standby, the family-run **Hotel Mexico** (Hidalgo 13, tel. 953/552-0086, $15 s or d, $23 t "old" rooms, $25 s or d, $29 t "new" rooms). Rooms in "new" (private bath) and "old" (shared bath) sections surround a rambling inside patio. All of the 20-odd rooms come with hot water, available only in the morning until 11am; credit cards are not accepted.

$25-50

Of Tlaxiaco's hotels, the semi-deluxe ★ **Hotel del Portal** (Constitución 2, tel. 953/552-0154, $23-28 s, d one bed; $26-35 d, t two beds), at the north-side plaza-front, affords a superb vantage for soaking in the market action and exploring the colorful town center. Inside, past the reception, you enter an elegantly restored grand patio, softly illuminated by an overhead skylight. The three stories of approximately 50 rooms encircle a back parking courtyard. The rooms come in two grades, standard and semi-deluxe and all are clean, comfortable, and well maintained, with hot-water shower-baths, TV, and parking; Visa and Mastercard are accepted.

Food

Taco stands and upstairs *fondas* (food stalls) at the covered **Mercado Benito Juárez** (one block south of the Plaza Constitución's southeast corner) are your best source of economical meals and snacks. Furthermore, a homey sit-down *comedor* (restaurant), the **Cocina Economica Doña Caro** (Morelos 13, no phone, 8am-8pm Mon.-Sat., $4-5), between Independencia and Hidalgo, two blocks east and three blocks south of the plaza's southeast corner, serves from a bountiful menu, for example, *huevos rancheros* and *mexicanos* for breakfast; and choice of either steaming chicken, turkey, or tamales smothered in mole, or savory pork and beef *guisados* (stews) for their all-inclusive four-course set lunch or supper.

Basic groceries are available at plaza-front *abarroterías* (grocery stores), notably at **Super Mega** (Constitución, tel. 953/552-0179, 8:30am-9pm Mon.-Sat., 8:30am-6:30pm Sun.), on the plaza's northeast side, two doors east of the Hotel del Portal.

For a leisurely *comida corrida* (set lunch) or a bountiful à la carte selection on a warm afternoon, go to refined, airy restaurant ★ **El Encanto** (Vásquez 6, tel. 953/552-0529, 8am-9pm Mon.-Sat., $3-7, set lunch $4), a block south and a block and a half east of the main plaza's southeast corner. Find them open also for à la carte breakfast and *cena* (supper).

Information and Services

Change money at Tlaxiaco's plaza-front **Banamex** (Colón 1, tel. 953/552-0166 or 953/552-0133, 9am-4pm Mon.-Fri., 9am-1pm Sat.) with ATM.

Alternatively, go to **Banorte** (at the plaza's southwest corner, tel. 953/552-0662, 9am-5pm Mon.-Fri.) for similar services and ATM.

Find the *correo* (tel. 953/552-2126, 9am-5:30pm Mon.-Fri., 9am-1pm Sat.), on the north side of the *jardín* in front of the church. Next door, at *telecomunicaciones* (tel. 953/552-0190, fax 953/552-0465, 8am-7:30pm Mon.-Fri., 9am-noon Sat.), you can send or receive a fax or money order.

Telephone long distance or send a fax at the big **SAM** *caseta larga distancia* (Constitución, on the plaza's north side, next to the Hotel del Portal, tel. 953/552-0313, 953/552-0314, or 953/552-0147, 7am-11pm daily). Alternatively (and more economically), buy a commonly available Ladatel telephone card and use it to call home in the United States, Canada, or Europe ($2 for four minutes).

If you need a doctor, ask at your hotel desk for a recommendation or contact one of Tlaxiaco's highly recommended physicians: such as Dr. Javier Noé Alavez Cervantes at **Sanatorio Mitzy** (Moctezuma 4, tel./fax 953/552-0058), a block and a half west from the plaza; or physician-surgeon **Dr. Geraldo Cruz Vela** (Aldama 6, tel. 953/552-0210).

For nonprescription medicines and drugs, try either **Farmacia La Merced** (corner of Morelos and Hidalgo, tel. 953/552-0483, 8am-9pm Mon.-Sat., 10am-2pm Sun.), downhill three blocks from the plaza, or **Farmacia Pronto** (Cinco de Mayo, tel. 953/552-0664, 9am-9pm Mon.-Sat.), half a block east of the plaza's southeast corner.

In police, fire, or medical emergencies call the *policía municipal* (tel. 953/552-1021) or hire a taxi to take you to them.

Tlaxiaco's friendly, family-owned laundry is **Lavandería Geminis** (Capitán José Herrera 20, tel. 953/552-0708, 8am-9pm Mon.-Sat.). Find it on Herrera: from the plaza's southwest corner, walk a block west, then three blocks south.

Mexican Names

Nearly every Mexican, from native country folks to pure Spanish bluebloods, goes by his or her Spanish-origin names. Outsiders, confounded by long handles, such as Doña Juana María López de Díaz, wonder how Mexican names got so complicated.

The preceding "Doña Juana" example is especially complicated, because it's a typical woman's name, which is generally more complex than that of a typical man.

So, let's explain a man's name first. Take the national hero, Vicente Ramón Guerrero Saldaña. Vicente is his first given name; Ramón, the second given name, corresponds to the "middle" name in the United States. The third, Guerrero, is customarily the father's first surname; and the last, Saldaña, his mother's first surname. Only on formal occasions are men referred to with all four of their names. Simply, "Vicente Guerrero" would do most of the time.

Now, back to "Doña Juana." I threw a curve at you by introducing "Doña." It's an honorific, used as "Dame," for a distinguished woman. ("Don" is the corresponding honorific for Spanish men.)

So, skipping the honorific, women's names start out like men's: First given name, Juana; second given name, María; and father's first surname, López.

Now, things get more complicated. For unmarried women, the naming is the same as for men. But when a woman gets married, she customarily replaces her second surname with her husband's first surname, preceded by "de," meaning "of." So, in the example, Juana is evidently a married woman, who has substituted "de Díaz" (her husband's first surname being Díaz) for her second surname, all adding up to Juana María López de Díaz.

Thankfully, however, informal names for women also are simplified. Juana, above, would ordinarily shorten her name down to her first given name followed by her husband's first surname: simply Juana Díaz.

All the above notwithstanding, many Mexican women do not go along with this male-dominated system at all and simply use their maiden names as they were known before they were married.

Getting There and Away

Long-distance service includes Sur and Omnibus Cristóbal Colón, from their bus station (Hipodromo 24 B, tel. 953/552-0182), half a block west of the Independencia corner. There, buses connect east and southeast with Teposcolula, Yanhuitlán, Nochixtlán, and Oaxaca City; and north with Tamazulapan, Huajuapan, Puebla, Cuautla (Morelos), and Mexico City.

Also, on Hipodromo, a few doors east, second-class Fletes y Pasajes (tel. 953/552-0432) long-distance buses connect east and southeast with Teposcolula, Yanhuitlán, Nochixtlán, and Oaxaca City; and north with Mexico City (Tapo terminal) by the expressway, via Coixtlahuaca, Tepelmeme, Tehuacán, and Puebla.

Furthermore, a pair of good van services provide fast and frequent connections. On Independencia, three blocks north of Hipodromo, Transportes Turística Mixteca Baja (Independencia, tel. 953/552-0308) connects very frequently with Oaxaca City, via Teposcolula and Nochixtlán, south with Putla (where connections are available for the Pacific coast), and Yosundua (around noon and 6pm daily). Alternatively, reliable RAMSA vans (Hipodromo 13), next to Omnibus Cristóbal Colón, connect frequently northeast with Oaxaca City, and south with Putla.

EAST OF TLAXIACO: SAN MARTÍN HUAMELULPAN

The community museum at Huamelulpan (oo-wah-may-LOOL-pahn), about two kilometers (1.2 mi) off Highway 125, five kilometers (3 mi) east of the Achiutla turnoff, was built partly to display the artifacts uncovered at the town's important archaeological

Duendes: Spirits of Mexico

Once upon a time, most everyone believed that the world was full of spirits that inhabited every object in creation: trees, rocks, animals, mountains, even the wind and the stars. World mythology is replete with examples, from the leprechauns of Ireland and the fairies of Mount Tirich Mir in Pakistan to the spirits who haunt old Hawaiian *heiaus* (temples) and the *duendes* of Mexico.

Such beliefs persist, especially in the Mixteca countryside. Eventually, many a campesino will take his children to his mountainside cornfield to introduce them to the *duendes*, the elfin beings who folks sometimes glimpse in the shadowed thickets where they hide from mortals.

Modernized city Mexicans, generations removed from country village life, often scoff at such antique beliefs. That is, until the family doctor fails to cure their weakened spouse or sick child. Then they often run to a *curandero* or *curandera* (folk healer).

"*Enduendado*," affliction by an angry *duende*, the *curandero* sometimes diagnoses. Often, the cure is simple and savvy: teas and poultices of forest-gathered herbs. Other times, it is mystical, such as "purifying" by passing an egg all over the afflicted one's body to draw out the illness, and then breaking the egg into a bowl. The shape the broken yolk takes, maybe of a snake, might determine the treatment, which may be long and intricate: massage with lotions of herbs and oils, followed by a *temazcal* (sweat bath) rubdown with rough maguey fibers, all consummated by intense prayers to the Virgin of Guadalupe to force the *duende* to cease the affliction.

Many times, the folk cure fails; other times, however, it succeeds, and with enough frequency to convince millions of Mexicans of the power of the village folk healer to purge a *duende*'s poisonous spell.

zone. The National Archaeology and History Institute (INAH) installed the museum's archaeological exhibits in 1978. Later, the local community took over and did its own oral history project during the late 1980s, which resulted in the museum's traditional medicine displays.

Note the sign on the post on the right as you reach the town plaza. It reads, roughly: "Please stop and register at the community museum and get a guide to show you the ruins." If you arrive when the museum is closed, ask around for someone to guide you.

Huamelulpan Museum and Archaeological Zone

The museum is officially called the **Museo Comunitario Ihitalulu** (ee-ee-tah-LOO-loo; Hwy. 125, tel. 951/510-4949, 10am-5pm Tues.-Sun., $1 admission), meaning "Beautiful Flower." Inside, on the left after you enter, you'll see the archaeological section first, with its especially notable monolith of Dzahui, the Mixtec god of rain, lightning,

and thunder (akin to the Zapotec god Cocijo). Also fascinating are burial remains, including a complete skeleton and bowls for portions of water, food, and *pulque* (alcoholic beverage) for the afterlife. On the museum's opposite side, find the equally intriguing traditional medicine exhibit, detailing methods that *curanderos* (curers), *yerberas* (herbal healers), and *parteras* (midwives) use to treat their clients.

EXPLORING THE ZONE

Leave time for a stroll around the archaeological zone. It was first visited in 1933 by Alfonso Caso of Monte Albán fame, and it has been intensively excavated and partly reconstructed by several others since the 1950s. Finds reveal that Huamelulpan was a small city occupied between 400 BC and AD 600, approximately the same epoch as Monte Albán.

Huamelulpan community museum volunteers lead visitors on tours of their archaeological zone, including Cerro Volado, for a fee of about $20. Arrive early and you may be able to arrange such a tour on the spot. Guides and **lodging** at Huamelulpan's tourist-house dormitory can also be reserved ahead of time by leaving a message, including time of arrival and number in your party, at the Huamelulpan long-distance telephone *caseta* (tel. 555/510-4949).

Getting There and Away

Get to Huamelulpan by car or Tlaxiaco-bound second-class Omnibus Cristóbal Colón Sur, Fletes y Pasajes, or van from Oaxaca City, Nochixtlán, Tamazulapan, or Teposcolula. Get off at the Huamelulpan turnoff on Highway 125, about half an hour (21 km/13 mi) past Teposcolula. In the reverse direction, drive or ride the same bus and van east from Tlaxiaco a similar 21 kilometers (13 mi), half an hour, and get off at the Huamelulpan side-road turnoff. Continue on foot, or by taxi, about two kilometers (1.2 mi) to the museum on the town plaza.

Northern Oaxaca

The vast, diverse northern Oaxaca landscape encompasses three of Oaxaca's traditional geo-cultural regions: the pine-tufted northern Sierra, the fertile, tropical Papaloapan basin, and the oases of the Cañada canyonland.

Here, travelers ready to venture north of the Valley of Oaxaca can find high mountains for camping, hiking, and climbing; tropical rivers and grand, glassy lakes for fishing, swimming, and boating; crystalline springs welling from the base of emerald mountains; and country markets where people wear colorful costumes and speak ancient traditional dialects.

This chapter is organized as a circular tour, initially exploring the mountain villages of Benito Juárez and Cuajimoloyas that perch at the first high crest north of Oaxaca City. Circling back and continuing north, deeper into the mountains, visitors will find the lushly forested, wildlife-rich country around Ixtlán and Guelatao, beloved president Benito Juárez's birthplace. The route continues north into the fertile Río Papaloapan basin to explore the cultural and natural riches of the Chinantec and Mazatec ancestral homelands. The road turns west, into the high

Mazateca, to Huautla de Jiménez, a mountain town made internationally famous by the hallucinogenic mushrooms of renowned *curandera* (indigenous medicine woman) María Sabina. Finally, returning west and south toward Oaxaca City, the route traces the tropical country of Teotitlán del Camino and Cuicatlán.

PLANNING YOUR TIME

You can enjoy Northern Oaxaca's varied sights and grand scenery in a circular excursion in three or four days, with a fair amount of driving on picturesque mountain roads that require your focused attention. The roads are in good condition for the most part, and there are countless spectacular views, but, alas, few if any turnouts where you can stop.

Nature enthusiasts might want to spend a couple of days and a night or two exploring the limestone cave, lush cloud forest,

---

Previous: mural of indigenous medicine woman María Sabina, Huautla de Jiménez; a pastoral scene along the lakeshore. **Above:** Cuicatlán.

Look for ★ to find recommended
sights, activities, dining, and lodging.

Highlights

★ **Balnearios Monte Flor and El Zuzul:**
Refresh yourself with a swim and a picnic, and
even camping overnight, at crystalline springs
(page 225).

★ **San Pedro Ixcatlán and the Islands:**
Ride an excursion boat to the rural, all Mazatec-
speaking Isla Soyaltepec and enjoy an overnight
in the charming Hotel Villa del Lago (page 228).

★ **Huautla de Jiménez:** This lovely mountain town is worthy of an overnight visit. Enjoy
the views and maybe even the vibes generated
by the psychedelic mushrooms growing in the
area. The strangely arresting mural on the town
hall depicts the mission of celebrated hallucinogenic healer María Sabina (page 230).

★ **Las Regaderas:** Take an excursion outside Huautla to enjoy the cooling spray of these
waterfalls, which plummet 100 feet into the wild,
tumbling river (page 234).

Northern Oaxaca

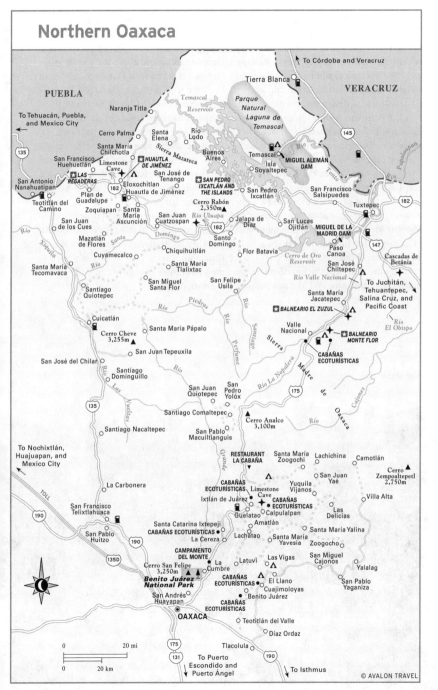

To Córdoba and Veracruz

Tierra Blanca

PUEBLA

VERACRUZ

Naranja Titla

Temascal Reservoir

Parque Natural Laguna de Temascal

To Tehuacán, Puebla, and Mexico City

Cerro Palma

Santa Elena

Río Lodo

Buenos Aires

Temascal

Isla Soyaltepec

MIGUEL ALEMÁN DAM

135

Santa María Chilchotla

Sierra Mazateca

San Francisco Huehuetlán

Limestone Cave

HUAUTLA DE JIMÉNEZ

San José de Tenango

SAN PEDRO IXCATLÁN AND THE ISLANDS

San Pedro Ixcatlán

San Francisco Salsipuedes

Tuxtepec

182

San Antonio Nanahuatipan

LAS REGADERAS

Eloxochitlan

Huautla de Jiménez

182

Teotitlán del Camino

Plan de Guadalupe

Zoquiapan

Santa María Ascunción

San Juan Cuatzospan

Río Uluapa

Jalapa de Díaz

San Lucas Ojitlán

MIGUEL DE LA MADRID DAM

San Juan de los Cues

Cerro Rabón 2,350m

182

Santo Domingo

147

Mazatlán de Flores

Santo

Chiquihuitlán

Flor Batavia

Cerro de Oro Reservoir

Paso Canoa

Cascadas de Betánia

Cuyamecalco

Domingo

San José Chiltepec

Santa María Tecomavaca

Río

Santa María Tlalixtac

San Felipe Usila

Río Valle Nacional

To Juchitán, Tehuantepec, Salina Cruz, and Pacific Coast

Santiago Quiotepec

San Miguel Santa Flor

Piedras

Santa María Jacatepec

BALNEARIO EL ZUZUL

Río El Obispo

Cuicatlán

Río

Santa María Pápalo

Río

Perfume

Valle Nacional

BALNEARIO MONTE FLOR

Cerro Cheve 3,255m

San Juan Tepeuxila

Santiago

CABAÑAS ECOTURÍSTICAS

San José del Chilar

Santiago Dominguillo

Río

San Juan Quiotepec

San Pedro Yólox

Río La Nopalera

175

Sierra

Madre

135

Las Nueltas

Santiago Comaltepec

Cerro Analco 3,100m

Río

de

Santiago Nacaltepec

San Pablo Macuiltianguis

Oaxaca

To Nochixtlán, Huajuapan, and Mexico City

RESTAURANT LA CABAÑA

Santa María Zoogochi

Lachichina

Camotlán

TOLL

La Carbonera

CABAÑAS ECOTURÍSTICAS

Limestone Cave

Yuquila Vijanos

San Juan Yaé

Cerro Zempoaltepetl 2,750m

190

San Francisco Telixtlahuaca

Ixtlán de Juárez

Guelatao

CABAÑAS ECOTURÍSTICAS

Calpulalpan

Villa Alta

San Pablo Huitzo

190

Santa Catarina Ixtepeji

CABAÑAS ECOTURÍSTICAS

Amatlán

Lachatao

Santa María Yavesia

Las Delicias

Santa María Yalina

Grande

La Cereza

Zoogocho

135D

CAMPAMENTO DEL MONTE

Latuví

Las Vigas

San Miguel Cajonos

Cerro San Felipe 3,250m

La Cumbre

CABAÑAS ECOTURÍSTICAS

El Llano

San Pablo Yaganiza

Yalalag

Benito Juárez National Park

Cuajimoloyas

Benito Juárez

San Andrés Huayapan

CABAÑAS ECOTURÍSTICAS

OAXACA

Teotitlán del Valle

Díaz Ordaz

0   20 mi

0   20 km

175

Tlacolula

131

To Puerto Escondido and Puerto Ángel

190

To Isthmus

© AVALON TRAVEL

and mountain meadows around **Ixtlán de Juárez,** perhaps tenting or lodging in local rustic forest *cabañas*. Alternatively, you could enjoy a bit of nearby forest walking and also have time to admire the graceful old colonial-era churches in Ixtlán and nearby **Capulalpam,** a designated *pueblo magico,* plus the President Benito Juárez shrine and museum, in his Guelatao birthplace, then spend an overnight in a comfy Ixtlán hotel or forest *cabaña*.

Heading north, over the Sierra summit and down into the lushly tropical Papaloapan basin, be sure to stop for a picnic and a swim at the crystalline natural springs **Balnearios Monte Flor** and/or **El Zuzul.** Continue north to Tuxtepec for lunch and perhaps a walk along the riverfront.

Continue west into the heartland of the indigenous Chinantec and Mazatec peoples.

Stop for a while at picturesque hilltop Ixcatlán village, and consider taking the boat excursion to isolated Isla Soyaltepec. Farther west, climbing along and above the scenic, green Cañon del Río Santo Domingo, arrive in the capital of the high Mazateca, Huautla de Jiménez, home of María Sabina of 1970s magic-mushroom fame. An overnight stay here will give you time to enjoy the views, and if you are adventurous, sample the local magic mushrooms that so inspired María Sabina and her followers. Continuing west, downhill, stop to bask in the cool spray of **Las Regaderas** twin waterfall.

With your grand circle tour nearly complete, coast downhill into the cactus-plumed, oasis-dotted Cañada country, for a stop at Cuicatlán, magnet for a host of Cuicatec mountain folks who crowd in daily for the big town market.

high Mazateca

Northern Sierra

The vast northern Sierra, the series of rugged mountain ranges that repeatedly rise and fall for a hundred miles, moving north from Oaxaca City, is a repository of a significant fraction of Mexico's increasingly scarce resources: unblemished pine and spruce-decorated mountain vistas, colonial-era mountain villages, and vanishing wildlife, including all of Mexico's wild cat species, from the jaguar and the ocelot to the *tigrillo* and jaguarundi. Their survival in the region is due to the sprinkling of northern Sierra communities that carefully husband their communal lands, harvesting their lumber at only a sustainable pace and guarding their holdings against poachers.

These communities welcome visitors. Among the best prepared are Benito Juárez in the south, on the first Sierra ridge above Oaxaca City, and Ixtlán de Juárez near the northern summit. The villagers in Ixtlán de Juárez offer cozy mountain *cabaña* lodgings, campsites, and guides for exploring their lands by bicycle, foot, or car. This relatively untouristed territory is a paradise for backpackers, campers, and lovers of the mountainous outdoors.

UP FROM THE VALLEY: BENITO JUÁREZ AND CUAJIMOLOYAS

This pair of mountain hamlets perch nearly a mile above the Valley of Oaxaca at the first towering crest of the cool, pine-tufted Sierra Juárez. The attraction here is not the towns themselves, but their gorgeous mountain environs and all that that implies: great billowing clouds, summer wildflowers, cool crystalline spring water, and the scent of spruce and pine.

Furthermore, the communities and the Oaxaca government, in their effort to develop the outdoor touristic resources of the northern Sierra, offer a number of food, lodging, and outdoor activity options in Benito Juárez, Cuajimoloyas, Llano Grande, and other villages.

(*Note:* These villages are part of a local network, known cooperatively as **Pueblos Mancomunados,** that welcomes visitors to enjoy and appreciate their wildlife-rich, pine-forested, mountain-top environment. Visitors can make accommodations and guide arrangements either directly through the communities, or more conveniently through their Oaxaca City agent, **Expediciones Sierra Norte.** *A further note:* These mountain villages are not on the main Northern Oaxaca route but on a separate access road through Tlacolula or, more scenically, through Teotlán del Valle. If your time is limited, you might pass on this trip since it has much of the same ruggedly beautiful mountain terrain you'll find around Ixtlán de Juárez, which lies on the main route north.)

Sights

The modest houses and farms of **Benito Juárez** village (pop. 1,000) are sprinkled along a single east-west ridge-crest road. The *cabañas ecoturísticas* lodgings and the community center, **Casa del Pueblo,** with the *comedor* (restaurant) and a cozy fireplace, are at the east end, uphill. At that point, signs direct you toward a number of possible diversions: You have your choice of a quarter-mile *tirolesa* (a forest canopy cable ride, $10); horseback riding ($16/hr); a stroll among the springs trickling downhill through the adjacent pine-shaded **Parque Recreativo**; or you can follow the sign marked Mirador, walking along the road (follow each uphill fork) about 2.5 kilometers (1.5 mi) north to the *mirador* (overlook) tower atop a craggy 3,100-meter-high (10,300 ft.) perch. Here, the view seems limitless. On clear days, early risers can even recognize the sunrise silhouette of Volcán de Orizaba (elev. 5,747 meters/18,856 ft.),

Mexico's tallest mountain, a hundred miles to the east.

Another possibility is to follow the 10-kilometer (six mi) *sendero peaton* walking trail, by mountain bike or on foot. The *cabañas ecoturísticas* manager rents the bikes ($10) and furnishes you with a guide ($12). For more information and cozy *cabaña* reservations, contact the **Benito Juárez tourism manager** (tel. 951/166-6313), or go through **Expediciones Sierra Norte** (tel. 951/514-3631, www.sierranorte.org.mx) in Oaxaca City.

Cuajimoloyas (kooah-hee-moh-LOY-ahs, pop. 1,000), six kilometers (four mi) east along the ridge road from Benito Juárez, is the metropolis of this part of the mountains. Besides lodging and restaurants, it has a pharmacy, health center, small grocery stores, and a long-distance telephone.

Your first stop should be the tourism headquarters on the right side of the road as you enter town, across from the small hotel Yacautzi (Place of the Maguey). The tourism manager can set you up with bicycles ($5/hour), a guide ($15 for three hours), or both. Reserve in advance by leaving a message via the **Cuajimoloyas tourism manager** (tel. 951/524-5024).

Mountain Guide

A very convenient option is to go with well-equipped Empresa Ecoturística Comunitaria (Community Ecotouristic Enterprise), also known as **Expediciones Sierra Norte** (210 M. Bravo, Oaxaca City, tel. 951/514-3631, www.sierranorte.org.mx). The efficient staff work with a dozen-odd Sierra Norte communities, called **Pueblos Mancomunados,** which include, besides the Benito Juárez-Cuajimoloyas-Llano Grande trio, Yavesia, Latuvi, Amatlán, and Lachatao. Jointly, they have established a 100-kilometer (60 mi) signposted hiking and mountain-biking trail network and offer accommodations in rustic village cabins and campsites.

Accommodations and Food

The three villages—Benito Juárez, Cuajimoloyas, and Llano Grande—offer many lodging choices. The busiest and best organized is Benito Juárez, which offers an assortment of rustic but comfortable lodgings, the most economical of which is the large original tourist accommodation, still called by its original label, **Tourist Yu'u** (dorms $12 pp, guest rooms $10 pp). It accommodates about 20 persons in a dormitory hall, with shared toilet and hot-water showers. The facility also has several four-person, bunk-bed, private-bath guest rooms that open onto the large common hall.

Additionally, Benito Juárez offers several detached private *cabañas* ($40 d, t, or q), sleeping four, with hot-water baths, fireplace, and kitchenette. For more information and reservations, call the **Benito Juárez manager** (tel. 951/166-6313, 8am-8pm daily) or **Expediciones Sierra Norte** (tel. 951/514-3631, www.sierranorte.org.mx).

Cuajimoloyas also offers accommodations, including three duplex *cabañas* uphill above the town, and a small, plain hotel, the **Yacautzi** (on the road, left side, as you enter town from Benito Juárez, $15 d hotel rooms, $40 d *cabañas*). Although the hotel offers five clean but unheated basic bare-bulb rooms with double bed, toilet, and hot-water shower, the three *cabañas,* a quarter mile uphill, are much cozier, each with two spacious duplex units sleeping four, with fireplace and a hot-water shower and toilet, shared by respective occupants of the duplex units. Reserve directly through the **Cuajimoloyas tourism office** (tel. 951/524-5024, 8am-2pm and 4pm-8pm daily) or through **Expediciones Sierra Norte** (tel. 951/514-3631, www.sierranorte.org.mx).

The latter-day ecotourist influx supports a sprinkling of modest local eateries. In Benito Juárez the best is the **Casa del Pueblo** community *comedor* (restaurant). In Cuajimoloyas choose between *comedores* **San Antonio** and **La Montaña,** run by friendly Gilda and Sergio Hilser; and in Llano Grande, you have *comedores* **La Curva** (good for both breakfast and groceries), **San Isidro,** and **Katy.** All are open approximately 8am-8pm daily, and provide breakfasts ($2-5), afternoon *comida* (set lunch; $3-5), and tacos, tamales, quesadillas, and hamburgers for supper ($3-5).

Campers should arrive with all food provisions in hand, especially fresh fruits and vegetables. Local stores may have only minimal supplies.

Getting There and Away

From Oaxaca City, the best route to Benito Juárez, Cuajimoloyas, and Llano Grande is via the buses of **Sociedad Cooperativa Flecha de Zempoaltépetl** (saym-poh-ahl-TAY-paytl) from the Oaxaca City second-class bus terminal, headed for Cuajimoloyas (and also Llano Grande). They leave approximately six times a day for Cuajimoloyas, via Tlacolula. (They go several places, so say *"¿A Cuajimoloyas?"* before getting on.) For Benito Juárez, get off at the mountain crest, at the junction where the Benito Juárez road splits left (west). Walk or catch a ride the six kilometers (four mi) to the Benito Juárez *cabañas* and Casa del Pueblo.

By car or RV, for experienced and fearless drivers only, it's quickest to drive to Benito Juárez via the spectacularly scenic route via Teotitlán del Valle. Turn left at the signed Teotitlán del Valle Highway 190 turnoff, about 30 kilometers (18 mi) east of Oaxaca City. Continue straight through town, uphill on an initially bumpy road. A mile or two later, past the Teotitlán dam, the graded gravel road gets better.

ALONG THE ROAD TO IXTLÁN

The main high road to northern Oaxaca winds far uphill, climbing over lush, pine-clad crests and descending into deep river canyons to the Sierra Juárez, the mountainous birthland of Benito Juárez, Oaxaca's beloved favorite son. Besides its historical significance, the Sierra Juárez's pristine, thickly forested ridges and shadowed stream valleys are a natural garden of springs, meadows, caves, and waterfalls—a de facto wilderness refuge for dozens of endangered species, including all of Mexico's wild cats.

The best hub for exploring the Sierra Juárez is the small town of Ixtlán de Juárez, easily reachable by bus or car, about 60 kilometers (37 mi) north from Oaxaca City via Highway 175.

17th-century Templo de Santo Tomás Apóstol, Ixtlán de Juárez

Benito Juárez: Mexico's President for All Seasons

Mexico's memory of Benito Juárez, its most revered president, is draped in legend. What's certain is that he was born on March 21, 1806, in the northern Oaxacan *municipio* of San Pablo Guelatao, at the hamlet of Santo Tomás Ixtlán. When his parents, of pure Zapotec origin, Marcelino Juárez and Brigida Garcia, died tragically when Benito was three, his uncle took him in. After a quiet childhood, mostly spent shepherding his uncle's flocks in the surrounding hills, Benito left for Oaxaca City in December 1818 to live with his sister, María Josefa.

For Benito, this was a lucky stroke. He became part of the Maza household, where María Josefa lived and worked as a cook. In the genteel, well-to-do Maza family surroundings, young Benito gained exposure to music, books, politics, and people—not possible for a poor boy in the country. Moreover, he met Margarita Maza, who, with the blessing of her parents, later became his wife.

While living with the Mazas, Benito immediately gained the attention of priest and bookbinder Antonio Salanueva, who, recognizing Benito's exceptional qualities, took him under his wing and sent him to school in town in January 1819. With Salanueva as his patron, Benito made rapid progress. He entered Oaxaca's new Scientific and Literary Institute in August 1828 to study law. Four years later, he was a practicing attorney. He entered politics, rapidly rose from state to federal legislator, then Supreme Court judge, finally being unanimously elected governor by Oaxaca's legislature on August 12, 1849.

From a successful term as governor, Juárez returned to national prominence. He was elected Mexico's president for two separate terms, both interrupted, first by civil war during the latter 1850s and then by the French Intervention from 1862 to 1867. Victory over the French finally brought peace, and Juárez was elected president for the third time in October 1871. He toiled day and night to realize his dreams for Mexico, but he died from exhaustion on July 18, 1872.

By bus, ride a Cuenca (koo-AYN-kah) first-class or ADO bus bound for Ixtlán (or Valle Nacional or Tuxtepec) from Oaxaca City's ADO-Cristóbal Colón first-class station, on Highway 190 at the north side of town. Drivers, set your odometer and head out from the junction where Highway 175 splits north from Highway 190, about five kilometers (three mi) east of the Oaxaca City center.

Campamento del Monte

About 34 kilometers (22 mi) north, 10 kilometers (6 mi) after La Cumbre, you arrive at an attractive chalet-style view restaurant perched on the right (east) side of Highway 175. Although **Restaurant del Monte** (tel. 951/518-6139, $5-7) is certainly worth a stop (especially for fresh trout or baked rabbit) all by itself, the **Campamento del Monte** (tel. 951/560-3052, local cell tel. 044-951/172-7277, delmontemx@hotmail.com, 9am-3pm Mon.-Sat., $15 pp, three person minimum per

cabin) across the road is the main attraction. The *campamento* includes several cabins that sleep up to six in dorm-style beds, as well as space for tent camping in the woods. There are hiking trails throughout the surrounding mountains.

AT THE SUMMIT: IXTLÁN DE JUÁREZ AND VICINITY

If a Mexican person told you that he or she lived in Ixtlán, you still wouldn't know where that is, for there are many Ixtláns in Mexico. The prefix *ix-* refers to *ixtle*, the Aztec word for the fibers of the maguey plant. The suffix *-tlan* means "land of" or "place of." The maguey plant is widespread in Mexico, and the Aztecs were so dominant at the time of the conquest that their names for local towns are still used today. So the many Ixtláns are all places that the Aztecs named Land of the Maguey. Oaxaca Ixtlán people gave their town a unique name, by naming it Ixtlán de Juárez, after their favorite son, revered President Benito Juárez.

Ixtlán de Juárez people grow a lot of wood, in the thick forests coating this part of the northern Sierra. Wisely, they don't cut too much of it, so their forests remain rich habitats for many wild creatures, including all species of Mexican native cats (notably the jaguar and mountain lion), spider monkeys, and tapirs, many of which have disappeared in other parts of southern Mexico. The diversity of species is so rich in Ixtlán de Juárez's woodlands that a panel of international experts convened by the World Wildlife Fund has rated the local forest as one of the world's 17 outstandingly biodiverse ecosystems.

Sights

Ixtlán de Juárez (pop. 8,000), despite being the capital of its own sprawling governmental district, feels like a village, where the main evening activity is to either watch or join the kids playing basketball on the courts in the central plaza, then get *cena* (supper) before the mom-and-pop *comedores* close around 8:30pm. Walk three blocks in any direction and you're in the woods.

Ixtlán de Juárez's main in-town sight is its treasured 17th-century **Templo de Santo Tomás Apóstol,** just northwest of the town plaza, behind the faithful, very proper plaza clock. The present *templo,* started by Dominican fathers around 1640, replaced an earlier all-adobe church. Construction was completed about a century later, in 1734. Decorating the baroque facade's summit is a bas-relief showing the dramatic confrontation of doubting Thomas with the risen Jesus. Inside, instead of the usual one golden *retablo* (altarpiece) behind the altar, several more decorate the nave walls, with gilded saints, angels, and masterfully pious 16th- and 17th-century oil paintings.

Treat yourself to a *moto* (motorcycle taxi, $4 one-way) ride 600 meters (2,000 ft.) uphill to the **El Mirador** mountaintop viewpoint, for a panoramic vista of the entire northern Sierra. While there, feast on fresh trout at the restaurant **Las Truchas** (tel. 951/166-5015, $7). (You can glimpse El Mirador, on the summit peak, visible far above the town plaza, to the northwest.)

Ecotours

Most of the natural sights around Ixtlán de Juárez are on communal land, so you must make arrangements for a guide from the community-run Ixtlán ecotour agency, **Viajes**

Ixtlán de Juárez has a lively *tianguis* with fresh produce from all over the region.

Ecoturísticos Schiaa Rua Via (Mountain Where the Clouds Are Born; Av. 16 de Septiembre, tel./fax 951/553-6075, www.ecoturixtlan.com, 9am-3pm and 5pm-8pm daily; tours from $25 pp per day, excluding transportation) to accompany you. Tours range widely over Ixtlán's grand 48,000-acre preserve. They include bird- and animal-watching, cloud forest hikes, mountain biking, rapelling, cave exploring, wilderness camping, and much more.

Especially interesting is their exploration of the eerie moss-draped cloud forest near Los Pozuelos camping shelter. The trail (part of the fabled **Camino Real,** route of long-vanished Aztec, Zapotec, and Mixtec traders who trekked between the Gulf Coast and the Valley of Oaxaca) leads past ice-age remnant wild begonia bushes, giant ferns, dwarf bamboo, and autumn-brilliant liquid amber trees.

stairs and a viewing platform in the forest at Ecoturixtlan

Accommodations and Food

The only recommendable in-town hotel is **Casa de Huéspedes La Soledad** (Calle Francisco Javier Mina, Barrio de la Soledad, tel. 951/553-6171, $10 s, $17 d), with about a dozen clean basic rooms (seven with private baths, the rest with shared bath). Reserve ahead. Get there by walking uphill, past the town plaza, two blocks; turn left at Zapata, turn right at the first street, continue another block north to the hotel on the right.

★ **Ecoturixtlan** (tel. 951/553-6075, ecoturixtlan@hotmail.com, $13 pp) invites visitors to stay in their forest *cabañas* near the Arco de Yagela cave about halfway down the road between Ixtlán and Capulalpam. Facilities include six duplex *cabañas;* each of the accommodation units sleeps four, with double bed, bunk bed, and fireplace with wood included. A hot-water shower-bath and toilet is shared between each pair of duplex units. The entire complex is set in an idyllic, pine-forested stream valley, and offers everything you might want for a day or two in the mountains: hiking, rock-climbing, caving, biking, *temazcal* sweat lodging, guided tours, a gondola ride, and all else ecotouristic,

along with those comfy *cabañas* and a good restaurant on site. If you've got your own wheels and you want to stop for a day or two and simply soak in the natural world, this is an ideal base.

Ixtlán de Juárez offers a sprinkling of food possibilities. Stock up on fruits and vegetables during the Monday **market,** on the town plaza. Otherwise, for some fresh items and a pretty fair grocery selection, go to **Abarrotes Jiménez** (tel. 951/553-6124), just downhill from the plaza's southwest corner.

Ixtlán de Juárez supports a few restaurants around the plaza. Very recommendable is **Comedor Jemima** (Sidencio Hernández 10, no phone, 6:30am-8pm daily, $4-6), half a block downhill from the plaza's southwest corner.

Another good choice is the popular *comedor* **Farolita** (corner of Zapata and 16 de Septiembre, two blocks uphill from the plaza, tel. 951/553-6441, 9am-9pm daily, $3-6) for hearty morning breakfasts and afternoon *comidas* (set meals).

Information and Services

Nearly all of Ixtlán de Juárez's services are available near the plaza. Change money at **Banorte** (corner of Revolución and 16 de Septiembre, tel. 951/553-6060 or 951/553-6217, 9am-4pm Mon.-Fri.) with ATM, a block uphill from the plaza. Also visit the town *biblioteca* (library) next door, south side from the bank.

Find the *correo* (9am-1pm and 3pm-6pm Mon.-Fri., 8am-noon Sat.) at the plaza's northeast corner. If you get sick, go to the *centro de salud* (on Revolución, behind the *presidencia municipal,* open 24 hours). Alternatively, consult one of the town's private doctors. Your choices are **Dr. Vicente Morales** (on the plaza, south side of the basketball court, tel. 951/553-6023, consultations: 5pm-8pm Mon.-Thurs.), or **Doctora Ofelia Maldonado Luis,** at her **Farmacia La Soledad** (16 de Septiembre 17A, tel. 951/553-6003, noon-6pm Mon.-Fri.), two blocks uphill from the plaza.

Both the *gasolinera* and the **bus station** are on Highway 175, about three blocks west of the plaza. Second-class Cuenca de Papaloapan buses provide several daily connections south with Oaxaca City and north with Valle Nacional, Tuxtepec, and intermediate destinations. Moreover **vans,** provide several daily fast Ixtlán-Oaxaca City connections, from their terminal on Highway 175, near the Cuenca bus stop.

EXCURSIONS AROUND IXTLÁN

Capulalpam, Pueblo Mágico

Picturesque **Capulalpam** (pop. 3,000) perches on its hillside about 12 kilometers (seven mi) east along the local road from Ixtlán. By virtue of its historic and cultural significance, Capulalpam was recently declared an official Pueblo Mágico, thus attaining the honored echelon of three-dozen-odd other uniquely typical Mexican villages.

Part of the reason for the town's pride is the **Templo de San Mateo,** completed by the Dominicans in 1718. Ordinarily serene, the church grounds overflow with merrymakers during the **Fiesta de San Mateo,** which climaxes yearly on September 21.

The church's renovated interior soars to a magnificent wooden ceiling. Charmingly naive designs painted by early native artisans decorate the front, below the choir, while a pair of angels, following Jesus's exhortation to become "fishers of men," dangle fish from opposite sides of the front altar.

ECOTOURS AND *CABAÑAS*

Riding the wave of its new Pueblo Mágico status, Capulalpam has also made itself into an **ecotourism center** (office in town center, lower floor of library, tel. 951/539-2168, www.turismocapulalpam.com.mx, *cabañas* $14 pp, camping $5 pp). They welcome visitors with a broad menu of outdoor activities (hiking forest trails, river crossing by hanging bridge, cave- and gold-and-silver-mine exploring, biking, trout-farm fishing) by day, and five comfortable duplex *cabañas,* with fireplaces, toilet and hot-water shower-baths to stay by night, plus a campground to boot.

Capulalpam's hillside plaza

ecotourist *cabañas*

Guelatao

A government-constructed monumental **Plaza Cívica** has converted this modest mountain town on Highway 175 three kilometers (two mi) south of Ixtlán de Juárez into a shrine for beloved President Benito Juárez, who was born nearby on March 21, 1806.

Juárez's timeless credo, *"El respecto al derechos ajenos es la paz"* ("Respect for the rights of all is peace"), marks the museum on the plaza, two blocks uphill from the town highway crossing. Inside, glass cases preserve a few precious mementos: a photograph,

Juárez's death mask, a letter, a diary, a graduation certificate from the seminary in Oaxaca, and a model of the renowned black carriage in which Juárez for years fulfilled his duties of office, one jump ahead of his enemies.

Also on the upper plaza above the lake (by the parking lot) is a bronze sculpture of Juárez's mother, Brigida Garcia, and, at the *presidencia municipal,* a bust of Juárez, together with the historic letter that Juárez wrote to his ambassador in the United States, opposing the meddling of the United States in Mexican affairs.

Into the Papaloapan

Humid, tropical air, moving gently westward from the Gulf of Mexico, cools, clouds, and drops a deluge of rain on the northern slope of the Sierra Madre de Oaxaca. The water collects and cascades down the mountains, gathering into great, rushing rivers that finally deepen and wind serenely through a grand tropical lowland plain called the Papaloapan (pah-pah-loh-AH-pahn), after the river system that drains it. The Tonto, the Santo Domingo, and the Valle Nacional join

near the town of Tuxtepec to form the Río Papaloapan.

The rivers are the region's prime asset. At high elevations on the Sierra's northern slope, the waters nourish vast, thick forests: pine-oak at the higher elevations and a lush, tropical hardwood rain forest that spreads downhill into the valleys. There, farmers have replaced the forest with rich fields of corn and tobacco, great thickets of rubber trees, and, in the shady underlay, plantations of shiny-leafed coffee bushes. The government, moreover, has tamed and harnessed the rivers, gathering them into a pair of immense reservoirs, Temascal and Cerro de Oro, for irrigation, recreation, and electric power.

★ BALNEARIOS MONTE FLOR AND EL ZUZUL

A few miles south of Valle Nacional town, a pair of *balnearios* (developed springs) are perfect for a relaxing afternoon picnic or a pleasant camping or *cabaña* overnight.

Idyllic **Balnearios Monte Flor** (at Cerro de Marín village, Km 43) is about 6 kilometers (3.5 mi) north of Valle Nacional and 27 kilometers (17 mi) south of Tuxtepec. On the river side of Highway 175 northbound, watch for the small Museo Comunitario sign and rough entrance driveway on the right, at the last village *tope* (speed bump).

Downhill, below the village, under grand, spreading trees, cool, crystalline water wells up beneath a great hillside monolith into a gorgeous natural bathing pool.

The community welcomes guests to stay at one of their invitingly rustic, lovingly handbuilt *cabañas* (tel. 200/123-0589, 200/123-0590, 200/123-0591, $30 for four) and take part in a menu of outdoor activities. These include biking, swimming, and guided wildlife-viewing walks in the surrounding luscious mountainside tropical forest. While you're there, be sure to take a look inside their **community museum** (tel. 200/123-0589, 200/123-0590, 200/123-0591, 9am-5pm daily, $1 adults, 0.50 kids) to see their collection of locally discovered archaeological artifacts.

The queen of the valley's bathing springs is the local favorite, **Balneario El Zuzul** (tel. 283/101-7078), a name everyone from Valle Nacional to Tuxtepec knows fondly. Part of the fun is getting there, because you have to cross the bridge over scenic, swift-flowing Río Valle Nacional. Once across, you see what the fuss is all about: a big, round, stone-edged blue pool of clear, cool spring water, which wells up from the depths for everyone's enjoyment, a perfect antidote for a hot afternoon.

Get there by driving or taking one of the *colectivo* taxis (less than $1) parked at the signed turnoff road, between Kilometers 36 and 37, about 11 kilometers (7 mi) north of Valle Nacional, or 24 kilometers (15 mi) south of Tuxtepec. Continue 0.5 kilometers (0.3 mi); bear left around the turn, and continue 1.2 kilometers (0.8 mi) over the river bridge to Vega de Sol village on the south bank. Turn right just after the bridge and continue three blocks and turn right into the El Zuzul entry driveway.

TUXTEPEC

Tuxtepec (pop. 140,000), Oaxaca's second-largest city, is the administrative and commercial center of the rich governmental district of the same name. For at least a millennium, the town, at its strategic river-junction location, has been an important trading center. Archaeologists believe that the Popoluca people, direct inheritors of the ancient Gulf Coast Olmec mother culture, first settled Tuxtepec perhaps 2,000 years ago. Today, Tuxtepec is a bustling, noisy little modern town. For a visitor, there is not much to do or see. The history is evident only in the small pyramid—not much more than a pile of rubble, really—so, unless you are devoted to seeing every last archaeological sight in Oaxaca, you can stop here for lunch or if the timing is right, overnight at one of the hotels along the river. There is little access to the river from the town even though it is built right on the riverbank, so if you get a room with a view, enjoy it.

The name Tuxtepec is the Spanish version of the town's Aztec label, Tochtepec, or Hill of the Rabbits, which probably describes the town's original site, atop some low hills about 2.5 kilometers (1.5 mi) west of present downtown Tuxtepec.

Orientation

Tuxtepec is a modern town that spreads for two or three miles along the steep bank of the broad Río Papaloapan, which flows nearly due east past Tuxtepec's busy downtown. The main business streets begin at the Highway

175 bridge at the west end and continue for about 1.5 kilometers (one mi) east to the town plaza. Moving away from the river, the main streets are Independencia, 20 de Noviembre, 5 de Mayo, and Libertad. A fifth street, quieter river-view boulevard El Muro, also runs parallel to the river, beginning at the east end of Independencia and gradually curving northerly, then westerly, until its course is completely reversed as it runs west along the north side of town.

Accommodations

Tuxtepec serves its many business visitors with a number of good hotels. Most of the fancier establishments lie along west-side Bulevar Benito Juárez (the northern prolongation of Highway 175), or in the quieter neighborhoods away from the downtown. The budget accommodations, most priced under $25, are in the busy downtown, either overlooking or near the river. In all cases, in warm and humid Tuxtepec, air-conditioning is worth the small extra charge.

UNDER $25

Right in the middle of town stands the attractively renovated **Hotel Mirador** (Independencia 531, tel./fax 287/875-0652, 287/875-0500, or 287/875-0797, $18 s or d one bed, $22 two beds, $25 t, add $4 for a/c) overlooking the river, next to the Paso Real ferry dock. Of the 51 attractively decorated rooms, reserve one of the 2nd-floor ones, numbers 219-223, along the quieter, upper river-view corridor. Rentals all include TV, phone, hot-water bath, and parking. Credit cards are not accepted.

$25-50

On the highway, a block from the bridge, stands one of Tuxtepec's most relaxing hotels, the spacious four-star **Hotel Hacienda** (Blv. Benito Juárez 409, tel. 287/875-1500, hhaciendatuxt@hotmail.com, $35 s or d, $40 t). Past the entrance and parking, relegated thoughtfully to the outer periphery, the reception leads to a cool, air-conditioned restaurant

(with TV; you can ask them to turn down the volume), bordering a relaxing pool patio and shady tropical garden. The 60 semi-deluxe rooms in three-story tiers are secluded, clean, and comfortable, though somewhat worn (but undergoing renovation). The most desirable rooms have small balconies overlooking the garden (ask for *"balcón con vista del jardín, por favor"*). Rates are quite reasonable for such amenities, which also include air-conditioning, warm-water baths, cable TV, phone, and parking; but credit cards are not accepted.

Food

Tuxtepec visitors enjoy plenty of good food. The two town markets, the river-view **central market** (on Independencia in the town center) and the west-side **Mercado Flores Magón** (on 20 de Noviembre, two blocks from the Hwy. 175 river bridge), are the best sources of groceries, fruits, and vegetables. At the central market, *fondas* (food stalls) upstairs serve economical, wholesome *comidas* (set meals) at luxuriously airy river-view tables. Especially recommended among the market *fondas* is ★ **Casita María Tere** (Independencia, 7am-8pm Mon.-Sat., 7am-4pm Sun., $3-6).

For fresh baked offerings, go early to the **Panificadora Principal** (on 20 de Noviembre, tel. 287/875-0755, 7am-9pm Mon.-Sat., 7am-noon Sun.), on the corner of Degollado, about five blocks east of Highway 175.

A good place to start the day is the relaxing, TV-free ★ **Restaurant Bla-Bla** (on 20 de Noviembre, between Morelos and Arteaga, local cell tel. 044-287/104-8570, 7am-6pm daily, $4-9) in mid-downtown, a block from the river. Choose from a dozen tasty breakfasts, soups, Mexican specialties, poultry, seafood, meats, and much more.

Information and Services

Tuxtepec has several banks, all with ATMs. The longer hours of **HSBC** (805 Independencia, tel. 287/875-2211, 9am-6pm Mon.-Fri.) make it a good choice. Find it between Degollado and Jiménez, about three blocks west of the town center. Alternatively, moving east, try Bancomer (Independencia 647, tel. 287/875-1959, 8:30am-4pm Mon.-Fri.), next to the market; or Banamex (at Independencia and Rayón, tel. 287/875-1974, 9am-4pm Mon.-Fri.), farther east.

Find the *correo* (corner of Libertad and Nicolas Bravo, tel. 287/875-0239, 9am-4:30pm Mon.-Fri., Sat. 9am-1pm) a block behind the town plaza church. *Telecomunicaciones* (corner of Carranza and Morelos, tel./fax 287/875-0202, 8am-7:30pm Mon.-Fri., 9am-12:30pm Sat.-Sun.) provides public fax and money orders. Find it by walking, from the downtown market, four blocks from the river, inland, along Morelos.

For nonprescription medicines and drugs, go to a *farmacia,* such as Farmacia Cruz Verde (Independencia 908, tel. 287/875-0774, 9am-9pm daily), across from HSBC bank.

Doctors are plentiful in Tuxtepec. Ask at your hotel desk for a recommendation or go to one of the several doctors downtown. Find some of them located in the office complex across Independencia from Scotiabank Inverlat. Here choices include a gynecologist (Eliseo Camacho Delgado, tel. 287/875-3878), ophthalmologist (Julio R. Sáchez), and more.

For more choices, or in an emergency, taxi to either the Hospital Regional Civil (Ortiz 310, corner of Calle Sebastian, tel. 287/875-0023) or the Hospital Seguro Social (Blv. Benito Juárez/Hwy. 175, tel. 287/875-1366), on the town side of the river bridge.

For police or fire emergencies, contact the municipal police (at the *presidencia municipal,* tel. 287/875-3166).

Get your laundry done at Lavanderia Lavasec (Independencia 1683, tel. 287/875-3706 or 287/875-5339, 9am-2pm and 4pm-8pm Mon.-Sat., 9am-2pm Sun.), downtown, on the far west side, two blocks from the Highway 175 river bridge.

Getting There and Away

Long-distance bus lines, from one major terminal and two minor terminals, provide many connections with both Oaxaca and national destinations.

The major bus station (near the corner of Matamoros and Libertad, tel. 287/875-0237 for reservations and information) for first-class Autobuses del Oriente (ADO) and Omnibus Cristóbal Colón (OCC) and mixed first- and second-class lines Autobuses Unidos (AU) and Cuenca de Papaloapan (Cuenca) is smack in the middle of downtown, three short blocks from the river.

ADO (ah-day-oh) offers broad service, covering much of southeast Mexico. Buses connect south with Oaxaca City via Valle Nacional and Ixtlán de Juárez; northwest with Orizaba, Puebla, Mexico City (Norte terminal), and Veracruz; and northeast with Minatitlán, Coatzacoalcos, Villahermosa, Campeche, Mérida, Cancún, and Chetumal, at the Belize border.

OCC buses connect southeast with Isthmus destinations of Juchitán, Tehuántepec, and Salina Cruz; and Chiapas destinations of Tuxtla Gutiérrez and San Cristóbal las Casas.

AU buses connect north with Puebla and Mexico City; and southeast with Isthmus destinations of Matias Romero, Juchitán, Tehuántepec, and Salina Cruz.

Cuenca buses connect south with Oaxaca City via Valle Nacional and Ixtlán de Juárez; and north and northwest with Loma Bonita, Temascal, Tierra Blanca, Orizaba, Córdoba, and Veracruz.

Additionally, AU and TRV second-class buses operate out of a second terminal (at the west-side Flores Magón market on 20 de Noviembre), on the downtown side of the Highway 175 ingress boulevard. Buses connect west several times daily with Mazateca destinations of Ixcatlán and Jalapa de Díaz (but, at this writing, not Huautla de Jiménez) and northwest with Temascal (Miguel Alemán dam and reservoir) and Tierra Blanca.

Small, second-class line Autobuses Trópico (Libertad 1215, tel. 287/875-2895), operating from a third terminal (a block and a half west of Matamoros), connects six times daily with Oaxaca City via Valle Nacional and Ixtlán de Juárez.

For **drivers,** mostly good paved roads connect Tuxtepec with both Oaxaca and national destinations. Highway 175 connects south with Oaxaca City via Valle Nacional and Ixtlán de Juárez, over the Sierra Madre, in about 213 kilometers (132 mi). However, steep, winding grades can sometimes slow traffic to a crawl. Allow about five hours for safety in either direction. You will discover this to be one of the most memorable drives in Oaxaca, with spectacular views around every bend, but maddeningly few safe places to stop and enjoy them. If you find a turnout, use it.

Combined Highways 147 and 185 connect Tuxtepec southeast with Tehuántepec, via Matías Romero and Juchitán. The nighttime robberies and hijackings that used to plague the lonely, northern Highway 147 leg of this route have fortunately abated. To be sure, stop at the Highway 175-Highway 147 intersection gas station to check if the highway remains secure. You can ask in Spanish, *"¿Es seguro la carretera a Matías Romero?"* Allow about five hours of road time, in either direction, for this 304-kilometer (189 mi) trip.

Highway 182, connects Tuxtepec west with Huautla de Jiménez in the high Mazateca, via Jalapa de Díaz. Allow about 3.5 daylight hours westerly, 3 hours easterly, for this spectacularly scenic 119-kilometer (74 mi) top-of-the-world trip. This is one great drive!

★ SAN PEDRO IXCATLÁN AND THE ISLANDS

One gateway to the vast Miguel Alemán reservoir shoreline is through **Ixcatlán,** a prime spot for a country stay. The town stands at the eastern boundary of the Mazateca, where many townspeople and virtually everyone in the surrounding countryside speak Mazatec, and women wear the bright blue-and-white horizontally striped local *huipil* (traditional embroidered dress). A number of Ixcatlán women embroider blouses and *huipiles.*

Along the Road

The major sight along Highway 182, about half an hour west of Tuxtepec, is the **Puente Pescadito,** which bridges the channel connecting the Temascal and Cerro de Oro reservoirs. *Palapa* restaurants at both ends of the bridge supply refreshments and bass dinners. Below, the riverbanks, accessible on foot or by negotiable dirt roads, are level

tranquil waters of the Temascal reservoir

Cerro Rabón

and invite fishing for *mojarra* (bass) and RV or tent camping.

The grand lake vista spreads for miles south and north. The southern arm, Reservoir Cerro de Oro, began to fill when the Miguel de la Madrid dam was built downstream during the 1970s. The reservoir level rose until it finally connected with the Temascal reservoir during the mid-1990s. In joining the two reservoirs, the channel consequently also connects the drainage basins of the Río Tonto, in the north, and the Río Santo Domingo, in the south. Although the Cerro de Oro reservoir is large, with about 260 square kilometers (100 sq. mi) of surface area, this is only a fraction of the size of the Temascal reservoir.

Isla Soyaltepec

If it's no later than 3pm, you're early enough for the last trip to Isla Soyaltepec. Once a small isolated town, Soyaltepec (pop. 500) is even more isolated since the reservoir has confined it to an island where most of its inhabitants speak only Mazatec. The only way

---

to go is by boat, for which you can bargain (figure $15-20 for a two-hour round-trip for up to about six people) at the embarcadero on Ixcatlán's west lakeshore (below the Ixcatlán church).

The 9.6 kilometer (six mi) crossing takes about half an hour. Along the way, butterflies flutter, herons stalk their prey, and clouds billow above the mirror-smooth lake surface. On the western horizon rises the gargantuan, loaf-shaped massif of Cerro Rabón, often cloaked in a blanket of clouds. You'll pass through a fleet of little islands, some with petite wooded crowns, perfect for an afternoon or overnight of soaking in the scenery and solitude.

At Soyaltepec, climb (one hour round-trip) to the old village and church on the island hilltop. Half a dozen kids will probably accompany you. Halfway up, you scale a pre-conquest-appearing ponderous stone staircase. At the top, take a look inside the venerable (1744) church, gaze westerly over the many-island-studded lake vista, and get a *refresco* (refreshment) at the hilltop store.

Accommodations and Food

★ Hotel Villa del Lago (Calle Benito Juárez, tel. 287/871-3090, $26 s or d) would be a pleasant surprise anywhere, but here, in little, out-of-the-way Ixcatlán, it seems a small miracle. The hotel is the labor of love of its friendly owner, Patricia Sarmiento Castillo, who rents six immaculate rooms with air-conditioning and hot-water shower-baths. She has made the hotel even more inviting with an elegantly lovely pool-patio downstairs and a top-level terrace from which guests can enjoy Ixcatlán's dramatic lake-view panorama. Señora Castillo also makes art-to-wear cotton clothing.

The reservoir, whose waters Ixcatlán escaped because of its hilltop perch, has brought fresh fish to Ixcatlán. A scattering of country *comedores* (restaurants) serve good lake bass dinners, notably the homey and clean El Paraíso *palapa* (Calle Benito Juárez, no phone, 8am-8pm daily, $4-8) in mid-town, next to the *larga distancia* sign. Best for breakfast is owner Lulu Salina's **el Vaquero** (no phone, 7am-9pm daily, $4-10), downhill, overlooking the lake, where, besides the good food, you can feast on the luscious lake view.

Information and Services

Visitors to Ixcatlán can also count on a number of basic services, including a highly respected doctor (known locally only as Doctor Hilario) in addition to Doctor Rene Hipolito Juárez, at the *centro de salud* (Gonzalo Ortega 36, near the town entrance). Other services include pharmacies, grocery stores, a post office, long-distance telephone, and Internet access.

Getting There and Away

Get to Ixcatlán by the **Autobuses Unidos** (AU) or **TRV** bus bound for Jalapa de Díaz, from Tuxtepec's west-side Flores Magón market. Ride to the Ixcatlán side entrance road, then taxi or walk the 6.4 kilometers (four mi) to town. An informal network of taxi cabs in the form of pickup trucks with canopied beds and benches also services this region; they stop to pick up anyone who flags them down.

Drivers: At Tuxtepec, turn left (west) from Highway 175 onto Highway 182 at the Jalapa de Díaz sign at the traffic circle, about three blocks north of the Río Papaloapan bridge. Continue along Highway 182 west 55 kilometers (34 mi) to the signed Ixcatlán right turn-off. Continue six paved kilometers (nearly four mi) to town.

★ HUAUTLA DE JIMÉNEZ

Huautla de Jiménez (pop. 40,000; elev. 1,800 meters/6,000 ft.), tucked on a lofty Mazateca mountainside, was put on the world map during the 1960s by María Sabina, a local Mazatec-speaking *curandera* (indigenous medicine woman) who, like many others, used hallucinogenic mushrooms as part of her bag of remedies. The word somehow got out, and a small army of Love Generation devotees of hallucinogens from the United States and Europe, known locally as *gippis* (HEE-pees), quickly descended on Huautla. With them, soon came a continuous stream of doctors, journalists, and anthropologists.

María Sabina seemed to enjoy her renown. She was invited far and wide to testify to the efficacy of her remedies at learned

Fried fish is a specialty along the shores of the Temascal reservoir.

Huautla de Jiménez

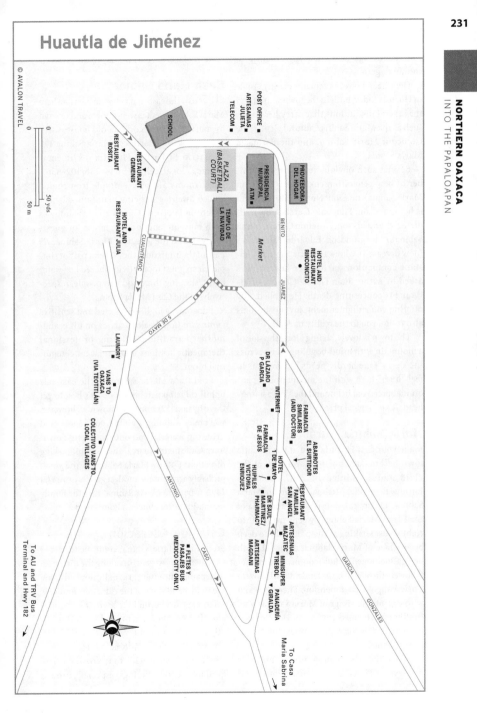

© AVALON TRAVEL

0   50 yds
0   50 m

SCHOOL

POST OFFICE
ARTESANIAS
JULIETA
TELECOM

RESTAURANT
ROSITA

RESTAURANT
GEMENIS

CUAUHTEMOC

HOTEL AND
RESTAURANT JULIA

PLAZA
(BASKETBALL
COURT)

PRESIDENCIA
MUNICIPAL
ATM

PROVEEDORA
DEL HOGAR

TEMPLO DE
LA NAVIDAD

Market

BENITO

JUAREZ

HOTEL AND
RESTAURANT
RINCONCITO

5 DE MAYO

LAUNDRY

VANS TO
OAXACA
(VIA TEOTITLAN)

COLECTIVO VANS TO
LOCAL VILLAGES

ANTONIO

DR LAZARO
P GARCIA

INTERNET

FARMACIA
DE JESUS

1 DE MAYO

HOTEL
VICTORIA
ENRIQUEZ

HUIPILES

DR SAUL
MARTINEZ/
PHARMACY

FARMACIA
SIMILARES
(AND DOCTOR)

ABARROTES
EL SURTIDOR

RESTAURANT
FAMILIAR
SAN ANGEL

ARTESENIAS
MAZATEC

MINISUPER
TREBOL

PANADERIA
GIRALDA

ARTESENIAS
MAGDANI

CASO

GARCIA

GONZALES

FLETES Y
PASAJES BUS
(MEXICO CITY ONLY)

To AU and TRV Bus
Terminal and Hwy 182

To Casa
Maria Sabrina

international medical conferences. But after a generation of fame, she passed away in 1985 at the age of 90, leaving Huautla to slumber again.

Her legacy, however, remains plainly visible in Huautla today, both in the town mural, and the several institutions that carry her name, such as the María Sabina Cultural Center, the Comedor María Sabina, and the Farmacia María Sabina.

Besides such obvious reminders, a number of new-generation *curanderos* carry on María Sabina's mission. Notable among them is her grandson, Filogonio Garcia, now middle-aged, and his son, Anselmo Garcia. María Sabina's older grandson, Eduardo Vallardares (now deceased), who was María Sabina's constant companion during her heyday, was asked by author Juan Garcia Carrera of his thoughts concerning death. He replied, "By offering you enlightenment, my mushrooms also resign you to the reality of death."

The town is lovely, strung along the side of a mountain with mind-boggling views across the sierra. One hardly needs mushrooms to feel "high" here with the mountainous panorama spread out below and the sky vast overhead. It's a magical place.

María Sabina Mural

Make your first Huautla stop at the Huautla town hall outside portico for a look at the vivid mural, painted in 2007 by Mario Enrique Fernández Medina, in honor of María Sabina. The mural, a dramatic panorama of the life of María Sabina, sweeps from left to right. Most striking is the panel of the deep brown face of María Sabina, depicted, with her hallucinogenic mushrooms, leading her followers through a transcendental window to a new, enlightened dimension. There they join with a saint-like visage of María Sabina, who, finally transformed into an eagle, cleanses (symbolized by the egg) the bodies and souls of her clients.

Inside the town hall, a modest museum displays artifacts, documents, photos, and mementos that illustrate Huautla's history from pre-Conquest through the excitement and fame of María Sabina's heyday to the present.

Casa María Sabina

El Fortín, the east-end ridgetop barrio where María Sabina lived, is well-known and revered by most all Huautlecos. Her old house, Casa María Sabina (Carretera María Sabina 149 A, Barrio El Fortín, Huautla de Jiménez, Oaxaca, local cell tel. 044-236/102-8567, guest rooms $10 pp), a simple iron-roofed stucco dwelling, is being maintained by her grandson Filogonio Garcia and his family as both museum and lodging house for guests interested in the legacy of María Sabina. As part of their mission, they offer a pair of simple, clean guest rooms (with shared hot-water bath), sleeping three and two people, respectively, in the Casa María Sabina.

Filogonio, a highly respected and sensitive *curandero* (folk healer) carries on his grandmother's tradition, offering professional therapeutic sessions in an adjacent ceremonial room.

Find Casa María Sabina in the east-side uphill ridgetop neighborhood. It's best to get there by taxi ($3) from downtown. If, however, you prefer walking (with hat, good shoes, and drinking water), head out east along downtown Calle Benito Juárez, always uphill, asking directions ("¿Casa María Sabina?") and you'll probably arrive at the modest grocery store (at 149A Carretera María Sabina) that the family maintains, after about an hour's walk.

Cerro de Adoración

From Casa María Sabina, continue to sacred site Cerro de Adoración along the dirt road, then path, continuing gradually upward along the right-hand slope of the ridgetop. Your destination is just beyond the highest hill visible ahead along the ridgetop, where, after another half-hour ascent, you'll reach the summit called Cerro de Adoración. Here, you'll find a monument with four crosses where local folks carry offerings, especially around

May 3, El Día de la Santa Cruz (The Day of the Holy Cross).

Shopping

Huautla offers some opportunities to shop for its prized, colorful textiles. Around the market, especially, you'll see the reason for the enthusiasm: women in handmade *huipiles* (traditional dresses) adorned with bright embroidered birds, fruits, flowers, and rainbows of pink-, yellow-, and blue-striped satin.

In addition to the *huipiles,* local women craft and embroider blouses, napkins, shirts, skirts, and tablecloths in floral and animal designs. For a multicolored selection of *huipiles, manteles* (embroidered tablecloths), and brightly costumed dolls, continue another few doors east to **Artesanías Magdani** (Benito Juárez 40, no phone, 8am-8pm Mon.-Sat., 8am-3pm Sun.).

Next, cross the street to **Artesanías de la Región Mazateca** (Benito Juárez 37, no phone, 9am-2pm and 4pm-8pm Mon.-Sat., 9am-2pm Sun.) for more lovely examples.

Accommodations

Newish ★ **Hotel Santa Julia** (Calle Cuauhtémoc 12, tel. 236/378-0586, $15 s or d, $17 s or d upstairs, $19 t) is a welcome addition for Huautla visitors. Twenty-one spacious, clean, and comfortably furnished rooms, with hot-water shower-baths, provide the basics, with TV, parking, and restaurant. The most pleasant are the upstairs rooms, some with awesome views, on the sunny south side. Find the hotel on the south, downhill side of the plaza.

Second choice goes to **Hotel Rinconcito** (Calle Benito Juárez 8, tel. 236/378-0136, 236/378-0243, or 236/378-0005, fax 236/378-0674, $16 s, $18 d in one bed, $25 d, t in two beds), across Benito Juárez from the market. Husband-wife owners Leonardo Altamirano and Catalina Casamiro rent eight plain but clean rooms with hot-water baths. The best are in front, with sunny views of the market below and the mountains in the distance.

Food

Go to the town market for the freshest fruits and vegetables. The best grocery selection is at **Minisuper El Trebol** (Calle Benito Juárez 41, tel. 236/378-0027, 9am-4pm and 6pm-9pm daily), across from the Hotel 1 de Mayo.

For fresh-baked goods, try the **Panadería Giralda** (Calle Benito Juárez 21, no phone, 7am-9pm Thurs.-Tues.). Find snacks, such as hamburgers, hot dogs, and *tortas* (sandwiches), at the stand in front of the Hotel Rinconcito, across Benito Juárez from the market.

Find the homey and reliable ★ **Restaurant Rosita** (tel. 236/378-0386, 7am-10pm daily, $3-6) below the plaza's southwest corner, a few doors down the lane that angles off of Cuauhtémoc. Its airy porch dining room with a view is an extra plus, especially for breakfast and lunch.

Information and Services

At this writing, Huautla now has an **ATM** located just to the right of the famed María Sabina mural.

A trio of doctors maintain offices on Benito Juárez. Moving east, first find **Dr. Lázaro Pérez Garcia** (Benito Juárez 12, upstairs, 8am-3pm and 5pm-8pm Mon.-Sat., also available on call). A block farther east, you'll find **Dr. Saul Martínez,** at his **pharmacy** (Benito Juárez, tel. 236/378-0257, pharmacy: 8am-10pm daily; consultations: 9am-1pm and 3pm-7pm Mon.-Sat.); he's also on call 24 hours a day. Also find **Dr. Flores Ramos** at his **Farmacia Similares** (Benito Juárez 21D, tel. 236/378-0857, 9am-3pm and 5pm-9pm Mon.-Sat.).

Nonprescription medicines and drugs are available at additional pharmacies on Benito Juárez, such as **Farmacia de Jesús** (Benito Juárez 16, 8am-2pm and 4pm-8pm daily).

The *correo* (8am-3pm Mon.-Fri.) and *telecom* (tel. 236/378-0397, 8am-3pm Mon.-Fri., 8am-1pm Sat.) stand side by side on the plaza's west side, above the shops, across the street (west) from the *presidencia municipal.*

The Hotel Rinconcito desk has a long-distance telephone (Benito Juárez 8, tel. 236/378-0136, 236/378-0243, or 236/378-0005, 8am-9pm daily).

Get your laundry reliably done at the small *lavandería* (tel. 236/378-0337, 9am-3pm and 5pm-9pm daily), half a block down the alley, adjacent to the Hotel Santa Julia, that runs downhill from Calle Cuauhtémoc.

Getting There and Away

Second-class Fletes y Pasajes buses (tel. 236/378-0406) operate out of a terminal on Calle Antonio Caso, which runs diagonally downhill from Calle Benito Juárez. They connect west with Teotitlán del Camino, thence south with Oaxaca City via Cuicatlán; and northwest with Mexico City via Tehuacán and Puebla. Furthermore, on Highway 182, both second-class TRV (tel. 236/378-0834) and Autobuses Unidos connect with Teotitlán, Puebla, and Mexico City. Additionally, Autotransportes Turísticos Cañada y Oaxaca (cell tel. 044-236/102-0530) vans connect, via Teotitlán and Cuicatlán, hourly during the day with Oaxaca City from their terminal at Calle Cuauhtémoc 23. Furthermore, from the street-side, just below the downhill intersection of Cuauhtémoc and Antonio Caso, a line of *colectivo* vans connect with a swarm of local villages, such as Eloxochitlán and San Agustín.

Note: Pick-up trucks with benches sheltered by canopies in their rear beds have emerged as one of the passenger vehicles of choice in these parts. You'll find them plying their trade, seeking your business, on most of the roads in the area, working on irregular schedules but heading in most directions.

For drivers, paved Highway 182 connects Huautla east with Tuxtepec via Jalapa de Díaz, along 122 kilometers (76 mi) of winding but breathtakingly scenic mountain road. For safety, allow 3 hours eastbound, downhill, or 3.5 hours westbound, uphill. In a westerly direction, Highway 182 connects Huautla east

with Teotitlán del Camino in 66 kilometers (41 mi) of paved, downhill, winding, scenic mountain road. (From Teotitlán, Highway 135 connects south an additional 161 kilometers (100 mi), about 3.5 hours, with Oaxaca City.) Allow 2 hours downhill (westerly) and 2.5 hours uphill (easterly). Take your time. This is another one of Oaxaca's spectacularly beautiful drives.

EXCURSIONS AROUND HUAUTLA

The area around Huautla, a verdant, dramatically folded landscape of mountains and deep valleys, hides a number of natural wonders, the best known of which include two spectacular limestone caves and a twin waterfall.

★ Las Regaderas

Easiest to get to and see is Las Regaderas, a pair of waterfalls not far west along Highway 182 from Huautla. Get there by car, AU or TRV bus, or local *colectivo* van to Puente de Fierro, marked by a big Santa María Chicotla sign and arch, about 6.6 kilometers (four mi) west, Teotitlán direction, from Huautla. Just before the bridge, turn right and continue past the arch to a side road. Turn and continue one kilometer (0.6 mi) downhill to the falls.

Las Regaderas (The Showers) plummet 30 meters (100 ft.) out of a jungly cliff into a wild, tumbling river. Great trees (apparently identical to California sycamores, *Platanus racemosa*) shade both banks. A steel-cable suspension walkway bridges the river next to a rustic riverside cabin. A short extension bridge accesses the cool spray at the foot of the falls.

Nindo-Da-Gé

Another spectacular site is the Nindo-Da-Gé (Broad Spring Mountain) cave, first explored completely in 1905, near the little town of San Antonio Eloxochitlán (ay-loh-shoh-CHEET-lahn). With a guide, you can explore several of the cave's 19 main galleries in half a day.

the waterfalls at Las Regaderas, near Huautla

The seemingly endless procession of dripping limestone formations, which have names such as The Infernal Hill, The Fort, The Snail, and Marimba, are even more fun if you dream up your own names.

The town invites visitors to camp locally (town stores can supply food and water) and explore their cave. Recently, authorities completed a road to the cave, which can be reached from town in about two kilometers (1.2 mi) by road, and only another one kilometer (0.6 mi) by foot trail.

The only obstacle to exploring the cave is the reasonable one that for safety reasons you must have a guide recommended by civic authorities. The guide receives no money; he or she serves as part of their community service obligation. However, do offer a donation, perhaps $20, in a sealed envelope, to the *ayuntamiento,* city government.

A town cave committee is in charge. The easiest procedure would be to arrive early enough (say, by 9am or 10am) to arrange for a guide. A good person to contact would be personable, former cave committee member and friendly schoolteacher, Professor Froilan Rios, whose house stands on the left side of the paved road as you enter town. The minimum excursion requires most of a day. Arrive early and bring at least two strong flashlights (four-celled or more, with extra batteries), good-traction shoes, and enough hard hats (hard plastic construction type) for everyone.

Get to San Antonio Eloxochitlán by bus or car 11 kilometers (seven mi) along the Teotitlán (west) direction on Highway 182, to the San Antonio turnoff gravel road on the right (north). Continue 7.7 kilometers (4.8 mi) to the town church, plaza, and *presidencia municipal.* (You can view some videos of recent explorations of the cave by logging "San Antonio Eloxochitlán You Tube" into Google.)

The Cañada: Canyon Country

Shadowed from rain by mountains on all sides, the dry, tropical Cañada canyonland comprises one of Oaxaca's major geo-cultural regions. It encompasses the Cuicateca—the land of the Cuicatecs—a Mixtec-related people who, for longer than anyone can remember, have hunted and farmed their homeland's cactus-plumed canyon bottoms and temperate upland valleys. Reclusive and traditional, Cuicatec people generally venture out from their home villages only infrequently, mostly to trade at the market towns—sometimes Teotitlán del Camino, more often at Cuicatlán. For visitors, this is a region most noteworthy for the drive-through, which is quite beautiful, coming down from the mountains around Huautla. Just watch out for random rocks in the road.

CUICATLÁN

Cuicatlán (pop. 10,000) is the commercial capital of the Cañada, the emporium for the entire high sierra hinterland that rises steeply, east of town. Cuicatlán, like Teotitlán, owes its wealth to abundant sunshine and water. In Cuicatlán, water is synonymous with the Río Grande, the river that passes just west of town. After nourishing a local oasis of fruit, vegetables, and grain, the Río Grande continues its good work downstream.

Sights

Cuicatlán (Place of Song) is home to a busy market, often packed with Cuicatec-speaking people, especially women, wearing their handmade *huipiles* (traditional embroidered dresses). Head there via the turnoff road from Highway 135, which, as it becomes Avenida Hidalgo, Cuicatlán's main north-south business street, leads 1.6 kilometers (one mi) north to the plaza at the town center. There stands the church, the **Templo de San Juan Bautista,** on the plaza's east side.

Back down on Juárez, across the street,

Templo de San Juan Bautista, Cuicatlán

south, from the *presidencia municipal* spreads the market. Although it's lively enough most days, the market is especially big on Saturdays and Sundays and overflowing around June 24, when merrymakers crowd the streets and celebrate the Fiesta de San Juan Bautista with costumes, parades and floats, community feasts, fireworks, and traditional dances.

Accommodations and Food

Cuicatlán best is the Hotel Sochiapan (Calle Hidalgo 40, tel. 236/374-0001, $22 s, d one bed, $26 d two beds, $30 t) with about 35 immaculate, attractively decorated rooms. Rooms come with hot-water shower-baths and cable TV.

As for food, you'll find the freshest fruit and vegetables in the market and the best grocery selection at the Super El Molino (tel. 236/374-0008, 7am-4pm and 5pm-10pm daily), at the plaza's southeast corner, across the street from the church.

Cuicatlán's best place to eat by far is the clean, seafood-specialty ★ Restaurant Boringuen (Juárez, tel. 236/374-0222, 8:30am-10pm daily, $3-5), uphill, two blocks east of the plaza. Here, from her spic-and-span kitchen, the proprietor puts out a stream of tasty breakfasts (like a cheese omelet), Mexican specialties (leg of pork tacos, *tlayuda*), and shrimp and calamari.

Information and Services

Most of Cuicatlán's service establishments are either on the town plaza or along Calle Hidalgo, the north-south Highway 135 ingress street. Although Cuicatlán still has no bank, you might be able to cash a $20 bill at the grocery store Super El Molino (tel. 236/374-0008, 7am-4pm and 5pm-10pm daily), at the town plaza's southeast corner. A long-distance telephone and Internet access is available at the small *caseta larga distancia* (tel. 236/374-0209, 7:30am-10:30pm daily), on the plaza at the east corner of Hidalgo.

Buy stamps or mail a letter at the *correo* (Leona Vicario, 9am-3pm Mon.-Fri., 9am-2pm Sat.).

For nonprescription medicines and drugs, cross to the north side of the plaza, to Farma Pronto (by the basketball court, tel. 236/374-0326, 7am-11pm daily).

For a medical consultation, see Dr. Rudolfo Reyes Escalante (Calle Centenario 30, tel. 236/374-0033). To get there from the plaza, walk two blocks down Hidalgo to Centenario, then turn right half a block. Alternatively, go to the 24-hour public *centro de salud* (on Hidalgo, tel. 236/374-0299), three blocks downhill from the plaza.

Getting There and Away

Autobuses Unidos (tel. 236/374-0014) second-class long-distance buses operate out of their terminal on Hidalgo, about four blocks downhill from the plaza. Buses connect, either north with Mexico City via Teotitlán, Tehuacán, and Puebla, or south with Oaxaca City.

For drivers, Highway 135 connects south with Highway 190 at Telixtlahuaca, thence with Oaxaca City, a total of 101 kilometers (63 mi). The route, paved and in good condition but winding, requires about two hours for safety.

In the northerly direction, Highway 135 connects with Teotitlán del Camino in about 60 kilometers (37 mi), 1.5 hours. From there, continue either east via Highway 182, 66 additional kilometers (41 mi), 2 hours, to Huautla; or north via Highway 135, another 63 kilometers (39 mi) to Tehuacán, 1.5 hours, and thence to Puebla (a total of 5 hours), and Mexico City (a total of 7 hours, or 5 hours total via the toll expressways 135 D and 150 D).

The Isthmus

A trip to the Isthmus of Tehuántepec sometimes seems like a journey to another country. At the Isthmus, the North American continent narrows to a scarce 160 kilometers (100 mi) in width; the mighty Sierras shrink to mere foothills.

The climate is tropical; the land is fertile and well watered. Luxuriant groves hang heavy with almonds, avocados, coconuts, mangos, and oranges. Rivers wind downhill to the sea, springs well up at the foot of mountains, and swarms of fish swim offshore. The Isthmus is a land of abundance, and it shows in the people. Women are renowned for their beauty, independent spirit, and their incomparably lovely flowered skirts and blouses, which young and old seem to wear at any excuse.

And they have excuses aplenty, for the Isthmus is the place of the *velas,* called fiestas in other parts of Mexico. But in the Isthmus, especially in the towns of Tehuántepec and Juchitán, *velas* are something more special. Most every barrio (neighborhood) must celebrate one in honor of its patron saint. A short list names 20 major yearly *velas* in Juchitán alone. The long list, including all the towns in the Isthmus, numbers more than 100.

If you're lucky to arrive during one of these *velas,* you may even be invited to share in the fun. Local folks dress up, women in their spectacularly flowered *traje* (traditional indigenous dress) and men with their diminutive Tehuántepec sombreros, red kerchiefs, sashes, and machetes. Sometimes entire villages or town barrios celebrate for days, eating, drinking, and dancing to the beautiful melody of "La Sandunga." Once you've been captured by its lovely, lilting strains, it will always bring back your most cherished Isthmus memories.

Wave chasers may want to slip down to the otherwise nondescript oil boomtown of Salina Cruz; though dominated by the petroleum industry, it is now a base of operations for a number of surfing expeditions. Sign up with one and they just might guide you to some of the best waves you'll ever ride.

PLANNING YOUR TIME

A circular side trip includes the vibrant market towns of Tehuántepec and Juchitán

---

Previous: beach near Salina Cruz; surfer at one of several great breaks near Salina Cruz. **Above:** *La Tejuana* sculpture, Tehuántepec.

The Isthmus

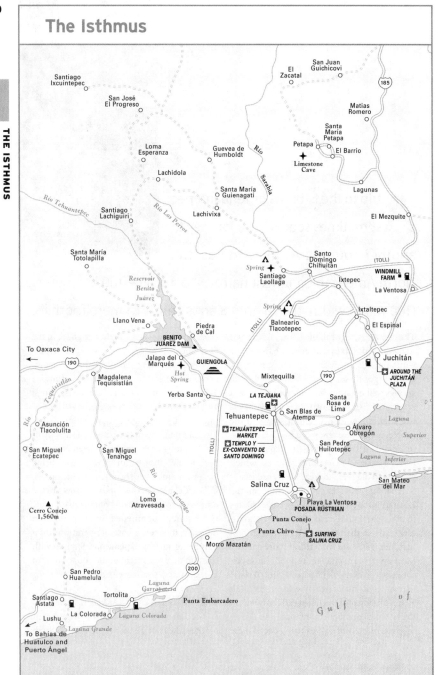

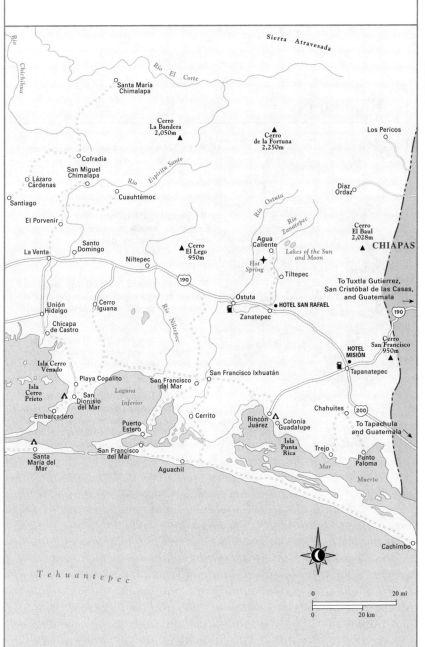

Sierra Atravesada

Río Chichihua

Río El Corte

Santa María Chimalapa

Cerro La Bandera 2,050m ▲

Cerro de la Fortuna 2,250m ▲

Los Pericos

Cofradia

San Miguel Chimalapa

Río Espíritu Santo

Lázaro Cárdenas

Santiago

Río

Cuauhtémoc

Diaz Ordaz

Río Ostuta

Cerro El Baul 2,028m ▲

CHIAPAS

El Porvenir

Cerro El Lego 950m ▲

Agua Caliente

Río Zanatepec

Lakes of the Sun and Moon

La Venta

Santo Domingo

Niltepec

190

Hot Spring

Tiltepec

To Tuxtla Gutierrez, San Cristóbal de las Casas, and Guatemala →

190

Ostuta

Unión Hidalgo

Cerro Iguana

Río Niltepec

Zanatepec

● HOTEL SAN RAFAEL

Chicapa de Castro

Cerro San Francisco 950m ▲

HOTEL MISIÓN

Tapanatepec

Isla Cerro Venado

Playa Copálito

San Francisco del Mar

San Francisco Ixhuatán

Isla Cerro Prieto

Laguna Inferior

Chahuites

200

San Dionisio del Mar

Embarcadero

Puerto Estero

Cerrito

Rincón Juárez

Colonia Guadalupe

To Tapachula and Guatemala →

Isla Punta Rica

Trejo

Santa María del Mar

San Francisco del Mar

Aguachil

Mar Muerto

Punto Paloma

Cachimbo

Tehuantepec

0   20 mi

0   20 km

© AVALON TRAVEL

Look for ★ to find recommended
sights, activities, dining, and lodging.

Highlights

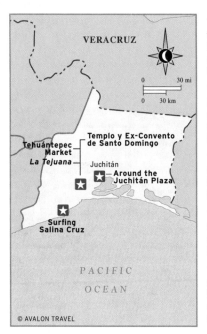

© AVALON TRAVEL

★ *La Tejuana:* This visually stunning sculpture of a Tejuana woman looms high above the highway just east of the metal bridge on the edge of Tehuántepec. Have a look at night when the lighting is strikingly dramatic (page 243).

★ **Templo y Ex-Convento de Santo Domingo:**. Be sure to see the recently discovered wall decorations painted by indigenous artists 450 years ago at this circa-1530 church (page 245).

★ **Tehuántepec Market:** This market is the best place to buy extravagant and colorful floral *huipiles* (traditional embroidered dresses) (page 245).

★ **Around the Juchitán Plaza:** The flowers, gold filigree, and embroiderered *huipiles* for sale are the main attraction on the Juchitán plaza (page 252).

★ **Surfing Salina Cruz:** Within a few miles of one of the largest oil refineries in Mexico, you'll find pristine point and beach breaks for surfers of every skill level. Kiteboarders will also find consistent afternoon winds (page 259).

between Oaxaca City and the Pacific resorts. For example, you could bus, drive, or fly south to the coast, spend some days basking in the ambience of the Pacific resorts, then begin your return to Oaxaca City east along the coast by either bus, car, or tour, enjoying four days along the way exploring the colorful markets, cuisine, and sights of the Isthmus. And, of course, check out the many surfing and kiteboarding beaches along the way.

Be sure to do plenty of strolling, and perhaps some shopping, in the colorful **Tehuántepec Market** hubbub, highlighted especially by the *tehuana* women in their colorful native dress. Later, don't miss enjoying at least one deliciously authentic Tehuántepec meal in the showplace Restaurant Scaru. After

dark, head up to the highway to take in the splendid sight of *La Tejuana*, the "made by the people" steel sculpture that stands guard over the entrance to town.

The next day, continue east half an hour to Juchitán. Here, stroll around the **Juchitán plaza** and market. Along the way, be sure to see the vibrant flower and handicrafts stalls, with riots of roses and lilies and their gold filigree, exquisite flowered *huipiles* (traditional embroidered dresses), bright hammocks, multicolored pottery, and much more. Take a break with lunch in the airy inner patio of the plaza-front Restaurant Casa Grande. In the late afternoon, head a few blocks west to enjoy the breeze and take a look at the monumental *Women Warriors* stainless steel sculptures overlooking the river.

Tehuántepec and Vicinity

Although both Juchitán and Salina Cruz are the Isthmus's big, bustling business centers, quieter, more traditional Tehuántepec remains foremost in the minds of most *istmeños* as the former pre-Columbian royal capital, the seat of Cosijopí, the beloved last king of the Zapotecs. Local people are constantly reminded of their rich royal history by virtue of the Templo y Ex-Convento de Santo Domingo, the construction of which was unique in Oaxaca because it was financed by an indigenous monarch, Cosijopí. Moreover, local people can directly see their ancestors' contribution to history by glimpsing the ancient (recently discovered) floral and animal decorations that their ancestors painted on the walls of the ex-convent nearly half a millennium ago.

The town of Tehuántepec is geographically the center of the Isthmus. Roads, like spokes of a wheel, branch out in all directions, south to Salina Cruz, northeast to Juchitán, and northwest to Oaxaca City. This means that travelers from Oaxaca City most easily reach both Juchitán and Salina

Cruz by passing through the fortunate town of Tehuántepec.

GETTING ORIENTED

Although the Río Tehuántepec splits the Santo Domingo Tehuántepec town (pop. 52,000) along a roughly north-south line, the west-side portion, across the river via the Puente Metalico (Metal Bridge), first built for locomotives around 1900, seems like a mere suburb of the town center, east of the river. On the central plaza itself, the *presidencia municipal* occupies the south side, along Calle 5 de Mayo; the main market, **Mercado Jesús Carranza,** lies on the plaza's west, river side, along Calle Juana C. Romero; and to the northeast, past the end of main north-south street Benito Juárez, about a block and a half northeast of the plaza, stands Tehuántepec's most venerable monument, the **Templo y Ex-Convento de Santo Domingo.**

SIGHTS
★ *La Tejuana*
The tall, steel-finished sculpture of a

Tehuántepec

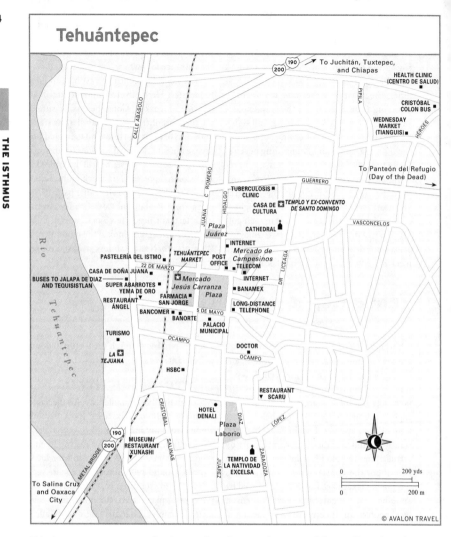

To Juchitán, Tuxtepec, and Chiapas

HEALTH CLINIC (CENTRO DE SALUD)

CRISTÓBAL COLON BUS

WEDNESDAY MARKET (TIANGUIS)

To Panteón del Refugio (Day of the Dead)

GUERRERO

VASCONCELOS

TUBERCULOSIS CLINIC

CASA DE CULTURA

TEMPLO Y EX-CONVENTO DE SANTO DOMINGO

CATHEDRAL

Plaza Juárez

INTERNET

Mercado de Campesinos

TELECOM

INTERNET

BANAMEX

LONG-DISTANCE TELEPHONE

PASTELERÍA DEL ISTMO

TEHUÁNTEPEC MARKET

POST OFFICE

CASA DE DOÑA JUANA

22 DE MARZO

BUSES TO JALAPA DE DIAZ AND TEQUISISTLAN

SUPER ABARROTES YEMA DE ORO

Mercado Jesús Carranza Plaza

RESTAURANT ÁNGEL

FARMACIA SAN JORGE

BANCOMER

BANORTE

5 DE MAYO

PALACIO MUNICIPAL

TURISMO

OCAMPO

DOCTOR

OCAMPO

LA TEJUANA

HSBC

RESTAURANT SCARU

HOTEL DENALI

Plaza Laborio

DIAZ

LÓPEZ

MUSEUM/ RESTAURANT XUNASHI

CRISTOBAL

SALINAS

JUAREZ

ZARAGOZA

TEMPLO DE LA NATIVIDAD EXCELSA

To Salina Cruz and Oaxaca City

METAL BRIDGE

CALLE ABASOLO

C ROMERO

HIDALGO

JUANA

DR LICEAGA

PIPILA

HÉROES

Río Tehuantepec

0   200 yds
0   200 m

© AVALON TRAVEL

Tehuántepec woman now dominates the scene as you cross the metal bridge and approach the busy east side of town, looming high above the tourist office located in the highway's central divider. In the 2000s, the sculpture was created by Miguel Hernández Urbán, an artist from Mexico City. The sculpture is made of local marble and fine wood along with stainless steel brought from Mexico City. A dramatic vision by day, *La Tejuana* is even more striking at night, when lit up, so be sure and do a walk or drive-by after dark.

Around the Plaza

First, take a stroll around the plaza, where you'll find some interesting sculptures, including noble likenesses of Miguel Hidalgo (the Father of Mexican Independence) and a pair of Tehuántepec heroes. On the north side, look for the bronze of a seated **Doña Juana Catalina Romero** (1855-1915), a

La Tejuana was created to honor the women of Tehuántepec.

broad fenced atrium, on the right. The aging landmark (to the left of the new church) is interesting partly because it was one of the few, if not the only, Christian churches in Mexico financed by a native ruler. Cosijopí, the last king of the Zapotecs, was baptized as Juan Cortés de Cosijopí after his friend and ally Hernán Cortés paid for the construction with both cash and the labor of thousands of his subjects. The building was erected under the supervision of Fray Fernando de Albequerque, vicar of Tehuántepec, between 1544 and 1550.

The ex-convent section, on the old church's north side, was abandoned not long after the Reforms of the late 1850s forced the Dominicans from Mexico. It had crumbled into a virtual ruin by the mid-20th century, when local people rolled up their sleeves and began restoring it in 1953. In 1982, with the restoration complete, the townsfolk christened their ex-convent as the **Casa de la Cultura** (tel. 971/715-0114, 9am-2pm and 5pm-8pm Mon.-Fri., 9am-2pm Sat.).

Tehuántepec legend. She is famous partly for her good works, establishing schools for Tehuántepec children during the days when public education was a rarity in Mexico.

On the plaza's west (market) side, you'll find the bronze bust of **A. Maximino Ramón Ortiz,** the first and only governor of the Isthmus, when it was separated from Oaxaca as the territory of Tehuántepec for a few years during the 1850s. Politics, however, were not Ortiz's first love. He is best remembered as the composer of "La Sandunga," Tehuántepec's beloved theme. His ageless melody seems to perfectly capture the essence of the Isthmus in a gracefully drowsy rhythm that swings slowly, yet deliberately, like the relaxed sway of lovers in a hammock beneath the deep shade of a Tehuántepec grove.

★ Templo y Ex-Convento de Santo Domingo

From the plaza's northeast corner, walk north along Calle Hidalgo one block to the venerable **Santo Domingo church,** behind its

★ Tehuántepec Market

The most colorful downtown action goes on at the **Mercado Jesús Carranza,** just across Romero from the plaza. At midday, the market overflows with life. The center of everything is the corridor street on the market's north side, which connects the plaza with the businesses along the railroad tracks behind the market.

The buzzing *motocarros* (motorcycle minitrucks) that you see depositing and picking up passengers by the railroad track seem to be a unique Isthmus invention. They mostly follow set round-trip routes around town for a fixed price of about $1 (13 pesos). When you get tired of walking, hop on for a breezy whirlwind tour of Tehuántepec's back streets.

Market vendors, especially women in *traje* (traditional indigenous dress), tend to be apprehensive of rubber-necking strangers with cameras in hand. A good strategy is to blend in, and if you want to take pictures, ask for permission first.

Get some relief from the heat and bustle inside the roofed market building itself. If you're

Frida Kahlo's Tehuántepec Connection

The Mexican artist Frida Kahlo and her husband Diego Rivera are perhaps the most important and assuredly the most renowned Mexican artists of the 20th century if not in all Mexican history. Though Rivera overshadowed Kahlo during their lives, in the end Kahlo's influence is ever present: Her iconic image has become as popular on shopping bags, T-shirts, coffee mugs, surfboards, and everything else as that of the ubiquitous Virgin of Guadalupe. Kahlo has emerged as a 20th-century Mexican saint. More importantly, the brilliant, penetrating paintings that she made, many of them profound self-portraits, have assumed a place high in the pantheon of 20th-century art.

Frida Kahlo is celebrated in Tehuántepec, her mother's home town.

Frida Kahlo possessed a decidedly feminist streak. This feminism was expressed most obviously in the simple fact of her being an independent and successful artist. But there is more to this feminist story, and this is where the Isthmus of Tehuántepec comes in. Tehuántepec is renowned above all for two things: the colorful brilliance of the elaborately embroidered clothing handmade here, and, perhaps more importantly, the fact that this region of Mexico is a matriarchy. The markets and shops and businesses and everything that goes on in Tehuántepec is under the control of women. The men work in the fields, and the women run the show. Frida Kahlo's mother came from Tehuántepec.

Kahlo always wore clothes from Tehuántepec, which she loved for their brilliant colors and instinctive, indigenous high style. She also wore them because she recognized in that matriarchal region of Mexico a space she could relate to and understand. Her dress aimed for style and self-protection but it also made a statement. Kahlo wanted to portray her Mexicanidad, and her political convictions, but her clothes also distinguished her as a female artist of the 1940s.

in the mood for shopping, plenty of handicrafts are available. On the bottom floor, stalls offer the gold filigree jewelry (at this writing, mostly faux-gold filigree, since gold is so expensive) that the Tehuántepec women love to wear. Look farther for lots of woven goods, such as baskets, string bags of *ixtle* fiber, hand fans, and hammocks.

Upstairs, via the stairway on the southwest corner by the railroad track, you'll find Tehuántepec's pride—the beautiful embroidered *tehuana* flowered blouses and skirts. Look around, decide what you want, then bargain for it. Asking prices for the prized, embroidered flower-design blouses run as much as $100, a whole outfit about $200, with bargaining.

Besides the aforementioned permanent daily markets near the plaza, country people flood into town for *tianguis* (native town market) on Wednesday and Sunday. Visit the **Wednesday tianguis,** set up along northside Calle Héroes, most easily reached by riding a *motocarro* from the plaza. The **Sunday tianguis** is much bigger, so much so that it's held on the west side across the river, beyond the big Oaxaca highway intersection, in the open space behind the Hotel Gueixhoba.

Casa de Doña Juana Catalina Romero

The railway track so intimately close to the market is due to the speculated intimate relationship between President Porfirio Díaz and

Tehunátepec's market

wooden looms, to an entire chapel of devotional memorabilia and a whole kitchen of great pottery jugs.

Welcoming owners Jose Manuel Villalobos and his wife Mari Carmen and their children offer a hearty Mexican *comida* (set meal) in their baronial river-view **restaurant** (noon-5pm daily, $6). Get there either by a short taxi ride from the plaza, or by walking two blocks south from the plaza's southwest corner. Turn right at the Hotel Donaji (corner of Plaza Laborio) and continue another two blocks, to the corner of Cristobal Salinas. Turn left one block, then turn right and continue a short block to the mansion, above, on the right.

ACCOMMODATIONS
Under $50
Downtown's best accommodation is the **Hotel Denali** (Juárez 10, tel. 971/715-0064, fax 971/715-0448, hoteldonaji@hotmail.com, $20 s, $25 d fan only, $30 s, $35 d with a/c), named for Oaxaca's beloved Apothecia heroine and located two blocks south of the plaza on quiet Plaza Laborio. This renovated hotel is very popular locally by virtue of its inviting, plant-decorated inner restaurant patio. The 48 rooms, in a big two-story block, are simply and invitingly decorated. Amenities include hot-water shower-baths, cable TV, a small pool-patio, and credit cards accepted.

Over $50
Tehuántepec's fanciest hotel is the four-star ★ **Hotel Guiexhoba** (ghee-ay-SHOW-bah; Carretera Panamericana Km 250.5, Barrio Santa María, tel./fax 971/715-1710 or 971/715-0416, guiexhoba@prodigy.net.mx, $45 s, $58 d, $70 t), which deserves extra points simply for its Zapotec label, the name of a locally abundant white flower with a fragrant scent reminiscent of jasmine. Find the hotel on Highway 190, inbound from Oaxaca City on the right before the bridge.

The Guiexhoba's 36 spacious, clean, and comfortable rooms, in two stories, enclose a parking courtyard that fortunately shields rooms on its north side from highway noise.

local beauty Doña Juana Catalina Romero (1837-1915). Doña Juana Catalina lived in the French-style mansion, now in faded white with fancy blue window awnings in need of serious renovation, which rises by the tracks.

Plaza Laborio
A number of smaller plazas dot Tehuántepec's several barrios. If you head south along Juárez two long blocks, you'll arrive at Plaza Laborio and its adjacent blue-trimmed, storybook **Templo de la Natividad Excelsa.** Before you go inside to look around, notice that the right bell tower is tilted at a crazy angle, not unlike the Leaning Tower of Pisa.

Museum and Restaurant Xunashi
Housed in a colonial-era family mansion-factory, **Museum Xunashi** (Callejon El Faro 1A, local cell tel. 971/129-7990, noon-5pm daily, $3) is decorated with a flock of antiques, which range from a giant portrait of the Virgin of Guadalupe and ancient

Juana Catalina Romero: Heroine of Tehuántepec

Why Tehuántepec's main downtown streets, which carry such nationally renowned labels as 5 de Mayo, Benito Juárez, and Hidalgo, should include Juana C. Romero among them is a question nearly all adult townsfolk can immediately answer. "Doña Juana," they say, is Tehuántepec's heroine because she "built schools and helped the children of Tehuántepec." Some go on to say that she "got lots of help for Tehuántepec from her friend, Presidente Porfirio Díaz."

Juana Catalina Romero did great work for the people of Tehuántepec.

When pressed, most Tehuántepec folks acknowledge that she had a close (some even say intimate) relationship with Porfirio Díaz. Juana Catalina was a 21-year-old Zapotec beauty when she was first introduced to Díaz in 1858. At that time, he was an ambitious young captain in the army of President Benito Juárez, struggling to win the bloody see-saw civil War of the Reform that pitted liberal against conservative forces everywhere in Mexico.

Although he must have been charmed by her at their first meeting, most certainly nothing immediate came of it, since, when he proposed to her, she turned him down. People say that she told him, "Yours is a liberal mission, with President Juárez, to save Mexico, while my mission is here in Tehuántepec, helping my people."

Whatever passed between them during later years has been the subject of endless gossip. What is certain, however, is that she never married, and they were certainly close confidantes. Moreover, Don Porfirio had the railroad tracks laid right past her house in downtown Tehuántepec, because, it is speculated, he could hop off the train and visit her any time with no fuss or muss.

Staff are generally attentive, competent, and courteous. Amenities include big pool, parking, cable TV, air-conditioning, hot-water shower-baths, credit cards accepted, in-house Internet, and the very good Restaurant Guiexhoba.

FOOD
Groceries and Treats

Tehuántepec's freshest fruit and vegetable sources by far are the luscious mounds of avocados, bananas, carrots, lettuce, mangos, pineapples, radishes, and much more in the plaza market. Likewise, find the best grocery sources, such as the **Super Abarrotes Yema** (tel. 971/715-0489, 8am-8:30pm daily), by the railroad tracks just west (river side) of the market.

Satisfy your sweet tooth with the baked offerings of the **Super Panadería y Pastelería del Istmo** (tel. 971/715-0808, 8am-8:30pm daily). Find it on the railroad tracks, just north of the market, on the left. For evening snacks, fill up at the taco stalls lined up behind the *presidencia municipal*.

Restaurants

Tehuántepec offers a sprinkling of good sit-down restaurants. By far the most colorful is the ★ **Restaurant Scaru** (at south-side cul-de-sac Callejon Leona Vicario 4, tel. 971/715-0646, 8am-11pm daily, $5-10). Here, in a graceful, airy setting, the owners lovingly portray picturesque aspects of traditional Isthmus life. Walls bloom with murals of fruit, festivals, and lovely *tehuanas* in their bright, flowery costumes, while patios are sprinkled with hammocks and sheltered overhead by luxurious handcrafted *palapas*. The menu features fresh seafood from the nearby gulf of Tehuántepec. Credit cards are not accepted.

Second choice goes to the good but more ordinarily picturesque restaurant at the **Hotel Guiexhoba** (Hwy. 190 Km 250.5, tel. 971/715-1710, 7:30am-10pm daily, $5-12), across the river. From a typical but tasty menu of breakfast (eggs and pancakes), lunch (hamburgers, soups, and stews), and dinner (meat, fish, fowl, and spaghetti), the food sometimes comes with a flaming crepe Suzette flourish. Credit cards are accepted.

INFORMATION AND SERVICES
Tourist Information

For travel recommendations and help in emergencies, go to the friendly **Turismo office** (on Hwy. 200 south, Salina Cruz direction, no phone, 9am-7pm daily), overlooking the Río Tehuántepec, two blocks west and two blocks south of the town plaza, before the river bridge, in the shadow of the sculpture *La Tejuana.*

Health and Emergencies

A number of town pharmacies provide both over-the-counter remedies and prescription drugs. Perhaps the best stocked is the town-center branch of the **Farmacia San Jorge** (Romero, 8am-8pm daily), located in a permanent street stall, right on Romero, on the market side of the town plaza.

If you need to consult a doctor, you can always find one at the big 24-hour **Hospital Materno** (Hwy. 190, tel. 971/713-7252) across from the bus station.

Alternatively, you have another highly recommended choice, **Dr. José Manuel Vichido** (Calle Ocampo, tel. 971/715-0862, 9am-2pm Mon.-Sat.). From the plaza's southeast corner, walk south one block along Juárez; turn left at the first street, Ocampo. The doctor's office is half a block farther on the left.

Police service is available from at least two sources in Tehuántepec. Call either the *policía municipal* (tel. 971/713-7000), or the **emergency number** (dial 066).

Money

Tehuántepec has some banks, all with ATMs. On the plaza's southeast side, go to up-and-coming **Banorte** (5 de Mayo, tel. 971/715-0140, 9am-4pm Mon.-Fri.) across from the market. Next door, also find **Bancomer** (5 de Mayo, tel. 971/715-1253, 8:30am-4pm Mon.-Fri.).

Communications

Both the *correo* (at the plaza's northeast corner, tel. 971/715-0106, 8am-4:30pm Mon.-Fri., 8am-noon Sat.), including rapid, secure **Mexpost** service, and *telecomunicaciones* (at the plaza's northeast corner, tel. 971/715-1197, 8am-5pm Mon.-Fri., 9am-noon Sat.-Sun.), for money orders and public fax, stand side by side at the plaza's northeast, Calle Hidalgo, corner.

Long-distance telephone, fax, and photocopies are available at **Papelería La Esfera** (at the plaza's southeast corner, tel. 971/715-0042, fax 971/715-2090, 8am-8pm Mon.-Sat., 9am-2pm Sun.).

GETTING THERE AND AWAY
By Bus

The vintage Tehuántepec bus station was supposed to be replaced years ago by a brand-new terminal, which remains yet unused. Meanwhile, on Highway 190-200, about a mile north of the town plaza, the old **bus terminal** (tel. 971/715-0108 for information and reservations for nearly all departures) still bustles with activity. Get there by taxi or *motocarro* (motorcycle mini-truck) from the plaza.

Four major bus lines, first-class **Autobuses del Oriente** (ADO) and **Omnibus Cristóbal Colón** (OCC), and mixed first- and second-class **Sur** and **Autobuses Unidos** (AU), offer many connections. Departures connect north and east via Juchitán with Tuxtepec, Villahermosa, Palenque, Minatitlán, Coatzacoalcos, Mérida,

Cancún, and Tulum; northwest with Oaxaca City, Puebla, and Mexico City; southwest with Salina Cruz, Bahías de Huatulco, Pochutla (Puerto Ángel), and Puerto Escondido; and east via Juchitán, Tuxtla Gutiérrez, San Cristóbal las Casas, and Tapachula at the Guatemala border.

In addition, from an adjacent terminal, a pair of independent second-class cooperating lines, **Oaxaca Istmo** and **Fletes y Pasajes** offer connections northwest with Oaxaca City and west with Bahías de Huatulco, Pochutla (Puerto Ángel), and Puerto Escondido, while Fletes y Pasajes also offers connections northwest with Oaxaca City, southwest with Salina Cruz, and northeast with Juchitán.

By Car

Good paved roads fan out from Tehuántepec in four directions. Highway 190-200 connects northeast with Juchitán (27 km/17 mi), then splits north as Highway 185 at La Ventosa and continues north, via Matías Romero and Minatitlán, all the way to the Gulf of Mexico at Coatzacoalcos, a total of 267 kilometers (166 mi). Allow about 4.5 driving hours, either way, for this relatively easy trip.

For Tuxtepec and northern Oaxaca, from cross-Isthmus Highway 185, turn onto Highway 147 at Matías Romero and continue northwest a total of 304 kilometers (189 mi) from Tehuántepec. Allow about five hours of driving time. *Note:* In the past, some robberies have occurred on the long (two-hour), lonely Highway 147 Matías Romero-Tuxtepec leg. Although security now appears to not be a problem, authorities still advise travelers to restrict their driving to *daytime only* on this stretch.

Highway 190 connects Tehuántepec northwest with Oaxaca City along 250 kilometers (155 mi) of well-maintained but winding highway. Allow about 5 hours in Oaxaca City direction (uphill), 4.5 hours in the opposite direction. This is yet another one of Oaxaca's

Scooting Around by *Motocarro*

Tehuántepec's public transportation system was long ago preempted by the town's regiment of *motocarros*—small, motorcycle-driven, flat-bed trucks that buzz, putt, squeal, and skid around town continuously. The center of the action is the railroad track behind the market, where all Tehuántepec *motocarros* faithfully return for passengers and cargo.

Motocarros have become the end-all answer to how to get around in Tehuántepec's heat. Long ago, everyone learned that too much midday walking can produce a considerable sweat at best and sunstroke at worst. If you get overheated, do as Tehuántepec people do and take a seat in the shade and cool down with an *agua* or *refresco*. Later, continue your breezy extended tour via *motocarro*. Fares run about $1 for an entire circuit of the town.

lovely drives, winding through mountains with maguey cactus plots (for *mezcal*-making) dotting the steep hillsides visible from the highway.

Highway 200 connects Tehuántepec west with the Oaxaca Pacific coast, via Salina Cruz (15 km/9 mi), Bahías de Huatulco (161 km/100 mi, three hours), Pochutla-Puerto Ángel (200 km/124 mi, four hours), and Puerto Escondido (274 km/170 mi, five hours) on paved, moderately traveled, secure highway.

Combined Highway 190-200 connects Tehuántepec east via Juchitán (27 km/17 mi) and Niltepec to Tapanatepec (126 km/78 mi) near the Chiapas border and beyond to Guatemala. Allow about 3.5 hours of driving time to Tapanatepec.

Drivers should fill up with gasoline at the Pemex *gasolinera* on the west side of the river, about two kilometers (1.2 mi) west of the bridge, where the road splits southwest to Salina Cruz, northwest to Oaxaca City.

Juchitán

Isthmus people associate the name Juchitán with both the town, Juchitán de Zaragoza, and the governmental district that it heads— a domain larger in extent than either the Distrito Federal or each of the four smallest Mexican states. The district of Juchitán (Place of Flowers) ranges from the Chimalapa, the roadless jungle refuge of dozens of Mexico's endangered species, south to the warm Pacific and the rich lagoons that border it.

But like any empire, Juchitán is the sum of its small parts: hidden slices of Mexico that few outsiders know, from the crystalline springs of **Tlacotepec and Laollaga** to the seemingly endless groves of the "world mango capital" at **Zanatepec** and the **vibrant market** and near-continuous **community festivals** *(velas)* of busy, prosperous Juchitán de Zaragoza.

GETTING ORIENTED

Juchitán (pop. 80,000) bustles with commerce all the daylight and early-evening hours. Main streets 16 de Septiembre and 5 de Septiembre steadily conduct a double stream of traffic to and from the north-side Highway 200

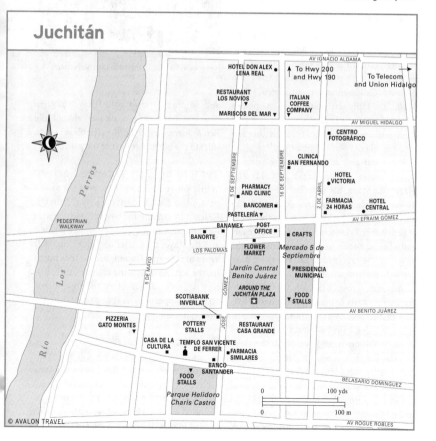

Juchitán

© AVALON TRAVEL

crossing. A few blocks to the west, the Río Los Perros (River of the Dogs, for the otters that hunt fish in the river) courses lazily southward, marking downtown Juchitán's western boundary. Traffic focuses about two kilometers (1.2 mi) south of the highway at the town plaza, the **Jardín Central Benito Juárez,** the town's commercial and governmental nucleus. On Calle 16 de Septiembre, on the plaza's east side, the long white classical arcade of the *palacio municipal* fills the entire block. Governmental offices occupy the upper floor of the *palacio municipal,* while businesses, crafts booths, and food stalls spread across the bottom. Behind the facade, taking up the entire city block east of the plaza, is the town market, Mercado 5 de Septiembre.

SIGHTS
★ Around the Juchitán Plaza

A fun spot to start off (or end) your day exploring Juchitán is at a table in the graceful old-Mexico patio of **Restaurant Casa Grande** (Calle Benito Juárez 12, tel. 971/711-3460, 7am-11pm daily, $6-12) on the plaza's south side. Here, a hearty breakfast or a cool lunch will invigorate you for yet another few hours of relaxed plaza sightseeing.

Stroll out and admire the fine busts of Benito Juárez on the plaza's east side and Margarita Maza, his wife, on the west side, by Calle 5 de Septiembre. On the plaza's north side, find the Monument to the Battle of September 5, 1866, where a Mexican eagle and a heroic Benito Juárez commemorate the victory of the ragtag local battalion over a superior French imperial force.

Step east, across Calle 16 de Septiembre, to the **crafts stalls** beneath the northerly (left) half of the *presidencia municipal* arcade. What you don't find downstairs you'll find in an upstairs market foyer. Stroll the aisles and choose from a host of excellent items, customarily including the famous Isthmus-embroidered skirts and blouses; handwoven *hamacas* (hammocks); leather huaraches and *bolsas* (purses); woven palm *tenates* (baskets) and reed *canastas* (baskets), *petates* (mats),

hammocks for sale in the Juchitán marketplace

and sombreros; and gold-filigree *joyería* (jewelry). For pottery, walk west along Calle Benito Juárez (which borders the plaza's south side) to the block just west of the plaza.

Templo de San Vicente Ferrer

While you're in the vicinity, visit the town's pride, the **San Vicente Ferrer church.** Reach it by circling the block: Continue west on Calle Benito Juárez, go immediately left at 5 de Mayo, then after one block turn left again at Belisario Domínguez, to the church on the left. Although the church's early history is shrouded in mystery, the present construction appears by its style to date from the mid-19th century.

The *Women Warriors*

As an interesting downtown side-street diversion, cross over the Río Los Perros for a look at the intriguing if somewhat the worse-for-wear *Women Warriors* sculptures on the west riverbank. Head west along Calle Benito Juárez. Two blocks west of the plaza, from the middle of the river bridge, notice the two tall sculptures of women (in Juchiteca skirts and blouses, of course), about two stories high, in what appears to be a small neighborhood park.

Few local residents seem to know much about them, except that "they are guarding the people from the river." Get a better view of the sculptures (which, close-up, you'll see are of stainless sheet steel) by accessing the west riverbank from the pedestrian bridge a block upstream (north) from Benito Juárez.

ENTERTAINMENT AND EVENTS

Juchitán's substantial excess wealth goes largely to finance an impressive round of parties, locally called *velas,* in honor of a patron saint or a historically or commercially important event. The *velas* are organized and financed by entire barrios, and led by *mayordomos,* usually a well-to-do male head of household, but also including his spouse, children, and all relatives and friends, who usually

Women Warriors sculptures

add up to a major fraction of the population of an entire Juchitán barrio.

Customary activities include blossom-decorated church masses, parties in the house of the *mayordomo,* community barbecues, a parade of fruit and flower-laden floats, from which the *capitanas,* dressed like brides in their stunningly embroidered Tehuántepec outfits, throw fruit and gifts to the street-side crowds.

Note: Although the *velas* are local affairs, everyone is invited, and can join the fun by paying a nominal entrance fee, customarily $5-10 per adult.

In all, Juchitecos celebrate 20 in-town *velas,* which fill streets with merrymakers during the last half of April, virtually the entire month of May, and several days each in June, July, August, and September—a total of about 50 days of celebrating for the entire year. This wouldn't be too excessive if it were not for the approximately 20 obligatory national holidays and the other 30 not-to-be-missed *velas* in neighboring Isthmus communities.

As much a night club as it is a restaurant, the **Restaurant-Bar Las Galias** (Efrain Gómez 15B, tel. 971-126-9005, dinner entrées $9-12) entertains guests with live Latin music, after 9pm Friday and Saturday nights. Arrive early for fish, chicken, or a good steak, then dance the night away.

ACCOMMODATIONS
Under $25

For a good downtown budget option, check out the 27-room **Hotel Victoria** (2 de Abril 29, tel. 971/711-1558, $17 s or d one bed, $19 d two beds with fan; add $5 for a/c), a block east and a block north of the town plaza's northeast corner. What you see is what you get: plain but clean rooms with private, hot-water shower-baths.

$25-50

Moving two blocks north from the plaza along 5 de Septiembre, past Miguel Hidalgo, you'll find the welcoming **Hotel Don Alex Lena Real** (16 de Septiembre 48, tel. 971/711-1064

Velas: Fiestas of the Isthmus

The Isthmus *velas* amount to a near-continuous regional party. People stay up all night, sometimes for days on end of feasting, drinking, dancing, and parading with family and friends, many of whom return from afar to renew cherished old relationships. What follows is a short list that includes only the most important Isthmus *velas*.

Date	Place	Festival
January 18-21	Jalapa del Marqués	San Sebastián de las Flores
First Friday of Lent	San Pedro Huamelula	Carnaval
February 20-25	Matías Romero	Vela San Matías
First days of April	San Pedro Tapanatepec	Feria de Mango
April 15	Juchitán	Vela Ique Guia
April 25	Juchitán	Vela Ique Guidxi
April 27	Juchitán	Vela Paso Cru
May 3	Juchitán	Vela Guzebenda
May 3-6	Salina Cruz	Santa Cruz
May 5	Juchitán	Vela Quintu
May 8	Juchitán	Vela Guigu Dixta
May 10	Juchitán	Vela San Pedro Cantarito
May 13	Juchitán	Vela San Isidro Guete
May 15	Juchitán	Vela Guela Bene
May 16	Juchitán	Vela Iguu
Last 15 days of May	Juchitán	Fiesta de San Vicente Ferrer
	Juchitán	Vela Biadxi
	Juchitán	Vela Calvario
	Juchitán	Vela Angelica Pipi
	Juchitán	Vela San Isidro Labrador

or 971/711-0989, fax 971/711-1064, hotedonalex@hotmail.com, $34 s, $40 d). The 14 very clean rooms with a choice of one king-size or a pair of double beds, come with air-conditioning, phone, cable TV, wireless Internet, and credit cards accepted.

Over $50

Juchitán's most relaxing hotel is the resort-style ★ **Gran Hotel Santo Domingo** (Crucero, Hwy. 200, tel./fax 971/711-1050, 971/711-3642, or 971/711-1959, www.hotelesdeoaxaca.com, $38 s, $52 d, $65 t), on the highway across from both the bus station and the ingress road to town. The Gran Hotel's choice attraction is an invitingly large pool and grassy patio, a welcome refuge for winding down from the heat and bustle. The approximately 60 rooms in a pair of long, double-storied tiers beyond a tropical entrance foyer, are spare but clean, spacious, high-ceilinged, and comfortable, with modern-standard bathrooms, air-conditioning, TV, phones, a good restaurant, parking, and credit cards accepted.

FOOD

Juchitán's downtown plaza food stalls do big business all day and half the night. Especially popular with local people are the market *fondas* (food stalls) at the bottom level, at the south (right) side of the *palacio municipal*. Another, more tranquil *fonda* spot is on the side plaza Helidoro Charis Castro, a block south of the main plaza, in front of the San Vicente Ferrer church.

Date	Place	Festival
	Juchitán	Vela San Vicente Chico
	Juchitán	Vela San Vicente Grande
	Juchitán	Vela de Cheguigo
Last week of May	Tehuántepec	Vela Sandunga
June 16	Juchitán	Vela San Antonio
June 24	Juchitán	Vela San Juan Bautista
	Juchitán	Vela Taberneros
	Juchitán	Vela Coheteros
June 24-30	San Pedro Huamelula	Fiesta del Apóstol San Pedro
June 27-30	San Pedro Tapanatepec	Fiesta Patronal de San Pedro
July 21-29	Santiago Laollaga	Fiesta de Santiago Apóstol
July	Juchitán	Vela de los Niños
August 13	Juchitán	Vela Asunción
August 15	Juchitán	Vela San Jacinto
August 13-16	Jalapa del Marqués	Fiesta de la Asunción
August 13-18	Tehuántepec	Fiesta Patronal del Barrio de Santa María Reoloteca
August 31-September 11	Tehuántepec	Fiesta del Laborio
September 3	Juchitán	Vela de la Familia Pineda
September 4	Juchitán	Vela de la Familia López
September 5	Juchitán	Vela del Triunfo del Batallón Juchiteco de 1866
	Juchitán	Vela Superior
October 1-4	San Francisco Ixhuatan	Vela del Santa Patrón
December 26	Tehuántepec	Vela Tehuántepec

For a snack (sandwich, pizza, salad) and delicious espresso coffee there is soft-seat, 21st-century hip **Italian Coffee Company** (corner of 15 de Septiembre and Hidalgo, tel. 971/711-0773, 9am-10pm daily, $2-5).

The pizza is hot, the spaghetti is tasty, and the salads are crisp at the **Pizzería Gato Montes** (Wildcat Pizza; Colón 7, tel. 971/711-3945, 5pm-midnight daily, $3-9). Add movies (starting around 7pm) and your evening will be complete. It's located a block west of the San Vicente Ferrer church, between Belisario Domínguez and Juárez.

The class-act plaza-front restaurant, fine for a midday break, is the refined ★ **Restaurant Casa Grande** (Benito Juárez 12, tel. 971/711-3460, 7am-11pm daily, $6-12) in the inner patio of an ex-mansion. Patrons choose from an international menu of soups, salads, sandwiches, meats, and pastas, and a number of Oaxacan regional specialties, such as *pechuga de pollo zapoteca* (breast of chicken, Zapotec style), *enchiladas de mole negro* (enchiladas with black mole sauce), and *chile relleno de picadillo* (chili pepper stuffed with spiced meat); credit cards are accepted.

On the other hand, local fish lovers frequent seafood restaurant **Mariscos del Mar** (corner of 16 de Septiembre and Hidalgo, no phone, 8:30am-7pm daily, $3-8), one block north of the plaza, for its menu of seafood and more. Have it all, including a plethora of clam, oyster, and shrimp cocktails; seafood soups, both clear and creamed; fish, octopus, squid, lobster, and shrimp (cooked 10 ways); and seven styles of *cucarachas* (small prawns).

INFORMATION AND SERVICES

Tourist Information

In Juchitán, try travel agent **Zarymar** (5 de Septiembre 100B, tel. 971/711-2867), several blocks north of the plaza, for information, airline tickets, and car rentals.

Health and Emergencies

A ready source of non-prescription medicines and drugs is the 24-hour **Farmacia 24 Horas** (corner of Efrain Gómez and 2 de Abril, tel. 971/711-0316), one block behind the north side of the *presidencia municipal*. Alternatively, go to **Farmacia Similares** (José F. Gomes, at the corner of 5 de Septiembre, tel. 971/711-3126, 9am-10pm daily), a block south of the plaza's southwest corner.

A number of doctors maintain offices near the plaza. For example, general physician-surgeons Dr. Ruben Calvo López and Dr. Carlos Alonso Ruiz and gynecologist Doctora Anabel López Ruiz hold regular consulting hours at **Clínica San Fernando** (16 de Septiembre, between Efrain Gómez and Hidalgo, tel. 971/711-1569), half a block north of the plaza's northeast corner.

In a medical emergency, follow your hotel's recommendation or hire a taxi to the **General Hospital Dr. Macedonio Benítez Fuentes** (Efrain Gómez, tel. 971/711-1441 or 971/711-1985), downtown, near the plaza.

In case of **police** or **fire** emergency, dial 066, the public crisis number.

Money

Change money or use the ATM at **Banorte** (Efrain Gómez 19, tel. 971/711-1160 or 971/711-3482, 9am-4pm Mon.-Fri., 10am-2pm Sat.), half a block west of the plaza's northwest corner. Second choice goes to **Banco Santander** (corner of Belasario Domínguez and José F. Gomes, tel./fax 971/711-2000, 9am-4pm Mon.-Fri.), a block south of the plaza.

Communications

The *correo* (tel. 971/711-1272, 8am-7pm Mon.-Fri., 9am-noon Sat.) is at the plaza's northeast corner, just west of the *presidencia municipal*. For a public fax or a money order, go to the **telecomunicaciones** (on Aldama, four blocks west of 16 de Septiembre, 8am-7pm Mon.-Fri., 9am-noon Sat.).

Photography and Cameras

A few downtown photo shops offer both digital and film cameras and supplies and services. The best is **Foto Alta Konica** (16 de Septiembre, east side, tel. 971/711-4428, 9am-9pm Mon.-Sat.), just north of the plaza.

Laundry

One of Juchitán's very few downtown **laundries** (2 de Abril 42, 9am-2pm and 4pm-7pm Mon.-Fri., 9am-6pm Sat.) is three blocks north of the plaza, between Obregón and Aldama.

GETTING THERE AND AWAY

By Bus

A modern long-distance *camionera central* (central bus station), at the Highway 190-200 crossing north of downtown, is the point of departure for all of the first-class and most of the second-class bus connections with both Oaxaca and national destinations. First- and second-class lines service customers from separate waiting rooms (first-class on the left, second-class on the right). The busy but clean station has snack stores and luggage-check service. Long-distance telephone and fax is available at a small office in the second-class waiting room.

Autobuses del Oriente (ADO; tel. 971/711-2565 or 971/711-1022) and affiliated lines offer direct first-class connections north with Gulf of Mexico destinations Minatitlán, Coatzacoalcos, Villahermosa, Palenque, Merida, Cancún, and Tulum; and northwest with Oaxaca City, Mexico City, Veracruz, and Tampico. Additionally, first-class carrier Omnibus Cristóbal Colón (OCC; tel. 971/711-2565) and its luxury-class subsidiary, Plus, offer connections northwest with Oaxaca City, Puebla, Mexico City, and Veracruz; southwest with Salina Cruz, Bahías de Huatulco, Pochutla (Puerto Ángel), and Puerto Escondido; and east with Chiapas destinations of Tuxtla Gutiérrez, San Cristóbal las Casas, and Tapachula, at the Guatemala border.

Second-class carriers include Autobuses del Oriente (ADO), which offers connections north with Coatzacoalcos; southwest with Tehuántepec and Salina Cruz; and east with Tapanatepec, including all intermediate destinations. Additionally, Autobuses Unidos (AU) offers second-class connections northwest with Tuxtepec, Puebla, Mexico City, Orizaba, and Veracruz; and southwest with Tehuántepec and Salina Cruz, including many intermediate destinations. Moreover, Sur offers second-class connections north with Coatzacoalcos; northwest with Oaxaca City; southwest with Bahías de Huatulco;

and east with Tapanatepec and Tapachula, including intermediate destinations.

Semi-local bus connections with adjacent towns are available via the Autotransportes Istmeños buses across the side street, south, less than a block toward town from the *camionera central*.

Mostly second-class Fletes y Pasajes buses operate out of a separate terminal, also at the Highway 190-200 crossing but on the west side, adjacent to the Restaurant Santa Fe. Buses connect east with Chiapas destinations of Tuxtla Gutiérrez, Tapachula, and the Guatemala border; northwest, with Oaxaca City, Puebla, and Mexico City; and north with Tuxtepec and Minatitlán.

By Car

Drivers have the same highway choices and destinations as they do for Tehuántepec. Simply subtract 30 minutes driving time (and 27 km/17 mi distance) for northerly and easterly trips; and add the same for northwesterly and southwesterly trips.

Salina Cruz and Vicinity

Salina Cruz was important long before the conquest. The *salinas* (salt-producing ponds), where untold generations of native folks had been harvesting salt for trade, attracted Hernán Cortés very soon after his arrival in Mexico. He also recognized Salina Cruz's strategic position on the Isthmus, where the long-sought route to China was accessible, not by a torturous trans-Sierra journey but by a short, easy passage over the narrow, low Isthmus. Cortés lost no time in acquiring the *salinas* as part of his personal domain and building ships on nearby Playa La Ventosa with which to explore the Pacific.

His efforts have been amplified by successive generations. Beginning in the 19th century and continuing to the present day, the Isthmus regularly tempts canal builders

wanting to carve a sea route between the Atlantic and Pacific. President Juárez's government settled for a rail connection, begun by the American Louisiana railroad company in Salina Cruz around 1870. President Porfirio Díaz presided over the project's climax, with up-to-date Salina Cruz port facilities built by the British company Iglesias, Pearson and Son, Ltd., around 1900.

Since the 1960s, Petróleos Mexicanos (Pemex) and other government authorities have greatly extended those early efforts with a hefty trans-isthmus pipeline funneling Gulf crude oil to a grand petrochemical complex as well as elaborate new shipping docks. From these, great loads of chemicals, crude oil, gasoline, and other fuels, minerals, fruit, and much more move out via truck, train, and

Salina Cruz

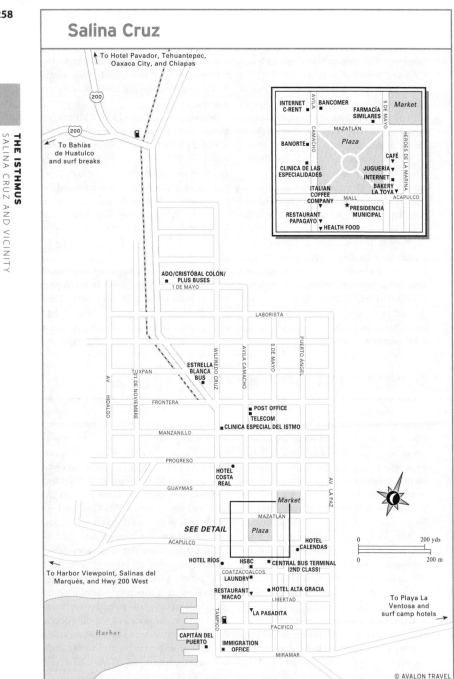

To Hotel Pavador, Tehuantepec,
Oaxaca City, and Chiapas

200

200

To Bahías
de Huatulco
and surf breaks

Detail map:

INTERNET C-RENT | BANCOMER | AVILA | 5 DE MAYO | *Market*
FARMACÍA SIMILARES
MAZATLÁN
CAMACHO
BANORTE | *Plaza* | HEROES DE LA MARINA
CAFÉ
CLINICA DE LAS ESPECIALIDADES | JUGUERÍA
INTERNET
BAKERY LA TOYA
ITALIAN COFFEE COMPANY | MALL | ACAPULCO
★ PRESIDENCIA MUNICIPAL
RESTAURANT PAPAGAYO
HEALTH FOOD

Main map:

ADO/CRISTÓBAL COLÓN/ PLUS BUSES
1 DE MAYO

LABORISTA

TUXPAN

AV HIDALGO

1 DE NOVIEMBRE

ESTRELLA BLANCA BUS

WILFREDO CRUZ

AVILA CAMACHO

5 DE MAYO

PUERTO ANGEL

FRONTERA

POST OFFICE
TELECOM
CLINICA ESPECIAL DEL ISTMO

MANZANILLO

PROGRESO

HOTEL COSTA REAL

GUAYMAS

AV LA PAZ

Market

MAZATLÁN

SEE DETAIL

Plaza

ACAPULCO

HOTEL CALENDAS

HOTEL RÍOS | HSBC | CENTRAL BUS TERMINAL (2ND CLASS)
COATZACOALCOS
LAUNDRY

To Harbor Viewpoint, Salinas del
Marqués, and Hwy 200 West

RESTAURANT MACAO
HOTEL ALTA GRACIA
LIBERTAD

TAMPICO

LA PASADITA

PACIFICO

Harbor

CAPITÁN DEL PUERTO

IMMIGRATION OFFICE

MIRAMAR

To Playa La
Ventosa and
surf camp hotels

0 — 200 yds
0 — 200 m

© AVALON TRAVEL

ship to Mexico and the Pacific. Salina Cruz has thus become the industrial engine of the southern Mexican Pacific, employing more than 10,000 workers whose wages directly and indirectly support many tens of thousands more. While this has delivered plenty of money and prosperity to the town, it has also transformed it into a large industrial port, complete with aroma de petroleo and massive infrastructure devoted to refining and transporting oil. These parts of Salina Cruz need not be on any traveler's itinerary, unless that traveler finds fascinating the complex machinery of the oil business.

However, beautiful pristine beaches can be found nearby, some of them sporting world-class surfing waves and winds high enough to get even the most jaded kiteboarders airborne.

GETTING ORIENTED

Salina Cruz (pop. 80,000), Oaxaca's third-largest city, outstrips both Juchitán and Tehuántepec in hustle and bustle. In Salina Cruz, enterprise reigns and people are working. Crowds with money to spend support a host of town-center markets, stores, offices, hotels, and restaurants. If you need to buy something, Salina Cruz is the place in the Isthmus where you're most likely to get it.

Salina Cruz's big downtown stretches in a two-kilometer (1.2 mi) rectangle north and south from the town plaza. Some of the north-south streets change names at the plaza, others don't. On the plaza's east side, 5 de Mayo becomes Héroes south of the plaza, while on the plaza's west side, Avila Camacho retains the same name its entire length. West another block and north of the plaza runs Wilfredo Cruz, which becomes Tampico on the south side, while a block east of 5 de Mayo, Puerto Ángel remains the same both north and south of the plaza. Thankfully, east-west streets do not change names. From a block north of the plaza, moving successively south, are Guaymas, Mazatlán, Acapulco, and, finally, Coatzacoalcos, a block south of the plaza.

Town activity focuses at the very pungent and busy **market,** northeast of the plaza, between Guaymas and Mazatlán. Several blocks south of the plaza are the container docks along the Calle Miramar, which leads to the drowsy beach village of **Playa La Ventosa.**

★ SURFING

From Salina Cruz, savvy surf-guides take surfers ranging from intermediate to expert on day trips to often empty breaks with some of the best waves on the west coast of

Salina Cruz features a long, lovely beach.

North America. These Oaxaca surf breaks are closely held secrets in the local surfing community. We highly recommend using one of the area's surf guiding groups, such as the guys from **Wavehunters.com** (Wavehunters Surf Travel, 6965 El Camino Real #105-573, Carlsbad, CA 92009, US tel. 760/494-7391, wavehunters@wavehunters.com) or the equally qualified **Las Palmeras Surf Camp** (local contact David Martinez, Calle el Pitayo s/n, Colonia Miramar, Salina Cruz, US contact Josh Mulcoy, josh@mulcoy-travel.com, US tel. 831/588-1306). There are more than a dozen local spots close by, including miles of Tehuántepec beach break, and great jetty and point break waves at Punta Conejo, Punta Coyotepec, Punta Coaixtlahuaca, and Punta Teotitlán.

Wavehunters just opened a small surf-camp/hotel, **Casa El Mirador** (salinacruz-surfcamp.com, seven-night packages priced from $1330 to $1630 per surfer, depending on numbers in the group), which overlooks the Gulf of Tehuántepec, and offers complete air/hotel/surf safari packages year-round. Prices do not include air or the 2.5-hour transfer by car from the Huatulco airport, but do include meals, one 8-hour trip or two 4- to 5-hour surf trips daily with a bilingual guide, and all hotel amenities. With four comfortable, air-conditioned rooms, Wi-Fi, shared kitchen, hammocks, satellite TV, and other amenities, this is a comfortable place to base a Mexican surf safari. This is not, however, a beach "vacation," rather a trip for serious surfers of intermediate to expert skill levels. Las Palmeras offers similar packages from their hillside home base on the south side of Salina Cruz.

ACCOMMODATIONS

The continuous flow of Salina Cruz visitors supports several hotels. With the exception of the beachfront hostelries in Playa La Ventosa, they are all (excepting one, Hotel Parador) near the town center. More recently, a couple of hotels have opened specifically for surfers bound for the many excellent surf spots between Salina Cruz and Huatulco.

Under $25

A good, low-budget choice is the **Hotel Ríos** (Wilfredo Cruz 405, tel. 971/714-0337, $12 s or d in one bed, $16 d, t, or q in two beds), a block west and half a block south of the

One of Mexico's largest oil refineries lies in Salina Cruz.

plaza. Here, the grandmotherly owner maintains three stories of about 20 plainly furnished but very clean rooms, arranged along corridors around an interior patio. Choose an upper room for more light and privacy. Rooms come with bath (tepid-water shower), fans, and street parking only; credit cards are not accepted.

$25-50

In the town center, the **Hotel Altagracia** (5 de Mayo 520, tel./fax 971/714-0726 or 971/714-6225, emarin_10949@hotmail.com, $30 s, $34 d, $38 t, $42 junior suite), just a block and a half south of the plaza, offers another good choice. The 18 rooms, in a compact but invitingly decorated two-story block, are clean, with either one king-size or two double beds. They are tastefully decorated in modern style, with tile floors and some marble baths. Amenities include hot-water shower-baths, air-conditioning, and Internet access. There is street-only parking and credit cards are not accepted.

Another downtown choice is the pricier **Hotel Costa Real** (Progreso 22, tel./fax 971/714-0293, $44 s, $47 d, $54 t), two blocks north, half a block west of the plaza. A plus here is the good restaurant, which is especially handy for breakfast. Upstairs, although the approximately 30 rooms are clean and comfortable enough, they do not appear particularly well-maintained. Make sure everything works before you pay. Amenities include hot-water shower-baths, air-conditioning, TV, and parking. Credit cards are accepted.

FOOD

Food is plentiful in downtown Salina Cruz. If you're on a tight budget, the *fondas* (food stalls) on the market's south and west sides will satisfy with hearty country-style soups, stews, rice, tamales, and seafood, with all the tortillas you can eat. For dessert, go to one of the close-in *panaderías* (bakeries). For example, try **La Toya** (on Acapulco, 8am-10pm daily), near the plaza's southeast corner.

Health food fanciers will appreciate the many shelves of grains, food supplements, vitamins, ginseng, herbs, and remedies at the **Centro Naturista Aquarius** (Avila Camacho, tel. 971/714-2180, 8am-8pm Mon.-Sat.); credit cards are accepted. Find it half a block south of the plaza's southwest corner, just past Restaurant Papagayo.

The first restaurant choice goes to locally popular seafood restaurant ★ **La Pasadita**

Perfect surfing conditions are not unusual around Salina Cruz.

(Avila Camacho, tel. 971/714-0356, 7am-10pm daily, $6-20), 2.5 blocks south of the plaza's southwest corner. Take a seat in their airy, tree-shaded dining room-patio and choose from a long menu that starts out with many breakfast packages, continues with salads and soups (oysters Rockefeller, oyster cream), and finishes with many styles of fish (breaded, with garlic, whole barbecued), and in season, even jumbo prawns (which they call *cucarachas*) and lobster. Credit cards are accepted.

For Chinese food, you have refined **Restaurant Macao Cantonesa** (Avila Camacho, tel. 971/714-3834, 9:30am-7:30pm daily, $3-7), which carries on Salina Cruz's Asian-food tradition, about two blocks south of the plaza's southwest corner. Diners choose from a long, very recognizable menu, including lots of meat, fish, and chicken dishes, such as almond chicken, pork chow mein, and spareribs.

Also among the town center's recommendable, sit-down eateries is locally popular **Restaurant Papagayo** (Avila Camacho 407, tel. 971/714-2084, 8am-10pm daily, $2-6), half a block south of the plaza's southwest corner. The Chinese-Mexican owners once offered some Asian food favorites, but now they've switched exclusively to Mexican and international specialties.

For dessert, try Starbucks look-alike **Italian Coffee Company** (corner of Acapulco and Avila Camacho, tel. 971/720-2840, 9am-11pm daily), on the southeast plaza-front corner. Take in the refined, air-conditioned ambience, while relaxing to soothing recorded melodies, sampling the rich espresso coffees, and snacking on sandwiches (*panini,* croissant) or desserts (cakes and brownies).

INFORMATION AND SERVICES
Health and Emergencies

A good choice for over-the-counter medications is **Farmacia Similares** (Generics Pharmcacy; Mazatlán, tel. 971/714-1670, open 24 hours daily), a few doors from the plaza's northwest corner.

Probably the most solid in-town medical clinic is the very professional **Clinica Especialidades Medica del Istmo** (Tampico 5, between Manzanillo and Frontera, tel. 971/714-5074). They have several specialists (internist, opthamalogist, pediatrician, gynecologist, pathologist,

This point break is a destination for Salina Cruz surf safaris.

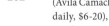

gastroenterologist, psychiatrist, and dentist) for office consultations and hotel calls.

Alternatively, right on the plaza's west side, the **Clínica de Especialidades Médicas** (Medical Specialties Clinic; Avila Camacho 306, tel. 971/714-4107, 9am-5pm Mon.-Sat.) offers consultations with a gynecologist, pediatrician, ophthalmologist, or dentist.

In a medical emergency, either follow your hotel's recommendation or have a taxi take you to **Sanatorio del Carmen** (clinic and pharmacy; Calle Francisco Villa 16, tel. 971/714-1180). In a police or fire emergency, contact the *policía municipal* (tel. 971/714-0523).

Money

Several banks, all with ATMs, serve downtown customers. A good first choice is **HSBC** (northeast corner of Avila Camacho and Coatzacoalcos, tel. 971/714-4476, 8am-6pm Mon.-Fri.), a block south of the plaza. Alternatively, also on Avila Camacho, try **Bancomer** (Avila Camacho, tel. 971/714-0032, 8:30am-4pm Mon.-Fri., 10:30am-2:30pm Sat.), on the east side of the street a few steps north of the plaza; or **Banorte** (tel. 971/714-4454 or 971/714-5898, 9am-4pm Mon.-Fri., 9am-2pm Sat.), on the west side of the plaza, near the plaza's northwest corner.

Communications

The town *correo* (east side of Avila Camacho, corner of Frontera, tel. 971/714-0040, 8am-7pm Mon.-Fri., 8am-4pm Sat.), with Mexpost secure mail service, and the *Telecom* (east side of Avila Camacho, corner of Frontera, tel. 971/714-0891, fax 971/714-0760, 9am-7:30pm Mon.-Fri.), stand side by side, four blocks north of the plaza. Moreover, a *larga distancia* **telephone office** (7am-midnight daily) serves customers at the plaza's southeast corner.

Immigration

Being a port of entry, Salina Cruz has a **Migración** (Immigration Office; tel. 971/714-1000 or 971/714-4531, 9am-1pm Mon.-Fri.), at the foot of Tampico, four blocks south of the plaza. Go there if you lose or need an extension on your tourist permit.

Car Rental

Rent a VW bug (minimum $40/day) at **Lone Star** (tel./fax 971/716-2650, bubistmo@hotmail.com, 9am-7:30pm Mon.-Sat.), on the north outskirts, along the Tehuántepec highway, about two kilometers (1.2 mi) from downtown.

Photography and Laundry

The best town source for cameras (Kodak, Konica, and Fuji), developing (both film and digital), and supplies is **Foto Discuento de Oaxaca** (Avila Camacho, tel. 971/714-4300, 9am-8pm Mon.-Sat.), half a block north of the plaza.

Get your laundry done at **Lavandería Carmel** (southeast corner of Avila Camacho and Coatzacoalcos, tel. 971/714-6105, 9am-9pm Mon.-Sat., 9am-noon Sun.), a block south of the plaza's southwest corner.

GETTING THERE AND AWAY

Three terminals serve Salina Cruz bus travelers. The two first-class terminals are on the north side of town. At Calle Laborista 2, corner of Highway 200, about seven blocks north of the plaza, computerized **Omnibus Cristóbal Colón** (OCC), **Plus,** and **Autobuses del Oriente** (ADO) (all bus lines contactable by local tel. 971/714-0703) offer first-class and luxury service that can also be booked and paid for by credit card via the **Ticket Bus** agency (toll-free Mex. tel. 800/702-8000).

OCC departures connect northwest with Mexico City (Norte and Tapo terminals) via Tehuántepec and Oaxaca City; west with Bahías de Huatulco, Pochutla (Puerto Ángel), and Puerto Escondido; and east with Juchitán, Zanatepec, Tuxtla Gutiérrez, San Cristóbal las Casas, and Tapachula on the Guatemala border. Its subsidiary line, Plus, offers luxury-class connections northwest with Oaxaca City, Mexico City, and Veracruz; and southwest with Bahías de Huatulco.

ADO offers luxury-class connections in three directions: northwest, via Juchitán and Puebla, with Mexico City Tapo terminal; northeast, via Villahermosa, with Mérida and Cancún; and west, via Tehuántepec, with Huatulco, Pochutla (Puerto Ángel), and Puerto Escondido.

At the other first-class terminal, also on Highway 200, five blocks north of the plaza, **Estrella Blanca** (tel. 971/714-5548) and its subsidiary lines offer first- and luxury-class connections along the Highway 200 corridor with Huatulco, Pochutla-Puerto Ángel, Puerto Escondido, and Acapulco (where connections may be made northwest, for Zihuatanejo, Puerto Vallarta, and the U.S. border), as well as Mexico City.

The **second-class bus terminal** (5 de Mayo, tel. 971/714-0259) is downtown, half a block south of the plaza. Here, **Autobuses Unidos** (AU) offers connections northwest with Oaxaca, Puebla, Mexico City, Orizaba, and Veracruz; and north with Tehuántepec, Juchitán, and Tuxtepec. **Sur** offers connections north, with Tehuántepec, Juchitán, and Coatzacoalcos; east with Zanatepec and Tapanatepec; and southwest with Astata and Bahías de Huatulco.

Drivers have the same highway choices and destinations as Tehuántepec. Simply add 20 minutes to the driving time (and 15 km/9 mi distance) for northerly, northwesterly, and easterly trips; subtract the same for southwesterly trips. Fill up with gasoline at the Pemex *gasolinera* on the highway, Tehuántepec direction, about six kilometers (four mi) north of downtown.

PLAYA LA VENTOSA

Playa La Ventosa is Salina Cruz's sleepy little beach village on the historic Bahía de la Ventosa (Windy Bay), where Hernán Cortés built his first caravels to explore the Pacific.

At about six kilometers (four mi) from downtown, you arrive at Playa La Ventosa. This is a good spot for kiteboarding as the wind is fairly strong and quite consistent, but you'll have to bring your own gear. There are surfboards available through some of the surf camps in town, but no kiteboarding gear as of yet.

Sights and Recreation

Wander the beach, rocky in the rainy summer and fall, sandy in the dry winter and spring. On the east side, by the river's mouth, collect shells and driftwood, watch the antics of the pelicans, seagulls, and cormorants, and, with your binoculars, look for rarer species. On the west side, explore the tide pools beneath the rocky headland, then head inland and hike the headland's forested arroyos up to the breezy hilltop for a close-up view of El Faro de Cortés.

On another day, go on a fishing excursion and catch a load of silvery *mojarra* (bass), *lisa* (mullet), and *sierra* (mackerel) for a feast for everyone in the neighborhood. Go in your own boat or hire a fisher (figure about $60) to take you out for half a day.

Surf, surf, surf and kiteboard, here and at half a dozen other beaches within 30 minutes' drive.

Accommodations

La Ventosa's rustic best is the sleepy **Posada Rústrian** (tel. 971/714-0450, $12 s, $24 d), so relaxing that it's worth reserving well ahead of time if you plan to arrive during high-occupancy times: around Christmas, Easter, weekends, and January-April. Posada Rústrian amounts to a downscale mini-resort, perched on a breezy rise with a palm-fringed beach view. Watch for the side road on the left (across from mini-store "Miscelanea de Diaz") as you're entering town. There are no TVs and no phones, simply about 20 basic rooms and a breezy, shaded restaurant with chairs and hammocks for resting, reading, and taking in the view. Rooms (check for maintenance and cleanliness before moving in) have fans and room-temperature private shower-baths.

Getting There and Away

Get there by car, taxi, or white or orange Ventosa-labeled bus running west along Calle Miramar next to the container docks, four blocks south of the plaza in Salina Cruz.

Drivers, bear left at the fork at the end of Miramar and continue winding over the hill toward the beach. After about three kilometers (two mi), you get a good view of the petrochemical plant on the left, belching a swirling, hellish plume of pollution. Fortunately for Salina Cruz (but not for other towns downwind), prevailing breezes blow the smoke in a northerly direction, away from town.

Background

The Landscape

On the map of North America, Mexico's state of Oaxaca (wah-HAH-kah) makes up the southern bulge of Mexico, the region where the Mexican coastline thrusts into the Pacific like the belly of a frolicking Pacific dolphin. Oaxaca is a sizable place—with 95,470 square kilometers (36,860 sq. mi)—and Mexico's fifth-largest state, as big as a midsize U.S. state, such as Indiana, or an entire small European country, such as Portugal.

As in Mexico as a whole, mountains rule Oaxaca's landscape. From the U.S. border, Mexico's grand pair of mother ranges, the Sierra Madre Oriental in the east and Sierra Madre Occidental in the west, sweep southward a thousand miles until they reach Oaxaca, where they bend eastward and practically merge. In Oaxaca, the ranges, respectively called the Sierra Madre de Oaxaca and the Sierra Madre del Sur, form a broad, rumpled, pine-tufted landscape, dotted with 20 peaks in excess of 3,000 meters (10,000 ft.). Only the mostly narrow southern coastal plain, one large valley, and a few scattered lesser vales provide enough level cropland to support large towns. From those few valleys, a handful of streams, blocked and forced by the mountains to twist through deep canyons, make their way to the sea.

CLIMATE

Despite its deep southern latitude, Oaxaca's elevation, cooling sea breezes, and summer rain showers moderate the heat. Most of the state,

excepting the remote mountain summits, basks in the tropics, never feeling the bite of frost.

The seashore and coastal plain, including all of the Isthmus, is a land of endless summer. Winter days are typically warm and rainless, peaking at 28-31°C (82-88°F) and dropping to 18-24°C (65-75°F) by midnight.

Summers on the Oaxaca beaches are warmer and wetter. Mornings are usually bright and balmy, warming to around 32°C (90°F). In the early afternoons, clouds often gather and bring short, sometimes heavy, cooling showers. Later, the sun reappears, drying the sidewalks and beaches and warming the breeze just in time to enjoy a dazzling Oaxaca puesta del sol (sunset).

Visitors to Oaxaca City experience similar but more temperate seasons. Midwinter days are typically mild to warm, usually peaking between 21°C and 24°C (70-75°F). Expect cool but frost-free winter nights between 9°C and 16°C (45-60°F). Oaxaca City summers are delightful, with afternoons typically 28-32°C (in the mid- to upper 80s) and pleasant evenings 24-26°C (in the mid-70s), perfect for strolling.

Visitors should take note that Oaxaca's rainfall, like all of Mexico's, is strongly seasonal. Most years, nearly all the rainfall accumulates during the summer and early fall. Rains taper off in October and November and don't usually return until June. May, before the rains, is typically Mexico's warmest month. Relief comes with the cooling summer showers.

Plants and Animals

Luxuriant tropical foliage is one of the reasons that visitors are pleasantly surprised when they visit Oaxaca during the rainy summer-fall season. Then, excursions through Oaxaca's coastal foothill forest can often reward travelers with a bounty of exotic verdure: Great leafy trees are swathed with mats of vines; giant-leafed **philodendrons** climb toward the canopy, while tropical hangers-on, such as spiny, pineapple-like red **bromeliads** and big, white-flowered **orchids** perch atop available branches. Wildflowers sprout everywhere, especially on temperate upland plateaus. There, summer rains bring carpets of roadside blossoms—purple daisies, blue and yellow lupine, morning glories, tiny magenta sweet peas, and dozens more.

The dry winter-spring season also brings rewards. Many trees, especially along the coast, having lost their leaves, flower in February. Hundreds of varieties of the **pea family** bloom in riotous red, pink, yellow, and white. Now and then visitors stop, attracted by something remarkable, such as a host of white flowers blooming from the apparently dead branches of the appropriately named *palo de muerto* (tree of the dead).

In dry country, cactus-like plants rule. Dotted all over the state, fields of **maguey** wait to be harvested for *mezcal*. Farmyards are fenced with bulging nopal (prickly pear) cacti, their thick leaves studded with red **tunas** (cactus apples).

VEGETATION ZONES

At least 8 of the 14 major vegetation zones in Mexico can be found in Oaxaca, and 6 of these zones can be visited along Oaxaca's major highways. Near the coast you'll find savanna, deciduous tropical forest, and pine-oak forest. Inland lie swaths of tropical evergreen forest, tropical rainforest, and arid tropical scrub. The more inaccessible mountainsides and peaks are home to the cloud forest and

Oaxaca Fast Facts

- **Land area:** 95,470 square kilometers/36,860 square miles (fifth largest among 31 Mexican states and the federal district)
- **Tallest mountain:** Cerro Quiexobra, 3,750 meters/12,300 feet
- **Population (2010):** 3,802,000 (10th largest among Mexican states)
- **Indigenous population:** 32 percent of the total
- **Population density:** 40 per square kilometer/103 per square mile

high coniferous forest, which can be reached only by climbing high mountain slopes and summits.

Savanna

The flat palm-dotted grasslands that can be found near Lagunas de Chacahua and along the Isthmus shoreline near Juchitán represent the last of Oaxaca's natural savanna, as much of this grassy terrain has been converted to farmland or pasture. The savanna lands are watery in summer, but go dry in winter and spring.

While grasses are the primary flora here, it is the variety of palms that lend the savanna character. The most prevalent is the **Mexican Fan Palm,** or *Palma Real*, with flat, spreading leaves and seasonal black fruits.

The most recognizable palm is the **coconut palm,** possibly the world's most useful tree, since every part of it can be put to work: fronds for thatch, mats, and baskets; lumber for construction, and the nut for drinking or making candy or oil. When you're sitting on the beach in the shade of a palm tree, most likely it's a coconut palm.

Vegetation Zones

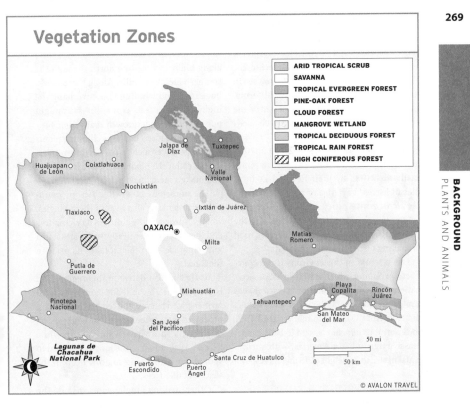

Legend:
- ARID TROPICAL SCRUB
- SAVANNA
- TROPICAL EVERGREEN FOREST
- PINE-OAK FOREST
- CLOUD FOREST
- MANGROVE WETLAND
- TROPICAL DECIDUOUS FOREST
- TROPICAL RAIN FOREST
- HIGH CONIFEROUS FOREST

© AVALON TRAVEL

The savanna is also home to the **gourd tree,** or *calabaza,* with grapefruit sized gourds growing from the trunk. Still in common use today, these gourds have been employed as eating and drinking vessels since Aztec times.

Tropical Deciduous Forest

You'll find this "short tree" forest along the Oaxaca coastline around Puerto Ángel and Huatulco. Deciduous trees shed their leaves in winter. However, their dreariness is countered by bright fall leaf colors and brilliant blooms of white, yellow, pink, and red flowers that burst forth in winter from the seemingly lifeless branches of several deciduous trees. These often-familiar flowering trees include the **Rosa Amarilla,** the **silk cotton tree,** the **frangipani** or **plumeria,** and the **poinsettia.** More unusual plants found here

are the lipstick tree, which contains a bright red-range dye within the pulp of its burrs, and the **mata raton,** or mouse killer, which offers fragrant swirls of pink and white blossoms in spring; its bark and leaves ground up and mixed with corn make an effective mouse and rat poison.

Pine-Oak Forest

About an hour inland from the coast, at elevations around 1,500 meters (5,000 ft.), the tropics give way to pine-oak forest, Oaxaca's most extensive vegetation zone.

Much of the forest that once covered half of Oaxaca has been cleared over the centuries to create farmland, especially in the central valley and surrounding mountainsides. Yet extensive upland tracts of pine-oak forest remain, storing moisture, anchoring soil, and providing food and shelter for a variety of animals.

The lower reaches of these forests are mostly composed of two types of oaks, called the **Encino,** a small-leafed evergreen, and the **Roble,** large-leafed and deciduous. These trees are much like the oaks you see in the United States, particularly in California. Clustered in the branches and scattered on the ground below, their acorns definitively identify them as oaks.

Up higher, above 1,800-2,100 meters (6,000-7,000 ft.), the oaks give way to pines, easily identified by their needle-like bundles of leaves. Varieties of pine include the **Mexican white pine,** similar to American white pine, the **Montezuma pine,** and the **Aztec pine,** with bright green needles used in making turpentine, tar, and soap.

Often found in this environs is the *ahuehuete,* or *Sabina,* which is known as Mexico's national tree. Every visitor to Oaxaca makes a pilgrimage to Santa María del Tule, a short distance from Oaxaca, to marvel at El Tule, the enormous *ahuehuete,* said to be the most massive tree in Latin America, with a trunk equal in size to its height of 46 meters (150 ft.).

Tropical Evergreen Forest

Marked by tall, leaf-crowned trees and lush undergrowth, this vegetation zone can be found in rainy foothills and low mountain areas, primarily along the northern Gulf slope, especially around Valle Nacional and along highways heading north through the southern Sierra foothills. Along these roads, huge trees and winding vines overhang the highway, and it feels as if a dinosaur might pop out of the undergrowth at any moment.

This dense forest contains climbing plants with huge leaves such as the **coriman.** Local people call it the *pinanona,* and eat its fruits and make a medicinal tea from its leaves.

The notorious **strangler fig,** or *matapalo* or killer tree, also lives in these jungles, where it sprouts in the crotch of its victim tree and then slowly, relentlessly, suffocates it in a viny embrace. And then it takes its place in the forest.

Coffee is also native to this region, and is grown beneath the shade canopy by local farmers, who harvest the red berries that are processed into coffee beans. The wild version of coffee, a shiny-leaved shrub with white flowers, is common in the jungle, but hard to spot as the plants tend to grow deep in the shade of taller trees.

Other striking jungle plants include the **African Tulip Tree,** notable for its large, bright red flowers, and the **heliconia,** one of

cactus hearts (called *piñas*) ready to be distilled into *mezcal*

the most strikingly beautiful of all flowers. A cousin of the banana, the heliconia's brightly colored bracts bear a strong resemblance to birds of paradise.

Tropical Rainforest

In these "forests primeval," heavy rains nourish enormous evergreen hardwoods up to 60 meters (200 ft.) in height, over layers of lesser trees and a luxuriant undergrowth of palms, bamboo, orchids, and bromeliads.

Oaxaca's rain forests once covered most of the region along its northern border with Veracruz, but ranches and farms have replaced much of it. Yet large swaths remain intact along Highway 175 near Valle Nacional, and also in the terrain on highways 185 and 147.

The grandest tree in this forest is the **mahogany,** highly valued for its beautiful, red-toned wood. Mahogany's beauty is its downfall: furniture makers love this wood, and so, everywhere it grows, Oaxaca included, loggers go after it. There are also rubber trees—if you see diagonal slashes on a trunk, it's a rubber tree, giving up sap for rubber. A similar tree, the **chicle** or chewing gum tree, is the original source for chiclets, the chewing gum that conquered the world in the early 20th century. The domesticated **rubber tree,** the source of Panama rubber, was once highly valued for its sap, which could be made into rubber. Synthetics replaced natural rubber in the 20th century, and the rubber tree faded in importance, but the wild version of this tree remains an integral part of the tropical forest.

The **chocolate tree** is also indigenous to the tropical rain forest. Cacao was once known as "the food of the gods," and its importance to Aztec culture is evident in that its seeds were used as currency. The cacao tree is a smaller tree and can be found beneath the canopy, its 25-centimeter (10 inch) pods sprouting directly from the trunk. Inside the leathery yellow pods lie the beans from which chocolate is made.

Arid Tropical Scrub

This desert-like zone, primarily found along the borders with Guerrero and Puebla, is completely dry in winter and spring; the rain falls only in summer. Here, succulents thrive. **Cacti** and **agaves** can store water in their fleshy leaves and trunks. The most well-known cactus is the **prickly pear,** known for its role in Aztec legend and its place on the national flag of Mexico. Today it is used for fencing, cattle food, and for eating—Mexicans love the *tunas,* or cactus apples that grow on the plant's leaves. This and several other types of cacti are jointly known as **nopal.** One spine-free type of nopal offers edible leaves—you'll see them in supermarkets all over Mexico—and once, in concert with a certain type of insect, was the source of bright red cochineal dye. Though synthetic dyes have replaced it for the most part, a few Oaxacan communities still make the real thing.

Another much-loved cactus is the **maguey,** or century plant, said to bloom after 100 years, and then die. The lifespan is more like 50 years. The maguey has a cousin, *mezcal,* the source of the liquor of the same name. This is Oaxaca's pride and joy, and one cannot visit Oaxaca without at least tasting some of the local brew. It's heady stuff. Other cacti provide material for various types of fiber, such as sisal and other useful materials. Providing a striking roadside attraction in this region, the **Bravo** cactus towers up to six meters (20 ft.) high.

Cloud Forest and High Coniferous Forest

Few tourists visit these two vegetation zones, for they are found on the slopes and summits of Oaxaca's highest mountains. The easiest access to these forests can be found in the mountains north of Ixtlán de Juárez along Highway 175, and atop the Mazatec holy mountain, Cerro Rabón. Should you wish to visit these remote regions, you'll need a guide. In the elevations between 900 and 1,800 meters (3,000-6,000 ft.), uou'll discover the little-seen plant and animal life of a region many botanists believe to be a remnant of the last Ice Age. This theory is supported by the similarity of many plants that are also found in Georgia and North Carolina in the United States: the brilliant reds and oranges of liquid amber, the white bark of beech, and white flowers of dogwood in summer.

You'll also see giant Mexican **tree ferns,** dating perhaps from the age of the dinosaurs, and **bromeliads,** cousins to the pineapple, high in the trees. Several types of **orchids,** also thrive here, especially the *bayoneta* or *pata de paloma,* recognizable by its dropping green leaves and white flowers which age to a mellow golden hue.

Above this region lies the mountaintop zone known as the **high coniferous forest,** roadless, cloud-wrapped alpine terrain, similar to the upper Rocky Mountains' higher slopes. Above 3,300 meters (10,000 ft.), stands of mixed pines, alders, and firs thrive, especially the **Montezuma pine.** Higher still live groves of **sacred fir,** locally known as *abeto* or *ayamel.* Finally, in the highest reaches of these peaks, bunchgrass and **Mexican juniper,** a bushy plant with edible blue berries, grow.

For more details of Oaxaca's marvelous plants, consult M. Walter Pesman's delightfully readable *Meet Flora Mexicana* (which, unfortunately, has been long out of print, but

major libraries often have a copy). Also informative is the more recent popular paperback *Handbook of Mexican Roadside Flora,* by Charles T. Mason Jr. and Patricia B. Mason.

MAMMALS

Although thousands of years of human hunting and habitat encroachment have generally reduced their numbers, many of Oaxaca's native animal species still thrive in the wild. While some animals, sensitive to human presence, such as **jaguars, howler monkeys,** and **tapirs,** are now rarely seen in Oaxaca, others, such as **foxes, coyotes, coatimundis,** and wild pig-like **jabalís,** seem unaffected by, and sometimes even appear to benefit from, human presence.

The excitement of seeing animals in the wild is the reward of visitors who take time to visit them in their own wilderness home grounds. Sylvan stretches, such as the pine-oak woodlands coating mountainsides northeast of Oaxaca City, the thick forests of the Huatulco preserve, or the rich mangrove wetland of Manialtepec near Puerto Escondido, are ripe with wildlife-viewing opportunities for those willing to get off the beaten track and quietly watch and wait.

a roadside attraction near Las Grutas

Armadillos, Coatimundis, Peccaries, and Bats

For the most part, **armadillos** and **coatimundis,** known in Mexico as *tejones,* have not been too adversely affected by the human encroachment on almost all wild animal habitat, and so you are likely to spot one of these critters without too much effort. The armadillo, of course is recognizable by its reptilian shell, while the coati resembles a skinny, more sleek version of a raccoon, with the same bandit mask but a more pointed face.

The pig-like **collared peccary** is one of Mexico's least endangered species. Called the *jabalí* locally, this American native ranges all the way from Canada into South America; it is recognizable by its whitish collar, which distinguishes it from the wild boars more recently introduced into the southeast and Pacific coast of the United States. The peccary is normally a shy animal, but when they congregate in packs, watch out: they can get very aggressive.

Oaxaca contains twice the **bat** species as the United States, and bats once were worshipped throughout much of Oaxaca. Today Oaxacans, like people everywhere, fear bats for their "vampire" reputation. Few bats actually dine on blood, while most help keep the ecosystem in balance—and people less plagued by bugs—by feeding on insects. They also pollinate flowers, rid cornfields of mice, and drop seeds, helping to restore forestlands.

Monkeys

If you're very lucky, willing to hire a guide, and ready to go a long ways to test that luck, you might spot a monkey or two in the remote reaches of the Chimalapa in the eastern Isthmus of Tehuántepec. Oaxaca's seldom-seen primates are the **spider monkey** and the **howler monkey,** and they are rare indeed. The spider monkey is known as a *mono* or a *chango* in Mexico, and is recognizable by its long skinny arms and legs, and its long, prehensile tail. The howler, with a voice box that makes it sound like King Kong, is even rarer, and has withdrawn deep into Oaxaca's

eastern jungles. Farther south, monkeys abound in Costa Rica, for example, but not up here: they've been hunted for food for centuries by poor indigenous peoples.

El Tigre

Not a tiger but the **jaguar,** *el tigre*'s cunning, stealth, and strength are legendary throughout Mexico. In ancient times, the jaguar was the source from whom kings, princes, and warriors thought they drew their power. At 150 kilograms and two meters in length (250 lbs., 6 ft.), the jaguar is the largest, most powerful cat in the Americas. With dark spots over a tan coat, the jaguar resembles a beefy, short-legged leopard. Once native to most of North America, jaguars have been driven by human encroachment and hunters—a jaguar pelt is worth a year's wages to a poor Mexican—into Oaxaca's deepest forests.

Today, there are jaguar restoration projects and laws to protect them, but jaguars remain few in number, each needing a fairly large chunk of terrain for hunting. Along with every kind of game, jaguars are known to hunt fish and to capture and devour turtles that have come ashore to lay eggs. They will attack if cornered, but are basically shy, and have never been known to be human-eaters.

Ocelots, Margays, and Jaguarundis

These three smaller Mexican cats, along with bobcats and mountain lions familiar north of the border, make their home in Oaxaca. From largest to smallest, first comes the **ocelot,** which looks like a miniature jaguar—hence the Mexican name, *jaguarillo.* Full-grown males measure about 10 kilograms (25 lbs.) in weight and one meter (3 ft.) in length. Ocelot fur is highly valued, meaning, of course, that it is fast disappearing from Oaxaca's forests. A **jaguarundi** is about the size of a large house cat—and it is definitely in the cat family, but its long body and tail lend it an otter-like appearance overall. The **margay** on first glance looks like a baby jaguar, spotted and diminutive size, but a closer look reveals the spots to be in orderly rows, unlike the jaguar. Margays can be domesticated and turned into house pets.

In spite of protections written into the law, all these wild cats are doomed to extinction if current hunting practices continue. They live in the wild, feasting on small game, birds, and fish. Rarely are they seen, for hiding from humans is a matter of self-preservation.

BIRDS

Oaxaca's coastal wetlands and upland forests straddle the southern zone of the great Pacific Flyway, the major western pathway for hosts of birds migrating south from the United States and Canada. These familiar winter visitors, such as Canada geese and ducks, including the Muscovy, black-bellied whistler, gadwall, baldpate, and shoveler, arrive and join an already-rich resident population of ibis, parrots, jacanas, egrets, herons, and anhingas, swelling the numbers into the millions.

Fairly common but always entertaining local birds include the cootlike, blackish **northern jacana,** known as the "lily walker" for its big-footed ability to do just that: walk on lily pads. At a glance, the bird appears to be walking on water. The **great blue heron** is also fairly common but always impressive, with a two-meter (6 ft.) wingspan and a proud head plume. Like the smaller and more numerous **snowy egret,** the heron lives in coastal wetlands. Both birds are fish, crab, and frog hunters, stalking their prey in slow motion, then snatching it up in a long beak. Similar in appearance but smaller in size is the **cattle egret,** originally African, and for the last 100 years plus a common Mexican bird.

Seabirds

Along with swarms of gulls, terns, sandpipers, and boobies, Oaxaca and most of the Mexican coast is home to a pair of larger, more impressive species: **brown pelicans** and **frigate birds.** Once threatened by DDT and other insecticides, the brown pelican has made a comeback, and large flocks of them abound in Oaxaca. They are distinguished by their large lower beaks of gullets, and especially by their feeding rituals: they swoop low over the water, like a squadron of jet fighters, until spotting a school of sardines or other fish. They then rise up and plummet into the sea, usually reappearing with a fresh catch in their beaks. The large, black and white frigate birds, with their architecturally crafted wings, ride high overhead, riding the thermals, then drop down to scavenge fish left behind by village fisherfolk, fighting over scraps; they also attack and eat baby turtles as they emerge from their nests and head for the sea. Though considered seabirds, frigates cannot land and take off on the water, for their feathers lack the water-resistant oil that allows other seabirds to do so.

Parrots

Flocks of parrots are everywhere around Oaxaca's coastal lagoons and tropical foothills, for they are very noisy creatures, squawking, chattering, and screeching as they race through the air from tree to tree. Half a dozen parrot species make their homes in Oaxaca, most of them green with various markings to distinguish one from the other. Two of the more common Oaxacan parrots are the **green parakeet,** distinguished by a long tail and a red throat, and the **Aztec parakeet,** green with an olive-brown throat. Alas, these and many other types of parrots are also to be found caged, for sale, in markets in almost every town in Oaxaca and indeed in all of Mexico.

Don't succumb to the temptation to buy a parrot in a cage. They are probably taken illegally, and they do not travel well (nor are they welcome on airlines, which will charge you a high fee to take one on a plane). They are difficult to get through customs as well. They are better off in the wild, in a flock, living as they are meant to live.

For superb color drawings and details, see *Bird-Finding Guide to Mexico* by Steve Howell (1999).

REPTILES AND AMPHIBIANS

Snakes

For the most part, Oaxaca's many snakes are harmless, shy, and will stay out of your way if you give them fair warning. That said, in the bush or jungle, carry a stick and beat the brush ahead, and don't stick your hand in dark holes. There are, after all, two families of notoriously poisonous snakes around: rattlesnakes and fer-de-lances. Both come in myriad types, and all are aggressive. Mexican rattlers, or *cascabeles,* have the same warning rattles that we find in diamondbacks in the United States. Their tropical viper cousins, the fer-de-lance, have half-a-dozen local names, and, at up to two meters (six ft.) in length, are fearsome indeed, particularly since they lack warning rattles. Wearing high boots and beating the brush is the best way to avoid being snake-bitten.

There are also poisonous sea snakes, *culebra marina,* in Oaxacan waters, although they are quite rare. They are small, ringed with yellow and black, and often live in groups. The venomous bite of a sea snake can be serious, even deadly. Their land counterpart is the coral snake, occurring in several species, with multicolored bands that always include red. Though small, shy, seldom seen, and with a tiny mouth hardly big enough to bite, if one does bite, it can be serious, even fatal.

Gila Monsters, Iguanas, and Geckos

The Gila Monster does not live in Oaxaca but in Sonora; however, its black and yellow tropical relative, the *escorpion,* does inhabit some Oaxacan terrain. It's a scary-looking critter, and the bite is poisonous but rarely fatal.

Oaxacan **iguanas,** or *garrobos,* like iguanas everywhere, are fiercely primeval in appearance but benign in intent. Oaxacans, like many Latinos, like to eat iguana (in Costa Rica they are called "chickens of the trees"). They are usually to be found in treetops, warming in the sun and munching on leaves and flowers, being strict vegetarians. Benign for sure,

but when you see a four or five footer, you definitely feel the need to step back. They look like dinosaurs!

Introduced from Europe decades back, the **gecko,** *guerita* (blondie) or *besucona* (the kissing one), adapted well and now lives in the wild from central Mexico all the way down into South America. Most common in coastal towns, they often take up residence in hotel rooms, where they make their unmistakable gecko sounds, and do their bit to rid the rooms of gnat and mosquitoes. If your room lacks a gecko, order one from room service.

Crocodiles

The noble **crocodile,** *cocodrilo* or *caiman,* was once hunted to near-extinction in Oaxaca due to demand for meat and hide, but today, well-enforced laws protect this fascinating creature, and with crocodile farms and hatcheries along the coast, the population is rebounding. A hatchery that can be visited by tourists is located in Lagunas de Chacahua, west of Puerto Escondido. There are two types found in Oaxacan lagoons: the true crocodile has a narrower snout than its local cousin, which is a type of alligator, or *lagarto.* They can get up to five meters (15 ft.) long, but are most often younger and only a few feet in length. If you see one in the water, don't go in to visit. They aren't necessarily aggressive but they can be opportunistic.

Sea Turtles

Sea turtles once swarmed ashore to lay eggs along the Mexican coastal beaches by the hundreds of thousands. However, they were prized for their meat, eggs, hides, and shells, and so, like the crocodile, nearly hunted into extinction. Now they have official protection, and while egg poachers and turtle hunters are still out there, most of the Mexican populace has embraced turtle protection. Volunteers walk the beaches to scare off poachers, and hatcheries are springing up everywhere. In Oaxaca, sanctuaries can be found in Bahías de Huatulco, near Puerto Escondido, and at Playa Escobillo and Playa Mazunte. At

Mazunte, in a dramatic turnabout, an aquarium and hatchery occupies the site of a former turtle processing factory.

The most common species of turtles in Oaxaca are the olive ridley, *tortuga golfina*, and the green turtle, *tortuga verde*. They can be seen from tour boats offshore of Puerto Escondido, Puerto Ángel, and the Bahías de Huatulco, grazing on sea grass. More rarely seen are the hawksbill turtle, *Tortuga carey*, and the occasionally sofa-sized but highly endangered leatherback, *tortuga laut*.

FISH

Four types of big game billfish abound in deep-sea grounds several miles offshore of Oaxaca's coast: swordfish, sailfish, blue marlin, and black marlin. While three-meter, 450-kilogram (10 ft., 1000 lb.) fish used to be brought in on occasion, fish half that size are more the rule these days. And after you win the fight, the rule these days is also to throw them back into the sea.

Other fish species thriving in Oaxacan waters include tuna-like jacks such as yellowtail, Pacific amberjack, pompano, and the roosterfish, a real fighter if you hook one. Excellent eating fish found locally include yellowfin tuna, mackerel, and dorado, also known as mahimahi. Closer in fishers find snapper, or *huachinango*, and sea bass, and in rocky areas right off the beach, croaker, mullet, and Goliath fish.

Sharks and rays are out there as well. Watch out for stingrays, lodged in the sand in shallow water. If you step on one it will inflict a painful, venomous lash with its barbed, stinger tail. Shuffle your feet when walking in the shallows to prevent this. Offshore, huge Pacific manta rays occasionally break the surface and leap skyward, flapping their great wings like birds. Just beyond the waves, fishers often reel in hammerhead, thresher, and leopard sharks. Beware of the leopard sharks, which are known occasionally to attack offshore swimmers and surfers.

History

Perhaps 20,000 years ago, small bands of people—descendants of the original humans who had crossed the Arctic land bridge from Siberia thousands of years earlier—found their way into the Oaxaca Valley, where they remained, foraging wild vegetables and fruits and hunting everything from squirrels and rabbits up to Ice Age camels and mammoths that inhabited the region in great herds. With such abundance easily available, the people multiplied.

By around 7000 BC, the climate had warmed a few degrees, and the big game were gone, extinct. Settling into a different kind of life, the people began to sow seeds of grains, legumes, vegetables, and fruits. These ancient Oaxacans then picked the best of the crop to plant for succeeding years; generations later, these ancient fields and farms bloomed with domesticated beans, squash, corn, and avocados.

EARLY CIVILIZATION
The Village Era

By 2000 BC the early Oaxacans had settled into village life, with hamlets usually numbering up to a dozen houses clustered together. Life in these earliest Oaxacan villages was fundamentally the same then as it is now, in smaller communities in Oaxaca valley: planting, harvesting, and preparing food was the primary task. Men worked the fields, women ground corn and made tortillas, utilizing less sophisticated versions of the same tools in use today. Family graves were made nearby, the dead buried with personal offerings.

The population grew, as did the villages. By 500 BC some villages such as San José El Mogote, north of Oaxaca City, grew into a small town, with up to 500 residents. Social classes began to appear, indicated by the presence of grander homes—as did specialization, evident in an excavation of a factory where mirrors were manufactured for trade.

Monte Albán

Roughly 2,500 years ago, ancestors of the Zapotec peoples of Oaxaca founded the first city in the Americas on a Oaxacan central valley plateau today known as Monte Albán. Here they erected monumental platforms, pyramids, palaces, and ceremonial ball courts. All were decorated with inscriptions in a language as yet undeciphered, telling the tales of their god-kings. Adobe homes for the lower classes occupied the hillsides below the palatial summit.

Monte Albán flourished for centuries: from an early population in the hundreds, the city expanded, with as many as 40,000 people living there at its height a thousand years later. By AD 500, Monte Albán encompassed seven square kilometers (three sq. mi) of homes, gardens, and monumental neighborhood sub-centers.

Other cities also thrived under Monte Albán's rule, including Yucuita and Monte Negro near Nochixtlán, in the Mixteca Alta; Cerro de las Minas in the Mixteca Baja; and Dainzu and Lambityeco in the central valley. Like Monte Albán, and in contrast to most village-era sites, these cities lay atop defensible hilltops, suggesting that war was a constant threat.

By AD 750, Monte Albán's power was fading, due to drought, disease, war, or overpopulation; nobody is really certain. By AD 1000, the city was abandoned, eclipsed by a crowd of tussling, battling, and scheming city-states. This state of affairs went on for several hundred years, notably with incursions from the Aztecs to the north in 1434; they went on to establish a presence in Oaxaca Valley in 1488. Their garrison at Huaxyacac marks the location of present day Oaxaca City.

All the diplomacy, wars, and seemingly consequential actions of this late pre-Colombian era disappeared into the vale of history with the arrival of the first Spaniards, in the person of Hernán Cortés and his ragged crew, who arrived on the Gulf Coast of Mexico in 1519.

THE CONQUEST

In one of the great if understandable blunders in world history, Quetzalcoatl was scheduled to show up, arriving from the east, at about the time Cortés made his appearance. Moctezuma II, lord of the Aztec Empire, mistook Cortés for the incarnation of the god. Moctezuma basically handed Cortés the keys to the Aztec kingdom, with its impossibly lavish treasures of gold, silver, and jewels. Thus, 550 half-starved Spanish pirate/conquistadors were able to conquer one of the greatest kingdoms in the history of the Americas.

Once Cortés secured his position in Tenochtitlán, the Aztec capital, he sent soldier emissaries in all directions, including south to Oaxaca. Soon, however, Spanish brutality caused a rebellion in Tenochtitlán. Alliances and battles went on for the next two years; by late in the year 1521, Cortés and his indigenous allies, eager to see the Aztec empire fall, had retaken the capital city. By March 1522, Oaxaca's mountains, valleys, and coastlines were under Spanish control. The Kingdom of New Spain of the Ocean Sea was established under the rule of Cortés.

NEW SPAIN

For Cortés, this was not enough. Having heard tales of the fertile valley of Oaxaca, he ordered all the Spanish settlers out of the valley and ventured south from Tenochtitlán in 1523, intent on claiming Oaxaca. Instead, he found Spanish squatters on land he had claimed for himself. This prompted him to disperse these settlers for the second time. Eventually, after several years of politicking and diplomatic back-and-forth, Oaxaca was his. In 1528 he traveled to Spain to obtain a queen for his kingdom, and to gain royal recognition. He returned triumphant, as the Marqués del Valle de Oaxaca, his noble young bride, Juana de Zuñiga, at his side. Cortés' holdings at the time, in addition to the 80,000 pesos a year he collected from thousands of indigenous subjects on three million scattered acres of Mexican lands, included 350,000 acres of Oaxacan valley farmlands, encompassing 34 villages and towns. The only place exempted from his valley domain was the town of Antequara, located on the site of the old Aztec garrison at Huaxyacac. Antequara would eventually evolve into Oaxaca City.

The Missionaries

On the heels of subjugation by the conquistadors, the indigenous people were passed into the hands of the missionaries, intent on healing, teaching them the ways of Christ, and baptizing them. In Oaxaca, the Dominicans led the way, with a convent in Antequara constructed in 1530. Other Dominicans spread the word throughout Oaxaca, followed by a host of other Christian sects. These missions were supported by King Charles V, of course, for it coincided with his political and economic goals.

Whatever harm they may have done, the missionaries did introduce new plants, flowers, and vegetables, and European crafts such as ironwork, glassmaking, pottery glazing, and wool processing. They learned native tongues and translated their bibles into Zapotec, Mixtec, and other local dialects. Soon there were churches everywhere.

The darker side of this missionary zeal was the rapid, rabid destruction of all signs of the previous culture, including temples, idols, paintings, and historical records. Such was manifest destiny. Native songs and dances were also banned, for fear that they kept alive old beliefs. In short, while they were kinder and gentler than the conquistadors—the Dominican father **Bartolomé de las Casas** spent his life fighting for the rights of indigenous peoples—the missionaries, too, did their bit to ensure the enslavement of the indigenous populations and the wholesale destruction of their cultures.

The King Takes Control

After 1530, the King of Spain decided to take control of Oaxaca in order to increase his tax base, and to "liberate" the enslaved natives from the brutal treatment they received at the hands of Cortés and his lieutenants, who ran the valley on his behalf through a system called **encomienda,** which granted these thugs the rights of feudal lords. Influenced by Father de la Casas, the crown passed the **New Laws of the Indies** in 1540, abolishing the rights of these Cortés cronies, abolishing the

an ancient tome from the library in the Museo de las Culturas de Oaxaca, Oaxaca City encomienda system, and outlawing enslavement of native peoples.

COLONIAL OAXACA
Congregación

In 1550, in spite of Spanish dominance of the valley, there were scarcely more than a thousand Spaniards in all of Oaxaca, while there were several hundred thousand indigenous people, mostly still ruled by the hereditary native nobility. In order to obtain more control over the population, the Spanish authorities began moving large numbers of indigenous people into new townships called *congregacións*, located in productive areas near mines, fertile valleys, and along established roads. This achieved its desired results, but it also further undermined the native cultures and traditions by taking people away from the land they had lived on for thousands of years. Today, many of Oaxaca's 570 government townships, *municipios*, derive from those early head towns, or *caberceras*, of these artificial divisions.

Along with their culture, the knowledge of the system of irrigation that fed their terraced fields was lost. Today, the consequences of forgetting this water-conservation tradition are evident in Oaxaca, as greater populations in the bottomland forces farmers uphill, where they lack the knowledge, common 500 years ago, of how to irrigate terraced hillsides.

Population Collapse

The destruction of indigenous culture was a tragedy, of course, but what killed off the native peoples of the Americas, here and everywhere else, was imported disease. By 1650, typhus, cholera, measles, smallpox, and other diseases had reduced the native population from an estimated 15-25 million to 1.3 million by 1650. In Oaxaca, the population around 1500 was estimated at roughly two million. By 1650, only 150,000 remained.

Contemporary Mexicans can look forward to the year 2019, the 500th anniversary of Cortés landing. It has taken these 500 years for the native-speaking peoples of Mexico to regain their pre-conquest population of 25 million.

The Changing Role of the Church

With their independent status derived directly from papal authority, the missionary orders promoted and protected the welfare of the native Mexicans. The established clergy,

fresco on a wall in the Museo de las Culturas de Oaxaca, Oaxaca City

Population Chages in New Spain

	Early Colonial (1570)	Late Colonial (1810)
peninsulares	6,600	15,000
criollos	11,000	1,100,000
mestizos	2,400	704,000
indígenas	3,340,000	3,700,000
negros	22,000	630,000

headed by bishops who were more interested in economic and political power than good works, often came into conflict with the missionaries. This battle came to an end in 1767, when the King of Spain expelled all the Jesuit missionaries from his New World colonies. The liberal, activist missionaries were understandably chilled, and the more conservative establishment church prevailed.

The church and its bishops and priests grew fat, lazy, and corrupt, collecting their biblically-ordained 10 percent tithe of everything from crops to mining profits. By the year 1800, the Catholic Church owned half of Mexico, and worked hand in glove with the ruling class to maintain their stranglehold on power, both political and economic.

The Colonial Economy

There was much at stake, economically. New Spain's vast riches poured into the coffers of Spain, which held a monopoly on everything: foreign goods and traders were absolutely prohibited. Thus, the crown could ensure that the colonies would always end up in deficit—to be made up in gold bullion.

This feudalist structure was even more pronounced in Oaxaca, and was even harder on the local populace due to the seasonal nature of much Oaxacan produce. This inevitably led to the need for cash advances, which bound the locals even more tightly to the system. This corrupt and unfair system led to a number of minor uprisings, portents of revolution to come.

Thanks to a monopoly on the cochineal trade, Oaxaca boomed. The population tripled to 20,000 during the 1700s, and Oaxaca City (the name was changed from Antequara in 1786) was New Spain's third largest city in 1800. Naturally, given the structure of the economy, the money all flowed to the wealthy elite, mostly Spanish-born, and the church officials and owners of large estates. A small merchant class got the trickle-down. The majority of the people, mixed and pure native descent—those who did all the work—got a very small share. Still, by the year 1800, Oaxaca was a prosperous place. The slaves were in place and increasing in numbers, and tons of gold, silver, and cochineal flowed across the Atlantic.

What Spain didn't realize is that New Spain—Mexico—had changed over 300 years.

Criollos: the New Mexicans

Nearly three centuries of colonial rule gave rise to a burgeoning population of more than a million criollos (kree-OH-yohs)— Mexican-born descendants of Spanish colonists, many rich and educated—to whom top status was denied.

High government, church, and military office had always been the preserve of a tiny but powerful minority of peninsulares— European-born Spaniards. Criollos could only watch in disgust as unlettered, unskilled peninsulares (derisively called gachupines— wearers of spurs) were boosted to authority over them.

Although the criollos stood high above the mestizo (mixed native-Spanish), indígena, and negro (African Mexican) underclasses, that seemed little compensation for the false

Cochineal: Nature's Richest Red Dye

Cochineal (*cochinilla*) is a prized, rich, scarlet dye, long cultivated in Mexico before the conquest. The Spanish, immediately seeing its export value, expanded production, especially in Oaxaca, where it became a major source of cash for native Oaxacans faced with increasing tribute demands. The rise of the textile industry in England, the Low Countries, France, and Spain further propelled demand for Oaxacan cochineal, renowned as the most brilliant, richest red dye in the world. The word spread, and, by its peak during the 17th and 18th centuries, Spain's cochineal trade extended as far as China. Although largely replaced by cheaper synthetic dyes by 1900, cochineal is still locally cultivated in the Valley of Oaxaca.

The actual source of the dye is the female of a type of scale insect, *Dactylopius coccus*, which feeds off of a variety of nopal (prickly pear) cactus. Typically, families or village cooperatives own patches of nopal, from which they brush the female beetles during the fall harvest. The beetles are then dried, ground, mixed with calcium or aluminum salts, and boiled in water. The resulting dye suspension is filtered and evaporated leaving pure crimson cochineal crystals, still preferred by many Valley of Oaxaca weavers.

smiles, the deep bows, and the costly bribes that *gachupines* demanded.

Mestizos, *Indígenas*, and African Mexicans

Upper-class luxury existed by virtue of the sweat of Mexico's mestizo, *indígena*, and black laborers and servants. African slaves were imported in large numbers during the 17th century after typhus, smallpox, and measles epidemics had tragically wiped out as much as 90 percent of the indigenous population. In Oaxaca, a small, African-born, black population of around 2,000 in 1650 rose gradually to approximately 10,000, both pure and mixed, by 1800. Although the African Mexicans contributed significantly (crafts, healing arts, dance, music, drums, and marimba), they had arrived last and experienced discrimination from everyone.

INDEPENDENCE

The chance for change came during the aftermath of the French invasion of Spain in 1808, when Napoléon Bonaparte replaced Spanish King Ferdinand VII with his brother, Joseph Bonaparte, on the Spanish throne. Most *peninsulares* backed the king; most criollos, however, inspired by the example of the recent American and French revolutions, talked and

dreamed of independence. One such group, urged on by a firebrand parish priest, acted.

El Grito de Dolores

"Viva Mexico! Death to the Gachupines!" These words, shouted by a firebrand revolutionary priest, Father Hidalgo, ignited the first of many revolutions that would take place in Mexico. Hidalgo succeeded in stirring the passions of the indigenous people, who managed to kill a number of *gachupines* (European-born Spaniards, derisively) and pillage their palatial homes. His army grew to 80,000. They assaulted Mexico City, but were no match for a 6,000-man Royalist army. They were routed, and Hidalgo fled north. Soon he was captured, defrocked, and executed, his head along with those of his three chief lieutenants hung from the walls of the Guanajuato granary (where his army had slaughtered 138 *gachupines*) for 10 years. Today, Hidalgo is an historic Mexican hero, and the day he shouted out *El Grito* is one of many celebrated revolutionary holidays in Mexico.

The 10-Year Struggle

There are a number of these holidays, reflecting Mexico's tangled political history. This would be the stuff of farce, of comedy, were it not so tragic, as one actor after another claimed the stage of Mexico's presidency and failed to lead the self-declared republic to the promised land of good, democratic government for the people. This is a fairly long and complicated tale, and there are many books that detail it well. The following is the abridged version.

After Hidalgo came José María Morelos, who took Oaxaca City from the Royalists in 1812. He declared a revolutionary government. Morelos's moment lasted about three years: he was captured and executed in December 1815.

Morelos was followed by his compadre Vicente Guerrero, who joined forces with a Royalist opportunist, Brigadier Augustin de Iturbide in 1821. Together they wrote up a document called the Plan de Iguala, promising Three Guarantees to the people: Independence, Catholicism, and Equality. At the head of an army called Trigarantes, after the three guarantees, they took Mexico City in 1921. Mexico, as of that moment, had attained independence.

But the country was broke after 10 years of war. Independence had achieved just one thing: the expulsion of the *peninsulares* (European-born Spaniards). The population was mostly illiterate and poor, with no experience in self-government. They yearned for a hero to lead them. Bring on the emperor!

The Rise and Fall of Agustín I

And so they got one: Iturbide, who called himself Emperor Augustín I, crowned in July of 1821, only to abdicate two years later when his former compatriots turned against him.

In 1823, Mexican leaders wrote up a constitution and created the republic of the Estados Unidos Mexicanos (United Mexican States), which Oaxaca soon joined. Oaxaca also created a state government structure and founded a university, from which a pair of Mexico's most memorable presidents, Porfirio Díaz and Benito Juárez, both graduated. Notably, they were both of indigenous descent.

The Disastrous Era of Santa Anna

After several years of anarchy, rebellions, failed coups, and other military and political machinations, in 1832 the military commander Antonio López de Santa Anna was declared president by a willing congress. Santa Anna had led several successful military operations, including the defeat of a Spanish invasion on the Gulf of Tampico, and had been called "Liberator of the Republic" and "Conqueror of the Spaniards" and was something of a national hero, at least to congress. Santa Anna soon resigned, not really interested in the office, but he would manage to pop in and out of the presidency like a jack-in-the-box 10 more times before 1855.

During his assorted reigns, he managed to lose Texas to the United States in 1836 (Remember the Alamo!), and worse, to declare war on the United States in 1847. A force of marines soon crushed the Mexican army and took Chapultepec Castle, where Mexico's beloved Niños Heroes cadets fell in the losing cause on September 13, 1847. As a result of this, in the treaty of Guadalupe Hidalgo, Mexico lost 40 percent of its territory—territory that today makes up the states of New Mexico, Arizona, California, Nevada, Utah, and Colorado.

To the south during this era, Oaxaca prospered under the leadership of Governor Benito Juárez. During his 1848-1852 term as governor, he opened hundreds of elementary schools and a number of teacher's academies. He improved roads and bridges, attracted foreign investment, and rebuilt the economy. The population of Oaxaca grew 25 percent between 1844 and 1854.

In Santa Anna's 11th and last term as president of Mexico, he sold off part of northern Mexico—southern New Mexico and Arizona—in what was known as the Gadsden Purchase. He used the $10 million to finance his last war again the Mexican liberals.

REFORM, CIVIL WAR, AND FRENCH INVASION
The Reforms

The era that followed the expulsion of Santa Anna was one of reform, as liberals such as Benito Juárez wrote new laws abolishing the tenets of privilege. While the intentions were good, the results did not always work out. For example, a law forcing the church to divest itself of massive land holdings simply moved these holdings into the hands of the only people who could afford to buy them: the already wealthy. In Oaxaca, fortunately, isolation from Mexico City allowed much of the land to stay in the hands of the indigenous peoples; many of the parcels sold by the church were bought by native Oaxacans.

Conservatives, generals, priests, and businesspeople opposed the law, and a reactionary uprising took place from 1858 to 1861, when the victorious liberal army paraded into the city on New Year's Day. Benito Juárez assumed the presidency of Mexico in March of 1861.

Juárez and Maximilian

Often compared to Abraham Lincoln, his contemporary to the north, Benito Juárez was a great president whose triumph lasted only a short while. Imperial France invaded Mexico in 1862, with a force numbering 60,000 soldiers. Yet the Mexican army and its bands of irregulars and guerrillas achieved several notable victories, including one at Puebla, where Oaxacan brigadier general Porfirio Díaz won fame as the "Victor of Puebla." That battle took place on May 5, Cinco de Mayo, now a well-known historical date and an excuse for a party. In spite of these victories, the French did take Mexico City and several state capitals, including Oaxaca City, by 1864. The French brought in an Austrian archduke, Maximilian, and his wife Carlota, and crowned them emperor and empress of Mexico.

Juárez carried on, in the mountains in exile, doing his presidential duties; by 1867, the Mexican army and its supporters, the Mexican people, had thrown of the yoke of the French emperor. In May, 1867, the liberal forces defeated Maximilian. A month later, Juárez ordered his death by firing squad on June 19, 1867.

Juárez Reelected, Díaz Rebels

Juárez easily won reelection in 1867, but Díaz soon accused him of violating the constitution. While Díaz stirred up trouble, Juárez continued the hard work of reform. Opposed by Díaz on his efforts to amend the constitution, Juárez was nevertheless reelected president in 1871. Exhausted, he died of a heart attack in July of 1872. Four years later, Porfirio Díaz was elected president in 1876. He ruled for the next 34 years.

ORDER AND PROGRESS
Pax Porfiriana

Although Porfirio Díaz's humble Oaxaca mestizo origins were not unlike Juárez's, Díaz was no democrat. When he was a general, his officers often took no captives; when he was president, his country police, the *rurales*, shot prisoners in the act of "trying to escape."

Order and progress ruled Mexico for 34 years. Foreign investment flowed into the country; new railroads brought the products of shiny factories, mines, and farms to modernized Gulf and Pacific ports. Mexico balanced its budget, repaid foreign debt, and became a respected member of the family of nations.

Oaxaca thrived during the Porfiriato, with public works improvements over three decades capped with the 1892 rail link with Mexico City. Manufacturing, coffee farming, mining, and a host of other industries made the state rich. The population of Oaxaca nearly doubled, to 40,000. But of course it was the rich that got richer, while most of the people, those who did the work, remained poor. While many in Oaxaca were able to hold onto their land, over 100 million acres of land ended up in the hands of rich Mexicans and foreign investors. By 1910, 90

Porfirio Díaz: Hero or Villain?

Porfirio Díaz, Mexico's most controversial and longest-serving president, was born in the city of Oaxaca on September 15, 1830. His parents, José de la Cruz Díaz and Petrona Mori, were of poor Mixtec-mestizo origin. Porfirio's father died when he was three, and he spent his childhood working at odd jobs to support his mother while attending public and parochial schools.

A seminal event occurred for young Díaz in 1854, when it was publicly announced that the entire faculty of the institute unanimously supported the notorious conservative dictator Antonio López de Santa Anna. Díaz asked that his abstention be recorded, and when publicly accused of siding with the liberal cause, he declared his support for General Juan Álvarez, leader of the liberal rebellion in Guerrero. The die was thus cast: For the next 50 years, Díaz never wavered from the image of a resolute, determined liberal, who possessed the courage of his convictions.

Forced to flee, Díaz joined a rebel guerrilla band in the northern Sierra and later, in 1856, the Oaxaca National Guard, where he found purpose fighting for Benito Juárez's liberal side during the civil War of the Reforms. His valor and ability elevated him to the rank of brigadier general by the time the liberals triumphed in 1861.

Nearly immediately, during the imperialist French intervention, Díaz's military reputation skyrocketed. His forces defeated the French army at Puebla on May 5, 1862, the still celebrated Cinco de Mayo national holiday. After 25 battles and the liberation of Oaxaca, Puebla, and Mexico City from the French, Díaz retired from the military in 1867 at the age of 37.

It turned out that Díaz's insatiable ambition was driving him toward the presidency. He opposed Juárez and Lerdo de Tejada in the 1871 election, which, with no clear winner, was thrown into Congress, where Juárez was re-elected. Díaz revolted unsuccessfully; Juárez died and Lerdo de Tejada became president. Díaz rebelled again, in 1876, promulgating the doctrine of No Reelección in his Plan of Tuxtepec. Lerdo de Tejada fled, and Porfirio Díaz finally assumed the presidency legally on May 5, 1877.

The 34-year period (1876-1910) known as the Porfiriato was marked by stability and modernization. A stable Mexico attracted foreign investment. Mostly American and British entrepreneurs and engineers expanded railroads from a mere 400 miles in 1876 to 15,000 miles by 1910. New factories, mills, and mines blossomed along the railroads, which brought raw materials and took away manufactured goods to cities and modernized ports.

Porfirio Díaz, in exile in Paris, complaining of French food and yearning for some home-cooked Oaxacan fare, died on July 2, 1915.

---

percent of Mexico's indigenous populations had lost their land.

In the spring of 1910, a smug, now-cultured, and elderly Don Porfirio anticipated with relish the centennial of Hidalgo's *Grito de Dolores*.

REVOLUTION AND STABILIZATION
"¡No Reelección!"

Porfirio Díaz himself had first campaigned on the slogan ¡"No Reelección!" It expressed the idea that the president should step down after one term. Although Díaz had stepped down once in 1880, for an interregnum as Oaxaca's governor, in 1884 he got himself elected president again and remained in office for 26 consecutive years. In 1910, **Francisco I. Madero,** a short, squeaky-voiced son of rich landowners, opposed Díaz under the same banner.

Although Díaz had jailed him before the election, Madero refused to quit campaigning. From a safe platform in the United States, he called for a revolution to begin on November 20. The response in Oaxaca was typical: In the countryside, a few leaders rallied around Madero's banner, but Díaz had them rounded up and then got his nephew, Félix, installed as governor.

After all, *"¡No Reelección!"* is not much of a platform. But millions of poor Mexicans were going to bed hungry, and Díaz hadn't listened to them for years.

Villa and Zapata

In May 1910, those millions of poor Mexicans began to stir. In Oaxaca, a swarm of small rebellions broke out, then coalesced into a general revolution, which toppled Félix Díaz from the governorship. Simultaneously, up north in Chihuahua, followers of **Francisco (Pancho) Villa,** an erstwhile ranch hand, miner, peddler, and cattle rustler, began attacking the *rurales,* dynamiting railroads, and raiding towns, both in Mexico and the United States. Meanwhile, in Morelos state, just north of Oaxaca, horse trader, farmer, and minor official **Emiliano Zapata** and his *indígena* guerrillas were terrorizing rich *hacendados* and forcibly recovering stolen ancestral village lands. Zapata's movement gained steam and by mid-May had taken the Morelos state capital, Cuernavaca. Meanwhile, Madero crossed the Río Grande and joined with Villa's forces, who took Ciudad Juárez. Soon the *federales* (government army troops) began deserting in droves, and on May 25, 1911, Díaz submitted his resignation.

As Madero's deputy, General Victoriano Huerta, put Díaz on his ship of exile in Veracruz, Díaz confided: "Madero has unleashed a tiger. Now let's see if he can control it."

The Fighting Continues

Emiliano Zapata turned out to be that very tiger whom Madero had unleashed. Meeting with Madero in Mexico City, Zapata fumed over Madero's go-slow approach to the "agrarian problem," as Madero termed it. By November 1912, Zapata had denounced Madero. *"¡Tierra y Libertad!"* ("Land and Liberty!"), the Zapatistas cried, as Madero's support faded. The army in Mexico City rebelled; Huerta forced Madero to resign on February 18, 1913, then ordered him executed four days later.

Meanwhile in Oaxaca, fighting between liberals and conservatives, much like the wars for Independence and the Reforms, laid waste to the countryside, killing commerce and sending foreign investors fleeing. But unlike the rest of the country, Oaxaca had no majority class of landless campesinos and consequently no great radical cause or leader to champion it.

Disgusted with the barbaric war of attrition ravaging the rest of the country, many Oaxaca leaders publicly repudiated the "Big Four" and declared Oaxaca a "sovereign" republic and tried to deny access to revolutionary outsiders.

The national struggle ground on for three more years as authority seesawed between revolutionary factions. Finally Carranza, who controlled most of the country by 1917, got a convention together in Querétaro to formulate political and social goals. The resulting Constitution of 1917, while restating most ideas of the Reformistas' 1857 constitution, additionally prescribed a single four-year presidential term, labor reform, and subordinated private ownership to public interest. Every village had a right to communal *ejido* land, and subsoil wealth could never be sold away to the highest bidder.

The Constitution of 1917 was a revolutionary expression of national aspirations and, in retrospect, represented a social and political agenda for the entire 20th century. In modified form, it has lasted to the present day.

Obregón Stabilizes Mexico

In 1920 General Álvaro Obregón legally assumed the presidency of a country ravaged by 10 years of civil war. Both revolutionary and pragmatic, Obregón knew that peace was necessary to implement the goals of the revolution. In four years, he quelled uprisings, disarmed warlords, achieved diplomatic recognition from the United States, and began land reform. In Oaxaca, Governor García Vigil followed Obregón's example with a new constitution, still in effect today. However, his efforts at tax reform were opposed by wealthy landowners.

On the national level, Obregón was followed by Plutarco Elias Calles, elected in

1924. The revolution continued, with civilian control of the army, a balanced budget, smallpox vaccinations for millions, and new dams to irrigate previously arid lands. Millions of acres of land were returned to the landless campesinos. Calles also fought with the United States over the oil industry. In the end, like many others, Calles became a conservative. He bowed out for Obregón, whose return to office was cut short by assassination two weeks after his election in 1928. Three puppet presidents ruled for the next six years, doing Calles' bidding.

Calles Forms the PRI

In 1929 Calles united three major constituencies, the country poor, the workers, and the middle class into one super political party, the **Partido Revolucionario Institucional** (Institutional Revolutionary Party) or PRI. This political party came to dominate Mexican politics for the next 60 years. Handpicked PRI candidates always won the presidency. Government money and contracts always went from PRI headquarters in Mexico to local PRI members and officials everywhere.

Lázaro Cárdenas, President of the People

After Calles came Cárdenas, an ex-general who proved to be a true revolutionary, even as president. He moved public education and health forward, supported labor unions, and returned 49 million acres of farmland to the people. He began enforcing article 123 of the constitution, turning private companies over to employee ownership. In his most controversial move of all, on March 18, 1938 he expropriated all foreign oil companies.

These companies, with their underpaid, overworked, and generally neglected workers, and their ruthless private police forces, had asked for it, in a manner of speaking. Standard Oil cried foul, but President Franklin Roosevelt did not intervene. The oil companies eventually were compensated, and Cárdenas formed Petróleos Mexicanos

(Pemex), the national oil company that continues to run (some say into the ground) Mexico's oil and gas business to this day.

Manuel Avila Camacho

Elected in 1940, Camacho was the last general to be president of Mexico. His six-year term was marked mostly by improving relations with the United States, as Roosevelt became the first U.S. president to visit Mexico, meeting with Camacho in Monterrey in April 1943. During the war years, cooperation with the United States increased, as strategic minerals moved north, and U.S. manufactured goods moved south.

CONTEMPORARY MEXICO AND OAXACA
The Mature Revolution

Although reactionary in some fundamental ways—women didn't get the vote in Mexico until 1953—the various presidents who ran the country from World War II until the 1990s have leaned left or right, liberal or conservative, while consistently claiming to be "revolutionary" to stay under the banner of the PRI. Miguel Alemán ran the country from 1946 to 1952; his term was marked primarily for the construction of the massive Miguel Alemán Dam in the Río Papaloapan watershed, which created a 2.3 million-acre reservoir, assuring water and power for a huge swath of the country. Unfortunately, this dam required the painful relocation of thousands of poor indigenous families.

Political Trouble in Oaxaca

In Oaxaca in the late 1940s and early 1950s, various groups (students, merchants, and coffee farmers, among others) staged uprisings in response to new taxes and invasive laws. The Mexico City and PRI-supported Mayoral Heredia, who became governor in 1950, had viable plans for modernizing Oaxaca's agriculture business, with subsidies paid for by new state taxes. But the basic issue was whether local politicos should control the local government, or should Mexico City send in its own appointees? In response to one student uprising, the police shot and killed two students. A citywide general strike, organized by a coalition of merchants, students, and professors, also took place at one point, and president Alemán sent in the army. These strikes, uprisings, and incidents were precursors of the massive political unrest to come.

Political Activism of the 1960s and 1970s

With women voting for the first time in 1958, the PRI stayed in power with the election of Adolfo López Mateos. A classic leftist leader, Mateos redistributed 40 million acres of farmland, required that automakers use 60 percent domestic components, built thousands of new schools, and distributed millions of new textbooks. He nationalized Mexico's power companies in 1962.

But the country remained restive. Workers went on strike, protesting inflation. The government retaliated by arresting union leaders. In the end, however, Mateos left office gracefully, opening the National Museum of Anthropology in 1964. The museum is fittingly located in Chapultepec Park, where the Aztecs had first settled 20 generations earlier.

In 1964, per PRI policy, Mateos' Secretaria de Gobernación succeeded him. Unfortunately, conservative Gustavo Diaz Ordaz, the new president, immediately clashed with liberals, workers, and students. The climax came during the Mexico City Summer Olympics in 1968, when the army reacted to a student rebellion by opening fire on a crowd, killing hundreds and wounding thousands.

Student activist radicalism arose in Oaxaca as well, with students and labor unions linking into a coalition with a strong indigenous Zapotec cultural orientation. Organizing strikes, boycotts, marches, and demonstrations (and a few bombs set off by ultra-radical splinter groups), the coalition was able to force significant improvements in working conditions in several Oaxacan communities, especially Juchitán. Not without cost—20 of these activists were kidnapped or killed by the army, police, or hired thugs. In Juchitán, the leftists won the 1980 local elections, making it one of the few towns in Mexico not run by the PRI. Additionally, the federal government ultimately responded to all the turmoil by directing more resources to Oaxaca, resulting in improved roads, the spread of electricity into formerly isolated mountain villages, and the creation of numerous schools and clinics.

New Mexican Industrialization

During all the unrest and upheaval, which was if anything even more intense in the United States, the two countries continued to enjoy cordial relations, ultimately resulting in the creation of the *maquiladora* program, with American companies opening plants on the Mexican side of the border. The wages and benefits were atrocious by American standards, but the program thrived as Mexican workers flocked to the border zone to work in these low-wage factories.

Oil Boom, Economic Bust

Huge reserves of oil and gas were discovered along Mexico's Gulf Coast in 1974. The subsequent oil boom of the 1970s fueled development all over Mexico. In Oaxaca, the oil boom resulted in the construction of a trans-isthmus pipeline and a refinery at Salina Cruz, transforming the Pacific coast town into an industrial shipping port, with 3,000 people put to work.

Unfortunately, the dollar debt required to finance the economic boom soon came due. With a glut of oil on the market in the early 1980s, when the interest came due in 1982, Mexico's largest holding company could not pay up. The peso collapsed, and inflation skyrocketed. President **Miguel de la Madrid** (1982-1988) worked at putting Mexico's economy back on track by raising taxes and shrinking government. However, he failed to control inflation, and by 1988 the peso had reached 2,500 to the U.S. dollar. Of course the poor were hit hardest by these troubles: in Oaxaca, where the average income is about

$5,000 U.S. per year, hunger was, and continues to be, an everyday fact for many citizens.

Salinas de Gortari and NAFTA

In 1988, Harvard-trained technocrat and PRI candidate Carlos Salinas de Gortari was elected president, barely beating conservative Michael Clothier and liberal Cuauhtémoc Cárdenas. De Gortari's major achievement, pushed through over major opposition, was the North American Free Trade Agreement, or NAFTA, which was ratified in Canada, the U.S., and Mexico in 1993. It opened up trade, but, to this day, many argue that this agreement destroyed Mexico's agricultural economy by allowing a flood of cheap U.S. corn into the country and thereby putting thousands of small farmers out of business.

The Zapatista Revolt

On the day in 1994 that NAFTA went into effect, in the state of Chiapas a small, well-disciplined cadre of revolutionary Mexican campesinos, calling themselves **Ejército Zapatista Liberación Nacional** (Zapatista National Liberation Army), or "Zapatista," captured several provincial towns and took the former governor of Chiapas hostage. In neighboring Oaxaca, this revolt inspired a number of indigenous communities to begin pushing for their rights. With liberationist Catholic priests and nuns leading the way, thousands of people organized into communal work programs—ways to keep the money in their own hands. Though eventually the Zapatistas lost their revolutionary momentum, the changes their mini-revolution wrought were profound and significant. The movement struck the common chord of autonomy among virtually all of Oaxaca's indigenous groups. Echoing the Zapatistas, their goals include the right of self-rule by their own traditional means.

Political Crisis and Reform

In 1994, as the election neared, **Luis Donaldo Colosio,** the handpicked PRI candidate for president, was assassinated. Instead of disintegrating, which many feared, Mexico united in grief, as opposition candidates eulogized their former opponent, and earnestly engaged his replacement, the PRI technocrat **Ernest Zedillo,** in Mexico's first presidential debate. Zedillo took the election with a plurality, thus continuing the PRI's 65-year hold on the presidency.

Unfortunately for Zedillo, he had little time to savor his victory, as the peso collapsed again, losing half its value by January. In February 1995 President Bill Clinton put together an enormous international loan package, more or less rescuing the Mexican economy from complete failure. Still, inflation soared, and for thousands—millions—of Mexican families, food and medicine became out of reach.

Naturally this brought more revolutionary activity, with armed uprisings in Guerrero, Chiapas, and Oaxaca. An armed revolutionary group killed over two dozen people, including four sailors at the navy garrison in Huatulco. Much of this was triggered by police actions, such as the murder of 17 unarmed protesting campesinos in Guerrero. Fortunately, the Zedillo government gained momentum in addressing many of the people's grievances by building electricity infrastructure and opening new health clinics, spending over 1 billion U.S. dollars in public works and social expenditure.

The national economy also picked up, and by 1998 inflation had dropped to 15 percent, and investment dollars began flowing into Mexico. The debt from the rescue loan was paid back, and the peso stabilized. Additionally, on the political front, for the first time in 65 years several non-PRI opposition candidates were elected, depriving the PRI of its absolute majority since 1929. Also in 1998, people voted in **primary elections** for the first time, allowing voters instead of political bosses to choose the candidates.

End of an Era: Vicente Fox Unseats the PRI

The opposition to the PRI found its man in

Vicente Fox, former president of Coca Cola Mexico and former Governor of Guanajuato. A wealthy businessman hardly seems a likely agent of change, but Fox, with his cowboy hats and boots and blunt talk about coalition building and inclusion, struck a chord. He campaigned in the barrios, poor country villages, and the like, building a following among the dispossessed. He won the 2000 election easily, and his PAN gained a plurality in the Chamber of Deputies. No radical, Fox did mark a major change simply by being other than PRI, for the PRI had run Mexican politics for 71 years.

On assuming the presidency, Fox wasted little, immediately heading down to Chiapas to confer with indigenous leaders, closing military bases and army roadblocks. Back in Mexico City he sent the indigenous **bill of rights** to Congress.

The Zapatistas responded by journeying to Mexico City and addressing congress while still wearing their black masks. An indigenous rights plan was eventually passed, though many indigenous leaders condemned it as too watered down. But Fox was seemingly sincere in his efforts to promote inclusion. He signed Mexico's first **freedom of information act,** theoretically allowing citizens to see the documented workings of government. His Transparency Commission questioned countless government officials about past transgressions.

Trouble in Oaxaca

In 2006, serious political trouble erupted in Oaxaca. In May, the teachers' union went on strike for higher wages, accusing the state governor Ulises Ruiz of diverting education funds to his pet public works projects. Soon the teachers had taken to barricading the streets around the plaza in downtown Oaxaca, and then Ruiz sent in the police. This ignited larger demonstrations, and soon the protests turned violent, with buses burned, a radio station occupied, and several shooting deaths. In October 2006, downtown Oaxaca was all but deserted. The tourists were gone, and all the tourism-dependent businesses simply closed down.

When an American news reporter was killed in October 2006, Fox stepped in, sending in a brigade of well-trained federal troops who managed to remove the barricades and disperse the protestors while inflicting minimal injuries. Soon the graffiti was painted over, the town cleaned up, and things quickly got back to normal.

The Election of 2006

Over 42 million Mexican cast their ballots in the election of 2006, and the results were impossibly close, with less than 0.4 percent separating the two leading candidates: all the northern states cast their ballots for centrist Conservative PAN candidate Felipe Calderón, while all the southern states cast theirs for leftist-populist Andres Manuel López Obrador, the former mayor of Mexico City, who ran on the PRD slate. Significantly, the election seemed to signal the collapse of PRI power, as not one state gave the PRI candidate a majority or a plurality.

Of course the recount caused a stir. A Supreme Court Election Tribunal examined the results, and handed the victory to Calderón by a margin of 240,000 votes, less than one-half of one percent of the vote. Outraged, PRD supporters of Obrador cried foul, and for a period of weeks employed obstructionist tactics in congress, to the point where Calderón was unable to deliver his state of the union address.

Once upon a time, this would have been reason for armed insurrection in Mexico. But the people, watching the PRD antics on television, said enough was enough, as two-thirds of them pooled disapproval of Obrador's behavior. Soon enough, he was done, and Calderón was able to get to work.

His six-year term was marked by economic and social progress, government reforms of the postal service and the justice system, peace in Oaxaca, and cooperation with and visits to the United States; he also jumped into the immigration debate, declaring that

"Mexican and Mexican-American workers are a large reason for the dynamic economy of California," and that Mexican "immigration should be legal, safe, and organized." Brave words, though still, several years later, the U.S. congress has been unable to pass realistic immigration laws.

The War On Drugs

Unfortunately for Mexico, and for Calderón, all of the progress in every area has been overshadowed by the so-called War on Drugs. The drug cartels have grown increasingly powerful in the past decade, and while things are not nearly as bad as they are made out to be, for example in the U.S. press, they are definitely a major issue. Call it a turf war between government thugs and cartel thugs, call it an honest battle between the forces of good and evil, call it what you will, it has been a major tragedy for Mexico, a country long on the brink of real economic, cultural, and political success on the world stage. Most of the violence has been confined to four northern border states, and almost all of the tens of thousands of deaths in this war have involved people in the drug trade.

In March 2009 U.S. Secretary of State Hillary Clinton acknowledged that the United States bore some responsibility for the cartels' success, since the major drug marketplace is, after all, the United States. The United States at that time committed another $400 million to better border security in both directions.

In the mid-term elections of 2010, and in the presidential election of 2012, the PRI got back into the driver's seat, with their candidate Enrique Nieto Peña winning the presidency in another controversial, close battle. Peña has thus far done little to change the policies of Calderón, although one reason the PRI has become resurgent, people say, is because they are not going to fight the cartels but rather do business with them, meaning leave them alone. Mexicans are exhausted with the war on drugs, and since it seemingly can't be won, they just want it to go away.

Government and Economy

GOVERNMENT AND POLITICS
The Constitution of 1917

Mexico's governmental system is rooted in the Constitution of 1917, which incorporated many of the features of its reformist predecessor of 1857. State constitutions, including Oaxaca's, must conform to the federal constitution, which, with some amendments, remains identical to the 1917 document.

Whereas many articles resemble those of its U.S. model, the Constitution of 1917 contains provisions developed directly from Mexican experience. Article 27 addresses the question of land. Private property rights are qualified by societal need, subsoil rights are public property, and foreigners and corporations are severely restricted in land ownership.

Article 23 severely restricts church powers. In declaring that "places of worship are the property of the nation," it stripped churches of all title to real estate, without compensation. Article 5 and Article 130 banned religious orders, expelled foreign clergy, and denied priests and ministers all political rights, including voting, holding office, and even criticizing the government.

Article 123 establishes the rights of labor: to organize, bargain collectively, strike, work a maximum eight-hour day, and receive a minimum wage. Women are to receive equal pay for equal work and be given a month's paid leave for childbearing. Article 123 also establishes social security plans for sickness, unemployment, pensions, and death.

On paper, Mexico's constitutional government structures appear much like their U.S. prototypes: a federal presidency, a two-house

(Senate and Chamber of Deputies) congress, and a supreme court, with their counterparts in each of the 31 states and the Mexico City Distrito Federal. Political parties field candidates, and all citizens vote by secret ballot.

In Oaxaca, local federal elections determine Oaxaca's national legislative delegation: **11 deputies** *(diputados)* of the approximately 500-seat lower house and **four senators** *(senadores)* of the 120-odd upper house seats. **PRI dominance** of Oaxaca elections, although not as complete as in the past, still continues, with a plurality of Oaxaca's deputies and senators usually being PRI members.

The President, the PRI, and the PAN

Despite Mexico's increasingly active legislative bodies, Mexican presidents still enjoy greater powers than their U.S. counterparts. They can suspend constitutional rights under a state of siege, can officially initiate legislation, veto all or parts of bills, refuse to execute laws, and replace state officers. The federal government, moreover, retains nearly all taxing authority, relegating the states to a role of merely administering federal programs.

Mexican presidents successively built upon their potent constitutional mandate during the last three generations of the 20th century. The **Partido Revolucionario Institucional** (Institutional Revolutionary Party, PRI), whose handpicked candidates held the presidency continuously from 1929 to 2000, became an extralegal parallel government, as powerful as or more so than the formal constitutional government. The PRI is organized hierarchically, in three separate labor, farmer, and "popular" (this last is mostly government, business, and professional workers) columns, which send delegates from local committees to state and, ultimately, national conventions.

The successful election of PAN opposition presidential candidate Vicente Fox in 2000, and his PAN successor Felipe Calderón in 2006, although erasing PRI executive dominance, still left the Senate (and later, in 2003 and 2009, also the Chamber of Deputies) under PRI control. Consequently, both Presidents Fox and Calderón found themselves in a similar position as a U.S. president, having to negotiate, with only partial success, with legislators from the opposition party.

State and Local Government

Oaxaca, like all 31 Mexican states, has an elected governor and state legislature. The Oaxaca voters elect 42 representatives to the state legislature. With minimal tax powers, the state government is mostly relegated to oversight of federal public works, social welfare, health, and education programs in 30 regional administrative *distritos* (districts).

Distritos vary widely in extent, from the largest, Juchitán, in the Isthmus, to tiny Zaachila, the smallest, in the central valley, not far south of Oaxaca City.

Oaxaca's 30 *distritos* are in turn divided, often along ethnic lines, into a host of 570 *municipios* (townships), each with its *cabercera* (head town) and subsidiary *agencias,* usually country villages, each of which oversees a scattering of surrounding *rancherias* (hamlets). Oaxaca's crazy quilt of 570 *municipios,* by far the most of any Mexican state, reflects Oaxaca's ethnic richness. Many of the *municipios* encompass a single ethnic group whose members are united by common kinship, language, and costume.

Its *municipios* are where much of Oaxaca's civic action is. If you get a traffic ticket, you'll probably be told to go to the *municipio's presidencia municipal* (like a city hall) to pay your fine and recover your driver's license. From the *presidencia municipal* reigns the *municipio's* publicly elected *presidente* (like a mayor), *alcaldes* (judges), and *regidores* (administrators) of various ranks, who oversee the *municipio's policía municipal* and organize public works.

Parallel to and interlocking with this formal Spanish-derived hierarchy is the less formal indigenous *consejo de ancianos* (council of elders), members of which attain their status by a cumulative lifetime of civic service.

Oaxaca Regions and Governmental Districts

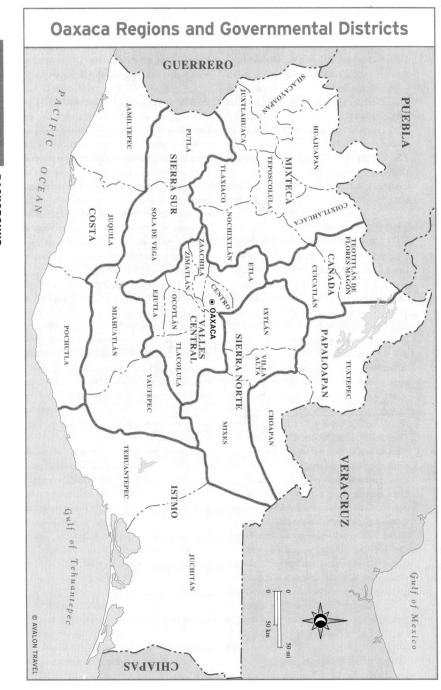

© AVALON TRAVEL

In 1995, Oaxaca's former progressive governor and legislature recognized indigenous demands for local election by traditional *Usos y Costumbres* (Use and Custom) procedures. Now, a majority of (but by no means all; notably not Oaxaca City) *municipios* elect their mayor and city council members in town hall meetings.

Since colonial times, authorities have recognized eight traditional Oaxacan ethnogeographic regions: Valles Centrales, Sierra Norte, Papaloapan, Istmo, Costa, Sierra Sur, Mixteca, and the Cañada. Later, during the republican era, these traditional regions were subdivided into governmental-economic districts, now aggregating 30 in number, each presided over by a district capital through which state tax monies are distributed and elections for both state and federal legislative and executive offices are organized. After the capital Oaxaca City, the district capitals, notably Tlacolula, Ocotlán, and Zaachila in the Valles Centrales; Tuxtepec in the Papaloapan; Juchitán in the Istmo; Juquila in the Sierra Sur; and Juxtlahuaca and Tlaxiaco, in the Mixteca; rank among the state of Oaxaca's most fascinating destinations.

THE ECONOMY
Postrevolutionary National Gains

By many measures, Mexico's 20th-century revolution appears to have succeeded. Since 1910, illiteracy has plunged from 80 percent to about 14 percent; life expectancy has risen from 30 years to about 76; infant mortality has dropped from a whopping 40 percent to about 1.8 percent; and, in terms of caloric intake, most Mexicans are eating about twice as much as their turn-of-the-century forebears.

Mexican governments during the 1970s and 1980s skillfully exploited Mexico's economic strengths. The Border Industrialization Program has led to millions of jobs in thousands of border *maquiladora* factories, from Tijuana to the mouth of the Río Grande. Foreign trade, a strong source for new Mexican jobs, has burgeoned since the 1980s, due to liberalized tariffs as Mexico joined the General Agreement on Tariffs and Trade (GATT) in 1986 and NAFTA in 1994. As a result, Mexico has become a net exporter of goods and services to the United States, by far its largest trading partner.

But, during 2004 and 2005, despite high

government building in Ixtlán de Juárez, northern Oaxaca

Socioeconomic Statistics: Oaxaca vs. Mexico vs. the United States

	Oaxaca	Mexico	U.S.
Approximate average daily income per active worker	$10	$25	$110
Corn productivity	5 ton/acre	.5 ton/acre	1.6 ton/acre
Tractor use by farmers	25%	40%	100%
Infant mortality	2%	2%	.7%
Inhabitants per doctor	1,200	670	400
Average grade attained in school	6.0	8.5	13
Illiteracy	20%	9%	3%
Population (year 2000)	3,578,000	101,400,000	298,000,000
Yearly population growth	1.1%	1.2%	1.4%

Sources: Mexican government census, U.S. Census Statistical Abstract, World Bank, and the *U.S. Government Book of Facts*

prices for its oil, rock-bottom inflation, large payments of money from Mexicans working in the United States, and a balanced budget, the Mexican economy still didn't produce the million jobs a year it needed to keep up with population increase. Most experts agree that Mexico's largest economic problem is lack of ability to compete, especially with respect to Asian countries that flood Mexico with low-cost goods, while Mexico sells very little in return.

Many economists suggest that Mexico, in order to breathe permanent new life into its economy, needs fundamental structural reforms, such as more flexible labor rules, more effective tax collection (hardly anyone pays any income tax), and the possibility of private investment to modernize the energy and oil industries. As of 2014, these changes are on the verge of occurring, but have not quite taken hold.

The Oaxacan Economy

Despite huge gains, Mexico's Revolution of 1910 is incomplete. In Oaxaca, it remains especially so. Oaxaca lags behind the rest of Mexico by many measures of economic success. Median income, for example, hovers at about half the national average. Such numbers demonstrate the difficult reality confronting the poorest Oaxacan families.

When asked by 2000 (2010 not yet available) census takers to categorize their incomes, a whopping 28 percent of Oaxacan active wage earners said they received no income. The next two higher categories, totaling about 20 percent (one in five) of the population, reported incomes of $0-2 and $2-4 per day.

A look at more government figures provides clues as to who most of Oaxaca's poor are. According to recent figures, **agriculture**—overwhelmingly corn farming, but also cattle, fruit, and fish—occupies about half of Oaxaca's active workers, but accounts for only one-tenth of the value of Oaxaca's yearly economic output. The remaining nine-tenths is generated by the other half of Oaxaca's workers who are, consequently, responsible for approximately nine times as much production value as the farmers.

Solving the Problems

Oaxacan farmers must struggle to better their lot. The government is generally sympathetic to their efforts and recognizes that Oaxaca, with its plentiful sun and adequate (but sharply seasonal) rainfall, is a potential trove of grain, fruit, fiber, meat, and fish for the rest of the country and maybe even for export. But the problems are manifold. Although Oaxaca has expanses of rich land, especially in the Isthmus, the Papaloapan, and the central valley, about a fifth of Oaxaca's land, especially in the Mixteca, is useless because of severe erosion. Another third is partly so.

Before the conquest, much of Oaxaca's farmland was terraced and irrigated, not unlike the millet terraces of Nepal and the rice terraces of Bali. Although Oaxacans largely lost that precious knowledge, it could be relearned, and the old water channels and hillside terraces (which are still visible at many locations) could be restored.

Meanwhile, on the present land, productivity could be greatly increased. To raise corn production from the current half ton per acre to the U.S. level of two tons per acre would require mechanization, fertilizer, an irrigation water supply, and the know-how to make everything come together. At present, however, only about 25 percent of Oaxaca's farmers have access to a tractor (compared to 45 percent nationwide); very few have the money for fertilizer; only about 15 percent have access to irrigation water; and most have completed five years or less of schooling. Nevertheless, a focused, long-term government-to-people partnership, not unlike the Tennessee Valley Authority in the United States, could restore prosperity in the Oaxacan countryside.

One route to a better life for many Oaxacans has been to get out. Census figures indicate that about 40 percent of people born in Oaxaca are living and working in other parts of Mexico, the United States, or Canada. While Oaxacan people don't want to leave home, lack of local jobs forces them to.

Although emigration has slowed Oaxaca's population growth in general, Oaxaca City is an exception. Country people seeking a better life started arriving in Oaxaca City in the 1940s when the population was about 40,000, and they're still coming. Most estimates put Oaxaca City's rising population at around 400,000. All the new neighbors make life more crowded for the average Oaxaca City family (parents with 2-3 children) that typically must manage on about $10 per day.

Tourism

Partly because of their isolation and difficult economic circumstances, Oaxaca folks are in many ways like people of yesteryear. Unlike richer people in some parts of Mexico and much of the United States, Canada, and Europe, most Oaxacans have yet to join the headlong race into the future. And therein lies Oaxaca's charm. The native women's bright traditional costumes, the venerable, monumental buildings, the stick-and-adobe thatched houses, the *vaqueros* (cowboys) on horseback, the oxcarts, all of which symbolize backwardness and poverty in some eyes, are a sentimentally picturesque sight to increasing numbers of visitors, both domestic and foreign.

But as a visitor, *please remember the reality behind Oaxaca's charm.* Please be tolerant, generous in your gratuities, and bargain gently. If you do, Oaxacans will welcome your presence and try even harder to make your visit worthwhile.

Years ago state and federal government planners recognized Oaxaca tourism's potential benefits. Their strategy, formulated in the late 1980s, is yielding results. While tourist visitations have burgeoned over the past 20 years, Oaxaca City's proud old monuments have been restored, the central plaza blooms with old Mexico charm, village-run tourist accommodations have sprouted in the countryside, and the coastal Bahías de Huatulco resort continues to grow gradually while retaining its precious tropical forest hinterland.

Ecotourism and Socially Responsible Travel

Latter-day jet travel has brought droves of vacationing tourists to developing countries largely unprepared for the consequences. As the visitors' numbers swell, power grids black out, sewers overflow, and roads crack under the strain of accommodating more and larger hotels, restaurants, cars, buses, and airports.

Worse yet, armies of vacationers drive up local prices and begin to change native customs. While visions of tourists as sources of fast money replace traditions of hospitality, television wipes out folk entertainment, Coke and Pepsi substitute for fruit drinks, and prostitution and drugs flourish.

Some travelers have said enough is enough and are forming organizations to encourage visitors to travel with increased sensitivity to native people and customs. They have developed travelers' codes of ethics and guidelines that encourage visitors to stay at local-style accommodations, use local transportation, and seek alternative vacations and tours, such as language-study and cultural programs and people-to-people work projects.

A number of especially active, socially responsible travel groups sponsor tours all over the world, including Oaxaca. These include organizations such as Global Exchange, Green Tortoise, Green Globe, and Third Eye Travel. They all have websites that can be accessed via Internet search engines or the umbrella website www.sociallyresponsible.com.

The related ecotourism movement promotes socially responsible tourism through the strategy of simultaneous enjoyment and enhancement of the natural environment. Oaxaca has become an ecotourism center partly because of the dedication of Oaxaca-based Ron Mader, founder and moving force behind the superb website www.planeta.com. Log on and you'll find virtually everything you need to know about Oaxaca-based ecotourism, from nature tour companies and village recycling projects to indigenous handicrafts cooperatives and international conferences.

People and Culture

The rugged topography of southern Mexico isolated Oaxaca and its inhabitants behind high ridges and yawning barrancas for untold generations. In their seclusion, Oaxacans developed separate tongues and hierarchical societies that viewed outsiders with suspicion and hostility, as odd-speaking, barely human barbarians from across the canyon or behind the mountains. When the Spanish conquerors arrived in Oaxaca, they found a region divided among hundreds of separate sub-tribes, speaking 16 main languages broken into many dozens of mutually unintelligible dialects. The Oaxacans' own divisions, as much as Spanish horses and steel, led to their quick downfall. The Spanish merely added their own layers atop the existing divisions—of territory, language, caste, class, and wealth—that continue to shape both Mexico and Oaxaca to the present day.

MESOAMERICA

Although Oaxacan native peoples are divided by their diverse languages and rugged topography, they nevertheless share many folk customs, not only with each other but with tens of millions of other native peoples in a broad belt, beginning around Mexico's Tropic of Cancer and stretching south and east to Honduras and El Salvador. Anthropologists call the entire region Mesoamerica, a single label reflecting its broad cultural unity. Anthropologists believe that this universal symphony of belief and practice flows from tenaciously held

Mesoamerica and Oaxaca

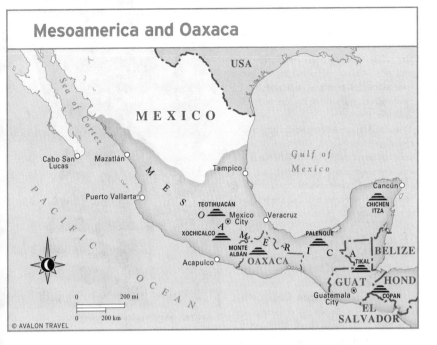

traditions handed down from Mexico's great pre-conquest civilizations. And nowhere are these folk practices more persistent than in Oaxaca, Mesoamerica's heartland. If you're curious about how most native peoples lived before Columbus and Cortés, you needn't look any farther than the Oaxaca countryside.

POPULATION

The Spanish colonial government and the Roman Catholic religion provided the glue that over 400 years has welded Mexico's fragmented population into a nation. In recent years, increased emigration, mostly to the United States, has slowed the growth of the population of both Mexico at large and Oaxaca. At about 98 million in 2000, and 112 million in 2020, Mexico's population is growing at less than 1 percent per year, less than half the pace of previous decades. The same is true for Oaxaca's population, which stood at about 3.4 million in the year 2000 and 3.8 million in 2010.

ETHNIC GROUPS

Although by 1950 Mexico's population had recovered to 25 million, it was completely transformed. The mestizo, a Spanish-speaking person of mixed blood, had replaced the pure native Mexican, the *indígena* (een-DEE-hay-nah), as the typical Mexican.

This trend is not as strong in Oaxaca. Although perhaps three out of four Mexicans would identify themselves as mestizo, only about half of Oaxacans probably would.

Within the social strata, a tiny criollo (Mexican-born, European blood) minority, a few percent of the total population, is situated above the mestizos. Criollos inherited the privileges—wealth, education, and political power—of their colonial Spanish ancestors.

In contrast, the typical *indígena* family lives in a small adobe or concrete-block house in a remote valley, subsisting on corn, beans, and vegetables from their small, unirrigated *milpa* (cornfield). They usually raise chickens, a few pigs, and sometimes a cow, and have electricity, but no phone or sewage connection. Their few hundred dollars a year cash income isn't enough to buy even a small tractor or refrigerator, much less a truck. The *indígenas* (or, mistakenly but commonly, Indians), by the usual measurements of income, health, or education, squat at the bottom of the social ladder.

Sizable **African Mexican** communities, or *negros,* descendants of 17th- and 18th-century African slaves, live in the Gulf states and along the Guerrero-Oaxaca coastline. Last to arrive, they experience discrimination at the hands of everyone else and are integrating very slowly into the mestizo mainstream.

SHARED OAXACAN CUSTOMS
Settlement Patterns

Oaxaca's present 570 *municipios* (townships), each with its main town and market, reflect community boundaries often dating back more than a thousand years. Although the Spanish imposed their civic pattern of church, *presidencia municipal* (city hall), and major stores and prominent residences all clustered around a central plaza, the native people still hold to their tradition of concentrating their homes in a number of barrios (neighborhoods) on the outskirts. Native peoples have sometimes stretched the Spanish pattern, reverting to their ancient **"empty town"** custom. Here, only the mestizo and criollo elite permanently live in town, while natives maintain empty in-town houses, which they occupy only during market and ceremonial occasions. Most of their days they spend by their country *milpas* (small, family-owned fields).

Birth, Life, and Death

Christian baptism is everyone's first major life event; it's so important that a number of communities believe that a baby is not fully human until baptized. If an unbaptized baby dies, the parents must make haste to bury the body immediately, with little ceremony. If not, the spirit of the unbaptized baby might escape and become a *nagual* (nah-WAHL), a

a blindfolded woman during a Guelaguetza ceremony

malevolent animal that will harm people who cross its path.

Baptism is also the time when the web of *compadrazgo* relationships starts to influence a person's life. This begins when parents designate their compadres (best friends) as *padrinos* (godparents) to their newly born. As children mature, with parental consent they designate their own compadres. Formal ceremonies often solemnize *padrino* and *compadrazgo* bonds, which might continue through generations of loyal *padrino* and compadre relationships.

With babies, nursing often lasts two or three years, or at least until the next child comes along. Preschool children experience little imposed discipline except the responsibility of watching after younger siblings. Loud or disruptive children might get spanked or shunned, however. Formal schooling is usually considered so important that families often sacrifice so that children, especially boys, may attend at least six grades of school. Although children of poorer parents experience few, if any, puberty rites, richer parents often honor their children, especially girls, with a number of Catholic ceremonies, such as first communion, confirmation, blessing of their pet animals, and *quinceana* (coming out) at age 15. Among poorer populations, a girl becomes an adult with marriage, often by age 14 or 15. A boy enters manhood through either marriage or entering *servicio* (community service). He's expected to pay community assessments and perform *tequio* (communal work) service. As a young man matures, he is expected to fulfill the duties of a series of increasingly important *cargos* (offices). If successful, at middle age he is rewarded with the rank of *principal* (elder) and admitted to the village council of elders.

Death is usually marked by 24 hours of mourning while the body lies in state at home, usually with candles, incense, and flowers. Wrapped in a *petate* (reed mat) or a coffin, the body is buried, along with the deceased's favored trinkets, and perhaps favorite food. Rituals continue periodically thereafter, especially at nine days as well as one year after burial.

Marriage, Family, and Inheritance

Traditional marriage is an alliance between families, initiated by the groom's parents, often through a go-between. Girls marry as early as 14, boys at 16 or 17. The more well-to-do marry later.

Although extended families generally encompass two, three, or four generations, couples often establish their own households after the birth of their first child. Even though both the wife's and the husband's relatives enjoy equal kinship status, couples are more likely to live near the husband's relatives. Other practices are male-weighted. Boys usually inherit more land than their sisters, and family names, nearly always Spanish, are inherited from the father.

Household Life

The basic house has a single room, a cleanly swept hard-dirt floor, stick-and-adobe walls, and a thatched roof. Better houses have more rooms, adobe or concrete walls, a concrete floor, and perhaps a flush toilet. Household goods hang on pegs and nails all around the walls. Overhead, rafters support grain and other heavy storage. Beds are either on floor mats or hammocks. A small altar with saint and candles occupies one corner, with the kitchen in the other. Cooking is either over open fire or on an adobe stove. Tortillas are heated on a flat adobe *comal* (griddle); beans, chilies, and stews are cooked in pottery jars *(ollas)* or metal pots over the open fire. Women grind corn by rolling with their stone *mano* on the *metate* basin. They grind chilies in their *molcajete* (mortar).

Men do the heavier outside work: clearing, burning, farming, building, repairing, plus fishing, hunting, and tending cattle and horses. If fields are far from the homestead, men sometimes take up temporary residence there during planting and harvest. Women cook, sew, wash clothes, gather fruit, flowers, and wild herbs, and tend household animals, such as pigs, goats, chickens, and turkeys. Women do most, if not all, of the marketing. Both men and women carry heavy loads.

Dress

Country people, especially in remote areas, still wear the traditional cottons that blend the Spanish and native styles. Men usually wear the Spanish-origin fiber **sombrero** (literally, shade-maker) on their heads, loose white cotton shirt and pants, and leather **huaraches** on their feet. Women's dress is often more colorful. It can include a *huipil* (long, sleeveless dress), often embroidered in bright floral and animal motifs, or a handwoven *enredo* (wraparound skirt that identifies the wearer with a particular locality). A very common addition is the Spanish-tradition, all-purpose woven shawl *(rebozo),* which can carry a baby, a bag of corn, or maybe even a chicken or two, as well as protect from the rain or sun. A *faja* (waist sash) and, in the winter, a *quechquémitl* (shoulder cape) complete the costume.

Mesoamerican Calendar

The Mixtec and Zapotec ancestors of present-day Oaxacans ordered their lives with the same calendric system as many Mesoamerican linguistic groups, including the Maya, the Aztecs (Nahuatl), the Tarascans (Purépecha), and many others. Their system combined two major calendric cycles. First, they used the agricultural calendar, tied to the seasons and derived from the approximately 365-day (more accurately 365.2422) cycle of the sun through the background of stars and constellations.

The Mesoamerican counting system was basic to the calendar's operation. The Mesoamericans didn't count by decimals, but rather used a vigesimal (20-count) system. They logically divided their agricultural year into 18 "months" of 20 days each, with a 5-day short month at the year-end. A given day, for example, might be called, instead of June 11 or June 12, 5-Deer or 6-Deer and so forth.

They tracked ceremonial dates, such as birthdays, with a separate ritual or divinatory calendar of 260 days that combined 20 separate named days with numbers one through 13. Succeeding days were identified as, for example, 2-Water, 3-Monkey, 4-Dog, and so on.

A given date was a unique coincidence of both calendars, which you can imagine as a pair of meshed cogwheels, turning in lockstep. As you picture the calendric cogwheels turning, at a given moment a certain cog (marked as 5-Deer, for example) in the solar calendar will always be meshing with some slot (marked as 3-Monkey, for example) in the ritual calendar, producing a unique combination of two numbers and two names (since the solar and the ritual calendars have different respective totals of cogs and slots: 365 vs. 260). For example, June 11, 1999, might be represented by the unique coincidence of cog 5-Deer and slot 3-Monkey; June 12, 1999, by 6-Deer and 4-Dog; June 13 by 7-Deer, 5-Water; and so on. (Note that the solar calendar progresses through named "months," such as "Deer" in the example, while the ritual calendar does not.)

In this system dates are unique, but only for a determined time period, because the entire calendric cycle repeats itself after all dual-number-dual-name combinations have occurred. This happens every 52 solar years (or, in days, 52 times 365, 18,980 days). During this time the intermeshed ritual calendar must pass through exactly the same number of days. Dividing 18,980 by

Making a Living

The great majority of Oaxacan indigenous people cultivate native corn, along with a number of other secondary crops, such as beans, squash, pumpkins, potatoes, chili peppers, and tomatoes. Depending upon soil and climate, they may also harvest potatoes, maguey (for alcoholic drinks), and fruits, such as mangos, papaya, chirimoya, *zapote,* and avocado. Other native crops might be cotton or maguey for *ixtle* fiber, and perhaps cocoa beans, *hule* (rubber), and chicle (chewing gum) for cash. Locally cultivated introduced cash crops include wheat, bananas, coffee, sugarcane, sesame seeds, and peanuts.

Many families or sometimes entire villages specialize in crafts, such as pottery, cloth weaving, or basketry. Although the appearance of cheap, machine-made cloth has weakened the tradition, many Oaxacan women still weave family garments with the ancestral backstrap loom. Treadle looms, introduced by the Spanish and operated by either men or women, are common around Oaxaca City. Potters, both women and men, practice their craft all over Oaxaca. Methods vary; they might confine themselves to the native hand-coiling or the Spanish-introduced potter's wheel, or use a combination of both.

Governmental and Religious Institutions

Although women exercise considerable behind-the-scenes influence, men customarily occupy the formal community leadership positions. Minor *presidencia municipal* (city hall) positions are usually appointive; senior its number of 260 cogs, you come up with the exactly 73 revolutions that the ritual calendar must undergo in the same 52 solar years.

Besides the Mixtecs and Zapotecs, all other Mesoamerican groups probably feared that cataclysmic events might occur at the end of each 52-year period, measured from some mythical beginning. High priests and presumably the populations at large observed solemn ceremonies, performed sacrifices, and watched the sky for auspicious portents, such as a bright overhead star, a conjunction of planets, or a comet, on the eve of their 52-year cyclical "millennium."

Knowledge of the Zapotec and Mixtec calendars is gradually being accumulated. Scholars believe that they have been used since at least the early urban stage, around 500 BC, approximately the founding of Monte Albán. Alfonso Caso, the discoverer of Monte Albán's earliest stages, associated a common but undeciphered Monte Albán glyph, of a headdress in profile, with the solar year. For Caso, this indicated that certain personages wearing such headdresses interpreted, read, or manipulated the calendar. The ritual calendar, called *piye* in Zapotec, was also certainly used at Monte Albán.

As in other parts of Mesoamerica, persons were named by their birth date, such as 8-Deer, 3-Dog, or 7-Monkey, in the ritual calendar. Such name-dates occur as glyphs associated with personages recorded in stone or on the surviving hieroglyphic paper books, called codices, such as the Codex Nuttall.

The Mesoamericans, as the Europeans, had to apply corrections to keep the solar calendar in correspondence with the seasons. This will happen only if the year averages, over the millennia, 365.2422 days. The presently used Gregorian calendar (which was instituted by Pope Gregory VIII in 1582) corrects the solar year approximately to 365.2425 days (compared to the actual 365.2422) by omitting the leap year every three out of four centuries. Therefore, although the years 1700, 1800, and 1900 were not leap years (that is, they were permitted only 365 days, instead of 366), the year 2000 was permitted 366 days. The Mayans, scholars believe, did a little better than this; they corrected the solar calendar to 365.2420 days.

positions, such as *regidor* (administrator), *alcalde* (judge), and *presidente* (mayor) are often elective. In-town native homes cluster in one or more barrios on the outskirts. A town *regidor* acts as a representative agent for one or more barrios.

Paralleling such formal civil institutions are the religious, which center on the *mayordomía*, the office responsible for the oft-elaborate ceremonial trappings and yearly fiesta of the barrio's patron saint. The barrio's *regidor* or one of its *cofradias* (religious fraternities) designates the *mayordomo* for a one-year *mayordomía* responsibility

RELIGION

Although the vast majority of Oaxacan *indígenas* consider themselves Catholics, their religion blends the catechism of the missionary fathers with ancient native beliefs. Deities in their age-old Mesoamerican pantheon assume thinly disguised identities among the host of Catholic saints. Besides paying obeisance at the village church altar, Oaxacan country folks also appease mountain, water, and underworld spirits with offerings and sacrifices at sacred summits, springs, and caves. Before killing a deer, for example, a hunter often asks permission of the *señor del monte* (lord, or spirit, of the mountain).

Other old beliefs persist. Many folks, especially in remote areas, believe that *animas* (spirits) of the dead, besides the Catholic God and the saints, influence the living. Appeasement of *animas* peaks on November 1 and 2, respectively, the Day of All Saints and the **Day of the Dead,** when many families gather all night at graves of their departed, with candles, flowers, incense, and the deceased's favorite foods.

Healers employ other remedies, such as consumption or avoidance of certain foods, sucking (to remove the mysterious object causing the illness), herbs and poultices, and also modern medicine. Especially common is a steam bath in the traditional *temascal,* a permanent wood or stone structure or temporary mat-covered brush hut, which many Oaxacan households maintain individually (rather than communally).

Every Mexican city, town, and village celebrates the cherished memory of their Virgin of Guadalupe on December 12. This celebration, however joyful, is but one of the many fiestas that Mexicans, especially the *indígenas,* rejoice in. Each village holds its local fiesta in honor of its patron saint, who is often a thinly veiled sit-in for some local pre-Cortésian deity. Themes appear Spanish (Christians vs. Moors, devils vs. priests), but the native element is strong, sometimes dominant. During Semana Santa (Holy Week) at Pinotepa Nacional in coastal Oaxaca, for example, Mixtec people, costumed as Jews, shoot arrows skyward, simultaneously reciting traditional Mixtec prayers.

LANGUAGE
Oaxacan Indigenous Languages

Linguists recognize 16 separate languages spoken in Oaxaca today. Experts identify each of them with one of five language families. North American language family names are conventionally derived by combining the names of the northernmost and southernmost languages of the group. Thus, Otomanguean, Oaxaca's most widespread language family, derives its label from Otomi, spoken northwest of Mexico City, and Mangue, spoken in southeast Mexico. All of Oaxaca's native language speakers occupy pretty much the same territories that they did at the time of the conquest. The Otomanguean, by location, moving generally west to east, are: **Amusgo, Chatino, Trique, Mixtec, Chocho, Ixcatec, Popoluca, Cuicatec, Mazatec, Chinantec,** and **Zapotec.** A language pair of eastern Oaxaca, **Mixe** (MEE-shay) and **Zoque** (SOH-kay), probably distantly related to Mayan dialects, are often lumped into a second family, the Mixe-Zoque family. Three other languages are the only representatives of their respective families: **Nahuatl** (the language of the Aztecs) of the Uto-Aztecan

The church has long played an important role in Oaxacan culture.

The Virgin of Guadalupe

Conversion of the *indígenas* was sparked by the vision of Juan Diego, a humble farmer. On the hill of Tepayac north of Mexico City in 1531, Juan Diego saw a brown-skinned version of the Virgin Mary enclosed in a dazzling aura of light. She told him to build a shrine in her memory on that spot, where the Aztecs had long worshipped their "earth mother," Tonantzín. Juan Diego's brown virgin told him to go to the cathedral and relay her instruction to Archbishop Zumárraga. The archbishop, as expected, turned his nose up at Juan Diego's story. The vision returned, however, and this time Juan Diego's brown virgin realized that a miracle was necessary. She ordered him to pick some roses at the spot where she had first appeared to him (a true miracle, since roses had been previously unknown in the vicinity) and take them to the archbishop. Juan Diego wrapped the roses in his rude fiber cape, returned to the cathedral, and placed the wrapped roses at the archbishop's feet. When he opened the offering, Zumárraga gasped: imprinted on the cape was an image of the brown virgin herself, proof positive of a genuine miracle.

In the centuries since Juan Diego, the brown virgin—La Virgen Morena, or Nuestra Señora La Virgen de Guadalupe—has blended native and Catholic elements into something uniquely Mexican. In doing so, she has become the virtual patroness of Mexico, the beloved symbol of Mexico for *indígenas*, mestizos, *negros*, and criollos alike.

In the summer of 2002, Pope John Paul journeyed to Mexico to perform a historic gesture. Before millions of joyous faithful, on July 31, 2002, the frail aging pontiff elevated Juan Diego to sainthood, thus making him Latin America's first indigenous person to be so honored.

family; **Chontal,** of the Hokan-Coahuiltecan family; and **Huave,** of its own family, Huave.

Understanding in Oaxaca is further complicated by a proliferation of **dialects.** Mixtec speakers from Jamiltepec, on the Pacific coast, for example, do not generally comprehend the Mixtec dialect of a town, such as Tlaxiaco, across half a dozen ridges 100 miles away. The same is true for Oaxaca's other major languages—Zapotec, Mazatec, Chinantec, and Mixe—and to a lesser degree, for the minor languages.

Few non-indigenous people, whether foreigners or Mexicans, have made the intense effort required to speak and understand a Oaxacan native language. All of the Otomanguean languages, like the Chinese dialects, are **tonal.** This means that a given word takes on different meanings depending upon the pitch—low, high, rising, or falling—with which it is enunciated. Consequently, in big market towns, Spanish is often the lingua franca of buying and selling. Nevertheless, at many country markets, aware visitors notice many people, usually older folks, who speak no Spanish at all.

INDIGENOUS GROUPS

Although anthropologists and census takers classify them according to language groups (such as Mixtec, Zapotec, or Nahua), *indígenas* typically identify themselves as residents of a particular locality rather than by language or ethnic grouping. And although as a group they are referred to as *indígenas* (native, or aboriginal), individuals are generally made uncomfortable (or may even feel insulted) by being labeled as such.

While the mestizos are the emergent self-conscious majority class, the *indígenas* remain mostly invisible, keeping to their country hamlets, except during town market days and fiestas. Typically, they are politically conservative, socially traditional, and tied to the land.

Their lot, nevertheless, has been slowly improving. *Indígena* families now often have access to a local school and a clinic. Improved health has led to a large increase in their population. Official census counts, however, probably run low. *Indígenas* are traditionally suspicious of government people, and census takers, however conscientious, seldom speak the local dialect.

Indigenous Languages

The 2000 national census figures list populations of those over five years old who speak an indigenous Oaxacan language:

Language	Population	Percentage of Total Oaxacans	Important Centers in Oaxaca
Zapotec	377,000	13.5%	Tlacolula, Juchitán, Pochutla
Mixtec	245,000	8.8%	Tlaxiaco, Huajuapan de León, Jamiltepec
Mazatec	174,000	6.5%	Huatla de Jiménez, Jalapa de Díaz
Chinantec	108,000	3.9%	Valle Nacional, Ojatitlán
Mixe	105,000	3.8%	Ayutla, Zacatepec
Chatino	40,000	1.4%	Nopala, Juquila
Trique	15,200	.55%	Tilapa
Huave	13,700	.49%	San Mateo del Mar, San Dionisio del Mar
Cuicatec	12,000	.43%	Cuicatlán
Nahuatl	11,000	.39%	Salina Cruz, Tuxtepec
Zoque	5,300	.19%	San Miguel Chimalapa, Santa María Chimalapa
Amusgo	4,800	.17%	San Pedro Amusgos
Chontal	4,600	.16%	Santiago Astata
Chocho	500	.018%	Coixtlahuaca
Popoluca	500	.018%	Santiago Chazumba
Ixcatec	200	.0072%	Ixcatlán
Totals	**1,076,000**	**38.7% of all Oaxacans**	

Recent figures nevertheless indicate that about 40 percent of Oaxacans are *indígenas*— that is, they speak one of Oaxaca's 16 native languages. Of these, about a fifth speak no Spanish at all. These fractions, moreover, are changing only gradually.

Once a year, in mid-July, thousands of indigenous people, from hundreds of ethnically distinct Oaxaca communities, converge on Oaxaca City for the **Guelaguetza** (gay-lah-GHET-sah) folk dance festival. Dazzled by the whirling color and spectacle, visitors begin to grasp the richness and sheer magnitude of Oaxacan folk tradition. Although their diversity is staggering, the simple fact is that the majority of indigenous Oaxacans (about three of every five) speak some dialect of one of two languages, Zapotec or Mixtec. Of these, the most numerous and visible are the Zapotecs, the people whom visitors encounter first in excursions from Oaxaca City.

Zapotecs

The Spanish label "Zapoteco" comes from Aztec, rather than Zapotec, tradition. The Zapotecs call themselves **Ben Zaa**, or "People of the Clouds." The Aztecs heard this as Tsapotécatl, or "Zapote People," a less-than-flattering "fruit eater" label.

Zapotec speakers, who number upward of 400,000, make up about one-third of Oaxaca's native people. The Zapotecs, moreover, are the most visible for more reasons than their numbers. In contrast to the Mixtecs, the Zapotecs,

Indigenous Peoples of Oaxaca

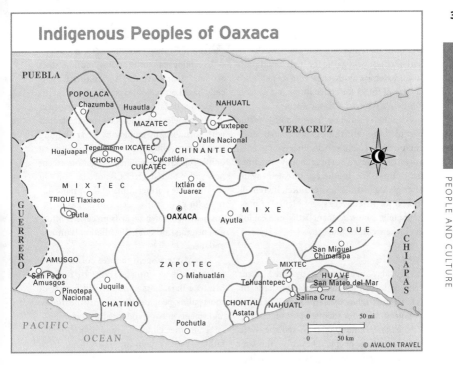

led by their kings Cosijoeza and Cosijopí, allied themselves with the Spanish right from the beginning. Nearly unique among Mexican indigenous groups, Zapotecs have figured prominently in national politics. Mexico's most beloved president, Benito Juárez, was of pure Zapotec origin. Zapotec influence is seen in other sectors as well. Although frequented by nearly all of Oaxaca's indigenous groups, a number of Oaxaca's largest native markets, such as Oaxaca City, Tlacolula, Tehuántepec, and Juchitán, are run by Zapotecs.

Individual Zapotec-speaking persons usually identify themselves more strongly with region or locale than language. (You might expect this, since the several Zapotec regional dialects are virtually separate languages, differing as much as French, Spanish, Italian, and Portuguese.) Living and work patterns, likewise, depend much more on locale—tropical coast, cool mountain, or highland valley—than ethnicity. Oaxaca's four Zapotec regions (and their important market centers), moving clockwise from Oaxaca's center, are the central valley (Oaxaca City, Tlacolula, Ocotlán), northern Sierra (Ixtlán, Yalalag, Villa Alta), Isthmus (Tehuántepec, Juchitán), and southern Sierra (Miahuatlán, Pochutla).

Zapotec communities, moreover, are generally skillful at resolving disputes. If informal means, like neighborly discussion, arbitration, or the council of elders, fail, then the argument will nearly always be resolved in the local court.

Although Zapotec speakers are gradually adopting new ways, many still remember the old gods, especially the god of rain, fertility, and lightning, known as Cocijo, in the central valley. On masks you may see him as a lizard. He controls the clouds and may even release *granizo* (hail) onto a wrongdoer's crops.

Other old beliefs persist. Influential animals are important actors in Zapotec fables. These animals include the *correcamino* (roadrunner), who brings good luck; the *tecolote* (small owl), who brings bad; and the *mariposa* (butterfly), who signifies death. Besides mysterious incantations, Zapotec traditional healers, both men and women, use a wealth of herbal cures: wild garlic for high blood pressure; cloves for toothaches; *rosa de fandango* (a type of mint) for conception; and *epazote morada* (a type of basil) for worms.

Although midwives traditionally preside over birthing, fathers are expected to be present to ensure a healthy baby. Pregnant women are often exhorted not to eat honey or mamey fruit. If possible, mothers are treated royally after giving birth. They traditionally remain in bed for three weeks, get plenty of massages, take *temascal* steam baths, and eat lots of chicken, chilies, and salt.

Mixtecs

It's probably not an accident that the Mixtecs' self-label, Nyu-u Sabi "People of the Rain" (or "Clouds"), has the same meaning as the Zapotecs' name for themselves. Linguists estimate that around 3,000 years ago, they were, in fact, the same people. They're not the same today, however. Their languages, although related, are mutually unintelligible, and their homelands are on opposite sides of Oaxaca.

The Mixtecs, who number around 350,000, comprise about a quarter of all Oaxacan native speakers. Nearly all live in three geographic zones in western Oaxaca: the Mixteca Baja, Mixteca Alta, and Mixteca de la Costa. The Mixteca Baja is the dry plateau-land basin of the Río Mixteco, which runs adjacent to the Puebla-Guerrero border, about 160 kilometers (100 mi) west by northwest of Oaxaca City. Major centers are Santiago Juxtlahuaca in the southwest and Huajuapan de León in the north. Bordering the Mixteca Baja to the southwest is the Mixteca Alta, a highland of pine-tufted peaks cut by lush deep canyons. Its major market centers, moving from north to south, are Tamazulapan, Teposcolula, and Tlaxiaco. Bordering the Mixteca Alta on the south is the Mixteca de la Costa, a roughly 160 square kilometers (50 by 50 mi) region of hills and valleys abutting the Guerrero border on the west and spreading southward from the foothills to the mangrove-fringed coastline. Its major centers are Pinotepa Nacional in the center and Santiago Jamiltepec to the east.

Exceptions notwithstanding, most Mixtecs are subsistence farmers. Agriculture is typically based on age-old slash-and-burn methods. Fields lie fallow for five years, then brush is burned, cleared, and the ground planted with corn, usually employing a *coa* (digging stick). Oxen, when they are used for plowing or hauling, are often rented. Irrigation, except near valley-bottom creeks, is not common. On the coast, the warmer climate allows more options for cash crops, such as bananas, mangos, *panela* (brown sugar from cane), cotton, and peanuts, although distribution is limited and local.

The Mixtecs seem to have cornered the palm-frond weaving market. In the dry Mixteca Baja, homeland to wild forests of short palms, people gather and dry the fronds, and whenever two hands are free, everyone—father, mother, children, grandmother, grandfather—weaves them into everything, from mats and hats to toys and baskets.

Coastal Mixtec women enjoy an unusual degree of autonomy. Besides often handling family purse strings and doing all the marketing, they typically keep their own family names and own property independently of their husbands. For some Mixteca Alta and Mixteca Baja men, traveling to the coast is believed to be dangerous, partly for fear that some Costa Mixteca women, through witchcraft, might steal (or disable) their penis. So, men, watch out for the women, especially around the Pinotepa Nacional market, where they often wear their best finery, which customarily includes an heirloom *pozahuanco* (wraparound skirt) of brilliant natural-dyed red cochineal and deep purple horizontal stripes. From afar, you'll easily recognize them, carrying themselves proudly, with their hat-like *jicara* (gourd bowl) tipped whimsically on their heads. Some women sell handloomed *pozahuancos* in the market. The authentic ones, by which coastal Mixtec women judge each other, sell for $150 or more.

Mazatecs

In contrast to the Zapotecs and Mixtecs, the Mazatec territory, the Mazateca, is relatively concentrated into a roughly 56- by 80-kilometer corner (35 by 50 mi) at Oaxaca's very northern tip. Mazatec villages and farms spread across two very fertile climatic zones: lush semitropical forested uplands and tropical rainforest river bottomland of the Río Papaloapan basin. Major market centers are Jalapa de Díaz and Huautla de Jiménez, both in the western highlands. Important subsidiary centers, many in the highlands around Huautla, are Cosolapa, Santa María Chilchotla, Huehuetlán, Eloxotitlán, San José Tenango, Mazatlán, Chiquihuitlán, and Ayautla. Although the Mazatecs' homeland spills over into neighboring Puebla and Veracruz states, around 170,000, or about 90 percent, live in Oaxaca.

The Mazatecs' own name for their homeland, Ampaad, which translates as the "Place Where the People Are Born," reflects their own creation myth. Legends say that the great tropical trees of Ampaad gave birth to three types of people: giants; ordinary-size humans, who became the present Mazatecs; and smaller people, who became the monkeys. The label "Mazatec" derives from the Aztec Nahuatl language and translates as "People of the Deer."

Left largely to themselves, the Mazatecs have retained many of their own traditions. Many of these they hold in common with their Chocho-, Popoloca-, and Ixcatec-speaking neighbors, whose tongues linguists sometimes lump into a Mazatec-language subfamily. Their isolation has left Mazatec speakers among the least Hispanicized of Oaxacans; as a group, as many as 40 percent speak little or no Spanish.

In 1944, government planners initiated the Papaloapan Project, which called for a huge hydroelectric works in the Mazatec heartland. The project's centerpiece, christened as the Miguel Alemán Dam and Reservoir in 1955, created a mammoth lake in the Mazatec lowland, drowning hundreds of thousands of acres of fertile Papaloapan basin forest and farmland. Although water and electric power were the projected benefits, the human cost turned out to be enormous. Mazatec society was torn by the forced removal of 22,000 poor Mazatec people to unfamiliar, often undesirable territory. Fortunately, the rest of the Mazatec population, largely in the western highlands around Huautla de Jiménez, remained undisrupted. Mexican authorities have since generally avoided such socially disruptive mega-projects.

Mazatec women are renowned for their costumes and adornments. At markets and festivals especially, watch for them in their famously bright *huipiles* (traditional embroidered dresses), horizontally striped in the middle, vertically on the sides. Beneath the *huipil* they often wear a loom-woven blue and white horizontally striped skirt. Their hair is also part of their decoration. They keep it soft and dark with a preparation called *pistle,* made from the core of the mamey fruit, and typically braid it with bright ribbons. Many women take pride in their home embroidery and handwoven cotton, silk, and wool, which they sometimes sell at markets.

As in the past, scarcity of priests weakens Catholic influence in the Mazateca. Priestly visits are so rare that many Mazatec campesino couples have two or three children by the time they enjoy a Catholic Church wedding ceremony. When a priest does arrive, rustic churches are customarily thronged with husbands and wives bringing children for baptism.

Mazatec people often gather for non-Catholic religious rites in fields and at sacred springs, caves, or mountains. Mazatec people especially venerate El Rabón peak, which towers over Jalapa de Díaz, and whose one-kilometer-high (0.6 mi) vertical rock wall is said never to have been scaled. There on that lofty summit live the *dueñes* (earth spirits), who must be appeased with prayers and *copal* incense for the return of lost souls. In the Mazateca lowland, *brujos* (witch doctors) carry out similar ceremonies at Cabeza de Tilpan cave near San José Tenango.

Curandero or *curandera* (traditional man or woman healers) are very busy in the Mazateca. Among their weapons against illness, many include natural forest-gathered hallucinogens, including *hongos alucinantes* (hallucinogenic mushrooms), *semillas de la Virgen* (seeds of the Virgin) or *ololiuhqui,* and *hojas de la pastora* (leaves of the shepherdess). These, used by either the patient or the healer, will induce enlightening visions that may lead to a cure.

Chinantecs

Although Oaxaca's approximately 100,000 Chinantec-speaking people live on some of Mexico's best-watered land, the majority are poor. Inaccessibility, tropical forests that were not easily tillable, and lack of gold or silver relegated the Chinantecs to the margin during colonial times. The Chinantecs' homeland, the Chinantla, is a 112- by 64-kilometer (70 by 40 mi) region around the important market town of Valle Nacional, in northeast Oaxaca. The Chinantla's natural division into eastern lowland (Chinantla Grande) and western upland (Chinantla Pichinche) was apparent to the first Spanish arrivals in the 1520s. For the Spanish conquistadors, the Chinantecs weren't pushovers. After years of seesaw skirmishes, the Spanish mounted their final push at Yetzelalag. Chinantec legend recounts that at the battle's height the Chinantec warriors invoked their gods, who opened the mountain, allowing them to escape. Nevertheless, the Chinantecs submitted to three centuries of labor on Spanish tobacco and sugarcane plantations and cattle ranches.

Although the Spanish colonial policy of *congregación* (the movement of indigenous people into townships) led to the abandonment of many original town sites, the upland Chinantla retained a number of important market centers. Among the most important and colorful are Sochiapan, Tlacozintepec, Usila, Quiotepec, and San Pedro Yolox in the western uplands; Valle Nacional and

San Lucas Ojitlán in the center; and Petlalpa, Lalana, and Jocotepec in the southwest lowlands.

During the 19th century, new colonists introduced coffee, pineapple, and rice agriculture, which, with the Papaloapan Project, continues in modern form today. Although the project forced painful relocations on thousands of lowland Mazatec and Chinantec peoples, it ended their isolation. Government jobs, schools, clinics, electricity, and sanitary and water systems changed life forever in the Chinantec lowlands. At the height of the disorder, swarms of protests erupted. Oaxacan bishops denounced government relocation efforts: "The *indígenas* continue to be the ones always exploited, those who must pay the price of any progress."

For good or bad, the Papaloapan Project lifted the native residents' health, literacy, and general standard of living at the expense of erasing many of their age-old ways of life. In contrast to the Chinantla highlands, few traditional markets function in the lower Chinantla. On the other hand, the government-planned communal and corporate plantations have greatly increased productivity. The Chinantla regularly produces the lion's share of Oaxaca's tobacco, rice, sugarcane, chilies, and pineapples. The workers, however, receive only a minimum of the benefits. Most profits flow to the government agencies, which control everything: seeds, planting, credit, harvesting, and marketing.

Nevertheless, tradition still rules in much of the upper Chinantla. In the minds of many Chinantec-speakers, the old fertility gods "Father and Mother Maize" still command the rain even though their prayers are Catholic. The cosmos is still a battleground between day, ruled by the young and vigorous sun, and night, ruled by the twinkling old stars. Some still believe that creation's original people, who refused to bow down before the god-sun, were changed to monkeys and banished to the forest forever for their error. In some villages, *rayos,* powerful members of lightning cults, are said to hurl lightning bolts against neighboring villages and know how to defend the home village against reverse attacks.

Mixes and Zoques

Their cultural and common Mayan linguistic linkages have led most experts to believe that the original Mixe and Zoque (MEE-shay and SOH-kay) people, together with the Popoloca of present Veracruz state, occupied a single territory. Invasions, first by the Zapotecs and Aztecs and then the Spanish, forced the present territorial divisions. The Mixes (pop. 100,000) occupy the mountainous belt that stretches about 160 kilometers (100 mi) from the central valley's eastern edge to the most easterly Mixe center, San Juan Guichicovi, several miles short of the cross-isthmus highway-rail line. Fifty-five kilometers (35 mi) farther east, Zoque territory (pop. 5,000), divided between two sprawling *ejido* grants, begins. From the Santa María Chimalapa-San Miguel Chimalapa line it spreads east, across the wild Chimalapa mountainous jungle to the Chiapas border. The few remaining Popoloca-speakers are limited to a few isolated villages in eastern Veracruz state.

Despite several costly campaigns, the Spanish force of arms never really conquered the Mixes. If they were conquered at all, it was by 16th-century Dominican missionaries who accomplished with kindness what Spanish guns and steel could not. By the end of the colonial era, they had established nine vicarages, among them Juquila Mixes, San Miguel Quetzaltepec, Asunción Puxmecatan, Ayutla, and San Juan Guichicovi, which all remain important Mixe market towns. Ayutla, closest to the central valley, is dominant.

Anthropologists generally describe Mixe traditions as "less developed" than other Oaxacan groups. They describe a "culture unsuited to the environment," as if the Mixe ways of life first flowered in fairer, more fertile lands and never completely adjusted to the cold, marginal mountainous regions where the Mixes fled in the face of foreign invasions. Such a speculation also explains the Mixes'

well-known wariness and avoidance of outside contact. The Zoque, by contrast, adapted relatively easily to Spanish ways and share little of the Mixes' shyness.

Spanish attempts to congregate the Mixes into towns were only minimally successful. Mixe people largely moved back into the countryside, leaving little-used empty houses in town. Today, most live in country hamlets clinging to mountainsides, with individual houses built on level stilt platforms.

Turbulence has marred the Mixes' recent history. In 1938, President Lázaro Cárdenas wanted to reward the Mixe people for their support of the Republic against the infamous 1865 French Intervention. He persuaded the Oaxaca legislature to award them semi-autonomous status in an all-Mixe district. However, a dispute broke out over the location of the district capital. The towns of Ayutla, Cacalotepec, and Zacatepec had their leading supporters, but Luis Rodríguez of Zacatepec was the most ruthless. While the others protested weakly, he led a four-year reign of terror with kidnapping, cattle rustling, torturing, murdering, and pillaging. This was done with the implicit support of Governor Vicente González. In 1943, Rodríguez cut off the feet and tongue of one prominent opponent and had another assassinated on the steps of the Government Palace in Oaxaca City. Enough was enough for Governor Sánchez Canom, who left Oaxaca City to intervene. But while he was gone, Rodríguez got him replaced. After that, Rodríguez was in complete control, murdering opponents with impunity, collecting tribute from towns and even 10 percent from religious fiestas and holding 500 prisoners in forced labor. Even after his death in 1952, his heirs tried to extend their reign until the 1970s. Despite Luis Rodríguez's notorious legacy, Zacatepec remains the Mixe district capital to the present day.

In 1972, partly in response to the trouble, Mixe people organized themselves into the grassroots social-political Federación Mixe. They soon coalesced with the already-existing local Worker's Federation of Chinantecs,

Zapotecs, and Mixes and the national General Union of Workers and Farmers of Mexico (UGOCM).

Mixe and Zoque social traditions closely follow Mesoamerican patterns. Mixe religion has striking parallels to those described in the Maya sacred book, the *Popol Vuh.* Their legends say that the Mixe god Kondoy was hatched from an egg, grew rapidly, and traveled, battling Aztec armies. He returned and arranged the world in the Mixe image, then retired to the Mixe sacred mountain, Zempoaltepetl, where he still lives.

Belief in the *nagual* persists among the Mixes. If an unbaptized baby dies, the parents must make haste to bury the body immediately, with little ceremony. If not, the spirit of the unbaptized baby might escape and become a *nagual,* a malevolent animal that will harm people who cross its path. Sometimes the *nagual* takes human form as a witch that can transform itself into an animal or other scary form and cause general mischief and illness by infusing some type of object into the victim's body. Traditional healers combine a number of remedies, such as *temascal* steam bathing, rubbing with herbs, prayers, sucking, and vision-inducing plants, to remove such infusions.

Chatinos

The southern Sierra country of the nearly 40,000 strong Chatinos is a 3,072-square-kilometer (1,200 sq. mi) enclave surrounded by Mixtecs on the west, Zapotecs on the north and east, and mestizos and African Mexicans on the south coast. Their language, part of the Zapotec subfamily, resembles Sierra Zapotec. Chatino market centers, besides the central and dominant Santa Catarina Juquila, are Panixtlahuaca, San Juan Quiahije, San Pedro Juchatengo, Nopala, and Zacatepec. Besides its commercial and political influence, Santa Catarina Juquila is a major pilgrimage center, especially for the hundreds of thousands of faithful who arrive on December 8 to honor their beloved Virgin of Juquila.

Most Chatino families are subsistence farmers; Zapotec and mestizo traders dominate commerce in the market centers. In addition to the customary corn, beans, and squash, farmers also cultivate coffee, either as day laborers or on their own land, in which case they sell the surplus for cash at the market.

Amusgos

The approximately 48- by 48-kilometer (30 by 30 mi) Amusgo territory straddles the Oaxaca-Guerrero border. Only about 5,000 of 40,000 Amusgo speakers live in Oaxaca, around the small centers of Cacahuatepec and San Pedro Amusgos, while the remainder live on the Guerrero side, near the centers of Ometepec, Xochistlahuaca, and Tlacoachistlahuaca.

Linguists reckon that the Amusgo language, a member of the Mixtec language subfamily, separated from Mixtec between 2000 and 1000 BC. Around AD 1000, the Amusgos came under the domination of the strong coastal Mixtec kingdom of Tututepec. In 1457 they were conquered by the Aztecs and, not long after, by the Spanish in the 1520s. Decimation of the Amusgo population by disease during the 16th century led to the importation of African slave labor, whose descendants, known locally as *negros* or *costeños,* live along the Guerrero-Oaxaca coastline.

Although the Amusgo population eventually recovered, many of the old colonial-era haciendas remained intact until modern times. The Amusgos, isolated from the mainstream of modern Mexican life, retain their age-old corn-bean-squash farming tradition. Moreover, they have received little attention from anthropologists or archaeologists, although several likely archaeological mounds exist near Amusgo villages.

Amusgo women are nevertheless famous for their hand-embroidered *huipiles* (dresses), whose colorful floral and animal designs fetch willing customers in Oaxaca tourist centers. Even better, Amusgo women often wear their *huipiles,* appearing as heavenly visions of spring on dusty small-town side streets.

Triques

About 80 kilometers (50 mi) farther north from the Amusgo territory, about 15,000 Trique (TREE-kay) people live in their 32- by 24-kilometer (20 by 15 mi) highland pocket of the Mixteca Alta. You'll see plenty of them in the Juxtlahuaca town market, especially Trique women, selling their brilliant red-striped wool *huipiles* (dresses) in the middle of the town square. Long ago, the Trique fled into the mountain vastness, from first Mixtec, then Aztec, and finally Spanish invaders. Some of their main centers are San Isidro Chicahuaxtla, San Juan Copala, and Tilapa, all south of Juxtlahuaca and north of Putla de Guerrero.

The Trique have only grudgingly accepted outside authority. Rebellions broke out often during the colonial era and later. In 1843 Trique forces rebelled against state and federal authorities, who needed five years to jail and execute the responsible leaders. Subsequently, during the later 19th and 20th centuries, coffee became a major Trique product and coffee beans became their money, which traders turned into alcohol and guns. Rebellion, which again required federal forces to suppress, broke out in Copala in 1956. The federal garrison remains in Copala to the present day.

Only at Chicahuaxtla, in the high Mixteca country (just off of Hwy. 125, about 40 km/25 mi west of Tlaxiaco), did Christianity have much effect. This was due to the compassionate persuasion of Father Gonzales Lucero hundreds of years ago. Consequently, much of the Trique's folklore survives to the present day. An oft-told creation myth describes the sun and the moon, and gods who once lived in a *calabaza* (calabash) but who broke out and rode a rabbit and a cat into the heavens to light the world. Around March 25, traditional *curanderos* (healers) lead services to appease the old gods at a sacred cave near Copala, about 20 kilometers (13 mi) down the highway south of Juxtlahuaca. They sacrifice a lamb and a goat while the gathered crowd offers incense and flowers.

Chochos, Ixcatecs, and Popolocas

Emigration and Spanish literacy are fast reducing the number of speakers of Chocho, Ixcatec, and Popoluca, three related tongues of the dry canyonlands of northwest Oaxaca. Of the three, the Chocho people are dominant in their extensive homeland around Coixtlahuaca and subsidiary centers of Tequixtepec and Tepelmeme. If you're going to hear any of the Chocho language, it will probably be in the market at Tepelmeme de Morelos, just off the Oaxaca-Puebla expressway about 24 kilometers (15 mi) north of Coixtlahuaca.

Defeated by the Mixtecs in the 1300s and the Aztecs a hundred years later, the Chochos were again subdued by Spanish conquistadors Orozco and Alvarado in 1522 and later converted by Dominican Father Fermín Abrego. Coixtlahuaca was a thriving Chocho and Ixcatec market until around 1900, but loss of topsoil to erosion has forced many families to emigrate.

If you're going to hear any Ixcatec at all, it will be in Ixcatlán, the sole Ixcatec *municipio*, accessible by dirt road about 32 kilometers (20 mi) northeast from Coixtlahuaca. The same is approximately true of Popoloca, whose few remaining speakers in Oaxaca live in the sliver of territory by the Puebla border, around Santiago Chazumba on Highway 125.

Cuicatecs

The Cuicatec language, by contrast, is holding its own, due to the isolation and richness of the homeland of the Cuicatecos ("People of Song"). About 15,000 Cuicatec people inhabit their present territory, mainly the *municipios* of Concepción Pápalo, San Juan Tepeuxila, San Pedro Teutila, and Santiago Nacaltepec in the mountains east of district capital Cuicatlán and south of the Río Santo Domingo canyon.

Archaeological digs around Concepción Pápalo and other sites reveal Toltec influences, hinting that the Cuicatec lands may have been a haven for some of the refugees from the fall of Tula, the Toltec capital in the north, around AD 1060.

Historians believe that Cuicatec speakers numbered about 60,000 before the conquest. They were defeated by both the Aztecs, around 1456, and Spanish soldiers, commanded by conquistador Martín Mezquita, in 1526. Nevertheless, during the colonial era, the Cuicatecs resisted both Catholic conversion and forced plantation labor by fleeing into the mountains, where they remain today. Although the Dominicans established a church in Pápalo in 1630 and tried to convert them, Catholic influence remains weak. The old gods, notably *jáiko*, the lord of their sacred mountain, Cerro Cheve, still live on in the hearts and minds of many Cuicatec people.

Today, you might hear some Cuicatec spoken at the busy market at Cuicatlán, where Cuicatec women come down from the mountains to sell their highland handicrafts: wool serapes and jackets, flower- and animal-motif embroidered *huipiles* (dresses), palm-leaf sombreros, *petates* (mats), and *cestas* (baskets).

Cuicatec people also earn cash collectively from the concession in which they allow the paper mill in Tuxtepec to harvest some of their forest trees. The money goes to finance community projects.

Huaves

The Isthmus territory of the Huave people encompasses the shoreline of the big tidal Lagunas Superior, Inferior, and the Mar Muerto. About 15,000 Huave-speaking people live there, notably around the villages of San Mateo del Mar, Santa María del Mar, San Dionisio del Mar, and San Francisco del Mar.

The Huave language, not clearly identified with any other language family, is generally classified in a family of its own. This is supported by studies by colonial historians, indicating that the Huave may have migrated from the Nicaraguan Pacific coast and settled around present-day Jalapa del Marqués on the Isthmus. The more-numerous Zapotecs, invading around 1375, forced them to the edges of the lagoons, where they now live.

Generally ignored and neglected by everyone, the Huaves hold on to many pre-conquest beliefs. In the absence of Catholic priests, native *curanderos* (healers) practice thinly veiled pagan rites in some village churches.

Although they subsist mainly on corn, beans, chilies, vegetables, and occasional meat, Huave-speaking people earn cash from their fish catches. Men sell fresh fish to wholesalers who arrive in the afternoons at the shoreline villages, while women sell the surplus as dried fish at Salina Cruz, Tehuántepec, and Juchitán markets.

Nahuas

Along the coast, in a 32-kilometer (20 mi) strip west of Salina Cruz and with the small town of Morro de Mazatán at its center, lies an enclave of Nahua (Nahuatl- or Aztec-speaking people). Besides this small region, several thousand more Nahuatl speakers live in two other small Oaxaca enclaves in the north, one around Tuxtepec and the other next to the Puebla border, wedged between Mazatec, Ixcatec, Chocho, and Popoluca territories. Such Nahuatl enclaves are probably remnants of early colonies established by the Aztec emperors after their armed expansion into Oaxaca in the 1400s.

Chontals

Finally, 30-40 miles farther west and north lies the Chontal (sometimes known as "Tequistlatec") territory. The Chontals are most visible on the coast, at Santiago Astata and San Pedro Huamelula. Today, about 25,000 speakers of Chontal, a language of the Hokan language family (widespread, from the north Gulf Coast to Central America), live in their approximately 2,560-square-kilometer (1,000 sq. mi) domain.

The Chontals are among the least modernized of Oaxaca indigenous groups. They have always tenaciously resisted invasion (though many in the zone due west of Tequisistlán have adopted the Zapotec language). Although many live near the coast, they do little fishing. Some live mostly by corn-based subsistence farming, and others emigrate to the Isthmus or elsewhere for cash employment.

Relatively unaffected by Catholicism, their traditions remain strong. A popular fable is of their folk-hero King Fane Kansini, whom, legend says, an elderly couple hatched as an infant from an egg that they had found. The old couple soon discovered that the infant had supernatural powers. As he matured, Fane Kansini acquired the burning desire to save his people from the Zapotecs. He invented body armor and a wondrous new kind of arrow, which he used to defeat the Zapotec king in battle and thus save the Chontal people from annihilation. The Chontal-Zapotec mutual enmity continues to the present time.

Festivals and Events

Urban families watch the calendar for midweek national holidays that create a *puente* (bridge) to the weekend and allow them to squeeze in a three- to five-day mini-vacation. Visitors should likewise watch the calendar. Such holidays (especially Christmas and Semana Santa/pre-Easter week) mean packed buses, roads, and hotels, especially around Oaxaca's beach resorts.

Country people, on the other hand, await their local saint's day or holy day. The name of the locality often provides the clue. For example, in Santa Cruz Papalutla, just east of Oaxaca City, expect a celebration on May 3, El Día de la Santa Cruz (Day of the Holy Cross). People dress up in their traditional best, sell their wares and produce in a street fair, join a procession, get tipsy, and dance in the plaza.

It's worth noting that Oaxaca, unique among Mexican states, has no bullfights. Benito Juárez, as governor during the 1850s, was instrumental in outlawing bullfights in Oaxaca. In his honor, they remain banned.

The following calendar lists national and notable Oaxacan holidays and festivals. For many more details, see the destinations cited. Call ahead to confirm dates. If you happen to be where one of these is going on, get out of your car or bus and join in!

JANUARY

• January 1: ¡Feliz Año Nuevo! (New Year's Day; national holiday), especially in Santiago Jamiltepec and Teotitlán del Valle.

• January 6: Día de los Reyes (Day of the Kings), especially in Santos Reyes Nopala, with traditional gift exchange; townsfolk perform favorite traditional dances.

• January 13-17: Fiesta del Dulce Nombre de Jesús (Festival of the Sweet Name of Jesus), in Santa Ana del Valle, Tlacolula, and Zimatlán. Troupes perform many traditional dances, including the Dance of the Feathers.

• January 17: Día de San Antonio Abad, decorating and blessing animals.

• January 20-21: Fiesta de San Sebastián, especially in San Pedro and San Pablo Tequixtepec, Pinotepa Don Luis, and Jalapa de Díaz.

• January 25: Fiesta del Apóstol de San Pablo (Festival of Apostle St. Paul), in Mitla: masses, processions, feast, fireworks, *jaripeo* (bull roping and riding), and dancing.

FEBRUARY

• February 2: Día de Candelaria, especially in Tututepec: plants, seeds, and candles blessed; procession and bullfights.

• February 5: Constitution Day (national holiday), commemorates the constitutions of 1857 and 1917.

• February 24: Flag Day (national holiday).

• February: During the four days before Ash Wednesday (46 days before Easter Sunday), usually in late February, many towns, especially San Juan Colorado, Putla, Pinotepa Don Luis, and Juxtlahuaca, celebrate Carnaval with Mardi Gras-style extravaganzas.

• February-March: Celebrations continue during Cuaresma (Lent), especially in Santiago Jamiltepec and Pinotepa Nacional, for several weeks.

MARCH

• Second Friday of Lent (nine days after Ash Wednesday): Fiesta del Señor del Perdón (Festival of the Lord of Forgiveness), in San Pedro and San Pablo Tequixtepec; big pilgrimage festival.

• Second Friday of Lent: Fiesta del Señor de Piedad, in Santiago Astata.

• Fourth Friday of Lent (23 days after Ash Wednesday): Fiesta del Señor de Misericordias, in Santa María Huatulco.

• Fourth Friday before Easter Sunday: Fiesta of Jesus the Nazarene, in Huaxpaltepec.

• Week before Palm Sunday: Week of Ramos, especially in Jamiltepec.

• Friday before Good Friday (11 days before Easter Sunday): Feria Comercial (Commercial Fair), in Huautla de Jiménez, with many traditional folk dances.

• March 18-19: Fiesta de San José, in Valle Nacional; on the weekend closest to March 10 in San José El Mogote.

• March 21: Birthday of Benito Juárez, the "Hero of the Americas" (national holiday), especially in Benito Juárez's birthplace, Guelatao; a whirl of traditional dances.

• March 21-31: Juegos Florales (Flower Games), in Oaxaca City.

APRIL

• April: Semana Santa (pre-Easter Holy Week, culminating in Domingo Santa—Easter—national holiday), in many locales, especially San Juan Colorado, Pinotepa Don Luis, and Pinotepa Nacional.

• Good Friday, two days before Easter

Sunday: Fiesta de la Santa Cruz de Huatulco (Festival of the Holy Cross of Huatulco).

• Saturday before Easter Sunday: Sábado de Gloria in San Miguel Tequixtepec. People, called *mecos,* don masks and do a kind of adult trick or treat for the occasion.

• First week in April: Feria del Mango (Mango Fair), in Tapanatepec.

• April 26-29: Fiesta de San Pedro Mártir de Verona, in San Pedro Yucunama.

MAY

• May 1: Labor Day (national holiday).

• May 3: Fiesta de la Santa Cruz (Festival of the Holy Cross), in many places, especially Salina Cruz, Tehuántepec, and Unión Hidalgo.

• May 5: Cinco de Mayo (national holiday), celebration of the defeat of the French at Puebla in 1862.

• May 10: Mothers' Day (national holiday).

• May 10-12: Fiesta of the Coronation of the Virgin of the Rosary.

• May 11-16: Fiesta de San Isidro Labrador (Festival of St. Isador the Farmer), in Ixcatlán.

• May 15-30: Velas de San Vicente Ferrer, in Juchitán.

JUNE

• June 2-3: Fiesta de San Antonio de Padua, in Jalapa de Díaz.

• June 23-24: Fiesta de San Juan Bautista (Festival of St. John the Baptist), especially in Tuxtepec, Valle Nacional, Cuicatlán, and Coixtlahuaca.

• June 25: Fiesta de San Pedro, in Santa María Huamelula; June 27-30 in San Pedro Tapanatepec; June 29 in San Pedro Amusgos; June 26-30 in Unión Hidalgo.

• June 29: Fiesta de San Pablo y San Pedro (Festival of St. Paul and St. Peter); June 21-28 in San Pedro Pochutla.

JULY

- **July 1-15: Fiesta of the Precious Blood of Christ,** in Teotitlán del Valle, featuring the Danza de la Pluma (Dance of the Feather).

- Usually on the two Mondays following July 16: **Lunes de Cerro** or **Guelaguetza** in Oaxaca City; all-Oaxaca dance extravaganza.

- **July 20-24: Fiesta de Santa María Magdalena** (Festival of St. Mary Magdalene), in Tequisistlán.

- **July 20-30: Fiesta de Santiago Apóstol** (Festival of St. James the Apostle), in Santiago Laollaga; July 22-27 in Suchilquitongo; July 23-26 in Jamiltepec and in Pinotepa Nacional; and July 25 in Juxtlahuaca.

AUGUST

- **August 1-5: Fiesta de Santo Domingo de Guzmán,** in Unión Hidalgo.

- August 13-18: **Fiesta del Barrio de Santa María Relatoca,** in Tehuántepec.

- **August 14: Fiesta de la Virgen de la Asunción** (Festival of the Virgin of the Assumption), in Tlaxiaco; August 15 in Nochixtlán; August 13-16 in Huazolotitlán.

- August 23-24: **Fiesta de San Bartolomé,** in San Bartolo Tuxtepec; August 24-27 in San Bartolo Coyotepec.

- August 26-September 2: **Fiesta de Santa Rosa de Lima,** in Salina Cruz; August 28 in Ojitlán.

- August 31-September 11: **Fiesta Laborio,** in Tehuántepec.

SEPTEMBER

- September 7-8: **Fiesta de la Virgen de La Natividad,** in Huautla de Jiménez.

- September 7-9: **Fiesta del Señor de La Natividad** (Festival of the Lord of the Nativity), in Teotitlán del Valle.

- September 11: **Fiesta de la Virgen de los Remedios,** in Jamiltepec.

- September 14: **Charro Day** (Cowboy Day), all over Mexico, rodeos.

- September 15-16: **Independence Day** (national holiday). Mayors everywhere reenact Father Hidalgo's 1810 *Grito de Dolores* from city hall balconies on the night of September 15.

- September 21: **Fiesta of San Mateo,** in Calpulalpan.

- September 23-30: **Fiesta de la Preciosa Sangre de Cristo** (Festival of the Precious Blood of Christ), in Tlacochahuaya, eight days of processions, dances, fireworks, and food.

- September 27-29: **Fiesta de San Miguel,** in San Miguel Tequixtepec and Teotitlán del Camino. Highlights include traditional dances, such as the Cristianos y Moros (Christians and Moors).

OCTOBER

- October 1-2: **Fiesta de San Miguel Arcangel,** in Puerto Ángel.

- First Sunday in October: **Fiesta de la Virgen del Rosario** (Festival of the Virgin of the Rosary), in San Pedro Amusgos.

- October 3-5: **Fiesta de San Francisco Asis,** in Salina Cruz.

- October 6-8: **Fiesta de San Dionisio,** in San Dionisio del Mar; pilgrimage.

- Second Sunday in October: **Fiesta del Santo Cristo de Tlacolula** (Festival of the Holy Christ of Tlacolula), in Tlacolula.

- Second Monday in October: **Fiesta de los Lunes del Tule,** in Santa María del Tule. Locals in costume celebrate with rites, folk dances, and feats of horsemanship beneath the boughs of their beloved great cypress tree.

- Third Sunday in October: **Fiesta de Octubre,** in Tlaxiaco, includes fireworks, basketball and *pelota mixteca* (traditional ball game) tournaments, and popular dances.

- October 12: **Día de la Raza** (Columbus

Day), national holiday that commemorates the union of the races.

NOVEMBER

- November: **Fiestas de Noviembre,** in Puerto Escondido, features the big folk dance festival **Fiesta Costéño.**
- November 1: **Día de Todos Santos** (All Saints Day), in honor of the souls of children. The departed descend from heaven to eat sugar skeletons, skulls, and treats on family altars.
- November 2: **Día de los Muertos** (Day of the Dead), especially in Tuxtepec and Cacahuatepec, in honor of ancestors. Families visit cemeteries and decorate graves with flowers and favorite foods of the deceased.
- November 11-16: **Fiesta de San Diego,** in Salina Cruz.
- November 13: **Fiesta de San Marcos,** in San Marcos Tlapazola (tourist Yu'u town in the Valley of Oaxaca).
- November 20: **Revolution Day** (national holiday), anniversary of the revolution of 1910-1917.
- November 22: **Fiesta de Santa Cecilia,** in Unión Hidalgo.
- November 25: **Fiesta de Santa Catarina,** in Santa Catarina Ixtepeji.
- November 29: **Fiesta de San Andrés,** in San Juan Colorado.

DECEMBER

- December 1: **Inauguration Day,** national government changes hands every six years: 2006, 2012, 2018 . . .
- December 8: **Día de la Purísima Concepción** (Day of the Immaculate Conception).
- December 8: **Fiesta de la Vírgen de la Soledad,** in Oaxaca and Juxtlahuaca.
- Late November-December 8: **Fiesta de**

Christmas *Posadas*

Christmas *posadas* are reenactments of Mary and Joseph looking for a place to stay at an inn in Bethlehem. In Mexico, they take place every night from December 16-24. There is a candlelit religious procession on each of those nine nights. The people (sometimes dressed up as Mary and Joseph) go to different individual homes each night and sing songs asking for shelter; and the people inside sing back and eventually let the visitors in to share food and drink.

la Virgen de Juquila, in Santa Catarina Juquila; Oaxaca's biggest fiesta.

- December 8-11: **Fiesta de Nuestra Señora de la Concepción,** in Santa María Huatulco.
- December 12: **Día de Nuestra Señora de Guadalupe** (Festival of the Virgin of Guadalupe), nationwide—processions, music, and dancing honoring the patroness of Mexico.
- December 16-18: **Fiesta de la Virgen de la Soledad,** in Oaxaca City.
- December 16-24: **Christmas Week.** Week of Christmas *posadas* (reenactments of Mary and Joseph looking for a place to stay in Bethlehem) and piñatas, with midnight mass on Christmas Eve.
- December 19-22: **Fiesta de Santo Tomás Apóstol,** in Ixtlán de Juárez.
- December 23: **Fiesta de los Rábanos** (Festival of the Radishes), in Oaxaca City.
- December 24: **Nochebuena** (Christmas Eve), in Oaxaca City and Yucunama.
- December 25: **¡Feliz Navidad!** (Christmas Day; national holiday); Christmas trees and gift exchange.
- December 26: **Vela Tehuántepec,** in Tehuántepec. Everyone in town dances to the lovely melody of "La Sandunga."
- December 31: **New Year's Eve.**

Arts and Crafts

Oaxaca abounds with attractive, reasonably priced handicrafts. A sizable fraction of Oaxacan families still depend upon homespun items: clothing, utensils, furniture, native herbal remedies, religious offerings, adornments, toys, and musical instruments. Many such traditions reach back thousands of years, to the beginnings of Mesoamerican civilization. The accumulated knowledge of manifold generations of artisans has in many instances resulted in finery so prized that whole villages devote themselves to the manufacture of a certain class of goods.

Shops and markets in Oaxaca City and the Valley of Oaxaca towns of Teotitlán del Valle, Santa Ana del Valle, Tlacolula, Mitla, San Bartolo Coyotepec, San Martín Tilcajete, Santo Tomás Jalieza, Ocotlán, Arrazola, and Atzompa are Oaxaca's most renowned sources of handicrafts.

Handicrafts (*artesanías,* ar-tay-sah-NEE-ahs) shoppers who venture away from the Oaxaca City center and the coastal tourist enclaves to the source villages and towns will most likely benefit from lower prices, wider choices, and, most importantly, the privilege of meeting the artisans themselves. There, perhaps in a patio shop on a dusty Teotitlán del Valle side street or an Arrazola family patio, you might encounter the people and perhaps view the painstaking processes by which they fashion humble materials—clay, wool, cotton, wood, metal, straw, leaves, bark, paper, leather—into irresistible works of art.

BARGAINING

Bargaining comes with the territory in Mexico and needn't be a hassle. On the contrary, if done with humor and moderation, bargaining can be an enjoyable path to encountering Mexican people and gaining their respect, and even friendship. The local crafts market is where bargaining is most intense. For starters, try offering half the asking price. From there on, it's all psychology: You have to content yourself with not having to have the item. Otherwise, you're sunk; the vendor will probably sense your need and stand fast. After a few minutes of good-humored bantering, ask for *el último precio* (the final price), in which, if it's close, you may have a bargain.

BASKETRY AND WOVEN CRAFTS

Weaving straw, leaves, and reeds is among the oldest of Oaxacan crafts traditions. Mat- and basket-weaving methods and designs go back as far as 5,000 years and are still used today.

The drier regions of Oaxaca are sources of fronds from the dwarf palms that populate the hillsides. In the Mixteca, in places such as Huajuapan de León and Coixtlahuaca and the east side of the Valley of Oaxaca around Tlacolula, you might see people sitting on a doorstep or at a bus stop or even walking down the street while weaving a *petate* (mat) or *tenate* (tumpline basket) of creamy white palm leaf, prized for its soft, pliable texture. All over Oaxaca, nearly everyone uses *petates,* from vacationers, for stretching out on the beach, to local folks, for keeping tortillas warm and shielding babies from the sun. *Tenates* have been raised to nearly a fine art in a number of Oaxaca localities, such as San Luis Amatlán, near Ejutla in the southern Valley of Oaxaca. There, craftspeople interweave dyed fibers with the natural palm, creating attractive, sensitively executed geometric designs.

Carrizo, a bamboo-like reed that grows on stream banks all over Oaxaca state, is the source of stronger, more rigid baskets, usually called *canastas* when they have handles, *tenates* when they don't. Well-known Valley of Oaxaca sources are San Juan Guelavía and Magdalena Teitipac, on the east side, and Santa Ana Zegache near Ocotlán in the south. Familiar variations include the prized *tenate para tortillas,* round at the top and tapering to square at the base, and *cajas para pájaros* (birdcages), sometimes fashioned in two, three, or four levels.

A third important weaving fiber in Oaxaca is **ixtle,** the dried strands from the leaves of maguey and related agave-family plants. Artisans all over Oaxaca craft ixtle into useful items, such as ropes for pulling, string bags for carrying, and hammocks for relaxing.

CLOTHING AND EMBROIDERY

Although *traje* (ancestral tribal dress) has become uncommon in Oaxaca City, significant numbers of Oaxacan native women make and wear *traje,* especially in the Mazateca, Chinantla, and Zapotec Sierra in the north, the Isthmus in the southeast, the coastal Mixteca in the southwest, and the Trique in the Mixteca Alta in the west.

The most common *traje* garment is the **huipil,** a full, square-shouldered, short- to mid-sleeved dress, often hand-embroidered with animal and floral designs and embellished with ribbons. Probably the most popular Oaxaca *huipiles* are the captivating designs from San Pedro de Amusgos (Amusgo tribe; white cotton embroidered with abstract colored animal and floral motifs). Others nearly as prized include the Trique styles from around San Andrés Chicahuaxtla (white cotton, richly embroidered red stripes, interwoven with green, blue, and yellow, and hung with colored ribbons); Mazatec, from Huautla de Jiménez (white cotton with bright flowers embroidered in multiple panels, crossed by horizontal and vertical purple and magenta silk ribbons); and Isthmus Zapotec, from Tehuántepec (brightly colored cotton densely embroidered with either geometric designs or a field of flamboyant, multicolored flowers).

Oaxaca shops and stalls also sell other, less common types of *traje.* These include the *quechquémitl* (shoulder cape), often made of wool and worn as an overgarment

in winter, and the **enredo,** a full-length skirt that wraps around the waist and legs like a Hawaiian sarong.

Mixtec women in Oaxaca's warm southwest coastal region around Pinotepa Nacional commonly wear the *enredo,* known locally as the **pozahuanco** (poh-sah-WAHN-koh), below the waist and, when at home, go barebreasted. When wearing their *pozahuancos* in public, they usually tie a **mandil,** a wide apron, around their front side.

Women weave the most prized *pozahuancos* using cotton thread dyed a light purple with secretions of tidepool-harvested snails *(Purpura patula pansa)* and silk dyed deep red with cochineal, an extract from the dried bodies of a locally cultivated scale insect, *Dactylopius coccus.* On a typical day, two or three women will be selling handmade *pozahuancos* at the Pinotepa Nacional market.

Ropa Típica

Colonial-era Spanish styles have blended with native *traje,* producing a wider class of dress, known generally as **ropa típica.** Lovely embroidered *blusas* (blouses), *rebozos* (shawls), and *vestidos* (dresses) fill shop racks and market stalls all over Oaxaca. Among the most popular is the so-called **Oaxaca wedding dress,** made of cotton with a crochet-trimmed riot of diminutive flowers hand-stitched about the neck and yoke. Some of the finest examples are made in San Antonino Castillo Velasco, just north of Ocotlán on the Valley of Oaxaca's south side.

GLASS AND STONEWORK

Glass manufacture, unknown in pre-Columbian times, was introduced by the Spanish. Today factories scattered all over Mexico turn out mountains of **burbuja** (boor-BOO-hah), bubbled-glass tumblers, goblets, plates, and pitchers, usually in blue, yellow, green, or red.

Artisans work stone, mostly near sources of supply. Puebla and Tequisistlán (in the Oaxaca Isthmus) are Mexico's main sources of decorative onyx (*onix,* OH-neeks). Factory shops turn out the galaxy of mostly rough-hewn, cream-colored items, from animal charms and chess pieces to beads and desk sets, which you'll see on some Oaxaca City curio shop shelves.

Cantera, a volcanic tufa stone, occurs in pastel shades from pink to green and is quarried in several locations in the Valley of Oaxaca. The most preferred is the light jade-green *cantera* from Magdalena Etla, northwest of Oaxaca City. It has replaced the original but exhausted green *cantera* source that supplied stone for most of Oaxaca City's original buildings. An open-air *cantera* workshop, with many examples of expertly sculptured *cantera* (by Hwy. 190 in Suchilquitongo, at the Valley of Oaxaca's northeast corner), welcomes visitors.

For a keepsake from a truly ancient Oaxacan tradition, don't forget the hollowed-out stone *metate* (may-TAH-tay, corn-grinding basin) and the three-legged *molcajete* (mohl-kah-HAY-tay), a mortar for grinding chilies. Most examples you'll see in Oaxaca are from Teitipac, in the west valley near Tlacolula (where you'll most likely see for-sale examples during the big Sunday market).

JEWELRY

Oaxaca has a healthy, local, jewelry-making tradition. The acknowledged leader in Oaxaca City is the family firm of Oro de Monte Albán. Their several city and coastal resort shops offer replicas of the ancient Mixtec designs, notably of many pieces found at Monte Albán's Tomb 7.

Tehuántepec women *(tehuanas)* have created a demand for elaborate gold filigree jewelry, made from fine wires and often decorated with pearls and precious stones. The finest, 10-18 karat (42-75 percent pure) gold, is more often kept in safe deposit boxes and used only on ceremonial occasions. Much more common is *chapa de oro,* gold look-alike filigree that contains no gold at all. Women sell this jewelry in Oaxaca City, at the north-central entrance of the 20 de Noviembre

market and in the Isthmus, at the Juchitán and Tehuántepec markets.

WOOD CARVING AND MUSICAL INSTRUMENTS
Masks

Spanish and Native Oaxacan traditions have blended to produce a multitude of masks—some strange, some lovely, some scary, some endearing, but all interesting. The tradition flourishes in Oaxaca and the strongly indigenous neighboring states of Michoacán, Guerrero, and Chiapas. Here campesinos gear up all year for the village festivals, especially Semana Santa (Easter week), early December (Virgin of Guadalupe), and that of the local patron, whether it be San José, San Pablo, San Pedro, Santa Barbara, Santa María, or a host of others. Every local fair has its favored dances, such as the Dance of the Conquest, Dance of the Feathers, the Christians and Moors, the Old Men, or the Tiger, in which masked villagers act out age-old allegories of fidelity, sacrifice, faith, struggle, sin, and redemption.

Although artisans craft Oaxaca masks of many materials (from stone and ebony to coconut husks and paper), wood, where available, is the medium of choice. For the entire year, workers carve, sand, and paint to ensure that each participant will be properly disguised for the festival. Although Oaxaca's larger municipalities usually have their cadres of mask makers, towns in the Mixteca region, notably Juxtlahuaca, in the Mixteca Baja, and Santa María Huazolotitlán and Pinotepa Don Luis, in the Mixteca de la Costa, are among Oaxaca's busiest authentic mask sources.

The popularity of masks has resulted in an entire made-for-tourist mask industry, which has led to mass-produced duplicates, many cleverly antiqued. Examine the goods carefully; if the price is high, don't buy unless you're convinced it's a real antique.

Alebrijes

Tourist demand has made zany wooden animals called *alebrijes* (ah-lay-BREE-hays) a

Oaxaca growth industry. Virtually every family in certain Valley of Oaxaca villages, notably Arrazola and San Martín Tilcajete, runs a factory studio. There, piles of copal wood, which men carve and women finish and intricately paint, become whimsical giraffes, dogs, cats, iguanas, gargoyles, dragons, and most of the possible permutations in between. The farther from the source you get, the higher the *alebrije* price becomes; what costs $5 in Arrazola will probably run about $10 in Oaxaca City and $30 in the United States, Canada, or Europe.

Musical Instruments

Virtually all of Mexico's guitars are made in Paracho, Michoacán (southeast of Lake Chapala), north of Uruapan. There, scores of cottage factories turn out guitars, violins, mandolins, ukuleles, and a dozen more variations every day. Products vary widely in quality, so look carefully before you buy. Make sure that the wood is well cured and dry; damp, unripe wood instruments are more susceptible to warping and cracking.

METALWORK

Several Oaxaca City family factories turn out fine cutlery, forged ironwork, and a swarm of bright tinware mirror frames, masks, and glittering Christmas decorations.

Cutlery tradition—knives, machetes, scissors, swords, and more—arrived in Oaxaca with the Spanish. Today, several family shops offer their wares in town shops and market stalls, notably at the Benito Juárez market in Oaxaca City.

Traditional **ironwork,** admittedly heavy to carry home in your luggage, is made to order, boxed, and shipped at a number of specialty shops in Oaxaca City. Some of the more commonly requested items, such as medieval-style lanterns and garden benches, are available on display.

Tinware (*hojalata,* oh-hah-LAH-tah), especially the colorfully lacquered Christmas decorations, including winsome angels, saints, Santas, butterflies, and fruits, constitute Oaxaca City's most sought-after metal craft. Running closely behind are the hosts of old-fashioned lead figures (soldiers, ballerinas, antique automobiles, angels) and fancy silvery mirror frames, metal boxes, birds, flowers, and much more. Many downtown handicrafts shops, in addition to stalls at the 20 de Noviembre market and the Mercado de Artesanías (Handicrafts Market), sell metal work.

Alebrijes are brightly painted imaginary animals made of wood.

Moreover, be sure to ask at the same shops and stalls for *milagros,* one of Mexico's most charming forms of metal work. Usually of brass, they are of homely shapes: a horse, dog, or baby, or an arm, head, heart, or foot. The faithful pin them, along with a prayer, to the garments of their favorite saint, whom they hope will intercede to cure the ailment or fulfill the wish designated by the *milagro.*

PAPER AND PAPIER-MÂCHÉ

Papier-mâché has risen to nearly a fine art in Tonalá, Jalisco. Many Oaxaca handicrafts stores stock small flocks of Tonalá-made birds, cats, frogs, giraffes, and other animal figurines, meticulously crafted by building up repeated layers of glued paper. The results, which are sanded, brilliantly varnished, and polished, resemble fine sculptures rather than the humble newspaper from which they were fashioned.

Other paper goods you shouldn't overlook include **piñatas** (durable, inexpensive, and as Mexican as you can get), available in every town market; colorful, decorative **cutout banners** (string overhead at your home fiesta) from San Salvador Huixcolotla, Puebla; and *amate,* wild fig tree bark paintings in animal and flower motifs, from Xalitla and Ameyaltepec, Guerrero.

POTTERY AND CERAMICS

The Valley of Oaxaca is the focus of a vibrant pottery tradition. Many of the most celebrated examples come from the village of Atzompa, a few miles northwest of the city. Traditionally popular for their green-glazed clay pots, dishes, casseroles, and bowls, Atzompa potters have evolved a host of fresh styles, from graceful vases and plates blooming with painted lilies to red clay pots and bowls inscribed with artfully flowing blossoms.

San Bartolo Coyotepec village, south of the city, has acquired equal renown for its **black pottery** *(barro negro),* sold all over the world. Doña Rosa, now deceased, pioneered the crafting of big round pots without using a potter's wheel. Now made in many more shapes by Doña Rosa's descendants, the pottery's celebrated black hue is produced by the reduction (reduced air) method of firing, which removes oxygen from the clay's red (ferric) iron oxide, converting it to black (ferrous) iron oxide. Workers burnish the result to produce an exquisite, pearly sheen.

Although most latter-day Oaxacan potters are aware of the health dangers of **lead pigments,** some for-sale pottery may still contain lead. The hazard comes from low-fired pottery in which the lead has not been firmly melted into the glaze. Acids in foods such as lemons, vinegar, and tomatoes dissolve the lead pigments, which, when ingested over a period of time, can result in lead poisoning. In general, the hardest, glossiest, high-fired stoneware that has been twice fired is the safest for dinnerware.

WOOLEN WOVEN GOODS

Mexico's finest wool weavings come from Teotitlán del Valle and the neighboring town of Santa Ana del Valle, less than an hour's drive east of Oaxaca City. Although they learned to work wool from the Spanish, the weaving tradition, continued by Zapotec-speaking families, dates back at least a thousand years before the conquest. Many families still carry on the arduous process, making everything from scratch. They gather the dyes from wild plants and the bodies of insects and sea snails. They hand-wash, card, spin, and dye the wool and even travel to remote mountain springs to gather water. The result, they say, is *vale la pena* (worth the pain): intensely colored, tightly woven carpets, rugs, and wall hangings that retain their brilliance for generations.

Although many handicrafts shops and a host of stalls in all the Oaxaca City markets sell the Teotitlán del Valle and Santa Ana del Valle weavings, a trip to Teotitlán del Valle (where Santa Ana del Valle weavers send most of their products for sale) is a must for Valley of Oaxaca first-time visitors.

Essentials

NSPORTE PRIVADO
AUTOMÓVIL

OAXACA
DE CARA A LA NACIÓN

TKP-1712

TKP-17-1

BICENTENARIO DE LA INDEPENDENCIA DE MÉXICO   2010   CENTENARIO DE LA REVOLUCIÓN MEXICANA

OAXACA

Transportation

GETTING THERE

Air

FROM THE UNITED STATES AND CANADA

The majority of foreign visitors reach Oaxaca by air, through the Mexico gateways of **Atlanta, Chicago, Dallas, Denver, Houston, Los Angeles, Miami, New York, Orlando, Phoenix, San Antonio, San Francisco, Tijuana, and Toronto.** Nearly all flights involve a plane change at the sprawling, super-busy Mexico City Airport, where connections are available, with Oaxaca destinations of either Oaxaca City, or Huatulco and Puerto Escondido, on the Oaxaca Pacific coast. For Oaxaca City, go by either **Aeromexico Airlines** (U.S. and Canada toll-free tel. 800/021-4000, www.aeromexico.com), **Volaris Airlines** (U.S. toll-free tel. 866/988-3527, answers in Spanish, wait to select English option, www.volaris.com.mx), or **Interjet Airlines** (U.S. toll-free tel. 866/285-9525, interjet.com.mx). If flying to Huatulco, go by either **Magnicharters** (www.magnicharters.com), Aeromexico, Interjet, or **Aeromar Airlines** (www.aeromar.com.mx); and, to Puerto Escondido go also via Aeromar.

Fortunately, **two air carriers provide direct Oaxaca connections** that bypass Mexico City completely. **Continental Airlines** (www.continental.com) offers two separate nonstop connections from Houston to Oaxaca City; and Aeromexico connects nonstop with Oaxaca City directly from Tijuana, just across the border from San Diego. The Tijuana connection from San Diego airport is straightforward: Take airport express bus 922 (or taxi) to the San Diego trolley terminal, where you board the blue line

trolley to Tijuana, walk across the border, and then taxi to the Tijuana airport.

Although only a few scheduled flights go directly to Mexico City from the northern United States and Canada, **charters** do, especially during the winter. In locales such as Boston, Buffalo, Calgary-Edmonton, Cleveland, Detroit, Minneapolis, Montreal, Ottawa, Seattle, Toronto, Vancouver, and Winnipeg consult a travel agent or website for charter flight options. Be aware that charter reservations, which often require fixed departure and return dates and provide minimal cancellation refunds, decrease your flexibility.

Air travelers can save money by shopping around, through websites such as www.cheaptickets.com and www.priceline.com, and through the airlines, both by telephone and the Internet. Don't be bashful about trying for the best price. Make it clear that you're interested in a bargain. Ask the right questions. Are there special incentive, advance-payment, night, midweek, tour-package, or charter fares? Peruse the ads in your Sunday newspaper travel section for bargain-oriented websites and travel agencies.

FROM EUROPE, LATIN AMERICA, AUSTRALASIA, AND ASIA

Some airlines fly across the Atlantic directly to Mexico City. These include **Lufthansa,** which connects directly from Frankfurt, and **Aeroméxico,** from Paris and Madrid.

From Latin America, **Aeroméxico** connects directly with Mexico City, from São Paulo, Brazil; Santiago, Chile; Lima, Peru; Buenos Aires, Argentina; and San José, Costa Rica. A number of other Latin American flag carriers also fly directly to Mexico City.

A few flights cross the Pacific directly

Airlines Serving Oaxaca

At this writing, two of the following scheduled airlines (Continental and Aeromexico) do connect directly (with no plane change) with Oaxaca City (OAX). The rest connect directly with Mexico City (MX), where connecting flights continue on to the Oaxaca destinations of Oaxaca City, Huatulco-Puerto Ángel, and Puerto Escondido. The following airlines are listed alphabetically, with their departure points in geographic order from west to east and south to north.

Airline	Origin	Destinations
Aeroméxico	Los Angeles	MX
tel. 800/237-6639	Ontario (California)	MX
www.aeromexico.com	San Diego	MX
	Seattle	MX
	Tijuana	MX
	Phoenix	MX
	San Antonio	MX
	Houston	MX
	New York	MX
	Atlanta	MX
	Orlando	MX
	Miami	MX
Air Canada	Toronto	MX
tel. 888/247-2262		
www.aircanada.com		
American	Dallas	MX
tel. 800/433-7300	Miami	MX
www.aa.com		
Continental	Houston	MX OAX HUA
tel. 800/231-0856	Newark	MX
www.continental.com		
Delta	Los Angeles	MX
tel. 800/221-1212	Dallas	MX
www.delta.com	Atlanta	MX
	New York	MX
U.S. Airways	Phoenix	MX
tel. 800/428-4322		
www.usairways.com		
Volaris	Tijuana	MX OAX
tel. 866/988-3527		
www.volaris.com.mx		

to Mexico, notably **Japan Airlines,** which connects Osaka-Tokyo to Mexico City, via Vancouver. More commonly, travelers from Australasia routinely transfer at Los Angeles, Phoenix, or San Francisco for connections to Mexico City, thence Oaxaca.

Bus

As air travel rules in the United States, bus travel rules in Mexico. Hundreds of sleek luxury- and first-class bus lines with romantic names such as Elite, Estrella de Oro (Star of Gold), and Estrella Blanca (White Star) roar out daily from the border, headed south.

Since U.S. bus lines ordinarily terminate just north of the Mexican border, you must usually disembark, collect your things, and, after having filled out the necessary but very simple paperwork at the immigration office, proceed on foot across the border to Mexico, where you can bargain with a local taxi driver to drive you the few miles ($2-4) to the *camionera central* (central bus station). (*Note:* Mexican border authorities require a valid passport to enter Mexico; United States authorities require a valid passport to return to the United States.)

Finally, after taking a taxi to the bus station, handy words to have in mind are *taquilla* (ticket booth), *guardaequipajes* (baggage checkroom), *llegada* (arrival), *salida* (departure), and *sanitario* or *baño* (toilet or bathroom).

First- and luxury-class bus service in Mexico is generally cheaper and better than in the United States. Tickets for comparable trips in Mexico cost less than half (as little as $100 for a 1,600-km/1,000-mi trip), compared to perhaps $200 in the United States.

In Mexico, as on U.S. buses, you often have to take it as you find it. *Asientos reservados* (reserved seats), *boletos* (tickets), and information must generally be obtained in person at the bus station, and credit cards are sometimes not accepted. Reserved bus tickets are typically nonrefundable; so don't miss the bus. On the other hand, plenty of buses roll south almost continuously. Two basic routes

are available, either through Mexico City or down the Pacific coast all the way.

PACIFIC COAST ROUTE

The route to Oaxaca along the Pacific shore, although the longest, requiring one or two transfers and at least three full 24-hour days, is the most scenic. Try to go luxury or first class all the way; the small additional cost is well worth it. Cross the border at **Tijuana, Mexicali,** or **Nogales,** where you can choose from at least three bus lines (the Estrella Blanca Group buses are best, with luxury-class **Futura** and first-class **Elite** buses) along the Pacific coast route, via combined National Highways 15 and 200, via Mazatlán, Puerto Vallarta, Zihuatanejo, Acapulco, and, finally, Puerto Escondido, in Oaxaca. At the border, get a bus as far south as you can, most likely **Elite** all the way to Acapulco; or if not, at least to Tepic or Puerto Vallarta, where you change to a bus headed south for, most likely, Lázaro Cárdenas, Zihuatanejo, or Acapulco, at the end of your second day. There, you catch a third bus, which will take you at least to Acapulco, and at most to Puerto Escondido by the end of your third day.

On the other hand, make it easy on yourself and stretch the trip to five days by resting

first-class bus

overnight in Puerto Vallarta and Zihuatanejo along the way. In Puerto Vallarta, stay on the beach at either **Hotel Rosita** (tel. 322/223-1033, tel./fax 322/223-2000, U.S. toll-free tel. 877/813-6712, www.hotelrosita.com, $50) or **Casa Corazon** (tel./fax 322/222-6364, U.S.-Canada toll-free tel. 866/648-6893, www.casacorazonvallarta.com, $40-50 d). In Zihuatanejo, stay on the beach at **Hotel Irma** (tel./fax 755/554-8003 or 755/554-8472, www.hotelirma.com.mx, $60-100 d) or budget **Posada Citlali** (tel./fax 755/554-2043, hotel-reserv@prodigy.net.mx, $35 d), a block from the beach.

MEXICO CITY ROUTE

This is the quickest bus route to Oaxaca, typically about 36 hours from the south Texas border, a day longer from California or Nogales, Arizona, via Guadalajara. From the western United States, cross the border at Tijuana, Mexicali, or Nogales (ride an Estrella Blanca bus, such as **Elite** or **Futura**). From the United States Midwest, Southeast, and East, cross the border at Laredo to Nuevo Laredo (ride an **Omnibus de Mexico** bus) or McAllen to Reynosa (ride either **Omnibus de Mexico** or **Grupo Senda** bus). For the most speed and comfort, at only a small extra cost, go by luxury-class bus to Mexico City.

Mexico City has four bus terminals: north, east, south, and west (respectively, Terminal Norte, Terminal Tapo, Terminal Sur, and Terminal Poniente). You will most likely arrive in the Terminal Norte, although a few buses from the west via Guadalajara might arrive at Terminal Poniente. For an overnight rest break, Guadalajara is especially handy. Stay at basic but clean and moderately-priced **Hotel La Serena** (tel. 33/3600-0910, fax 33/3600-1974, reservas@aranzazu.com.mx, $38 d), with pool and restaurant, conveniently adjacent to the bus station.

In any case, at Mexico City, if you're heading to Oaxaca City, from Terminal Norte, board an **Autobuses del Oriente (ADO)** or **Cristóbal Colón** bus, via the Puebla expressway (*autopista* or *corta*) to Oaxaca City.

If you're heading for the Oaxaca Pacific coast, best board an **Estrella Blanca** affiliate (such as **Turistar** or **Futura**) or an **Estrella de Oro** bus bound for Acapulco, where you can transfer to a Puerto Escondido-bound bus.

If somehow the above connections are not available at Terminal Norte (or Terminal Poniente), share a taxi (don't try it by public transit) to Terminal Sur (or Terminal Tapo for Oaxaca City via ADO) and catch an Estrella Blanca subsidiary (such as Elite, Turistar, Futura, Flecha Roja, or Transportes Cuauhtémoc) all the way to Puerto Escondido via Acapulco. If you miss the direct Puerto Escondido connection, settle for an express connection to Acapulco, where plenty of local departures head out southeast for Puerto Escondido.

Get across town to your continuing bus terminal via *taxi especial* (private taxi) or *colectivo* (collective taxi). Although such a trip is possible by public transportation, don't try it. If you do, you're either a Mexico City veteran traveling light and know what you're getting into or are willing to bear a load of frustration, pain, and the dirty looks from fellow passengers as you unwittingly poke them with your bulging backpacks and luggage in a crowded subway or local bus.

Car or RV

If you're adventurous and like going to out-of-the-way places, but still want to have all the comforts of home, you may enjoy driving your car or RV to Oaxaca. On the other hand, considerations of cost, risk, wear on both you and your vehicle, and the congestion hassles in towns may change your mind.

MEXICAN CAR INSURANCE

Mexico does not recognize foreign insurance. When you drive into Mexico, Mexican auto insurance is at least as important as your passport. At the busier crossings, you can get it at insurance "drive-ins" just north of the border. The many Mexican auto insurance companies are government-regulated; their numbers keep prices and services competitive.

Mexico City Driving Restrictions

To reduce smog and traffic gridlock, authorities have limited which cars can drive on which days in Mexico City, depending upon the last digit of their license plates. If you violate these rules, you risk getting an expensive ticket. On Monday, no vehicle may be driven with final digits 5 or 6; Tuesday, 7 or 8; Wednesday, 3 or 4; Thursday, 1 or 2; Friday, 9 or 0. On weekends all vehicles may be driven.

Sanborn's Mexico Insurance (Sanborn's Mexico, P.O. Box 310, McAllen, TX 78502, toll-free tel. 800/222-0158, tel. 956/686-3601, www.sanbornsinsurance.com), one of the best-known agencies, certainly seems to be trying the hardest. It offers a number of books and services, including the *Recreational Guide to Mexico,* a good road map, "smile-by-mile" *Travelog* guide to "every highway in Mexico," hotel discounts, and more. Much of this is available to members of Sanborn's Sombrero Club.

Alternatively, look into **Vagabundos del Mar** (tel. 800/474-2252, local tel. 707/374-5511, www.vagabundos.com), an RV-oriented Mexico travel club offering memberships that include a newsletter, caravaning opportunites, discounts, insurance, and much more.

Mexican car insurance runs from a bare-bones rate of about $8 a day for minimal $10,000/$50,000 (property damage/medical payments) coverage to a more typical $14 a day for more complete $20,000/$100,000 coverage. On the same scale, insurance for a $50,000 RV and equipment runs about $30 a day. These daily rates decrease sharply for six-month or one-year policies, which run from about $200 for the minimum to $400-1,600 for complete, high-end (SUV, trailer, boat) coverage.

If you get broken glass, personal effects, and legal expenses coverage with these rates, you're lucky. Mexican policies often don't cover them.

You should get something for your money, however. The deductibles should be no more than $300-500, the public liability per occurrence/medical payments per person/per occurrence should be about double the ($25,000/$25,000/$50,000) legal minimum, and you should be able to get your car fixed in the United States and receive payment in U.S. dollars for losses. If not, shop around.

A SINALOA NOTE OF CAUTION

Although bandidos seldom menace Mexican roads (but loose burros, horses, and cattle often do), be cautious in the infamous marijuana-and-opium-growing region of Sinaloa state, north of Mazatlán. It's best not to stray from Highway 15 (or the 15D toll expressway) between Culiacán and Mazatlán or from Highway 40 between Mazatlán and Durango. Curious tourists have been assaulted in the hinterlands adjacent to these roads.

THE GREEN ANGELS

The Green Angels have answered many motoring tourists' prayers in Mexico. Bilingual teams of two, trained in auto repair and first aid, help distressed tourists along main highways. They patrol fixed stretches of road at least twice daily by truck. To make sure that they stop to help, pull completely off the highway and raise your hood. You may want to hail a passing motorist or trucker with a Mexican cell phone to call the **Mexico Tourism-Green Angels hotline** (tel. 800/903-9200, or all-purpose emergency direct tel. 078) for you.

If, for some reason, you have to leave your vehicle on the roadside, don't leave it unattended. Hire a local teenager or adult to watch it for you. Unattended vehicles on Mexican highways are quickly stricken by a mysterious disease, the symptoms of which are rapid loss of vital parts.

MEXICAN GASOLINE

Pemex, short for Petróleos Mexicanos, the government oil monopoly, markets diesel fuel and two grades of unleaded gasoline:

ESSENTIALS TRANSPORTATION

Driving Distances

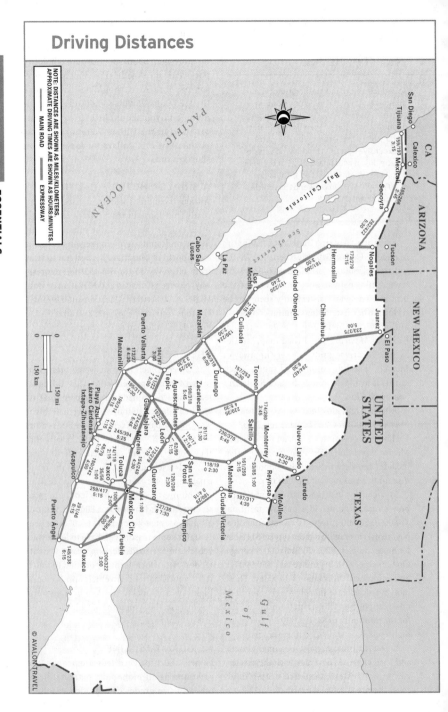

NOTE: DISTANCES ARE SHOWN AS MILES/KILOMETERS.
APPROXIMATE DRIVING TIMES ARE SHOWN AS HOURS:MINUTES.
——— MAIN ROAD ——— EXPRESSWAY

© AVALON TRAVEL

Road Safety

Hundreds of thousands of visitors enjoy safe Mexican auto vacations every year. Their success is due in large part to their frame of mind: Drive defensively, anticipate and adjust to danger before it happens, and watch everything: side roads, shoulders, the car in front, and cars far down the road. The following tips will help ensure a safe and enjoyable trip.

- **Don't drive at night.** Range animals, unmarked sand piles, pedestrians, one-lane bridges, cars without lights, and drunk drivers are doubly hazardous at night.

- Although **speed limits** are rarely enforced, *don't break them.* Mexican roads are often narrow and shoulderless. Poor markings and macho drivers who pass on curves are best faced at a speed of 64 kph (40 mph) rather than 120 kph (75 mph).

- **Drive on sand only sparingly.** Even with four-wheel-drive, you'll eventually get stuck if you drive either often or casually on beaches. When the tide comes in, who'll pull your car out?

- Watch with an eagle eye and **slow down** at the *topes* (speed bumps) at the edges of towns and for *vados* (dips), which can be dangerously bumpy and full of water.

- Extending the **courtesy of the road** goes hand-in-hand with safe driving. Both courtesy and machismo are more infectious in Mexico; on the highway, it's much safer to spread the former than the latter.

92-octane *premio* (PRAY-mee-oh) and 87-octane Magna (MAHG-nah). Magna is good gas, yielding performance similar to that of U.S.-style regular unleaded gasoline. It runs about $3.64 per gallon at this writing. Higher octane premium gas (*rojo* at the station) runs about $3.82. On main highways, Pemex makes sure that major stations (typically spaced about 30 miles apart in the countryside) stock Magna.

GAS STATION THIEVERY

Although the problem has abated considerably in recent years (by the hiring of young female attendants), boys who hang around gas stations to wash windows are notoriously light-fingered. When stopping at the *gasolinera,* make sure that your cameras, purses, and other moveable items are out of reach. Also, make sure that your car has a lockable gas cap. If not, insist on pumping the gas yourself, or be super-watchful as you pull up to the gas pump to make certain that the pump reads zero before the attendant pumps the gas. Some of these guys and gals like to start the pump at 100 or 200 pesos, and pocket the difference.

A HEALTHY CAR

Preventive measures spell good health for both you and your car. Get that tune-up (or that long-delayed overhaul) *before,* rather than after, you leave.

Carry a stock of spare parts, which will be more difficult to get and more expensive in Mexico than at home. Carry an extra tire or two, a few quart bottles of motor oil, oil and gas filters, fan belts, spark plugs, tune-up kit, ignition points, and fuses. Be prepared with basic tools and supplies, such as screwdrivers, pliers including Vice-Grip, lug wrench, jack, adjustable wrenches, tire pump, tire pressure gauge, steel wire, and electrical tape. For breakdowns and emergencies, carry a folding shovel, a husky rope or chain, a gasoline can, and flares or red highway markers.

BRIBES (MORDIDAS)

The usual meeting ground of the visitor and Mexican police is in the visitor's car on a highway or downtown street. To the tourists, such an encounter may seem mild harassment by the police, accompanied by vague threats of going to the police station or impounding the car for such-and-such a violation. The tourist often goes on to say, "It was all right, though... we paid him $20 and he went away...Mexican cops sure are crooked, aren't they?"

And, I suppose, if people want to go bribing their way through Mexico, that's their business. But calling Mexican cops crooked isn't exactly fair. Police, like most everyone else in Mexico, have to scratch for a living, and they have found that many tourists are willing to slip them a $20 bill for nothing. Rather than crooked, I would call them hungry and opportunistic.

Instead of paying a bribe, do what I've done a dozen times: Remain cool, and if you're really guilty of an infraction, calmly say, "Ticket, please." *("Boleto, por favor.")* After a minute or two of stalling, and no cash appearing, the officer most likely will not bother with a ticket, but will wave you on with only a warning. If, on the other hand, the officer does write you a ticket, he will probably keep your driver's license, which you will be able to retrieve at the *presidencia municipal* (city hall) the next day in exchange for paying your fine. Obviously your decision about paying the bribe will be influenced by your travel schedule as well as the hassle or lack thereof of finding the city hall, paying the ticket, and getting your license back.

CROSSING THE BORDER

Squeezing through the border traffic bottlenecks during peak holidays and rush hours can easily take two or three hours. Avoid crossing 7am-9am and 4:30pm-6:30pm. Moreover, with latter-day increased U.S. homeland security precautions, the return, northbound border crossing, under the best of conditions, generally takes at least an hour waiting in your car, along with a hundred or more other frustrated drivers. (*Note:* Mexican officials require a **valid passport** upon entry into Mexico for everyone in your party except babes in arms. A valid passport is likewise required by U.S. officials upon your return to the United States.)

HIGHWAY ROUTES FROM THE UNITED STATES

If you've decided to drive to Oaxaca, you have your choice of four general routes. At safe highway speeds, from the Mexican border these routes require as many as five days or as few as two days, depending on your route.

The longest but most scenic route is the **Pacific route,** which starts out as Mexican National Highway 15 from the border at Nogales, Sonora, an hour's drive south of Tucson, Arizona. Soon you join Highway 15D *cuota autopista* (toll expressway)—or continue along old *libre* (free) Highway 15— proceeding southward smoothly, over cactus-studded plains mountains that give way to irrigated farms and groves and palmy tropical coastal plain by the time you arrive in Mazatlán. Follow the *periféricos* (peripheral bypasses) that conduct traffic past the congested downtowns of Hermosillo, Guaymas, Culiacán, and Mazatlán. Between these centers, you can speed along via the *cuota* Highway 15D expressway virtually the entire way. If you prefer not to pay the high tolls (around $60 total for a passenger car, much more for multiple-wheeled RVs) you should stick to the old *libre* Highway 15. Hazards, bumps, and slow going might force you to reconsider, however. The cuota bypasses all the major cities these days, so you need not even see, much less drive through, some of the larger, more congested cities.

At **Tepic,** the Pacific route leaves Highway 15-15D and continues south via Highway 200, winding past tobacco farms and mango orchards, through lush forest, climbing vine-hung canyons, crossing a score of rivers, past a host of palm-tufted beaches, and passing the renowned vacation lands of **Puerto Vallarta, Manzanillo, Ixtapa-Zihuatanejo,** and **Acapulco.** Finally, several days after you crossed the border, you arrive at the heart of the tropical Oaxaca coast at Puerto Escondido or Puerto Ángel.

A speedier variation on the Pacific route is the **Pacific-Mexico City route,** which starts out as the Pacific route but departs from the

Highway Routes from the U.S. Border to Oaxaca

Route	Via	Miles/Km	Hours at the Wheel	Travel Days
Pacific	Nogales-Mazatlán Puerto Vallarta Acapulco-Puerto Ángel	1,911/3,075	46	5
Pacific-Mexico City	Nogales-Mazatlán Guadalajara-Mexico City Puebla-Oaxaca City	1,749/2,814	34	3
Central	Ciudad Juárez-Chihuahua Torreón-Zacatecas Querétaro-Mexico City Puebla-Oaxaca City	1,370/2,204	29	3
Eastern	Reynosa-Ciudad Victoria Tampico-Pachuca-Mexico City Puebla-Oaxaca City	967/1,556	22	2

Pacific coast, eastward, at Tepic, continuing along Highway 15 or 15D past Guadalajara, via Toluca to Mexico City.

Across town, at the Los Reyes southeast-side suburb, pick up the Puebla-Veracruz expressway Highway 150D, where you continue about an hour past Puebla to a fork. Follow the south fork expressway, via Tehuacán and Nochixtlán, to Oaxaca City. This nearly all-expressway route minimizes the road time from the western U.S. border to three very long, or, to be safe, four days to Oaxaca. Note: Be sure to arrive in Mexico City on a day of the week when driving restrictions (determined by the last digit of your license plate) do not apply to your car.

If, however, you're driving to Oaxaca from the central United States, go via the **central route,** crossing the border at El Paso to Ciudad Juárez, Chihuahua. There, National Highway 45, preferably via the *cuota* multi-lane expressway (or, if not, the old *libre* two-lane highway), leads you southward past high, dry plains and the cities of Chihuahua and Jiménez (use *periféricos* to bypass downtowns). Continue via Highway 49 southwest,

through Gómez Palacio and the silver colonial cities of Zacatecas to San Luis Potosí, where you connect with Highway 57 expressway, via Querétaro, to the northern outskirts of Mexico City.

At that point, best use the east-bound *periférico* expressway via Carpio and Tezcoco instead of trying to fight your way through downtown Mexico City. At Los Reyes on the southeast side of town, pick up Highway 150D, the expressway east to Puebla, where you continue southeast via the toll expressway to Oaxaca. To be safe, allow three daytime-only driving days for this route.

Folks heading to Oaxaca from the eastern and southeastern United States probably save the most time by crossing the border from McAllen, Texas, to Reynosa and taking the **eastern route** to Oaxaca. Continue south, via Highway 97 then Highway 101, to Ciudad Victoria, bypassing the downtown by the *periférico*. Then connect with Highway 80 to Tampico. There, again bypass the downtown and pick up Highway 105 south headed for Tempoal de Sánchez. After a long, winding, mountain climb via Huejutla de Reyes, you reach Pachuca and continue southward via expressway Highway 85 to Mexico City. At Carpio in the northern suburb, take the east bypass expressway, via Tepexpan and Tezcoco, continuing to east-bound expressway 150D for Puebla. There, you continue southeast to Oaxaca City. If you start off at dawn each morning, you could probably get to Oaxaca safely in two driving days, under optimal conditions. It's best to do it in three leisurely days, including two overnights.

GETTING AROUND
Air

Travelers on tight time budgets find it useful to save a half or full day by flying, instead of driving or busing, over the Sierra between Oaxaca City and the Pacific resorts of Puerto Ángel, Bahías de Huatulco, and Puerto Escondido.

A pair of light charter airlines (found in the general aviation terminal, the building to the right as you face the main terminal) connect Oaxaca City with Huatulco and Puerto Escondido on the Pacific coast. Contact **Aerotucan** (in Oaxaca City, Calle Emilio Carranza 303, corner of Eucaliptos, tel. 951/502-0840, toll-free outside Oaxaca City tel. 800/640-4148, www.aerotucan.com.

mx) or **Aerovega** (in Oaxaca City, Alameda de León No. 1, Centro, tel. 951/516-4982).

Bus

The bus is the king of the Oaxaca road. A host of lines connect virtually every town and most villages in Oaxaca. Three distinct levels of service—luxury or super-first class, first class, and second class—are generally available. **Luxury-class** (usually called something like Primera Plus or Ejecutivo, depending upon the line): super-deluxe express coaches speed between major towns, seldom stopping en route. In exchange for somewhat higher fares (about $70 Oaxaca City-Puerto Escondido, for example, compared with $50 for first class), luxury-class passengers enjoy rapid passage and airline-style amenities: plush reclining seats, air-conditioning, on-board toilet, video, and aisle attendant.

Although less luxurious, **first-class** service costs less, is frequent, and always includes reserved seating. Additionally, passengers usually enjoy soft reclining seats and air-conditioning (if it's working). Besides making regular stops at or near most towns and villages en route, first-class bus drivers, if requested, will usually stop and let you off anywhere along the road.

art outside the airport, Huatulco

Second-class bus seating is unreserved. In outlying parts of Oaxaca, there is a class of buses even beneath second class, but given the condition of many second-class buses, it usually seems as if third-class buses wouldn't run at all. Such buses are the stuff of travelers' legends: the recycled old GMC, Ford, and Dodge school buses that stop everywhere and carry everyone and everything to the smallest villages tucked away in the far mountains. As long as there is any kind of a road to it, such a bus will most likely go there.

TICKETS, SEATING, AND BAGGAGE

Online and telephone ticketing has arrived in Oaxaca. The up-and-coming agency **Boletotal** (formerly Ticket Bus, toll-free tel. 800/702-8000, or 800/009-9090, Oaxaca City tel. 951/514-6655, www.boletotal.com. mx), with offices in Oaxaca City, sells tickets for long-distance routes all over the state of Oaxaca, reaching as far west as Acapulco and Mexico City, north to Veracruz, and east to Mérida, Cancún, and the Guatemala border. Participating bus lines are ADO (Autobuses del Oriente) and its affiliates OCC (Omnibus Cristóbal Colón), AU (Autobuses Unidos), Sur, and Cuenca. Otherwise, other first-class (notably Estrella Blanca along the Pacific

coast) and second-class bus lines don't issue tickets online in Oaxaca.

Nevertheless, plenty of buses usually leave daily, so the easiest way to go is to get to the bus station early enough on your traveling day to ensure that you'll get a bus to your destination. You can make this almost foolproof by calling (or asking your desk clerk to call) the bus station ahead for departure information.

At the station, you'll find that although some first-class bus lines accept credit cards and issue computer-printed tickets at their major stations, many reserved bus tickets are sold for cash and handwritten, with a specific *número de asiento* (seat number) on the back. If you miss the bus, you lose your money. Furthermore, airlines-style automated reservations systems have not yet arrived at the smaller Oaxacan bus stations. Consequently, you can generally buy reserved tickets only at the *salida local* (local departure) station. (An agent in Tehuántepec, for example, cannot ordinarily reserve you a ticket on a bus that originates in Oaxaca City, a day's travel down the road.)

Request a reserved seat number, if possible, from numbers 1–25 in the *delante* (front) to *medio* (middle) of the bus. The rear seats are often occupied by smokers, drunks, and

The bus is Oaxaca's most popular form of public transportation.

Driving Distances Within Oaxaca

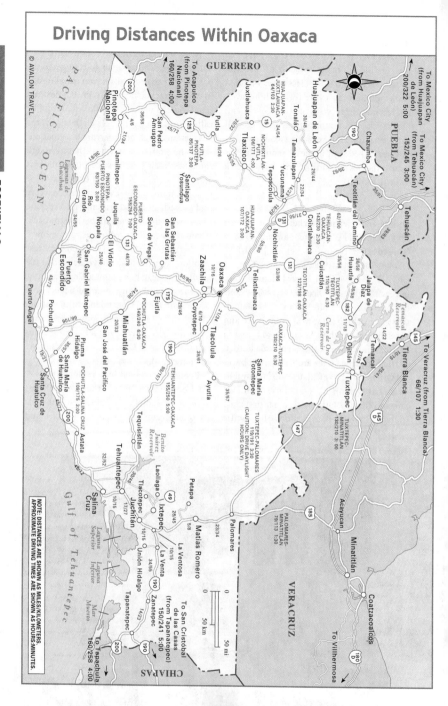

© AVALON TRAVEL

NOTE: DISTANCES ARE SHOWN AS MILES/KILOMETERS.
APPROXIMATE DRIVING TIMES ARE SHOWN AS HOURS:MINUTES.

general rowdies. At night, you will sleep better on the *lado derecho* (right side) away from the glare of oncoming traffic lights.

Baggage is generally secure on Oaxaca buses. Label it, however. Overhead racks are often too cramped to accommodate airline-size carry-ons. Carry a small bag of your crucial items on your person; pack clothes and less essential items in your checked luggage. For peace of mind, watch the handler put your checked baggage on the bus and watch to make sure it is not mistakenly taken off the bus at intermediate stops.

If, somehow, your baggage gets misplaced, remain calm. Bus employees are generally competent and conscientious; if you are patient, recovering your luggage will become a matter of honor for many of them. Baggage handlers are at the bottom of the pay scale; a tip for their mostly thankless job would be very much appreciated.

On long trips, carry food, drinks, and toilet paper. Station food may be dubious and the sanitary facilities ill-maintained.

If you are waiting for a first-class bus at an intermediate *salida de paso* (passing station), you often have to trust to luck that there will be an empty seat. If not, your best option may be to ride a usually-much-more-frequent second-class bus.

Car

Getting around by car in Oaxaca has its pluses and minuses. On the minus side, cars are expensive to rent and roads are often narrow and usually shared with pedestrians, horses, cows, and burros. On the plus side, driving allows you to go where you want on your own schedule.

RENTAL CAR

Car and jeep rentals are an increasingly popular transportation option for Oaxaca travelers. They offer mobility and independence for local sightseeing and beach excursions. (However, street congestion makes for slow and frustrating driving in downtown Oaxaca City. It's best to get around via taxi, $2-3, for anywhere in downtown.) Agents stationed regularly at both the Oaxaca City airport and downtown are Economy, Alamo, and Europcar; in Puerto Escondido, Budget; and in Huatulco, Thrifty, Europcar, and Dollar. Rental car agents also do business in Salina Cruz and Juchitán in the Isthmus, Tuxtepec in Northern Oaxaca, and Huajuapan de León in the Mixteca.

During the winter high season, especially, make reservations in the United States and Canada prior to departure.

Rental agencies generally require drivers to have a valid driver's license, passport, a major credit card, and may require a minimum age of 25.

Oaxaca car rentals are not cheap. With a 15 percent or more "value added" tax tacked on and mandatory Mexican car insurance, they run more than in the United States. The cheapest possible rental car, usually a vintage, well-used, stick-shift VW Beetle, runs $30-50 per day or $200-400 per week, depending on location and season. Prices are steepest during Christmas-New Year's and pre-Easter weeks. Before departure, use the international agencies' (Thrifty, Hertz, Alamo, Budget, and Europcar) toll-free numbers to shop around for availability, prices, and reservations. During non-peak seasons, you may save lots of pesos by waiting till arrival and renting a car through a local agency. Shop around, starting with the agent in your hotel lobby or the local yellow pages (under "Automóviles, renta de").

Car insurance that covers property damage, public liability, and medical payments is an *absolute must* and is required by Mexican law. Although it is customarily included in the price of your rental car, make certain that you're covered before signing the deal. **Collision insurance** may not be included and costs extra. However, major credit cards do furnish coverage that supplements your personal car insurance. Double-check your coverage with both your auto insurance agent and your credit card company before leaving for Mexico.

If you get into an accident in Mexico

without insurance, you will be in deep trouble, possibly jail. Safe driving in Oaxaca requires more caution and less speed than back home.

TAXIS

The high prices of rental cars make taxis a viable option for local excursions. Cars are luxuries, not necessities, for most Oaxacan families. Travelers might profit from the local money-saving practice of piling everyone in a taxi for Sunday park, beach, and fishing outings. You may find that an all-day taxi and driver (who, besides relieving you of driving, will become your impromptu guide) will cost less than a rental car.

The magic word for saving money by taxi is *colectivo:* a taxi that you share jointly with other travelers. Your first place to practice getting a taxi will be at the airport, where *colectivo* tickets are routinely sold from booths at the terminal door.

If, however, you want your own private taxi, ask for a *taxi especial,* which will probably run about three or four times the individual tariff for a *colectivo.*

Your airport experience will prepare you for in-town taxis, which in Oaxaca do not have meters. **You must establish the taxi price before getting in.** Bargaining comes with the territory in Mexico, so don't shrink from it, even though it may seem a hassle. If you get into a taxi without an agreed-upon price, you are letting yourself in for a more serious, potentially nasty hassle later. If your driver's price is too high, he'll probably come to his senses as soon as you hail another taxi.

After a few days, getting taxis around town will be a cinch. You'll find you don't have to take the high-ticket taxis lined up in your hotel driveway. If the price isn't right, walk toward the street and hail a regular taxi.

In town, if you can't seem to find a taxi, it may be because they are all hanging around waiting for riders at the local stand, called a taxi *sitio.* Ask someone to direct you to it: Say *"Excúseme. ¿Donde está el sitio taxi, por favor?"* ("Excuse me. Where is the taxi stand, please?").

Tours and Guides

For many Oaxaca visitors, locally arranged tours offer a hassle-free alternative to rental car or taxi sightseeing. Hotels and travel agencies, many of whom maintain front-lobby travel and tour desks, offer a bounty of sightseeing, water sports, bay cruise, fishing, and wildlife-viewing tour opportunities.

Visas and Officialdom

PASSPORTS, TOURIST CARDS, AND VISAS
Your Passport

Your passport is your positive proof of national identity; without it, your status in any foreign country is in doubt. Don't leave home without one. In fact, Mexican border inspection officials require that everyone (except babes in arms) must have a valid passport to enter Mexico; U.S. immigration rules require that everyone, including **U.S. Citizens, must have a valid passport in order to re-enter the United States.** United States citizens may obtain passports (allow 4-6 weeks) at local post offices. For a fee, private passport agencies can speed this process and get you a passport within a week, maybe less.

Entry into Mexico

For U.S. and Canadian citizens, entry by air into Mexico for a few weeks could hardly be easier. At the check-in desk agents immediately inspect your passport. During the flight, airline attendants hand out tourist cards *(tarjetas turísticas)* en route and officers make them official by glancing at passports and stamping the cards at the immigration gate. Business travel permits for 30 days or fewer are handled by the same simple procedures.

Canadian residents must similarly show a valid passport upon entry to Mexico. Nationals of other countries (especially those such as Hong Kong, which issue more than one type of passport) may be subject to different or additional regulations. For advice, consult your regional **Mexico Tourism Board Office** (U.S./Can. tel. 800/446-3942, www. visitmexico.com) or local Mexican consulate. Very complete and up-to-date Mexico visa and entry information for nationals of virtually all of the world's countries is available at the Toronto, Canada, **Consulate website** (www.consulmex.com, select "visa and consular services" on the left of the homepage).

More Options

For more complicated cases, get your tourist card early enough to allow you to consider the options. Tourist cards can be issued for multiple entries and a maximum validity of 180 days; photos are often required. If you don't request multiple entry or the maximum time, your card will probably be stamped single entry, valid for some shorter period. Request the maximum (180 days is the absolute maximum for a tourist card; long-term foreign residents routinely make semiannual "border runs" for new tourist cards).

Student and Business Visas

A visa is a notation stamped and signed on your passport showing the number of days and entries allowable for your trip. If you need to stay in Mexico more than 180 days, you may apply (sometimes by enduring considerable red tape) at the consulate nearest your home. However, an ordinary 180-day tourist card may be the easiest student or business visa option, if you can manage it.

Entry for Children

Mexican rules for traveling children are very specific: Children under 18 traveling in Mexico must have their own tourist cards and be accompanied either by their parents or by adults carrying an affidavit that gives permission (including relevant dates and locations), notarized by the children's parents. Parents can avoid such difficulties with red tape by getting a passport and a Mexican tourist card for each of their children.

Oaxaca travelers should hurdle all such possible delays far ahead of time in the cool calm of their local Mexican consulate rather than the hot, hurried atmosphere of a border or airport immigration station.

Entry for Pets

A pile of red tape may delay the entry of dogs, cats, and other pets into Mexico. Be prepared with veterinary-stamped health and rabies certificates for each animal. For more information, contact your regional Mexico Tourism Board or your local Mexican Consulate.

Don't Lose Your Tourist Card

If you do, be prepared with a copy of the original, which you should present to the nearest federal Migración (Immigration) office (on duty at Oaxaca City, Puerto Escondido, and Huatulco airports) and ask for a duplicate tourist permit. Lacking this, you might present some alternate proof of your date of arrival in Mexico, such as a stamped passport or airline ticket. Savvy travelers carry copies of their tourist cards while leaving the original safe in their hotel rooms.

Car Permits

If you drive to Mexico, you will need a permit for your car. Upon entry into Mexico, be ready with originals and copies of your proof-of-ownership or registration papers (state title certificate, registration, or notarized bill of sale), current license plates, and current driver's license. The auto permit fee runs about $30, payable only by non-Mexican bank MasterCard, Visa, or American Express credit cards. (The credit-card-only requirement discourages those who sell or abandon U.S.-registered cars in Mexico without paying

Mexico Tourism Board Offices

More than a dozen Mexico Tourism Board (Consejo de Promoción Turístico de Mexico, CPTM) offices and scores of Mexican government consulates operate in the United States, Canada, Europe, South America, and Asia. Consulates generally handle questions of Mexican nationals abroad, while Mexico Tourism Boards serve travelers heading for Mexico.

For straightforward questions and Mexico regional information brochures, contact the Tourism Board (U.S./Can. tel. 800/446-3942, www.visitmexico.com). If you need more details and read a bit of Spanish, you might find visiting www.cptm.com.mx helpful also. Otherwise, contact one of the North American, European, South American, or Asian Mexico Tourism Boards directly for guidance.

IN NORTH AMERICA

From Alaska, Arizona, California, Colorado, Hawaii, Idaho, Montana, Nevada, Utah, Washington, and Wyoming, contact the Los Angeles office (2401 W. Sixth St., 4th Fl., Los Angeles, CA 90057, tel. 213/739-6336, fax 213/739-6340, losangeles@visitmexico.com).

From British Columbia, Alberta, Saskatchewan, and the Yukon and Northwest Territories, contact the Vancouver office (999 W. Hastings St., Suite 1110, Vancouver, BC, V6C 2W2, tel. 604/669-2845, fax 604/669-3498, mgarcia@visitmexico.com).

From Arkansas, Colorado, Louisiana, New Mexico, Oklahoma, and Texas, contact the Houston office (4507 San Jacinto, Suite 308, Houston, TX 77004, tel. 713/772-2581, fax 713/772-6058, houston@visitmexico.com).

From Alabama, Florida, Georgia, Mississippi, Tennessee, North Carolina, Puerto Rico, and South Carolina, contact the Miami office (5975 Sunset Dr. #305, Miami, FL 33143, tel. 786/621-2909, fax 786/621-2907, miami@visitmexico.com).

From Illinois, Indiana, Iowa, Kansas, Kentucky, Michigan, Minnesota, Missouri, Nebraska, North Dakota, Ohio, South Dakota, and Wisconsin, contact the Chicago office (225 North Michigan Ave., 18th Fl., Suite 1800, Chicago, IL 60601, tel. 312/228-0517, fax 312/228-0515, chicago@visitmexico.com).

From Connecticut, Delaware, Kentucky, Maine, Maryland, Massachusetts, New Hampshire, New Jersey, New York, Pennsylvania, Rhode Island, Vermont, Virginia, Washington D.C., and West Virginia, contact the New York office (400 Madison Ave., Suite 11C, New York, NY 10017, tel. 212/308-2110, fax 212/308-9060, mmora@visitmexico.com).

From Ontario, Manitoba, and the Nunavut Territory, contact the Toronto office (2 Bloor St.

customs duties.) Credit cards must bear the same name as the vehicle proof-of-ownership papers.

The resulting car permit becomes part of the owner's tourist card and receives the same length of validity. Vehicles registered in the name of an organization or person other than the driver must be accompanied by a notarized affidavit authorizing the driver to use the car in Mexico for a specific time.

Border officials generally allow you to carry or tow additional motorized vehicles (motorcycle, another car, large boat) into Mexico but will probably require separate documentation

and fee for each vehicle. If a Mexican official desires to inspect your trailer or motor home, go through it with him.

Accessories, such as a small trailer, boat shorter than six feet, CB radio, or outboard motor, may be noted on the car permit and must leave Mexico with the car.

For more details on motor vehicle entry and what you may bring in your baggage to Mexico, you might also consult the AAA (American Automobile Association) *Mexico TravelBook*. Since Mexico does not recognize foreign automobile insurance, you must buy Mexican automobile insurance.

West, Suite 1502, Toronto, Ontario M4W 3E2, tel. 416/925-0704, fax 416/925-6061, toronto@visit-mexico.com).

From New Brunswick, Newfoundland, Nova Scotia, Prince Edward Island, and Quebec, contact the Montreal office (1 Place Ville Marie, Suite 1931, Montreal, Quebec H3B2C3, tel. 514/871-1052 or 514/871-1103, fax 514/871-3825, montreal@visitmexico.com).

IN EUROPE

From England, Wales, Scotland, Ireland, Sweden, Estonia, Lithuania, and Latvia, contact the London office (Wakefield House, 41 Trinity Sq., London EC3N 4DJ, England, UK, tel. 207/488-9392, fax 207/265-0704, uk@visitmexico.com).

From Hungary, Poland, Slovenia, Slovakia, Germany, Austria, German Switzerland, and the Czech Republic, contact the Frankfurt office (Taunusanlage 21, D-60325 Frankfurt-am-Main, Deutschland, tel. 697/103-3383, fax 697/103-3755, germany@visitmexico.com).

From France, Belgium, Luxembourg, Monaco, Russia, and French Switzerland, contact the Paris office (4 Rue Notre-Dame des Victoires, 75002 Paris, France, tel. 1/428-69612 or 1/428-69613, fax 1/428-60580, france@visitmexico.com).

From Spain and Portugal contact the Madrid office (Carrera San Jeronimo 46, 28014 Madrid, España, tel. 91/561-3520 or 91/561-1827, fax 91/411-0759, spain@visitmexico.com).

From Italy, Turkey, Israel, Cyprus, and Malta, contact the Rome office (Via Barbarini 3-piso 7, 00187 Roma, Italia, tel. 06/487-4698, fax 06/487-3630 or 06/420-4293, italy@visitmexico.com).

IN SOUTH AMERICA

From Brazil, contact the São Paulo office (Alameda Administrativo, Rocha Azevedo 882, Conjunto 31, Tercer Andador, São Paulo, Brazil, 01410-002, tel. 3088-2129 or 3082-3981, fax 3083-5005, brasil@visitmexico.com).

From Argentina, contact the Buenos Aires office (Av. Reconquista 1056, piso 11, 1003 Barrio Retiro CABA, Buenos Aires, Argentina, tel. 1/4139-6670, fax 1/4139-6771, argentina@visitmexico.com).

IN ASIA

From Japan, Korea, India, Indonesia, Malaysia, Singapore, Thailand, Taiwan, and Vietnam, contact the Tokyo office (2-15-1-3F, Nagata-Cho, 2-chome, Chiyoda-ku, Tokyo, Japan 100-0014, tel. 335/030-290, fax 335/030-643, japan@visitmexico.com and pnajar@visitmexico.com).

Crossing the Border and Returning Home

Squeezing through border bottlenecks during peak holidays and rush hours can be time-consuming. Avoid crossing 7am-9am and 4:30pm-6:30pm.

Just before returning across the border with your car, park and have a customs (aduana) official remove and cancel the holographic identity sticker that you received on entry. If possible, get a receipt (recibo) or some kind of verification that it's been canceled (cancelado). Tourists have been fined hundreds of dollars for inadvertently carrying uncanceled car entry stickers on their windshields.

At the same time, return all other Mexican permits, such as tourist cards and hunting and fishing licenses. Also, be prepared for Mexico exit inspection, especially for cultural artifacts and works of art, which may require exit permits. Certain religious and pre-Columbian artifacts, legally the property of the Mexican government, cannot be taken from the country.

If you entered Mexico with your car, you cannot legally leave without it except by permission from local customs authorities, usually the Aduana (Customs House) or the Oficina Federal de Hacienda (Federal Treasury Office).

All returnees are subject to U.S. immigration and customs inspection. These inspections have become generally more time-consuming since September 11, 2001. The worst bottlenecks are at busy border crossings, especially Tijuana and, to a lesser extent, Mexicali, Nogales, Juárez, Nuevo Laredo, and Matamoros, all of which should be avoided during peak hours.

United States law allows a fixed value ($800 at present) of duty-free goods per returnee. This may include no more than one liter of alcoholic spirits, 200 cigarettes, and 100 cigars. Up to 10 percent duty will be applied to the first $1,000 (fair retail value, save your receipts) in excess of your $800 exemption. You may, however, mail packages (up to $100 value each) of gifts duty-free to friends and relatives in the United States. Make sure to clearly write "unsolicited gift" and a list of the value and contents on the outside of the package. Perfumes (over $5), alcoholic beverages, and tobacco may not be included in such packages.

Improve the security of such mailed packages by sending them by Mexpost class, similar to U.S. Express Mail service. Even better (but much more expensive), send them by Federal Express or DHL international couriers, which maintain offices in Oaxaca City, Puerto Escondido, Huatulco, Tuxtepec, Salina Cruz, Juchitán, and other larger Oaxaca towns.

U.S. Government Customs and Wildlife Information

For more information on U.S. customs regulations important to travelers abroad, read or download the useful pamphlet *Know Before You Go* by visiting the **U.S. Customs and Border Patrol** website (www.cpb.gov). Click on "Travel" at the top of the homepage, then scroll down to *Know Before You Go.*

For more information on the importation of endangered wildlife products, contact the **Fish and Wildlife Service** (1849 C. St. NW, Washington, DC 20240, toll-free tel. 800/344-9453, www.fws.gov).

Recreation

SNORKELING AND SCUBA DIVING

Many exciting clear-water sites, such as the **Bahías de Huatulco** and **Playa Estacahuite** near Puerto Ángel and **Playa Angelito** near Puerto Escondido, await both beginner and expert snorkelers and divers. Veteran divers usually arrive during the dry winter and early spring when river outflows are mere trickles, leaving offshore waters clear. In Huatulco and Puerto Escondido, professional dive shops rent equipment, provide lessons and guides, and transport divers to choice sites.

While convenient, rented equipment is often less than satisfactory. To be sure, serious divers bring their own gear. This might include wetsuits in the winter, when some swimmers begin to feel cold after an unprotected half hour in the water.

SURFING, SAILING, AND KAYAKING

Oaxaca has the Mexican Pacific's acknowledged best (but most challenging) surfing beach, the renowned **Playa Zicatela** "pipeline" at Puerto Escondido. The surf everywhere is highest and most exciting during the July-November hurricane season, when big swells from storms far out at sea attract platoons of surfers to favored beaches.

Other lesser but still popular intermediate-level surfing spots are **Playa Zipolite** near Puerto Ángel, **La Boca** at Huatulco, and Playa Chacahua, in the national park, an hour's drive west of Puerto Escondido.

Between Huatulco and Salina Cruz, surfers have discovered over a dozen breaks in recent years, including the now-well-known Barra de la Cruz, with its endless right point barrel.

Sailboarders, sailboaters, and kite surfers can often find the moderately breezy conditions that they love during the Oaxaca winter or spring. At that time they gather to enjoy the near-ideal conditions at many coves and inlets near the resorts.

Kayakers who, by contrast, are happiest in tranquil waters, also do well in the winter and spring in sheltered coastal bays and coves, notably the **Bahías de Huatulco.** Mangrove lagoons, furthermore, especially **Laguna Manialtepec** near Puerto Escondido, and Laguna Chacahua farther west, or Laguna Corrallero, near Pinotepa Nacional, near Oaxaca's western border, offer abundant kayaking opportunities.

Stand-up paddleboarders can explore the tranquil waters of the Bahías de Huatulco and/or the mangrove lagoons. Those in search of wave-riding thrills need only follow the surfers' trails to find great waves for stand-up paddleboard surfing. Do not try this at Puerto Escondido!!!

While "serious" surfers will likely be traveling with their own boards, several sales and rental surf shops have opened along the Oaxaca coast. They offer high-quality rental gear for surfing and stand-up paddling. Given the exorbitant cost of shipping oversized baggage, for example surfboards, unless you're planning on doing nothing but surfing, these rental shops are a good deal. Kiteboarders and kayakers should still plan on bringing their own gear.

POWER SPORTS

Power sports, such as water skiing, parasailing, and personal watercraft riding, are not widespread on Oaxaca beaches. In parasailing, a motorboat pulls while a parachute lifts you, like a soaring gull, high over the ocean. After 10 minutes, they deposit you (usually gently) back on the sand. Personal watercraft are like snowmobiles except they operate on water, where, with a little practice, even beginners can quickly learn to whiz over the waves. They may be fun for some but they are also noisy and intrusive. If you must do this, try to find a deserted place to indulge.

Although the luxury hotels at the Bahías de Huatulco provide experienced crews and equipment for such activities, it is recommended that you practice while sober and with caution. Moreover, you, as the paying patron, have a right to expect that your providers and crew are themselves both cautious and sober besides being well equipped.

BEACH BUGGIES AND ATVS

Some visitors enjoy racing along the beach and rolling over dunes with beach buggies and ATVs (all-terrain vehicles, *motos* in Mexico); balloon-tired, three- or four-wheeled motor scooters; and mini-jeeps. While certain resort rental agencies cater to the growing use of such vehicles, limits are in order. Of all the proliferating high-horse-power beach pastimes, these are the most intrusive. Noise, exhaust and gasoline pollution, injuries to operators and bystanders, and scattering of wildlife and destruction of their habitats have led to the restriction of beach buggies and ATVs on beaches and in forest habitats.

FISHING

Experts agree that the Oaxaca coast is a world-class deep-sea and surf fishing ground. Sportfishing enthusiasts routinely bring in dozens of species from among the several hundred that have been identified in Oaxaca waters.

Surf Fishing

Most good fishing beaches away from the immediate resort areas will typically have only a few locals (mostly with nets) and fewer visitors. Oaxacans do little sportfishing. Most either make their living from fishing or do none at all. Some local folks catch fish for supper with nets. Consequently, few Oaxaca shops

Fish

A bounty of fish dart, swarm, jump, and wriggle in Oaxaca's surf, reefs, lagoons, and offshore depths. While many make delicious dinners (albacore, dorado, pez gallo), others are tough (sailfish), bony (bonefish), and even poisonous (puffers). Some grow to half-ton giants (marlin, Goliath fish, sunfish), while others are diminutive reef-grazers (parrot fish, damselfish, angelfish) whose bright colors delight snorkelers and divers. Here's a sampling of what you might find underwater or on your dinner plate.

The **best-eating** of the bunch are albacore, dolphinfish *(dorado)*, red snapper, roosterfish, snook *(robalo)*, triggerfish *(pez Puerco)*, wahoo, yellowfin tuna, and yellowtail *(jurel)*.

- **albacore** *(albacora, atún):* 2-4 feet in size; blue; found in deep waters; excellent taste

- **angelfish** *(angel):* one foot; yellow, orange, blue; reef fish

- **barracuda** *(barracuda, picuda):* two feet; brown; deep waters; good taste

- **black marlin** *(marlin negro):* six feet; blue-black; deep waters; good taste

- **blue marlin** *(marlin azul):* eight feet; blue; deep waters; poor taste

- **bobo** *(barbudo):* one foot; blue, yellow; found in surf; fair taste

- **bonefish** *(macabi):* one foot; blue or silver; found inshore; poor taste

- **bonito** *(bonito):* two feet; black; deep waters; good taste

- **butterfly fish** *(muñeca):* six inches; black, yellow; reef fish

- **chub** *(chopa):* one foot; gray; reef fish; good taste

- **croaker** *(corvina):* two feet; brownish; found along inshore bottoms; rare and protected

- **damselfish** *(castañeta):* four inches; brown, blue, orange; reef fish

- **dolphinfish, mahimahi** *(dorado):* three feet; green, gold; deep waters; excellent taste

- **grouper** *(garropa):* three feet; brown, rust; found offshore and in reefs; good taste

- **grunt** *(burro):* eight inches; black, gray; found in rocks, reefs

sell fishing equipment. Plan to bring your own, including hooks, lures, line, and weights.

In any case, the cleaner the water, the more interesting your catch. On a good day, your reward might be *sierras, cabrillas,* porgies, or pompanos pulled from the Oaxaca surf.

You can't have everything, however. Foreigners cannot legally take Mexican abalone, clams, coral, lobster, rock bass, sea fans, seashells, shrimp, or turtles. Nor are they supposed to buy them directly from fisherfolk.

Deep-Sea Fishing
Santa Cruz de Huatulco, Salina Cruz, and, to a lesser extent, Puerto Escondido and Puerto Ángel are well-known jumping-off spots for the big prize marlin and sailfish.

A deep-sea boat charter generally includes the boat and crew for a full or half day, plus equipment and bait for 2-6 people, not including food and drinks. The full-day price depends upon the season. Around Christmas and New Year's and before Easter (when reservations will be mandatory), a boat can run $400 at the Bahías de Huatulco, less during low season and at the other spots.

Renting an entire big boat is not the only choice. *Pangas* (outboard launches seating up to six passengers) are available for as little as $50, depending on the season.

- jack *(toro):* 1-2 feet; bluish-gray; offshore; good taste
- mackerel *(sierra):* two feet; gray with gold spots; offshore; good taste
- mullet *(lisa):* two feet; gray; found in sandy bays; good taste
- needlefish *(agujón):* three feet; blue-black; deep waters; good taste
- Pacific porgy *(pez de pluma):* 1-2 feet; tan; found along sandy shores; good taste
- parrot fish *(perico, pez loro):* one foot; green, pink, blue, orange; reef fish
- puffer *(botete):* eight inches; brown; inshore; poisonous
- red snapper *(huachinango, pargo):* 1-2 feet; reddish pink; deep waters; excellent taste
- roosterfish *(pez gallo):* three feet; black, blue; deep waters; excellent taste
- sailfish *(pez vela):* five feet; blue-black; deep waters; tough, poor taste
- sardine *(sardina):* eight inches; blue-black; offshore; good taste
- sea bass *(cabrilla):* 1-2 feet; brown, ruddy; reef and rock crevices; good taste
- shark *(tiburón):* 2-10 feet; black to blue; in- and offshore; good taste
- snook *(robalo):* 2-3 feet; black-brown; found in brackish lagoons; excellent taste
- spadefish *(chambo):* one foot; black-silver; found along sandy bottoms; reef fish
- swordfish *(pez espada):* five feet; black to blue; deep waters; good taste
- triggerfish *(pez puerco):* 1-2 feet; blue, rust, brown, black; reef fish; excellent taste
- wahoo *(peto, guahu):* 2-5 feet; green to blue; deep waters; excellent taste
- yellowfin tuna *(atún amarilla):* 2-5 feet; blue, yellow; deep waters; excellent taste
- yellowtail *(jurel):* 2-4 feet; blue, yellow; offshore; excellent taste

Bringing Your Own Boat

If you're going to be doing lots of fishing, your own boat may be your most flexible and economical option. One big advantage is you can go to the many excellent fishing grounds the charter boats do not frequent. Keep your equipment simple, scout around, and keep your eyes peeled and ears open for local regulations and customs, plus tide, wind, and fish-edibility information.

Fishing Licenses and Boat Permits

Anyone, regardless of age, who is either fishing or riding in a fishing boat in Mexico is required to have a fishing license. Although Mexican fishing licenses are obtainable from certain bait and tackle stores and car insurance agents or at government fishing offices everywhere along the coast, save yourself time and trouble by getting both your fishing licenses and boat permits by mail ahead of time from the Mexican Department of Fisheries. Call at least a month before departure and ask for (preferably faxed) applications and the fees (which are reasonably priced, but depend upon the period of validity and the fluctuating exchange rate). On the application, fill in the names (exactly as they appear on passports) of the people requesting licenses. Include a cashier's check or a money order for the exact amount, along with a stamped, self-addressed envelope. Address the application to the **Mexican Department of Fisheries** (Oficina de Pesca, 2550 5th Ave., Suite 15, San Diego, CA 92103-6622, U.S. tel. 619/233-4324, fax 619/233-0344).

Freshwater Fishing

Oaxaca has four large reservoirs: Yosocuta, in the Mixteca near Huajuapan de León; Cerro de Oro and Miguel Alemán, in the north near Tuxtepec; and Benito Juárez Reservoir, in the Isthmus not far from Tehuántepec. Their shorelines are scenic and easily accessible, and their waters are home to several varieties of fish, mostly *mojarra* (bass), plentiful enough for local folks to make a living cooking fish dinners.

Accommodations

Oaxaca has lodgings to suit every style and pocketbook: world-class resorts, small beachside hotels, bed-and-breakfasts, homey *casas de huéspedes* (guesthouses), friendly trailer parks, community-maintained tourist lodgings, and many miles of breezy beaches, ripe for camping.

In Oaxaca City, the busy **high seasons,** when hotel reservations are generally necessary, are July, Day of the Dead (late Oct.-early Nov.), and mid-December-Janurary 6, the Day of the Kings. On the coast, high seasons are also mid-December-January 6, plus mid-February-Easter, and the months of July and August. Excellent, quiet **low-season** times to visit anywhere in Oaxaca are November after the Day of the Dead and the month of January after January 6, when prices are low and the weather is consistently temperate and dry.

Hotel Rates

The rates listed in this book are U.S. dollar equivalents of peso prices, taxes included, as quoted by the hotel management at the time of writing. They are intended as a general guide only, and probably will only approximate the asking rate when you arrive. Some readers unfortunately try to bargain by telling desk clerks that, for example, the rate should be $30 because they read it in this book. This is unwise, because it makes hotel managers and clerks reluctant to quote rates for fear readers might hold their hotel responsible for such quotes. As private businesses, hotels are free to raise their rates; conversely, if the price is too high, customers are entitled to take their business elsewhere.

In Oaxaca, hotel rates depend strongly upon inflation and season. To cancel the effect of the fluctuating Mexican peso, rates are reported in U.S. dollars. However, when settling your hotel bill, you should always insist on paying in pesos by cash or by credit card, which by law must be marked in pesos.

Saving Money

The hotel prices quoted here are **rack rates:** the maximum tariff, exclusive of packages and promotions, that you would pay if you walked in off the street and rented an unreserved room for one day. Savvy travelers seldom pay the maximum. Since most hotel clerks will tell you that their hotel doesn't give **discounts** (*discuentos*), it's best not to use that forbidden word. Instead, always inquire if there are any **promotions or packages** (*promociones o paquetes,* proh-moh-see-OH-nays oh pah-KAY-tays). At any time other than the high seasons, you can generally bargain for a lowered price. Don't be shy; if the hotel asking price is $60, offer $40. At best, you'll get what you want; at worst, you can always take your business elsewhere. Often discounts (shh!) come as one or two free days for a one-week stay. Promotional packages available during slack seasons sometimes include free extras, such as breakfast, a car rental, a boat tour, or a sports rental. A travel agent and/or Internet travel site can be of great help in shopping around for such bargains.

You will virtually always save money if you deal in pesos only. Insist on booking your lodging for an agreed price in pesos and paying the resulting hotel bill in pesos, rather than dollars. The reason is that dollar rates quoted by hotels are often based on the hotel desk exchange rate, which is sometimes as much as 10 percent less favorable than the bank exchange rate. For example, if the desk clerk tells you your hotel bill is $1,000, instead of handing over the dollars, ask him or her how much it is in pesos. Using the desk conversion rate, the clerk might say something like 10,000 pesos (considerably less than the 11,000 pesos that the bank might give for your $1,000). Pay the 10,000 pesos or have the clerk mark 10,000 pesos on your credit card slip, and save yourself $90.

GUESTHOUSES, BED-AND-BREAKFASTS, AND HOMESTAYS

A significant fraction of Oaxaca City lodgings fall into these categories. On city residential side streets, often several blocks removed from the tourist zone, are many of the *casas de huéspedes* (guesthouses), bed-and-breakfasts, and homes where increasing numbers of families are renting rooms to visitors.

Such lodgings vary from scruffy to spic-and-span, humble to luxurious. At minimum, you can expect a plain room, a shared toilet and hot-water shower, and plenty of atmosphere for your money. Rates are highest in Oaxaca City and the Bahías de Huatulco, ranging between $20 and about $100 for two. Discounts are often available for long-term stays.

Note: Oaxaca bed-and-breakfasts are generally rather expensive, since they are a lodging style sought out by mostly North American travelers accustomed to paying high prices. If you want to save money, check out the Mexican version of the same thing, the homier *casa de huéspedes.*

In addition to the guesthouse, bed-and-breakfast, and homestay-style lodgings listed

in the destination chapters of this book, you should also consult the many classified advertisements of the local tourist newspapers, especially in Oaxaca City and Puerto Escondido. Moreover, Spanish Language School, common in Oaxaca City, usually recommends a list of homestays (family accommodations) to their participants.

APARTMENTS AND HOUSE RENTALS

For longer stays in Oaxaca City, many visitors prefer the convenience and economy of an apartment or house rental. Choices vary, from spartan studios to deluxe homes big enough for entire extended families. Prices depend strongly upon season and amenities, from $350 per month for the cheapest to around $1,000 for the most luxurious.

At the low end, you can expect a clean, furnished apartment with kitchen and bathroom and once- or twice-a-week housecleaning service. Higher up the scale, houses vary from moderately luxurious homes to sky's-the-limit mansions, blooming with built-in designer luxuries, such as a swimming pool or tennis court, and including at least a gardener, cook, and maid.

Shopping Around

You can find many guesthouses, bed-and-breakfasts, and apartment rentals through on-the-spot local contacts, such as the tourist newspapers' want ad sections, websites, neighborhood For Rent *(Renta)* signs, and local listing agents. If you prefer making rental arrangements prior to arrival, you can usually email, fax, or telephone managers directly; many of them speak English.

COMMUNITY *CABAÑAS ECOTURÍSTICAS*

More than a dozen rural communities, mostly on the east side of the central Valley of Oaxaca, the Northern Sierra, and the Mixteca, encourage visitors to come and stay in their tourist lodges, called *cabañas ecoturísticas* (ecotouristic cabins). These are government-built, rustic but comfortable, modern-standard cabins, managed and maintained by a community-appointed *gerente* (manager). *Cabañas* typically have two separate one-room units that sleep up to six people each and share a single flush toilet and shower-bath between them. Units rent for about $10-20 per night per person, or $30-50 per group, with towels, blankets, flush toilets, and hot-water showers.

LOCAL HOTELS

Locally owned and operated hotels make up most of the recommendations in this book. Many veteran travelers find it hard to understand why people come to Oaxaca and spend $200 a day for a super-luxury hotel room when simpler but comfortable alternatives can run as little as $30.

In Oaxaca City, many such hotels are within easy walking distance of the town center, with its lovely plaza, restored old monuments, restaurants, and shops. In the Puerto Escondido and Puerto Ángel resorts, most of them are either right on the beach or very near it. Local hotels, which depend as much on Mexican tourists as foreigners, generally have clean, large rooms, often with private view balconies, ceiling fans, and toilet and hot-water bath or shower. What they often lack are the plush extras—air-conditioning, cable TV, phones, tennis courts, exercise gyms, spas, and saunas—of the luxury resorts.

Booking local hotels is straightforward. Many of them can be emailed and all of them can be dialed or faxed directly (from the United States, dial 011-52, followed by the telephone or fax number) for information and reservations. If your Spanish is rusty, ask for someone who speaks English (ask, in Spanish: "*¿Por favor, hay alguien que habla Inglés?*"—por fah-VOR, AY ahhl-ghee-AYN KAY AB-lah een-GLAYS?). Always ask about money-saving packages (pah-KAY-tays) and promotions (proh-moh-see-OH-nays) when reserving.

INTERNATIONAL-CLASS RESORTS

Oaxaca visitors enjoy several beautiful, well-managed, international-class resort hotels in Oaxaca City and the Bahías de Huatulco. Their super-deluxe amenities, moreover, need not be overly expensive. While high-season room tariffs ordinarily run $100-300, low-season packages and promotions sometimes cut these prices by half. Shop around for savings through travel agents, and by calling the hotels directly through their toll-free 800 numbers.

CAMPING, PALAPAS, AND TRAILER PARKS

Although Oaxaca has only a sprinkling of formally maintained places for camping, many inviting beach and inland country spots are customarily used informally.

Beach Camping

Camping at beaches is popular among middle-class Mexican families, especially during the Christmas-New Year's week and during Semana Santa, the week before Easter. During other times of the year, tent and RV campers usually find prospective camping spots not crowded. The best beach spots typically have a shady palm grove for informal camping and a *palapa* (palm-thatched) restaurant that serves drinks and fresh seafood. (Heads up for falling coconuts, no joke, especially when it is windy.) Cost for parking and tenting is often minimal, typically only the price of food at the restaurant.

As for **camping on isolated beaches,** opinions vary, from dire warnings of bandidos to bland assurances that all is peaceful along the coast. The truth is probably somewhere in between. Trouble is most likely to occur in the vicinity of resort towns, notoriously, on the outskirt beaches of Puerto Escondido, where a few local thugs have harassed isolated campers.

When scouting out a place to camp, a good general rule is to arrive early enough in the day to get a feel for the place. Buy a soda at the *palapa* or nearby store and take a stroll around. Say *"Buenos dias"* to the people along the way; ask if the fishing is good: *"¿Pesca buena?"* Use your common sense. If the people seem friendly, ask if it's *seguro* (safe). If so, ask permission: *"¿Es bueno acampar acá?"* ("Is it OK to camp around here?"). You'll rarely be refused.

Beach *Palapas*

Visitors can still rent beachfront *palapas* (thatched houses) in Puerto Escondido; west of Puerto Escondido, at Playas Zipolite, Mazunte, and Ventanilla (near Puerto Ángel); and east of Puerto Escondido, at Roca Blanca and Playa Chacahua. Amenities typically include beds or hammocks, a shady thatched porch, cold running water, a kerosene stove, and shared toilets and showers, for about $10 per day per person.

The bad news is that security has been a problem in some *palapas,* notably at Puerto Escondido. The good news is that the Puerto Ángel area has some of the better *palapas,* such as Lo Cósmico and Shambhala. The best news of all is that *palapas* are usually right on the beach, so you can walk right out your front door onto the sand, where surf, shells, and seabirds will be there to entertain you.

Mountain and Backcountry Camping

Oaxaca's mountain and rural backcountry offer many additional camping opportunities. Private owners and communities maintain picnic areas and informal campgrounds at choice sites, such as springs, waterfalls, caves, *sabineras* (giant cypress groves), and on rivers and reservoir shorelines.

Invariably, camping sites are on private (*particular,* par-tee-koo-LAHR) or communal land. As a courtesy, you should obtain permission to set up camp either from the site manager, the closest neighboring restaurant or house, or at the nearest *presidencia municipal* or *agencia.* Such permission, sometimes for a small fee, is usually granted almost automatically. Please reciprocate by keeping your campfire, if permitted, modest and under control, respecting local etiquette (don't swim or sunbathe in the nude), cleaning up thoroughly, and carrying away all your trash.

For an informative and entertaining discussion of camping in Mexico, check out *The People's Guide to Mexico* by Carl Franz.

RV Trailer Parks

Campers who prefer company to isolation usually stay in trailer parks. Oaxaca has five modest but recommendable RV trailer parks: two in Oaxaca City; two in Zipolite by the beach, near Puerto Ángel; and one in Puerto Escondido, on the beach.

Food and Drink

Some travel to Mexico for the food. True Mexican food is old-fashioned, homestyle fare requiring many hours of loving preparation. Such food is short on meat and long on corn, beans, rice, tomatoes, chilies, spices, onions, eggs, and cheese.

Mexican food is the unique end-product of thousands of years of native tradition. It is based on corn—*teocentli,* the Aztec "food of the gods"—called *maíz* (mah-EES) by present-day Mexicans. In the past, the typical Mexican woman spent much of her time grinding and preparing corn: soaking the grain in limewater (which swells the kernels and removes the tough seed-coat) and grinding the bloated seeds into meal on a stone *metate.* Finally, she would pat the meal into tortillas and cook them on a hot, baked mud griddle.

Fewer women these days make tortillas by hand. The gentle pat-pat-pat has been replaced by the whir and rattle of automatic tortilla-making machines in myriad *tortillerías,*

ESSENTIALS
FOOD AND DRINK

where women and girls line up for their family's daily kilo-stack of tortillas.

A Mexican family meal, more often than not, is some mixture of sauce, meat, beans, cheese, and vegetables wrapped in a tortilla, which becomes the culinary be-all: the food, the dish, and the utensil all wrapped into one.

This most Mexican style of meal usually includes one or two of a number of specialties known by Mexicans as *antojitos* and known to everyone else as "Mexican food." These are the familiar burritos, chiles rellenos, enchiladas, guacamole, nachos, quesadillas, refried beans, tacos, tamales, and other combinations of beans, cheese, corn, eggs, meat, sauces, and spices that make up the menus of Mexican restaurants in the United States and Canada.

HOT OR NOT?

Much food served in Mexico is not "Mexican." Eating habits, as most other Mexican customs, depend upon social class. Upwardly mobile Mexicans typically shun the corn-based native food in favor of the European-style food of the Spanish colonial elite: chops, cutlets, fish, clams, octopus, omelets, pasta, potatoes, rice, soups, salads, and steaks.

Such fare is often bland. *"No picante"* (not spicy) is how the Mexicans describe bland food. *"Caliente"* or *"Calor,"* the Spanish words that describe "hot" water or weather, do not, in contrast to English usage, also imply spicy *(picante)*.

VEGETARIAN AND ORGANIC FOOD

Strictly vegetarian cooking is the exception in Mexico, although a few macrobiotic-vegetarian restaurants and health-food stores have opened in Oaxaca City, Puerto Escondido, Puerto Ángel, and the Bahías de Huatulco. Meat is such a delicacy for most Oaxacans that they can't understand why people would give it up voluntarily. If vegetable-lovers can manage with beans, cheese, corn, eggs, fruit, and *legumbres* (vegetables) and not be bothered by a bit of *manteca de cerdo* (pork fat), Mexican (and Oaxacan) cooking will suit them fine.

Although much Oaxacan produce would probably qualify north of the border as de-facto organic, a system for classifying food as organic is just beginning in Oaxaca City and the coastal tourist resorts of Puerto Escondido and the Bahías de Huatulco.

If all you require is strictly vegetable fare, Oaxaca is a snap. Most restaurants, all the way down to a humble Mexican *comedor* or *fonda* (food stall) will almost always be able to fill up

Oaxacans eat these locusts like Americans eat popcorn.

reflect high worldwide demand, even at the humblest seaside *palapa.* The freshness and variety, however, make even the typical dishes seem like bargains at any price.

FRUITS AND JUICES

Squeezed vegetable and fruit juices (*jugos,* HOO-gohs) are among the widely available delights of Oaxaca. Among the many establishments—restaurants, cafés, and *loncherías*—willing to supply you with your favorite *jugo,* the **jugerías** (juice bars) are often the most fun. Colorful fruit piles usually mark *jugerías.* If you don't immediately spot your favorite fruit, ask anyway; it might be hidden in the refrigerator.

Besides your choice of pure juice, a *jugería* will often serve **licuados.** Into the juice, they whip powdered milk, your favorite fruit, ice, and sugar to taste for a creamy afternoon pick-me-up or evening dessert. One big favorite is a cool banana-chocolate *licuado,* which comes out tasting like a milk shake, minus the calories.

ALCOHOLIC DRINKS

The Aztec chiefs often sacrificed anyone caught drinking alcohol without permission. The later, more lenient, Spanish attitude toward getting *borracho* (soused) has led to a thriving Mexican renaissance of alcoholic beverages: aguardiente, Kahlua, *mezcal,* pulque, and tequila.

Mezcal, distilled from the fermented juice of the maguey (century) plant, was introduced by the Spanish colonists in Oaxaca, where the best *mezcals* are still made. *Mezcal* and **tequila,** the best of which is made near Guadalajara from the blue agave subspecies of maguey, both come 76 proof (38 percent alcohol) and up. A small white worm, endemic to the maguey plant, is often added to each bottle of factory *mezcal* for authenticity.

Raicilla is a cruder, more potent form of *mezcal,* usually over 100 proof, that many workers indulge in on Saturday night after a week on the job.

Pulque, Mexico's ancestral alcoholic

cactus pears and mangos, standard Oaxacan fare

some hot corn tortillas with fresh diced tomatoes, avocados, beans, and onions, add some piquant fresh *salsa,* and serve it all up as several tasty and nutritious hot tacos.

SEAFOOD

Early chroniclers wrote that Aztec Emperor Moctezuma employed a platoon of runners to bring fresh fish 480 kilometers (300 mi) from the sea to his court every day. On the Oaxaca Pacific coast, fresh seafood is fortunately much more available from scores of shoreline establishments, ranging from thatched beach *palapas* to five-star hotel restaurants.

Oaxaca seafood is literally there for the taking. When strolling on the beach, I have seen well-fed, middle-class local vacationers breaking and eating oysters and mussels right off the rocks. Villagers up and down the coast use small nets (or bare hands) to retrieve a few fish for supper, while communal teams haul in big nets full of silvery, wriggling fish for sale right on the beach.

Despite the plenty, Oaxaca seafood prices

Catch of the Day

- *Ceviche* (say-VEE-chay): a chopped raw fish appetizer as popular on Oaxaca beaches as sushi is on Tokyo side streets. Although it can contain anything from conch to octopus, the best ceviche consists of diced young *tiburón* (shark) or *sierra* (mackerel) fillet and plenty of fresh tomatoes, onions, garlic, and chilies, all doused with lime juice.

- *Filete de pescado:* fish fillet breaded *(empanizada)*, sautéed *al mojo* (ahl-MOH-hoh) with butter and garlic, or smothered in mole.

- *Pescado frito* (pays-KAH-doh FREE-toh): fish, pan-fried whole; if you don't specify that it be cooked *a medio* (lightly), the fish may arrive well done, like a big, crunchy french fry.

- *Pescado veracruzana:* a favorite everywhere. Best with *huachinango* (red snapper) smothered in a savory tomato, onion, chili, and garlic sauce. *Pargo* (snapper), *mero* (grouper), and *cabrilla* (sea bass) are also popularly used in this and other specialties.

- Shellfish: *ostiones* (oysters) and *almejas* (clams) by the dozen; *langosta* (lobster) and *langostina* (crayfish), *asado* (broiled), *al vapor* (steamed), or *frito* (fried). Pots of fresh-boiled *camarones* (shrimp) are sometimes sold on the street in markets by the kilo; restaurants will make them into *cóctel* (cocktail) or prepare them *en gabardinas* (breaded) at your request.

beverage, although also made from the sap of the maguey, is locally brewed (but not distilled), to a small alcohol content, between beer and wine. The brewing houses are sacrosanct preserves, circumscribed by traditions that exclude both women and outsiders. The brew, said to be full of nutrients, is sold to local *pulquerías* and drunk immediately. If you are ever invited into a *pulquería,* it will be an honor you cannot refuse.

Aguardiente, by contrast, is the notorious fiery Mexican "white lightning" of locally fermented and distilled cane juice, and is a dirt-cheap ticket to oblivion for poor Mexican men.

While pulque comes from an age-old indigenous tradition, **cerveza** (beer) is the beverage of modern mestizo Mexico. Full-bodied and often tastier than "light" U.S. counterparts, Mexican beer enjoys an enviable reputation.

Those visitors who indulge usually know their favorite among the many brands, from light to dark: Superior, Corona, Pacífico, Tecate, Carta Blanca, Modelo, Dos Equis, Bohemia, Victoria, Indio, Tres Equis, and Negra Modelo. Nochebuena, a flavorful dark brew, becomes available only around Christmas. The lighter beers are almost always served with a slice of lime.

Mexicans have yet to develop much of a taste for *vino* (wine), although some domestic wines, such as the Baja California labels Monte Xanic, Domecq, and Cetto, are always quite drinkable and sometimes excellent.

BREAD AND PASTRIES

Excellent locally-baked bread is a delightful surprise to many first-time visitors to Oaxaca. Small bakeries everywhere put out trays of hot, crispy-crusted *bolillos* (rolls) and sweet *panes dulces* (pastries). They range from simple cakes, muffins, cookies, and doughnuts to fancy fruit-filled turnovers and puffs. Half the fun occurs before the eating: Grab a tray and tongs, peruse the goodies, and pick out the most scrumptious. With your favorite dozen finally selected, you take your tray to the cashier, who deftly bags everything up and collects a few pesos (two or three dollars) for your entire mouthwatering selection.

A Trove of Fruits and Nuts

Besides carrying the usual temperate fruits, *jugerías* (juice bars) and traditional markets are seasonal sources of many delectable, exotic (followed by an *) varieties.

· **avocado** *(aguacate,* ah-wah-KAH-tay): Aztec aphrodisiac

· **banana** *(platano):* many kinds—big and small, red, purple, and yellow

· *chirimoya*:* green scales, white pulp, sometimes called an *anona*

· **ciruela*:** looks like (but tastes better than) a small yellow-to-red plum

· **coconut** *(coco):* coconut "milk," called *agua coco,* is a delicious-nutritious thirst quencher

· **grapes** *(uvas):* August-November season

· *guanabana*:* looks, but doesn't taste, like a green mango

· **guava** *(guava):* delicious juice, widely available canned

· **lemon** *(lima real,* LEE-mah ray-AHL): uncommon and expensive; use lime instead

· **lime** *(limón,* lee-MOHN): abundant and cheap; douse salads with it

· *mamey** (mah-MAY): yellow, juicy fruit, excellent for jellies and preserves

· **mango:** king of fruit, April-August. Grown in profusion in Tapanatepec, Oaxaca, the mango "world capital."

· **orange** *(naranja,* nah-RAHN-ha): often greenish-yellow skin, but much sweeter than most California oranges

· **papaya:** said to aid digestion and healing

· **peach** *(durazno,* doo-RAHS-noh): delicious and widely available as canned juice and fruit

· **peanut** *(cacahuate,* kah-kah-WAH-tay): home roasted and cheap

· **pear** *(pera):* fall season

· **pecan** *(nuez):* for a treat, try freshly ground pecan butter

· *piña anona*:* looks like a thin ear of corn without the husk; tastes like pineapple

· **pineapple** *(piña):* huge, luscious, and cheap

· **strawberry** *(fresa,* FRAY-sah): local favorite

· **tangerine** *(mandarina):* sweet, juicy, and common around Christmas

· **watermelon** *(sandía,* sahn-DEE-ah): perfect on a hot day

· **yaca*** (YAH-kah): relative of the Asian jackfruit, with pebbly green skin, round, and as large as a football; yummy mild taste

· *zapote** (sah-POH-tay): yellow, fleshy fruit, said to induce sleep

· *zapote colorado*:* brown skin, red, puckery fruit, like persimmon; commonly, but incorrectly, called *mamey*

Travel Tips

WHAT TO TAKE

Everyone should bring or plan to buy a hat for sun protection and a light jacket or sweater for the occasional cool evening. Loose-fitting, hand-washable, easy-to-dry clothes make for trouble-free tropical vacationing. Leave showy, expensive clothes and jewelry at home. Stow valuables in your hotel safe or carry them with you in a sturdy zipped purse or a waist pouch on your front side.

ACCESS FOR TRAVELERS WITH DISABILITIES

Mexican airlines and hotels (especially the large ones) have become sensitive to the needs of travelers with disabilities. Open, street-level lobbies and large, wheelchair-accessible elevators and rooms are available in nearly all Pacific Mexico resort hotels (and some smaller, especially boutique, hotels). Furthermore, nearly all street-corner curbs accommodate wheelchairs.

Both Mexico and United States law forbids travel discrimination against otherwise qualified people with disabilities. As long as your disability is stable and not liable to deteriorate during passage, you can expect to be treated like any passenger with special needs.

Make reservations far ahead of departure and ask your agent to inform your airline of your needs, such as a boarding wheelchair or in-flight oxygen. Be early at the gate to take advantage of the pre-boarding call.

For many helpful details to smooth your trip, get a copy of *Survival Strategies for Going Abroad* by Laura Hershey, published in 2005 by **Mobility International USA** (132 E. Broadway, Suite 343, Eugene, OR 97401, tel. 541/343-1284 voice/TTY, fax 541/343-6812, www.miusa.org). Mobility International is a valuable resource for many lovers of Mexico, for it encourages travelers with disabilities with a goldmine of information and literature and can provide them with valuable Mexico connections. They publish a regular newsletter and provide information and referrals for international exchanges and homestays.

Similarly, **Partners of the Americas** (1424 K St. NW, Suite 700, Washington, D.C. 20005, tel. 202/628-3300 or 800/322-7844, fax 202/628-3306, www.partners.net), with chapters in 45 U.S. states, works to improve understanding of disabilities and facilities in Mexico and Latin America. It maintains communications with local organizations and individuals whom travelers with disabilities may contact at their destinations.

TRAVELING WITH CHILDREN

Children are treasured like gifts from heaven in Mexico. Traveling with kids will ensure you are welcome most everywhere. On the beach, take extra precautions to make sure they are protected from the sun.

A sick child is no fun for anyone. Fortunately, clinics and good doctors are available even in most small towns. When in need, ask a storekeeper or a pharmacist, *"¿Dónde hay un doctor, por favor?"* ("¿DOHN-day eye oon doc-TOHR por fah-VOHR?"). In most cases, within five minutes you will be in the waiting room of the local physician or hospital.

Children who do not favor typical Mexican fare can easily be fed with always-available eggs, cheese, *hamburguesas,* milk, oatmeal, corn flakes, tomatoes, avocados, bananas, cakes, and cookies. Quesadillas (two tortillas with melted cheese between) are always popular with kids; they're like the Mexican equivalent of a grilled cheese sandwich.

Your children will generally have more fun if they have a little previous knowledge of Mexico and a stake in the trip. For example, help them select some library picture books and magazines so they'll know where they're going and what to expect, or give them responsibility for packing and carrying their own small travel bag.

Be sure to mention your children's ages when making air reservations; child discounts of 50 percent or more are sometimes available. Also, if you can arrange to go on an uncrowded flight, you can stretch out and rest on the empty seats.

For more details on traveling with children, check out *Adventuring with Children* by Nan Jeffries.

SENIOR TRAVELERS

Age, according to Mark Twain, is a question of mind over matter: If you don't mind, it doesn't matter. Mexico is a country where whole extended families, from babies to great-grandparents, live together. Elderly travelers will benefit from the respect and understanding Mexicans accord to older people. Besides these encouragements, consider the number of retirees already in havens in Puerto Vallarta, Guadalajara, Manzanillo, Oaxaca, and other regional centers.

Certain organizations support and sponsor senior travel. Leading the field is **Road Scholar** (formerly Elderhostel; 11 Ave. de Lafayette, Boston, MA 02111-1746, toll-free tel. 800/454-5768, www.roadscholar.org). Check out their list of Mexico programs, which has regularly included a 10-day Oaxaca-based Spanish-language and culture program.

Some books also feature senior travel opportunities. One of the pithiest is *Unbelievably Good Deals and Great Adventures You Can't Have Unless You're Over 50,* by Joan Rattner Heilman, published by McGraw Hill (2008). Its 200 pages are packed with details of how to get bargains on cruises, tours, car rentals, lodgings, and much, much more.

The Internet is full of senior-oriented travel information. Near the top of the list is the **Transitions Abroad** site (www.transitionsabroad.com), which offers a gold mine of useful resources for seniors inerested in traveling and living abroad.

GAY AND LESBIAN TRAVELERS

The great majority of visitors find Oaxaca people both gracious and tolerant. This extends from racial color-blindness to being broad-minded about sexual preference.

As a result, both Oaxaca City and, to an equivalent extent, the coastal resorts have acquired a growing company of gay- and lesbian-friendly hotels, bars, and entertainments. For Oaxaca City hotel, restaurant, and nightlife details, visit the gay-oriented travel website www.go-oaxaca.com; for a list of gay-friendly bars, nightclubs, and businesses, log on to www.go-oaxaca.com/lifestyles.html.

Some gay- and lesbian-oriented Internet and print publishers also offer excellent travel guidebooks. One of the most experienced is **Damron Company** (tel. 415/255-0404 or 800/462-6654, www.damron.com), which publishes, both in print and by Internet subscription, the *Damron Women's Travel Guide* and *Damron Men's Travel Guide* guidebooks, containing a wealth of gay and lesbian travel information, including more than a dozen listings in Oaxaca City.

If you're interested in more gay and lesbian travel information, advice, and services, check out the San Francisco **Purple Roofs** Internet agency (www.purpleroofs.com). They offer lesbian and gay-friendly Oaxaca hotel and travel agent listings, plus a multitude of services, from tours and air tickets, to travel insurance and hotel reservations.

TOUR-STUDY PROGRAMS

Oaxaca's rich archaeological and cultural heritage provides a focus for some noteworthy tour-study programs.

Road Scholar (11 Lafayette Ave., Boston, MA 02111, 800/454-5768, www.roadscholar.org), formerly known as Elderhostel, offers tours leading participants on Oaxaca explorations emphasizing local traditions, food, and fiestas, plus lots of practice in conversational Spanish. Their Dia de Los Muertos tour focuses on the happy Mexican tradition of celebrating the beloved departed in joyous gravesite, food, flower- and candle-festooned family fiestas. Programs include visits to the archaeological sites of Monte Albán and Mitla and appreciation of indigenous tradition through visits to pottery, weaving, and woodcraft villages and evening excursions to enjoy Oaxacan food and folkloric music and dance. Accommodations can include both hotel rooms and homestays with Mexican families.

Birding tour outfitter **Field Guides** (9433 Bee Cave Rd., #1-150, Austin, TX, toll-free tel. 800/728-4953, www.fieldguides.com) leads tours focusing on the two dozen species endemic to Oaxaca as well as other migratory species. Along the way, trips often include archaeological and historical sites and colorful native markets.

Adventuresome travelers hankering for something unusual should check out **Manos de Oaxaca** (Oaxaca tel. 951/571-3695, www. traditionsmexico.com), led by artisan-guide and Oaxaca-lover Eric Mindling. His bliss is leading like-minded folks in explorations of clay and fiber arts by country artisans in the Valley of Oaxaca. The approach is people-to-people, the accommodations sometimes rustic, the prices reasonable, and the rewards potentially great. Other options include a "Flavors of Oaxaca" culinary tour, and a Oaxaca photography workshop.

Health and Safety

STAYING HEALTHY

In Oaxaca as everywhere, prevention is the best remedy for illness. For those visitors who confine their travel to the beaten path, a few basic common-sense precautions will ensure vacation enjoyment.

Resist the temptation to dive headlong into Mexico. It's no wonder that people get sick— broiling in the sun, gobbling peppery food, guzzling beer and margaritas, then discoing half the night, all in their first 24 hours. An alternative is to give your body time to adjust. Travelers often arrive tired and dehydrated from travel and heat. During the first few days, drink plenty of bottled water and juice, and take siestas.

Immunizations and Precautions

A good physician can recommend the proper preventatives for your Oaxaca trip. If you are going to stay pretty much in town, your doctor will probably suggest little more than updating your basic typhoid, diphtheria-tetanus, hepatitis, and polio shots.

For camping or trekking in remote tropical areas—below 1,200 meters (4,000 ft.)—doctors often recommend a gamma-globulin shot against hepatitis A and a schedule of chloroquine pills against malaria. While in backcountry areas, use other measures to discourage mosquitoes, fleas, flies, ticks, no-see-ums, "kissing bugs," and other tropical pesties from biting you. Common precautions include sleeping under mosquito netting, burning *espirales mosquito* (mosquito coils), and rubbing on plenty of pure DEET (n,n dimethyl-meta-toluamide) "jungle juice," mixed in equal parts with rubbing (70 percent isopropyl) alcohol. Although super-effective, 100 percent DEET dries and irritates the skin.

Sunburn

For sunburn protection, use a good sunscreen with a sun protection factor (SPF) rated 15 or more, which will reduce burning rays to one-fifteenth or less of direct sunlight. Better still, take a shady siesta-break from the sun during the most hazardous midday hours. If you do get burned, applying your sunburn lotion (or one of the "caine" creams) after the fact usually decreases the pain and speeds healing. So-called "waterproof" sunscreens are not waterproof after an hour, and should be reapplied.

Safe Water and Food

Although municipalities have made great strides in sanitation, food and water are still potential sources of germs in some parts of Oaxaca. Although water is nearly always safe everywhere, except in a few upcountry localities, it's still probably best to drink bottled water only. Hotels, whose success depends vitally on their customers' health, generally provide *agua purificada* (purified bottled water). If, for any reason, the available water is of doubtful quality, add a water purifier, such as Potable Aqua brand (get it at a camping goods store before departure) or a few drops per quart of water of *blanqueador* (household chlorine bleach) or *yodo* (tincture of iodine) from the pharmacy.

Pure bottled water, soft drinks, beer, and fresh fruit juices are so widely available it is easy to avoid tap water, especially in restaurants. Ice and *paletas* (iced juice-on-a-stick) may be risky, especially in small towns.

Washing hands before eating in a restaurant is a time-honored Mexican ritual that visitors should religiously follow. The humblest Mexican eatery will generally provide a basin to *lavar las manos* (wash the hands). If it doesn't, don't eat there.

Hot, cooked food is generally safe, as are peeled fruits and vegetables. These days milk and cheese in Mexico are generally processed under sanitary conditions and sold pasteurized (ask, *"¿Pasteurizado?"*) and are typically safe. Mexican ice cream used to be both bad-tasting and of dubious safety, but national brands available in supermarkets are so much improved that it's no longer necessary to resist ice cream while in town.

In recent years, much cleaner public water and increased hygiene awareness have made salad, once shunned by Mexico travelers, generally safe to eat in tourist-frequented Oaxaca cafés and restaurants. Nevertheless, lettuce and cabbage, particularly in country villages, are more likely to be contaminated than tomatoes, carrots, cucumbers, onions, and green peppers. In any case, you can try dousing your salad in *vinagre* (vinegar) or plenty of sliced *limón* (lime) juice, the acidity of which kills most bacteria. Many markets now sell iodine for raw food washing in their fruit and vegetable departments. Look for the blue bottles labeled BacDyn. They come in small sizes for travelers as well as liter-sized bottles for long-term visitors.

First-Aid Kit

In the tropics, ordinary cuts and insect bites are more prone to infection and should receive immediate first aid. A first-aid kit is a good precaution for any traveler and mandatory for campers. Equip your first-aid kit with aspirin, rubbing alcohol, hydrogen peroxide, water-purifying tablets, household chlorine bleach or iodine for water purifying, swabs, bandages, gauze, adhesive tape, Ace bandage, chamomile *(manzanilla)* tea bags for upset stomachs, Pepto-Bismol, acidophilus tablets, antibiotic ointment, hydrocortisone cream, mosquito repellent, knife, and good tweezers.

HEALTH PROBLEMS
Traveler's Diarrhea

Traveler's diarrhea (known in Southeast Asia as "Bali Belly" and in Mexico as *turista* or "Montezuma's Revenge") sometimes persists, even among prudent vacationers. You can suffer *turista* for a week after simply traveling from California to Philadelphia or New York. Doctors say the familiar symptoms of runny bowels, nausea, and sour stomach result from normal local bacterial strains to which newcomers' systems need time to adjust. Unfortunately, the dehydration and fatigue from heat and travel reduce your body's natural defenses and sometimes lead to a persistent cycle of sickness at a time when you least want it.

Time-tested protective measures can help your body either prevent or break this cycle. Many doctors and veteran travelers swear by Pepto-Bismol for soothing sore stomachs and stopping diarrhea. Acidophilus, the bacteria found in yogurt, is widely available in the United States in tablets and aids digestion. Warm *manzanilla* (chamomile) tea, used widely in Mexico (and by Peter Rabbit's mother), provides liquid and calms upset stomachs. Temporarily avoid coffee and alcohol, drink plenty of *manzanilla* tea, and eat bananas and rice for a few meals until your tummy can take regular food.

Although powerful antibiotics and antidiarrhea medications such as Lomotil and Imodium are readily available over *farmacia* counters, they may involve serious side effects and should not be taken in the absence of medical advice. If in doubt, consult a doctor.

Chagas' Disease and Dengue Fever

Chagas' disease, spread by the "kissing" (or, more appropriately, "assassin") bug, is a potential hazard in the Mexican tropics. Known locally as a *vinchuca,* the triangular-headed, two-centimeter (0.75-inch) brown insect, identifiable by its yellow-striped abdomen, often drops upon its sleeping victims from the thatched ceiling of a rural house at night. Its bite is followed by swelling, fever, and weakness and can lead to heart failure if left untreated. Application of drugs at an early stage can, however, clear the patients of the trypanosome parasites that infect the victims' bloodstreams and vital organs. See a doctor immediately if you believe you're infected.

Most of the precautions against malaria-bearing mosquitoes also apply to dengue fever, which has become a fairly persistent, if not quite epidemic, problem in parts of coastal Mexico in recent years. The culprit here is a virus carried by the mosquito species *Aedes aegypti.* Symptoms are acute fever, with chills, sweating, and muscle aches. A red, diffuse rash frequently results, which may later peel. Symptoms abate after about five days, but fatigue may persist. A particularly serious, but fortunately rare, form, called dengue hemorrhagic fever, afflicts children and can be fatal. See a doctor immediately. Although no vaccines or preventatives are available, other than

generally deterring insects, you should nevertheless see a doctor immediately.

Scorpions and Snakes

While camping or staying in a *palapa* or other rustic accommodation, watch for scorpions, especially in your shoes, which you should shake out every morning. Scorpion stings and most snake bites are rarely fatal to an adult but are potentially very serious for a child. Get the victim to a doctor calmly but quickly.

Tattoos

All health hazards don't come from the wild. A number of Mexico travelers have complained of complications from black henna tattoos. When enhanced by the chemical dye PPD, an itchy rash results that can lead to scarring. It's best to play it safe: If you must have a vacation tattoo, get it at an established, professional shop.

MEDICAL CARE

For medical advice and treatment, let your hotel (or if you're camping, the closest *farmacia*) refer you to a good doctor, clinic, or hospital. Mexican doctors, especially in medium-size and small towns, practice like private doctors in the United States and Canada once did before health insurance, liability, and group practice. They will come to you if you request it; they often keep their doors open even after regular hours and charge reasonable fees.

You will receive generally good treatment at the many local hospitals in Oaxaca's tourist centers and larger towns. If you must have an English-speaking, American-trained doctor, the **International Association for Medical Assistance to Travelers (IAMAT)** (1623 Military Rd., #279, Niagara Falls, NY 14304, tel. 716/754-4883; or 2163 Gordon St., Guelph, Ontario N1K 1B5, tel. 519/836-0102, or 1287 St. Clair Ave. W, Toronto, Ontario M6E 1B8, tel. 416/652-0137, www.iamat.org) publishes an updated booklet of qualified member physicians, some of whom practice in Oaxaca City, Puerto Escondido, and

Medical Tags and Air Evacuation

Travelers with special medical problems should consider wearing a medical identification tag. For a reasonable fee, **Medic Alert** (2323 Colorado Ave., Turlock, CA 95382, California 95382, tel. 209/668-3333, toll-free tel. 888/633-4298, www.medicalert.org) provides such tags, as well as an information hotline that will inform doctors of your vital medical background.

In life-threatening emergencies, highly recommended **Aeromedevac** (Gillespie Field Airport, 681 Kenney St., El Cajon, CA 92020, toll-free tel. 800/462-0911, from Mexico 24-hr toll-free tel. 800/832-5087, www.aeromedevac.com) provides high-tech jet ambulance service from any Mexican locale to a U.S. hospital for roughly $20,000.

Alternatively, you might consider the similar services of **Med-Jet Assist** (Intl. Airport, 4900 69th St., Birmingham AL, 35206, toll-free U.S. tel. 800/527-7478, www.medjetassist.com; in emergencies, world-wide, call U.S. tel. 205/595-6626 collect).

Huatulco. IAMAT also distributes a very detailed *How to Protect Yourself Against Malaria* guide, together with worldwide malaria risk and communicable disease charts.

For more useful information on health and safety in Mexico, consult Drs. Robert H. Paige and Curtis P. Page's *Mexico: Health and Safety Travel Guide* (Tempe, AZ: Med to Go Books, 2004) and Dirk Schroeder's *Staying Healthy in Asia, Africa, and Latin America* (Berkeley, CA: Avalon Travel Publishing, 2000).

WATER SAFETY

As viewed from Oaxaca beaches, the Pacific Ocean usually lives up to its name. Many protected inlets, safe for children's play, dot the coastline. Unsheltered shorelines, on the other hand, can be deceiving. Smooth water in the calm forenoon often changes to choppy in the afternoon; calm ripples lapping the shore in March can grow to hurricane-driven walls of water in November. Such storms can wash away sand, changing a wide gently sloping beach into a steep rocky one plagued by turbulent waves and treacherous currents.

Undertow, whirlpools, crosscurrents, and occasional oversized waves can make ocean swimming a fast-lane adventure. Getting unexpectedly swept out to sea or hammered onto the beach bottom by a surprise breaker are potential hazards.

Never attempt serious swimming when tipsy or full of food; *never* swim alone where someone can't see you. *Always* swim beyond the breakers (which come in sets of several, climaxed by a big one, which breaks highest and farthest from the beach). If you happen to get caught in the path of such a breaker, avoid it by diving straight under it and letting it roll harmlessly over you. If you do get caught by a serious breaker, try to roll and tumble with it (as football players tumble) to avoid injury.

Poisonous sea snakes, although rare and shy, do inhabit Oaxaca waters. Much more common, especially around submerged rocks, is the toothy **moray eel** that sometimes inflicts a painful bite. Don't stick your fingers or toes anywhere you can't see.

Now and then, swimmers get a nettle-like **jellyfish sting.** Furthermore, take care around **coral reefs** and beds of **sea urchins; corals** can sting (like jellyfish), and you can get infections from coral cuts and sea-urchin spines. Shuffle along sandy bottoms to scare away stingrays before stepping on one. If you're unlucky, its venomous tail-spines may inflict a painful wound.

If you suffer a coral scratch or jellyfish sting, experts advise you to wash the afflicted area with ocean water and pour alcohol (rubbing alcohol or tequila) over the wound, then apply hydrocortisone cream available from the *farmacia.*

Injuries from sea-urchin spines and stingray barbs are painful and can be serious. Physicians recommend similar first aid for both: remove the spines or barbs by hand or with tweezers, then soak the injury in as-hot-as-possible fresh water to weaken the toxins and provide relief. Another method is to rinse the area with an antibacterial solution—rubbing alcohol, vinegar, wine, or ammonia diluted with water. If none are available, the same effect may be achieved with urine, either your own or someone else's in your party. Get medical help immediately.

CRIME AND PERSONAL SAFETY

Occasional knifepoint robberies and muggings have marred the once-peaceful Puerto Escondido nighttime beach scene. Walk alone and you invite trouble, especially along Playa Bachoco and the unlit stretch of Playa Principal between the east end of the *adoquín* and the Hotel Santa Fe. If you have dinner alone at the Hotel Santa Fe, avoid the beach and return by taxi or walk along the highway to Avenida Pérez Gasga back to your hotel.

Fortunately, such problems seem to be confined to the beach. Visitors are quite safe on the Puerto Escondido streets themselves, often more so than on their own city streets back home.

Safe Conduct

Mexico is an old-fashioned country where people value traditional ideals of honesty, fidelity, and piety. Crime rates are low; visitors are often safer in Mexico than in their home cities.

This applies even more strongly in Oaxaca. Don't be scared away by headlines about kidnappings and drug-related murders in border cities such as Tijuana and Ciudad Juárez, or car hijackings in bad Mexico City neighborhoods. Violent crime is nearly unknown in Oaxaca City. Around the *zócalo*, women are often seen walking home alone at night. Nevertheless, some Oaxaca neighborhoods are friendlier than others. If you find yourself walking in a locality at night that doesn't feel too welcoming, do not hesitate to hail a taxi.

Although Oaxaca is very safe with respect to violent crime, you should still take normal precautions against petty theft. Stow your valuables in your hotel safe, don't wear showy jewelry or display wads of money, and especially at a crowded market, keep your camera and valuables protected in a waist belt, secure purse, or zipped pockets. If you're parking your car for the night, do it in a secure garage or a guarded hotel parking lot.

Even though four generations have elapsed since Pancho Villa raided the U.S. border, the image of a Mexico bristling with bandidos persists. And similarly for Mexicans: despite the century and a half since the *yanquis* invaded Mexico City and took half their country, the communal Mexican psyche still views gringos (and, by association, all white foreigners) with revulsion, jealousy, and wonder.

Fortunately, the Mexican love-hate affair with foreigners does not usually apply to individual visitors. Your friendly *"buenos dias"* ("good morning") or *"por favor"* ("please"), when appropriate, is always appreciated, whether in the market, the gas station, or the hotel. The shy smile you will most likely receive in return will be your small, but not insignificant, reward.

Women

Your own behavior, despite low crime statistics, largely determines your safety in Mexico. For women traveling solo, it is important to realize that the double standard is alive and well in Mexico. Dress and behave modestly and you will most likely avoid harassment. Whenever possible, stay in the company of friends or acquaintances; find companions for beach, sightseeing, and shopping excursions. Ignore strange men's solicitations and overtures. A Mexican man on the prowl will invent the sappiest romantic overtures to snare a gringa. He will often interpret anything but a firm "no" as a "maybe," and a "maybe" as a "yes."

Men

For male visitors, alcohol often leads to trouble. Avoid bars and cantinas; and, if given

Mexico's excellent beers, you can't abstain completely, at least maintain soft-spoken self-control in the face of challenges from macho drunks.

The Law and Police

While Mexican authorities are tolerant of alcohol (and marijuana in some tourist destinations), they are decidedly intolerant of other substances such as psychedelics, cocaine, and heroin. Getting caught with such drugs in Mexico usually leads to swift and severe results.

Equally swift is the punishment for nude sunbathing, which is both illegal in public and offensive to Mexicans. Confine your nudist colony to very private locations.

Although with decreasing frequency lately, traffic police in Oaxaca sometimes seem to watch foreign cars with eagle eyes. Officers seem to inhabit busy intersections and one-way streets, waiting for confused tourists to make a wrong move. If they whistle you over, stop immediately or you will really get into hot water. If guilty, say *"Lo siento"* ("I'm sorry") and be cooperative. Although the officer probably won't mention it, he or she is usually hoping that you'll cough up a $20 *mordida* (bribe) for the privilege of driving away. Don't do it. Although the officer may hint at confiscating your car, calmly ask for an official *boleto* (written traffic ticket), if you're guilty, in exchange for your driver's license (have a copy), which the officer will probably keep if he or she writes a ticket. If after a few minutes no money appears, the officer will most likely give you back your driver's license rather than go to the trouble of writing the ticket. If not, the worst that usually will happen is you will have to go to the *presidencia municipal* (city hall) the next morning and pay the $20 to a clerk in exchange for your driver's license.

The customarily tranquil state of Oaxaca has occasionally experienced episodes of public unrest. Recent conflicts have been the result of the longstanding backlog of unsettled grievances that run from local land disputes and protest strikes by underpaid teachers, such as the teacher strike that paralyzed Oaxaca City for several months during 2006, all the way up to unsolved political kidnappings and assassinations.

Since 2006, aggrieved, often local community delegations have petitioned local authorities for redress and set up camp in plain view for visitors to see in the Oaxaca *zócalo*. There is no reason for visitors to be alarmed about such lawful demonstrations as long as they remain as peaceful as they have been for the past eight years.

Pedestrian and Driving Hazards

Although Oaxaca's potholed pavements and "holey" sidewalks won't land you in jail, one of them might send you to the hospital if you don't watch your step, especially at night. "Pedestrian beware" is especially good advice on Mexican streets, where it is rumored that some drivers speed up rather than slow down when they spot a tourist stepping off the curb. Falling coconuts, especially frequent on windy days, constitute an additional hazard to unwary campers and beachgoers.

Driving along Mexican country roads, where slow trucks and carts block lanes, campesinos stroll the shoulders, and horses, burros, and cattle wander at will, is hazardous, and doubly so at night.

Information and Services

MONEY

Whatever the circumstance, your travel money will usually go much further in Oaxaca than back home. Despite the national 15 percent ("value added" IVA) sales tax, local lodging, food, and transportation prices will often seem like bargains compared to the developed world. In both Oaxaca City and the Oaxaca Pacific resort towns, hearty restaurant dinners run $4-10, while basic, but comfortable and clean hotel rooms go for as little as $30.

The Peso: Down and Up

Overnight in early 1993, the Mexican government shifted its monetary decimal point three places and created the "new" peso (now known simply as the "peso"), which, at this writing, trades between 11 and 13 per U.S. dollar. Since the peso value sometimes changes rapidly, U.S. dollars are a more stable indicator of value than pesos, and are therefore used in this book to report prices. You should, nevertheless, always use pesos to pay for everything in Mexico.

Since the introduction of the new peso, the centavo (one-hundredth of a new peso) has reappeared, in coins of 5, 10, 20, and 50 centavos. Incidentally, the dollar sign, "$," also marks Mexican pesos. Peso coins *(monedas)* in denominations of 1, 2, 5, and 10 pesos, and bills, in denominations of 20, 50, 100, 200, 500, and 1,000 pesos, are common. Since banks like to exchange your dollars for a few crisp large bills rather than the often-tattered smaller denominations, ask for some of your change in 50- and 100-peso notes. A 500-peso note, while common at the bank, may look awfully big to a small shopkeeper, who might be hard-pressed to change it.

Banks, ATMs, and Money-Exchange Offices

Mexican banks, like their North American counterparts, have lengthened their business hours. Hong Kong Shanghai Banking Corporation (HSBC) maintains the longest hours: some branches as long as 8am-6pm Monday-Saturday. Banamex (Banco Nacional de Mexico), generally the most popular with local people, usually posts the best in-town dollar exchange rate in its lobbies, for example, *Tipo de cambio: venta 11.799, compra 11.933,* which means it will sell pesos to you at the rate of 11.799 per dollar and buy them back for 11.933 per dollar.

ATMs (automated teller machines), or *cajeros automáticos* (kah-HAY-rohs ahoo-toh-MAH-tee-kohs), have become the money sources of choice in Mexico. Virtually every bank has a 24-hour ATM, accessible by a swarm of U.S. and Canadian credit and ATM cards, with proper "PIN" ("NIP," pronounced "NEEP" in Spanish) identification codes. *Note:* Some Mexican bank ATMs will "eat" your ATM card if you don't retrieve it within about 15 seconds of completing your transaction. Retrieve your card *immediately* after completing your transaction.

Since one-time Mexican bank charges (typically $2-3 per transaction) do not depend on the amount you withdraw, you might as well save on fees by withdrawing the maximum ($300-500). A word of warning: as of this writing, ATMs not located in banks have become notorious, all over Mexico, for scams and frauds. People withdraw money, some criminal somehow gets their card information and their PIN, and helps himself to their cash. We recommend only withdrawing money from an ATM that is located in or adjacent to a bank.

Even without an ATM card, you don't have to go to the trouble of waiting in long bank service lines. Opt for a less-crowded bank, such as Bancomer, Banco Serfín, BaNorte, or a private money-exchange office *(casa de cambio).* Often most convenient, such offices often offer long hours and faster service than the banks, for a fee (as little as $1 or as much as $4 per $100).

Keeping Your Money Safe

In Oaxaca as everywhere, from Paris to Perth, **thieves** circulate among the tourists. Keep valuables in your hotel *caja de seguridad* (security box). If you don't particularly trust the desk clerk, carry what you cannot afford to lose in a money belt. Pickpockets love crowded markets, buses, and airport terminals where they can slip a wallet out of a back pocket or dangling purse or a camera from its belt case in a blink. Guard against this by carrying your wallet in your front pocket, your camera in your purse or daypack, and your purse, waist pouch, and daypack (which clever crooks can sometimes slit open) on your front side.

Don't attract thieves by displaying wads of money or flashy jewelry. Don't get sloppy drunk; if so, you may become a pushover for a determined thief.

Don't leave valuables unattended on the beach; share security duties with trustworthy-looking neighbors, or leave a bag with a shopkeeper nearby.

Tipping

Without their droves of visitors, Mexican people would be even poorer. Deflation of the peso, while it makes prices low for outsiders, makes it rough for Mexican families to get by. The help at your hotel typically get paid only a few dollars a day. They depend on tips to make the difference between dire and bearable poverty. Give the *camarista* (chambermaid) and floor attendant 20 pesos every day or two. And whenever uncertain of what to tip, it will probably mean a lot to someone—maybe a whole family—if you err on the generous side.

In restaurants and bars, Mexican tipping customs are similar to those in the United States. Tip waiters and bartenders about 15 percent for satisfactory service.

Credit Cards

Credit cards, such as Visa, MasterCard, and, to a lesser extent, American Express and Discover, are widely honored in the hotels, restaurants, crafts shops, and boutiques that cater to foreign tourists. You will generally get better bargains, however, in shops that depend on local trade and do not so readily accept credit cards. Such shops sometimes offer discounts for cash sales.

COMMUNICATIONS
Using Mexican Telephones

Although Mexican phone service has improved in the last decade, it's still sometimes hit-or-miss. If a number doesn't get through, you may have to redial it more than once. When someone answers (usually *"Bueno"*), be especially courteous. If your Spanish is rusty, say, *"¿Por favor, habla inglés?"* (¿POR fah-VOR, AH-blah een-GLAYS?—"Please, do you speak English?"). If you want to speak to a particular person (such as María), ask, *"¿María se encuentra?"* (¿mah-REE-ah SAY ayn-koo-AYN-trah?).

Since November 2001, when telephone numbers were standardized, Mexican phones operate pretty much the same as in the United States and Canada. In Oaxaca City, for example, a complete telephone number is generally written like this: 951/514-4709. As in the United States, the "951" denotes the telephone area code, or *lada* (LAH-dah), and the 514-4709 is the number (except in the case of a cell phone) that you dial locally. If you want to dial this number **long distance** *(larga distancia),* first dial "01" (like "1" in the United States and Canada), then 951/514-4709. All Mexican telephone numbers, with only three exceptions, begin with a three-digit *lada,* followed by a seven-digit local number. (The exceptions are Monterrey, Guadalajara, and Mexico City, which have two-digit *ladas* and eight-digit local numbers. The Mexico City *lada* is 55; Guadalajara's is 33; Monterrey's is 81. For example, a complete Guadalajara phone number would read something like 33/6897-2253.)

Although **Mexican cellular telephones** are as universally used as those in the United States and Canada, at this writing they operate a bit differently. In order to call a local cellular number, for example, the Oaxaca local number 951/514-4709, you must prefix it with "044." Thus, in Oaxaca City and in the Valley of Oaxaca, dial 044-951/514-4709. However, outside of Oaxaca City and the Valley of Oaxaca, for example, in Puerto Escondido, you call a cellular number in Oaxaca City by first dialing "045." Thus, from Puerto Escondido calling Oaxaca, simply dial 045-951/514-4709.

In Oaxaca towns and cities, direct long-distance dialing is the rule from hotels, public phone booths, and efficient private computerized telephone offices. The cheapest, often most convenient, way to call is by buying and using a public telephone **Ladatel telephone card** *(tarjeta telefónica)*. Buy them in 30-, 50-, and 100-peso denominations at the many outlets (minimarkets, pharmacies, liquor stores) that display the blue and yellow Ladatel sign.

Another equally economical option is to do your phoning in a *caseta larga distancia* (local phone office). Typically staffed by a young woman and often connected to a store or café, the *larga distancia* becomes an informal community social center as people pass the time waiting for their phone connections.

The most convenient but **costliest telephoning option** is to use your hotel room telephone, which can run as much as $0.50 per minute to call locally, and $5 per minute to call the United States, Canada, or Europe.

Getting your own cell phone adapted for Mexico at home before you leave and using it on your trip probably won't help much, since it will probably run about $80 per month stateside cost, plus about $100 or more in Mexico, for say, 400 monthly minutes.

Buying and using a Mexican cell phone in Mexico is a good alternative. They are reasonably priced ($25-50), and you can buy minutes in increments of 100 pesos.

Calling Mexico and the United States

To call Mexico direct from the United States, first dial 011 (for international access), then 52 (Mexico country code), followed by the Mexican area code and local number. For example, from the United States, call a Oaxaca local number such as 951/514-4709 by dialing 01152-951/514-4709. Again, you must **dial cellular phone numbers a bit differently,** by entering a "1" before the area code. Thus, if Oaxaca City local number 514-4709 were a cellular number, from the United States you must dial 01152-1-951/514-4709.

For station-to-station **calls to the United States and Canada from Mexico,** dial 001 plus the area code and the local number. For example, to call San Diego (area code 619) local number 388-5390, from Mexico, simply dial 001-619/388-5390. For calls to other countries, ask your hotel desk clerk or see the easy-to-follow directions in the local Mexican telephone directory.

Beware of certain private "To Call Long Distance to the U.S.A. Collect" (or "by Credit Card") telephones installed prominently in airports, tourist hotels, and shops. Tariffs on these phones often run as high as $10 per minute (with a three-minute minimum), for a total of $30, whether you talk three minutes or not. Always ask the operator for the rate, and if it's too high, buy a 30-peso ($3) Ladatel phone card for a (six-minute) call home.

Post, Telegraph, and Internet Access

Mexican *correos* (post offices) operate similarly, but more slowly and much less securely, than most of their counterparts all over the world. (Hopefully this may improve, due to the recent Mexican post-office reform measures.)

Mail services usually include *lista de correo* (general delivery, address letters *"a/c lista de correo"*), *servicios filatelicas* (philatelic services), *por avión* (airmail), *giros* (postal money orders), and Mexpost secure and fast delivery service, sometimes from separate Mexpost offices.

Mexican ordinary (non-Mexpost) mail has been sadly unreliable and pathetically slow. If, for mailings within Mexico, you must have security, use the efficient, reformed government Mexpost (like U.S. Express Mail) service. For fast and absolutely secure private mailings inside Mexico, use the excellent, widely available Estafeta courier service. For international mailings, check the local Yellow Pages for widely available (but very expensive, $30 for a letter to the United States) DHL, Federal Express, or UPS courier service.

Telégrafos (telegraph offices), usually near the post office, send and receive *telegramas* (telegrams) and *giros* (money orders). *Telecomunicaciones* (Telecom), the new high-tech telegraph offices, added computerized telephone and public fax to their available services.

Internet and computer services, including personal email access, has arrived in Oaxaca cities and towns, large and small. Internet "cafés" are becoming increasingly common, especially in the Oaxaca City, Huatulco, Puerto Escondido, and Puerto Ángel resort centers. Online rates run $1-2 per hour. Most hotels now offer Internet access in lobbies and often in guest rooms as well.

Electricity and Time

Mexican electric power is supplied at U.S.-standard 110 volts, 60 cycles. Plugs and sockets are generally two-pronged and nonpolar (like the pre-1970s U.S. ones). Bring adapters if you're going to use appliances with polar two-pronged or three-pronged plugs. A two-pronged polar plug has different-sized prongs, one of which is too large to plug into an old-fashioned nonpolar socket.

The entire state of Oaxaca and all surrounding states operate on U.S. Central Time, the same as Mexico City and central U.S. states such as Nebraska, Illinois, Tennessee, and Louisiana.

Resources

Glossary

Many of the following words have a socio-historical meaning; others you will not find in the usual English-Spanish dictionary.

abarrotes: groceries, grocery store

aguardiente: Mexican "white lightning": cheap distilled liquor made from sugarcane

aguas: watch out!

alcalde: mayor or municipal judge

alebrije: fanciful wooden animal, mostly made in Arrazola and Tilcajete villages

alfarería: pottery

andador: walkway, or strolling path

antojitos: native Mexican snacks, such as tamales, chiles rellenos, tacos, and enchiladas

artesanías: handicrafts

artesano, artesana: craftsman, craftswoman

asunción: the assumption of the Virgin Mary into heaven (as distinguished from the *ascención* of Jesus into heaven)

atole: a popular nonalcoholic drink made from corn juice

audiencia: one of the royal executive-judicial panels sent to rule Mexico during the 16th century

autopista: expressway

ayuntamiento: either the town council or the building where it meets

balneario: hot springs; can refer to a natural feature, a recreational spa, or a resort

barrio: a town or village district or neighborhood, usually centered around its own local plaza and church

bienes raices: literally "good roots," but popularly, real estate

bola: small crowd of people

boleto: ticket, boarding pass

brujo, bruja: male or female witch doctor or shaman

caballero: literally "horseman," but popularly, gentleman

cabaña ecoturísticas: bungalow lodging for tourists

cabercera: head town of a municipal district, or headquarters in general

cabrón: literally, a cuckold, but more commonly, bastard, rat, or S.O.B.; sometimes used affectionately

cacique: local chief or boss

calenda: procession, usually religious, as during a festival

camionera: bus station

campesino: country person; farm worker

canasta: basket, traditionally made of woven reeds, with handle

cantera: local volcanic stone, widely used for colonial-era Oaxaca monuments

Carnaval: celebration preceding Ash Wednesday, the beginning of the fasting period called Lent. Carnaval is called Mardi Gras in the United States.

casa de huéspedes: guesthouse, often operated in a family home

cascada: waterfall

caudillo: dictator or political chief

centro de salud: health center/clinic

charro: gentleman cowboy

chingar: literally, to "rape," but also the universal Spanish "f" word, the equivalent of "screw" in English

Churrigueresque: Spanish baroque architectural style incorporated into many Mexican colonial churches, named after José Churriguera (1665-1725)

científicos: literally, scientists, but applied to President Porfirio Díaz's technocratic advisers

coa (estaca): digging stick, used for planting corn

Cocijo: Zapotec god of rain, lightning, and thunder

cofradía: Catholic fraternal service association, either male or female, mainly in charge of financing and organizing religious festivals

colectivo: a shared public taxi or minibus that picks up and deposits passengers along a designated route

colegio: preparatory school or junior college

colonia: suburban subdivision/satellite of a larger city

comal: a flat pottery griddle, for cooking/heating tortillas

comedor: restaurant

comida casera: home-cooked food

comida corrida: economical afternoon set meal, usually with four courses: soup, rice, entrée, and dessert

compadrazgo: the semi-formal web of village and barrio *compadre* and *padrino* relationships that determine a person's lifetime obligations and loyalties

compadre: a semi-formalized "best friend" relationship that usually lasts for life

comunal: refers to the traditional indigenous system of joint decision-making and land ownership and use

Conasupo: government store that sells basic foods at subsidized prices

correo: mail, post, or post office

criollo: person of all-European, usually Spanish, descent born in the New World

Cuaresma: Lent (the 46 days of pre-Easter fasting, beginning on Ash Wednesday, and ending on the Saturday before Easter Sunday)

cuota: toll, as in *cuota autopista,* toll expressway

curandero, curandera: indigenous medicine man or woman

damas: ladies, as in "ladies room"

Domingo de Ramos: Palm Sunday

ejido: a constitutional, government-sponsored form of community, with shared land ownership and cooperative decision-making

encomienda: colonial award of tribute from a designated indigenous district

farmacia: pharmacy or drugstore

finca: farm

finca cafetelera: coffee farm

fonda: food stall or small restaurant, often in a traditional market complex

fraccionamiento: city sector or subdivision, abbreviated "Fracc."

fuero: the former right of Mexican clergy and military to be tried in separate ecclesiastical and military courts

gachupin: "one who wears spurs"; a derogatory term for a Spanish-born colonial

gasolinera: gasoline station

gente de razón: "people of reason"; whites and mestizos in colonial Mexico

gringo: once-derogatory but now commonly used term for North American whites

grito: impassioned cry, as in Hidalgo's *Grito de Dolores*

hacienda: large landed estate; also the government treasury

hamaca: hammock

hechicero: a "wizard" who often leads native propitiatory ceremonies

hidalgo: nobleman or noblewoman; called honorifically by "Don" or "Doña"

hojalata: tinware, a popular craft of Oaxaca

huarache: popular dish consisting of a fried masa base with a variety of toppings

huipil: traditional emroidered dress

indígena: indigenous or aboriginal inhabitant of all-native descent who speaks his or her native tongue; commonly, but incorrectly, an *indio* (Indian)

jacal: native label for thatched, straw, and/or stick country house

jaripeo: bull roping and riding

jejenes: "no-see-um" biting gnats, most common around coastal wetlands

judiciales: the federal "judicial," or investigative police, best known to motorists for their highway checkpoint inspections

jugería: stall or small restaurant providing a large array of squeezed vegetable and fruit *jugos* (juices) *juzgado:* the "hoosegow," or jail

lancha: launch (a small motorboat)

larga distancia: long-distance telephone service, or the *caseta* (booth or office) where it's provided

licencado: academic degree (abbrev. Lic.) approximately equivalent to a bachelor's degree in the United States

lonchería: small lunch counter, usually serving juices, sandwiches, and *antojitos*

machismo; macho: exaggerated sense of maleness; person who holds such a sense of himself

manañita: early-morning mass

mano: a hand, or the stone roller used to grind corn on the flat stone *metate*

mayordomo: community leader responsible for staging a local Catholic religious festival

mezcal: alcoholic beverage distilled from the fermented hearts of maguey (century plant)

mestizo: person of mixed native and European descent

metate: a slightly concave, horizontal stone basin for grinding corn for tortillas

milagro: literally a miracle, but also a small religious wish medal, often pinned to an altar saint by someone requesting divine intervention

milpa: a small, family-owned field, traditionally planted in corn, beans, and squash

mirador: viewpoint, overlook

molcajete: a stone mortar and pestle, used for hand-grinding, especially chilies and seeds

mordida: slang for bribe; "little bite"

olla: a pottery jug or pot, used for stewing vegetables, meats, beans, coffee

padrino, padrina: godfather or godmother, often the respective compadres of the given child's parents

palapa: an open, thatched-roof structure, usually shading a restaurant

panela: rough brown cane sugar, sold in lumps in the market

panga: outboard motor-launch *(lancha)*

papier-mâché: the craft of glued, multilayered paper sculpture, centered in Tonalá, Jalisco, where creations can resemble fine pottery or lacquerware

Pemex: acronym for Petróleos Mexicanos, the national oil corporation

peninsulares: the Spanish-born ruling colonial elite

peón: a poor wage-earner, usually a country native

periférico: peripheral boulevard

petate: all-purpose woven mat, from palm fronds

piciete: native tobacco, widely cultivated in Northern Oaxaca state

piñata: papier-mâché decoration, usually in animal or human form, filled with treats and broken open during a fiesta

plan: political manifesto, usually by a leader or group consolidating or seeking power

Porfiriato: the 34-year (1876-1910) ruling period of president-dictator Porfirio Díaz

posadas: Christmas, especially on Christmas Eve, procession, in which participants, led by costumed Holy Mary and Joseph, knock on neighborhood doors and implore, unsuccessfully, for a room for the night

pozahuanco: horizontally striped hand-woven wraparound skirt, commonly worn in Oaxaca's coastal Mixtec district

pozole: stew of hominy in broth, usually topped by shredded meat, cabbage, and diced onion

presidencia municipal: the headquarters, like a U.S. city or county hall, of a Mexican *municipio*, county-like local governmental unit

preventiva: local, state, or federal police, especially charged with directly foiling crooks

principal, anciano: a respected elder, often a member of a council of elders, whom the community consults for advice and support

pronunciamiento: declaration of rebellion by an insurgent leader

pueblo: town or people

puente: literally a "bridge," but commonly a long holiday weekend, when resort hotel reservations are highly recommended

pulque: the fermented juice of the maguey plant, approximately equivalent in alcoholic content to wine or strong beer

puta: whore, bitch, or slut

quinta: a villa or upscale country house

quinto: the colonial royal "fifth" tax on treasure and precious metals

ramada: a shade roof, usually made of palm fronds; in coastal Mexico, *ramadas* often shelter homes or restaurants

regidor: a community official, often a town council member, responsible for specific government functions, such as public works

retablo: altarpiece, often of ornately carved and gilded wood

retorno: cul-de-sac

ropa típica: traditional dress, derived from the Spanish colonial tradition (in contrast to *traje,* traditional indigenous dress)

rurales: former federal country police force created to fight bandidos (bandits) and suppress political dissent

Sabi: Mixtec god of rain

sabino: "Mexican" or "Montezuma" bald cypress tree, *Taxodium mucronatum*

Semana Santa: Holy Week, the week preceding Easter Sunday

servicios: the indigenous ladder of increasingly responsible public tasks that, if successfully performed, leads to community approval, prestige, and leadership for a given individual by middle age

tapete: wool rug, made in certain east-side Valley of Oaxaca villages

taxi especial: private taxi, as distinguished from *taxi colectivo,* or collective taxi

telégrafo: telegraph office, lately converting to high-tech *telecomunicaciones (telecom),* that also offers computerized telephone and public fax services

temazcal: traditional indigenous sweat room, rock-enclosed and heated by a wood fire, usually used for healing, especially by women after childbirth

tenate: basket of woven palm leaf, with tumpline instead of a rigid handle

tepache: a wine, fermented from *panela* (sugarcane juice)

tequio: an obligatory communal task, such as local road work, street sweeping, or child care, expected of all adult villagers from time to time

tianguis: literally "awning," but now has come to mean the awning-decorated native town market

tlacoyos: fired or toasted cakes made of masa; similar to corn tortillas but fatter

tono: a usually benign animal guardian spirit

topil: lowest municipal job, of messenger, filled by youngest teenage boys

traje: traditional indigenous dress

vaquero: cowboy

vecinidad: neighborhood

yanqui: Yankee

zócalo: the popular label originally for the Mexico City central plaza; now the name for central plazas all over Mexico, including Oaxaca

Spanish Phrasebook

Your Mexican adventure will be more fun if you use a little Spanish. Mexican folks, although they may smile at your funny accent, will appreciate your halting efforts to break the ice and transform yourself from a foreigner to a potential friend.

Spanish commonly uses 30 letters—the familiar English 26, plus four straightforward additions: ch, ll, ñ, and rr, which are explained in "Consonants," below.

PRONUNCIATION

Once you learn them, Spanish pronunciation rules—in contrast to English—don't change. Spanish vowels generally sound softer than in English. (*Note:* The capitalized syllables below receive stronger accents.)

Vowels

a   like ah, as in "hah": *agua* AH-gooah (water), *pan* PAHN (bread), and *casa* CAH-sah (house) e   like ay, as in "may:" *mesa* MAY-sah (table), *tela* TAY-lah (cloth), and *de* DAY (of, from)

i   like ee, as in "need": *diez* dee-AYZ (ten), *comida* ko-MEE-dah (meal), and *fin* FEEN (end)

o   like oh, as in "go": *peso* PAY-soh (weight), *ocho* OH-choh (eight), and *poco* POH-koh (a bit)

u   like oo, as in "cool": *uno* OO-noh (one), *cuarto* KOOAHR-toh (room), and *usted* oos-TAYD (you); when it follows a "q" the u is silent; when it follows an "h" or has an umlaut, it's pronounced like "w"

Consonants

b, d, f, k, l, m, n, p, q, s, t, v, w, x, y, z, and ch   pronounced almost as in English; h occurs, but is silent—not pronounced at all

c   like k as in "keep": *cuarto* KOOAR-toh (room), Tepic tay-PEEK (capital of Nayarit state); when it precedes "e" or "i," pronounce c like s, as in "sit": *cerveza* sayr-VAY-sah (beer), *encima* ayn-SEE-mah (atop)

g   like g as in "gift" when it precedes "a," "o," "u," or a consonant: *gato* GAH-toh (cat), *hago* AH-goh (I do, make); otherwise, pronounce g like h as in "hat": *giro* HEE-roh (money order), *gente* HAYN-tay (people)

j   like h, as in "has": *Jueves* HOOAY-vays (Thursday), *mejor* may-HOR (better)

ll   like y, as in "yes": *toalla* toh-AH-yah (towel), *ellos* AY-yohs (they, them)

ñ   like ny, as in "canyon": *año* AH-nyo (year), *señor* SAY-nyor (Mr., sir)

r   is lightly trilled, with tongue at the roof of your mouth like a very light English d, as in "ready": *pero* PAY-doh (but), *tres* TDAYS (three), *cuatro* KOOAH-tdoh (four)

rr   like a Spanish r, but with much more emphasis and trill. Let your tongue flap. Practice with *burro* (donkey), *carretera* (highway), and Carrillo (proper name), then really let go with *ferrocarril* (railroad)

Note: The single small but common exception to all of the above is the pronunciation of Spanish y when it's being used as the Spanish word for "and," as in "Ron y Kathy." In such case, pronounce it like the English ee, as in "keep": Ron "ee" Kathy (Ron and Kathy).

Accent

The rule for accent, the relative stress given to syllables within a given word, is straightforward. If a word ends in a vowel, an n, or an s, accent the next-to-last syllable; if not, accent the last syllable.

Pronounce *gracias* GRAH-seeahs (thank you), *orden* OHR-dayn (order), and *carretera* kah-ray-TAY-rah (highway) with stress on the next-to-last syllable.

Otherwise, accent the last syllable: *venir* vay-NEER (to come), *ferrocarril* fay-roh-cah-REEL (railroad), and *edad* ay-DAHD (age).

Exceptions to the accent rule are always marked with an accent sign: (á, é, í, ó, or ú), such as *teléfono* tay-LAY-foh-noh (telephone), *jabón* hah-BON (soap), and *rápido* RAH-pee-doh (rapid).

BASIC AND COURTEOUS EXPRESSIONS

Most Spanish-speaking people consider formalities important. Whenever approaching anyone for information or some other reason, do not forget the appropriate salutation—good morning, good evening, etc. Standing alone, the greeting *hola* (hello) can sound brusque.

Hello. *Hola.*
Good morning. *Buenos días.*
Good afternoon. *Buenas tardes.*
Good evening. *Buenas noches.*
How are you? *¿Cómo está usted?*
Very well, thank you. *Muy bien, gracias.*
Okay; good. *Bien.*
Not okay; bad. *Mal or feo.*
So-so. *Más o menos.*
And you? *¿Y usted?*
Thank you. *Gracias.*
Thank you very much. *Muchas gracias.*
You're very kind. *Muy amable.*
You're welcome. *De nada.*
Goodbye. *Adios.*
See you later. *Hasta luego.*
please *por favor*

yes *sí*
no *no*
I don't know. *No sé.*
Just a moment, please. *Momentito, por favor.*
Excuse me, please (when you're trying to get attention). *Disculpe* or *Con permiso.*
Excuse me (when you've made a boo-boo). *Lo siento.*
Pleased to meet you. *Mucho gusto.*
How do you say . . . in Spanish? *¿Cómo se dice . . . en español?*
What is your name? *¿Cómo se llama usted?*
Do you speak English? *¿Habla usted inglés?*
Is English spoken here? (Does anyone here speak English?) *¿Se habla inglés?*
I don't speak Spanish well. *No hablo bien el español.*
I don't understand. *No entiendo.*
How do you say . . . in Spanish? *¿Cómo se dice . . . en español?*
My name is . . . *Me llamo . . .*
Would you like . . . *¿Quisiera usted . . .*
Let's go to . . . *Vamos a . . .*

TERMS OF ADDRESS

When in doubt, use the formal *usted* (you) as a form of address.

I *yo*
you (formal) *usted*
you (familiar) *tu*
he/him *él*
she/her *ella*
we/us *nosotros*
you (plural) *ustedes*
they/them *ellos* (all males or mixed gender); *ellas* (all females)
Mr., sir *señor*
Mrs., madam *señora*
miss, young lady *señorita*
wife *esposa*
husband *esposo*
friend *amigo* (male); *amiga* (female)
sweetheart *novio* (male); *novia* (female)
son; daughter *hijo; hija*
brother; sister *hermano; hermana*

father; mother *padre; madre*
grandfather; grandmother *abuelo; abuela*

TRANSPORTATION

Where is . . . ? *¿Dónde está . . . ?*
How far is it to . . . ? *¿A cuánto está . . . ?*
from . . . to . . . *de . . . a . . .*
How many blocks? *¿Cuántas cuadras?*
Where (Which) is the way to . . . ? *¿Dónde está el camino a . . . ?*
the bus station *la terminal de autobuses*
the bus stop *la parada de autobuses*
Where is this bus going? *¿Adónde va este autobús?*
the taxi stand *la parada de taxis*
the train station *la estación de ferrocarril*
the boat *el barco*
the launch *lancha; tiburonera*
the dock *el muelle*
the airport *el aeropuerto*
I'd like a ticket to . . . *Quisiera un boleto a . . .*
first (second) class *primera (segunda) clase*
roundtrip *ida y vuelta*
reservation *reservación*
baggage *equipaje*
Stop here, please. *Pare aquí, por favor.*
the entrance *la entrada*
the exit *la salida*
the ticket office *la oficina de boletos*
(very) near; far *(muy) cerca; lejos*
to; toward *a*
by; through *por*
from *de*
the right *la derecha*
the left *la izquierda*
straight ahead *derecho; directo*
in front *en frente*
beside *al lado*
behind *atrás*
the corner *la esquina*
the stoplight *la semáforo*
a turn *una vuelta*
right here *aquí*
somewhere around here *por acá*
right there *allí*
somewhere around there *por allá*
road *el camino*

street; boulevard *calle; bulevar*
block *la cuadra*
highway *carretera*
kilometer *kilómetro*
bridge; toll *puente; cuota*
address *dirección*
north; south *norte; sur*
east; west *oriente (este); poniente (oeste)*

ACCOMMODATIONS

hotel *hotel*
Is there a room? *¿Hay cuarto?*
May I (may we) see it? *¿Puedo (podemos) verlo?*
What is the rate? *¿Cuál es el precio?*
Is that your best rate? *¿Es su mejor precio?*
Is there something cheaper? *¿Hay algo más económico?*
a single room *un cuarto sencillo*
a double room *un cuarto doble*
double bed *cama matrimonial*
twin beds *camas gemelas*
with private bath *con baño*
hot water *agua caliente*
shower *ducha*
towels *toallas*
soap *jabón*
toilet paper *papel higiénico*
blanket *frazada; manta*
sheets *sábanas*
air-conditioned *aire acondicionado*
fan *abanico; ventilador*
key *llave*
manager *gerente*

FOOD

I'm hungry. *Tengo hambre.*
I'm thirsty. *Tengo sed.*
menu *carta; menú*
order *orden*
glass *vaso*
fork *tenedor*
knife *cuchillo*
spoon *cuchara*
napkin *servilleta*
soft drink *refresco*
coffee *café*
tea *té*

drinking water *agua pura; agua potable*
bottled carbonated water *agua mineral*
bottled uncarbonated water *agua sin gas*
beer *cerveza*
wine *vino*
milk *leche*
juice *jugo*
cream *crema*
sugar *azúcar*
cheese *queso*
snack *antojo; botana*
breakfast *desayuno*
lunch *almuerzo*
daily lunch special *comida corrida (or el menú del día depending on region)*
dinner *comida (often eaten in late afternoon); cena (a late-night snack)*
the check *la cuenta*
eggs *huevos*
bread *pan*
salad *ensalada*
fruit *fruta*
mango *mango*
watermelon *sandía*
papaya *papaya*
banana *plátano*
apple *manzana*
orange *naranja*
lime *limón*
fish *pescado*
shellfish *mariscos*
shrimp *camarones*
meat (without) *(sin) carne*
chicken *pollo*
pork *puerco*
beef; steak *res; bistec*
bacon; ham *tocino; jamón*
fried *frito*
roasted *asada*
barbecue; barbecued *barbacoa; al carbón*

SHOPPING

money *dinero*
money-exchange bureau *casa de cambio*
I would like to exchange traveler's checks. *Quisiera cambiar cheques de viajero.*

What is the exchange rate? *¿Cuál es el tipo de cambio?*
How much is the commission? *¿Cuánto cuesta la comisión?*
Do you accept credit cards? *¿Aceptan tarjetas de crédito?*
money order *giro*
How much does it cost? *¿Cuánto cuesta?*
What is your final price? *¿Cuál es su último precio?*
expensive *caro*
cheap *barato; económico*
more *más*
less *menos*
a little *un poco*
too much *demasiado*

HEALTH

Help me please. *Ayúdeme por favor.*
I am ill. *Estoy enfermo.*
Call a doctor. *Llame un doctor.*
Take me to ... *Lléveme a ...*
hospital *hospital; sanatorio*
drugstore *farmacia*
pain *dolor*
fever *fiebre*
headache *dolor de cabeza*
stomach ache *dolor de estómago*
burn *quemadura*
cramp *calambre*
nausea *náusea*
vomiting *vomitar*
medicine *medicina*
antibiotic *antibiótico*
pill; tablet *pastilla*
aspirin *aspirina*
ointment; cream *pomada; crema*
bandage *venda*
cotton *algodón*
sanitary napkins use brand name, e.g., Kotex
birth control pills *pastillas anticonceptivas*
contraceptive foam *espuma anticonceptiva*
condoms *preservativos; condones*
toothbrush *cepilla dental*
dental floss *hilo dental*
toothpaste *crema dental*

dentist *dentista*
toothache *dolor de muelas*

POST OFFICE AND COMMUNICATIONS

long-distance telephone *teléfono larga distancia*
I would like to call ... *Quisiera llamar a ...*
collect *por cobrar*
station to station *a quien contesta*
person to person *persona a persona*
credit card *tarjeta de crédito*
post office *correo*
general delivery *lista de correo*
letter *carta*
stamp *estampilla, timbre*
postcard *tarjeta*
aerogram *aerograma*
air mail *correo aereo*
registered *registrado*
money order *giro*
package; box *paquete; caja*
string; tape *cuerda; cinta*

AT THE BORDER

border *frontera*
customs *aduana*
immigration *migración*
tourist card *tarjeta de turista*
inspection *inspección; revisión*
passport *pasaporte*
profession *profesión*
marital status *estado civil*
single *soltero*
married; divorced *casado; divorciado*
widowed *viudado*
insurance *seguros*
title *título*
driver's license *licencia de manejar*

AT THE GAS STATION

gas station *gasolinera*
gasoline *gasolina*
unleaded *sin plomo*
full, please *lleno, por favor*
tire *llanta*
tire repair shop *vulcanizadora*
air *aire*

water *agua*
oil (change) *aceite (cambio)*
grease *grasa*
My ... doesn't work. *Mi ... no sirve.*
battery *batería*
radiator *radiador*
alternator *alternador*
generator *generador*
tow truck *grúa*
repair shop *taller mecánico*
tune-up *afinación*
auto parts store *refaccionería*

VERBS

Verbs are the key to getting along in Spanish. They employ mostly predictable forms and come in three classes, which end in *ar, er,* and *ir,* respectively:

to buy *comprar*
I buy, you (he, she, it) buys *compro, compra*
we buy, you (they) buy *compramos, compran*

to eat *comer*
I eat, you (he, she, it) eats *como, come*
we eat, you (they) eat *comemos, comen*

to climb *subir*
I climb, you (he, she, it) climbs *subo, sube*
we climb, you (they) climb *subimos, suben*

Here are more (with irregularities indicated):

to do or make *hacer* (regular except for *hago,* I do or make)
to go *ir* (very irregular: *voy, va, vamos, van*)
to go (walk) *andar*
to love *amar*
to work *trabajar*
to want *desear, querer*
to need *necesitar*
to read *leer*
to write *escribir*
to repair *reparar*

to stop *parar*
to get off (the bus) *bajar*
to arrive *llegar*
to stay (remain) *quedar*
to stay (lodge) *hospedar*
to leave *salir* (regular except for *salgo,* I leave)
to look at *mirar*
to look for *buscar*
to give *dar* (regular except for *doy,* I give)
to carry *llevar*
to have *tener* (irregular but important: *tengo, tiene, tenemos, tienen*)
to come *venir* (similarly irregular: *vengo, viene, venimos, vienen*)

Spanish has two forms of "to be":

to be *estar* (regular except for *estoy,* I am)
to be *ser* (very irregular: *soy, es, somos, son*)

Use *estar* when speaking of location or a temporary state of being: "I am at home." *"Estoy en casa."* "I'm sick." *"Estoy enfermo."* Use *ser* for a permanent state of being: "I am a doctor." *"Soy doctora."*

NUMBERS

zero *cero*
one *uno*
two *dos*
three *tres*
four *cuatro*
five *cinco*
six *seis*
seven *siete*
eight *ocho*
nine *nueve*
10 *diez*
11 *once*
12 *doce*
13 *trece*
14 *catorce*
15 *quince*
16 *dieciseis*
17 *diecisiete*
18 *dieciocho*
19 *diecinueve*

20 *veinte*	
21 *veinte y uno* or *veintiuno*	
30 *treinta*	
40 *cuarenta*	
50 *cincuenta*	
60 *sesenta*	
70 *setenta*	
80 *ochenta*	
90 *noventa*	
100 *ciento*	
101 *ciento y uno* or *cientiuno*	
200 *doscientos*	
500 *quinientos*	
1,000 *mil*	
10,000 *diez mil*	
100,000 *cien mil*	
1,000,000 *millón*	
one half *medio*	
one third *un tercio*	
one fourth *un cuarto*	

TIME

What time is it? *¿Qué hora es?*
It's one o'clock. *Es la una.*
It's three in the afternoon. *Son las tres de la tarde.*
It's 4 a.m. *Son las cuatro de la mañana.*
six-thirty *seis y media*
a quarter till eleven *un cuarto para las once*
a quarter past five *las cinco y cuarto*
an hour *una hora*

DAYS AND MONTHS

Monday *lunes*
Tuesday *martes*
Wednesday *miércoles*
Thursday *jueves*
Friday *viernes*
Saturday *sábado*
Sunday *domingo*
today *hoy*
tomorrow *mañana*
yesterday *ayer*
January *enero*
February *febrero*
March *marzo*
April *abril*
May *mayo*
June *junio*
July *julio*
August *agosto*
September *septiembre*
October *octubre*
November *noviembre*
December *diciembre*
a week *una semana*
a month *un mes*
after *después*
before *antes*

(Courtesy of Bruce Whipperman, author of *Moon Pacific Mexico*.)

Suggested Reading

Some of these books are informative, others are entertaining, and all of them will increase your understanding of both Mexico and Oaxaca.

HISTORY

Blanton, E. Richard, Gary M. Feinman, Stephen A. Kowaleski, and Linda M. Nicholas. *Ancient Oaxaca*. Cambridge, New York, and Melbourne: Cambridge University Press, 1999. A scholarly account of pre-Columbian Oaxaca history, for the serious reader.

Brunk, Samuel. *Emiliano Zapata: Revolution and Betrayal in Mexico*. Albuquerque, NM: University of New Mexico Press, 1995. A detailed narrative of the renowned revolutionary's turbulent life, from his humble birth in Anenecuilco village in Morelos through his de facto control of Mexico City in 1914-1915 to his final betrayal and assassination in 1919. The author authoritatively demonstrates that Zapata, neither complete hero nor complete villain, was simply an incredibly determined native leader who paid the ultimate price in his selfless struggle for land and liberty for the campesinos of southern Mexico.

Calderón de la Barca, Frances. *Life in Mexico, with New Material from the Author's Journals.* Charleston, SC: Bibliobazaar, 2006. A new copyright and printing of the humorous original 1843 book, by the brilliant, celebrated Scottish wife of the Spanish ambassador to Mexico.

Casasola, Gustavo. *Seis Siglos de Historia Gráfica de Mexico (Six Centuries of Mexican Graphic History).* Mexico City: Editorial Gustavo Casasola, 1978. Six fascinating encyclopedic volumes, in Spanish, of Mexican history in pictures, from 1325 to the present. Now out of print, but large city and university libraries may have copies.

Chance, John K. *Conquest of the Sierra.* Norman, OK: University of Oklahoma Press, 1989. Professor Chance uses archival sources to trace the evolution of colonial society, principally the northern Sierra Zapotec communities and how they adapted their religion, customs, and settlement patterns in response to the pressures of Spanish rule.

Collis, Maurice. *Cortés and Montezuma.* New York, NY: New Directions Publishing Corp., 1999. A reprint of a 1954 classic piece of well-researched storytelling. Collis traces Cortés's conquest of Mexico through the defeat of his chief opponent, Aztec Emperor Montezuma. He uses contemporary eyewitnesses, notably Bernal Díaz del Castillo, to revivify one of history's greatest dramas.

Cortés, Hernán. *Letters from Mexico.* Translated by Anthony Pagden. New Haven, CT: Yale University Press, 1986. Cortés's five long letters to his king, in which he describes contemporary Mexico in fascinating detail, including, notably, the remarkably sophisticated life of the Aztecs at the time of the conquest.

De las Casas, Bartolome. *A Short Account of the Destruction of the Indies.* New York, NY: Penguin Books, 1992. The gritty but beloved Dominican Bishop, renowned as Mexico's "Apostle of the Indians," writes passionately of his own failed attempt to moderate and humanize the Spanish conquest of Mexico.

Díaz del Castillo, Bernal. *The Discovery and Conquest of Mexico.* New York, NY: Da Capo Press, 2003. A fascinating, still-fresh, soldier's tale of the conquest from the Spanish viewpoint.

Garfias, Luis. *The Mexican Revolution.* Mexico City: Panorama Editorial, 1985. A concise Mexican version of the 1910-1917 Mexican revolution, the crucible of present-day Mexico.

Gugliotta, Bobette. *Women of Mexico, the Consecrated and the Common.* Encino, CA: originally published by Floricanto Press, 1989. Lively legends, tales, and biographies of remarkable Mexican women, including several from Oaxaca. Libraries, Amazon.com, and others have used copies.

León-Portilla, Miguel. *The Broken Spears: The Aztec Account of the Conquest of Mexico.* New York, NY: Beacon Press, 1992. Provides an intriguing contrast to Díaz del Castillo's account.

Meyer, Michael, and William Sherman. *The Course of Mexican History.* New York, NY: Oxford University Press, 2003. An insightful, interestingly written, 700-plus-page college textbook in paperback. A bargain, especially if you can get it used.

Novas, Himlice. *Everything You Need to Know About Latino History*. New York, NY: Penguin Group, 2007. Chicanos, Latin rhythm, La Raza, the Treaty of Guadalupe Hidalgo, and much more, interpreted from an authoritative Latino point of view.

Ridley, Jasper. *Maximilian and Juárez*. London: Orion Pub. Group, 2001. This authoritative historical biography breathes new life into one of Mexico's great ironic tragedies, a drama that pitted the native Zapotec "Lincoln of Mexico" against the dreamy, idealistic Archduke Maximilian of Austria-Hungary. Despite their common liberal ideals, they were drawn into a bloody no-quarter struggle that set the Old World against the New, ending in Maximilian's execution, the insanity of his wife, and the emergence of the United States as a power to be reckoned with in world affairs.

Ruíz, Ramon Eduardo. *Triumphs and Tragedy: A History of the Mexican People*. New York, NY: W. W. Norton, Inc., 1992. A pithy, anecdote-filled history of Mexico from an authoritative Mexican American perspective.

Shorris, Earl. *Life and Times of Mexico*. New York, NY: W. W. Norton, 2006. A grand, 750-page narrative of the divided soul of Mexico, driven by 3,000 years of history, as told by Mexicans, from the ancient Olmecs, Benito Juárez, and Emiliano Zapata, to maquiladora laborers, prostitutes, and a movie director.

Simpson, Lesley Bird. *Many Mexicos*. Berkeley, CA: University of California Press, 1962. A much-reprinted, fascinating, broad-brush portrait of Mexican history.

ARCHAEOLOGY

Flannery, Kent, and Joyce Marcus. *The Cloud People*. New York, NY: Academic Press, 2003. Eminently authoritative authors trace the divergent evolution of the Zapotec and Mixtec peoples as revealed by the archaeological record.

Marcus, Joyce, and Kent Flannery, contributor. *Zapotec Civilization*. London and New York, NY: Thames and Hudson, 1996. The distinguished authors elegantly illustrate and trace the evolution of the Valley of Oaxaca civilization, from 10,000 BC to the conquest, using the results from recent finds and hundreds of maps, drawings, and photos.

Winter, Marcus. *Oaxaca, the Archaeological Record*. Mexico, D.F.: Minutiae Mexicana, 1992. A distinguished Oaxaca resident archaeologist skillfully traces a concise history of Oaxaca's pre-conquest inhabitants, based on finds at Monte Albán, Mitla, and many other sites. Dozens of maps and site descriptions make this 100-page pamphlet an especially useful guide.

UNIQUE GUIDE AND TIP BOOKS

American Automobile Association. *Mexico TravelBook*. Heathrow, FL: American Automobile Association, 2003. The American Automobile Association (tel. 800/922-8228, www.aaa.com) offers short but sweet summaries of major Mexican tourist destinations and sights. Also includes information on fiestas, accommodations, restaurants, and a wealth of information relevant to car travel in Mexico. Available in bookstores, or free to AAA members at affiliate offices.

Church, Mike and Terry. *Traveler's Guide to Mexican Camping*. Kirkland, WA: Rolling Homes Press (order by tel. 800/922-8228, or through www.rollinghomes.com). This is an unusually thorough guide to trailer parks all over Mexico, with much coverage of the Pacific coast in general and Oaxaca region in particular. Detailed maps guide you accurately to each trailer park cited and clear descriptions tell you what to expect.

Forgey, Dr. William. *Traveler's Medical Alert Series: Mexico, A Guide to Health and Safety.* Merrillville, IN: ICS Books, 1991. Useful information on health and safety in Mexico. Out of print, but available through Amazon.com.

Franz, Carl. *The People's Guide to Mexico.* Emeryville, CA: Avalon Travel Publishing, 13th edition, 2006. An entertaining and insightful A-to-Z general guide to the joys and pitfalls of independent economy travel in Mexico.

Gilford, Judith. *The Packing Book.* New York, NY: Ten Speed Press, 2006. The secrets of the carry-on traveler, or how to make everything you carry do double and triple duty, all for the sake of convenience, mobility, economy, and comfort.

Graham, Scott. *Handle With Care: Guide to Socially Responsible Travel in Developing Countries.* Chicago, IL: The Noble Press, 1991. Should you accept a meal from a family who lives in a grass house? This insightful guide answers this and hundreds of other tough questions for people who want to travel responsibly in the third world. It's out of print, but available through Amazon.com.

Jeffrey, Nan. *Adventuring with Children.* Ashland, MA: Avalon House Publishing, 1996. This unusually detailed book starts where most travel-with-children books end. It contains, besides a wealth of information and practical strategies for general travel with children, specific chapters on how you can adventure—trek, kayak, river-raft, camp, bicycle, and much more—successfully with the kids in tow.

Werner, David. *Where There Is No Doctor.* Berkeley, CA: Hesperian Foundation, 1992. This guide instructs on how to keep well in the tropical backcountry.

Whipperman, Bruce. *Moon Acapulco, Ixtapa & Zihuatanejo.* Berkeley, CA: Avalon Travel, fourth edition, 2008. The most comprehensive guidebook, with an abundance of detail of not only the famous resorts but the little-known untouristed treasures, from the mountains to the sea, of Oaxaca's neighboring state of Guerrero.

FICTION

Bolaño, Roberto, *The Savage Detectives* and *2066.* New York, NY: Farrar, Straus, Giroux, 2007 and 2008. These are a pair of masterworks, great, deeply tragic, surreal, at times humourous, and experimental novels set in Mexico in the late 20th century. Bolaño, who died of liver failure at the age of 50 in 2003, was Chilean-born but considered by many to be a challenger to Fuentes as the greatest Mexican novelist of the past 50 years.

Bowen, David, ed. *Pyramids of Glass.* San Antonio, TX: Corona Publishing Co., 1994. Two dozen-odd stories that lead the reader along a month-long journey through the bedrooms, the barracks, the cafés, and streets of present-day Mexico.

Boyle, T. C. *The Tortilla Curtain.* New York, NY: Penguin-Putnam, 1996; paperback edition, Raincoast Books, 1996. A chance intersection of the lives of two couples, one affluent and liberal Southern Californians, the other poor homeless illegal immigrants, forces all to come to grips with the real price of the American Dream.

Cisneros, Sandra. *Caramelo.* New York, NY: Alfred A. Knopf, 2002. A celebrated author weaves a passionate, yet funny, multigenerational tale of a Mexican-American family and of their migrations, which, beginning in Mexico City, propelled them north, all the way to Chicago and back.

De la Cruz, Sor Juana Inez. *Poems, Protest, and a Dream.* New York, NY: Penguin, 1997.

Masterful translation of a collection of love and religious poems by the celebrated pioneer, Mexican feminist-nun Sor Juana Inez de la Cruz (1651-1695).

De Zapata, Celia Correas, ed. *Short Stories by Latin American Women: The Magic and the Real.* New York, NY: Random House Modern Library, 2003. An eclectic mix of more than 30 stories by noted Latin American women. The stories, which a number of critics classify as "magical realism," were researched by editor Celia de Zapata, who got them freshly translated into English by a cadre of renowned translators.

Doerr, Harriet. *Consider This, Señora.* New York, NY: Harcourt Brace, 1993. Four expatriates tough it out in a Mexican small town, adapting to the excesses—blazing sun, driving rain, vast untrammeled landscapes—meanwhile the local folks observe them with a mixture of fascination and tolerance.

Finn, María, ed. *Mexico in Mind.* New York, NY: Vintage Books, 2006. The wisdom and impressions of two centuries of renowned writers, from D. H. Lawrence and John Steinbeck to John Reed and Richard Rodríguez, who were drawn to the timelessness and romance of Mexico.

Fuentes, Carlos. *Where the Air Is Clear.* New York, NY: Farrar, Straus, and Giroux, 1971. This is the seminal work of Mexico's celebrated novelist.

Fuentes, Carlos. *The Years with Laura Díaz.* Translated by Alfred MacAdam. New York, NY: Farrar, Straus, and Giroux, 2000. A panorama of Mexico from Independence to the 21st century through the eyes of one woman, Laura Díaz, and her great-grandson, the author. One reviewer said that she, "as a Mexican woman, would like to celebrate Carlos Fuentes; it is worthy of applause that a man who has seen, observed, analyzed and criticized the great occurrences of the century now has a woman, Laura Díaz, speak for him."

Jennings, Gary. *Aztec.* New York, NY: Atheneum, 1980; reprinted by Forge Books, 2006. Beautifully researched and written monumental tale of lust, compassion, love, and death in pre-conquest Mexico.

Nickles, Sara, ed. *Escape to Mexico.* San Francisco, CA: Chronicle Books, 2002. A carefully selected anthology of 20-odd stories of Mexico by renowned authors, from Steven Crane and W. Somerset Maugham to Anaïs Nin and David Lida, who all found inspiration, refuge, adventure, and much more in Mexico.

Perez-Riverte, Arturo. *Queen of the South.* New York, NY: Plume Books, 2005. In a gripping good read, the author tackles the dangerous world of Mexican drug trafficking. The story immediately races along with protagonist Teresa Mendoza, fleeing for her life from Mexico to Morocco. There, learning from her every step, threading her way through a snake nest of dangerous men, she finally triumphs as the ringleader of a big drug trafficking ring.

Peters, Daniel. *The Luck of Huemac.* New York, NY: Random House, 1981. An Aztec noble family's tale of war, famine, sorcery, heroism, treachery, love, and, finally, disaster and death in the Valley of Mexico.

Traven, B. *The Treasure of the Sierra Madre.* New York, NY: Hill and Wang, 1967. Campesinos, *federales,* gringos, and *indígenas* all figure in this modern morality tale set in Mexico's rugged outback. The most famous of the mysterious author's many novels of oppression and justice in Mexico's jungles.

Villaseñor, Victor. *Rain of Gold.* New York, NY: Delta Books (Bantam, Doubleday, and Dell), 1991. The moving, best-selling epic of the gritty travails of the author's family. From humble rural beginnings in the Copper Canyon, they flee revolution and certain death, struggling through parched northern deserts to sprawling border refugee camps. From there they migrate to relative safety and an eventual modicum of happiness in Southern California.

ARTS, CRAFTS, AND ARCHITECTURE

Baird, Joseph. *The Churches of Mexico, 1530-1810.* Berkeley, CA: University of California Press, 1962. Mexican colonial architecture and art, illustrated and interpreted, with many monumental examples from Oaxaca.

Chibnik, Michael. *Crafting Tradition: The Making and Marketing of Oaxaca Wood Carvings.* Austin, TX: University of Texas Press, 2003. Authoritative study of the phenomenally popular growth of *alebrijes,* Oaxaca's fanciful wooden animals. This carefully researched work covers all you need to know about the history, crafting, artistry, and the social and economic ramifications of Oaxacan woodcrafts in particular and handicrafts in general.

Fishgrund, Andrea Stanton. *Zapotec Weavers of Teotitlán.* Santa Fe, NM: University of New Mexico Press, 1999. Authoritative, richly color-illustrated description of the history, economics, and techniques, both traditional and contemporary, of the textile weavers of Teotitlán del Valle, in the Valley of Oaxaca.

Martínez Penaloza, Porfirio. *Popular Arts of Mexico.* Mexico City: Editorial Panorama, 1981. An excellent pocket-sized exposition of Mexican art and handicrafts.

Morrill, Penny C., and Carol A. Berk. *Mexican Silver.* Atglen, PA: Shiffer Publishing Co., 2001. Lovingly written and photographed exposition of the Mexican silver

craft of Taxco, Guerrero, which was revitalized through the initiative of Frederick Davis and William Spratling in the 1920s and 1930s. Color photos of many beautiful museum-quality pieces supplement the text, which describes the history and work of a score of silversmithing families who developed the Taxco craft under Spratling's leadership. This book greatly adds to the traveler's appreciation of the beautiful Taxco silver crafts.

Mullen, Robert J. *The Architecture and Sculpture of Oaxaca, 1530s to 1980s.* Tempe, AZ: Arizona State University, 1995. An informative stone-by-stone guide to Oaxaca's monumental buildings, mostly churches. The author's solid commentary vivifies visits to every church of note in Oaxaca and transforms what might be humdrum sightseeing for the reader-traveler into recognition, understanding, and appreciation.

Sayer, Chloë. *Arts and Crafts of Mexico.* San Francisco, CA: Chronicle Books, 1990. All you ever wanted to know about your favorite Mexican crafts, from papier-mâché to pottery, toys, and Taxco silver. Beautifully illustrated by traditional etchings and David Lavender's crisp black-and-white and color photographs.

PEOPLE AND CULTURE

Castillo, Ana, ed. *Goddess of the Americas.* New York, NY: Riverhead Books, 1997. Here, a noted author has selected from the works of seven interpreters of Mesoamerican female deities to provide readers with visions of the Virgin of Guadalupe that range as far and wide as Sex Goddess, the Broken-Hearted, the Subversive, and the Warrior Queen.

Casumano, Camille. *Mexico, a Love Story: Women Write About the Mexican Experience.* Berkeley, CA: Seal Press, 2006. A dozen-odd writers share stories, some poignant, some entertaining, and all endearing, that express their love for Mexico and its people.

Chinas, Beverly Newbold. *Isthmus Zapotecs: A Matrifocal Culture of Mexico.* Forth Worth, TX: College Publishing, 1997. In a detailed academic study, the author explains how an indigenous, female-dominant culture functions in Oaxaca.

Cohen, Jeffrey. *Cooperation and Community: Economy and Society in Oaxaca.* Austin, TX: University of Texas Press, 2000. A pithy, authoritative account of the history, economy, politics, and folkways of the Santañeros—the people of the weaving village of Santa Ana del Valle, in the Valley of Oaxaca. Here, time-honored customs—*compadrazgo, guelaguetza, promesas*—fuse with latter-day realities to produce a culture simultaneously modern and traditional.

Cordrey, Donald, and Dorothy Cordrey. *Mexican Indian Costumes.* Austin, TX: University of Texas Press, 1968. A lovingly photographed, written, and illustrated classic on Mexican native peoples, including many Oaxacan groups.

Edinger, Steven T. *The Road from Mixtepec.* Fresno, CA: Asociación Cívica Benito Juárez, 1996. A compassionately researched and photographed account of the people of San Juan Mixtepec, in the Mixteca Alta region of Oaxaca. The author, through his solid anecdotal narrative, relates the story of how a people whose means of existence have been gradually degraded for the past 400 years maintain their lives, spirit, and traditions only by repeated emigration to work as marginal farm laborers in northern Mexico and the United States.

Finerty, Catherine Palmer. *In a Village Far From Home.* Tucson, AZ: University of Arizona Press, 2000. After a successful Madison Avenue career, the author packed up and eventually found herself the volunteer nurse in an isolated western Mexico village. From her eight-year diary, she shares the joys and sorrows of a cast of village characters, from a valiant Catholic padre and his frowning bishop, to Chuy, her indigenous housekeeper, and Chila, her landlord.

Greenberg, James B. *Blood Ties: Life and Violence in Rural Mexico.* Tucson, AZ: University of Arizona Press, 1993. The author reveals, with a wealth of personal anecdotes, the cultural underpinnings beneath decades of deadly feuding between two leading Chatino towns in Oaxaca's southern Sierra.

Haden, Judith Cooper, and Matthew Jaffe. *Oaxaca, the Spirit of Mexico.* New York, NY: Artisan, division of Workman Publishing, Inc., 2002. Simply the loveliest, most sensitively photographed and crafted coffee-table book of Mexico photography yet produced. Photos by Haden, text by Jaffe.

Leslie, Charles M. *Now We Are Civilized.* Detroit, MI: Wayne State University Press, 1960. A now-classic anecdotal study of the worldview and ways of the Zapotec people of Mitla, Oaxaca.

Martinez, Zarela. *The Food and Life of Oaxaca.* New York, NY: Macmillan, 1997. Martinez, a New York restaurateur, leads her readers on an intriguing tour of Oaxacan folkways by way of the palate. Features chapters on Oaxaca's seven moles, 150 recipes, and two dozen photos of finished gastronomical creations.

Nader, Laura. *Harmony, Ideology, Justice, and Control in a Zapotec Mountain Village.* Palo Alto, CA: Stanford University Press, 1990. How some northern Sierra Zapotecs solve disputes using religion-based ideas of harmony to achieve justice and social control.

Palmer, Colin A. *Slaves of the White God: Blacks in Mexico.* Cambridge, MA: Harvard University Press, 1976. A scholarly study of why and how Spanish authorities imported African slaves into the Americas and how they were used afterward. Replete with poignant details taken from Spanish and Mexican archives describing how the Africans struggled from bondage to eventual freedom.

Romney, Kimball, and Romaine Romney. *The Mixtecans of Juxtlahuaca.* Huntington, NY: Robert E. Krieger Publishing Co., 1973. The authors study the contemporary Mixtec culture of the western Mixteca. Pithy examples, especially of the organization of fiestas, still ring true despite the two generations that elapsed since the research was done.

Stephen, Lynn. *Zapotec Women.* Durham, NC: Duke University Press, 2005. Study of how women run much of the local economy and a significant fraction of the politics in the Oaxaca Isthmus districts of Tehuántepec and Juchitán.

Toor, Frances. *A Treasury of Mexican Folkways.* New York, NY: Bonanza Books, 1947; reprinted 1985. A lovingly illustrated encyclopedia of vanishing Mexicana—costumes, religion, fiestas, burial practices, customs, legends—compiled during the celebrated author's 35 years' residence in Mexico in the early 20th century.

Sabina, María. *María Sabina Selections.* Berkeley, CA: University of California Press, 2003. María Sabina (1894-1985) was the celebrated traditional healer and tutor to an entire new age generation, from mellow hippies, to straight-laced psychiatrists, seeking cures through María's magic mushrooms. Although she was not a poet, she has nevertheless left behind a poetic legacy of essays and chants, compiled by her family and followers in her Northern Oaxaca mountaintop hometown of Huautla de Jiménez.

Trilling, Susana. *Seasons of My Heart.* New York, NY: Ballantine Publishing Group, 1999. The celebrated Oaxaca author, chef, and cooking teacher leads her readers on a culinary journey of the seven regions of Oaxaca. Along the way, they stop by market towns, mountain hamlets, shoreline villages, and lush highland valleys, visiting the friends with whom she refined the dozens of recipes that introduce the best of Oaxacan cooking. *Seasons of My Heart* is the companion volume to Trilling's National Public Television series on Oaxacan cooking.

Wauchope, Robert, ed. *Handbook of Middle American Indians.* Volumes 7 and 8. Austin, TX: University of Texas Press, 1969. Authoritative, fascinating, but aging studies of important native-speaking groups in northern, central (vol. 8), and southern (vol. 7) Mexico.

GOVERNMENT, POLITICS, AND ECONOMY

Campbell, Howard. *Zapotec Renaissance: Ethnic Politics and Cultural Revival in Southern Mexico.* Albuquerque, NM: University of New Mexico Press, 1994. A history of how the Zapotecs around Juchitán, Oaxaca, fought city hall and won.

Dillon, Samuel, and Preston, Julia. *Opening Mexico: The Making of a Democracy.* New York, NY: Farrar, Strauss and Geroux, 2005. Former Mexico City *New York Times* bureau chiefs use their rich personal insights and investigative journalistic skill to tell the story of the latter-day evolution of Mexico's uniquely imperfect democracy. Their story begins during the 1980s, tracing the decay of the 71-year-rule of the PRI, to its collapse, with the election of opposition candidate Vicente Fox in 2000.

Murphy, Arthur D., and Alex Stepick. *Social Inequality in Oaxaca.* Philadelphia, PA:

Temple University Press, 1993. A sociopolitical history of grassroots underclass activism in Oaxaca City during the 1960s, 1970s, and 1980s.

Poleman, Thomas T. *Agricultural Development in the Mexican Tropics.* Palo Alto, CA: Stanford University Press, 1964. The successes, failures, and consequences of Mexico's great dam project in Oaxaca's Papaloapan basin.

Rubin, Jeffry W. *Decentering the Regime.* Winston-Salem, NC: Duke University Press, 1997. Ethnicity, radicalism, and democracy in Juchitán, Oaxaca.

FLORA AND FAUNA
Goodson, Gar. *Fishes of the Pacific Coast.* Stanford, CA: Stanford University Press, 1988. More than 500 beautifully detailed color drawings highlight this pocket version of all you ever wanted to know about the ocean's fishes (including common Spanish names) from Alaska to Peru.

Howell, Steve N. G., and Sophie Webb. *A Guide to the Birds of Mexico and Northern America.* Oxford: Oxford University Press, 1995. All the serious bird-watcher needs to know about Mexico's rich species treasury.

Includes authoritative habitat maps and 70 excellent color plates that detail the males and females of around 1,500 species. (For a more portable version, check out Steve Howell's *Bird-Finding Guide to Mexico,* 1999.)

Mason Jr., Charles T., and Patricia B. Mason. *Handbook of Mexican Roadside Flora.* Tucson, AZ: University of Arizona Press, 1987. Authoritative identification guide, with black and white illustrations, of all the plants you're likely to see in the Oaxaca region.

Morris, Percy A. *A Field Guide to Pacific Coast Shells.* Boston, MA: Houghton Mifflin, 1974. The complete beachcomber's Pacific shell guide.

Pesman, M. Walter. *Meet Flora Mexicana.* Globe, AZ: D. S. King, 1962. Delightful anecdotes and illustrations of hundreds of common Mexican plants. Out of print.

Wright, N. Pelham. *A Guide to Mexican Mammals and Reptiles.* Mexico City: Minutiae Mexicana, 1989. Pocket-edition. Lore, history, descriptions, and pictures of commonly seen Mexican animals.

Internet Resources

A number of websites may be helpful in preparing for your Oaxaca trip.

GENERAL TRAVEL
Internet Travel Sites
www.travelocity.com, www.expedia.com, www.priceline.com, www.orbitz.com
These are four of the many major sites for airline and hotel bookings.

Travel Insurance
www.travelinsure.com, www.worldtravelcenter.com
Both sites are good for general travel insurance and other services.

Mexico Car Insurance
Sanborn's Insurance
www.sanbornsinsurance.com
Sanborn's Insurance is the long-time, very reliable Mexico auto insurance agency, with the

only north-of-the-border adjustment procedure. Get your quote online, order their many useful publications, and find out about other insurance you many have forgotten.

GAY AND LESBIAN

Go Oaxaca
www.go-oaxaca.com/overview/gay.html
A small page that lists a number of gay-friendly bars, restaurants, nightclubs, and a few gay-friendly hotels in Oaxaca City.

Purple Roofs
www.purpleroofs.com
One of the best general gay travel websites is maintained by San Francisco-based travel agency Purple Roofs. It offers, for example, details about several gay-friendly Oaxaca hotels, in addition to a wealth of gay-friendly travel-oriented links worldwide.

TRAVELERS WITH DISABILITIES

Mobility International
www.miusa.org
Mobility International website is expertly organized and complete, with a flock of services for travelers with disabilities, including many people-to-people connections in Mexico.

STUDY TOURS

Road Scholar
www.roadscholar.org
Site of Boston-based Road Scholar, Inc. (formerly Elderhostel, Inc.), with a very popular program of ongoing study tours, including a Oaxaca program of Spanish Language and Oaxacan culture.

U.S. GOVERNMENT

U.S. State Department
www.state.gov/travelandbusiness
The U.S. State Department's very good travel information site, includes lots of headings and links to a swarm of topics, including Mexican consular offices in the United States, U.S. consular offices in Mexico, travel advisories, and links to other government information, such as importation of food, plants, and animals, U.S. customs, health abroad, airlines, and exchange rates.

MEXICO IN GENERAL

MexConnect
www.mexconnect.com
This is an extensive Mexico site, with dozens upon dozens of subheadings and links, especially helpful for folks thinking of traveling, working, living, or retiring in Mexico, including Oaxaca.

Mexico Desconocido
www.mexicodesconocido.com.mx
This is the site of the excellent magazine *Mexico Desconocido* (Undiscovered Mexico) that often features unusual, untouristed destinations, many in the state of Oaxaca. It links to a large library of past articles, which are not unlike a Mexican version of National Geographic Traveler, featuring solid, hard-to-find information, in good English translation, if you can get it. (The site is so voluminous that the automatic translator tends to bog down at the effort.)

On the initial homepage, find the small magnifying glass and dialog box, labeled "buscar" ("find") at the upper right. I typed in "Oaxaca" and got 206 informative hits about places and things in Oaxaca, each linked to an article in the magazine.

Mexico Online
www.mexonline.com
Very extensive, well-organized commercial site with many subheadings and links to Mexico's large and medium destinations, and even some small destinations. For the state of Oaxaca, they cover Oaxaca City, Huatulco, and Puerto Escondido. For Oaxaca, their linked page www.mexonline.com/cityguide-oaxaca.htm is typical, with manifold links about many dozens of accommodations, from luxury hotels to modest bed-and-breakfasts. It's excellent.

Mexico Tourism Board
www.visitmexico.com
The public-private Mexico Tourism Board (Consejo de Promoción Turítica de Mexico) maintains a moderately helpful general site for destination travel information. It has lots of summarily informative subheadings, not unlike an abbreviated guidebook. If you can't find what you want here, call the toll-free information number (tel. 800/446-3942) or email contact@visitmexico.com.

If you can read some Spanish, its Spanish-language version, www.cptm.org.mx, is much more specific and detailed.

On the Road in Mexico
www.ontheroadin.com
This helpful site, with regularly updated information and photos of Mexico trailer parks and campgrounds, includes accurate and very usable maps to lots of out-of-the-way locations, many along the Pacific coast, including Puerto Escondido, Puerto Ángel, and Huatulco.

OAXACA CITY AND OAXACA IN GENERAL

Ecoturism in Oaxaca
www.ecoturismoenoaxaca.com
A good up-and-coming site with broad partial coverage of outdoor recreation sites, ripe for hiking, climbing, rapelling, bicycle riding, rafting, and more. Includes hotels, cabins, camping sites, and restaurants.

Oaxaca Bed-and-Breakfasts
www.oaxacabedandbreakfast.org
Modest but helpful site of the Oaxaca Bed-and-Breakfast Association. The dozen-odd accommodations of English-savvy owner-operators run $65-100 per night. A number of them are recommended in this book.

Oaxaca Mio
www.oaxaca-mio.com
Excellent commercial site, with lots on history, culture, sights, hotels, and services in Oaxaca City and Valley. Oaxaca coast coverage,

including Puerto Escondido and Huatulco, is still informative, but not so extensive.

Oaxaca Secretary of Tourism
www.oaxaca.travel
Very detailed website of the Oaxaca Secretary of Tourism. Good Tourist Guide section with archaeological sites, recipes, churches, museums, festivals, myths and legends, murals, handicrafts, and more. The site goes the extra step farther and provides extensive detailed information.

Oaxaca Times
www.oaxacatimes.com
The website of the *Oaxaca Times* newspaper has links to restaurants, galleries, handicrafts shops, services, plus a handy classified section usually including a long list of Oaxaca City apartment, house, homestay, and bed-and-breakfast rentals.

Planeta.com
www.planeta.com
Superb life project of Latin America's dean of ecotourism, Oaxaca resident Ron Mader, who furnishes a comprehensive English-language clearinghouse of everything ecologically correct, from rescuing turtle eggs on the Oaxaca coast to preserving the cloud forests in the Oaxaca's northern Sierra Juarez. Contains dozens of pages competently linked for maximum speed. Check out www.planeta.com/oaxaca.html for a block-long list of information-packed links to everything you need to know about Oaxaca.

Vacation Rentals
www.vrbo.com, www.choice1.com,
airbnb.com
A trio of very useful sites for picking a vacation rental house, condo, or villa, with information and reservations links to individual owners. Prices vary from moderate to luxurious. Coverage extends over much of the Mexican Pacific, and, especially in www.vrbo.com (Vacation Rentals by Owner), many

listings are in Oaxaca City, Puerto Escondido, and Huatulco.

OAXACA COAST

El Sol de la Costa
www.elsoldelacosta.com

Extensive and authoritative commercial site of the excellent Puerto Escondido bilingual tourist newspaper *El Sol de la Costa* (Warren Sharpe, editor and publisher). It's especially useful for restaurants, sights, and services and also includes much cultural background, especially on local indigenous culture and traditions. A handy classified section usually lists a number of vacation rentals by owner.

Huatulco Hotel Association
www.hoteleshuatulco.com.mx

Useful site of the Huatulco Hotel Association, with links to about four dozen hotels, ranging from modest to plush (but mostly plush), including prices for some of the hotels. The remaining information (restaurants, events, tour operators, water sports, and land sports) would be more useful if it were in English.

Huatulco Magazine
www.huatulco.magazine.net

Site of the reliable, local, free tourist magazine, with a plethora of links to its advertisers, from real estate and rental cars to handicrafts shops and three-, four-, and five-star hotels.

Own Mexico
www.ownmexico.org

Ex-pat Canadian Brent May runs this Huatulco-based real estate company. He's helpful, gregarious, and truly loves the Huatulco region and all things Mexico. Even if you aren't looking to buy, he's a fount of worthwhile information.

Puerto Real Estate
www.puertorealestate.com

Very good website of Puerto Escondido Real Estate; besides home sales, it lists and photo-illustrates many vacation rental villas, condos, and apartments ($300-3,000/week) and offers trip-planning services.

Tomzap
www.tomzap.com/oaxaca.html

This project of Mexico lover Tom Penick is a very informative site, especially for down-scale corners of Oaxaca. It's unusually detailed about Puerto Escondido, Puerto Ángel, Zipolite, Mazunte, and the Bays of Huatulco. Information includes hotels, travel, history, surfing, scuba and snorkeling, and much more, with much helpful advice on what to enjoy and what to avoid. It's very Good. (*Note:* Be aware, however, that some information is out of date.)

Zicatela Properties
www.zicatelaproperties.com

Excellent site of Puerto Escondido's Zicatela Properties real estate company. It's especially good for moderately priced apartment, condo, and vacation home rentals (as low as $250/week). It also lists a number of services to help newcomers settle into Puerto Escondido.

Index

WXYZ

List of Maps

Photo Credits

Title page: masks and costumes for Guelaguetza dancers © Kirsten Wardman; pg. 4: a wild Oaxacan beach © Justin Henderson; pg. 5: Interior courtyard at Oaxaca's museum of culture © Justin Henderson; pg. 6 top-left: © Kirsten Wardman; top-right and bottom: © Justin Henderson; pg. 7 top: © Kirsten Wardman; bottom left and right: © Justin Henderson; pg. 8: © Justin Henderson; pg. 9 top: © Kirsten Wardman; bottom-left: © Kirsten Wardman; bottom-right: © Justin Henderson; pg. 10: © Justin Henderson; pg. 12: © Justin Henderson; pg. 13: © Donna Day; pg. 15: © Justin Henderson; pg. 16: © Justin Henderson; pg. 17: © Justin Henderson; pg. 18 left and right: © Justin Henderson; pg. 19: © Justin Henderson; pg. 20: © Justin Henderson; pg. 22: © Kirsten Wardman; pg. 23: © Justin Henderson; pg. 24: © Justin Henderson; pg. 25: © Kirsten Wardman; pg. 26: © Galyna Andrushko/123RF; pg. 27: © Kirsten Wardman; pg. 28: © Justin Henderson; pg. 29 top and bottom: © Justin Henderson; pg. 31: © Justin Henderson; pg. 37: © Justin Henderson; pg. 38: © Justin Henderson; pg. 40: © Justin Henderson; pg. 41: © Justin Henderson; pg. 42: © Justin Henderson; pg. 44: © Justin Henderson; pg. 46: commons.wikimedia.org; pg. 56: © Justin Henderson; pg. 57: © Justin Henderson; pg. 65: © Justin Henderson; pg. 78 top and bottom: © Justin Henderson; pg. 79: © Justin Henderson; pg. 84: © Justin Henderson; pg. 86: © Justin Henderson; pg. 87: © Justin Henderson; pg. 88: © Justin Henderson; pg. 89: © Justin Henderson; pg. 91: © Justin Henderson; pg. 92: © Justin Henderson; pg. 93: © Justin Henderson; pg. 94: © Justin Henderson; pg. 97: © Justin Henderson; pg. 98: © Justin Henderson; pg. 99: © Justin Henderson; pg. 100: © Justin Henderson; pg. 101: © Justin Henderson; pg. 103: © Justin Henderson; pg. 105: © Justin Henderson; pg. 107 top: © Kirsten Wardman; bottom: © Justin Henderson; pg. 109: © Kirsten Wardman; pg. 112: © Justin Henderson; pg. 113: © Justin Henderson; pg.

118: © Justin Henderson; pg. 122: © Justin Henderson; pg. 132: © Justin Henderson; pg. 134: © Justin Henderson; pg. 135 : © Justin Henderson; pg. 138: © Justin Henderson; pg. 139: © Justin Henderson; pg. 141: © Justin Henderson; pg. 143: © Justin Henderson; pg. 156: © Justin Henderson; pg. 158 : © Justin Henderson; pg. 159: © Kirsten Wardman; pg 163: © Gioppi/Dreamstime.com; pg. 180 top and bottom: © Justin Henderson; pg. 181: © Justin Henderson; pg. 185: © Justin Henderson; pg. 187: © Justin Henderson; pg. 188: © Justin Henderson; pg. 191: © Justin Henderson; pg. 193: © Justin Henderson; pg. 194: © Justin Henderson; pg. 196: © Justin Henderson; pg. 199: © Justin Henderson; pg. 200: © Justin Henderson; pg. 203: © Kirsten Wardman; pg 212 top and bottom: © Justin Henderson; pg. 213: © Justin Henderson; pg. 216: © Justin Henderson; pg. 219: © Justin Henderson; pg. 221: © Justin Henderson; pg. 222: © Justin Henderson; pg. 223: © Justin Henderson; pg. 224: © Justin Henderson; pg. 228: © Justin Henderson; pg. 229: © Justin Henderson; pg. 230: © Justin Henderson; pg. 235: © Justin Henderson; pg. 236: © Justin Henderson; pg. 238 top and bottom: © David Ramirez; pg. 239: © Justin Henderson; pg. 245: © Justin Henderson; pg. 246: © Justin Henderson; pg. 247: © Justin Henderson; pg. 248: © Justin Henderson; pg. 252: © Justin Henderson; pg. 253: © Justin Henderson; pg. 259: © Justin Henderson; pg. 260: © Justin Henderson; pg. 261: © Justin Henderson; pg. 262: David Ramirez; pg. 266 top: Kirsten Wardman; bottom: © Justin Henderson; pg. 270: © Justin Henderson; pg. 272: © Justin Henderson; pg. 278: © Justin Henderson; pg. 279: © Justin Henderson; pg. 293: © Justin Henderson; pg. 298: Kirsten Wardman; pg. 302: © Justin Henderson; pg. 320: © Justin Henderson; pg. 322 top: © Justin Henderson; bottom: © Kirsten Wardman; pg, 325: © Justin Henderson; pg. 332: © Justin Henderson; pg. 333: © Justin Henderson; pg. 348: © Kirsten Wardman; pg 349: © Justin Henderson

Acknowledgments

I'd like to thank my wife Donna Day and my daughter Jade Henderson for all their love and support, and Ziggy the Dog for his friendship and amusing personality. More generally speaking, *muchas, muchas gracias* to all my ex-pat gringo and Mexican friends and acquaintances everywhere in Mexico, but especially in Oaxaca in this instance, for all their guidance, insight, and patience with my abominable Spanish. You Oaxacans are very lucky, for you live in an utterly magical place.

MAP SYMBOLS

≡≡≡	Expressway	○	City/Town	✈	Airport
≡≡	Primary Road	◉	State Capital	✈	Airfield
≡	Secondary Road	⊛	National Capital	▲	Mountain
⋯	Unpaved Road	★	Point of Interest	✦	Unique Natural Feature
―	Feature Trail	•	Accommodation		
------	Other Trail	▼	Restaurant/Bar		Waterfall
⋯⋯	Ferry	■	Other Location	▲	Park
≡	Pedestrian Walkway	⋀	Campground	⊡	Trailhead
▥▥▥	Stairs			⛷	Skiing Area

⚑	Golf Course	
Ⓟ	Parking Area	
⬛	Archaeological Site	
⛪	Church	
⛽	Gas Station	
⬡	Glacier	
▦	Mangrove	
▨	Reef	
▤	Swamp	

CONVERSION TABLES

$°C = (°F - 32) / 1.8$
$°F = (°C \times 1.8) + 32$
1 inch = 2.54 centimeters (cm)
1 foot = 0.304 meters (m)
1 yard = 0.914 meters
1 mile = 1.6093 kilometers (km)
1 km = 0.6214 miles
1 fathom = 1.8288 m
1 chain = 20.1168 m
1 furlong = 201.168 m
1 acre = 0.4047 hectares
1 sq km = 100 hectares
1 sq mile = 2.59 square km
1 ounce = 28.35 grams
1 pound = 0.4536 kilograms
1 short ton = 0.90718 metric ton
1 short ton = 2,000 pounds
1 long ton = 1.016 metric tons
1 long ton = 2,240 pounds
1 metric ton = 1,000 kilograms
1 quart = 0.94635 liters
1 US gallon = 3.7854 liters
1 Imperial gallon = 4.5459 liters
1 nautical mile = 1.852 km

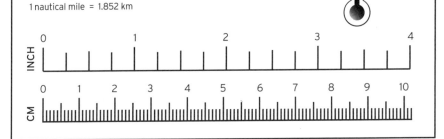

MOON OAXACA
Avalon Travel
a member of the Perseus Books Group
1700 Fourth Street
Berkeley, CA 94710, USA
www.moon.com

Editor: Erin Raber
Series Manager: Kathryn Ettinger
Copy Editor: Naomi Adler Dancis
Graphics and Production Coordinator:
  Lucie Ericksen
Cover Design: Faceout Studios, Charles Brock
Moon Logo: Tim McGrath
Map Editor: Albert Angulo
Cartographers: Brian Shotwell
Indexer: Greg Jewett

ISBN-13: 978-1-61238-896-0
ISSN: 1533-3949

Printing History
1st Edition — 2000
7th Edition — May 2015
5 4 3 2 1

Text © 2015 by Justin Hendersen and Avalon Travel.
Maps © 2015 by Avalon Travel.
All rights reserved.

Front cover photo: Skeleton dressed for the Day of
  the Dead Festival in Oaxaca © Richard l'Anson/
  gettyimages
Back cover photo: restaurant on Playa Zipolite © Uli
  Danner | Dreamstime.com

Printed in Canada by Friesens